ROCK ME ON THE WATER

A LIFE ON THE LOOSE

Written and illustrated by Renny Russell

Foreword by David Brower

Animist Press

First Edition

An Animist Press Book
Renny Russell, publisher
P.O. Box 726
Questa, New Mexico 87556
Visit Renny at www.rennyrussell.com

Any similarity of this book's title to that of a song, movie, or any other artistic endeavor is coincidental.

Design and layout by John Cole GRAPHIC DESIGNER, www.johncolegrf.com
and Renny Russell
Printed and bound in China by Midas Printers on 128 gsm
Chinese Gold East FSC matte art paper.
Cover and inside pages composed in QuarkXpress 7 on a Macintosh
Text type ITC Leawood

PUBLISHER'S CATALOGING-IN-PUBLICATION
(Provided by Quality Books, Inc.)
Russell, Renny.
Rock Me on the Water: A Life on the Loose / written and
illustrated by Renny Russell; foreword by David Brower. — 1st ed.
p. cm.
LCCN 2004096769

Hardcover: ISBN 0-9760539-0-X
Softcover: ISBN 0-9760539-1-8
Slipcase: ISBN 0-9760539-2-6

1. Green River (Wyo.-Utah)—Pictorial works.
2. Boats and boating—Green River (Wyo.-Utah)—Pictorial works.
3. Russell, Renny—Travel—Green River (Wyo.-Utah)—Pictorial works. I. Title.

F767.G7R87 2007 779'.9917925
QBI04-200471

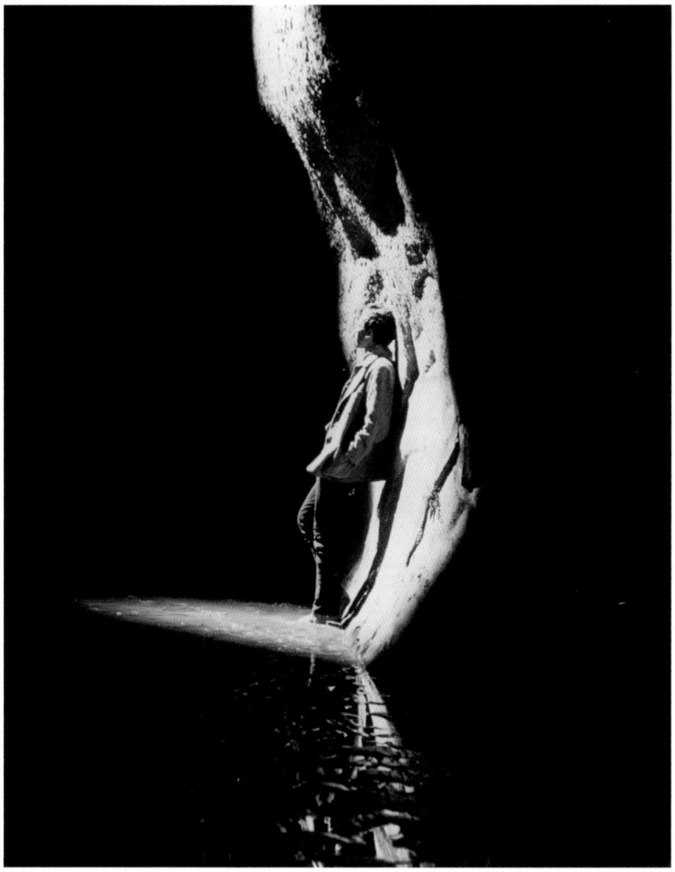

In memory of Terry Russell taken by water June 17, 1965

QUEM DI DILIGUNT ADOLESCENS MORITUR

Contents

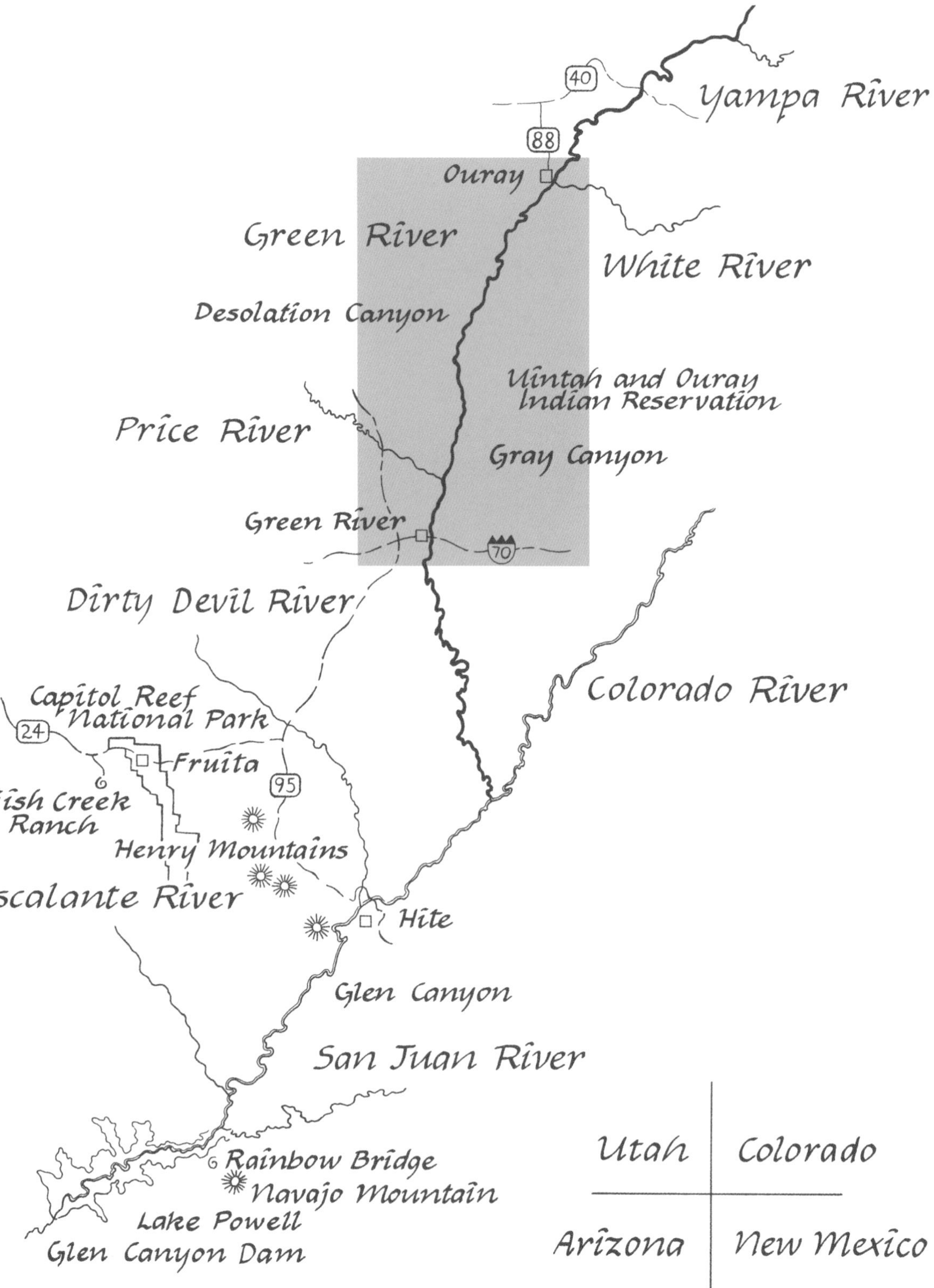

40
Yampa River
88
Ouray
Green River
White River
Desolation Canyon
Uintah and Ouray
Indian Reservation
Price River
Gray Canyon
Green River
70
Dirty Devil River
Colorado River
Capitol Reef
National Park
24
Fruita
95
Fish Creek
Ranch
Henry Mountains
Escalante River
Hite
Glen Canyon
San Juan River
Utah
Colorado
Rainbow Bridge
Navajo Mountain
Lake Powell
Glen Canyon Dam
Arizona
New Mexico

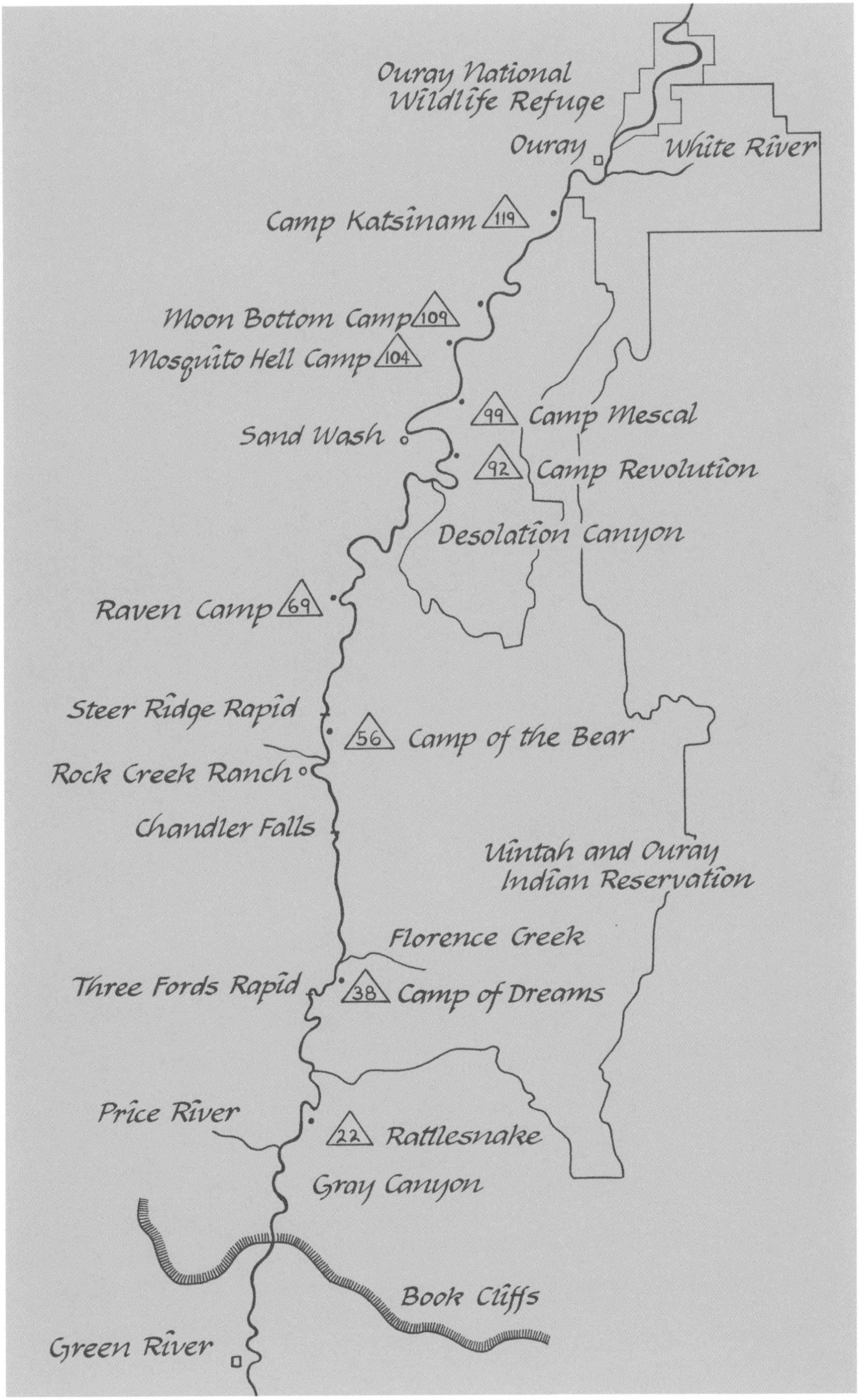
Ouray National
Wildlife Refuge
Ouray
White River
Camp Katsinam
119
Moon Bottom Camp
109
Mosquito Hell Camp
104
99
Camp Mescal
Sand Wash
92
Camp Revolution
Desolation Canyon
Raven Camp
69
Steer Ridge Rapid
56
Camp of the Bear
Rock Creek Ranch
Chandler Falls
Uintah and Ouray
Indian Reservation
Florence Creek
Three Fords Rapid
38
Camp of Dreams
Price River
22
Rattlesnake
Gray Canyon
Book Cliffs
Green River

Reader, thou hast here an honest book. I desire therein to be viewed as I appear in my own genuine, simple and ordinary manner, without study or artifice: for it is myself I paint.

— Michel de Montaigne

Foreword

BY DAVID R. BROWER

When he was nineteen, Renny Russell took a trip down the Green River with his big brother, Terry. It was a coming-of-age celebration for Terry, a celebration of adventurous youth and of a brotherly bond—one that already had led the Russell brothers to explore and enjoy most of the best wilderness in the West—and perhaps especially, a celebration of wild rivers.

Their photographs—they too modestly called them "drugstore" photographs—were the basis for an unusual Sierra Club book, *On the Loose,* with its inspired text, all of it in painstaking calligraphy that must have taken more time than the recorded adventures. Fifteen thousand copies, hardbound and slipcased, introduced the book three decades ago, when young readers needed it. The book was not yet off the press when Renny and Terry put in on the Green River, their wildest adventure yet, in Utah. Several miles downstream, in Desolation Canyon, they encountered an unexpected rapid and their boat doubled over and dumped them. Terry was lost. Renny swam alone out of the rapid and walked for three days across the desert before finding help. He has worked alone, in the years since, to make life a celebration of the beauty and mystery of wild places, especially free-flowing rivers, according to the pattern set when he and his brother were two kids on the loose.

"If there is a magic on the planet," speculated Loren Eiseley, "it is contained in water." Anyone who has experienced a desert river—like the Green—knows that magic. For while any raindrop or rivulet has power, a big river, flowing through time and a timeless desert, fills the canyon it has created with something as magical as you are likely to encounter.

Down that magical river Renny Russell floats in these pages. The river has memories in its channels, and Renny carries himself back to their common memories, past the tamarisk, sparse forests, sculptured canyon walls, and wildlife, including a bear he didn't care for (nor will you). We are carried along in recollections and insights of a life once enriched, now saddened, by the disappearance of wild places. In his dory, *Seedskeedee*, named for the Green River's headwater reach, Renny finds the eddies and bends a little strange, like the tamarisk, an alien invader that doesn't belong in this part of the world. But Renny belongs here, dearly and poignantly, and wants Terry back here too, and he reveals a brotherly love not often witnessed these days. The Sierra Nevada, where I first met them, wants them back as well.

I remember Terry's encounter with the Free Speech Movement in Berkeley but only vaguely. There's nothing vague here about Renny's encounter with it and what it meant to both of them, including the music of the times, which Renny remembers in ways I didn't, not just because of our age difference but because I never had perfect pitch, as he does. Perhaps he knew what Li Po, some seven hundred years ago, told anyone who would listen: "We never grow tired of each other, the mountain and I." Renny listened well.

David R. Brower

in Berkeley as 1999 ends

Acknowledgments

Rock Me on the Water would never have been published without the support of friends to whom I am eternally grateful.

At the launch site on the Green River, writer, guide, and historian Herm Hoops understood why I had returned and generously shared his knowledge and love of wild rivers.

Valerie Cohen, who grew up "jealous of my cousins' mysterious journeys into Western mountains and deserts," critiqued my cryptic early journal entries and brought perspective to the craft of writing and the work involved in getting it right.

Without the financial support of Nat and Sarah Cobb, Fred St. Goar, Dave Kingsley, Nancy Maynard, Tom Udall, Bill Wayne, and Carol Wiley, *Rock Me on the Water* would not have been published. My river friend Curt Crowther shared my love for the Green River and offered his support, compassion, and wisdom.

Special thanks to Paul Anderson and Vi Ann for their suggestions, and to my copyeditor extraordinaire Linda Bevard, who endured the many drafts of my work. Serendipity connected me with graphic artist John Cole, who, with his keen sense of design and killer eye, brilliantly combined my illustrations and photographs with text.

The magic, the power and the unfathomable mystery of the Green River have been the inspiration, indeed the very corner stones that built the book. And for that I am forever grateful. Many times Coyote stole my words and scrambled my mind, until after seven trips down the Green River he finally let me get my story right. Thanks to Raven for his guidance and to Bear for his power and tenacity.

I wish to thank authors Craig Childs, David James Duncan, Derrick Jensen, Jon Krakauer, the late Ellen Meloy, Terry Tempest Williams, and Ann Zwinger, who generously endorsed *Rock Me on the Water.*

My love and appreciation run deep for the *On the Loose* family, who helped keep the vision of this book alive and the fire burning, and for my brother Terry's spirit that illuminates every page.

Introduction

My brother's body was found circling in an eddy above Florence Creek Rapid. The discovery came after an exhaustive search of the Green River in Utah. Terry had just turned twenty-one and did not leave this world easily. When the boat that retrieved his body arrived at the eight-foot-high diversion dam at Tusher Rapid, a six-inch gash had been cut in her bottom. Another rescue boat wrecked a motor. The following day, the hearse carrying my brother from Green River, Utah, to the crematorium in Ogden had engine failure and had to be towed. There seemed to be a kind of cosmic resistance to his untimely departure.

This last thought mingles with the steam from my cup of tea as it rises and dissipates in the air. I glance out the window and notice more new houses under construction on the valley floor below my home in the Sangre de Cristo Mountains of New Mexico. Has it really been nearly four decades since the world lost Terry?

On June 11, 1965, my brother and I launched our small rubber boat in the flood-swollen waters of the Green River. Five days later, a rapid surprised us and our raft flipped. I was washed up on a beach in Desolation Canyon, one of the most isolated regions in the West. I made my way downriver to an abandoned ranch, where I scrounged for food and clothes among dust, snakes, rats, and cobwebs. With a blanket and a pair of boots, enveloped in a cloud of despair, I began a seventy-mile walk to the town of Green River.

I finish my tea as the early sun strikes the high ridges of Ute Mountain, an extinct volcano that rises from the high-desert plateau. It looks like the back of a giant whale. I'm awake early because I have a mission. Next to me on the table is a worn leather-bound manuscript. On its spine, in gold lettering, is embossed "On the Loose." It is the original bound manuscript of calligraphy and photographs that Terry and I created in the mid-'60s. This solitary volume of two brothers' wilderness rambles spawned a million copies when the Sierra Club published it. It became an anthem for our generation. I had not been ready to revisit the book since Terry died, keeping it wrapped in blue velvet.

On this morning, I put it in my backpack and begin walking up the mountain behind my house. I pass through the dense piñon and juniper forest and then, higher on the mountain, into aspen groves dotted with clumps of subalpine fir. Finally, I break through into open tundra, where ravens play on the thermals. On the bare-boned summit, massive cumulus clouds gather, smelling of rain, with the ominous rumblings of distant thunder.

I remove the book from its velvet covering as if it were the Gutenberg Bible and reverently open the leather cover. I touch the title page and am transported to a different time and place. I spend the afternoon with our book, slowly turning its pages, reveling in all the good humor and love that went into its making. Through the clouds, sun spills across the pages, with their photographs still firmly attached, and reveals the faint pencil markings that guided Terry's hand as he lettered the text. In memory I walk the trails Terry and I traveled. Was it all a dream? With each turn of the page, my brother's spirit leaps into the high alpine air and is set free.

On top of the mountain, I realize it is time to write a new book. In the decades since Terry's death, I have distilled enough of life to shine a new light on our journey and gain a clearer perspective of the past.

So consumed am I by the thought that I fail to notice a ridge is no place to be in a thunderstorm. Hurriedly, I wrap *On the Loose* in its velvet cover and return it to my pack. I move quickly down the mountain, among lightning bolts, seeking shelter in the timber. Back home, I go to the oldest part of my house—the first room I built as a bulwark against life's storms. To terminate the mindless wandering I had done in search of solace after Terry died, I had bought a piece of wilderness. Now, rather than merely visiting wild places, as Terry and I had done, I make my home in wilderness; it beckons irresistibly, as it always did, just beyond my door.

I was seduced by the light of northern New Mexico—the pure, clear, golden light of mountains named for the blood of Christ. The landscape took hold of me—its mesas and high rolling hills, its sensuous round-topped peaks. I found my home in country that is neither desert nor mountain, but a composite—where cactus grows among the aspen; where ground cover is dense with oak, piñon, and juniper; where the undergrowth conceals the wanderings of fox, raccoon, elk, coyote, mountain lion, and bear. I found a home where sweet spring water rises from the heart of the mountain. Tall pines guard entrances to canyons where jagged granite spires loom. The savanna stretches northwest for a hundred miles to the high peaks of Colorado's San Juan Mountains, where distant blue-gray volcanoes rise up and merge with the horizon.

Here I built an octagonal room that over the years metamorphosed into the heart and soul of my home. Each subsequent room branched out from the original, like limbs of my body—testimonials to my growth and folly. Some rooms I've torn down, others I've had to rebuild. In the center of the octagon, a large ponderosa log supports the roof. Beams radiate from it, connecting the corners and forming a chambered nautilus. Each chamber has borne witness to a life of triumphs and follies, forged in large part by the immense legacy of living *On the Loose.*

On one wall hangs an eclectic collection of photographs and calligraphy, diligent and watchful testimonials to a brotherly bond forged by our mutual love and passion for wilderness. I move a stack of my own paintings to get a closer look.

In a delicately carved gold frame Terry immortalized in calligraphy the words of Henry David Thoreau, as a gift for my high school commencement in 1964: "Remember thy Creator in the days of thy youth. Rise free from care before the dawn, and seek adventures. Let the noon find thee by other lakes, and the night overtake thee every where at home. There are no larger fields than these, no worthier games than may be here played . . ."

Next to it, an intricate pen-and-ink drawing, reminiscent of the work of the finest Old World engravers, reads "Happy Birthday. With Love Forever. To Ma. From Terry." Another calligraphy piece celebrates the words of Arthur Rimbaud: "The goal in life is the transformation of the self into a maker of poetry or beauty. This is more important than anything done along the way." The words are centered in a swirling pattern in gold-leaf design. Below that is a snapshot of Terry playing his autoharp, a touchstone image that found its way into our book. Terry scribed these words to accompany it: "It's a shame that a race so broadly conceived should end with most lives so narrowly confined."

My eyes linger last and longest on a picture of my brother that I took on top of Mount Whitney in the Sierra Nevada in 1963, culminating our grueling record-breaking walk on the John Muir Trail. Silhouetted against a cobalt-blue sky,

Terry seems larger than life. He fills most of the frame, so large that he dwarfs the distant horizon and the dim shadow of the Salton Sea far to the southeast. On our rambles through the Sierras, Terry merged with wilderness so completely that he became one with it. Captured in this picture, his tan face and full smile radiate all the joy, confidence, and light of one who knows who he is and knows his place on the planet. I give Terry a wink and feel an urgency to return to the Green River, to retrace our fateful journey, and to begin writing.

My plan to return to the river has been brewing for some time, and the dream to build my own boat in which to run it is nearly realized. In my shop I put the finishing touches on the dory that will take me down the Green River and complete the circle Terry and I began on that June day in 1965. Gluing a last section of the gunwale, I concentrate on getting the proportions of resin and hardener just right. Too little hardener and the epoxy will never set up. Too much and it may possibly catch fire or turn rock-hard before I can use it.

During the five years I would spend writing *Rock Me on the Water,* I would have to be certain that I mixed just the right proportion of resin to hardener. I knew Terry would be looking over my shoulder to make certain the mix was right. He would let me know when the interface between past and present was a true bond, resilient and enduring. Late that afternoon, as the glue dries, I sit quietly in the light and admire the graceful lines and curves of my boat. An adventure down the Green River will take me back in time, just as it will propel me forward into the future. I begin to comprehend the enormity of my return.

At Steer Ridge Rapid, where Terry drowned and where I was, in a sense, reborn, I will complete the circle. There the river will reveal that the last note of a song is merely the beginning of another. At the end of my childhood, when the rapids released me to that river beach, I began another song. With the writing of this book, that song is now complete.

Nearly forty years after Terry disappeared in the river, I can hear both the dissonant and the melodic notes more clearly than before. I can feel the rhythm in a deeper place, a beat that resonates in my soul. As my generation will attest, it is harder being on the loose now than it was in our youth. It seems to take greater courage to find new trails. The prophetic warnings in *On the Loose* are coming to pass. Terry wrote: "The weed will win in the end, of course. Thine alabaster towns will tumble, thine engines rot into dust. Man will break his date with the future."

Freedom was and still is close to the heart of it. Indeed, freedom is what *On the Loose* was all about, a freedom born of wild places where nature shouts—or whispers—freedom. *Rock Me on the*

Water has revived in me what *On the Loose* was written for. It recalls the Free Speech Movement launched at the University of California at Berkeley, where Terry was arrested and thrown in jail. Revisiting that era serves as a reminder that our civil liberties are threatened today more than ever, that complacency breeds apathy which in turn kills the spirit, and that care and vigilance are vital.

Rock Me on the Water is a philosophical journey, a fresh new painting for which *On the Loose* has primed the canvas. This book tries to both illuminate and bring to life some of the mysteries and insights behind the veil of *On the Loose* and to come to terms with some of its ideological naiveté. It's a furtherance of seminal ideas for those of us who came of age when *On the Loose* first appeared. But more than being a nostalgic look backward, *Rock Me on the Water* is for the future—for succeeding generations who may feel adrift in cyberspace and wish to return to the real world, to wilderness. They are the ones who must continue fighting for all the right things our battered planet needs to keep turning.

But as *On the Loose* reminded us, "These are human things; the point of it all is Out There, a little beyond that last rise you can just barely see, hazy and purple on the sky." I've been out there beyond that last ridge and back again. I have learned that rivers, like souls, are pure magic, and that they endure. The Green River has flowed like a timeless melody through my soul for most of my days, our life forces merging in a ceaseless current. Generations come and go, but rivers are constant, their lessons invaluable and their flow never ending.

RENNY RUSSELL

THE SANGRE DE CRISTO MOUNTAINS

NEW MEXICO

SUMMER 2007

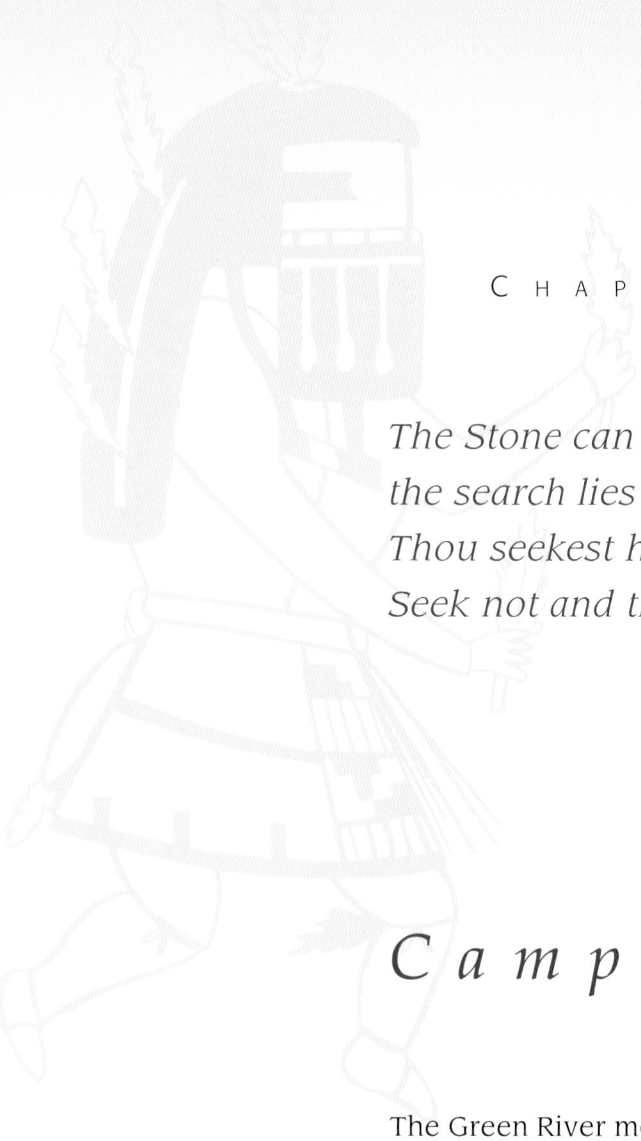

CHAPTER ONE

The Stone can only be found when
the search lies heavily on the searcher.
Thou seekest hard and findest not.
Seek not and thou wilst find.

— FROM AN ALCHEMIST'S ROSARIUM

Camp Katsinam

The Green River moved like a powerful serpent, its waters swollen with melted snow from the Wind River Mountains and its main tributary, the Yampa. I stood in the water, placed my hands in the current, and paid my respects. I was greeted with the sweet smell of saturated earth awakening to spring and the pungent aroma of sage, of moldy old roots, of willows and yucca, of minerals, of cougar and bear scat. Deer carcasses, uprooted trees, raven feathers, damselflies, bat wings, cicadas were carried in this silty concoction of life and death that was the collective memory of a thousand miles of myriad creeks and streams. Above me, cottonwood leaves exploded in green, their seeds spilling into the sky. This is the place where I began my river journey as a child, and where I will complete the circle.

I backed the trailer into the river and christened my boat *Seedskeedee* with a liquor distilled from the blue agave plant. As I

Ouray ferry, Utah, 1930s.

watched her gently bob in the current, I recalled a day in June 1965 that has been burned into my being. I traveled back to this exact spot along the river on the outskirts of Ouray, Utah. The clear light of that spring morning became an amber glow of memory.

A Land Rover, with its canvas top flapping in the wind, passed over the bridge at Ouray and rolled to a stop. It had been a long two-day drive from Berkeley, California. My brother, Terry, aged twenty-one, had just graduated from the University of California. Tall and lanky, he carried himself like an arrow. His large green eyes scrutinized the world through his horn-rimmed glasses. As an English major, he had read most of the great literary works and could speak five languages, but he had not yet distilled all he had learned. The ink had hardly dried on the pages of our hand-lettered manuscript, *On the Loose*, and we had left the work in the hands of environmental icon David Brower, who insisted that it be published by the Sierra Club.

I was a couple of years younger, about as tall, hardly an intellectual, and voraciously consumed the landscape—the colors, the light, the smells, the moment. Terry kept a watchful eye on me, knowing I was a trickster. After a year at the San Francisco Art Institute, I doubted art could be taught, and had yet to know the skeptical philosophy and moral dualism that would come to cloud my metaphysical take on life. There were no prophets, saints, grace, evil, secular humanism, and nationalism. There were no "rewards in heaven"—wilderness was heaven, and we were truly in heaven, about to run the Green River!

We hadn't known anyone who had run the river through Desolation and Gray Canyons, so we hadn't a clue what lay downstream. We didn't expect to see anyone because this was when the river still belonged to the ravens, coyotes, and wild horses. Experience we lacked, but we did have an ample supply of idealism and a belief we were invincible. The pulse of the river was the pulse in our veins.

The amber glow of memory deepened . . . amorphous shapes materialized and dissipated, and I heard the murmuring of voices . . .

Terry and I unloaded our ragged World War II ten-man boat, designed for assault landings on the coast of Japan. It came equipped with a survival kit that included fishhooks and patches to repair bullet holes from enemy fire. More than likely, the boat would have sunk from the weight of Terry's books. There was no room for his recent acquisition, *The Wonders of Nature and Art,* in its four leather-bound volumes, dated MDCCL ("Being an account of whatever is most curious and remarkable throughout the world").

I sawed the legs off a rickety old rocking chair and lashed it to the deck, just as Major John Wesley Powell had done on his boat, the *Emma Dean,* on his expedition from Green River, Wyoming, to the Grand Wash Cliffs.

A pair of ravens cackled, startling me back, and I ran down the bank to the boat to get in sync with the present. Everything was just as I had left it—my life jacket snapped to the bowline; my journal on the deck, its pages fluttering in the wind—just me and a boat against the backdrop of a timeless river in a land of immeasurable horizons.

I untied *Seedskeedee*, put on my life jacket, and slid the oars into their locks. I stood for a long time, rope coiled in hand, wondering what my brother would have thought of my returning to the river; wondering how Tristan felt when he cast

Ouray today.

Building a dory is a beautiful madness.

off alone in his tiny boat upon an infinite ocean. The ravens circled low, demanding my attention, performing somersaults and half rolls. I cackled back. Ravens had answered my cries when I searched along the river for Terry. They would be my allies.

I hopped into the boat, and she came alive as I pulled hard on the oars, pointing her stern toward the deepest channel. Yes! I had set the oarlocks in the proper places and the footwell at the right depth. I leaned back, savoring the moment, and then rowed from one side of the river to the other, just to feel the water beneath me. She skimmed across the water like lightning; she gained momentum and sustained it; she turned on a dime. And because she had a rigid hull, the ride in the rapids would be a wild one. I spun *Seedskeedee* in circles until all was a blur—a wonderful dream—and felt the spirits of the Crow and the Shoshones who once lived at the headwaters of the Green and imagined how the river mingled with their souls and crept into their songs. Their name for the Green was *Seeds-kee-dee Agie,* or Prairie Hen River.

I ran my hands along her ash rails, feeling their smoothness, and admired the graceful arc of her gunwales, joining at the bow post, and recalled the three-year epic to build her. Building a dory requires fourteen sheets of plywood, fifteen gallons of epoxy resin, and a mountain of hinges, latches, nuts, bolts, and screws, a love of aesthetics, and a bit of madness.

And it's an endurance event requiring hundreds of hours of precise cutting and gluing. The intensity of the project has been known to destroy relationships and cause severe headaches, dizziness, and nausea. Some builders on a budget will forgo buying food in order to acquire materials. But when the boat has its final coat of paint, and the gunwales have their final coat of oil, and at last you're on the water, it's all worth it. There's absolutely nothing like rowing a wooden boat on a wild river—a boat with heart, soul, and spirit; a boat that will take you to places you've never been. Cook on her, sleep on her, or dance on her—your boat is home. To those who know them, there's something magical about the boats.

I asked the wind, "Oh, Don Bernardo Miera y Pacheco, where is your mythological river, the San Buenaventura?" Miera was the cartographer with Spanish explorers Fathers Francisco Dominguez and Silvestre Vélez de Escalante, who, in 1776, were the first Europeans to encounter the crossing of the Green River. Miera drew the river running west, and for nearly a century following, mapmakers perpetuated the myth that the river flowed across the Great Basin. Fur trappers, miners, and missionaries searched in vain for a river that flowed west to the Pacific Ocean. Miera named their imaginary river the San Buenaventura. John Wesley Powell shattered the myth in 1869 when he discovered that the Green River indeed traveled south. What a time to be alive—before every corner of the West had been mapped, before every drop of river water had been allocated!

I passed beneath the bridge at Ouray—the last river crossing for the next one hundred twenty-eight miles. That such sheer volume of water

Wooden boats with heart, soul, and spirit.

Herons and cormorants occupy the same biological niche.

could pass so silently was eerie. But the silence was broken as I neared the Ouray National Wildlife Refuge. Ducks, cranes, herons, and myriad waterfowl use the Green as a flyway during their annual migrations. Canada geese, flying by radar, passed in overdrive, their cries altering slightly as they made subtle changes in direction.

Since I was traveling at maybe a mile an hour, I had plenty of time to speculate on a large blue-and-white umbrella on the east side of the river. When I passed, a gent with a white beard, his pants tucked into his cowboy boots, stomped down to the river in an obvious state of agitation. Waving his hands wildly in the air, he yelled, "Ya oughta get a motor for that thing! You'll be lucky to get down to Sand Wash [30 miles distant] in a week!" He paused, as if he were waiting for me to say something, and then he said, "Ya should have someone help you row." Truth of the matter was I couldn't row fast enough away from him.

I stopped for lunch and skirted an anthill, where a lizard was feasting. Condemned by many as lowly and insignificant, the ant is a lot like man. Ants wage war, cooperate with one another, bury their dead, capture prisoners of war, use propaganda and surveillance, and are nomadic hunters. I peered into the entrance of their hill. All the ants seemed busy working for the common good. Was there a lesson to be learned here? Bread crumbs, held fast in their mighty mandibles, disappeared into the communal caverns. Locked in their world of pheromones, they act and react in a world of chemicals that dictate their every move. The ant has memory of only the previous hour and no concept of the future. Could this be true enlightenment? Their micro-wilderness probably will outlast our own ecosystems; maybe they know something we don't.

I rowed on, brushing the stowaway ants off my pants down the footwell and condemning them to a lonely death. Ghost-gray cottonwood trees appeared around the bend, their branches reaching skyward like bony witches' fingers clawing the sky. Perched on a pile of sticks were dozens of herons, along with their unlikely bedfellows, the black cormorants, who occupy the same biological niche. Young heron hatchlings, with their rubbery necks, peered from beneath their mothers at a sky into which they soon would fly. Nature was busy "being," while I, the rogue primate with my "big brain," seemed a spectator. Although still in the sun, I was surrounded by storms in an immense sky of endless horizons. Blue-black clouds concealed the Hopi *katsinam*, who danced and worked their magic, bringing rain to the thirsty desert. I hoped they would dance through my dreams tonight and sing a laconic chant. And then the rain came. The boat hugged the shore and I leaned back, surrendering myself to the river, peering into the dense growth where birds with wings of sky blue flashed and where the vireo eye saw all.

The wind blew me to camp in late afternoon at mile 119—that is, the number of miles north of the town of Green River, as indicated in Belknap's definitive guide to Desolation and Gray Canyons. In the lush grass, gnarly old cottonwoods stood like wise men—they had seen my brother's restless spirit adrift above the river, ridges, and mesas, unaware of the ruins and rubble his untimely departure left behind: A mother was unable to reconcile his loss, failed a suicide attempt, and never spoke of him again; an aunt turned away and turned to stone. A cynical uncle referred to me only as "the unlovely brother," believing Terry gave me equal credit as coauthor of *On the Loose*, but doubting I could "write a note to a milkman that would make sense." And an entire family who believed I was somehow responsible for my brother's death.

I emerged from their shadow with a greater sense of who I was, stronger than ever, and with a deepened awareness of the gift of life. Trouble was, I sank ever deeper into the heart of *On the Loose,* where Terry was frozen in time along with a wilderness that had disappeared. I tried to live the legacy but failed because I was a child of the '60s. I denied growing old and wanted wilderness to remain

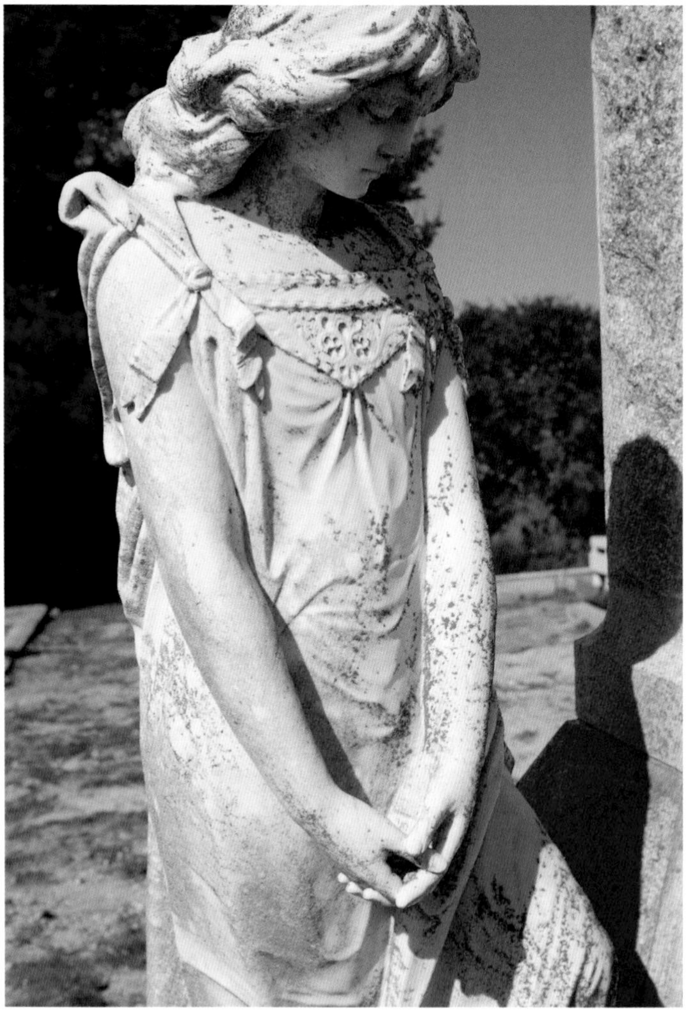

Cemetery, Marin County, California, 1963.

unchanged. I wanted freedom without responsibility, for the miraculous to reveal itself eternally as in a vial of LSD. How well the book was received seemed irrelevant, its success meaningless.

I hopped to shore with *On the Loose,* tied the boat, dashed toward a cotton-wood, threw my arms around it, and bellowed through the branches, BROTHER, WHERE ARE YOU? For decades I avoided probing too deeply into the book—hell, it was written in an age of innocence by a couple of goofy kids—let it go . . . and over time was able to celebrate it. Now, after more than three decades of distilling its contents, I began scrawling notes in the margin where the story needed to be re-examined, and put stars next to all that had endured. "Dag nab it, Terry," I said with a grin, "let's sort some things out this trip, let's do a little investigative work and follow a thread back into the labyrinth and see what we find! Just maybe the past will lead to the future . . ."

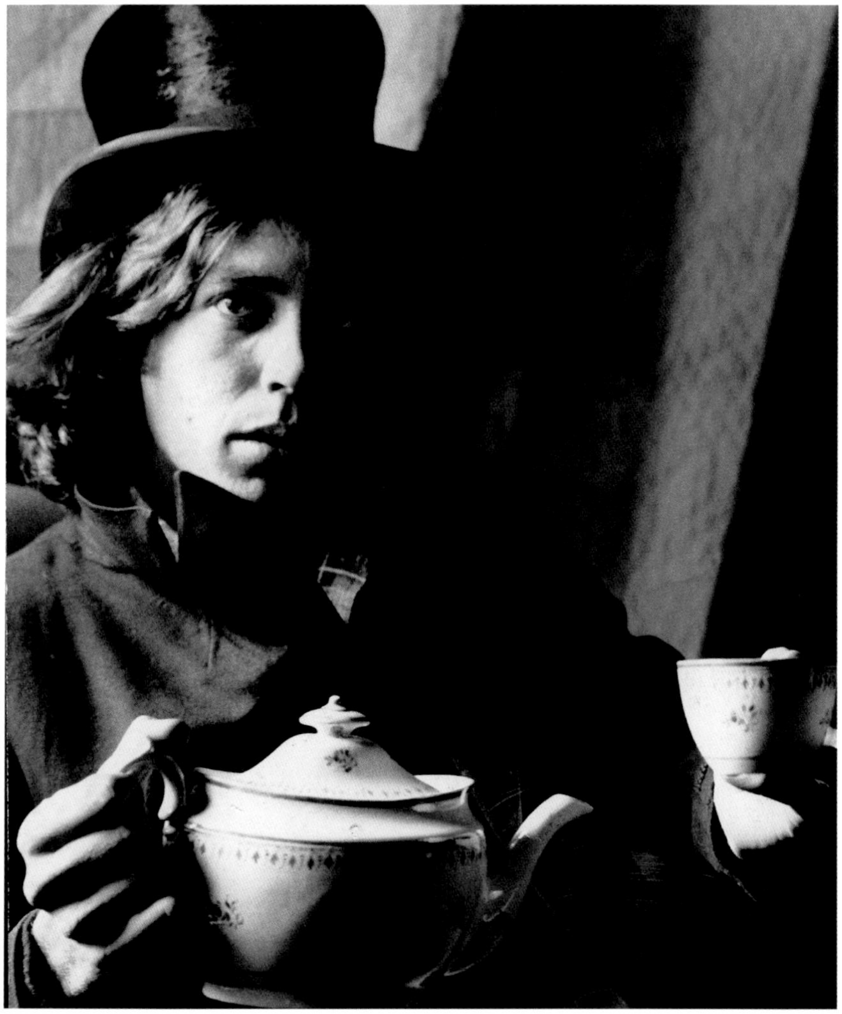

Mill Valley, California, 1966.

To the east, shafts of sun shot from beneath brooding clouds, dashing across the landscape with great urgency, bathing the land in brilliant, immaculate light. I sat on a cottonwood log, feeling powerless to do anything but watch the show. Bolts of lightning darted about, framed within a rainbow that spanned the horizon. I was drenched to the bone, but it didn't matter—the river was welcoming me home.

Chapter Two

Its substance reaches everywhere; it touches the past and prepares the future; it moves under the poles and wanders thinly in the heights of air. It can assume forms of exquisite perfection in a snowflake or strip the living to a single shining bone cast up by the sea.

– Loren Eiseley

Red Moon Camp

I poked my head from the tent. Last night's storm had passed and offered the day a promise. Droplets clung to the spring grass, and with the first rays of the sun they sparkled like facets from a thousand diamonds. A tangled mass of cottonwood limbs and leaves swayed above. The only marker to gauge time's passing was the sunlight working its way down a cottonwood, illuminating the leaves against a brilliant sky of cerulean blue.

In the river channel, an immense amount of water passed silently and urgently, keeping pace with the pulse of the planet, seeming out

A new beginning.

of place in this harsh, parched landscape—eighteen thousand one-foot-square cubes of water passing every second—so much water that it was hard to fathom that there wasn't enough water to supply downstream water needs.

The Yampa joins the Green about seventy-five miles upriver, colored by the land from its source in the mountains, south of the Colorado town that bears its name. The river miraculously escaped the noose of the Army Corps of Engineers and Bureau of Reclamation as a trade-off for building Glen Canyon Dam; it is the last major free-flowing river in the entire Colorado River Basin. A few miles upriver yesterday, I had passed the White River, its chocolate-brown water tinged by its journey from the headwaters above Trapper's Lake in Western Colorado's Flattop Mountains. Yesterday I drifted on the fine waterline where two rivers join, one oar in the Green, the other in the White—the two stubbornly refusing to mingle for several miles.

The flocks of birds that peppered the sky didn't care one way or another about dams or human concerns. I, like them, was on the wing. Ducks dove for breakfast; geese bowed low, their long necks thrust forward to the ground, and tiptoed into the protective cover of willows with their young. A lone western grebe passed on the water and gave me a hard look with his piercing red eye. Their songs needed no words. John Livingston wrote that to contemplate the possibility of "a non-human ethic" (i.e., wildlife) would literally mean turning Western metaphysics inside out.

In my imaginings, Archaeopteryx bore down on me. I cringed below this feathery reptile with its terrible claw and felt the wind from its thunderous wings. Paleontologists believe this creature is related to songbirds that chattered above, and had evolved from the dinosaurs that had survived the smoke of a meteor that exploded in the Yucatán some one hundred fifty million years ago.

Just as swiftly as he had come, he vanished, leaving me contemplating the concept of time. Dinosaurs ruled supreme for around a hundred million years and humans for only a hundred thousand. If the age of the earth is represented by a twenty-four-hour clock, man's written history represents only one second—and in North America, only one-tenth of that.

With precious little time on my hands, I crawled out of my sleeping bag and picked my way through the fallen cottonwood limbs and into the womb of my boat in search of the makings for coffee. I leaned over the gunwales and washed my face and felt the calm water's unspoken power gently move my hand. Water! From the blue waters of Havasu Creek in the Grand Canyon, rich in calcium carbonate, to the thick, orange, frothing waters of a flash flood. From the translucent blue-green waters carving their way through the heart of glaciers to the silty droplets drying on my face. Water can sing lullabies or can kill babies in a tidal wave. Your fluid force runs beneath my boat—as it runs through my veins. Oh water! You are milk and honey, you are redeemer and slayer. Your endless flow carries me on and on . . . neither now nor then . . . the moment eternal . . . wash me down.

Like a mosquito unnoticed until it starts drilling, I heard it now—the distant rumbling of diesel motors, sucking and throbbing, as they pounded their way through the siltstone and sandstone, ripping open the Gilsonite veins like bloated ticks drunk on greed—pop, pop . . . pop . . . pop, pop. The wells are visible from any ridge along the river—2,280 oil wells and 1,270 gas wells in the Uinta Basin. A drop in the bucket compared with what may be on the horizon. In three days, I will float the Green River where it cuts though the Tavaputs Plateau, the largest remaining wild and roadless area in the Western states. Four wilderness areas are proposed there, where the largest deer and elk herds roam. Many endangered species live there as well. The area is under siege by loggers, and in Utah there are few environmental regulations. These two million pristine acres of federal, state, and tribal lands are being considered for gas and oil development.

But the ducks and geese couldn't give a damn about this either, and I follow their cries into the dense growth along the shore, where waterways meander in a maze, filling small ponds. Here I find spoonbills, cormorants, mallards—some deep green, others black and white—and ducks of gold, shimmering in the sun. Scores of dabbling and diving ducks demonstrate landing and departure techniques: The divers take off from the water by first running across it, while the dabbling ducks spring into the air at takeoff. So many birds lay hidden in the grass that they flew up in waves as I passed.

With spring's high water come frogs and crickets with their mesmerizing drones—a pandemonium of pure primeval sound shreds the air that, in the middle of the night, is unsettling. Water, always the catalyst, spins a thread of life that has flourished here without interruption since time immemorial.

I coiled the bowline and shoved off, ravenous for a new chapter of a book I couldn't put down. *Seedskeedee* would carry me into the heart of the next chapter. To the north, lavender clouds boiled and rolled over the high ridges of the Uinta Mountains, trailing curtains of rain. River islands dreamily appeared and disappeared around graceful bends in the river. They demanded exploration. Great piles of driftwood came to rest on the islands—roots, gnarly limbs, and entire trees were intertwined, sculpted and weathered by sun, wind, and water. The variety in form, texture, and color, and the perfection in their unpretentious simplicity, made works of art created by mortal man seem vain. I picked up a driftwood root shaped like a snake that revealed its subterranean

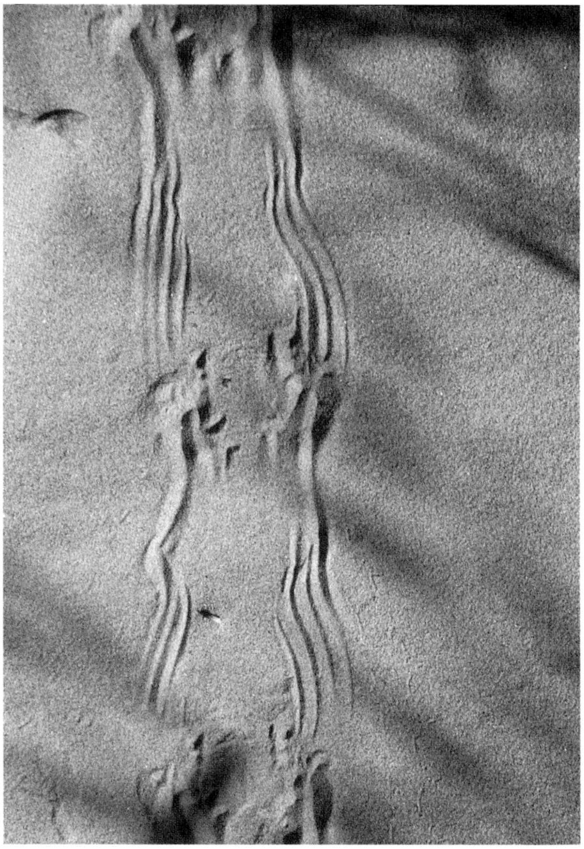

past. In its tenacious struggle for water, it had twisted and turned its way around stones worn smooth like giant marbles by the river.

Uprooted trees covered the beach, their roots entangled like lovers. My imagination turned these old silvery gray cottonwoods into griffins, into chimeras—a fire-breathing monster with a lion's head, goat's body, and serpent's tail. I grabbed onto him and wrestled him to the ground . . . but the creature vanished like my dreams.

The sand was covered with beaver and deer tracks, and I traced their edges with my bare feet. It was slow going through the dense cottonwoods, where beaver had felled trees over a dry channel in the hope that floods would fill it. The Army Corps of Engineers has much to learn.

When I returned to the river where I remembered tying *Seedskeedee,* there was nothing but sand, driftwood, and river. Boatless and stranded on the island, I probably would perish—or would I sharpen sticks with stones and go hunting, wrapping myself in animal hides? I didn't even know how to build a fire without matches. The idea didn't sit well. I had put a star beside a line from *On the Loose* the night before, and it snuck up on me now: "At least if the species has lost its animal strength, its individual members can have the fun of finding it again." Fun indeed, and what's animal strength?

My Pleistocene origins clashed with my domesticated self. Where was the intuitive metaphysical realm of my forebears, and their knowledge of myth and its connection in understanding life's cycles? Still, my genes have an expectation that insists I live close to wilderness. The memory lives on—an imprint that strikes a chord despite the times in which I live.

For sixty million years! our ancestors outsmarted and killed predators in the veldt of southern Africa. We owe much to this intense drama—our minds, our memory, even our consciousness, and the very origins of myth itself. Without the hunt, we would not have developed or been able to reason abstractly; indeed, man would not have survived.

I broke into a run. Where was my boat, my lifeline back to the supermarket, back to shelter, back to love? Around the bend I found *Seedskeedee,* exactly where I had tied her. I felt foolish. Back on the river, no wind stirred. The clouds had moved away from the Uintas, and all bird activity subsided; even the river was silent. No beginning, no end. I was timelessly adrift, adjusting to the awesome silence—that fearful tranquility—as the current washed me down.

Seedskeedee willingly would have drifted through the night, but I reined her in at mile 109 to camp, across the river from where Red Moon, the last warring Ute Indian, had retreated with his followers to avoid capture. It was a wretched and miserable time for a proud people. The expanding Mormon empire had touched off an extended conflict with the Utes. After Brigham Young had satisfied himself that the land surrounding this camp for hundreds of square miles was (as noted in the Salt Lake *Deseret News*) no more than a "vast contiguity of waste fit only for nomadic purposes," the northern Utes were rounded up and confined to the Uintah Valley Reservation, designated as such by Abraham Lincoln in 1861. This land contained some two million acres, minus a 7,004-acre strip of land removed by Congress in 1888 because it contained valuable Gilsonite deposits. Pop . . . pop . . . pop, pop go the gas wells.

I pulled into camp. A heron flew so close I could hear the rush of air through its wings. Across the river, a solitary figure dressed in white appeared and slowly waved. I waved back, and then the figure disappeared into the dense growth. Possibly it was the ghost of Red Moon or my brother's apparition, both restlessly adrift in the spirit world. I waited for the figure to reappear across the river, but all was silent; all was still.

If Terry had survived and I had drowned, would he have returned to the Green River, tormented by the loss of his brother? If the deck had been cut before the cards were dealt on our trip in 1965, it might have been a different game altogether. I cracked open an ale, leaned back on the deck, and recalled a time of running and seeking.

After Terry died, my family's reticence became unbearable. I packed a few belongings, and for the next three years, home was behind the wheel of our Land Rover. After returning Terry's ashes to the river, I drove to Jackson Hole, Wyoming, to tell our father, Harvey, that his son had drowned. I rolled into the parking lot of his "Teton Mystery House." I wandered through the house—it sat askew, creating optical illusions—but discovered no mystery. Harvey met me at the exit gate. I hadn't the heart to tell him about Terry right off. He took me to a small trailer that housed a $10,000 pair of Tony Lama boots studded with gold and jewels. I stared blankly at the display case. Then he took me to a room above the garage, where in long rows of cages, chinchillas cowered as if they knew they were destined to become fur coats.

Nels and Guri Finkelson.

At the house, I thumbed through an album of Finkelson family history, collected by an aunt I'd never met. My great-grandparents Nels and Guri Finkelson gazed sternly at me from an old photograph taken in Slidre, Valdres, Norway, in the mid-1850s. On another page I discovered a newspaper clipping of

Climbing Mount Eisenhower, Canadian Rockies, 1967.

my grandfather Peter Finkelson and bride, Clara, smiling, in their wedding clothes. The caption told how they celebrated for three days, built a pavilion, invited three hundred guests, butchered several steers and dozens of chickens, made their own beer, and cooked two hundred fifty pies. An orchestra had played, and the dancing went on late into the evening. I hardly felt like celebrating or dancing or eating pies. My thoughts were of my brother and how best to tell my father what had happened.

La Paz, Baja, 1970s.

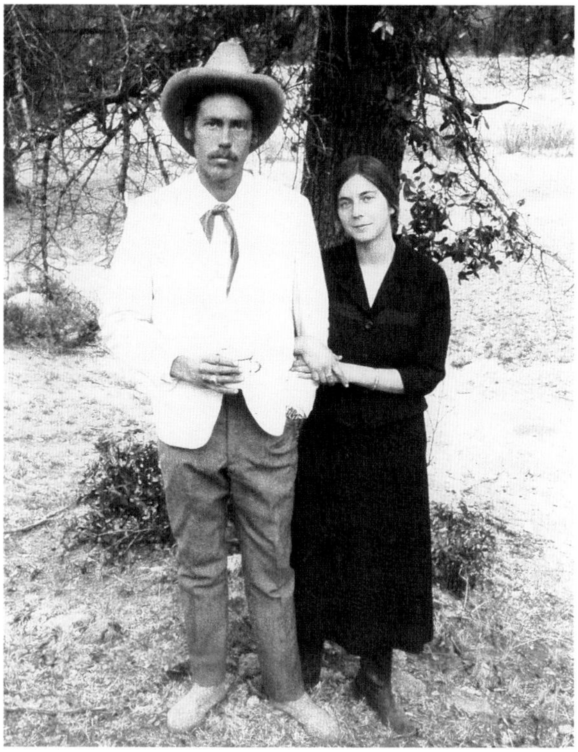

Crossing the border at Nogales.

During breakfast Harvey asked about Terry. I stared blankly at my eggs and burned bacon and then out the window at the cumulus clouds building along the ridge above the Snake River. Then I told my father that Terry had drowned. I'd never seen my father cry before.

Next morning, I headed north to Canada to where the road ends at Prince Rupert, British Columbia. Then without a pause I turned around and burned down the highway to Oaxaca, Mexico—and then did it again. At highway junctions I consulted the *I Ching*—a prophetic Chinese book of fortune—for guidance.

Along the way I ate peyote (getting high, then sick), read Kerouac, took chances, had affairs, and was deluded. In the Canadian Rockies, while waiting for the clouds to lift to climb Mount Eisenhower, I ran out of steam. I would never find my brother and could no longer run from myself. I craved something solid to hold on to. I pointed the Rover south, with one eye cocked for a place to call home.

But that was a long time ago. I perched on an outcropping. The river had me in its spell. The water seemed alive, with a thousand luminescent fish reflecting the sun, and moved like an eye-dazzler Navajo blanket with its intricate designs. As the sun edged its way toward the horizon, the water turned from reddish-brown to silver-gray. Downstream, a long avenue of cottonwoods swept around the bend. Paradise! So full was I on color and light I had little need for dinner. The river didn't release me until dusk.

The last glimmerings of day hung in the western sky. I built a fire. Flames shot into the night sky awash with a zillion stars. I put a log on the fire and closed my eyes. Memories dislodged like driftwood in flood and began to stir. If only I could swim into the current and climb onto a driftwood log—some chimera—where would it take me?

CHAPTER THREE

The more I distrust my memory, the more confused it becomes. It serves me better by chance encounter; I have to solicit it nonchalantly. For if I press, it is stunned; and once it has begun to totter, the more I probe it, the more it gets mixed up and embarrassed. It serves me at its own time, not mine.

— MICHEL DE MONTAIGNE

The Early Years

My father, Harvey Finkelson, was an MP in the army. He was recovering from a gunshot wound in a hospital in Modesto, California, where my mom, Phoebe, was a nurse during the Second World War. Phoebe's biological clock was ticking, and the alarm went off. She wanted children, maybe to help her forget about the war. After a brief romance, they married.

My brother was born in Rochester, Minnesota, where my father had grown up. Soon after, at my grandmother Alice Russell's urging, my parents packed up and moved west, their destination Pasadena, California. But Jackson, Wyoming, was as far west as my father would travel.

Phoebe and Harvey Finkelson.

Elk Springs Ranch, Jackson, Wyoming, 1945.

Harvey found home where the Snake River meanders through the Tetons that rise like granite fangs from the valley floor.

Just south of Jackson, they bought a log home surrounded by five small log cabins on one hundred eighty acres. They named it Elk Springs Ranch. A cabin without plumbing, electricity, or telephone may have been too severe for my mom and her baby, or maybe she just wanted children but was too selfish to accommodate a husband. At any rate, with the spring thaw Phoebe fled, with Terry in her arms and me in her belly, back to her mother in South Pasadena. Harvey knew she was gone for good.

My mother, Phoebe Anne Russell, and sister Elizabeth had a wild childhood. In early photographs my mom has a credulous faraway look, like one who spends much time staring at the moon and dreaming. Raised partly in Jamaica, she was more at home outside than indoors. She spent her summers at Switzer's Camp in California and from there explored the Sierra Madre Mountains. Phoebe first saw the Sierra Nevada at age seven, and at twelve she went on a two-week pack trip through Sequoia National Park. She worked summers in Yosemite, covering all the park within walking distance, and she did her first solo climb of Mount Lyell.

Phoebe was an avid rock climber and president of the rock-climbing section of the Sierra Club. And she was a skier extraordinaire—she remarked once that, like Yosemite, she was famous for her falls. Her devotion to and love of skiing were shared in a biweekly magazine she helped launch, *The Mugelnoos.*

She contributed to the *Sierra Club Bulletin* and in the June 1950 bulletin wrote "The Last Citadel" about a secret place she used to frequent, a hideaway in the Sierras that she shared with us: "Here is a different wealth from that which most men understand. It may not be gained by blasting these rocks, felling these trees, damming this stream; it could be lost in an hour. To try to take this treasure is to lose it. Leave it unchanged: The gain will not be yours alone, but every man's. You who have walked otherwise through all the earth, walk gently here." Phoebe was complex, feisty, independent, and a mystery—even to her sons.

Phoebe Anne Russell in South Pasadena, California.

Phoebe in Yosemite.

Dinner from the Snake River.

My emergence is dimly remembered: The rush, the falling, the light entering my retinas, amorphous soft shapes—the arrival, the awakening, and the *scream*. Without fanfare, my eight-pound, ten-ounce self emerged on July 31, 1946.

It may have been when I crawled down the steps of my grandmother's back porch into the cool Southern California evening and saw the planets and stars for the first time. Or perhaps it was when an owl was trapped in the back porch—his yellow eyes like two fiery suns burning into my soul, while his wings pounded and his talons ripped at the screen window. Or it may have been a few years later when I roamed the pine and eucalyptus groves in the rolling hills with my brother above the Bay in Berkeley, California. It was somewhere back then I was aware of something colossal, something so much larger than myself. Those pine forests stood like great protectors, like divine beings that allowed my imagination to entwine with their roots that connected to a wondrous labyrinthine underworld. I followed. It was a time before socialization tried to beat my anthropomorphic self to a pulp, when I could still feel the spirits of animals, in the natural world that was to become the fundamental source for creativity. A childhood of wandering began at that dimly remembered house on Panoramic Way in the Berkeley hills. Pursued by her mischievous hallucinations, my mother created a peculiar mythology

The brothers, 1946.

In the Berkeley Hills, California, 1951.

A life that sets all things in rhyme. The Sierras, California, 1952.

that manifested in her portraying our father as anything from a wicked ogre to a winged phantom. Fleeing from her imagination, we moved from here to there and back again for the next twelve years. From the Berkeley hills we moved down into the city. Terry and I rode bicycles to every corner of the county—to the towering monument at the Campanile at the University of California. There, we took the elevator to the top and watched the tiny ant-people making their way to class, just as my brother would in another decade.

With her Leica 35mm camera, Phoebe documented anything and everything we did outdoors, even the stiff little bodies of bluegill I caught at nearby Lake Temescal. Her Leica captured Terry and me on our first pack trip into the high country of the Sierra Nevada, when we were hardly old enough to know one end of a horse from the other. Her photographs swelled the pages of her Sierra Nevada album. Under a photograph of my brother sleeping in a meadow by a river, she wrote these words by Christopher Morley: "And Life, that sets all things to rhyme, May make you poet, too, in time—But there were days, O tender elf, When you were Poetry itself!"

When I wanted to play the banjo and guitar, Phoebe bought the instruments and found the teacher. When I wanted to be an octopus for Halloween, she sewed an elaborate costume with moving tentacles, operated by a maze of ropes and pulleys. The outfit made quite a hit with the girls, who were curious how I was able to move my tentacles with such finesse.

On our first trips to Yosemite in the mid-'50s, we tormented our mother when we disappeared up the long granite cracks by Half Dome. Under the roof of the sky, we camped in the deserts of Death Valley and on the beaches of Point Reyes National Seashore. In the redwood groves of Northern California, Terry and I lost track of the number of arm lengths encircling these giants. Arching backward, I saw branches disappear in the fog. This was a time when my brother and I still believed that some treetops actually reached to touch the stars.

In our '48 Pontiac coupe, we burned down the road from Berkeley to Pasadena, visiting family. At dawn we rolled down Highway 101, passed the Soledad Mission, cut east at Paso Robles on Highway 46 through Lost Hills and Wasco, joined Highway 99, then streaked down the San Joaquin Valley through Bakersfield. The Pontiac labored over Grapevine Pass and rolled into the driveway of our grandmother Alice's house—a solid place providing continuity in our transient young lives.

The old brown-shingled house had a screened-in back porch where Terry and I slept. Each night without fail, our grandmother brought glasses of ice water and gave us big wet grandmother kisses that sent us squirming under the covers. In the morning the forlorn notes of the

Packing into the Sierras.

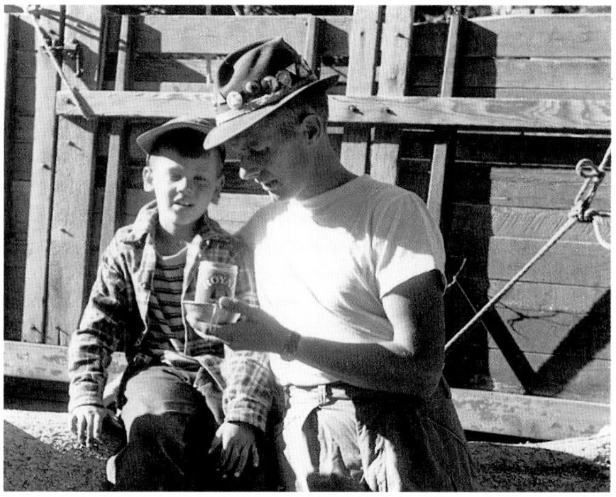

Terry with David Brower.

doves ushered in a new day, their song mingled with the fog that bridged the gap between dream and day.

Alice weighed less than one hundred pounds, never learned to drive, and wore high-top black leather shoes that she shuffled along the hardwood floors. She would nurse her morning cup of black coffee while reading the *Los Angeles Times,* then rummage through the pill drawer for the medications that kept her heart pumping.

I had seen my grandfather Bert Russell only in pictures—a handsome man with a boyish face in a three-piece suit. Arthritis deformans crippled him, and rather than cause his family to suffer, he left, alone, for Washington, D.C., checked himself into a sanitarium, disposed of his few belongings, and wrote the family "serene and loving letters." With swollen and painful hands he managed to complete the final drafts of two original astronomical theories, containing beautiful and intricate drawings; these he left to his daughters. He then took poison and died.

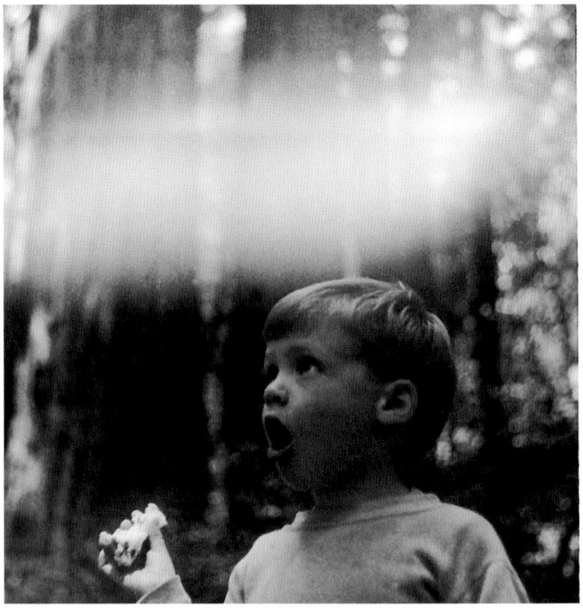

"The light" and the wonder.

The author as octopus.

The magic of books.

Bert's spirit may have been lingering outside that old brown-shingled house where Terry would—if I'd been harassing him—pin me to the ground with his knees, and while glaring down at me, grind his knuckles into my jaw and slowly—ever so slowly—drool on my face. Brotherly love, I suppose, but it drove me nuts. I was faster than he was, so when I wiggled free, Terry could only wish he could catch me. On the lawn we'd engage in open warfare with water pistols and garden hoses, fights that wouldn't always end pleasantly, while we eagerly waited for the music of the Good Humor Man's ice-cream truck, reminding us of what was important.

What was even more important than ice cream was spending time in my Aunt Elizabeth's studio. She and her husband Max lived in the Altadena foothills in a

Brotherly love.

rambling house called Sage Hill. In her studio I watched her paint in oils, drawn to her quiet, aloof ways. Canvases lined the wall in her studio. Her table was covered with lithographic stones. Her print "Nameless Errand" depicts an empty buggy pulled by a single black horse, trotting through a ghost town somewhere in the Mojave Desert. "Spook Town" shows a night scene in which a single light illuminates through a drawn curtain, and a black cat darts across the street. Others were titled "Where Lost Years Are," "Terminal Vision," and "Cloud Ocean."

She had no patience for small talk, was bored at parties, and thought solitude an addictive drug. Death meant nothing to her, but she was fearful of what she called "the desert"—a meaningless place without boundaries, feelings, or direction that she referred to as a "continuum of time's pace." She recoiled at the thought of publicity and recorded her inward path in a little black book on whose cover she scrawled, "This is a very private book; please respect it until I am dead." She concluded that her work was not really unique and was only

'48 Pontiac coupe.

Grandparents Bert and Alice Russell.

Aunt Elizabeth at work.

good material for a psychoanalyst. The fact is, she remains one of the most unrecognized and gifted Western landscape painters of her generation—a sort of Georgia O'Keeffe who never found her Alfred Stieglitz.

In her studio were stacks of books, some in glass cabinets with sliding doors. I'd thumb through volumes of Edward Weston's photographs, Michelangelo's paintings, and Van Gogh's work, but I was especially drawn to the work of Hieronymus Bosch and Max Ernst. Moss, lichen, and twisted roots of bristlecone pine lay next to slabs of thinly cut dinosaur bone and petrified wood that leaned against the windows, inviting light to illuminate them.

Brothers in studio.

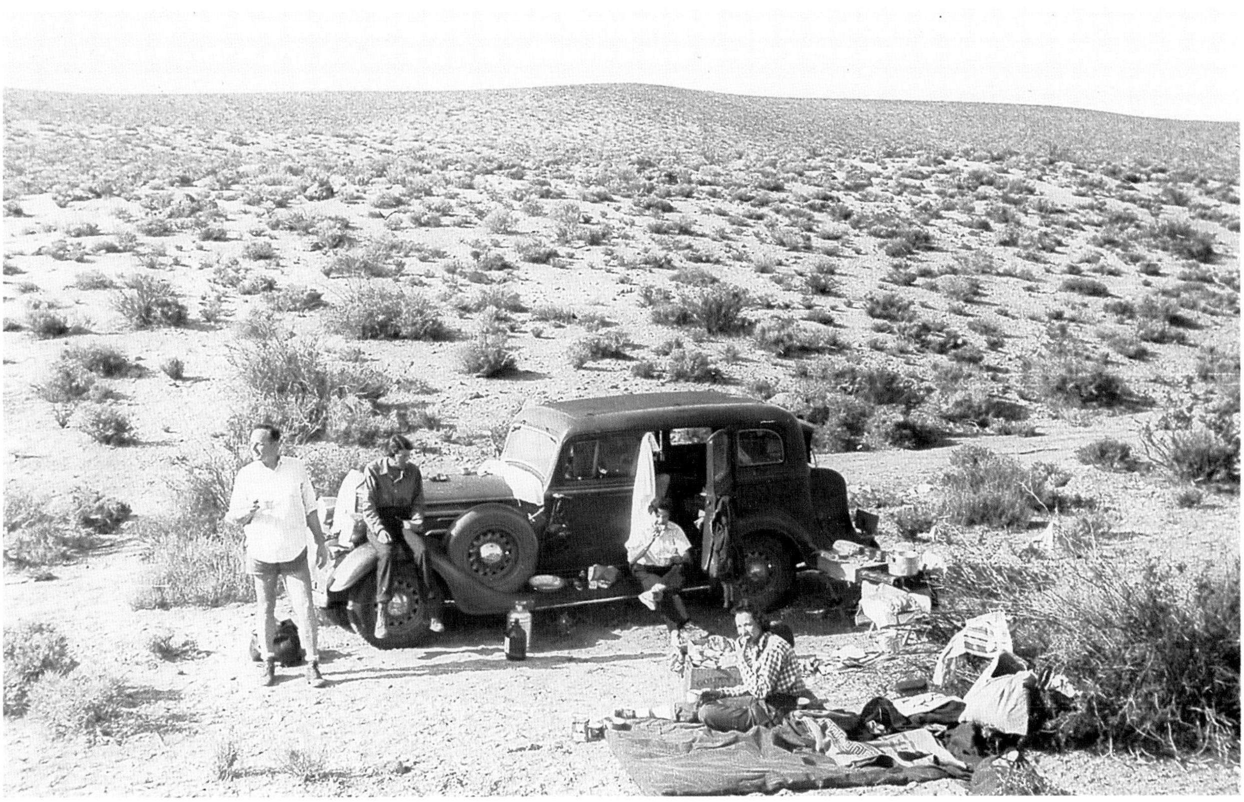

Car camping, Mojave Desert, 1930s.

Uncle Max was a mystery.

Our aunt surrendered a corner of her studio to us, where we fooled around with paint and clay. We were of an age when the subconscious flowed freely and uninterrupted from the mind to the hand holding the paintbrush—those early years of expression before intellect subdues instinct. She teasingly spoke of gnomes and goblins and such that hide out in cavernous interiors of pine roots, in solitude, in dim light, in cool quiet, seen only by believers.

Elizabeth married Max Lewis, most notably remembered for his ability to eat an entire chicken (bone and all), for patenting a vitamin supplement called "Vital," for crushing several of my grandmother's ribs while giving her a hug, and for founding the company Microdot, which made electronic components for the emerging space program.

In their home at Sage Hill hung paintings by Maynard Dixon and sketches by

Richmond–San Rafael Bridge, California, 1954.

Diego Rivera and Conrad Buff. Buff's large canvases of the Southwest landscape, painted with thousands of tiny brush strokes, captured its distance and space as seen through the picture windows overlooking the rolling foothills of Altadena. Beneath the windows, on old Navajo rugs, Terry and I played chess, and he would always win, perhaps because my mind wandered through the intricate designs of the rugs with their soft shades of the desert.

In the afternoon we followed our aunt down to the barn. Her horses Pearl and Triggs were good company. While Elizabeth hitched up her fastest horse, Witch, for a buggy ride, my brother and I played with Pearl's soft mouth. We leaned over the corral fence and fed Camel cigarettes to the sheep at the risk of losing our fingers. Elizabeth disappeared in the dust, seeming to ride into the clouds billowing up over the mountains. She left behind in the dust the indelible imprint of one who had an intrinsic knowledge for what lay beyond the world of man. I admired her for her love of books, her talent as a painter, her passion for wilderness; for her independence and craving for solitude.

Our vacations were cut short when Phoebe felt the proximity of one of her phantoms, which were, more often than not, a father hot on our trail. We loaded up the Pontiac and headed back over

Elizabeth hitching Witch.

Grapevine Pass, down into the San Joaquin Valley on that long, dead-level road, an endless horizontal plane that seemed to radiate forever out in all directions. To the west lay the dark, brooding outline of the Coast Range, and to the east loomed the "Range of Light," the luminous blue-and-white ramparts of the Sierra Nevada. I was learning math by counting the tires on the semi-trucks as we blew by them and learning how to read from the Burma Shave signs on Highway 101.

We arrived in Berkeley before school began to move our meager belongings into a cramped apartment on College Avenue. I'd walk into the starry night and stare down the centerline of the street, hoping to catch a glimpse of my phantom father flying by or of our neighbor's Oldsmobile with its chrome hood ornament—an emblem of the world that reflected in the streetlights. The West was a big place then, and every fiber of my being ached to see it.

Chapter Four

I can't say I was ever lost, but I was bewildered once for three days.

— Daniel Boone

Where Mountain Meets Desert

From a mountain of photo albums, I take one from the shelf that offers clues to when Terry and I began a life on the loose. I blow off dust, revealing "The Santa Rosa Mountains January 1944–1954." I open to the title page with a picture of San Jacinto and San Gorgonio Mountains taken from Santa Rosa. A quote by Hart Crane reads, "Yes, tall, inseparably, our days pass sunward."

It was summer, 1954. We would spend the better part of the next two years in the deserts of Southern California and in the Santa Rosa Mountains. This rugged range was remote compared with the more formidable peaks to the northwest in the San Jacinto Mountains—San Gorgonio Peak, San Jacinto, and Baldy. It was a place of silence—a landscape forever reinventing itself with the subtleties of changing light.

Max and Elizabeth bought eighty acres of land in the Santa Rosa Mountains and renovated a small cabin they called Nightingale, which was home, at least for a little while. We arrived in a thunderstorm. At the porch steps, Phoebe's screams stopped me cold. She ran toward

Santa Rosa String Band.

me, shovel in hand. A rattlesnake under the back porch step was coiled and ready to strike. A decisive blow, and the rattlesnake lost his head. I couldn't sleep that night, haunted by writhing snakes, and at dawn went outside and found his body in knots. His headless body lunged toward my hand. Terror mingled with fascination, awakened an awareness of the mystery. Nature had begun to supply a cunning alphabet, selecting and combining letters as she pleased. Words like beauty, adventure, and spirit were what this summer was all about.

My mom turned the event into an epic poem immortalizing her courage:

Old snake he crawled back
towards his bed,

"Better watch out!" those rattles
said.

A shovel smashed down behind
his head,

And mister snake was as good
as dead.

His fangs dripping with poison,
old snake fought back.

But Phoebe's iron nerves could
never crack.

With all the power her punch
could pack

She smashed in his head with
a deadly whack.

Against the backdrop of high-desert mountain crags, our cabin nestled in the shadows of ponderosa pines. We had no electricity, and the refrigerator was a wooden box covered with burlap perched on two-by-four legs. As long as the burlap was kept wet and the wind blew, it worked. The fireplace was large enough to walk into, and a Victrola record player scratched songs like "Frankie and Johnny were lovers, and lordy, lordy, how they

The Santa Rosa cabin. Southern California, 1954.

could love." We made our own music too—my brother played the cello, my aunt the guitar, I doubled on the recorder and drum, and my mom played the autoharp. We were the fabulous Santa Rosa String Band. The racket drove game deep into the brush, and Max followed.

Terry and I were up at the crack for our first mountain ascent—Toro Peak. As I reached the cabin door, I was reminded that in the past year I had narrowly escaped death when my wagon sped out of control beneath the wheels of an oncoming car, that I had been swept out to sea in a riptide at Huntington Beach in California, that I fractured my wrist, and had to be rescued in the dark when Terry and I rode our bikes to the far horizon. Caution was not yet a word offered to us in nature's "cunning alphabet." We bolted out the door.

We found a game trail that led to Toro Peak. Watching from the 8,700-foot summit, we saw fog rising from the desert far below, snaking its way up the precipitous ravines that slash the north slope of the mountain, engulfing the cedar, white fir, and sugar pine. A mosaic of light and color swept across the desert floor. The wildness struck a chord that has resonated since. We had found our church; the sermon was omnipresent and omnipotent. Our church was filled with light and joy, not redemption and eternal damnation. No banal heaven with its silly saints. No golden women and apple trees, but the here and now, the idyllic and corporeal

Toro Peak summit.

The earth shook and the sky burned.

real earth on which we stood. Paradise! We felt the force that blew through the trees; we saw it in the eyes of the deer we surprised; it was in the creeks we passed. Elizabeth wrote "Toro At Dawn":

> *Bright morning star has found me on*
> *the mountaintop alone, I've climbed*
> *up the stairs of thunder and seized*
> *from the eagles their throne.*
>
> *Three hundred miles lie spellbound*
> *and gauzy under the haze.*
>
> *The secret breezes are bringing attar*
> *of pine boughs and sage.*
>
> *Oh where is the world that will focus*
> *the dream and the real into one?*
>
> *The lazy earth rotates a little, and over*
> *the rim comes the sun.*

That day on the mountain, my world came into focus when the dream became real, and the real seemed a dream. Terry and I found the cabin too small, its air too musty, and the family too loud, so we spent most of the summer camping in the woods. We explored all directions—got lost, went hungry, and got caught in thunderstorms. The music of the pines was a melody the Santa Rosa String Band could never play, and the sweet vanilla aroma from the bark of the ponderosa was our elixir. We climbed the smooth granite boulders and hoarded rocks glittering with mica that we believed was gold. But food shortages brought us back to the cabin, where at dinner we devoured meat like true carnivores. We were rapidly becoming more than our mother could handle and may well have contributed to her aging prematurely.

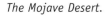

The Mojave Desert.

Toward the end of summer the monsoons arrived, and I discovered more words from nature's cunning alphabet—the power of storms. The earth shook and the sky burned. Lightning slashed into two yellow pines six hundred feet from the cabin, starting a blazing fire, with flames twenty-five feet high shooting up from the base of the trees. The *Pasadena Star News* reported:

> *With the nearest telephone an hour away and no other residents atop the mountain, the two women and boys grabbed shovels, brooms, and water pails, and raced to battle the flames. They fought the flames during the evening hours and through the night. By morning the blaze had been knocked down and was under control. Rangers credited the vacationers with saving the area from a serious forest fire.*

As I revisited Elizabeth's album, our time on the mountain came to life:

> *Got stuck in the truck below mouth of Martinez canyon, flat tire, no spare . . . threw ourselves in muddy Palm Canyon stream with clothes on, also drank the water . . . took horses 4 miles from end of road, a wonderful gallop in the evening light, below a nearly new moon over Santa Rosa. . . . We made a leisurely camp, climate is wonderful, spring water is divine, mosquitoes are b-29's . . . bed at dark. Coyote seen near camp early A.M. I was woozy from falling off a tree while getting moss yesterday . . . we had a leisurely brunch of flapjacks . . . left in the rain, and just barely got down off the mountain . . . it was hair-raising.*

The characters came and went that summer, but none were etched in my mind more than a certain Steve Ragsdale, a prospector turned preacher. I still see his long flowing white beard and his hair tucked under his silver-gray Stetson. He put the fear of God in me. His pale blue eyes looked through and beyond Terry and me, and he declared, as if he were in direct communion with Jesus Christ Himself, "I can see God in those kids' eyes."

What put the fear of God in Phoebe was her irreconcilable dilemma of how to deal with our father. She sensed him near. My uncle accompanied her on long walks to calm her, to chase away her apparitions. Where would we move next? We packed the Pontiac and headed for one of my uncle's holdings to the north on the other side of Gorgonio Peak—the Crawford Ranch in Lucerne Valley. It was more "out in the middle of nowhere" than I could possibly have imagined.

I slept during the long school-bus ride from Lucerne Valley to the ranch. Terry gave me a sharp poke in the ribs. "Wake up; we're home." Home? As much as anywhere was home in the '50s. The bus rolled to a stop. We were the last kids off and still had a half-mile to go. The Crawford Ranch was seventy-five miles east of Los Angeles, off the highway linking Victorville and Lucerne Valley. It was a land of dry lakes, dust storms, and the bony, desolate peaks of the Granite Mountains with the names Mount Ord, Fry, and Stoddard.

When I knew Max was coming to visit, I ran out on the dirt track to greet him, waiting for the rumble of his V-8

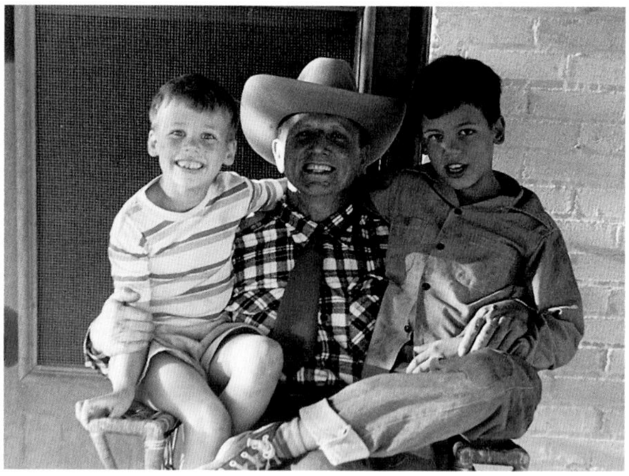

Uncle Max and nephews at the Crawford Ranch.

Firepower Chrysler Imperial as he came roaring back into our lives. He gave his nephews his usual rib-crunching hug and launched us into the air. Like persons in exile we devoured his boxes of delicatessen goodies, like pickled frog legs, European pastries, snails, halvah, and Swiss chocolate.

I watched Max and Phoebe—their heads down, lost in thought and conversation—walk slowly off and disappear into the desert. I had grown accustomed to it. Perhaps they spoke of Terry and me, of life, maybe whether she was happy living so far from town—grown-up stuff. Then Max would vanish as he had come, in a dust cloud. We'd watch his car until it was a speck melting into the horizon, not sure if his coming had been a dream or an awakening.

The elementary school in Lucerne Valley was small. I had the distinction of being the only boy in the third grade. But my classes were held out in the open. With meat tied to the end of a string, I learned

how to catch crawdads in the irrigation ditches that brought water to Max's alfalfa fields. I learned how to survive dust storms when caught out in the open. We explored abandoned mines, built pens for our tortoises and horned toads, made a bow with arrows, and hunted jackrabbits. In a mirage, Terry's image would distort, disappear, and reappear while great cities rose and then merged with sand. Tumbleweeds rolled and slammed against the barbed-wire fences, where they remained until dust claimed them. Amorphous clouds hung above the peaks with no intention of bringing rain. My brother and I became so much a part of that landscape, we could have dissolved into a mirage and never returned.

Coaxing memory to dislodge pearls that explain past events, I wonder if Phoebe was running from the mischievous fantasies that tormented her, or maybe she was a malcontented misanthrope. At any rate, Terry and I were on our own trail that summer, oblivious to her inner workings. We had found in wilderness a continuum, something solid that would prove a touchstone—a foundation for our adventures that would culminate in writing *On the Loose*. When I saw that faraway look darken my mother's face, I knew it was time to move on. We loaded the Pontiac coupe, locked the door at the Crawford Ranch, and headed back to Berkeley—never to return.

C h a p t e r   F i v e

What is life but a series of inspired follies?

— George Bernard Shaw

Mosquito Hell Camp

A rattlesnake's nostrils are so sophisticated that the snake can sense a change in one degree of temperature from thirty feet away, and though earless, it can feel vibrations from a hundred yards away. It is so deadly that its head, when severed, can still bare its fangs and bite. After a rattlesnake injects the venom, it is able to track its prey, using its tongue to transport microscopic particles from the environment to the roof of its mouth.

On an early-morning walk across from Moon Bottom, I thrashed through a dense grove of cottonwoods and tamarisk and stepped directly on a midget faded rattlesnake that was deep in rattlesnake dreams. I lurched one way and the snake slithered the other. Saturated with adrenaline, I watched it disappear into the brush. There was no need for coffee that morning. The stage was set for a

day of light and dark and the unpredictable.

I broke through a wall of brush and began walking up a long ramp that I hoped would take me to the canyon rim. I picked my way through desert primrose that had bloomed during the night and offered their fragile, paper-thin petals to the new day. The flowers would wither by noon. I pressed my nose into the heart of them, where dozens of red spiders the size of pinheads climbed over one another, deep in pollen.

I left the main drainage and crunched onward toward the rim. I followed the tracks of deer and bighorn sheep and noticed where they had struggled in the mud, up through a notch in the cliff. They knew this was the only route to the rim, and I trusted their wisdom. The sun melted me as I followed one false summit after another.

The bone-white tips of an enormous pair of elk antlers marked the summit. Partly buried in the sand, they lay symmetrically parted like the pages of a book. I read the story of an elk's life of wanderings by their polished-smooth tips and their markings. I sat between them and contemplated packing them back to the boat but resisted the temptation even to touch them. Their beauty lay in where they were on this high plateau. Away from the rim in the junipers, I found more antlers and a snake's skin wrapped delicately around a boulder—a place to let go. This would be a good place to shed my skin, to let my antlers fall, to cut loose the entanglements of life, and live with the knowledge of the datura plant, which creates its flower from the most parched and barren soil and blooms for only a single night.

I walked to a point where boulders balanced precariously on the rim's edge, rocking one that weighed several tons and that rumbled like thunder from the heart of the earth. They defied gravity and were poised to tumble through five hundred feet of space. I sat down and assimilated the 360-degree panorama. Far below, slices of river appeared and disappeared through a maze of canyons, the country so interwoven it was nearly impossible to tell in which direction the river was flowing. I spent a good part of the afternoon wandering through the junipers, where I found rusted artifacts of a cowboy camp. In the American tradition, these good old boys let go too—their .25-.35 and .44 caliber brass casings littered the ground among bits of charcoal and broken purple glass.

Long shadows reminded me the sun was slipping toward the western horizon, and I began the long descent to the river. Back in the main drainage I startled a couple of western whiptail lizards. The male had immobilized the female's front legs in his jaws. She seemed blasé about the whole affair until a beetle appeared from a crack. Then, bang! She nabbed him. Seeming oblivious to her partner's advances, she maneuvered the insect until its kicking legs were pointed down her throat; then it simply walked into her stomach. She closed her eyes. She had just accumulated enough sperm to allow her to produce young for a year and had enjoyed a gourmet meal, all in a matter of five minutes. Life was good for this whiptail, or so it seemed.

Pages are windows, and windows are to see through.

The closer I got to the river, the thicker their swarms—the Green River mosquito is legendary and has driven more than one person to the brink of madness. I broke camp and headed downstream with the illusion that I could escape them.

What I couldn't escape was *On the Loose.* Being on the Green flooded me with memories of my brother that prompted me to revisit our book. I opened to the title page and noted a prophetic quotation by George Bernard Shaw that had marked my path more than Terry could have possibly imagined: "What is life but a series of inspired

Chasing rainbows below Venado Peak.

follies?" My brother would have been dumbfounded had he known the follies his younger brother would encounter, especially during the decade of the '70s. I recalled how, on my eighty-acre piece of land in the Sangre de Cristos of northern New Mexico, I began a building project that after more than thirty years remains unfinished.

I knew nothing about construction and blindly commenced to throw up a shelter in the winter of 1970 with just a chain saw, a hammer, spikes, and a few crude tools. I camped in the center of my octagonal shell, and when November arrived the roof was only half complete and the snow piled up in the roofless part of the house. I crawled out of my sleeping bag, forced my feet into frozen boots, built a bonfire, put a scratchy old 78-rpm record on my Brunswick Victrola, shoveled the snow out of the room, and began another day of building. But I neglected to pour a foundation, so after a few years the nine monolithic pine trees I had cut to mark the corners and center of the room had rotted. I had to jack up the corners and pour a foundation.

The homestead. New Mexico, circa 1969.

I knew nothing about relationships. Linda—whom I had met at UC Cal—foolishly turned down a scholarship to study classical piano in Europe and moved in with me. She courageously endured the hardships on the mountain, possibly supported by the strength and guidance she received from her great-grandfather Geronimo's concho belt, which she placed under her pillow at night. I respected its power. Her father Frank visited. His first comment was that it would be easy to hold off an army from the rocky crags above my house. Contrary to folklore and songs, Geronimo didn't drive a Cadillac, but a Buick, as did Frank. He didn't stay long. What passed through his mind while he slowly—ever so slowly—added a quart of oil to his Buick the morning he left remains a mystery.

When Linda could endure me no more, she slipped away in the night, only returning to claim her belt, her loom, and her Steinway piano.

I knew nothing about horses. I tried raising Appaloosas, even though there was no pasture on my eighty acres of scrub oak and rocks. One particularly obstinate horse that I was breaking broke me. I was thrown, trampled, and humbled. Fractures were common as my

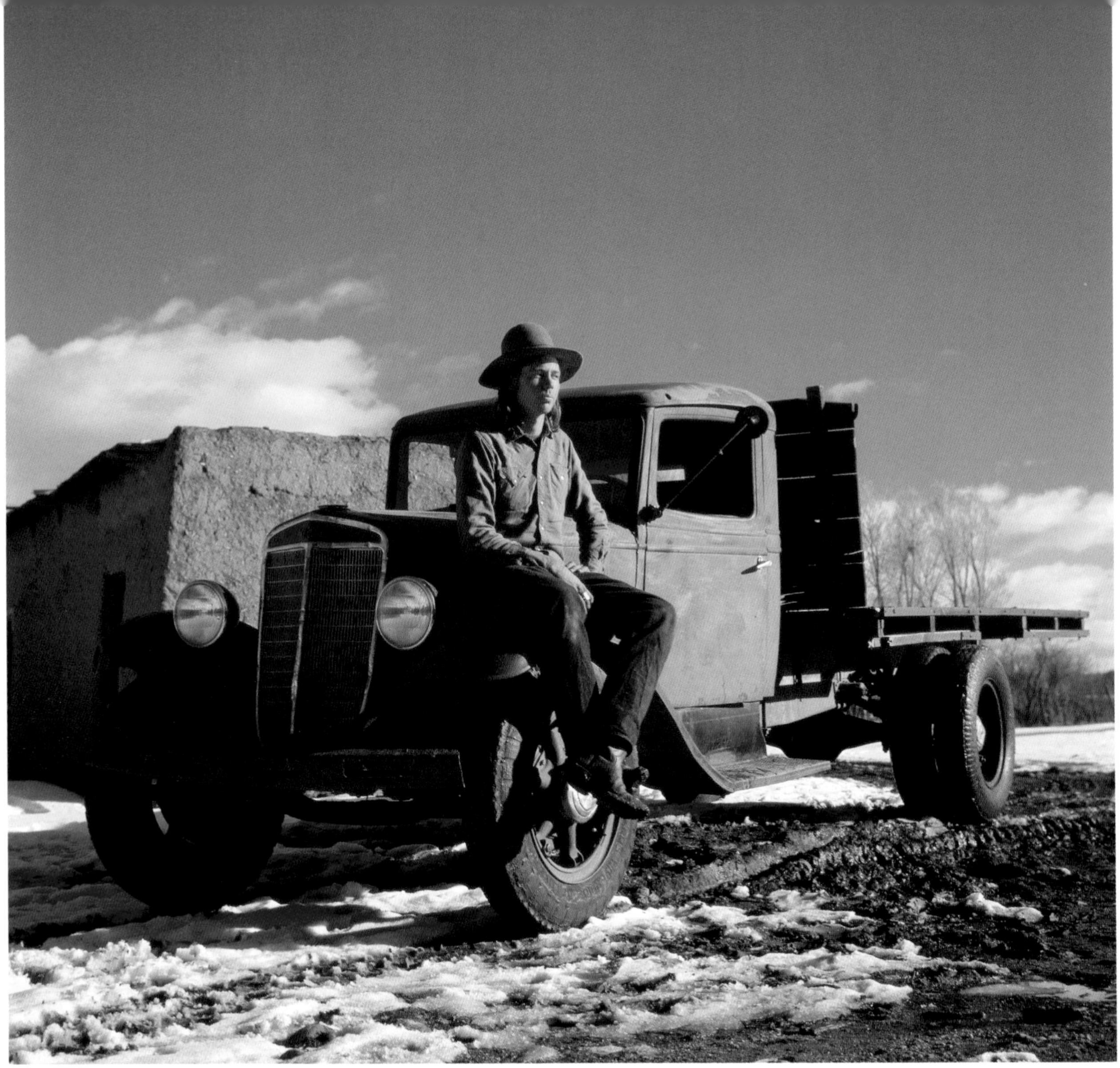

J. Martinez Ranch, Peñasco, New Mexico, 1968.

dreams of horses evaporated. The final straw of my quixotic business was when a couple of horses broke through the fence, got out on the highway, and were run over. My last brood mare, Sugar Blues, gave me no colts and I sold her.

This series of follies pursued me to Mexico, where I spent winters. What remained of my brother's Land Rover took me there. The canvas top was torn to shreds, and sections of the front fenders flapped in the wind. On one occasion, my departure was delayed when, on a subzero morning, I built a fire under the oil pan that got a little out of hand and burned most of the electrical wiring. While driving down the beach outside Escondido, I bogged down in sand and tore up the rear differential. I disconnected the drive shaft and limped back to the states on

Linda in the Badlands of South Dakota, 1971.

the front two wheels. At the border crossing in Nogales, I was forced to pour two gallons of perfectly good Oaxacan mezcal down the toilet. Then I was pulled over for driving in an erratic manner, accused of being an illegal alien and of stealing the Rover. When I made it home, I parked the old war pony and eventually traded it for an Edward Weston photograph and a chain saw.

The wind fluttered the pages of *On the Loose* to a photograph of Stevens Arch taken in the canyon country of the Escalante. The accompanying caption read, "A man is never lost, he has only been mislaid." These lines took on new meaning in the late '60s and '70s and begged for a new interpretation. Man was mislaid in a big way that Terry could never have imagined and that challenged the book's and my ideological innocence. On April 4, 1968, the world lost Martin Luther King, and the assassination of Robert Kennedy followed two months later. I could never return to the pristine arch Terry and I had come upon up Stevens Canyon. And as the war in Vietnam ground down, a lot of soldiers returning home were lost, betrayed, and adrift in a country divided. The disenfranchised have always been lost and always will be, and mislaid beyond redemption. In the context of the times, these lines from *On the Loose* seem merely prophetic rather than philosophical. The truth was that the only times my brother and I were lost and mislaid were when we didn't have gas money to get out of town and into wilderness, when our truck broke down, or when school interrupted our adventures.

But now I lived in wilderness; I no longer ventured in and out of it as Terry and I had done. The change was a challenge, especially since I lived a solitary ascetic life and had no mentor or brother to lead the way down the trail. I had to reinvent myself and build a new life. By the end of the '70s, my octagonal abode had a floor and was insulated, but it would be another ten years before there was wiring and the walls were plastered. The house seemed to grow organically on its own schedule, not mine. I no longer stacked mountains of firewood inside by the stove, patented in 1868 and brought across the country by wagon.

And I had discovered the carpenter's level, and I had a few power tools and even a couple of electrical outlets connected to a gasoline generator that was always breaking down. I started building a hexagonal room that would evolve into a kitchen. But through the whine of the power tools, I heard the distant roar of rapids. The Colorado River through the Grand Canyon was calling and would be my other home for the next two decades.

The mosquitoes were a nightmare on the water, but when I stopped to camp at mile 104 they were swarming. In dense sheets they blew by, pelting the boat; the high-pitched sound of their wings was like the screams from an asylum. And when I hopped on shore they were ready for me, and immediately clouds of them started to feed. It was dinnertime and I was the main course.

The mosquito causes more human suffering than any other organism, and more than a million people a year die from the deadly diseases these insects carry. West Nile virus arrived in the Western Hemisphere at the end of the millennium as the insect enlarges its range of misery and death. It's only the female that requires a protein blood meal for egg production; the male prefers flower nectar. Mosquito "boats" passed on the water, where females had laid three hundred eggs at a time. Each female can produce three thousand young during her two-week lifetime.

The receding waters of the Green left ponds of stagnant water, where mosquitoes reproduced in numbers unimaginable by those who haven't witnessed them firsthand. Against these odds I didn't have a chance. I imagined that the combined weight of the mosquitoes along the Green River at this time of year was greater than the weight of all humankind.

Determined to finish my beverage and enjoy the evening, I sat on the deck of the boat, flyswatter in hand, wearing long pants and a long-sleeved shirt and drenched in repellents that didn't work.

1965 Land Rover model 109.

I swatted mercilessly at the mosquitoes. The bloated insects rolled into the footwell of the boat, where I finished them off, their blood-filled bodies bursting like ripe grapes. It was not a pretty sight. Others flew off so drunk on blood they could hardly navigate.

I cooked a quick meal and made a dash for the tent, food in hand, with the *zancudos* in hot pursuit. I zipped the netting, and immediately the mesh was darkened by thousands of them, now driven to hysteria by the smell of my dinner. The tent was unbearably hot. My clothes were covered with blood and reeked of insect repellent and sweat. That night, in a restless sleep, I dreamed of Mexico, old Land Rovers, and mosquitoes with heads the size of bowling balls, drilling their way through the tent lining as I lay there, unable to move or defend myself.

Dean Brimhall caught in a flood on the Fremont River.

peach, pear, mulberry, and plum trees was legendary. One of the realities of life in Fruita was that the river that brought life to the land sometimes washed away entire orchards, along with pigs and houses, and buried farmland in foot-deep silt.

Max and Elizabeth bought an orchard along Sulphur Creek in 1954, planning to move there. But cancer snatched Max, and our aunt remarried a gent named Dick Sprang. They built a house and operated a modest fruit business, which they aptly called Ripple Rock Ranch. Phoebe, Terry, and I spent the summer of 1958 mingling with Fruita's eccentric inhabitants and merging with the slickrock wilderness surrounding the park.

Max left me a bucket of silver dollars for the sole purpose of buying a horse. Joe was no thoroughbred—just a worn-out old cow pony that a local film crew had ridden nearly to death. I rode him along Sulphur Creek—past the old cottonwood tree where the locals used to gather to get their mail before there was a post office; past the schoolhouse built in 1896 that served as a place of worship, as well as a place for dances and the town hall; past petroglyph panels of the Fremont Indians—and then followed the trail along the Fremont River. In a few years, the gorge would be gutted by State Highway 24, which would claw its way through thirty miles of wilderness to the town of Hanksville.

I was learning that in the canyon country, the sky could be blue above, but on a distant mesa a thunderstorm could be raging. Floodwater, filthy with desire and urgency, cascaded over the cliff wall and down into the Fremont River. Entire juniper trees and house-size boulders thundered down cliffs. Debris tumbled in a maelstrom of thick, churning, orange water. My horse had seen it all before and was more concerned about the grain back at the barn and getting me off his back, but I had this peculiar desire to put a boat into the foaming torrent and see where it would take me.

I brushed Joe, grained him, and headed back to the house but made the mistake of walking by my uncle's studio windows.

Our aunt preferred the company of horses.

Dick was hard at work at his drafting table, and gave me the evil eye. My uncle was tall and solidly built, with large pale-blue eyes like moons that swam in his head and an immense forehead that reflected the sun. Like many of that generation, he wouldn't be caught dead wearing anything but khaki pants and shirts.

Although Dick once said that my Aunt Elizabeth was "a far better and noted artist than I ever was," he was to become a legend drawing *Batman* and *Superman* comics. Dick drew the characters in such a bold and exciting way that he overshadowed the dozens of artists who tried to imitate him. Nobody ever drew a more sinister Riddler or a more expressive and convincing Batman.

During the '30s and '40s, Dick lived in New York City, made connections, was hired on by DC Comics, and for two decades turned out some of the finest comic-book art ever created. At dawn Dick would disappear into his studio, with a cup of coffee to drown the Jim Beam whiskey he'd had the night before. A good workday for Dick was to complete a page of the strip. His talent was too valuable to spend inking, so he sent his pencil work off to ink-master Charles Paris in New York.

I was curious to watch Dick at work, but made my second mistake of approaching him from behind, where he sat trancelike at his drafting table, waiting for Batman to materialize. Dick

Dick Sprang was a historian, artist, and misanthrope.

cut loose a curse, and I ducked a book that whizzed over my head. In his old woody station wagon, my uncle mysteriously came and went. I wouldn't have been surprised to see him flying over the ranch with Lois Lane. A twelve-year-old's imagination can be very active, especially when I watched him clean and oil the Colt .45 he kept on the dresser.

If I couldn't watch Dick work, at least I had his stack of *Batman* and *Superman* comic books. In the center of the pile I came upon a *Playboy* magazine, and for the first time, for better or worse, I became familiar with female anatomy.

Our uncle's knowledge of the West was considerable, and his book collection was unparalleled in Wayne County, Utah. After dinner, with whiskey for dessert, he became animated and launched into long discourses on whatever topic popped into his head—Colorado River lore, life in New York City in the '30s (and how it had gone to hell since), or how the Mormons were dangerous. He also made a good case for leaving Capitol Reef as a national monument, saying that if it became a national park it would be ruined.

Dick knew every mile of Glen Canyon intimately—every placer claim, every sandbar, every trail, the name of every cowboy who rode the trails, and even the names of their horses.

Our uncle's eccentric friends who visited included surrealist painter Max Ernst, who fled Europe after World War II and found refuge in Sedona, Arizona. Sprang wrote: "Max would ask me how I ever drew all those little panels so well, and I told him I did it the same way he slammed a paint roller across a canvas and sold it for $75,000. He would roar with laughter and grab me around the shoulders in a big European hug. We knew the score."

Like brilliant artists who suffer from a fire within, Dick could be an aloof nihilist one minute and a gregarious entertainer the next. He moved ghostlike through life—secretive and anonymous. He was a mulish and stubborn man who never forgave or forgot. Still, my difficult uncle's love of rivers and the canyon country of southeast Utah, his

Aunt Elizabeth in Glen Canyon.

knowledge of the West, his talent as an artist and calligrapher, and his aloof independence rubbed off on us. Dick was in the shadows, watching, while we wrote *On the Loose.*

Terry and I befriended one of the hired hands and worked in the orchards loading fruit on a flatbed truck to take to Richfield. I careened through the orchards on a Ferguson tractor, snatching succulent peaches, apples, pears, and apricots.

We had the dismal task of removing mashed apricots from the driveway and quickly learned the difference between a Moorpark and a Sweet Pit apricot. We cranked a machine that turned apricots into slush. We drank it by the gallon, put it on ice cream, and bottled it. At night I dreamed of apricots. On days off, Terry and I hiked down to where Sulphur Creek joined the Fremont River and disappeared into the gorge, where it joined Muddy Creek, becoming the Dirty Devil,

Fruita once "blossomed like a rose."

Doc A. L. Inglesby in Glen Canyon.

eventually combining its silty waters with the Colorado River. The peculiar names of these rivers tugged at my imagination.

Days in ecstasy passed at our favorite swimming hole, where we stretched out on the hot rocks like two chuckwallas, Terry lost in a book and I in a dream. At Capitol Reef Lodge we watched slide shows on geological wonders like Goblin Valley or Glen Canyon. When the lights went out the bats flew in. This was cause for more excitement than the slides generated, especially when bats were caught in a fishnet.

World War II brought electricity, and telephones finally arrived in 1962. A trickling of newcomers began to appear after the war. Although Fruita's population never grew much beyond ten families, the word was out—Fruita had been "discovered." One character in this new wave of outsiders was Dr. Arthur Leroy Inglesby.

Doc was short and stocky, wore thick glasses, chomped on the tail end of a cigar, and wore overalls caked with grease. At the entrance of his home were two signs. One read "Fruita, Elevation 5416." It had arrows that pointed in two directions; one pointed to "Hanksville, 45 miles" and the other to "Torrey, 12 miles." The second sign read "A. L. Inglesby, Rocks and Minerals." Vines and trees obscured his house, constructed from logs and chunks of petrified wood, from the road. Slabs of ripple-marked sandstone were bolted together and formed a fence that enclosed the rich green of his property. He rented out a couple of cabins, mainly to fellow rock hounds.

Inglesby invited us in for lunch. In his musty bedroom a soft tawny light filtered in through the curtain, casting an amber glow on his brass bed, which was nestled among shelves of stones—flowered obsidian, cut spherically to the size of bowling balls; cross sections of dinosaur thighs; bookends made of malachite; and slabs of azurite. Inglesby taught me to cut geodes, showing that hidden inside a rough exterior of a stone can be a sparkling universe of crystals.

One afternoon, while Inglesby was cutting stones and keeping a watchful eye on his rock tumblers, Dean Brimhall stopped to visit; he was another outsider who'd discovered Fruita in the early '50s. Dean spent most of his time rooting around the backcountry with his collapsible aluminum ladders. Some, which were permanently fixed with bolts and spanned great blocks of sandstone, allowed him to reach the high benches overlooking Capitol Reef National Monument. He scoured the alcoves and caves in search of artifacts of the Fremont Indians. Though he was in his seventies, we could barely keep up with his powerful stride. Dean taught that you can't know the desert until you get it into your muscles, and that's just what we did. We explored the monument with him from one end to the other.

In the Moenkopi Formation, dinosaurs once pounded their way through the slime and ooze along the edge of a lagoon or coastal floodplain, when the earth's climate was wet and tropical. The tracks had dried and filled with mud. Dean delicately wedged a crowbar between the layers and tapped with his hammer. After two hundred twenty-five million years in darkness, the tracks of the primitive reptile Chirotherium were revealed in the sun, expanding my adolescent concept of time. We loaded Dean's flatbed truck with tracks.

Dean Brimhall scoured the alcoves for artifacts.

By today's standards, that would have been our fourth federal offense—driving off the road, hammering bolts into a cliff, disturbing archaeological sites, and removing dinosaur tracks. Charles Kelly, the only national monument employee, looked the other way.

Like the other characters in Fruita, Charles Kelly left an indelible mark. A printer by trade, he was an amateur archaeologist, a historian, a geologist, and Capitol Reef's first custodian. Kelly belonged to no organization whatsoever, never went out socially, wasn't interested in politics, and hated radios. Rather misanthropic by nature, he harbored a particular contempt for Mormons. He wrote: "I really ought to move to California, but if I did the Mormons would say they ran me out of Utah—so I stay just to spite them."

Georgie White and Harry Aleson swim the Colorado River.

I'd watch Kelly drive by the ranch in his beat-up pickup on his way to work. Sometimes he would stop for coffee and speak with Dick about the sorry condition of the world, the Mormon problem, the uranium boom, and all those damn people who kept pouring into what the two men considered was their private paradise. He gave me a copy of the book he wrote, *The Outlaw Trail: A History of Butch Cassidy and His Wild Bunch*, which detailed the men who rode through these parts raising hell.

There were those who passed through Fruita, though not on horseback, who still were contrary to ordinary. Harry Aleson drove a turquoise-blue Plymouth. And through its windshield, Terry and I first saw the slickrock wilderness that surrounded the monument. Aleson explored the canyons of the Colorado Plateau and recounted his travels in letters, journals, and snapshots, although most were out of focus, and his notes were so nebulous that following his trail has been nearly impossible.

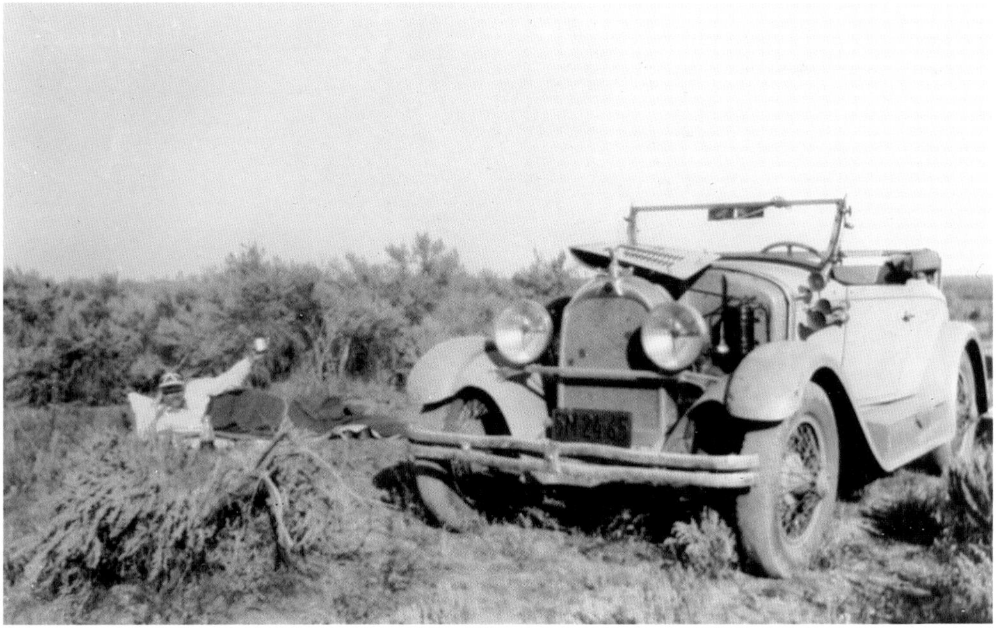

Harry Aleson, breakfast in the desert.

Aleson introduced Georgie White to the Colorado River, and she, in her leopard-skin swimsuit and hard hat, introduced commercial river running, as we know it today, to the Grand Canyon. In life jackets, she and Harry swam fifty miles of the flood-swollen Colorado River above Lake Mead, bringing with them only a few meager rations.

When everyone else was going downriver, Harry navigated a powerboat up the Colorado through Grand Canyon. He bent propellers on rocks, sheared pins, rolled boats, and beat himself up. His quixotic "Up Colorado River Expedition," as he called it, made headlines in the early 1940s.

When things got desperate, Harry survived by splitting open barrel cactus and chewing "a little evil-tasting dampness out of its white pith." He suffered scorpion and snake bites and subsisted for days on sugared tea when his food ran out. Death seemed like a good-natured jab in the side, bestowed by some unseen jolly prankster.

Aleson loathed civilization, preferring instead to live in a cave nestled in the travertine formation at the lower canyon of the Colorado above Lake Mead. His cave overlooked a waterfall and had a private lagoon. In his journals, capital letters always identified people and places he considered personally or historically significant. Harry called his cave "MY HOME" and even considered glassing in the entrance to create what he called a modern-day cliff dwelling.

The brothers explore the Henry Mountains.

Through dust kicked up by Harry's Plymouth, we caught glimpses of the Henry Mountains—peaks that in 1869 J. W. Powell named the Unknown Mountains—the summits of which begged to be climbed. Even before Harry's Plymouth rolled into the yard at Ripple Rock Ranch, Terry and I were making plans to return. In the coming years, Aleson's influence marked every page in *On the Loose,* and he would be my ally when Terry died.

In 1901, it took the Mormon bishop in Torrey ninety minutes to travel to Fruita. Mudslides often closed the road entirely. I watched the highway department straighten out the bends and pave twelve miles of road that snaked down to the monument from Torrey to the west. I walked on the new blacktop highway to the ribbon-cutting ceremony that commemorated its completion. Highway engineers and politicians concluded that the improved road would be the best thing that ever happened to Fruita.

I wondered. The locals wondered, too, if the new road possibly was the beginning of the end. In the next decade, their homes in Fruita would be leveled for the new national park. Toward the end of the function, Miss Cora Smith stepped to the microphone with her big ol' hollow-bodied Gibson guitar and belted out an Everly Brothers tune: "Bye bye love; bye bye happiness; hello loneliness; I think I'm a-gonna cry . . ."

We studied Dick's topographical maps of the Henry Mountains. In the Cold War climate of the 1950s, the Atomic Energy Commission encouraged the exploration for and milling of uranium on the Colorado Plateau. Charles Kelly wrote, "Prospectors' jeeps passing through are averaging forty a day. They drive with the throttle wide open in order to beat the other fellow to those million-dollar claims." The upside was that by the late '50s the rush had subsided, and this wilderness of mountain and canyon was more accessible.

Two brothers left their tracks along the scant game trail leading to the summit of Mount Ellen, and in the blue-gray Chinle Formation soil, searching for petrified wood and dinosaur bones at the base of the Factory Butte monolith. Two brothers nearly lost their lives trying to climb up a forty-foot band of rock to the summit, when better judgment prevailed. We left our tracks at the Wolverton Mine with its waterwheel still intact. I tucked myself into one of the huge wooden spokes and Terry rocked the wheel until I hung head down, pleading for mercy. And our tracks mingled with those of the buffalo that still roam in the Henrys. Bulls with blazing red eyes hung back in the herd and shook the earth with their hooves, daring us to come closer.

Toward the end of summer our father, Harvey Finkelson, arrived in Fruita in the dark of night, while Terry and I slept. Phoebe had sensed his impending arrival and fled the day before. Perhaps after twelve years, her illusory phantoms grew weary of tormenting her, so we could now meet our father.

We awoke to a knock on the door of the guesthouse, and from the shadows our dad emerged. Harvey was tall and lean and wore a mustache, a silver-gray Stetson, and cowboy boots. He was right out of a western movie, but I couldn't tell if he was a good guy or a bad guy. Harvey lingered uneasily outside while Terry and I eyed him curiously, and felt the glow of his smile that lit up the night. He gave me a hug that I didn't know quite what to do with.

In the morning, we packed for Elk Springs Ranch in Wyoming. Reluctantly, I got into the car with a man who claimed to be my father. Dick waved good-bye and smiled, his gold fillings reflecting the sun. I didn't believe that smile for a minute—he couldn't wait to get rid of us.

Harvey's sedan rolled west over the new blacktop, past Dean Brimhall's ladder, past Torrey's Mormon Church, where I'd attended services with my aunt. I'd eaten the bread and drunk the water and had the hell scared out of me by a fire-and-brimstone preacher. Then we passed Boulder Mountain; I'd caught my first cutthroat trout in its high lakes. On we sped, past Bicknell and Loa, past Thousand Lake Mountain, and north to unknown places. We traveled mostly in silence, my dad occasionally pressing my leg, struggling for words to express the agony of not having seen us grow up. We arrived late, and I woke up early at Elk Springs Ranch in the cabin where I had been conceived. In the living room, bearskins and trophy elk and antelope heads hung from the walls. Their glass eyes seemed to follow me. I wondered what my life would have been like, had I grown up at the ranch. On the woodstove in the kitchen were enough bacon, eggs, and pancakes to feed half of Wyoming. Harvey was under contract to provide meals for the highway department.

I ran down to the Snake River in a cloud of grasshoppers. I filled a jar with them and spent the rest of the day catching trout that rose from the deep to take my bait, like amorphous apparitions—luminescent, elusive, and magical. Terry was bored and suspicious of Harvey and thought ranch life was crude. He'd brought about every book Mark Twain ever wrote, and had begun

Roughing It. What the West had been seemed more interesting to him than what the West had become.

Deep in books, Terry read while I helped Harvey butcher a steer and whack heads off chickens for dinner. He read while I rode bareback along Horse Creek, following its waters up from the Snake River, and he disappeared into the woods while I helped Harvey saddle horses for tourists.

Harvey's property extended across the highway, where he operated a gas station and a small store that sold plastic grizzly bears and other such stuff, and I helped pump gas and sell pop. While Terry began Twain's *Mysterious Stranger,* I was out on the back porch overlooking the emerald waters of the Snake River, listening to tunes by Hank Williams and Patsy Cline gush and throb heartache from the Wurlitzer jukebox, a glowing, bubbling, pulsating sculpture that flashed brilliant rainbow colors that reflected dreamily off the polished hardwood floors. "Your cheatin' heart will tell on you" didn't make much sense to a twelve-year-old, but I couldn't get enough of Hank's voice, and the twang of his guitar drove me wild.

We drove to Yellowstone, and one thing that Terry and Harvey did agree on was that the Tetons, rising up from the valley floor like sharks' teeth, were about as beautiful as mountains get. Harvey took us up the Snow King Mountain chairlift and to the Million Dollar Cowboy Bar in Jackson, then north to the park to see Old Faithful. The aspen were turning in the high country, ushering in a long Wyoming winter. It was time to return to Berkeley and school.

Through the window of the plane at the Jackson airport, Harvey seemed small and intangible, like a fading dream. I waved but was uncertain if he saw me. It would take a while to distill the summer of '58, and the liquor that came was bittersweet but strong. Terry and I were well on our way to laying out the world and planting ourselves in it.

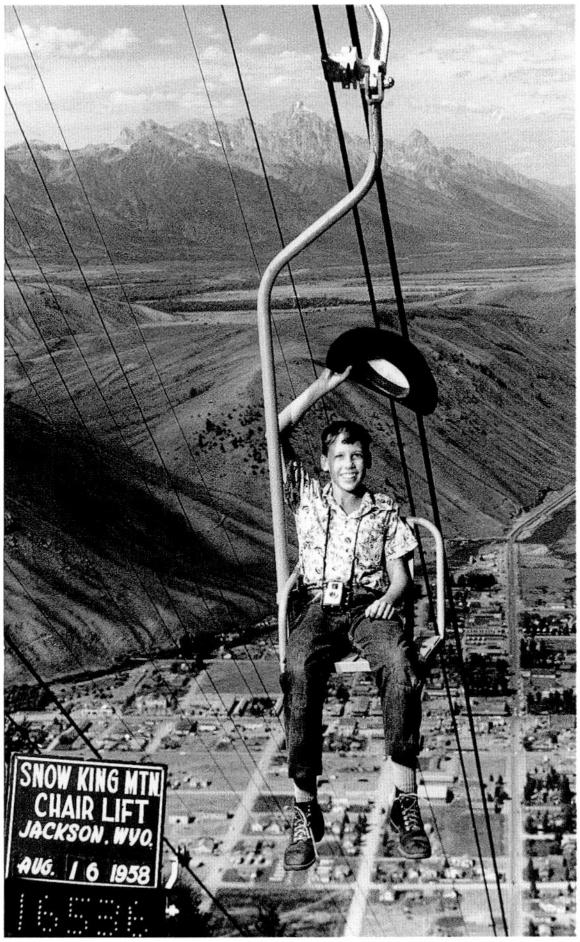

The author in Jackson, Wyoming.

C H A P T E R   S E V E N

The flow of the river is ceaseless and its water is never the same. The bubbles that float in the pools, now vanishing, now forming, are not of long duration: So in the world of man and his dwellings. . . . People die in the morning, they are born in the evening, like foam on the water.

— Kamo no Chomei, 1212

Camp Mescal

Listless mosquitoes, hung over from last night's drinking, paid me no attention as I loaded the espresso maker. I jumped into the river and washed yesterday away. I was on the water early and drifted in total silence. It was so quiet I imagined the river was dreaming.

The country was immense, its horizons infinite. To get a feel for just how big it is, I had to climb to high places—the perspective is completely different there than it is from river level. I rowed to shore just as the sun struck the high ridges and began to climb. Just short of the rim, I startled a golden eagle, who ascended, making ever-enlarging circles directly overhead. The edges of his wings seemed transparent as

the sun illuminated them, and I felt more alive than I had for a long time.

My thoughts took me to uncharted places. Time: Then as now—now as then. Occurrence—reoccurrence. This morning, time stood still while I passed through infinite space. I had no tools to comprehend the great epochs that created this landscape. Author Edward Wilson suggests that the mind was never designed to understand such things as time or, for that matter, even itself. He contends the brain is merely a device to ensure survival and reproduction; and love, pride, and anger in the end only help perpetuate the cycle. How callous, Mr. Wilson! What of man's limitless capacity for love, for joy, for hope; his biological need to share the agony and ecstasy of life through art and music? The eagle passed again, reminding me what was important.

On this bare-boned rocky outcropping, the land, the light, and the river offered a banquet for the senses, and if I were to die gorging myself on the ineffable beauty, then I would die content. Here, my mind quieted and returned to its origins—my spirit merged with sunlight, water, and air. For an instant, time ceased to exist, and nothing separated me from the landscape. The two fused. Perhaps my evolutionarily hardwired "mythic-mind" was informing me that I shouldn't separate subject from object? It insisted on a flow between the two and that I bond with both. Without wild places to inspire, to heal, where I could feel a part of something larger than myself, I would wither and die.

I was five hundred feet above and a mile away from the river, but the Green may have once flowed here at my feet. Smooth river-worn stones—purple, red, and shiny black—lay in what was once a river channel. I was in no hurry. I sat on a boulder and let small, smooth, warm stones slide slowly through my fingers. I picked up a deep-purple cobble that fit nicely in my palm. With its pale orange rings it looked like the fiery birth of planet Earth, hurtling through the cosmos. I felt its warmth and ancient smoothness, then put it in my mouth. If I swallowed it, would I be hurled back in time to when the river first carved through these canyons? Would I feel the glacial waters of melting ice caps flowing over me? Would I be buried beneath volcanic ash? Would I recall a zillion sunrises and sunsets? I wondered how many more sunrises I had been allocated. I hiked my mortal human self with its very large brain back to the river—suppressing its craving to ask questions that have no answers.

Seedskeedee wanted to hug the shore and that was fine by me. We were in stealth mode, positioned to see wildlife. The boat collided with a dozen Canada geese, and their cries shattered the stillness. The young streaked for cover in the tamarisk; others washed down with the current. I moved into their beach for lunch and to scribble lines in my journal. A shoveler duck arrived with family. When they caught wind of me, ducklings scrambled onto their mother's back, while others paddled in her wake as if connected by an invisible elastic cord. They made a direct line to the other side of the river, disappearing in the willows—small dramas on a big river.

After lunch, I followed a streambed up a side canyon, then scrambled up a talus slope to a ridge that led to the rim. I was starved for this landscape—hungry for the big picture. The lush green tamarisk along the river far below is a nonnative plant—an "alien" species, in the sense that God didn't put it there; humans did. In the early 1900s, it was introduced to California from the eastern Mediterranean as an ornamental plant and to stabilize the soil and prevent erosion. It spread frighteningly quickly along every river tributary in the Southwest, crowding out native plants and sucking up a phenomenal amount of water. Sitting under this plant on a hot day, you can feel a fine mist falling from its leaves. The plant is so prolific that it has taken root in the concrete at the base of Glen Canyon Dam in Arizona. Its tenacious roots may one day crack the dam and set the Colorado River free.

Though science has brought about amazing achievements, it seemed insignificant this afternoon. Man the meddler. Man the manipulator. Man the interpreter who assigns value to all things nonhuman. His annihilation of the mystery and his quest for universal domestication have evolved into a social disorder. Author and mystic Richard Jefferies saw nature void of "contracted order," rather, as "divine chaos," rich with limitless hope and possibilities.

I wondered which species was more alien—man or the tamarisk—as I picked

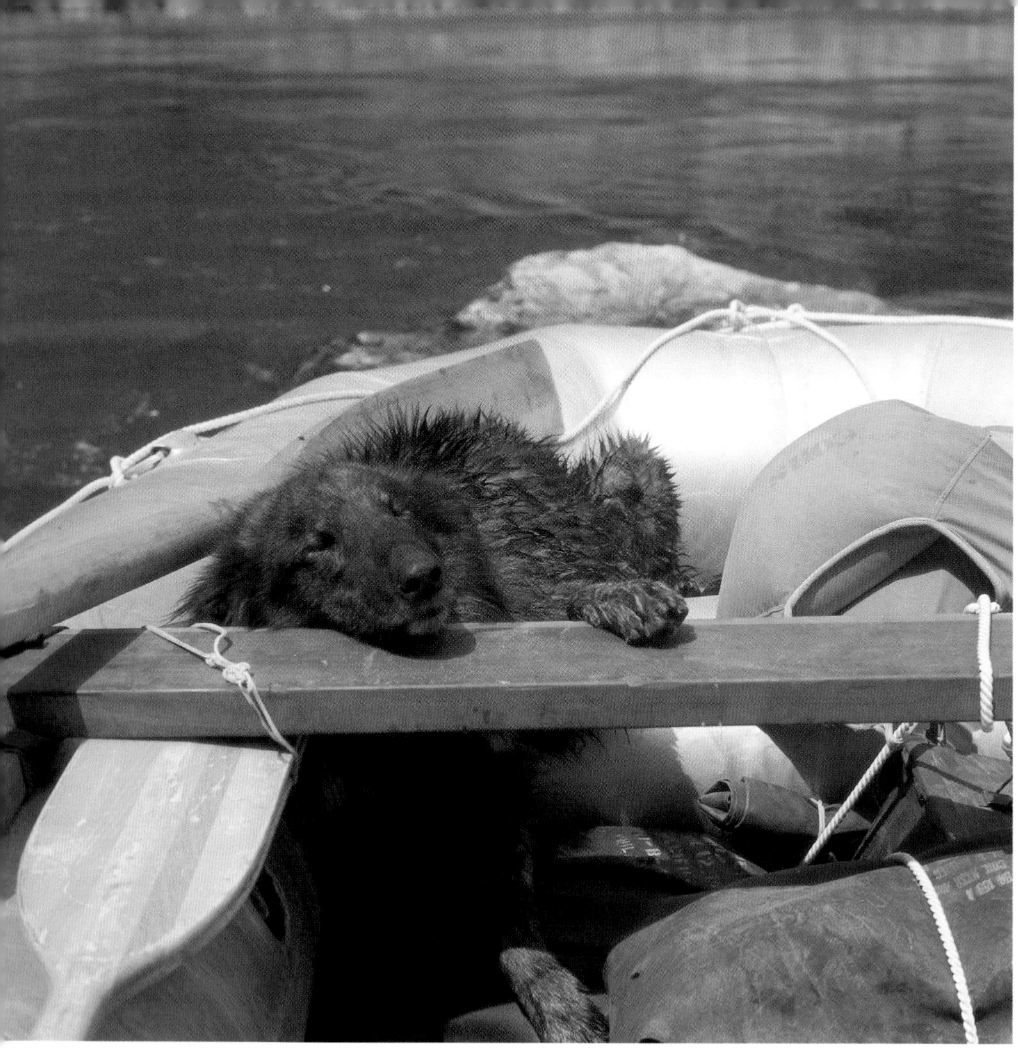

Smoky takes on the rapids of Idaho's "River of No Return."

and the region had undergone cycles of uplift and submergence. The land once had been beneath the waters of a shallow north/south seaway nearly a thousand miles wide that had deposited a mile-thick layer of sediment. I would have had to wait twenty million years for the seaway to retreat before I would feel the sun. As the Uinta Range rose, the area to the south was forming the Uinta Basin. Streams and rivers began to fill Lake Uinta, depositing sand and silt to a depth of two thousand feet. For five million years, I would have had to remain under this immense shallow lake that turned the Uinta Mountains into an island. Then fifty million years ago, the lake filled with sediments and vanished. Walking on that much geological time puts a human life span in perspective.

In the cross section of the Green River Formation that lay before me, water scoured the creek, revealing fossils of shellfish and insects. Rough-edged boulders covered with ripple marks, raindrop indentations, and bone fragments lay in jumbled piles, as though they had been

my way down a talus slope on feet that would be useless without shoes, in skin not designed for the sun and easily pricked by thorns and spines. My progress to the river was slowed by a gash in the earth, ripped open by flash floods, revealing secrets that geologists continue to discover and interpret.

I oscillated between scientific inquiry and Jefferies' divine chaos, trying to explain the crazy geology that tore at my senses. Geological theories are intriguing. I was in the heart of the intertonguing Wasatch and Green River Formations, thrown into God's cement mixer with some aggregate as an experiment. Some of the fossils were the size of my fist, polished smooth by water.

An insect the length of a fingernail dashed across the fossils. He had no head, as we know it, but was all legs that moved wave-like. Two long probes protruded from his body, moving to a slightly different beat than his legs. I wondered how he filled his days among the fossils. I didn't need to know his Latin name or study him under a microscope—he was what he was, and what he was made me smile.

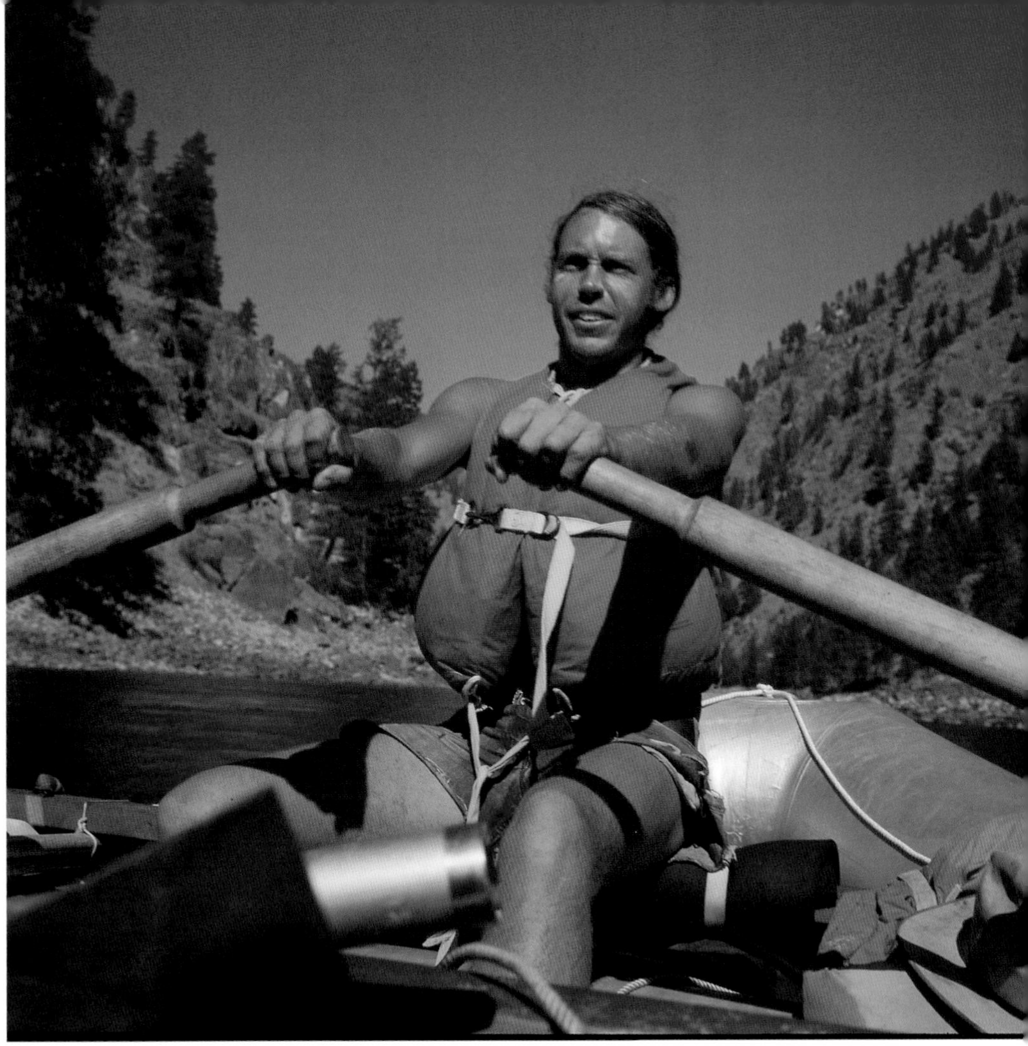

The author returns to the river. The Main Salmon, 1972.

Seedskeedee bucked and lurched in gale-force winds and scowled at me for parking her so close to the rocks that were grinding away on her chine. I apologized. As I rowed into the current, the thought struck that I was required by the Bureau of Land Management to show my permit at Sand Wash today. But where was Sand Wash? Visibility was reduced to zero by blowing sand and spray from the river, so I could have easily passed it by. And what did it matter if I showed my permit today, tomorrow, or next month? I searched in a hatch for *Belknap's Desolation River Guide* but grabbed another guidebook—my dog-eared copy of *On the Loose.*.

I had been pondering one of the book's observations: "We fear what we don't know. . . . Cut the root and the plant dies. Learn wilderness and you don't fear anything." In 1965, the Green River had all but destroyed my desire to even see a

Montana's South Fork of the Flathead.

river again. I feared it—the root had been nearly severed, and the plant was dying. Though the decade of the 1970s was mostly one of folly, I made one smart move: I returned to the river. On July 27, 1972, I bought a six-valve Yampa rubber boat, five ten-foot oars, one pump, two yards of patching material, and one gallon of Gaco paint, all for $967.23. The Land Rover had been replaced with a '57 Chevy truck. I threw the boat in back, called my half-coyote dog, Smoky, packed some provisions, and headed north to run the Main Salmon River in Idaho. Terry and I had run the river in 1961, and I had vivid memories of hot springs, of sandy beaches among the ponderosa pines. At the launch, little had changed—there were no boats and no pesky rangers, just me and Smoky and the river. I was terrified at Salmon Falls, but by the time I neared the end of my trip, above Riggins, rivers had become my friend again, and confidence returned. The South Fork of the Flathead left an indelible mark. The rivers of the North speak a different language than desert streams and rivers. Their dance is not encumbered with silt—their waters are clear and playful and offer up secrets more readily. Wranglers loaded boats and supplies on packhorses, and we rode to the headwaters of the Flathead in the Lewis and Clark National Forest. Deadfall choked the river, necessitating portages. Grizzlies passed like shadows through the woods. Around the fire we cooked native cutthroat trout so large we had to cut them in half to fit the pan. We sipped whiskey, picked guitars, sang old Louvin Brothers songs, and howled at the moon. Life was good—this was truly God's country.

In the early '80s, I began guiding on the Colorado River in Grand Canyon. Like many guides I flipped my share of boats, broke oars, got sucked down in whirlpools, narrowly escaped rockfalls and flash floods, stepped on rattlesnakes, got bit by scorpions, broke bones, saved lives, rescued passengers from the water with throw-lines, and nursed the sick,

maimed, and injured, removing cactus spines, treating victims for dehydration, for heat stroke, for alcohol poisoning, and loading people into helicopters for emergency evacuations. Some passengers suffered from vertigo, others from insomnia and nymphomania.

At one time or another, a river guide must be a psychiatrist, a geologist, a doctor, and an entertainer—sometimes a clown, other times a fool. A guide may be a doctor, a Vietnam vet, a builder, a lawyer, a teacher, an artist, or a writer. But the common current that braids them together is their love and respect for the river. It's a love so intense and a life lived so intensely on the edge that at the end of

Grand Canyon river guide entertains passenger.

The author as an Arizona Raft Adventures guide.

a river season, reentry into the world they left behind can be overwhelming and intimidating. Leading a "normal" life again is nearly impossible, and the result may be living with depression, alcoholism, fragmented relationships, and suicide. The Colorado River is a powerful, uncompromising brown god that can either kill you or give you a reason to live.

I told passengers that Glen Canyon Dam had been the single worst ecological disaster of the century. I'd pull over in the heart of Marble Canyon, where the Bureau of Reclamation, which had proposed building a dam, had drilled exploratory holes in the limestone. Seemed like every trip someone had heard of *On the Loose,* and I was little prepared then as now for the notoriety. No place was more fitting than in Marble Canyon to ask one of the book's most challenging questions—"Could we create if we could not destroy? Would we want knowledge without control? Beauty without rape? Was I just born too late?"

There's no better place than on a boat in the Grand Canyon to allow silence to work its magic, or to cultivate an ecological awareness, or to simply offer one's own theories of nature as divine chaos. But it's always the river that transforms lives, and the boatman is simply a conduit.

The easygoing lackadaisical years of river guiding in the Grand Canyon vanished toward the end of the '80s. Park

Guides up Matkatamiba Canyon, 1970s.

politics, regulations, and the concerns of "private boaters," who wanted more opportunity to run the river without a concessionaire, turned the Grand Canyon into a battleground. Companies, often run by greedy river czars, carved out their empires—squeezing as much profit as they could out of so-called "user days" handed out by National Park Service bureaucrats. Many of the best guides quit in disgust or were fired for defiance.

Beaches were eroding, trails were cut through archaeologically sensitive areas, and native fish species were on the decline. Staples were attached to hump-back chub in the Little Colorado River. Tags were wired to bones in the most remote caves in the Redwall Limestone

Robert Cruikshank. I noticed that a first edition of Mark Twain's *Mysterious Stranger*, illustrated by N. C. Wyeth, was still on the shelf. I had recently lusted after it, but, penniless, I had left the shop with that familiar unfulfilled longing.

On this particular day we had business with the Dawson brothers. From a brown paper bag I pulled out a couple of leather-bound books that our grandmother had given us—early editions of *Gulliver's Travels* and *The Adventures of Robinson Crusoe.* Reluctantly, we had decided to sell them. We explained to Muir and Glen our mission, and with a wink, they gave us more money than the books probably were worth. Cash in pocket, we caught a bus to Glendale, where Kelty backpacks were being manufactured. The packs lined the showroom wall, beckoning, alluring, emanating possibility, freedom, and adventure. We were on our way to where sky and horizon merged.

While most high school kids craved fast Impalas and fast girls, Terry thought being snowbound in a remote cabin with a four-month supply of kerosene and an armful of books was all the romance he needed. We devoured *Adventures in the Unknown Interior of America* by Cabeza de Vaca, *Mountaineering in the Sierra Nevada* by Clarence King, *Wildlife in America* by Peter Matthiessen, and Wallace Stegner's *Beyond the Hundredth Meridian.* We read government reports on remaining wilderness areas and pored over maps of southern Utah in the heart of what Stegner called the Plateau Province. We studied maps of what remained of wild America, represented by tiny dots scattered through Idaho, California, Washington, Wyoming, and Utah. They were pitifully few. Within those tiny dots we would discover the slickrock wilderness of Escalante, Glen Canyon, the Wind River Mountains, the Cascades, the Sierras of California, and Idaho's Salmon River.

Phoebe could no longer keep up with us on the trail and may have been glad to be rid of us so she could follow her own path. She resumed painting and working in her darkroom. By the summer of 1962, we were more or less on our own. We read everything we could get our hands on about the Sierras and the John Muir Trail and hummed down the highway toward Yosemite. We would discover the same trails Muir had, leading to sharp ice peaks, and "see God making the world." We would, as he wrote, "interpret the rocks, see alpine glow set fire to the monolithic granite domes, learn the language of flood, storm and avalanche."

We organized supplies and put food in metal containers to cache at Red's Meadow, the halfway point on the trail. Freeze-dried, lightweight food had just been invented but not perfected. On a package of "pork chops," the cooking instructions read: "To prepare, add water with 'powdered enzymes,' soak meat ten minutes and fry." They were uneatable.

In ten days we hiked the entire trail to the summit of Mount Whitney, some two hundred fifty miles to the south, and saw no one until the last day. At timberline, on our way down to Whitney Portal, a man labored slowly up the trail. Lashed to his makeshift wooden pack frame were a mattress, an axe, and a coffeepot. He was a curious sight—we had never seen anyone like him on the trail. He paused briefly and gasped, "Is it worth it?" We didn't know what to tell him.

Perhaps Terry knew he wouldn't live long; he was, at times, obsessed with exploring as much of

The Sierras, California, 1962.

On the summit of Mount Whitney, 1962.

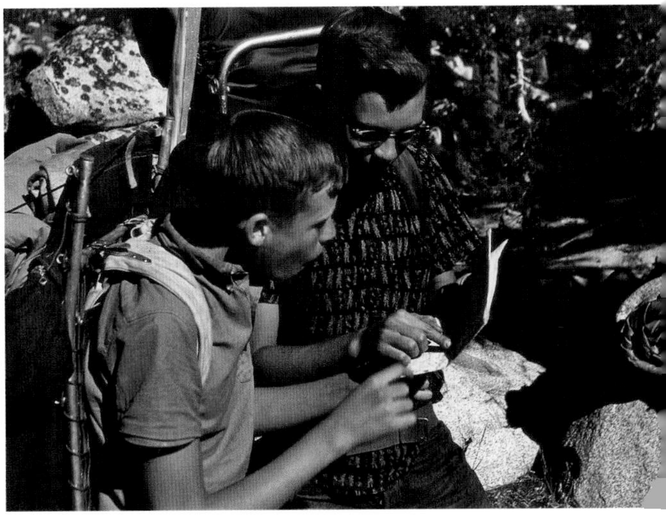

Hiking the John Muir Trail, 1962.

the West as was humanly possible. I was overpowered by his sense of urgency. I exhausted myself trying to keep up with him, so when he suggested we hike the length of Death Valley the following spring, I told him he'd have to go alone. I was listening to my own muse, which led me to the south rim of the Grand Canyon. I dropped Terry off in the Cottonwood Mountains in the northern part of Death Valley and headed for Arizona.

The Hermit Trail had been buried under rock slides, and a sign at the trailhead read "Primitive—Not Recommended." An invitation to descend. I was swallowed up in the blue-violet depths of the canyon, arriving at Hermit Rapid. The days merged, so oblivious was I to time passing. I spent three days mesmerized, hardly able to leave my sandy perch. The color, the light, the rock forms, exploded in my retina. I had brought a copy of Oliver La Farge's *Laughing Boy*, but reading seemed absurd. The Little Colorado River was flooding. It ran red with the Supi, with Hermit Shale, tinged with the color of crushed red chilies, thickened by silt and stone. I could not shout over the roar. My senses jerked back and forth. I was dragged into the heart of the legendary fifth wave that crests at twenty feet, exploding into a frothy mist. Did boats really pound through this maelstrom? As I walked back up the trail and drove back to meet Terry in Death Valley, I felt my foundation had shifted. Waters would come to possess and haunt me.

The following summer, in a Rambler station wagon, we rambled out of town, heading north for our first river trip. The Main and the Middle Fork of the Salmon River were swollen with spring runoff and moved with urgency, sculpting granite boulders into sensuous shoulders and bottoms, just as they would shape our imperishable love for wild places. I felt the unforgiving power of water when I tumbled overboard for my first white-water baptism, and an appreciation for life when Terry grabbed me by the collar and saved my life, dragging me back into the boat. Driftwood fires lit the night sky and my imagination, and I followed the sparks until they became stars. I plunked tunes on my banjo and sang songs with the guides late into the night. They were my mentors. They were strong brown gods.

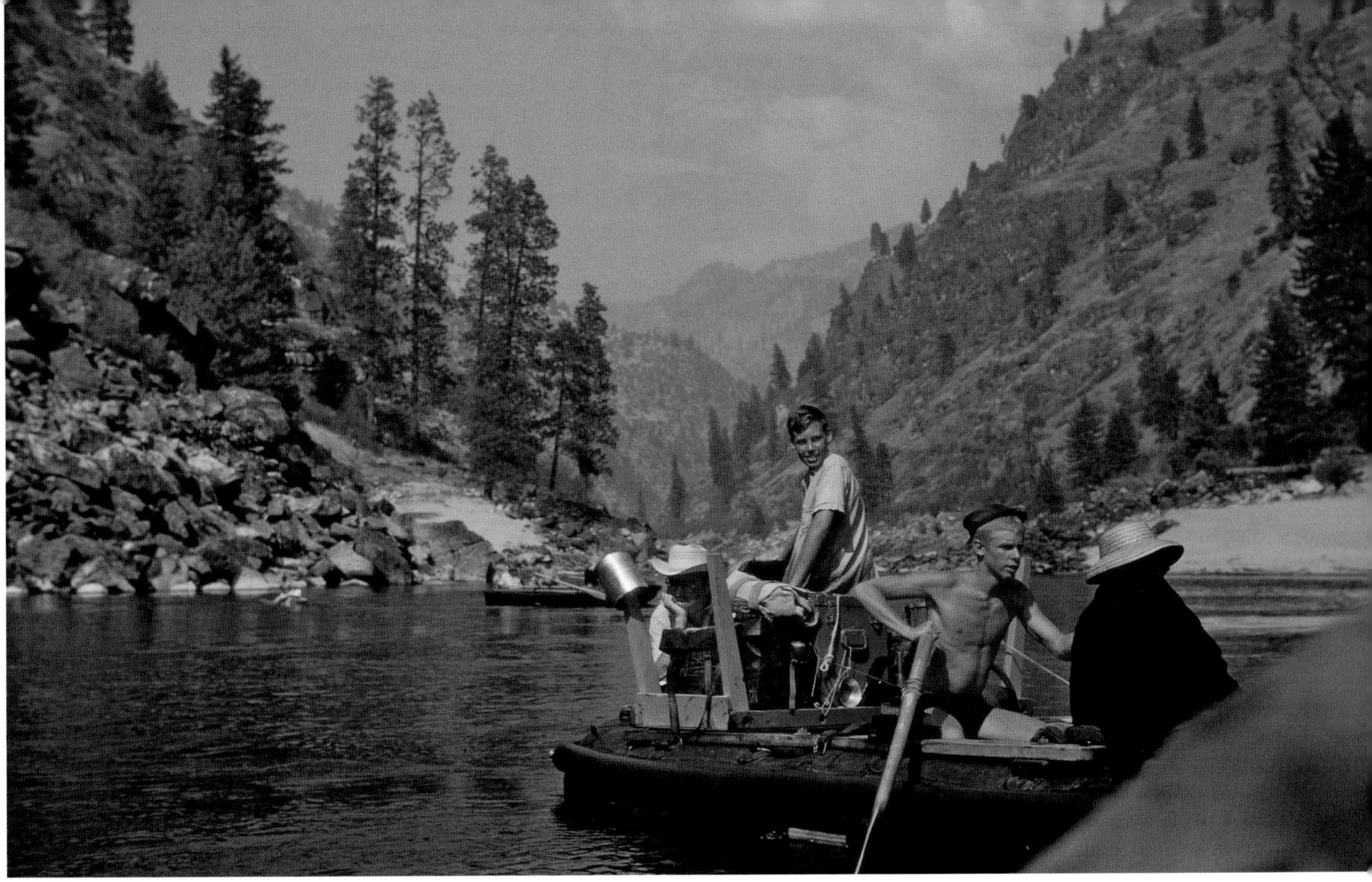

Middle Fork of the Salmon, Idaho, 1961.

The fact was that in less than a year we had driven the Rambler into the ground. Terry had taken the car to New York after reading Kerouac's *On the Road* and getting an itch to travel cross-country, and someone had taken a crowbar to the door and stolen all his belongings. He returned, loathing big cities more than ever. We needed a vehicle that could take the punches. I found a Willys truck in a classified ad. The beast had no speedometer, so Terry drew a portrait of Theodore Roosevelt and glued it to the dashboard where the gauge had been. It was a rough-ridin' truck. We pointed the Willys toward the canyons of Escalante in southeastern Utah—a blank area on the map.

In this remote slickrock wilderness, a kid named Everett Ruess had wandered the mesas and canyons in the 1930s with his burro and dogs, in search of the very things Terry and I craved: peace, adventure, wildness. Ruess wrote in his last letter to his family that he had known too much of the depths of life and preferred anything to what he called

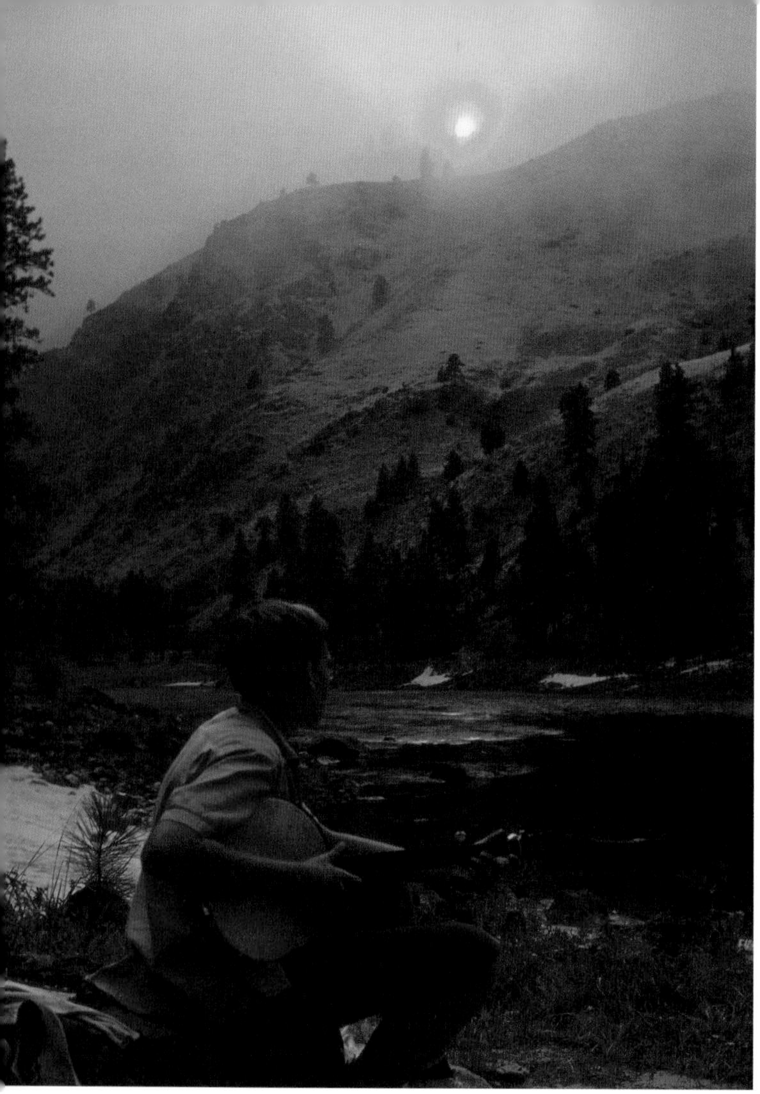

was never seen again. Everett left no trace and no clues.

We parked our truck at the head of Harris Wash and started walking. We followed the drainage down to the Escalante River and explored its side canyons—Fence, Stevens, Davis, and Soda. A thousand years earlier, the Ancestral Puebloans had prospered, covering a vast area of what is now southern Utah and northern Arizona. They built houses of stone and earth, grew crops on the canyon floor, and painted intricate designs on clay pots. On cliff walls streaked with a dark patina of manganese and iron, they scratched and painted their cosmologies.

The meanings of these petroglyphs and pictographs remain beyond reach. Just as the Ancestral Puebloans' arti-

an anticlimax, and that he did not wish to taste but to drink deep. Perhaps he was prophesying his own death when he wrote, "I have seen more beauty than I can bear."

Twenty-eight years after Everett, Terry and I arrived, ready to drink deep from the same spring and to be "drunk on the elixir of beauty." I imagined Everett in an intoxicated Dionysian frenzy, scratching "NEMO"—the Latin word meaning "nobody"—on sandstone cliffs and in caves, just as my brother wrote in the sand: "Terry Loves Wilderness." The canyons swallowed young Ruess, and he

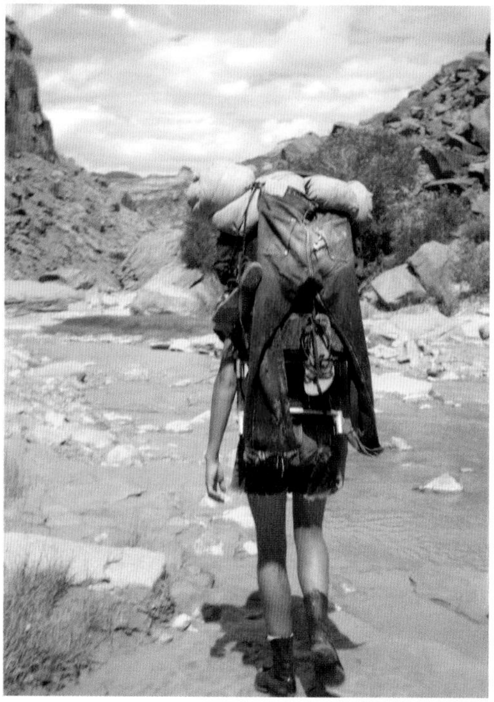

Packing into the Escalante.

facts—like the split-twig figurines made of willow twigs—have been radiocarbon-dated as being four thousand years old, so were their petroglyphs and pictographs, and the woven sandal fragments have been dated at eight thousand years.

My brother and I were on the lookout for evidence of their passing. We could spot a metate—used for grinding corn—by its shape, even though centuries ago it had been placed upside down to prevent water from freezing and cracking it. Coyote tracks around a ruin were significant and led us to an axe head, still dangerously sharp. It's an indescribable rush, discovering a delicately chiseled obsidian arrowhead in the pink sand, or coming upon a yucca basket exposed by a flash flood, or discovering a clay vessel in a niche, embellished with elaborate geometric designs, right where it had been left a thousand years earlier.

We explored cliff houses, where the Indians had cut steps in sandstone up vertical walls to their dwellings. On stairways worn thin by time and erosion, we'd walk the fine line between satisfying our curiosity and peeling off the wall to our deaths. Adding to the drama, we dared one another to go just one step farther.

Under the overhangs, granaries were built to protect corn from moisture and rodents—and the builders' fingerprints were preserved in

Davis Gulch, off the Escalante, Utah.

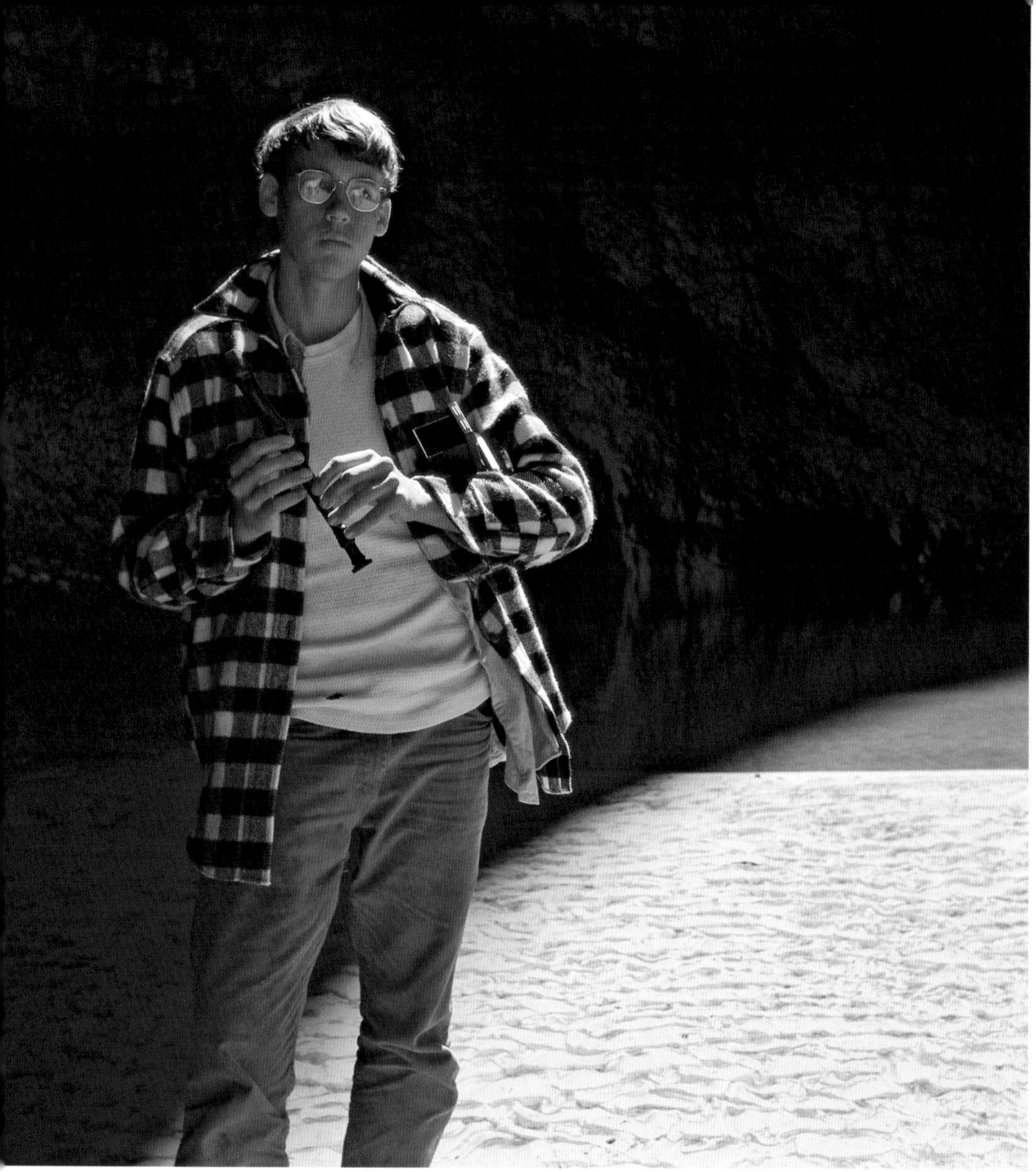

Brothers in Cathedral in the Desert, 1963.

a .33-caliber Winchester slug in Wetherill's head. The spirits have their ways. I wondered if the Ancestral Puebloans lived in an atmosphere of desperate fear of persistent and devilish enemies—imagined or real—who drove them to live like swallows and eagles in small cracks and niches in the cliffs. Their lives may have been conservative, cautious, and constricted, and their petroglyphs could have been manifestations of a terrible fear of "the enemy."

What became of the Ancestral Puebloans is anyone's guess. It is speculated that around 1250 A.D., drought, depleted resources, and encroaching Indian tribes forced them from their cracks in the cliff. Similar stresses may, someday, force the current inhabitants of large cities in the Southwest to move. Perhaps their imaginings finally caught up with them, and they were eaten by those red-horned, hollow-eyed, wide-shouldered monsters they depicted in their pictograph panels. These

the dried mud between the stones, as if the granaries had been constructed yesterday. Rock slabs covered the entrance, where inside we hoped to find pottery jars that still contained corn.

Rancher turned quasi-archaeologist Richard Wetherill may have rooted around the same ruins that we had. In Chaco Canyon in northwestern New Mexico, he plundered the ruins, selling artifacts abroad to collectors. It is speculated that on June 22, 1910, a Navajo put

anthropomorphs, with their sunken eyes and antennae, haunt the canyon country, suggesting that the Puebloans all were dancing to the same drum—whatever music that was.

The canyon deepened as we neared Glen Canyon and the Colorado River. Walls of Navajo sandstone—shaped by wind, water, and time—towered above. Desert varnish left its mark where water, seeping over the canyon walls, leached minerals from the rock and oxidized, turning the stone a lustrous, metallic black. We lounged in the shade of cottonwoods during the heat of the day, or plunged into the bottomless *tinajas* and swam in the river still cold from its journey down Boulder Mountain, where the Escalante is born.

A few miles above the confluence of the Escalante and the Colorado Rivers, we entered Cathedral in the Desert, once the very heart and soul of the canyon country. Until now, the creator had only been practicing—playing with form, color, and light—but when he went to work on his Cathedral, he began his masterpiece. Any one of the great cathedrals of Europe would fit inside the massive alcove.

The architects of the sixteenth century designed their cathedrals with spires that reached toward the heavens, so as to be closer to God. The desert's Cathedral was built of towering, interlocking walls that rose from the consecrated sand floor so high that only a slice of sky was visible.

The music that filled the Cathedral in the Desert was not polyphonic but the sound of water over stone as it cascaded into sacrosanct fern-lined pools on its way to the Colorado River.

I slithered deep into a crack of an undercut bank overlooking the Cathedral and lay there most of the afternoon. The place was awash in golden light. In a few years the Cathedral, along with Glen Canyon, would vanish beneath the waters of Lake Powell.

We trudged up Coyote Gulch, exhausted and nearly out of food. Where the canyon narrowed, a mule deer charged by so close I could see the sheen of her eye and feel the wind of her passing. Terry and I both felt an eerie presence—perhaps Everett's spirit, driven to madness at having seen too much beauty, or maybe one of those red-horned hollow-eyed petroglyph spirits had metamorphosed into a deer. We hoped to catch a ride back to our vehicle at Harris Wash to complete our loop. But not a car passed that day or the next, and we ended up walking more than fifty miles on the Hole-in-the-Rock Road, a dirt track that passed between the remote town of Escalante and the overlook above the Colorado River at the Crossing of the Fathers.

On our second day without water, Terry rambled on in a delirious fashion about Fray Escalante and Fray Dominguez, the first nonindigenous people to travel through these parts, venturing into terra incognita in 1776. These missionaries hoped to discover a northern trail connecting the New Mexico settlements with California. As the snow fell, they decided to head back to Santa Fe, which meant crossing the Colorado. At what is now Lee's Ferry—just south of the confluence of the Escalante and Colorado Rivers—Fray Escalante built a crude raft, and they set out to pole their way across the river. He lost contact with the bottom of the river, and they were blown back to shore. They lost their clothes trying to swim the river and were repeatedly turned back by "extremely perilous ledges of rock that finally became impassable." Finally, the river let them go, and they were able to cross at Padre Creek Canyon. Escalante captured the crossing of the Colorado River with one word: *salsipuedes*—get out while

Anthropomorphs haunt the canyons.

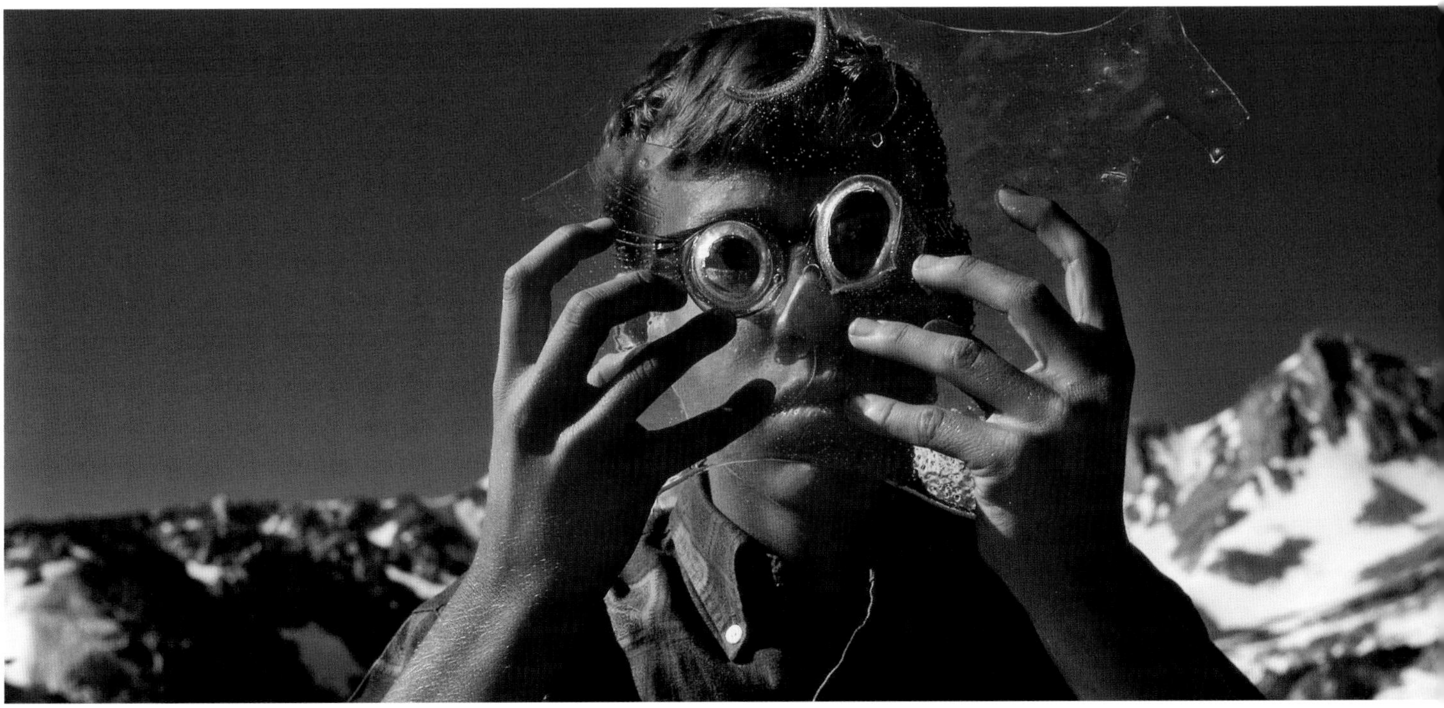

The Sierras.

you can. After many more perils, they arrived back in Santa Fe in January 1777.

Our food was gone, our situation desperate. We drank the slime from the bottoms of stock tanks. Exhausted and weak from hunger, we arrived back at Harris Wash, completing the last leg of our journey. We had parked in the middle of the drainage, and a flash flood had left a high-water mark on the tire up to the axle. We dislodged tree limbs and debris from underneath the chassis and were relieved when the engine turned over. *¡Salsipuedes!* Our mud-stained tires reluctantly spun us back to California.

Terry's winter of 1962 at Carleton College drove him wacko. "We've got to get into the mountains this spring and disperse the shocking amount of flab, unsteady nerves, and general absurd and laughable physical condition this Minnesota winter has got me into. I hope our trip to the Cascades will disperse this pathetic, hideous, chalk-white pallor that comes from constantly huddling indoors by the radiator."

Our blisters had healed from our escapade in the canyons of the Escalante, and we drove the Willys northward to the Cascades of Washington to hike the backcountry in the Chelan Mountains. A toll ferry up Lake Chelan brought us to the trailhead. The

second day out, bad weather moved in. Rather than head down to lower elevations like smart campers, we pushed on, hoping to make it over a pass en route to Cardinal Peak and beat the brunt of the storm. But the storm hit us hard at timberline. With zero visibility and numb fingers we set up tube tents—lightweight, seamless plastic tubes, suspended by a rope attached at both ends to trees. In the wind and snow they were totally useless.

It snowed off and on that night and the next day and snow continued on into the following night. By the second morning we were on the verge of hypothermia; we made our way down into the timber and stumbled upon an unlocked cabin, where we built a fire and burned holes in our sleeping bags trying to dry them. We aborted the expedition. Back at the truck, a freeze had cracked

Chelan Mountains, Washington.

the engine block. We drove it anyway—a thousand miles back to California. Even Teddy Roosevelt had enough of that rough ride.

By today's standards of "the extreme," our adventures seem benign. We were just a couple of goofy brothers who never thought twice that we were doing anything out of the ordinary—that our exploits were to be immortalized. It was unimaginable. We believed that wilderness was a given, like air, like water, and that she would always be there when we needed her. But during the next decade, wild places would be threatened and inundated with people, dams would be built and rivers throttled. The innocence of childhood was passing and clouds were gathering on the horizon, and for the first time I would see the dark side of the moon.

CHAPTER NINE

In the canyon itself the days flow through your consciousness as the river flows along its course. . . . The current becomes the time on which you move. The river supplies and in a sense supplants the need to measure time . . . there is no more liberating or healing experience. It penetrates to the very core of being, untangling knots and recreating the spirit.

— ELIOT PORTER

Glen Canyon

"Should we flood the Sistine Chapel so tourists can get nearer the ceiling?" asked David Brower in 1967, when the Bureau of Reclamation was moving forward with plans to flood the Grand Canyon. Brower was executive director of the Sierra Club from 1952 until 1969 and was able to stop the dam project cold in Marble and Bridge Canyons, but Glen Canyon didn't fare as well.

Shortly after World War II, the Bureau of Reclamation located potential dam sites in the upper Colorado River Basin for electrical generation and irrigation. The Yampa, a major tributary of the Green, carved Dinosaur National Park into a spectacular natural wonder. The Yampa remained a

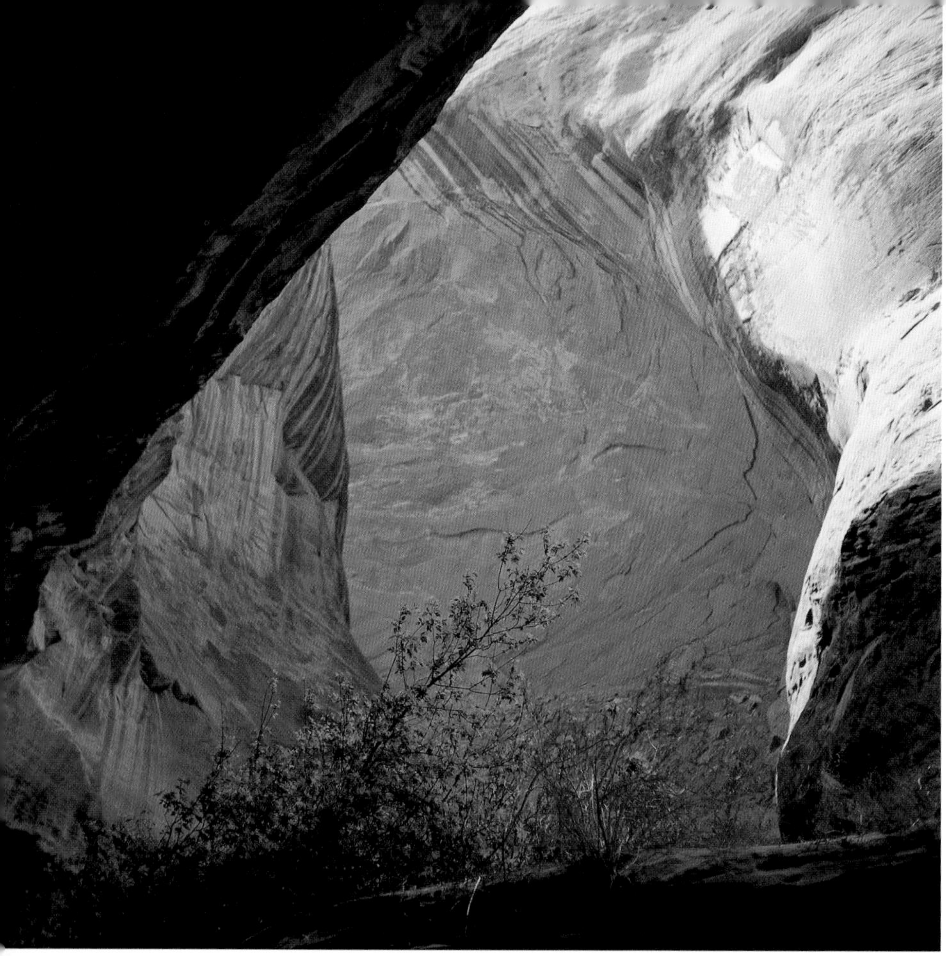

Cathedral in the Desert, 1964.

free-flowing river, largely because of media attention that the Sierra Club instigated. Sierra Club was one of the first groups that offered commercial trips through canyons. These trips in the early 1950s demonstrated that river running could be a safe proposition, but more importantly, it got the word out that Dinosaur was on the hit list as a centerpiece for the Bureau of Reclamation's proposed dam sites. The tide of public opinion turned toward preservation, and the hotly disputed proposals for Split Mountain and Echo Park Dams were withdrawn.

Under the leadership of David Brower, the Sierra Club defeated all but one of these proposals. Dinosaur National Park would be created, but only if Glen Canyon Dam was built. It was a political swap that haunted Brower the rest of his life.

What made Glen Canyon special was what killed it—it was remote and hidden from the world. Writers, scientists, explorers, painters, and photographers had tried to capture the Colorado Plateau, but few had heard of one of its crown jewels—Glen Canyon—and fewer still had been down the river. Eliot Porter was one of the few who shared Glen Canyon with the world through his photographs and writings, but it was too late.

Consequently, on January 21, 1963, the steel gate dropped at Glen Canyon Dam, beginning the destruction of one of the planet's most sacred wild places. A grassroots effort is under way to restore Glen Canyon and has gained wide support, but nature itself is doing a good job of decommissioning the dam: A quarter century's worth of silt from the Colorado River is trapped behind the dam, in perfect harmony with the drought that's lowered Lake Powell. Twenty-seven million tons of sediment is dumped into the reservoir every twenty-four hours. The annual flow of twelve million acre feet can fluctuate from 1,600 cubic feet to a torrent of 300,000 cubic feet per second—not surprising, considering the upper Colorado River Basin drains 110,000 square miles.

As the surface area of Lake Powell increases with silt, so does evaporation, adding to the saline content of the water, so that by the time it reaches Mexico it is even ill suited for irrigation. Today, the waters of the Colorado, which once sustained a vibrant ecosystem, rarely reach the ocean; the ecosystem may never recover. Six percent of the average flow of the river is lost by evaporation and by water seeping into the sandstone, and what's left generates a pitiful three percent of electricity used in the four states it serves. The river's ecosystems—the native fish, plants, and animals, all the way to the Gulf of California—want the river back. Because of Lake Powell's diminished capability to store water, another year of high runoff could bring about a catastrophic flood, as in 1983. That year, the dam nearly failed. So much water backed up behind the dam that house-sized chunks of concrete broke loose from the diversion tunnel. In response, plywood was placed across the entire length of the dam to hold back the water—a short-sighted solution to a boondoggle.

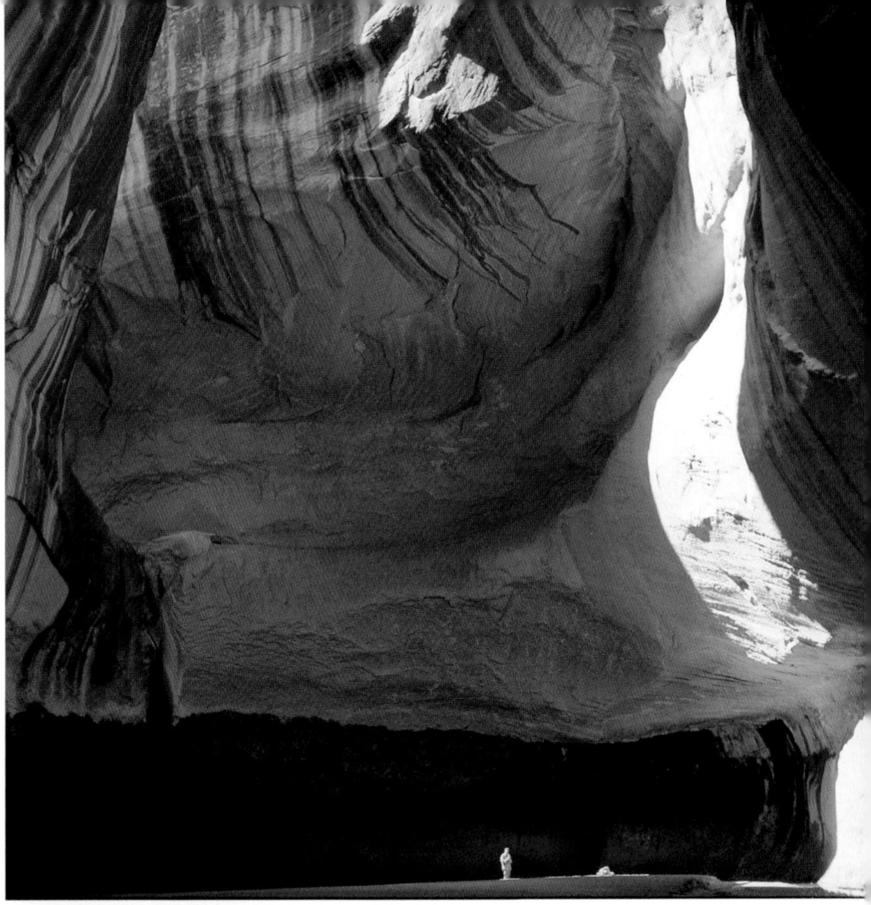

Hite ferry; Harry Aleson at the oars.

I was thumbing through a *Sierra Club Bulletin* in my junior year in high school when the offer of a trip down Glen Canyon caught my eye. It was the last chance to see the canyon before it was lost to the rising waters of Lake Powell. The trip through Glen Canyon began at a small settlement called Hite and ended at Kane Creek, one hundred twenty miles downriver—four hundred miles away by road. At Hite, the Neilsens operated a ferry across the Colorado River and weren't very excited about the Bureau of Reclamation's plan to remove their ranch house and evict them. Soon, the orchards, cottonwoods, willows, pomegranates, and grapes of their land would be two hundred feet beneath the waters of Lake Powell. The blue herons, porcupines, bobcats, mule deer, beavers, and foxes would be homeless.

In Glen Canyon we entered a wonderland of stone, light, and water, where the Colorado River relaxes and stretches over long, sensuous sandbars and takes a deep breath before plunging into the maelstrom of the Grand Canyon. Deep red-brown Wingate Sandstone loomed high above, and below rested the purple-green Chinle Formation, with Navajo Sandstone domes trailing off in the distance. This was the geology through which the Colorado River cut its way.

At camp, under towering cottonwood trees set aglow by driftwood fires, I learned the art of cooking with a Dutch oven. Mornings revealed evidence of the nocturnal carousing of reptiles, small rodents, insects, and birds, their tracks crisscrossing the sand in crazy patterns. I struggled with the oars, learning the rudiments of rowing, and was hired on the spot as a guide.

Below Ticaboo, we passed for one dreamy river mile beneath a massive sandstone wall, stained by desert varnish, that rose a thousand feet straight up from the river. At Olympia Bar we found remnants of a gold-mining operation—a waterwheel used to coax the precious metal from the silt and sand. But Glen Canyon gave the miners no gold.

A canyon no one knew.

We explored Forgotten Canyon, Hidden Passage, Music Temple, and Twilight Canyon. We walked through a landscape that was both beautiful and terrifying—what Wallace Stegner called "a lovely and terrible wilderness." Few places on earth offered such a variety of geographic delights as did Glen Canyon. There, sandstone was sculpted into convoluted folds, ridges, chasms, domes, buttes, grabens, benches, mesas, synclines, monoclines, and anticlines. Seen on hikes from the high ridges, the whole country opened up—Navajo Mountain, the Kaiparowits Plateau, and the Henry Mountains rose blue on the horizon.

In her book *Good Bye River,* my Aunt Elizabeth wrote:

> *In the mirror glass-like water are reflected faraway cliffs, and beyond them distant blue peaks of the Waterpocket Fold—far, far away, so far, so tiny, so perfectly drawn, that like a cloud castle on a summer's day, they seem to hold all the magic of that unattainable land of dreams where everything is peace and perfection.*

The largest fault in Glen Canyon made it possible for a group of Mormon pioneers, who were en route to settle along the San Juan River in Utah, to blast a road down to the Colorado. We camped at what's

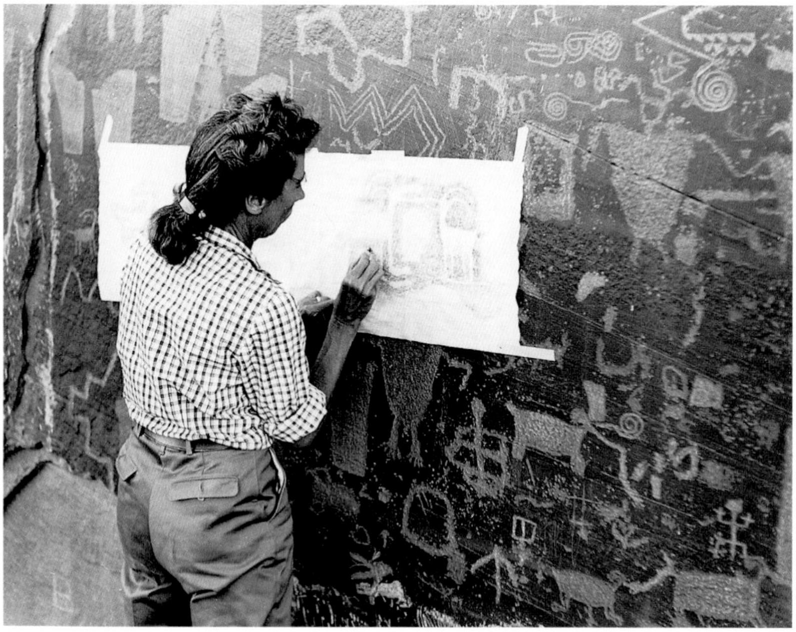

Aunt Elizabeth at Smith Fork, 1961.

called the Crossing of the Fathers. Under a full moon, we hiked up the crack in the fault, a thousand feet up to the rim. Here, eighty-three Mormon wagons once passed. I imagined ghostly silhouettes of their torn canvas coverings flapping in the wind; the blasts of dynamite opening a road down to the Colorado; the smell of sweat mingling with the cries of the babies born on the journey; and the sound of livestock groping and gouging the sandstone down the 45-degree descent to the river. Here, the fervent pioneers built a raft, crossed the river, and traveled one hundred fifty miles of nearly impassable country before collapsing in Bluff, Utah.

The ghostly wagon train passed. The old Mormon road was a reminder that, for centuries, rivers were only obstacles—nightmarish impediments to travel—where nature was neither forgiving nor glorious. The Indians, Escalante, and the Mormons all were on a mission and were exploring in the true sense of the word—risking disaster and overcoming. We can no more understand their mind-set than they could comprehend commercial river running.

At the end of our Glen Canyon trip at Kane Creek, the waters of the reservoir were rising; time was running out for Glen Canyon. Dave Brower agonized its loss and wrote, "Glen Canyon died and I was partly responsible for its needless death." He was planning one last trip. Terry and I would join him.

In the fall of 1963, Terry enrolled at the University of California at Berkeley to finish the last two years of his bachelor's

Crossing of the Fathers.

degree, while I plodded along in my senior year at high school at Pasadena. On his beat-up Royal typewriter, he wrote me long, illustrated letters, vital and alive, often reprimanding me for not writing more often. Terry wrote:

> *Yesterday's slide show on Glen Canyon showed some stupendously gorgeous color shots. Included were a number of before-and-after shots, making the flooding look like a senseless, maniacal catastrophe, which it is: beavers swimming hopelessly about with no place to go, monstrous piles of driftwood choking the side canyons, and most of all, the bland, broad, level, totally alien water surface, which broods like a hardened murderer over the holy beauty, which it has erased for the remainder of our civilization. Included in the show were some pictures taken during a winter trip. Can you imagine spending Christmas Eve in a warm red cave in the cliff, then waking up to a brilliant morning with snow frosting all the formations around you? I buzzed over to David Brower's to see if I could pin him down on precise plans for a Glen Canyon trip, rang the bell, and there I was, shaking hands with "The King"! I listened as Dave's friends talked about dams and power and water; about Glen mostly, and how a few years ago they almost had it saved but someone "caved"; about the Bureau of Wreckla-mation "playing fast and loose"; about Stewart Udall. Brower and his wife, Anne, remembered me right off from*

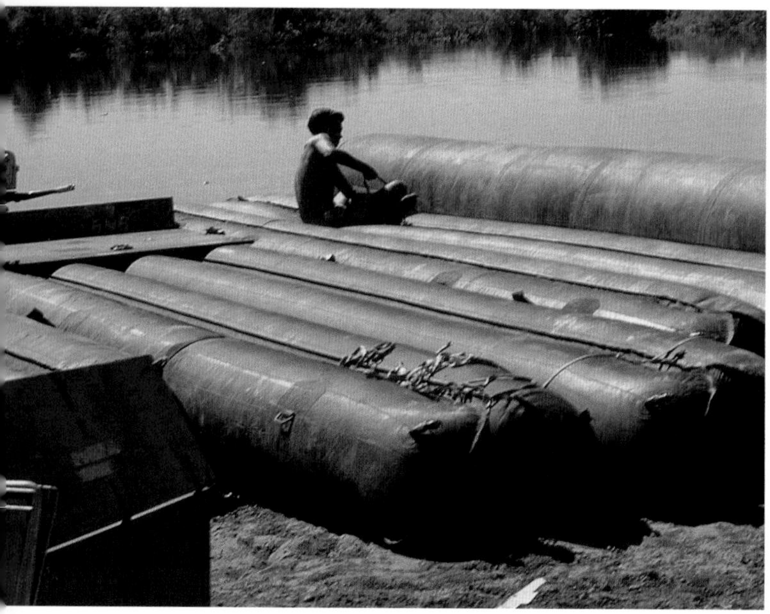

our Sierra trip in 1951; they even saved some of my drawings. By about 11:00 the guests had all gone home. I sat around 'til 1:00 talking about things and pouring tiny glass after glass of this slurpy green booze.

Dave reminisced about ol' Phoebe Russell, the university in his youth, the Club and the worries of the directors, etc. It was really heady. We also talked about the trip, which was what we came for. The main problems were getting equipment and getting enough people. Already there were four "deadheads" like us. Also there'll be an Argentine poet, the Hydes (but not the Porters), and the New York printer of Porter's In Wildness Is the Preservation of the World, Glen Canyon, *etc.*

The hitch on our Jeep can be welded on Wednesday; we'll test the outboards in the bay before we leave. Hold onto your hat because when the trip is over we may go down the Grand Canyon, Escalante, Gray, and Desolation, etc. afterwards. Check out whether our air mattresses are okay—there's no sandbars anymore, so we'll sleep on the slickrock. Tell Ma to send twenty-five more dollars . . . classes end tomorrow.

When I heard that Dave Brower was organizing a trip to document the rising waters of Lake Powell and needed help driving equipment from Oakland to

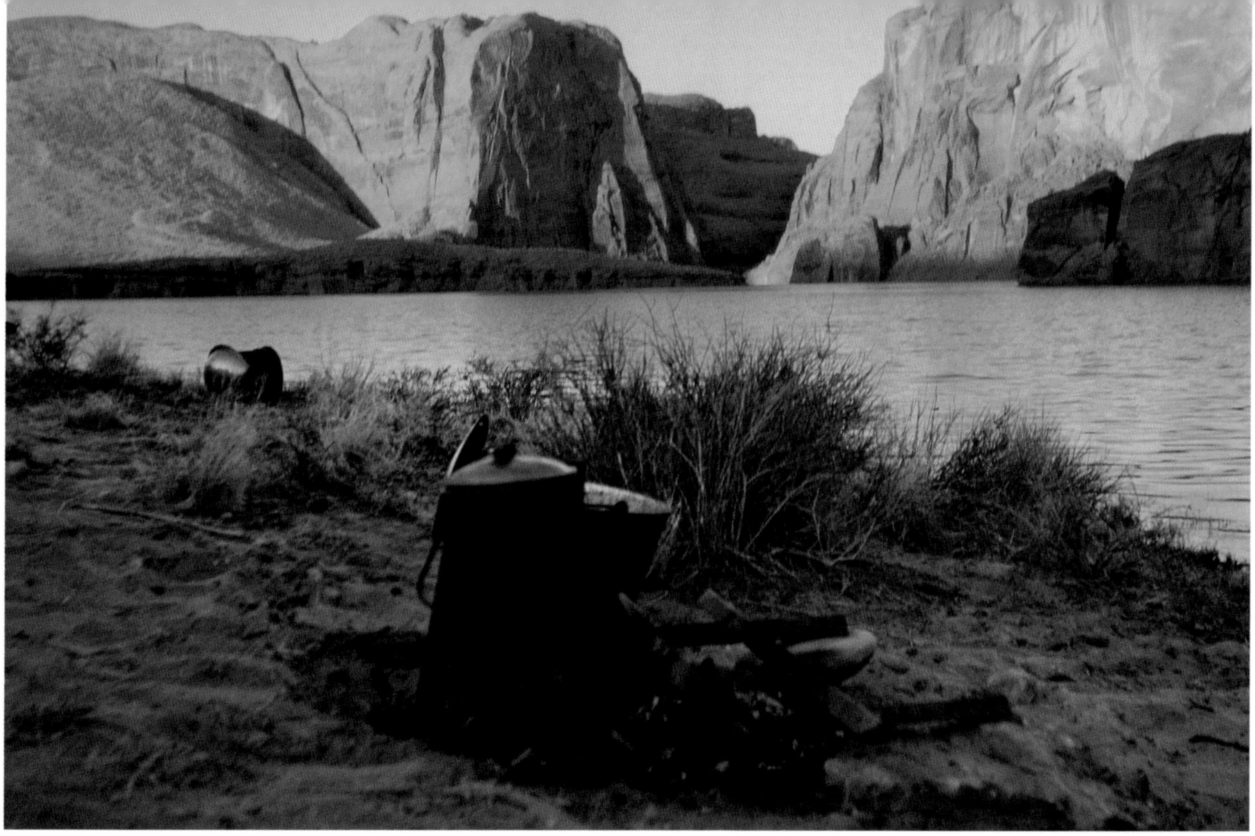

Arizona, I didn't hesitate. I finagled an early diploma and left for the Bay Area. Terry was "glad to hear" of my "triumph of ploy and maneuver."

Our trip began at Wahweap, not far from Glen Canyon Dam. We planned on going up the reservoir as far as possible in eight days, then back in four or five days. It was a somber time. At night I lay in my sleeping bag, unable to sleep. Sand dunes saturated by water thundered down into the water. The water already had backed up into the lower canyons of the Escalante—Soda and Davis—and the cottonwood trees, where Terry and I had camped, were partially inundated, with only the tops of the trees remaining. The air was heavy with the pungent, sweet, sickly smell of their drowning. We documented, cursed, and photographed our way up the lake. By the time we returned to Wahweap we realized the enormity of what had been lost—just as Bureau of Reclamation commissioner Floyd Dominy, who had masterminded and pushed for the dam, was celebrating the throttling of another river. Like a recovering alcoholic, Dominy now acknowledges the downside of "reclamation" and the failure of subsidized water sales, mistakes he equates with the government's "atrocious treatment of Indians."

Some believe it's time to restore the river and the canyon, not for us but for future generations. Others find it difficult to feel any emotion at all with respect to

how future generations will view the environment, much less feel any responsibility toward them, despite how portentously and rhetorically we speak of how the unborn "should" view wilderness. Will we learn from our mistakes? Will wisdom prevail? I wonder how long it will take the Colorado to flush out forty-five years of silt, slime, sunken house-boats, batteries, bodies, tires, and who-knows-what. It will take tens of thousands of years to truly "restore" Glen Canyon, and, by then, will there be anyone who cares?

I recalled an observation from *On the Loose* that accompanied a photograph of the Colorado River in Glen Canyon, which helps put its flooding in perspective. On the top of the page, in large, bold numerals, is written the distant year 19963. Below this are the imagined thoughts of a deer:

> "No, it wasn't always this nice. Most always, yeah, but for a little while the water didn't flow." He shook his antlers and went back to browsing.

CHAPTER TEN

In the desert there is all and there is nothing. God is there and man is not.

— HONORÉ DE BALZAC

Camp Revolution

Deer grazed on spring grass just outside my tent, and flying wedges of gray-and-white geese peppered the early morning sky. My thoughts flew with them . . . Sure, wilderness had changed, and so had I. No revelation there. The pure will, pure desire, pure intention that inflamed my youthful meanderings had given way to a more blasé worldview. Like many of my generation, I never really grew up. Even though the swift blow from the archangel struck down Terry, and wilderness was transformed, and even though I ate from the Tree of Knowledge that can confound and corrupt, the pulse of those early golden years still beats strong.

I felt compelled to write an elegy for Terry—to release a torrent of feelings, or risk drowning in them. My journal molded perfectly to my knee, its edges frayed and worn by remembrance.

Your pack hangs on the wall of memory—its aluminum frame protrudes from worn places in the fabric, like the delicate bleached bones of a bird.
Did it topple from a boulder on Forester Pass in the Sierras?

The nylon string attached to the zipper of its rear compartment—where you kept the topographical maps and books—is frayed and thin.
You never admitted that we were lost, or the distance too great.

Your pack smells of a thousand campfires, of sardines, of smoky green pea soup, of bread and cheese, of insect repellent and sweat.
You always carried more than your share.

On warm summer evenings your old pack stirs in the wind, and in my mind's eye I see you on a far ridge afire with alpenglow.
I wonder what it's like where you are, and if you did win the game by playing for more than we both could afford to lose.

Thus I mused as I packed the boat and drifted across the river to climb the high ridges to the rim that had seemed so inviting yesterday evening. But in the hard flat light of a new day, the land was stark and inhospitable. I tied *Seedskeedee* and pointed my feet toward the highest point on the ridge. As Desolation Canyon deepens, climbing becomes more of a chore because an impenetrable rock wall guards the rim.

The land was so dry and desolate that even the hearty greasewood shrub and prickly pear cactus seemed stunted and deformed. Ants wandered listlessly. I crunched through the crusty alkaline soil where an occasional flower offered hope. Courageously, they made a brief spring appearance, unknowing that the merciless summer sun would scorch and shrivel them. I wanted to live this day as they did, oblivious that it could be my last—I wanted not to be trapped by the past, or anxious about the future, so that the present never arrives.

The moonlike landscape pulled me onward up the long, rolling ridges. The morning's peace steadily eroded. The flowers wilted. In the desert one risks sensory overload: sounds, landforms, too much space, too little water, too much sky, and the fixed qualities of landscape can be unsettling. In the desert one's awareness of the duality of all things comes into focus: the contrasts of light and dark, of sky and earth, of water and mirage, and of life and death, where things unseen but heard demand some logic or interpretation.

I felt detached from the landscape and failed to see how I fit into it. For an uncomfortable moment I felt my soul separate from my body and drift toward the horizon. I cried out, wanting to reclaim it, but my voice sounded hollow and empty and rattled like seeds in a dried gourd.

The landscape forced upon me visions of soulless bodies wandering aimlessly. I saw Sisyphus push his rock up the hill, only to see it roll it down again ad infinitum. Where was my tribe, that in stories and art once linked past, present, and future with the eternal cycles and sacred places? Where were the cosmologies that explained life's contradictions, provided meaning, and alleviated fear? Where was my guide to tell me what one life is worth without this connection, juxtaposed against a gargantuan landscape of endless horizons—this maze of absolute silence except for the ringing in my ears, like the drone of a million locusts?

I didn't like this corner of my mind and pushed it away with a long drink of water and continued my walk. Nearly every ridge had a trail cut deep into chalk soil where generations of wild horses eked out a living, surviving on dust and parched weeds. Every hundred yards, mounds of manure lay in neat, orderly piles, as if some spirit had swept it into place. Strange; where were all the horses? And what would explain the piles of long, narrow rocks, some as long as myself? The slabs had been fired by the sun for eternity and were textured with squiggly imprints of tiny lake creatures that once navigated through the slime and ooze of retreating waters. I struck the slabs together and they echoed with a hollow sound—like plates rattling about in a cloister.

A sheer wall blocked my progress to the summit. Flirting with danger, I carefully worked my way up a crack, climbing the last fifty feet over crumbly rock. The landscape from up high seemed even more unfathomable—too large, too complex with its maze of interwoven mesas and ridges leading off into infinity. Thin horizontal bands of sepia cut through a landscape of subtle blues and gray-greens interspersed with layers of pale orange that capped the distant ridges. To the south, I traced the long meandering ribbon of the Green to where it was swallowed up by Desolation Canyon.

John Wesley Powell wrote a more levelheaded description of Desolation Canyon in his July 6, 1869, journal entry, although there must have been moments when he reckoned with things beyond science:

> *We pass through a region of the wildest desolation. The Canyon is very tortuous, the river very rapid, and many lateral canyons enter on either side. These usually have their branches, so that the region is cut into a wilderness of gray and brown cliffs. Piles of broken rock lie against these walls; crags and tower-shaped peaks are seen everywhere; and away above them, long lines of broken cliffs, and above and beyond the cliffs are pine forests, of which we obtain occasional glimpses, as we look through the vistas of rocks.*
>
> *The walls are almost without vegetation; a few dwarf bushes are seen here and there, clinging to the rocks, and cedars grow from the crevices—not like the cedars of a land refreshed with rains, great cones bedecked with spray, but ugly clumps, like war clubs, beset with spines. We are minded to call this the Canyon of Desolation.*

Far below, a herd of wild horses stood like statues, then slowly, one step at a time, moved down a ridge toward the river. It was the pitiless, rugged land that made them the animals they were—lean, wily, and skittish. Could I get near one?

A thin slab of sandstone about the size of a fist caught my eye and stopped me in my tracks—it was covered with intricate designs. Short lines were incised horizontally, possibly representing clouds, and superimposed over myriad zigzag lines, possibly mountains. Why was it here? There were no potsherds, arrowheads, or other artifacts. It had withstood the elements for centuries and had been placed there by a hand long since turned to dust, when craft bore a humbler, more ancient relationship with nature in a nonlinear world.

My imaginings drifted across the mesas and I followed . . . Were fear and chaos the fountainhead of myth and ritual? Or did myth and ritual emerge peacefully through a visionary and intuitive understanding of place, where plants and animals shape cosmologies? I felt the burden of knowledge—cheated by technology, corrupted by science that explains away the mystery, calculates numbers, and collects data and confines it to tidy bundles of logic. When hypotheses fail, like good soldiers, scientists hop back on the treadmill. There are those who cannot mistrust science, even though it may someday prove that we do not exist. Taoist Chang writes that knowledge that stops at what it cannot know is the ultimate, and those who do not subscribe to this will be worn down by the celestial potter's wheel. Maybe the rudimentary scratchings on the beautiful little stone I held in my hand were created as part of a human's need to leave a message behind before he passed through the great wall to oblivion. Someday, perhaps, someone or something will hear the music of J. S. Bach played by Glenn Gould resounding inside *Voyager* as it drifts beyond our solar system. With a telescopic lens the size of a Kansas cornfield, will we see something we wish we hadn't—some looming shape at the far end of our galaxy with the *Voyager* spacecraft clutched in its claw?

George Bradley, the melancholy hypochondriac who kept a secret journal on Powell's expedition in 1869, felt compelled to leave something of himself behind and wrote of the peculiar piles of rocks that I had stumbled upon:

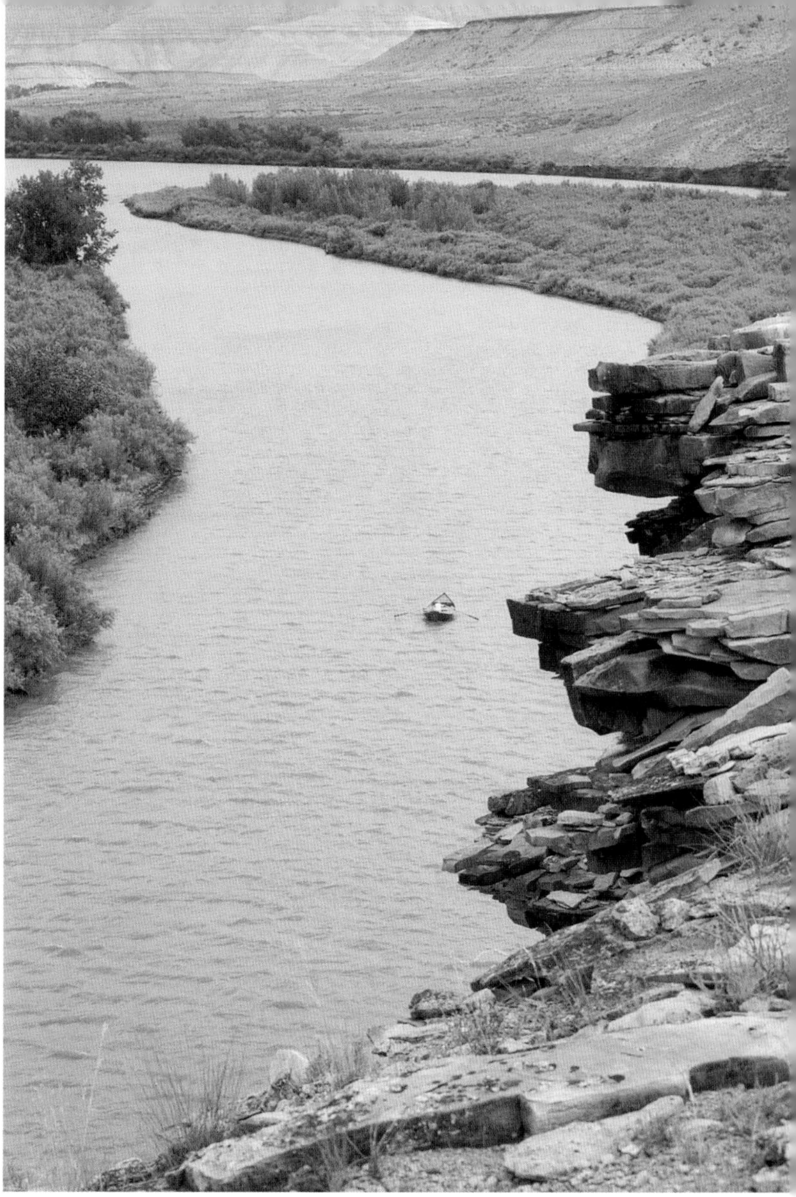

I think it was the work of Indians, for I could not find names or letters on any of the rocks. I re-piled them and added a long rock, over seven feet, which I placed on end and made very secure. I also put my name on a flat stone with name of expedition and date and fastened it up very strong. I think it will stand many years.

I dashed down the ridges laughing like a lunatic, not wishing to be worn

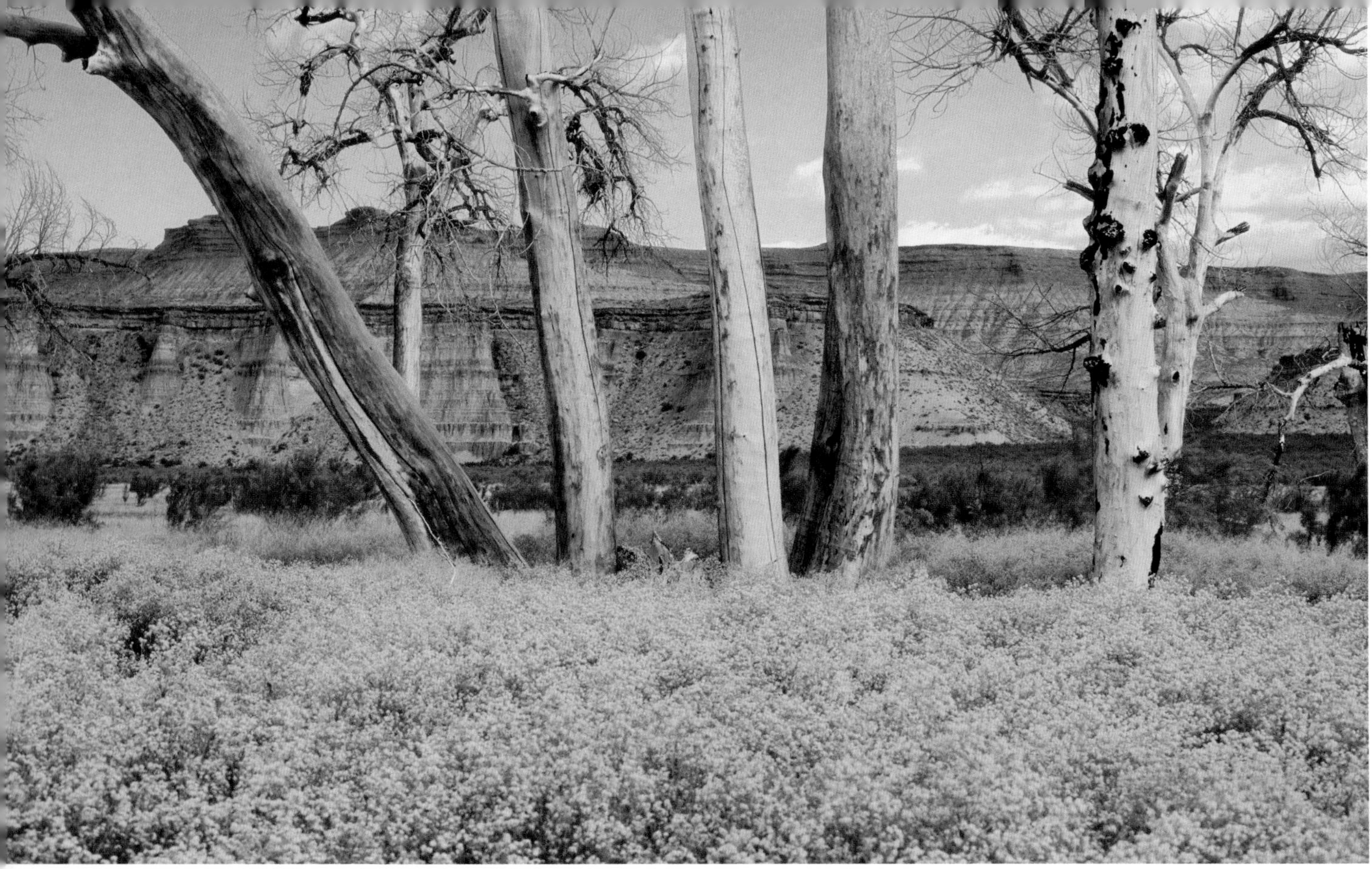

down by Chang's celestial potter's wheel by asking too many questions. I followed deep ruts of wild horses' tracks, hoping to catch a glimpse of them. But by the time I arrived at the boat, they had vanished. I wouldn't have been surprised, after the places my mind had taken me on my walk, to have seen Pegasus fly overhead—wings pounding against the sky, fire shooting from his nostrils—with Terry on his back. If my brother asked me to hop on behind to fly off to Mount Helicon, would I have gone with him?

I looked upstream and there were no boats in sight. There were no airplanes. There was no wind. Just one man, a boat, and a river. I untied and rowed relentlessly until I saw the unmistakable pattern of sixteen buzzards headed directly toward me. I dropped my oars. They circled low, and for an uncomfortably long time their beady eyes glared down at me. Their paperlike wings moved like no other bird's—stiff, irregular, and convulsive—and conjured images of famines, and plagues, and the recurring cycles of life and death. Was I no more than a piece of meat? I stood on the deck cackling, mimicking their flight . . .

Around the bend, I saw what the buzzards had been up to. A deer had tried to swim the river, had perhaps miscalculated the distance, drowned, and was snagged on a submerged limb, his antlers cutting the water like a knife. I heard the high-pitched drone of countless millions

of winged insects that blew upstream in mindless swarms. They battered the boat, flew into my mouth and eyes, and made pilgrimages deep into my ears. Wave after wave passed, conjuring apocalyptic images of flesh-eating insects.

To brighten up the day, a flock of great white pelicans cruised in from the south. In a perfectly orchestrated ballet, they rose, fell, and skimmed the water in unison and swooped down next to me. They seemed prehistoric with their black-tipped wings, bright orange bills, and large pouches.

I passed a grove of cottonwoods killed by fire amid fields of waist-high white flowers. The contrast was abrupt. I had to get closer. Some trees were coal-black, others bone-white, and every shade of gray between, silhouetted against a Persian-blue sky where shafts of sun played hide-and-seek with clouds on the run. My fingers traced trees textured like snakeskin; felt the sleek smooth surfaces

Sand Wash ferry, 1930s.

a maximum of thirty people per group. During the "peak season"—May until October—on a five-day trip covering eighty-four miles, there can be as many as seven hundred fifty people on the river. That's a hypothetical 27,000 people a year.

I searched the shore for a slot to land between two groups of thirty people who were chattering excitedly. A dozen kayakers formed a circle on the beach next to their boats and were doing yoga, while the trip leader barked out rules and regulations. When I rowed in, an assemblage stared blankly at me from their partly submerged lawn chairs.

"Good afternoon," I said, with the biggest smile I could muster. "Could this be Sand Wash?" I added in my most cheerful voice, "How far to the Sea of Cortez?" This drew blank looks. "Seen the river ranger?" I asked.

They grunted in unison and pointed toward a sterile double-wide trailer. I knocked on the door and shuffled my feet. Rock-and-roll music boomed against the walls. On the third knock, an attractive young seasonal ranger appeared and told me to wait while she changed into her government shirt. Together, we walked down to the launch site. Her name was Jessica.

"Not many folks start up at Ouray like you," she said. "Never done it myself. In

of others. Sun cut across the hollowed-out trunks and bare-boned limbs, stark and angular, that clawed at the sky. In the center of these ghostly giants was a single tree that the fire hadn't taken. I sat beneath him and paid my respects.

I untied *Seedskeedee* and drifted. Where the river made a sharp left turn, in country I thought roadless, a pickup truck was parked. Only then did I realize I hadn't passed Sand Wash yesterday in the sandstorm. Except for the apparition of Red Moon, I hadn't seen anyone in four days, or was it five? Anyway, I was on river time that contracts, protracts; collapses, elongates, and eventually stands still.

At Sand Wash, the Bureau of Land Management channels river travelers through Desolation and Gray Canyons—the most popular section of the Green River, where the canyon deepens and rapids begin. Rangers "release" six groups of river runners from Sand Wash daily, allowing the fall there'll be a few duck hunters."

"That's too bad," I replied, "I mean, for the ducks."

I invited her on board for a cup of tea, offering her a chunk of ginger candy that she pretended to like. With clipboard in hand, she methodically checked my cargo to make certain I had all the equipment required of a boater in the latter part of the twentieth century. Jessica said she was in her senior year at the University of Georgia, majoring in outdoor recreational management. I wanted to ask her what she thought people did before recreation was "managed."

I mentioned that there were sure a lot of people at the launch today, and she replied it was quieter than it had been earlier in the day, when a cluster of CEOs flew in to be coddled by a river company "targeting" the affluent. Jessica said each executive is issued his own personal guide, gourmet food is served, and mattresses with sheets are provided, accompanied with a mint on the pillow each night.

Never having seen a wooden boat on the river before, she asked, "And where's your repair kit?" This new breed of recreational specialist laughed when I whipped out my cordless drill and pointed it at her, warning her to "be careful 'cause it's loaded."

I gave her a copy of *On the Loose* and told her it was written by a couple of brothers who were about her age, who had roamed the West, snapped photos, and written about their love of wild places. In jest, I asked if she wanted to come along with me. With a shy smile, she politely declined. I was impatient to get back on the river and leave the menagerie. So with my papers in order, and with official clearance from the United States Government, I said good-bye, untied *Seedskeedee*, and rowed on.

I'd lost track of the date—it made little difference, and since my watch had sunk, time still had passed, and what river mile it was seemed irrelevant. What was plain was that river running on the Green had gone through a few transformations since I had last been here. Was I an anachronism—an anomaly out of step with the times? Did I expect the character of the river to remain as in the days of *On the Loose*? No, but the diminished sense of adventure raised a pang of nostalgia—no more venturing into the unknown without a global positioning system with barometric altimeter, elevation computer, odometer, electronic compass, and a celestial information page.

Still, it's not necessary to be a Shackleton to have an adventure. There's more to a climb than reaching the summit, and heroic tales of man battling nature are giving way to stories of those exploring the inner landscape.

On the Loose had an uncanny way of sneaking up on me. So did an H. G. Wells

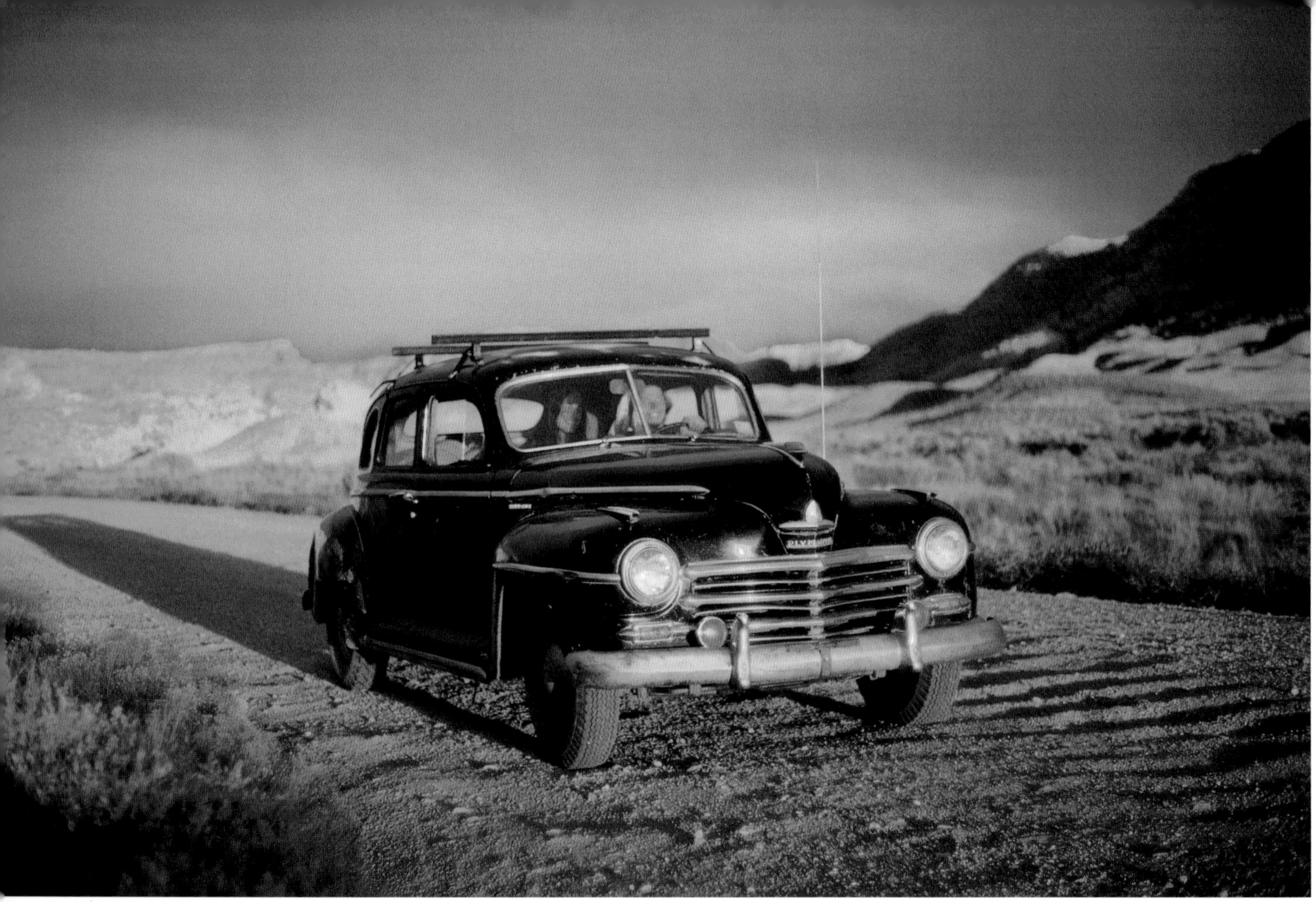

Utah's Canyonlands National Park.

quote from the book that spoke of the human condition in these "plethoric times," when the majority go through contemporary life "fudging, evading and slacking, never really frightened nor passionately stirred." . . . Bet my brother would have concluded that the majority of the race has become flabby and lobotomized, adrift in the sheepish calm of cyberspace, estranged from its roots—an animal who has evolved culturally and biologically into an ecological misfit, whose own existence is a problem that he has to solve and from which he cannot escape.

As I passed the broad, sweeping bend at Sumner's Amphitheater, I reflected on another quote from *On the Loose*: "Hurry and take the road to a roadless area, because it won't be roadless long. Too much demand . . . And so we push the big wheel nearer the edge . . . the land of the free and the home of the auto dump." Terry never saw the "big wheel" go over the edge, but his predictions have come to pass. Where do you stop the big wheel? Where's the edge? Where did all the "roadless areas" go? I asked the wind how *On the Loose* could demean the automobile yet manage to justify it when it was driven to a "roadless area."

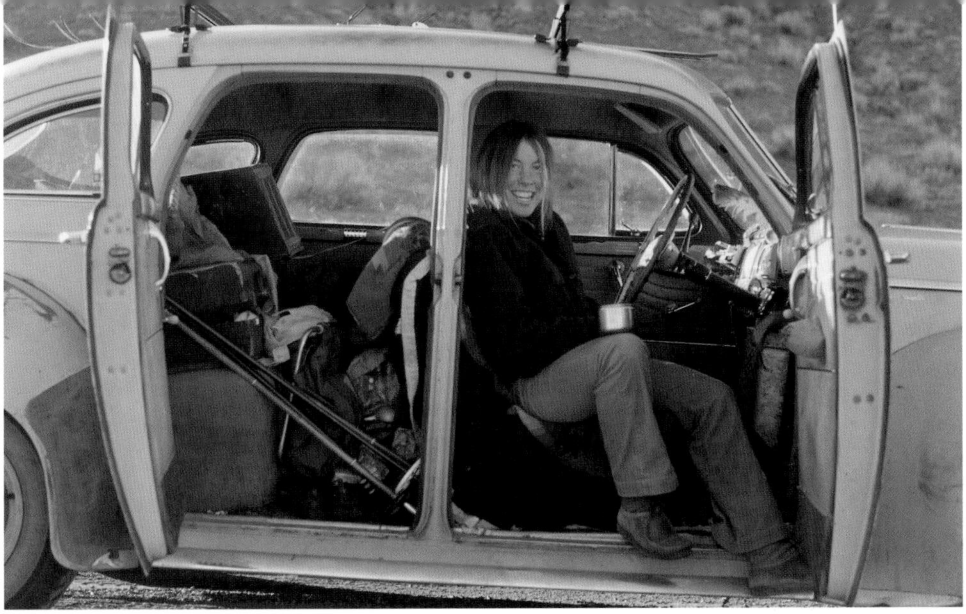

Ramblin' fever.

Once upon a time, camping in Organ Pipe Cactus National Monument was easy. But in 1992 when I revisited the monument to climb Mount Ajo, it was overcrowded and had become a mini–police state, where armed border patrol and monument cops interrogated from shiny and new white trucks.

On my way to the monument in southern Arizona, I tried to camp along the Salt River east of Phoenix, and found a different sort of river than I remembered. Walking downstream, I felt the smooth river cobbles beneath my feet where the Salt River once flowed—Phoenix and agricultural interests had all but sucked the Salt dry. I picked my way through a maze of discarded items from a consumer society: television sets, screens blown out by shotgun blasts; refrigerators, doors swinging in the wind, riddled with bullet holes. Entire mobile homes lay on their sides, their thin walls ripped open like sardine cans, their grotesque contents spilling into stagnant, polluted waters.

I crossed the floodplain to the crack of automatic-pistol fire. The bullets ricocheted around me. It was the weekend—time to go to the river and shoot television sets. I made a dash back to the truck, passing two sad-eyed fishermen

Civilization once depended on fossil fuel . . .

slumped over in lawn chairs. There was no camping here. The wheel had been pushed over the edge.

Robert Frost asked us, "What do we make of a diminished thing?" The scarlet globemallows still poked their heads out of the sand to bloom, and I knew the river would one day return. I wondered if my disillusionment with society and the loss of wild places was selfish. I, too, was a consumer and part of the problem. What had I done lately to heal a diminished wilderness? It's endemic to grumble, a challenge to inspire. Often I find myself eagerly anticipating the next cataclysmic event to wash the planet clean. All things said, it's apathy that kills. Wilderness will endure. Man will find his way.

Despite a culture in decline and the bullets, I held fast to this belief as I streaked south on Highway 85. I stopped for lunch at a "recreation area" with a locked gate. The discharge of a large-caliber hunting rifle echoed off the canyon walls. For the next forty miles, I apprehensively drove through Luke Bombing and Gunnery Range, and turned south at a town appropriately named Why.

There was no camping in Organ Pipe Cactus National Monument without a reservation, and I had none. Just outside the monument I caught sight of the scratchings of an old road and crossed an abandoned railroad track. I followed the road until it ended in a garden of creosote, paloverde, and mesquite. I had

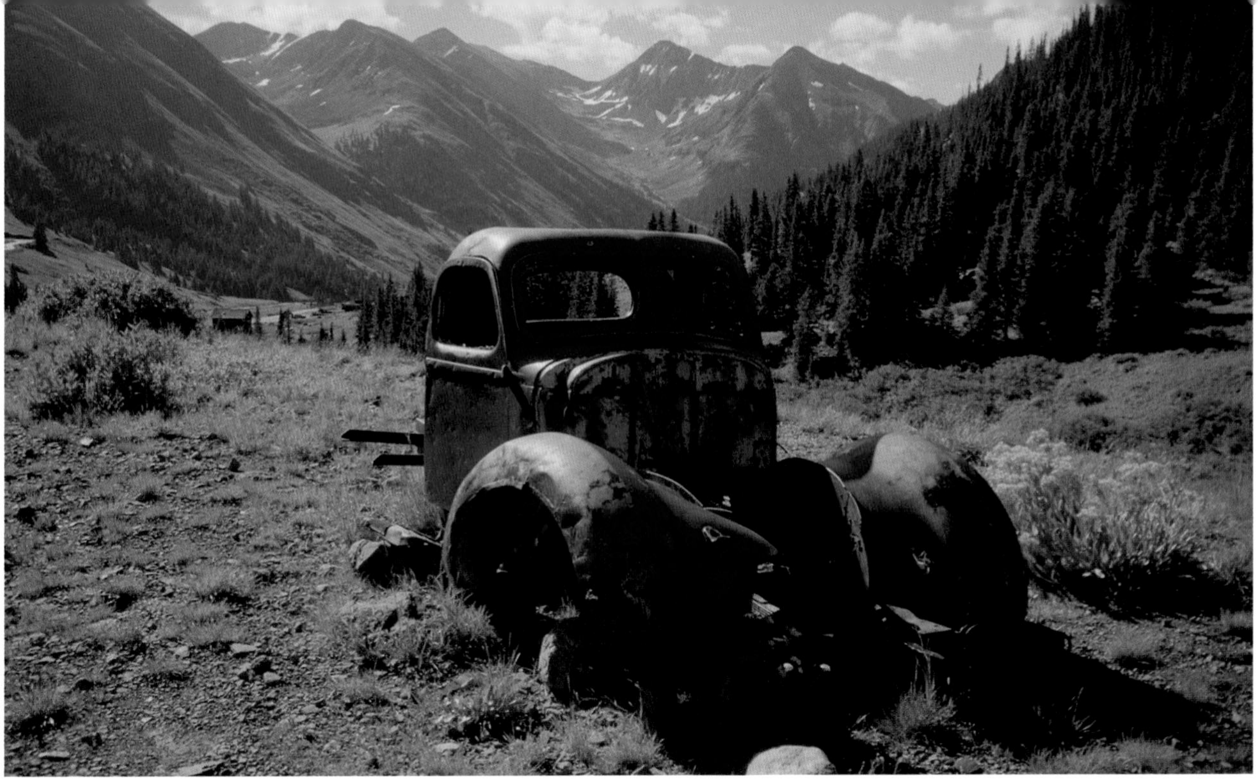

arrived! Was this the mythological place that Terry and I had known—that interface between the road and paradise? I grabbed my camp chair, Martin guitar, and a book of short stories by Wallace Stegner. Then the slam of a truck door jerked me from paradise. A heavily armed border patrol officer approached and asked me to leave, or I'd be fined for driving a few feet off the road. I put my chair, guitar, and book back in the truck and retreated down a dirt track where footprints of Mexican migrants had cut a deep trail in the sand—each footprint a mystery no one can define as desperate souls search for the American dream in the broken promise land . . .

Two miles north, I drove through a sea of Winnebagos—a sort of overflow encampment of retirees who couldn't fit into the monument's campground. Twenty miles later I parked under a saguaro and camped. The sun was going down, but the pilots at the gunnery range were just waking up. All night, fighter jets thundered overhead, and the sky to the west was afire with rockets and the boom of artillery.

Early the next morning, I drove toward Mount Ajo and began climbing. The springtime desert was never more beautiful, and the air was filled with sweet fragrance and renewal. The murkiness of the past few days washed away down the arroyo. From the summit I saw the Diablo Mountains directly to the west, and the rolling hills of the Sonora

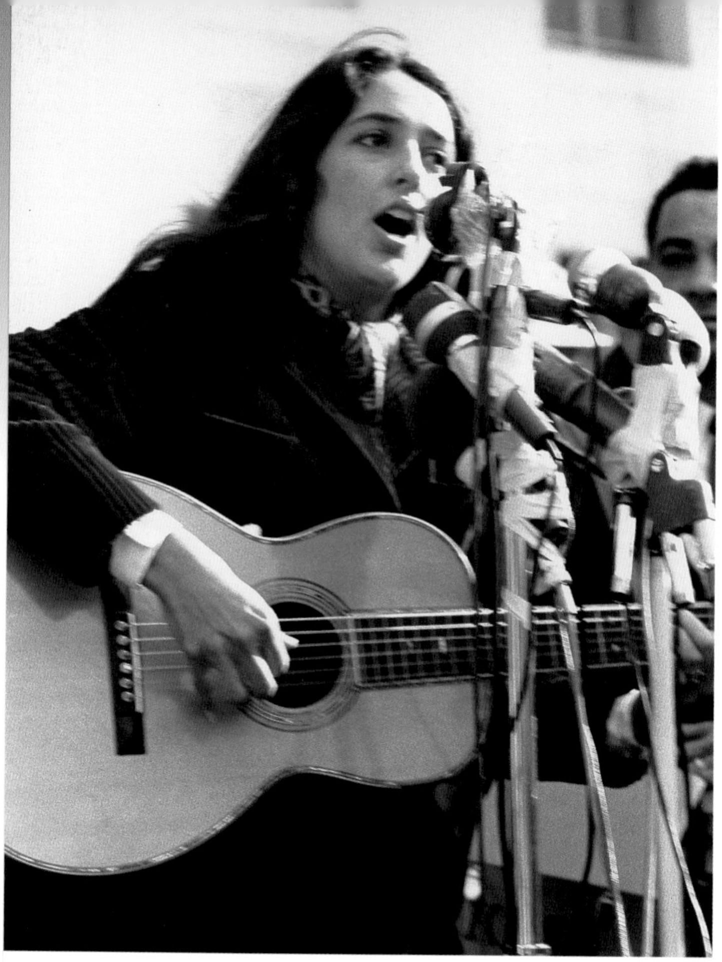

Joan Baez at Free Speech rally, Berkeley, California, 1964.

Terry and I sat with our backs to the wall inside Sproul Hall along with hundreds of students who were fed up with university bureaucracy. The protesters demanded more of a voice in administrative decisions. A showdown with the uncompromising administration was inevitable. Terry, like many of the other protesters, was a staunch Jeffersonian—intent on upholding the United States Constitution. He wasn't interested in the destruction of democracy and was hardly a wild-eyed revolutionary.

I weighed the options, nervously nudged my brother, and told him my political convictions fell just short of going to jail. Noticing that the door was still open, I delicately picked my way through a tangle of protesters' legs, and tripped over the feet of Joan Baez, who was singing, "Oh freedom, oh freedom—and before I'll be a slave, I'll be buried in my grave, and I'll fight for my right to be free."

I burst through the door surrounded by a wall of six hundred policemen hell-bent on beating down five hundred passively resisting students. A passerby zeroed in on me and launched into an invective tirade about being weary of paying taxes for bums and beatniks like me and said I deserved a sentence of hard labor. An angry crowd swelled around me in the plaza, filled the steps of Sproul Hall, and pressed toward the barricaded doors. I was certain we were moments away from a riot. Hysteria and pandemonium prevailed and the tension was indescribable.

Terry remained inside the building—stubborn and steadfast. I watched as students were dragged from Sproul Hall on their backs—arms and wrists twisted—down a long staircase, much to the amusement of the police. Jeering at the protesters, the cops threatened to beat my brother senseless if he resisted. I restrained myself.

On December 3, 1964, five hundred demonstrators were hauled

Outside Sproul Hall the tension was indescribable.

away and arrested for trespassing, booked behind covered windows where no reporters were allowed, and thrown in jail. My brother stood tall that day. He would have been the pride of our ancestor Elizabeth Dyar, who mixed paint and applied it to the men of the Boston Tea Party to disguise them. Story goes she melted her pewter spoons for bullets, casting them in a mold her father had brought to the American colonies from France.

Terry spent three years at Carleton College in Minnesota, recovered from being rejected by Yale and Harvard. He returned to the West, where he belonged, to finish his degree at the University of California. That year he wrote:

All in all, going to school with sandaled weirdies, zoot-suited graduate students, and sari-ed Moslems [sic] seems more like the real thing than going to school with 1,365 Bill Mitchells. It's hard to explain the sense of a serious permanent enterprise which distinguishes education at a university; the buildings are larger and more majestic, the bookstore is bigger and more crowded, even the trees seem bigger and more firmly rooted in the soil. The powerful hum of the machinery of education at Cal isn't overpowering, it's vastly reassuring. It looks like a good year.

I recall the awkward silence, our unspoken sadness, and the solid farewell handshake at the San Francisco airport before Terry left for Carleton. I watched until his plane was a speck against a sky that would forever be a different shade of blue. His absence made me realize how interwoven our lives had been, and I began the struggle to define myself beyond my brother's power.

After Terry left for Carleton, Phoebe and I moved to Pasadena, California, to take care of my grandmother for the remainder of her days. Adrift in the mist of memory, I grab cloud fragments to recall the storm and the light of that distant time: I ran. Mr. Swift, our track coach, suggested we lie down and listen to Beethoven's Fifth Symphony before a competition, to focus. It worked—we were fast. But not as fast as the Afro-American students I had run with in Berkeley. Pasadena's high school was segregated. In English class, I offered book reviews of John Griffin's *Black Like Me* and Richard Howard's *Black Cargo*. I can't say I was very popular. My heart and soul were far away in wilderness with my brother—pounding through the rapids on the Salmon River or climbing the high ridges of the Sierras, where long feathers of clouds streaked across the cobalt-blue sky and luminous arrows of light pierced the glassy air.

My art instructor, Jack Dalton, threw me a life jacket. Gay, rambunctious, vivacious, and feisty, he offered a fresh palette of colors and new ways of seeing. He took his favorite students to dinner, to movies; snuck us into college-level anatomy classes; and took us to shows at the Los Angeles Art Museum to view Gaston Lachaise's bronze nudes. Jack had lived and studied with the French impressionist Raoul Dufy during his last years, and I can still hear Dalton quoting Dufy: "Man was created to complete the work of God, and the painter to put order in nature. The best way for the painter to find order is to proceed like the Creator, and separate dark from light." But since I believed God's work was already complete, and nature was perfect order, I didn't know how to proceed separating dark from light.

But light arrived when Dalton offered me a storage room in which to paint and study— encouraging me on my own path. I checked out books on the lives and work of Heironymus Bosch and Albrecht Dürer. I traveled so far into Bosch's painting *The Garden of Earthly Delights* that I lost my way. His work was a far cry from that of Conrad Buff, a landscape painter of the Southwest, who became my mentor and teacher. Neither Jack Dalton nor Conrad taught that the creation of art and money were in any way related. I outgrew my workspace at high school and turned my grandmother's garage into a studio and began painting a surreal conglomerate of images inspired by these artists. In the back of the garage my ramblin' friend Bill Wayne and I tuned up our beloved Martin D-21 guitars and played about every song the New Lost City Ramblers ever recorded—soulful music from Appalachia, songs from the Prohibition and Depression days. The high lonesome sound of Roscoe Holcomb gave me goose bumps, and I studied *How to Play the Five-String Banjo,* taught by Pete Seeger. I thought Earl Scruggs was God.

In my makeshift studio, my record player spun the Country Gentlemen's *Tobacco Road;* Spider John Koerner, Ray, and Glover sang *Blues, Rags, and Hollers*. I drank my first beer and tried but failed at rolling a Bull Durham cigarette. I graduated from South Pasadena High in 1964 and was accepted to the San Francisco Art Institute. I packed for Berkeley and never looked back.

The Berkeley I remembered had vanished—or maybe the lens through which I viewed the world had changed, especially what it revealed along Telegraph Avenue, the main artery leading to the university. Familiar landmarks, like the Mediterranean Coffeehouse, Kip's Restaurant, and

Cody's Books remained. But the Campanile at the University didn't seem as tall, and the bells in its tower had a new ring. There was unrest on all fronts: The Vietnam War was raging, and the new environmental movement was defining itself as a major political force. Vast tracts of wilderness were being threatened by logging, and rivers were being throttled. So small acts of defiance were not uncommon. In the dark of night Terry and I yanked survey stakes for a proposed road through the heart of old-growth redwoods in Northern California.

Electricity crackled along Telegraph Avenue. The hipsters and beatniks described by Allen Ginsberg had metamorphosed into hippies. It seemed the entire city was either climbing or crashing on drugs. On the Avenue, the illegitimate sons and daughters of Woody Guthrie pounded out songs on beat-up guitars for their dinners. Craftsmen slept under trees and chained their goods to streetlight poles to keep the police from confiscating them. Smoke from incense and pot filled the air. Groups of disheveled kids wearing bells, beads, and bangles huddled together, speaking in a rhapsodic drone. They turned on, freaked out, were stoned, tripped, had their minds blown, were groovy, crashed, had flashes, felt the vibes, saw the great white light while doing their thing, were sometimes uptight or wiped out, but were always where it's at. Incongruous kids with painted faces pushed one another down the streets in shopping carts. Others passed trance-like, their wings singed, like Icarus who had flown too close to the sun. Shops sold books on astrology, the *I Ching,* tarot cards, the occult, magic exotic rituals, and mysticism. Religions were devoured like sugar cubes—Zen, Sufism, shamanism, and Gnosticism. Jack Kerouac's characters from *On the Road* roamed the streets, jammed the coffee-houses, and packed the clubs—"the ones mad to live, to talk, to be saved, desirous of everything at the same time who burned like Roman candles exploding like spiders across the stars and in the middle you see the blue centerlight pop and everybody goes 'Awww.'"

Psychedelic bands like the Grateful Dead, the Jefferson Airplane, Quicksilver Messenger Service, the Family Dog, and Sopwith Camel appeared. Music surged and pulsated from apartments above the shops and into the streets. The Airplane pounded out the anthem of the times, how one pill can make you larger and another make you small—go ask Alice, when she's ten feet tall. The music's energy and drive made a powerful potion: there had been nothing like it before, least of all for me, who had grown up listening to Hank Williams and the Kingston Trio. There I was, living in the very heart of a new Babylon—and it blew the top off my head.

I lived in Berkeley my first semester, a short hop across the Bay from the San

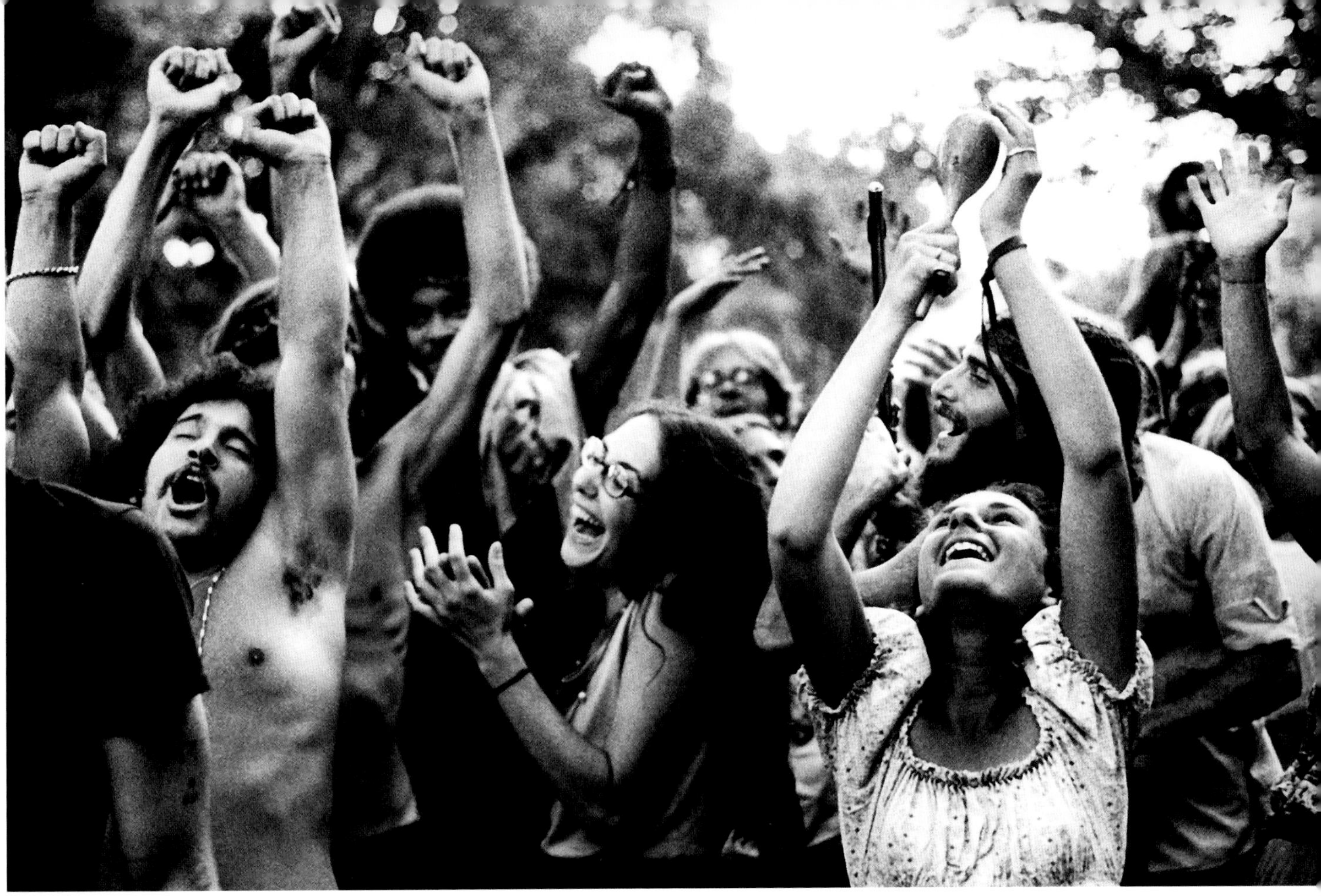

Alas! The forbidden fruits were eaten, and thereby the warm life of reason congealed.

Francisco Art Institute, where I studied sculpture, anatomy, art history, experimental motion pictures, lithography, and oil painting, and audited UCB classes that Terry recommended. I found an apartment above a hamburger joint on Bancroft Way, just off Telegraph Avenue. The room was permeated by the odor of decades of grease. The brouhaha downstairs, the racket of dishes and clanging pots, combined with the mayhem of the fraternities across the street, made sleeping nearly impossible. But I didn't have much time for sleep, not with studying, weekend trips with Terry to Yosemite or Point Reyes, or simply walking the streets.

From my greasy apartment window, I watched the street scene below as though it were a movie whose actors called me to join the dance. But the psychedelic wonderland seemed as alluring as it was alien and terrifying. Even my record player didn't know if it should spin Alan Hovhaness, Bill Monroe, Bach, or the Grateful Dead. Unsure, I lashed myself to my easel, as Odysseus had bound himself to the mast

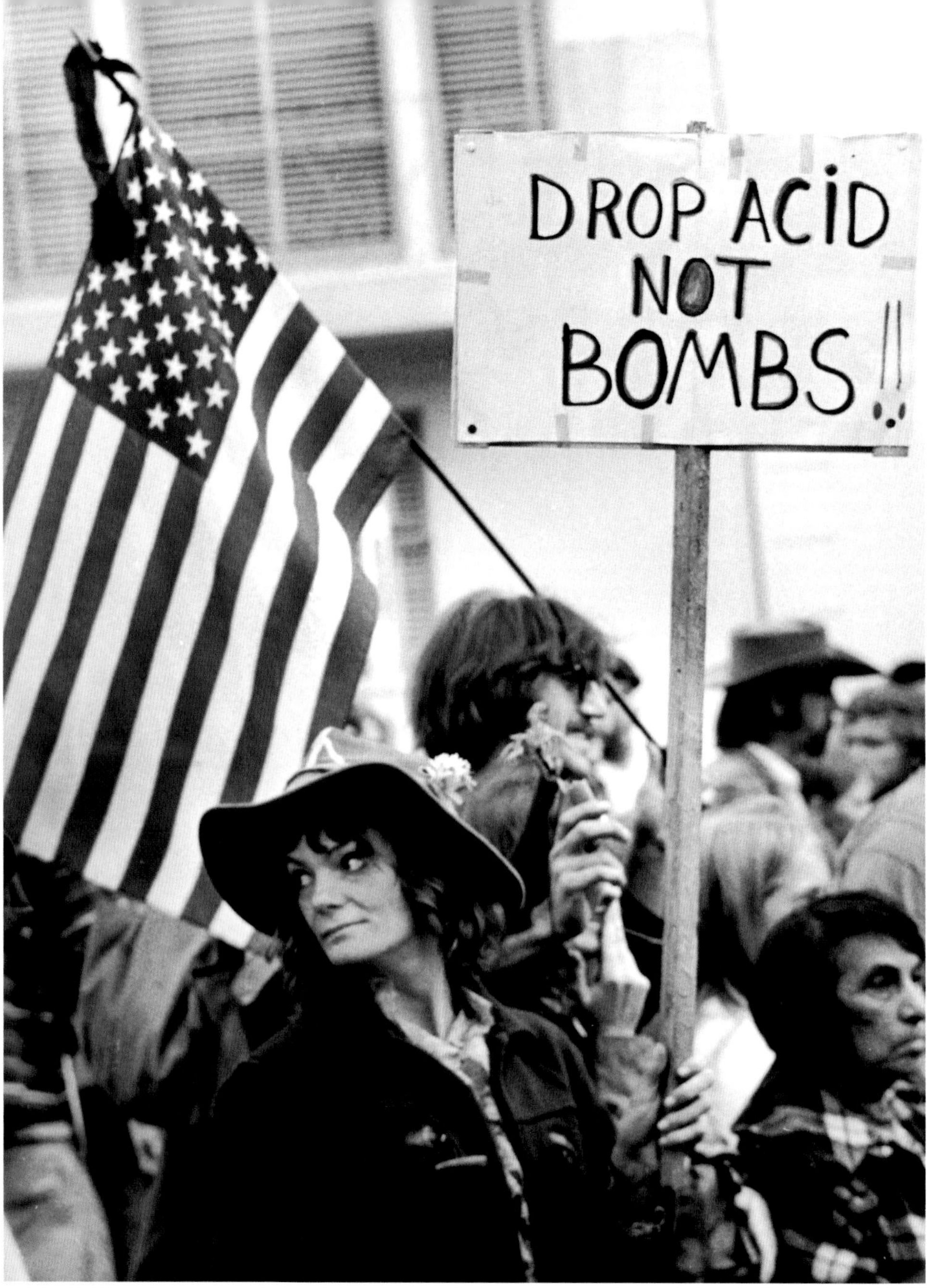

Each man's morals shape his destiny . . .

of his ship to save himself from being seduced by the sirens. But to no avail. Rumi wrote, "Alas! the forbidden fruits were eaten, and thereby the warm life of reason congealed. A grain of wheat eclipsed the sun of Adam, like as the Dragon's tail dulls the brightness of the moon."

I walked to the plaza outside the student union building, where it was relatively quiet after the Free Speech rallies. A crowd gathered around local musicians Country Joe and the Fish, who sang, "One, two, three, what are we fighting for? Don't ask me, I don't give a damn, next stop is Vietnam." I nervously fingered a vial of pure LSD that renowned chemist

Augustus Owsley Stanley III had concocted in his notorious illicit laboratory across the Bay. A fellow art student told me that if I took the drug I would become the Buddha or Einstein, or God. I was game. The powder went down with a gulp and the world I had known vanished forever.

A fleet of ships appeared through a misty rainbow of color, and from their masts, banners and spangles gently moved in the breeze . . . jewels hung in a cobalt-blue sky, their facets brilliantly reflecting the sun. Country Joe's voice trailed off . . . "But now . . . there is . . . no place to run to." I felt like Jell-O.

The ships returned and I boarded, walking the thin line between weakness and courage, sanity and madness. As the gangplank was pulled away, I realized I had brought no luggage and had no idea where I was going. My fellow passengers just smiled and said, "Have faith, man—try some of these. We're all heading down the same river together, to an ocean of eternal peace and love." But the voice of reason cautioned: "Like Ferdinand Magellan, you may succeed in circumnavigating the globe, discover the Spice Islands, and return to Portugal a hero. But first you may spend a hellish winter in your boat locked in ice, and eat the leather rigging, sawdust, and rats to survive." I shuddered. My friends saw I was having a bad trip—they smiled, held my hand, and away we sailed to Haboola Land. We visited Dante's *Inferno* and Milton's *Paradise.* Sometimes on our journey we were bathed in warm golden light, and at other times we wandered about aimlessly in a Gustave Doré landscape of perpetual twilight, where it's impossible to tell the good angels from the bad.

The ships sailed away, and the chimes of the Campanile brought me back to the bench at the UC campus, though I never returned entirely. Country Joe had packed his guitar and was gone. I tucked my brain under my arm and headed back to my greasy apartment.

No matter how "free" love was in the '60s, or how strong the belief that the moment was all there was, the psychedelic revolution took its toll. Lost souls, permanent cripples, failed seekers, runaways, and expatriates in exile huddled together in darkened doorways, overwhelmed by a world that no longer made sense—a world that one moment was beautiful beyond words and the next was a chaotic, grotesque nightmare. The early explorers who opened Pandora's pillbox and experimented with psychedelics discovered that no one can live in paradise forever. Some returned with incredible stories, but others were washed overboard and eaten by sharks. My fellow travelers, whom I will never see again, have long since scattered far and wide.

Psychedelics left me with an inarticulate sense that something irrecoverably significant existed beyond my understanding, and that I had lost or missed a unique opportunity for transcendence. But the drug-induced dream never can be carried over into daily life. Where there is no discipline and hard work, there is no lasting meaning. The lingering mist of chemical agents only masks what author Peter Matthiessen calls the true experience of the infinite in us.

Among those who remained on solid ground was Terry. He walked the hard and wiry line of rectitude, watching the emerging drug culture from the windows of the university library, where the orderly world of books and logic prevailed. Terry mastered Russian, Latin, Spanish, French, and German. Though at times social, he was indifferent, detached, and aloof. He possessed an inner wisdom and awareness that transcended his studies—as though he had studied these subjects before in another life. His humor always prevailed:

> *Some glowing scholastic reports: I got an "A" on the Zoology quiz, second highest in the class, and on a Geography test I got the highest grade in the entire 200-student class: 96%. We got math tests back Thursday. I got a "D." 36%. . . . I just went into the bathroom, slashed my wrists, took an overdose of sleeping pills and tried to hang myself with a towel from the ceiling. What's the use of living after you've almost flunked a math test?*
>
> *Today I really had a fine trip. The weather has been sparkling clear lately, the sun was warm, the breeze brisk. Up along Skyline Boulevard I had the road all to myself. About halfway up two dogs appeared from nowhere and started following me. After five miles they were still romping along behind, and since I knew I couldn't leave them, I took them all the way to Redwood Regional Park, fed them dried beef and cheese for lunch midst the pines, and then took them home. I got a flat tire, like a bonehead, over an awful dirt road, and since I had to be back by 3:00 to pre-enroll for French 1, I hurried down gingerly on the rim. Boy, did I look like an idiot coasting down Claremont on a flat tire with two panting dogs stopping traffic in the rear.*

The heat and noise in my apartment above the burger joint were unbearable, and I was suffering from visual and sensory overload—the feeling one might get after eating a half dozen Lindt chocolate bars. Serendipity brought me to a cabin that was for rent in the town of Canyon. The abode was hidden in a dense forest of redwood, and it suited me fine. A few ridges east of Berkeley, Canyon was inhabited by a motley mix of artists, outlaws, writers, and assorted misfits. The cabin smelled of damp, decaying wood and was heated by antiquated electric heaters, whose coils were situated in the center of a concave copper plate. The heaters cast a soft orange light through the house and were always blowing fuses. Away from the city, I found peace to create, study, and just be.

Music cooled the fire that raged through me. The haunting, soulful music of Bach's cello suites mellifluously flowed from my battered stereo. The notes ascended to the high branches of the redwoods in the fog where they hung suspended, then descended, circling around the trees. Pierre de la Rue's mass *Dolores Gloriose Recollentes* lured me into the sweet, sorrowful world of polyphonic music, evoking feelings intangible—those things beyond human understanding. The Latin texts meant nothing, but the music brimmed over with emotion transcending language.

But there was no escaping the madness over the ridge to the west in Berkeley, or the sad-eyed ladies of the lowlands that Bob Dylan sang about. With a bottle of Liebfraumilch, the sad-eyed lady and I would cruise the back roads in a 1939 Packard that I had bought for two hundred dollars. The car was a bargain, even though it grumbled when I used second gear. The long graceful hood covering its straight-eight engine seemed even longer when reflecting a full moon. We cranked up the radio, and from the Packard's one gigantic speaker the Righteous Brothers pleaded, "Baby, baby, I'd get down on my knees for you," and the Stones sang, "Hey—you—get off of my cloud!"

Just as Terry's skirmish with the Free Speech Movement led him far from the trails we had walked, I also found myself exploring new realms. Fellow students teased me without mercy—"Oh, come on, Renny, it's really fun. You'll like it—just take a little puff and we'll go hear B. B. King at the Fillmore." The more I pulled away, the more they pushed. Finally, in a moment of weakness, alone in my Canyon hideaway, I lit up the tail end of a marijuana cigarette that my friend Emily

There was something in the wind . . .

books, papers, an old typewriter, mementos from our adventures, art supplies, and a life-size black bust of Ajax—the fleet-footed Greek hero in the Trojan War—gazing into eternity. During one of my visits there, the thought occurred to organize photos of our rambles and match them with quotations. Terry began toying with design ideas for the title page. During dinner we came up with a name for our book—*On the Loose.*

While Terry consumed books, I could be found at the Cinema Guild movie house, watching Marlene Dietrich, in *Blue Angel,* callously rip the heart from her obsessed lover, or absorbed by the intrigue and passion in Marcel Carne's *Children of Paradise.* Emily and I sneaked into the Elmwood Theater and watched *Woman in the Dunes*, with its masterful black-and-white cinematography and film score by Toru Takemitsu that has haunted me since. We gripped our chairs and witnessed raw, unadulterated sex. I wanted to hold Emily so bad it hurt as we walked home along the lamp-lit streets of College Avenue—but I was a coward.

When I should have been studying, I spent late nights at the Cabale, watching my favorite folk heroes get inebriated—like Ramblin' Jack Elliott, who sang about a Tennessee stud that was long and lean, the color of the sun and his eyes were green. So I could make it over the hill and back home to Canyon, I'd have a café au lait at the Mediterranean Cafe.

Against the intense backdrop of music, psychedelics, and school, a war was going on that was tearing America apart. By the end of March 1964, President Johnson stepped up the bombing of North Vietnam and sent in U.S. ground troops, igniting major protests at universities across the country. I was involved with the anti–Vietnam War movement: I attended rallies and painted antiwar posters depicting Uncle Sam wrapped in an American flag, a black cloth concealing his face. The flag's stripes turned to serpents that writhed around his neck.

The Selective Service was desperate to provide manpower for the military, as the supply of volunteers ready to serve the U.S. armed forces was running short. I wore a black armband while leading protesters from the UC campus to the Oakland Induction Center, and shortly thereafter was ordered to appear there myself.

We were herded like cattle into a stock pen—pushed and prodded from one room to the next for interviews and exams. I stood in a circle with my compatriots in a pen where scales were rigged to assure that the overweight and underweight could be drafted. My naiveté was crushed that day when I witnessed a military theater of the grotesque, a spectacle of the deviant, men in uniform estranged from their roots and natural context, barking out orders and committing the most aberrant acts. Naked and stripped of pride and dignity, I bent over and let them have their way.

In a locked room with an army psychologist, I told my interrogator I was dangerous and a deviant. After filling out a questionnaire, I was grilled about my alleged involvement with Students for a Democratic Society, then detained and threatened by military police, who were prepared to induct me immediately. But the draft board let me go, and I soon received word that I had received the highest honor attainable: I was classified 4F—not qualified for military service. I was bad cannon fodder, indeed.

From jail to Point Reyes.

I was swept downstream, not knowing what lay around the bend. The big wave

And what were we fighting for?

of the mid-1960s seemed so powerful it would never break. Terry and his compatriots planted a seed of dissension at Sproul Hall that would grow and spread to other universities, providing generations to come with a model for empowerment. I had laid a solid foundation for artistic expression and had come to believe that nothing is as it seems.

Through the storms and the sun that darkened and illuminated life in Berkeley, Terry and I held fast to our own private world. We were of one mind. Of one heart. My brother was my rock, always there to lean on, and I was his confidant, his ally, his crazy kid brother. We cultivated what was important and knew what endured—art, love, beauty, and our passion for wild places. During our last year together, these pursuits were deeply ingrained.

In the tradition of the ascetic scribes, Terry immortalized in his calligraphy the words of French poet Arthur Rimbaud and placed them in a gold frame that hung above his desk while we wrote *On the Loose.* The frame now hangs above mine. Rimbaud's imperishable philosophy marked our trail then, as it marks mine now.

> *The goal of life is the transformation of the self into a maker of poetry or beauty. This is more important than anything done along the way.*

THE goal of life is the transformation of the self into a maker of poetry or beauty. This is more important than anything done along the way. Rimbaud
Terry to his mother · 1962

CHAPTER TWELVE

Time is a sort of river of passing events, and strong is its current; No sooner is a thing brought to sight than it is swept by and another takes its place, and this too will be swept away.

— MARCUS AURELIUS

Raven Camp

I awoke with a nostalgic longing to return to the Berkeley of the 1960s—to strike sparks and ride again the crest of that high beautiful wave, though the era had passed. The carnival had long since left town, leaving only an empty popcorn box blowing in the wind.

The wind can never blow away the war that haunts America. What horrendous images must have flashed through the minds of our classmates who, upon returning from Vietnam, took their lives. How benign the era of McCarthyism and the Free Speech Movement seem through the lens of history. How innocent the bloodbath at the University of Wisconsin, when police with billy clubs attacked students who were peacefully protesting the Vietnam War, seems now—in the era of the so-called Patriot Act and of a government that has more information on its citizens than did the worst tyranny in history. America is sharply divided. Again, disheartened patriotic citizens—like ancestor Elizabeth Dyar of the American Revolution—are melting down their pewter for bullets, fighting for freedom and an America whose people will be proud of it and the world will respect.

Terry never could have imagined the extent to which corporations and media conglomerates would infect the planet, creating an ethos in which money is the only index of a person's value and the techno-machine shepherds us down meaningless paths, frustrates our talents, and diminishes our internal lives. Although police beat my brother during the Free Speech Movement, he never could have dreamed that social, economic, and political institutions would become a scary sort of domesticated pathology—a system antithetical to the behavioral blueprint of our genes, against nature itself.

As far back as 1751, French intellectuals bashed the Calvinistic notion that man is innately evil and believed that he was "naturally good," that there exist hope and redemption, that it's man's institutions that keep him bound in chains. As Terry quoted passages from the Bible in *On the Loose,* could he have been aware that for 2,500 years, Western religious institutions had been demolishing the true unity that is manifested through love between man and man and the oneness between nature and man—principles found in religions such as Taoism and Buddhism? How easy it was for us then—to put on a backpack and head down the trail when life got too complicated in search of our own religion; to live a life that Solomon speaks of in Ecclesiastes—from whence the rivers come and where all rivers run into the sea . . .

I watched a sunrise tinged with toxins from unregulated power plants, a reminder of how political institutions are sacking and pillaging the last of wild America. I made my way to the coffeepot and contemplated a walk to bring my thoughts back into sync with the river—to let its current dissolve the ideological quagmire that threatened to pollute my soul. Keep it simple, I reminded myself . . . keep it simple . . . "Man is never lost, he is only . . ."

A cave high on the canyon rim had caught my eye yesterday afternoon. Perhaps it would contain Fremont pots filled with beads, or frogs carved from jet, or perhaps a necklace of hematite, or sandals of yucca fiber. Would I find obsidian arrowheads still attached with sinew to their shafts, or perhaps clay figurines, or ceremonial pipes? When removed by archaeologists and hidden away in basements or imprisoned in bulletproof, climate-controlled display cases, unclassifiable items lose their context. Captions describing them often read "Archaeologists do not understand these objects." Artifacts are found when one is not consciously looking for them. When the mind is quiet and detached from self, magic happens. You may discover a vessel tucked away in a niche that has been there perhaps a thousand years, waiting to be discovered by only you. What's important is context—remove the artifact, you remove the soul. Leave it—and hope that a "pot hunter" won't take it and sell it on the black market.

Remove the artifact and remove its soul.

But after my climb to the cave, I found no treasure, only a pack-rat midden—assemblages of ancient plants and animals held in place by a matrix of crystalline urine called *ambrette*. Their nests often reach five feet in depth and can cover hundreds of square feet. The William Lewis Manly party of 1849 came across some middens in southern Nevada that resembled variegated candy. Some of the party took it for "sweet but sickish food" and were later troubled by nausea. Middens have been dated in the West as far back as twenty thousand to forty thousand years, predating human occupation of the continent.

Iron-prowed skiff at Gold Hole.

Elusive and secretive, pack rats are rarely seen. *Neotoma cinerea* may one day inherit the earth.

On my return to the river, my feet followed tracks of deer and wild horses that covered nearly every square inch of ground of a steep hillside, where boulders balanced precariously. I hoped to catch sight of a wild horse or two, but all I found were pits where they had rolled in the dirt. I longed to get close to a herd, to feel their steamy heat and see the fire in their eyes. Had I spent too much of my life searching for something just out of reach?

Without the burden of history, could I create my own Pegasus, not from the blood of Medusa? Could I throw my own sparks across the sky and find my place in new constellations? Like Michelangelo, could I find my own angel in stone and carve until I set her free? Was my return to the Green River in search of my brother yet another dream?

I gathered up all the lingering theoretical, philosophical ruminations and chucked them in the river—at least for the moment—and walked to the boat for breakfast.

I devoured a mound of strawberries, melons, grapes, and kiwis topped with raisins, walnuts, yogurt, and maple syrup—a far cry from the 1965 trip, when Terry and I ate moldy bread and braunschweiger sausage, gnawed on Ohio Farms beef sticks and crackers, and washed it down with Tang orange drink.

After breakfast I flipped through the guidebook. I estimated I had eighty miles to the takeout, and just enough food—it was time to get moving. Without an oar stroke, *Seedskeedee* pointed her bow downstream and found the current as though she had a mind of her own. I pulled over at Gold Hole and followed a path leading to an overhang, where a miner or rancher had stashed a boat. It was built of tongue-and-groove pine with a metal bow. A small wave would flip it like a feather. Perhaps it belonged to a rancher who used it to cross the river. I sat inside the little boat and imagined I was a gold miner in the early 1900s, that I'd built the boat to bring supplies down from Ouray to my diggings, and had abandoned it when the bears moved in, or maybe when my food ran out. I never did discover gold, or perhaps my horses drowned while crossing the river, and I had to hike out of the canyon, only to die of thirst. My body was never found. Even today, it's a long hike from the canyon to any road or town. As the crow flies, it's nearly fifty miles east to Rangely, Colorado.

Seedskeedee seemed like a barge compared with that fragile little boat, and it felt good pulling on the oars and hearing the hull cut the water.

Long before Europeans swarmed over the West, indigenous peoples moved like shadows in and along the river, weaving their mysterious way in and out of side canyons. Then, in 1825, along came trapper and trader General William Ashley, who led the first recorded boat trip from Wyoming to the lower Uinta Basin in his circular "bull boats" made of hides stretched over willow branches. About the same time, explorer Dennis Julien left five inscriptions along the Green marking his passing.

Through a lens clouded with controversy and intrigue, John Wesley Powell's amorphous figure appears. On May 24, 1869, Powell and his motley crew of Civil War veterans and mountain men left the town of Green River, Wyoming, to explore the Green and Colorado Rivers—the last unmapped rivers in the United States. Powell's four boats were each twenty feet in length, four feet wide, double-ribbed, made of oak, and could carry two thousand pounds of cargo. The oarsmen plowed backwards into danger, erroneously believing there was safety in speed. Early on, the expedition lost a boat, the *No Name*, at Disaster Falls, when it piled into a boulder, broke in half, and sank with much of their food and clothing. It was a hellish trip. They swamped, swam, swore, and sweated downriver, eating moldy bread and rancid bacon. The men continually patched the battered planking on their boats. They broke all their oars and made new ones from driftwood. They went hungry and boiled in the sun; their boots were worn to shreds. They portaged their boats around many of the rapids and existed in a perpetual state of toil and danger. Powell wrote, "The men talk cheerfully as ever; jests are bandied about freely this morning; but to me the cheer is somber and the jests ghastly."

Things went steadily from bad to worse. Toward the end of the expedition, they arrived at what Powell would later name Separation Rapid—a churning maelstrom in a boulder-strewn channel, offering no chance to portage. Three members of the party thought it would be madness and suicide to try to go on. The next morning, after an emotional parting, the three men began their walk out of the canyon. They may have starved to death or been killed by Indians, but more than likely they were murdered by Mormons who feared that Powell's discoveries would bring on a wave of settlers and infringe on their empire. At any rate, the three were never seen again. The rest of the party plunged into the rapid and soon arrived at Grand Wash Cliffs. The next day they completed their journey at the confluence with the Virgin River. They were the first to run the Green and Colorado Rivers.

Whether Powell was obsessed with ambition and prone to exaggeration or was a sensitive visionary steeped in art and poetry, his bravery and contribution to science and ethnology are undisputed.

Seedskeedee and I sped past Powell in his boat, the *Emma Dean*, and from his observation chair lashed to the deck, he gave me a hard look. Just ahead lay the ghostly outline of another boat—the *Panthon,* captained by George Flavell and his sidekick Ramón Montez. They were the next to venture down the Green River after Powell, although there's speculation that before Flavell's trip, a gentleman named James White lashed himself to a log and survived the Colorado through Grand Canyon. In 1896, Flavell and Montez left Green River, Wyoming, and

went all the way to Yuma, Arizona. Flavell's boat of two-by-four Oregon pine was only fifteen feet long, flat-bottomed and square-sterned, with a five-foot beam. To help protect his boat from the rocks, Flavell straightened steel wagon wheels and fastened them along the sides. Flavell wrote in his journal, "We must expect some accidents and expect to hit some rocks. There is only one stone we must not hit . . . our tombstone." Montez sat on the stern of the boat, looking troubled, as I sped past.

It was more difficult catching up with the next boat. I was gaining on Nathaniel Galloway, who was building a whole new generation of river boats in the 1930s. They were light, sixteen feet long, and, unlike other river boats on the Green River, were built with a rake—deepest at the midsection and rising toward the bow and stern. Galloway popularized the new technique of rowing bow first and facing obstacles. He influenced boat design for decades to come.

Out of the mists of river lore and boats, I passed Bus Hatch with his sons Don and Ted, who pioneered commercial river running, and then Buzz Holstrom, who seemed lost in a dream. Loners and misfits see different colors than those who follow the herd. River runner Holstrom, in 1937, was the first to run the river by himself from Green River, Wyoming, to Lake Mead in Nevada. As an act of completion and defiance, Buzz rowed across Lake Mead and bumped up against Hoover Dam. What thoughts he may have had during those solitary nights under the stars, or how he felt above the maelstrom of Lava Falls, or what the river really meant to Buzz, we'll never know for certain—nor why, on May 18, 1946, he bumped up against another kind of dam and shot himself in the temple.

In 1938, Zee Grant rowed the first inflatable rubber boat, called *Charlie,* through the Grand Canyon, and the first kayak would appear in 1941. What river boats lie ahead a hundred years hence stretch the limits of imagination.

I pointed *Seedskeedee* toward a grove of box elders to have lunch. I tied the boat to a clump of trees that shared a common root. Their trunks fanned out in all directions, covering a fifty-foot diameter. I leaned back in the center and followed their branches skyward and out over the water. The box elder appeared along the river corridor for the first time today. It's a relative of the maple and produces a low grade of maple-like syrup. The tree is so prolific it creates a dense, impenetrable thicket for miles. Birds hidden deep in its branches fill the air with chattering. The land and water were bathed in ephemeral light that not even the painter Albert Bierstadt could have captured.

I built a hearty roast beef sandwich with all the extras, grabbed a bag of blue corn chips, and stretched out on a carpet of leaves. A gentle breeze blew upriver and the temperature was perfect. Writing in my journal, I dug deep for words to describe the quality of light illuminating the leaves. "The luminous electric green leaves of the box elders exploded in my retina and shot through me like . . ." No good.

"The place was awash with an ethereal glow that only God could have . . ." No, that didn't do it either. Adjectives waged war with nouns while the verbs sabotaged my best intentions. Words resisted and fought stubbornly with the paper. I put down my pen in defeat.

I rowed away with this paradise tucked in a safe place deep inside, and felt all the richer for having been in the presence of a Deity. We can only admire in humility the beauty and mystery of this world as far as we can grasp it—that is all.

Most birds fly in flocks, but a few, like the heron and the cormorant, are loners and fly alone. I had reveled in solitude on the upper stretches of the river, but that was about to change. When I rounded a bend, a troupe of thirty or so folks milled about onshore, while others lounged in tents. The party was crammed together so tightly you couldn't have put a brick between them. One group chanted, hands above their heads, circling slowly. I couldn't tell if they were partaking in a quasi–Native American ritual, if it was drivel, or if they were speaking with the Buddha.

The peace continued to erode as the drone of tour and shuttle planes that infest the canyon most of the day drowned out the chanting. Next I encountered the cluster of CEOs who had launched just before me at Sand Wash. At the sight of *Seedskeedee,* one of them turned away from his cell phone and called, "Nice boat." I was glad to be on the river early before the multitudes, wind, and heat. A commercial river party roared by in a cloud of blue exhaust. The guide, wearing the latest designer river garb, glanced my way and waved halfheartedly. The congestion was unbelievable. The river permit system in the West has become so encumbered with bureaucratic red tape, and the demand is so great, that there's a decade's wait to run some rivers.

Next to pass were three bright-orange boats, lashed together with a motor mounted in the middle. Everyone on board wore matching orange hats. I was about to run Jack Creek Rapid but rowed into an eddy to watch the show. They cut their motor, untied, and then rowed through the rapid. Just below it, they retied, fired up their motor, and disappeared around the bend, leaving behind a reeking, incongruous haze of exhaust.

At mile 69 a tent is dwarfed beneath a cottonwood.

I exited off the interstate and sat on the deck, reading in the shade of a cottonwood as the afternoon rush-hour traffic passed. Someone yelled, "Now *you're* doing it the *right* way!" I was tempted to yell back, "Long live anachronism! Power to the misanthrope! God bless anomalies!" I muttered a line of Montaigne's—"He who follows another follows nothing . . . He finds nothing, indeed he seeks nothing"—but concluded as Montaigne did, *que sais je?* What do I know?

And yet, despite all the people, the river itself remained the same enigmatic force it had been in 1965. In the depths of this gorge, boats and people seemed insignificant. The canyon now was massive, and its walls of deep reds and browns were streaked with dark desert varnish. It has been noted that the canyons of the Green are deeper in places than the Grand Canyon, and this afternoon I was in the very heart of them. Seen from the rim, I would appear as a dot—less than an iota of a particle. I leaned back, tilting my head skyward, and let *Seedskeedee* take over. Tenacious pines clung to the rock face in the long, nearly vertical gullies below the rim, standing like sentinels overseeing their domain in a land where no man will venture.

At last I saw them! A motley herd of mustangs had come to the river for an evening drink—horses that will never feel the cut of a bridle in their mouths or the pull of cinch straps. They remain vestiges of the untamable, icons of the romanticized fantasies of the Old West. Author Frank Dobie captured their essence when he wrote, "Coyote duns, the smokies, the blues, the blue roans, the snipnosed pintos, the flea-bitten grays, and black-skinned white, the shining blacks, the rusty browns, the red roans, the toasted sorrels, the cream-maned palominos, and others in shadings of colors as various as the hues that show and fade on the clouds at sunset."

One mustang drank alone. I thought of my brother. The horse's ears followed me like radar, perhaps even before he was fully aware of my presence. His color was burnt umber, and he had a white star on his forehead and two white rear legs. Scars covered his hindquarters. His matted mane was thick with burrs and hung in dreadlocks down his powerful neck. His tail nearly touched the ground. He was powerfully lean and built for speed and endurance.

With a jerk he threw his head back. Maybe he sensed I was trying to reach inside his mind. He seemed to telepathically signal the other horses that there was danger. Then sixteen wild-horse eyes and ears locked onto me with such force that I melted into the boat. They bolted up a ravine, protecting a colt in the middle of the herd. I thought I'd seen the last of them, but they returned, one by one, in defiance—they'd be damned if anything would keep them from their evening drink. They finished and disappeared into the dust.

It was hard to imagine that the bloodline of these horses could be traced back to the 1500s, to the golden age of Spain, when Queen Isabella supplied her invaders with Iberian horses, considered the finest in the world. Many escaped and became known as *musta-os,* and then mustangs. The horses grazed and thrived in country where other breeds couldn't. They became renowned for their speed, agility, endurance, and incredible will to survive. The Apaches in Arizona plundered the mustangs from the Spanish and used them for trade with tribes farther north. The Utes were also excellent horse thieves and ran them north to trade with the Plains Indians and the Nez Perce.

General George Crook, notorious for slaughtering indigenous people, once remarked, "If troops can't overtake a band of Indians in two hours, it's better to give up the chase. . . . Their horses can go ninety miles without water and can wear out every Cavalry horse we have on the frontier." Along with introducing the tribes to smallpox and killing off the buffalo, the United States government continued its campaign of genocide by eradicating the mustangs.

Dust from the thundering herd settled by the time I passed, as though the mustangs had been a dream. The sun was high on the canyon wall before I camped at mile 69, where the stout limbs of a lone cottonwood stretched over the water, inviting me to come ashore for the night. I placed my bedroll beneath the branches of the old warrior, whose lower trunk had been battered by rocks and debris during high water. I rested under a canopy of lush spring foliage among the dead limbs and buds. We would be soul mates for the night.

I feasted on green chile and chicken posole, then walked down to the river in the lingering light. Just a dozen miles downstream was the notorious rapid where my brother drowned and whose roar I had heard for more than thirty years.

I rummaged through my river library. Beneath Bill Beer's book about swimming the Colorado through the Grand Canyon—"a cheap vacation that got a little out of hand"— I grabbed a battered copy of *On the Loose.* Tonight I wanted to sink deep into it. The firelight darted across the pages of an early edition from 1967. Its tattered and stained pages were stuck together by water from many rivers and remnants of meals cooked out in the open, along with my recent scribblings in the margins. It was a wonder this copy had survived. I felt my brother near.

CHAPTER THIRTEEN

If you would not be forgotten as soon as you are dead, either write things worth reading or do things worth writing.

— BEN FRANKLIN

On the Loose

The origins of *On the Loose* can be traced to our grandmother's den and her love for books. Terry and I grew up with them, we slept with them, and we inhaled them. I spent countless hours reading in her cool, darkened den that smelled of old leather bookbindings and musty Persian carpets. On a round clawfoot table, *The Atlantic, Harper's*, *National Geographic,* and *Life* were laid out, according to date, in long, neat rows. Behind the sliding glass doors of her bookcases were treasures like Mark Twain's collected works and the eleventh edition of the *Encyclopedia Britannica.* I randomly opened one of its twenty-nine volumes and submerged myself in an era of great peace and sanity, before the Great War tore the world apart . . . or so said the frayed article, "The World That Was," clipped by my grandmother, celebrating the edition. I hadn't discovered that the volumes mainly chronicled man's quest for wealth, empire, and fame. "The world that was" before recorded history was not to be found between the encyclopedia's pages—it had been annihilated. The *Britannica* is an

South Pasadena, California, 1963.

intriguing fairy tale of recorded events because they are irretrievable as personal experience.

As the years passed in my grandmother's den, I grew weary of the weight and burden of history contained in those twenty-nine volumes. The more I learned of Western civilization, the stranger my life became, and invariably I turned to leather-bound books like my grandmother's 1902 edition of Ralph Waldo Emerson's essay *Self-Reliance*. "Cast the bantling on the rocks / Suckle him with the she-wolf's teat / Wintered with the hawk and fox / Power and speed be hands and feet." Emerson pointed me toward *On the Loose*, and I never looked back.

Alice wrote mystery books and articles for *John Martin's Book,* a children's magazine. She read to us late into the night, sometimes from her book *Strangers in the Desert,* a tale of suspense, kidnapping, and adventure in the Mojave Desert. She planted seeds that grew into our love of and passion for collecting old rare books. It wasn't the kind of infatuation most teenagers would understand, but Terry and I became fanatic bibliophiles. A half-dozen years later, Terry wrote from Carleton College:

> *Thanks for the vivid description of your last acquisitions. With some of them (such as* Walton's Lives*), I was tempted*

to ask when you were ever going to read these books, but I realized that true, dyed-in-the-wool rare-book collectors never ask each other that kind of absurd question. Once we have succeeded in building a mammoth library whose walls are lined with glass cases full of glittering old leather bindings, then perhaps we'll take one from the shelves on a quiet evening, sink into a soft armchair, and read it.

Terry sent long, illuminated letters about how he missed the West; the bleak and frigid Northfield, Minnesota, winters; his scholastic achievements; and plans for our next wilderness adventure. I was scolded for not writing more often, but events like near-fatal bike crashes and girl troubles prevented me. I told Terry that to ease my broken heart, I had found a new love—a Martin D-28 guitar that I even slept with.

We competed ruthlessly for vintage books. I had an edge because I was closer to the bookshops in Los Angeles and to my grandmother's purse strings. Far away at Carleton, all Terry could do was drool with envy at the rare and out-of-print books just out of reach in a locked room on the third floor of his college library. On one occasion he finagled a key to the room and when no one was looking, sneaked in, opened the glass cases, and thumbed through the books. He reported his discovery:

There was an unbelievably keen set of eighteenth-century dictionaries! One was in English, five volumes, 1738, with fantastic frontispieces and ornaments. One was in Dutch, 1740, in a gorgeous red and gold binding. And finally, a first edition of the famous French encyclopedia by Diderot, about twenty volumes in blue and gold, each with an accompanying volume of fabulous plates!!!! This set is the most beautiful I have ever laid my eyes upon, utterly incomprehensible, fantastic, stupendous, wondrous, and indescribable. My book collector's spine is still shivering.

He also mentioned a beautifully illustrated work on medicine that I bet he wanted to stick inside his jacket. Written by an Aztec Indian in the fifteenth century, it listed herbs to cure various ills. He said reading it made him a confirmed manuscript addict, and he was determined to learn Latin.

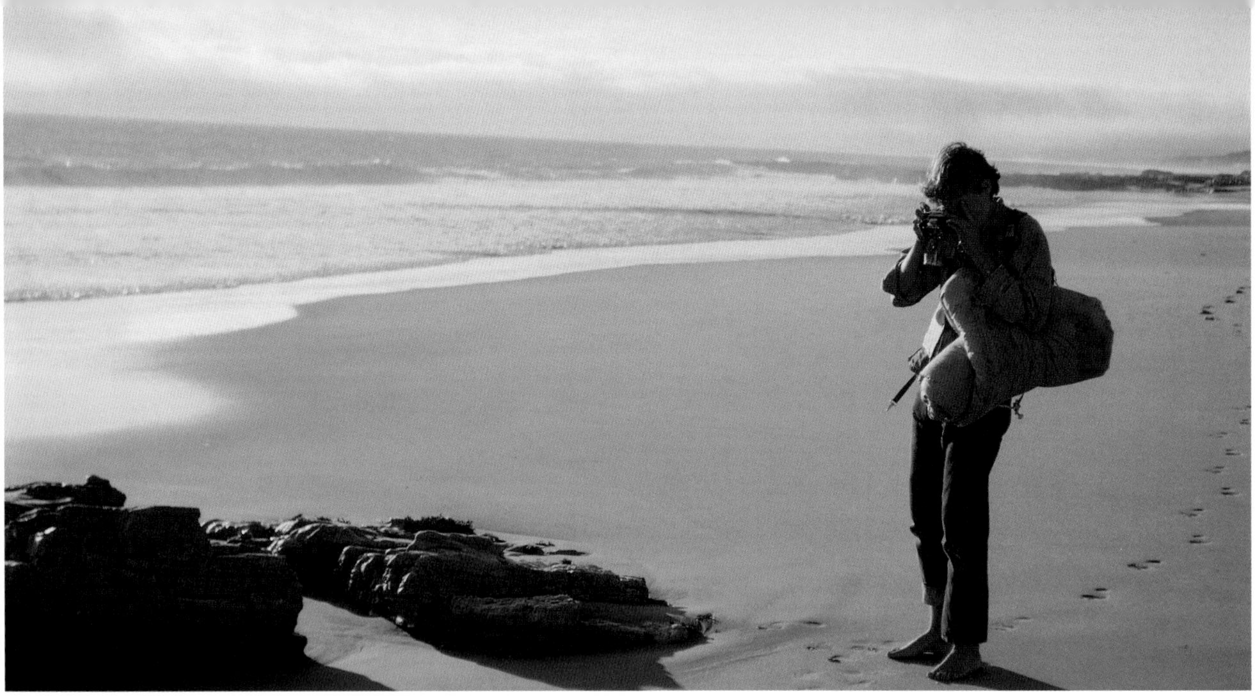

On the loose in Point Reyes, California, 1964.

In our letters we enclosed our latest artistic creations, each trying to outdo the other. Terry wrote:

> *A quaintly lettered wrapping in a familiar hand gave me an inkling that this was going to be something really big. My hands were shaking so badly when I opened your package that twice I had to stop and sustain myself with long swigs of apple-jack brandy. Finally, with the tissue off, I saw your magnificent work. All I could do was stare for long minutes in rapturous awe, occasionally emitting a gasp of wonder or a groan of artistic jealousy—the crosshatched cherubs, the opulent angels, the animals, and all the delicately shaded script, and the various touches of ornament added at key points throughout.*
>
> *My roommate admitted it was as good as anything that I'd ever sent home, and I was seriously considering having it immediately framed but decided it was too rich for Northfield's cultural diet. I don't have to tell you it's the best lettering I ever received from any mortal pen. It's great with a mile-high G. Only ten days until spring break!*

Terry enclosed an early print of a Dürer engraving, done in 1497, titled *The Four Sorceresses*, which depicted four naked women huddled together, up to no good. The sorceresses glared down on me while I tried my hand at

ink and cross-hatching with the finest of crow-quill pen points.

Edward Johnston's *Writing & Illuminating & Lettering* taught my brother the art of manuscript writing, calligraphic styles and techniques, and the use of the correct pens, papers, and equipment. My brother was obsessed by illuminated texts that would soon possess him as he began work on his own manuscript. By 1964, we had accumulated thousands of slides of our rambles through the West, taken with cameras that, despite our best intentions, we invariably destroyed. We dropped cameras into the ocean, subjected them to sandstorms, and more than once accidentally mangled them in our backpacks. The 35mm Kodak Pony was the workhorse of choice because it was inexpensive and easily replaced.

Terry wrote, "I've been trying out new films. A sample roll of Agfachrome came out in delicious colors, but it seems to have trouble with bright surfaces and sky. I'm now trying Ansco/100." I was less particular about film than my brother and preferred imprinting the landscape on my senses directly.

Our mom had moved to Mill Valley, just north of San Francisco, and spent free time in her darkroom. Perhaps in her trays of developer she was searching for an image of the person she was before motherhood. She had every large-format book the Sierra Club published, with their photographs of wilderness driving home the club's potent message.

We thumbed through her coffee-table books—*Words of the Earth* by Cedric Wright, *The Eloquent Light* by Nancy Newhall. A decade earlier, Phoebe had taken us to meet Cedric, who explained the workings of our first box camera. Photographs of the Sierras lined his walls; they were so inviting I wanted to walk into them and down the trail.

Though the books published by the Sierra Club were beautiful and the text inspiring, they seemed lofty and impersonal, destined to collect dust on a coffee table. Still, they lit the spark that started the fire behind *On the Loose*. The times were right for a fresh take on wilderness that was simple, direct, and accessible—and seen through the eyes of our generation. In a sense, Terry and I stood in relation to our natural world as Homer or Thoreau stood in relation to theirs—that is, we felt modern achievement could rival that of the ancients. It was the same "nature" that we all walked in. Terry especially saw the classics not as a burden, but rather as a promise that he could also achieve. In fact, he identified so much with Homer that he began the section "Triumph" with Homer's thoughts: "For afterwards a man finds pleasure in his pains, when he has suffered long and wandered long. So I will tell you what you ask and seek to know."

However, it was hard to be a Homer when wilderness was under siege. Terry wrote in a rage that when all the projected state, federal, and local water projects—dams—were completed in California, there would not be one free-flowing river in the Coast Range or Northern Sierra. And he concluded with a somber "God help us all."

We sifted through slides that had escaped damage from sand and sun and had prints made at a local drugstore. In the introduction, Terry wrote, "The photographs in this book are of the lowest fidelity obtainable. They are as far from the photographer's vision as cheap cameras, mediocre film, and drugstore processing can make them."

We matched our best photographs with Terry's soulful writing, combined with quotations—from the Bible to Steve McQueen. In my wanderings through UC Berkeley, I had discovered a recreational facility where students escaped academia. There I found a darkroom with a Beseler enlarger. When the darkroom was vacant, I'd sneak in with my negatives. In a tray of developer I watched the dreamy, amorphous images appear—a photograph of a wagon wheel taken in the

Terry's desk where On the Loose *was written.*

ghost town of Bodie, California, during a snowstorm, or of my brother playing his autoharp on the running board of a Model A Ford. Matching this photograph with text, Terry wrote, "It's a shame that a race so broadly conceived should end with most lives so narrowly confined." Then I attached the photographs to the pages using a dry-mount press, all the while looking over my shoulder, hoping I wouldn't be discovered and booted off campus.

While studying for finals and being in the eye of the hurricane during the Free Speech Movement, Terry found time to hand letter the entire text of *On the Loose.* To appease the restless spirit that tore at him and begged to escape the city, he wrote, "Adventure is not in the guidebook and beauty is not on the map. Seek and ye shall find." In the autumn of 1964 the writing of *On the Loose* began, and in less than three months it was complete.

The manuscript was bound in green Moroccan leather, and in gold lettering "On The Loose" was stamped on the spine. The title was upside-down, so it read from the bottom up, but it didn't matter and somehow seemed fitting.

On the Loose was about to take on a life of its own and strike a universal chord, a joyous resonance that has lingered in the air since, continuing to vibrate long after the last note was struck. David Brower, then executive director of the Sierra Club, heard our music and liked the song.

Dave, in the coming decades, would help pass the Wilderness Act, and when he became too radical for the Sierra Club, he began Friends of the Earth and later, the Earth Island Institute. Renowned nature writer John McPhee wrote that Dave was the Sierra Club's "leader, its principal strategist, its preeminent fang." He was known to be feisty, uncompromising, and sometimes arrogant.

On a whim we showed Dave our book. My brother and I arrived at the Browers' house in the Berkeley hills. We knocked, and Dave let us in. His daughter Barbara was shy, mysterious, and reclusive, but her pet monkey wasn't. He snapped at us as we passed into the living room. Dave's son Bob was adrift in a cloud of pot, beating on drums in the basement, and Kenneth, Dave's eldest, reminisced how we got thoroughly lost in the canyon country of southeast Utah while packing our boat on our backs to run the lower section of the Escalante River down to the Colorado. It turned into an all-night moonlight escapade. We ended up tearing holes in our boat and had to abandon it.

Dave poured a drink and showed us a copy of *The Place No One Knew,* Eliot Porter's legendary book on Glen Canyon that he had just finished editing. I felt like a total nerd . . . why should a larger-than-life icon care about the rambles of a couple of goofy brothers? Still, we handed Dave our book. While he slowly turned the pages, I studied his face for clues to his thoughts. He revealed nothing. Then, without finishing, he flashed his sky-blue eyes at us and simply said, "We have to publish this." I melted.

Dave poured another drink. Barbara shyly glanced at my brother, plainly smitten by this tall, handsome young man. Contradictions rattled me as Barbara's monkey banged around in its cage. Dave used hydroelectric power. Dave drove a car that polluted. He was forced to compromise his beliefs behind closed doors. His indecisiveness drowned Glen Canyon.

Still, Dave was a brilliant visionary who stood for what he believed, and he was determined to publish *On the Loose.* It began appearing in bookstores in 1968. It's the Sierra Club's most successful publication, if the success of a book is measured in numbers sold. It has weathered half a dozen printings and sold more than a million copies.

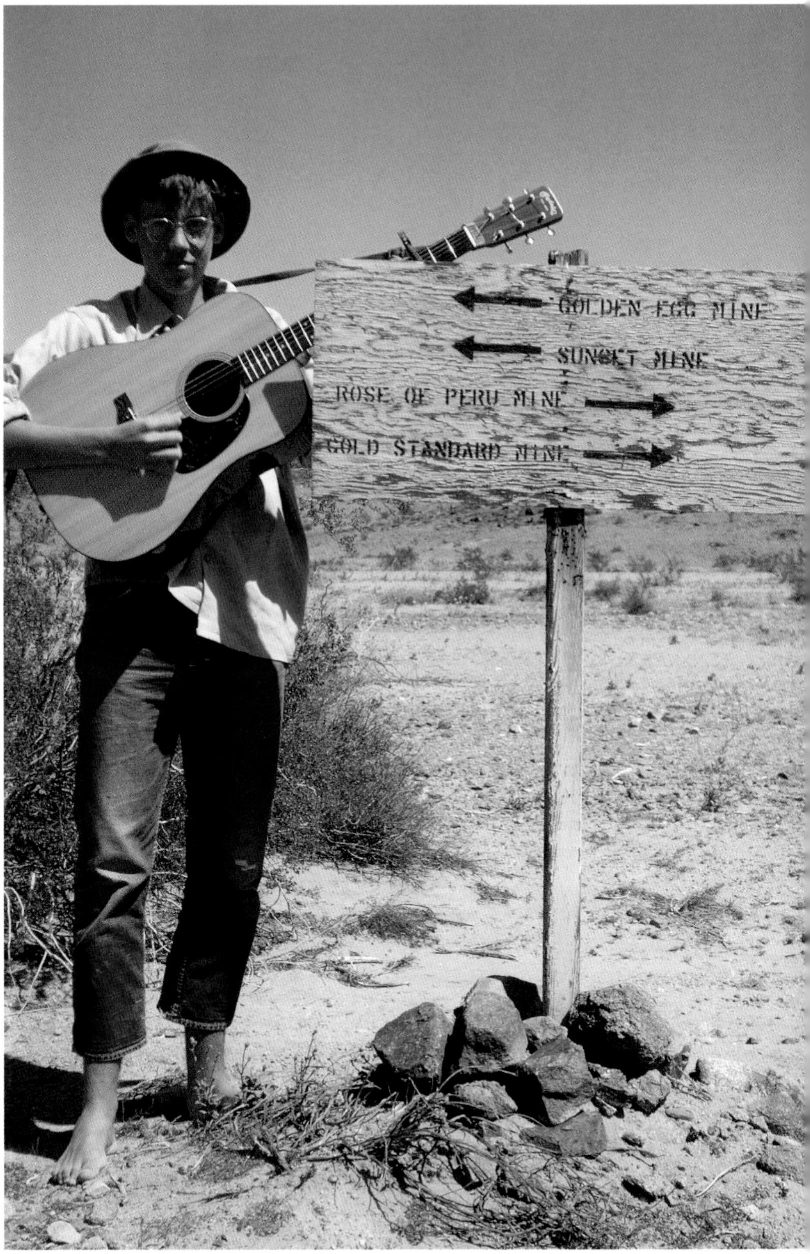

Ken Brower, the Sierra Club board of directors, and photographer Ansel Adams vehemently opposed the publication of *On the Loose*. Adams scoffed at us for not taking photography seriously. But his black-and-white world would soon give way to one of color. A young generation was in search of new trails, and in their backpacks they would be toting *On the Loose*.

Publishing the book presented a dilemma. Selfishly, I considered the wild places we had explored to be "ours," and if the book were published, our connection to them would be trivialized. It would become just another commercial enterprise. Terry and I were anomalies. We wanted to share the book but had no idea it would be instrumental in leading to the inundation of the very places we thought sacrosanct.

Though defending Terry as the main architect of the work, I've borne the challenge of celebrating it without him and defining myself beyond it. I never imagined I would become, as Ken Brower remarked, "a prisoner of the book." Some are surprised that I no longer look as I did at

age eighteen. I sometimes feel myself trapped inside its pages, destined to journey with it through life, like Annie Dillard's image of a bleached-white weasel skull attached to the talons of an eagle—together forever.

The *On the Loose* phenomenon: Readers who came of age in the '60s may identify the book with some pivotal moment in their lives. When between the pages of the book, we follow the same trail we walked in our youth through fields of columbines swaying gently in the breeze, or we hop in a boat and run a pristine river before it's dammed. Since life is basically an illusion and because of the times in which we live, any hope gleaned from recalling a simpler, more coherent time is a gift to be treasured.

My, how times have changed: When Terry and I climbed Mount Whitney, how could we have imagined the concept of an "environmental impact assessment"—the human hallucination that all things

in nature are predictable and controllable, that wildlife and resources exist solely for the benefit of man?

How could we have known that once a thing is perceived as having some utility for human consumption, it's only a matter of time until it's destroyed? As we swam the rapids on Idaho's Salmon River, how could we have visualized the need for a so-called Environmental Protection Agency that some believe is a fraud and an illusion with little interest in restoring ecosystems and is, in reality, a technologically arrogant bureaucracy propagating the interests of big business? How could we have envisioned a government that would open wildlands to drilling, mining, and commercial logging, putting 58.5 million acres of national forest in peril? Walking along the high alpine lakes in the Evolution Basin of the Southern Sierra, Terry and I never would have believed that an administration would reverse a thirty-year effort to clean up our nation's waters, or that a president would be capable of uttering these words: "It isn't pollution that's harming the environment, it's the impurities in our air and water that are doing it."

That night at the Brower home, my brother and I severed the cord connecting us to *On the Loose*. Terry would never see the book again. In a few months, he would graduate from the University of California. We were both weary of the city, and every fiber in our bodies pleaded for wilderness. For our summer rambles, we bought the remains of a World War II ten-man army surplus boat, set to work patching it, and began packing gear for our biggest adventure yet. We were going to run the Green River through Gray and Desolation Canyons.

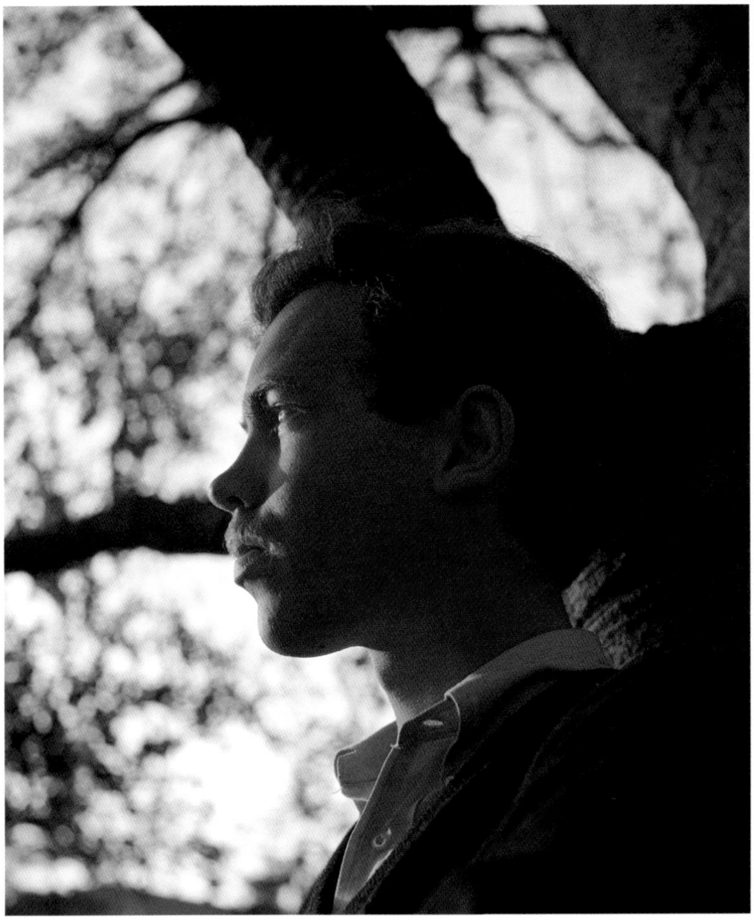

Last picture of Terry Russell.

CHAPTER FOURTEEN

Nature is no sentimentalist. . . . We must see that the world is rough and surly, and will not mind drowning a man or a woman; but swallows your ship like a grain of dust. The cold . . . tingles your blood, benumbs your feet, freezes a man like an apple. . . . The elements, fortune, gravity, lightning, respect no persons.

— RALPH WALDO EMERSON

Apocalypse

At dawn I stood by the smoldering remains of last night's fire. I threw on dry juniper branches, and the coals exploded to life and cast a warm, rosy glow on the sand. I walked down to the river. The canyon walls loomed like giant bat wings silhouetted against a deep-ultramarine sky. I sat on *Seedskeedee*'s deck until stars were consumed by the new day. There was a copy of *On the Loose* on the deck—odd; I didn't remember putting it there.

The new day brought with it a fresh slant on the book. It was impossible to live between the pages like an artifact. In my imaginings I take off my backpack at a fork in the trail and rest awhile. I look around for my brother. The pines stir . . . I take out a copy of *On the Loose* and lay it on a boulder—I must travel fast and light now; no time

to wallow in the past, no place for cynicism or wandering lost in that epistemological thicket . . .

I see a post with three signs pointing different directions. The first points toward a well-worn trail to TERMINAL CITY. It's where man has all but exhausted the planet's resources, wages war, tolerates insufferable arrogance among elected officials, and travels down an information highway leading to a labyrinth of "networked" illusions that knows not the difference between electronic gibberish and wisdom. In Terminal City, prosthetic devices of all kinds alienate and create a barrier between man and man, mask the oneness between man and nature. I shudder. That place has all but killed me and tried to take my soul, too. I turn away.

On a trail less traveled, a sign points toward the recently incorporated community of ALTERNATIVEVILLE, where man makes courageous decisions to heal the planet. There is no fear, no vanity, no hatred or crime—everyone has enough. Solar energy is no longer a dream; everybody uses it. Our rivers, the air, and the land are restored. Man is rebuilding failed political institutions and has addressed overpopulation and global warming. In ALTERNATIVEVILLE, there is a modest certainty about the meaning of things. Work has again become meaningful; there is vigilance of spirit, gratitude for the gift of life, and the courage to take responsibility for it. I hesitate . . . should I head down that trail?

The paint on the third sign is nearly indecipherable; the sign dangles from the post. I blow off dust and read LAND OF AUTOCHTHONS. The trail is overgrown with vegetation but has recently been traveled. Perhaps here man has reclaimed the very best expressions of his humanity—those invented not by civilization, but by cultures that came before history. Heading down this trail, will I rediscover my origins, where time and space once mingled with animals, humans, and gods, weaving an enduring fabric of fertility and death and the sacredness of all living things? Will I find lost cosmologies that, in stories and art, link past, present, and future with eternal cycles and sacred places? Could I find that nonlinear place where souls are attributed to inanimate objects—the world of animism from which all things emerge and to which all return? I hoist my backpack, leaving *On the Loose* on a boulder, and head down the trail. It's a long walk back home to the Pleistocene.

This rush of imagined destinations, which had teased and tormented me for years, evaporated like the steam from my coffee. It was time to get on the water and face the beast—to make peace with Steer Ridge Rapid. I wanted to look into the heart of it and acknowledge that this was, indeed, where Terry had drowned. With the passing of time, the wave of my life had moved forward, yet elements remained here. I had never left the river entirely, and today I would come full circle. The terror of being thrown into the river and my desolate passage out of these canyons seemed as remote and buried as the fossils beneath Lake Uinta. Would the churning turbulence of the rapid unearth fragments of memory to reconstruct the event? Would I look into the eyes of God and find peace and redemption, or would I behold an unforgiving and uncompromising demon, its corona ablaze, who would pull me beneath the waves to finish me off this time?

With the last of my coffee, I sat on a sandbar that would soon be covered by the rising pulse of the Green. I looked upriver—waiting for a sign, heart pounding. The sun crept down the canyon wall and transformed the dew on *Seedskeedee* to vapor. Within the steamy mist, Terry and I swept around the bend in our ten-man rubber boat, having just run Jack Creek Rapid without incident. It was June 17, 1965, and I was bellowing a tune and picking my Martin guitar for the last time. I could barely make out the words of the old Greenbriar Boys song I'd just learned . . . "I see a distant stir and I hear a reckless sound . . . and something seems to say I'm bound for higher ground. So now I'll swim ashore for I must make it, though I'm up to my neck in high muddy waters . . ." Terry was at the oars, strong and in command. In the swift current we quickly vanished downriver and I, in memory, followed.

> *On June 11 we put on the river, planning to take about ten days for the trip down. The river turned out to be higher than it had been for twenty years. We traveled fast. We got out and inspected nearly every rapid before running it. The weather was beautiful except for a storm the first night.*
>
> *— R. Russell, June 1965*
>
> *(Direct quotes from author's journal, resurrected 2003 from the Harry Aleson Collection at the Utah Historical Society.)*

Remains of Russell boat pulled to shore at Rock Creek Ranch.

I didn't know if Terry had survived the rapid or how far upriver I was from the town of Green River. I called for my brother, searching along shore and in the water for movement—a cry, a sign. Sharp rocks tore at my bare feet. After about three miles I came to a ranch, tucked back a few hundred yards from the river among the cottonwoods. I later learned that it was Rock Creek Ranch. I made my way through the weeds and found it was abandoned. Inside it was dark and musty. I searched for food and clothes where for decades, pack rats and snakes had had the run of the place.

I found a pair of stiff leather work boots and a moth-eaten red and black blanket. I clung to a sliver of hope that I would survive, and was convinced that this discovery was more than a coincidence. I walked down to the river and continued my search for Terry. My cries sounded hollow and were swallowed up in the roar of the river. Ravens circled above who had seen it all, but would tell me nothing. At dusk I returned to the ranch. I hung my shirt over a chair with one missing leg, wrapped myself in the blanket, and tried to sleep. My shirt fluttered in the breeze above me and in the moonlight took flight like a winged phantom.

I headed downriver calling for my brother. I had to do some rock climbing to get past the cliff at some places. Before evening I sighted a ranch a little way back from the river. There were fruit trees from an old orchard and berries, which I ate. I walked into one of the buildings. A sign said: "Keep cupboard door closed!" I found a can of peanut butter, some dried prunes, coffee, an old pair of shoes, and an old blanket. I spent the night there.

Early next morning I stuffed rags into the oversized boots and began walking downriver, certain I would catch up with my brother just around the bend. Morning became afternoon and there was no sign of him. I crawled under the shade of boulders during the heat of the day, and when it cooled down, walked until dark, and then curled up in my blanket.

It was day two and still no Terry. It was slow going. More than once the sliver of a game trail along the shore would dead-end—pinched off where the cliff face met the water. I'd backtrack to where I could climb up and around the cliff, eventually working my way back to the river. The days ran together like a long string of empty boxcars that seemed to go nowhere. The Green had become a river with no beginning or end. The blurred image of the winged phantom that had haunted my sleep the night before flew through the juniper trees, and he stared at me with huge red eyes. It's an image that has never entirely departed. I had yet to rediscover Stegner's "geography of hope."

I walked on, believing I would wake up at any moment to find it had all been a dream—but I didn't. Eighteen miles north of the town of Green River, I came to the Price River and hesitated—should I follow it upstream, or continue along the Green? Did it matter? I continued downriver.

> *Next day I put on my shoes and continued down river, carrying the blanket and prunes, climbing along the steep canyon walls, sometimes over talus, sometimes having to go a long distance around the head of a side canyon. Then I would hit a side canyon entering* that *canyon, and have to go around that. Around midday I would curl up and rest in a shady spot. One day I climbed a high mesa and thought if I could get to the top of that, I could see where I was headed. But there was just another talus slope down the other side, and the river was way out of sight. I dropped my blanket and let the stuff roll out over the ground. I sat down with my head in my hands and thought, "What the hell am I doing here?"*

The day was comfortably warm, and the new spring leaves of the cottonwood trees danced in a breeze that sent clouds of seeds skyward.

Fish Creek Ranch at the base of Boulder Mountain, Utah, 1965.

The churning turbulent maelstrom of Desolation and Gray Canyons was now a calm, playful river meandering its way through the Book Cliffs, stretching out and relaxing over a thirsty desert. Entire trees, uprooted by high water, moved lazily in the current like giant serpents, twisting their long necks as they passed into open farm country and then down through Stillwater and Labyrinth Canyons. But in Cataract Canyon, the huge logs came to life, plummeting over rocks and pounding through waves. A golden eagle glided effortlessly, lizards did push-ups on hot rocks to the tune of a new season, and I was on my third day—having walked some forty-five miles from Rock Creek Ranch.

It was a perfect day for a picnic. A young couple sat in the shade of a cottonwood whose limbs reached into a cloudless, cerulean-blue sky. All was peace and harmony. On the picnickers' embroidered tablecloth lay a basket that held foods for a feast.

I couldn't make out what they were saying—only their laughter, like distant bells, was carried by the wind. Was I watching a movie in slow motion, or dreaming a dream? Their laughter stopped abruptly as I approached—I scared the hell out of them with my tattered blanket, disheveled appearance, and feet raw and bleeding from boots that had lost their soles. When I found my voice, I explained as much as words could that there had been a boating accident and my brother was lost.

They offered me food and wanted to drive me into Green River and then to my aunt and uncle's Fish Creek Ranch at the base of Boulder Mountain, a four-hour drive to the southwest on Highway 24.

When I arrived that evening, there was no family and the house was locked. The plan had been for Terry and me to rendezvous here after the trip and catch a ride back to Ouray for our vehicle. I thanked the couple and watched their taillights merge into the night. The darkness and the cold mountain air enveloped me like death. A lone coyote's call cut the cool high-desert air as I curled up in the grass to sleep.

> *Sunday afternoon I found a road and was slogging along about two miles from Green River, when two people appeared ahead of me. Their figures seemed strange and unreal. I was in my old ragged clothes that had been soaked in the river and slept in, and the couple hesitated when they saw me coming: I noticed the woman kind of got behind her man. When I came up to them I said, "How far to Green River?" The man said, "About two miles." Then he asked what was the matter, or what happened. I said, "There's been a boat wreck." I told him about it. He immediately became concerned. They gave me a lift to Green River. I told the sheriff about the accident. He acted like a stupid cop, cross-examined me, asked questions like—"What were you* doing *there?" etc.*
>
> *The men at the gas station collected some money to buy me a hamburger, which was kind. Then my friends drove me all the way into Wayne County—to Fish Creek Ranch. In the morning a neighbor, LaVell Morrill, showed up and I explained what happened. He took me to his ranch and fed me a tremendous breakfast: I ate six eggs and a dozen pieces of bacon, with four pieces of toast, and coffee.*

The next morning at 10:30, Phoebe and Elizabeth arrived at Fish Creek Ranch. There was excitement, hugs, and smiles. Mom asked, "Where's Terry?"

An irrigation ditch ran like a snake through the yard—a thick carpet of spring grass encircled by gigantic poplar trees so old Brigham Young could have planted them. The lively mountain water plunged over river cobbles that my aunt had collected from Glen Canyon and fell into deep pools. The water was singing a different song than the roar of the rapid still pounding in my head. Chairs were invitingly placed in the shade under a willow tree where Terry and I had played music together, passing long, lazy summer days. Cats lounged and my favorite dog, Sage—now stiff with arthritis—gave me a big, slobbering kiss.

My mom asked again, "Where's your brother?" I glanced at the massive cumulus clouds lumbering over Boulder Mountain like giants and heard the distant sound of thunder, and I knew it would soon rain, and it would rain, and rain. I took hold of the freshly painted white fence surrounding the yard and replied simply, "Terry is lost."

Dreamily, I watched my family as though they were in a play and I was in the audience. I watched my uncle split mountains of firewood, day after day, and knew that concealed behind each swing of his axe were feelings that would remain unshared. I watched him put away his pencils and paper—Superman and Batman would have to wait. I noticed the construction on the largest and most extravagant house ever built in Wayne County shut down and the workmen drive away. Then, the lights dimmed and my Aunt Elizabeth walked on stage. I saw a storm pass through her, eroding her stoic facade. I watched her clean her brushes and cover her easel. From the darkness, I heard my mother's wailing and bolted from my seat. The house lights came on and the theater dissolved. I held her, calmed her, and offered hope that Terry would be found.

But the family was paralyzed. I held fast to hope and drove to nearby Teasdale to see Harry Aleson. He threw me a lifeline. Cool-headed Harry had the gift of knowing when to speak and when not to. I was wrestling with having been at the oars when the stars fell from the sky. How could Terry, so young, strong, and passionately alive, simply vanish? Had this fire and light really gone out? Harry and I both refused to believe that Terry had drowned. The day after I arrived at Fish Creek Ranch, Harry swung into action. He wrote:

> *After a quick bowl of soup and tea and cake—I got a map—and with ARTH CHAFFIN drove to the Sprangs'—phoned the*

Harry Aleson threw me a lifeline.

Green River sheriff—found that no search had been instigated. Then I phoned Utah State Aeronautics, and the Carbon County sheriff at Price—who got things moving. . . Young Renny determined the exact place of upset on the 1918–1919 U.S.G.S. river maps Burt Loper had given me at rapid at 56.6 from zero at Green River Utah . . . then I got ahold of Jim Hurst at Green River Airport. At 3:45 he picked Renny and me up at Torrey—we flew straight through to the river.

– *Aleson letters*

Hurst was a tall, lean pilot with piercing eyes. His overalls were stained and stiff with grease. He didn't waste words. We boarded his plane. Harry had a quart of milk to ease the pain of the stomach cancer that would later kill him. I brought a bedroll, ready to drop to my brother, containing food, juices, matches, can opener, and so on, rolled in a sheet. Harry kept saying over and over, "If Terry is alive—we'll find him."

Recd 7 JULY 65 from ES by HLA
8 JULY 65 loaned to DOCK ORMAR

Crews Hunt Californian Missing in Green River

Special to The Tribune

PRICE—A search was launched Monday for a 21-year-

and told of their rubber raft overturning in rapids.

Carbon County Sheriff Albert

The plane coughed and sputtered, then came to life, and we barreled down the runway, heading north toward a notch in the Book Cliffs where the Green River emerges from Gray Canyon. The Book Cliffs are one of the longest continuous escarpments in the world, stretching two hundred fifty miles through Utah and Colorado.

Fifty-seven river miles from the airport, we were directly above Rock Creek Ranch. Two miles north of the ranch Hurst put his plane into a nosedive, and we were circling over Steer Ridge Rapid—so low I could see game tracks in the wet sand. My stomach went through the floorboards, and Jim shot me a smile that didn't restore my confidence. Harry wrote his wife Dotty on June 24:

> *We flew down inside the canyon, sixty miles right above the water—saw no sign of Terry—or tracks on the sandbars—found the boat five miles below capsize—no one around—flew down the river about 100 feet above—on quiet water you could see a twig five inches long. At mile 52, Left Bank, we shot over the boat—maybe two wing-spans below us. At Mile 56 RENNY recognized the upset rapid and place where he crawled out. Less than two miles further up river JIM HURST swung about in a canyon mouth, and we headed*

down river—searching every foot of silted bar, bank—
bushes—ledges—plus circling the abandoned buildings at the
McPherson Ranch—but, without a trace of Terry. It was really
rough flying—my eyeglasses jumped out of my shirt pocket—
landing in my lap. We had not the slightest trace
or sign of the missing brother.

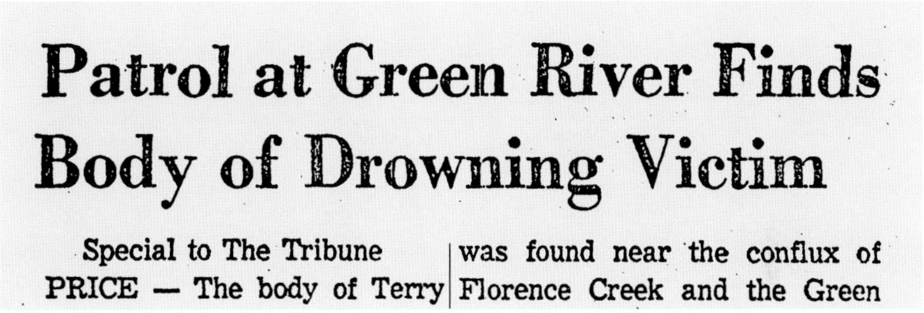

Patrol at Green River Finds Body of Drowning Victim

Special to The Tribune
PRICE — The body of Terry was found near the conflux of Florence Creek and the Green

We reluctantly headed back to Green River, where Harry and I spent the night at the Uranium Motel, room 1. I stared blankly at the plaster flaking from the motel walls while Harry phoned his river friend Bus Hatch to see if he could spare a boatman to join the search. But Bus was attending a funeral for one of his boatmen who had drowned on the Yampa. Then Harry phoned river guide Ken Sleight, who had pulled our collapsed boat out of the river at Rock Creek, thinking he might have clues as to Terry's whereabouts. But Sleight had continued downriver through Cataract Canyon.

Then the police arrived. For two hours, folks from the sheriff's posse and Utah State Highway Patrol, and curious locals, heard details of the disaster. Next day, June 22, Harry and I stopped by the American service station in Green River to question Sheriff Wilcox of Emery County, the arrogant cop who hadn't believed what had happened when I arrived in Green River. Harry concluded that Wilcox was "a young man under thirty—little experience—and a do-nothing."

The search continued. Sheriff's deputies and Ouray Indians launched a boat at McPherson Ranch, fourteen miles below Rock Creek, and searched upstream. Another boat would launch from Sand Wash and motor downstream. Harry and I had done all we could, so Jim Hurst flew us back to the airport at Torrey.

On June 25, Search and Rescue found Terry's body at Florence Creek, eighteen miles below Steer Ridge Rapid. The current slows here; big eddies form and swirl about; water flows upstream, defying logic. Just as Terry's death defied logic. Driftwood logs pause and rest before heading downriver through Wire Fence and Three Fords Rapids. In this eddy, Terry's body came to rest. Harry returned from Teasdale to Green River to make funeral arrangements, and wrote:

> *Two deputy sheriffs found me at the Uranium Coffee Shop—brought me in their car to the sheriff's office—paper work—maps—showed me boats they used on search—one 10-man with a motor—and a 7-man used in towing body.*

Harry recalled my family's strength: The two women were accepting the situation with more courage than I believe I've ever known two women to show." Phoebe wrote, just days after we lost Terry,

Even today there is a beauty in the rock, the wave, / There is a glory in the flowing stream. / We by perceiving beauty, shall be saved, / And enter, too, the glory of his dream.

I had to find peace with my own God. I went on long walks by myself behind the family's ranch in the high rolling hill country and into the cove where white Navajo Sandstone cliffs butt up against the soft shoulder of Boulder Mountain. To the west the land falls gently away to Capitol Reef. I walked along the creeks that flow from the mountain where I caught my first brook trout and shot my first jackrabbit, where Terry and I found arrowheads, manos, and metates. In this high-desert country among the piñon and juniper trees I screamed like an angel whose wings were being torn off, and then cried a river.

In water we are conceived; water nourishes the embryo, and water is ninety percent of our body weight. The arrangement of atoms is the same whether the water is lulling you off to sleep beside a river or drowning you. And even after a devastating flood, it leaves life behind—as if it had intelligence and knew exactly what it was doing.

My life since has been a search for the knowledge and secrets that have offered hope and strength after the flood.

In reconciling death, some find comfort in reincarnation or astrology. Others turn to Christ, to the Buddha, to Krishnamurti. Some turn to the stoic philosophers for peace, while others just turn away, or turn on, or simply take an aspirin. Solace is where you find it. I have found it by returning to wilderness and in the austere immensity of the universe, where galaxies dance, where questions are asked and answers are given that are not always easily interpreted. I invariably seek out a star brighter than the rest, the ineffable light of my brother's spirit that had been my guide.

I got a call from Harry. He had just returned from Green River and wanted to speak with me alone. On the mantle above his fireplace was a box containing Terry's ashes. Harry slipped a Swiss army knife and a tube of Blistex into my hand, the items found in Terry's shorts. I gripped them tightly and felt acid creep up my stomach and fill my mouth. We stood a long while together in silence. I told Harry what I wanted to do but he already knew. I had to take Terry back to the river to set his spirit free. It was a task the family neither understood nor wanted any part of. My aunt left a cryptic note that read, "Good luck on your mission."

I caught a ride back to the boat launch where Terry and I had left the Land Rover. The Rover seemed like a lost soul, like its motor had been stolen, like its lights had been blown out. A Ute Indian in Ouray had moved it to higher ground—otherwise it could have washed away in the flood. When I fired up the Rover, the realization hit hard that I had begun a new journey—one without a brother. A quote from *On the Loose* pricked with new meaning: "Play for more than you can afford to lose, and you will learn the game." But what had I learned?

I brought a topographical map of my destination—the maze of canyons west of Rock Creek Ranch. I can no more recall in detail the next few days than a sleepwalker can tell where he's been. Maybe my brain disconnected, becoming selective with memory—choosing what to remember, what to bypass, and what to forget in order to protect its vulnerable places. I parked the Rover above a drainage that would take me to Steer Ridge Rapid. With Terry's ashes on my back, I started down to the river.

Warm sands, mysterious sands, drifting and shifting sands. Sand undergoing metamorphism for eternity, each grain shaped by its journey from a faraway place. Fine sand, coarse sand, sand of every color that's carried by water and deposited—only to be washed away again. In a dry creek bed just below the high-water line of the river, I prepared a place for my brother, feeling the sand's warmth as it slipped between my fingers. Terry's spirit now fills the entire depth and breadth of the deepest and wildest parts of one of the most beautiful and powerful canyons in the world. He is everywhere, and he is nowhere. I knew Terry would like this place to rest awhile, before the floodwaters released him to begin another journey.

And though I close my eyes and
cover my heart entirely, I see a muffled waterfall,
in big muffled raindrops.
It is like a hurricane of gelatine,
like a waterfall of sperm and jellyfish.
I see a turbid rainbow form.
I see its waters pass across the bones.

— Pablo Neruda

Chapter Fifteen

I am the daughter of Earth and Water,
And the nursling of the Sky;
I pass through the pores of the ocean and shores,
I change but I can never die.

— Percy Bysshe Shelley

Camp of the Bear

But that was a long time ago—dreamlike and intangible. My empty coffee cup from earlier that morning brought me back to the river, so deep was I in musing. I grabbed a handful of sand and tossed it in the air—it was good to be on solid ground. A solitary raven flew low on a reconnaissance mission. Upon seeing me he gained altitude, tucked his wings, and free-fell, performing daring acrobatics, somersaults, and half rolls. He gave a cackle, then landed in a cottonwood tree, eyeing me curiously.

No bird can match the raven for being resourceful and clever. Myths from every corner of the planet recognize his power. He disobeyed Noah during the Great Flood and failed to return to the ark with news he had discovered land. The Haida and the Inuit Indians believe the raven created the world and placed the sun in the sky, that

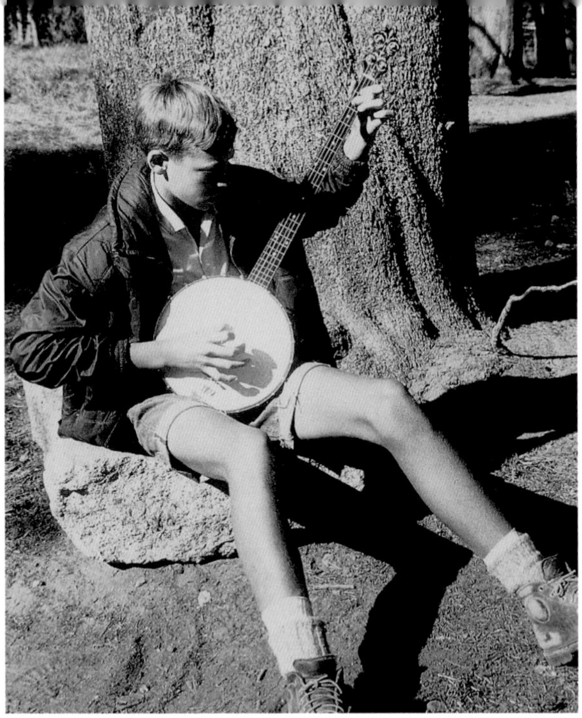

he brought fire and offered salmon and sacred cedar to the people. Some believe Raven foreshadows darkness, depression, and death. The Norse god Odin had two ravens, Hugin (thought) and Munin (memory), that he used as messengers.

Raven glared down at me, knowing much more than I could fathom. Raven remained on his perch peering into my mind. If he was wise, he would know I was on edge and alone. If he had the gift of prophecy, he wasn't surprised to see me return to the river. If he could move between the realms of past and present to pierce life's illusions, he would help me fuse the two and crush illusion.

When I searched for my brother, a raven had answered my cries, and he had been following me since. Sometimes as a jester, other times as a prophet, ravens had an uncanny way of appearing when I needed them. Our eyes locked, and with a *"KAW–KAW–KAW!"* he flew downriver.

I broke camp. Concerns about running Steer Ridge alone ravaged me. I pushed off from shore and spun the boat, searching for Raven, and felt a sensation I hadn't felt for a long time—that the boat stands still while the canyon walls pass. These canyon walls had witnessed Terry and me spending our last morning together. In memory we climbed Toro Peak and felt the joie de vivre of our first summit climb. Terry rescued me from the surf when I was caught in a riptide. His hand grabbed my collar when I was trapped under a boat on the Salmon River in Idaho. I leaned on him when I broke my arm catapulting over the handlebars delivering the *Oakland Tribune.* I leaned on him again in the Sierras after my appendix nearly ruptured. I endured his brotherly wrath when, by mistake, I put the Rambler station wagon in reverse at high speed and careened into a ditch. I saw him mimicking Jackson Pollock, sloshing paint

on a canvas and then rolling in it. I heard him bellow audacious diatribes at dam builders as we drove over Glen Canyon Dam for the first time, and melted whenever he praised my artistic creations. As the canyon walls dreamily passed, I moved close to the countless times he guided me through the maze of teenage delusion and indecision with wisdom, humor, and grace.

I recalled the times behind the photographs in *On the Loose*—misjudging the tides at Point Reyes, being trapped in a cove by the surging waters, and having to swim for our lives. Walking in circles for days in the slickrock wilderness of Escalante, trying to get back to our Jeep after our overinflated rubber boat blew up in the sun. I reined in the times spent with my brother that were beyond knowing—listening for the sound that rises out of the earth, searching for that primitive authentic joy that is contained in the closeness of fire, wind, and water. And all those moments in wilderness, dazzled by the miracle of a thousand glimmers of light on the water and by the awesome beauty of a thousand sunsets.

I snapped back to the river and rowed into an eddy just above Steer Ridge Rapid for lunch. The current swung the boat around while I nervously made a sandwich, tightened the straps on my life jacket for the hundredth time, and made certain the latches on the hatch doors were secure. I rowed back into the current and soon heard the roar of Steer Ridge, which appeared with little warning around a sharp left-hand bend in the river.

I pulled over on the west side of the river just above a small drainage.

I walked it, searching for clues as to what created the rapid, to see if it had been scoured by a flash flood that may have flushed rocks and debris into the river channel, constricting and altering it. The drainage didn't look as though it ever carried a large volume of water. I was dumbfounded. A raven glided upstream; its shiny coal-black back carried the sky. On the east side of the river I tied *Seedskeedee* and walked to a ledge above the rapid, just as Terry and I had done. I searched the landscape, trying to find amorphous bits of memory that I could piece together that would confirm I had been here. But the pieces didn't fit. The past was severed from the present. It hardly seemed the same river, just as the Renny arriving here in 1965 with his brother in their soggy, underinflated rubber boat seemed a stranger to me now.

But when I climbed the hill overlooking the rapid, past and present fused. This was the place. My eyes bored deep into the crashing hole that flipped our boat. I didn't see the eyes of God, nor did I see a demonic apparition—simply water passing over stones.

It was hard to believe that this rapid had taken my brother. I felt estranged. I had since run rapids that could have easily swallowed this one. I had expected a Niagara Falls—something with the grandeur and power to match the stature of my brother.

Still, the waves, the holes, boulders, and logjams at Steer Ridge are something to be reckoned with as the river pounds and surges relentlessly, scouring and grinding rocks to sand and silt. The rapid probably looked about as it had in 1965, or for that matter as it did when John Wesley Powell passed here in the *Emma Dean* more than one hundred thirty years earlier. Powell wrote of his encounter with Steer Ridge Rapid in his journal on July 11, 1869:

> *Standing on the deck, I think it can be run. Coming nearer, I see that at the foot it has a short turn to the left, where the water piles up against the cliff. . . . We shoot by a big rock; a reflex wave rolls over our boat and fills her. I see the place is dangerous, and quickly signal the other boats to land where they can. . . . Another wave rolls our boat over, and I am thrown some distance into the water. The boat is drifting ahead of me twenty or thirty feet, and, when the great waves have passed, I overtake it, and find Sumner and Dunn clinging to her. . . . Dunn loses his hold and goes under . . . we have drifted down stream some distance, and see another rapid below. How bad we cannot tell, so we swim toward shore, pulling the boat with us, with all vigor possible. At last we reach a huge pile of driftwood. The guns and barometer are lost . . . two rolls of blankets are lost, and sometimes hereafter we may sleep cold.*

The waves, rocks, and logjams had shifted slightly since Powell's journey, like pieces on a chessboard awaiting another game. I longed for a miraculous event—to see the sky crack open and William Blake's evangelic figures tumble to earth to offer meaning for us mere mortals. To witness my brother's form weaving through the waves, or see him walking up the trail toward me with his big smile; to share with him a lifetime of joys, follies, and sorrows. I offered my best yodel from the depths of my soul—just as Terry and I did when we were separated on the trail, or when we felt the joy of just being alive. But the roar of the rapid swallowed it. I reached skyward trying to frame something that the snake's throat while the serpent's head swayed trancelike back and forth, muscles rippling with anticipation. Nature knows nothing of sympathy or cruelty—it just is. The thought arrived unsolicited that I was the snake and my brother the frog, and it didn't sit well. I considered the notion that Terry had possibly exhausted himself trying to save me, a debt I could never repay.

The frog was a reminder that we are at the mercy of nature's capricious moods. The Greek dramatist Aeschylus was killed by the shell of a tortoise that slipped from the talons of an eagle in flight. I looked toward the sky, wondering what one life was worth, aware that there was something monstrously larger than myself at the helm. I had an unsettling feeling that if I remained below the rapid I would be swept away. Hastily I coiled the bowline, pulled the anchor in, and with a rapid at my back that had foreshadowed my destiny, I rowed downriver. The circle was complete.

I had been on the water late into the afternoons most of the trip, which meant dinner in the dark and little time to read and write. Today I wanted to camp early, to digest the day and see if I could find the notes to finish old songs and compose new ones. I thought of the Martin guitar that had sunk with our boat and wondered how long it had taken the river to grind it into the silt. I wanted to camp between Steer Ridge Rapid and Rock Creek Ranch—perhaps at the very place where the river had released me.

I could feel the river's pull as it edged me toward the east bank, where sand dunes rolled among old junipers. Upstream winds deposited their cargo of sand on the outside bends along the river and created rolling dunes. It was an unlikely site. The landing was rocky and thick with cactus, camouflaged by the grass, and I would have to climb a hill to reach camp. But it suited me just fine—it felt fresh and untrodden and offered a sweeping panorama of the river.

At the top of the eddy, I remained in the boat a long while, suspended between exhaustion and elation. The water on one side

of the boat sped by powerfully and urgently, while the water on the other side was in the calm of the eddy. Like my boat, I was somewhere between—savoring a moment of peace in calm water, knowing that the moment could dissolve.

I explored camp and came to rest in the sand in the shade of a juniper tree with blanket, journal, and guitar. Brand-new melodies found me, but I failed to find words for my journal. The easygoing afternoon eroded and I felt restless—something was brooding beyond the dark cumulus clouds gathering to the east.

I set out the makings for dinner—buffalo burgers with green chile and cheese, with a side order of squash that I would fry with mountains of garlic and ginger—and then went for a stroll upriver. Little did I know, as I felt the warm sand between my toes and sipped an ice-cold ale, savoring the late-afternoon light on the water, that the Ute Indians, high on the east rim of the canyon, were conjuring powerful spirits that would shake my foundation.

My eyes scoured the landscape for Bear. He was gone but I felt him near just the same. Remnants of adrenaline congealed and honed my senses. Perhaps I had camped on sacred Ute land that he protected from the intrusions of white people.

I dreaded catching what Navajos call bear sickness. The tribe believes that all you have to do is pass a bear path or pick up ants that a bear has slept on, and you'll develop "mental troubles," overwhelming fatigue, swelling of the arms and legs, vomiting, and diarrhea. The only cure is to sit alone for a day, fast, and sing bear songs. Could I become Bear—as the Zunis believe—if I painted my body red, tied yucca around my waist, chest, and head, tied a red eagle feather to my hair, and wrapped myself in

Todo es según el color del cristal con que se mira.

bearskins? Why hadn't Bear laid me open? Why had he appeared at the exact spot where my brother had drowned, and why hadn't I calmly sat down and spoken words he could understand? What I did know was that Bear would return . . .

I skipped breakfast and hurriedly threw camping gear on *Seedskeedee*'s deck and untied the boat. I would store the gear in her hatches once I was in the current. Although the cruel wind was picking up, the storm had passed, and the morning offered a new beginning—it was good to be alive below Steer Ridge Rapid!

A few miles downriver I rowed to shore directly across from Rock Creek Ranch, the same place that thirty-three years earlier had seemed the most lonely and isolated place on the planet. A couple dozen boats lined the shore, drawn to the clear waters of Rock Creek and the crumbling remains of a once prosperous ranch. A group sat around a smoldering fire, chatting and sipping coffee. I was struck by the normalcy of it all and smiled and waved. I tied *Seedskeedee* downriver from the crowds and made my way through a field of parched cheatgrass to what remained of the old Rock Creek Ranch.

In the rubble of the ranch I awakened spirits, who recognized me and scurried for cover. I stood in the center of the structure, feeling vacant and transparent—unable to recognize anything familiar. Cottonwood limbs grew through the windows and doors, reclaiming the site. In 1910, the misanthropic Seamounton brothers cleared several hundred acres, constructed an elaborate irrigation system, built corrals, and planted orchards and alfalfa. I asked the wind, "Where are you, Eugene Eraud?" "Frenchy," as he was called, fled Europe rather than risk conscription into the army that had taken his father and two brothers. Five years later, fate delivered him to the Seamounton ranch, and he was put to work rebuilding it in the 1920s after it was partially destroyed by fire. The blocks were superbly cut and edged so straight that they remain so to this day. Frenchy's ghost scurried under a burned-out beam. Fire had finally claimed the building shortly after I had first been there in 1965.

I entered one of the dilapidated outbuildings. Solid workbenches remained and were cluttered by shriveled remains of leather halters with rusted buckles. Nails, nuts, bolts, and cans filled with dust lay among the chunks of collapsed roof that covered the floor. Snakes slithered beneath the rotting floorboards. I froze at the sight of high-top leather boots highlighted by a shaft of sun that streamed through a hole in the roof. They were identical to the ones I'd found after the accident. I left the decay to the pack rats, spiders, and snakes.

My last stop was at the old orchard, the only living vestige of the ranch. I leaned back in the branches of the largest and oldest apple tree and found that my limbs conformed perfectly with the tree's.

A breeze rustled the grass as the vicissitudes of past and present mingled. The solid and stately ranch house still stands—but the rubble discloses little evidence of its former elegance. The young Renny who rummaged through the cupboards for food would not know me now. These resilient old trees that had endured a half century of neglect still blossomed, but produced less fruit. And through their branches I saw a river that once terrified me but now seemed peaceful and offered strength. No easy task stepping into the same river twice when the waters were ever flowing over me.

The Spanish proverb says, *Todo es según el color del cristal con que se mira*—"Everything partakes of the color of the crystal through which it is seen." The color of our crystal is ever changing, depending on the light of our life's experiences. When I was last in this orchard, my credulous eyes saw only the primary colors through the crystal; the colors had not yet been mixed by my having lived.

The colors that mingled on my palette through the '90s were especially deep and vibrant. I built dories—boats whose gunwales were inlaid with silver, turquoise, jet, and coral—and painted them all the colors of the rainbow. Art ruled supreme! I inherited the contents of my aunt's studio, moved her gigantic easel into my studio, and began

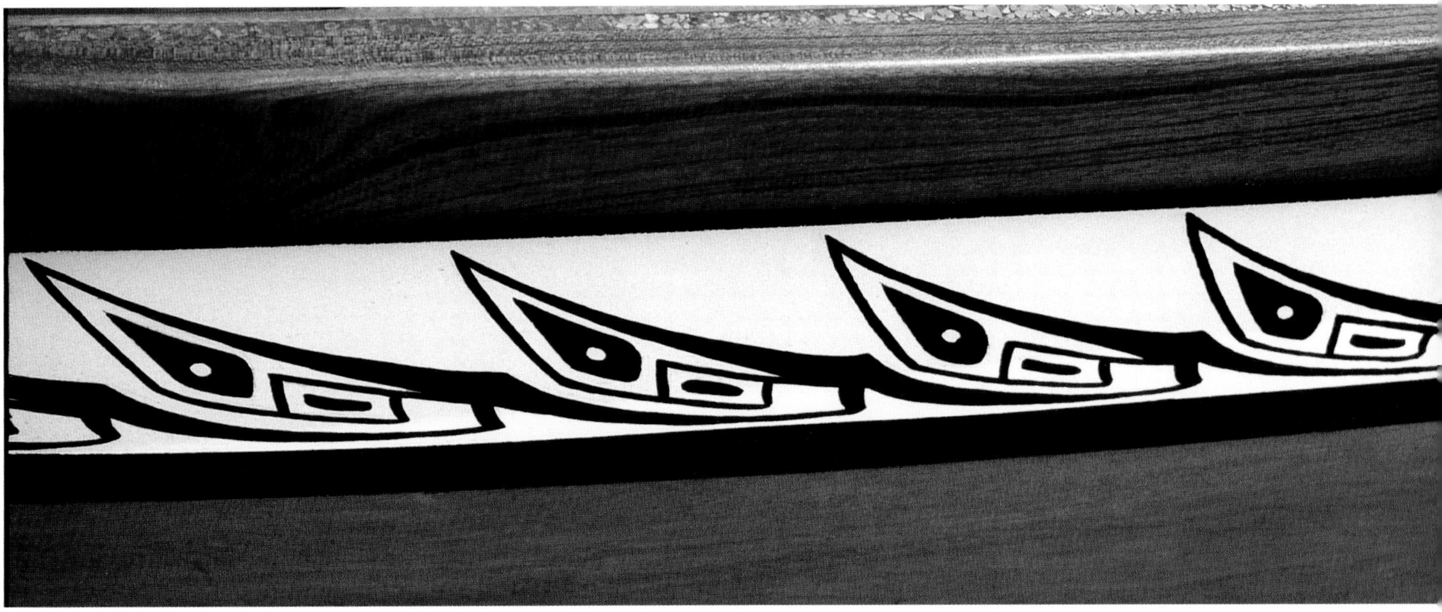

Hear that high lonesome sound?

painting with oils. Elizabeth's lithographs had survived. Her "Nameless Errand, "Spook Town," and "Where Lost Years Are" had changed meaning for me since I was a child watching, mesmerized, as she painted haunted images on stone. Life had since been filled with "Nameless Errands," some determined by choice, others by fate. "Where Lost Years Are" seems a somewhat ambiguous place that I haven't found, nor do I want to. And America is filled with "Spook Towns," but not the ones my aunt depicted in her Mojave ghost town lithographs. With those of like mind, I went on winter trips in wooden boats down the Colorado River in the Grand Canyon, skied along the Continental Divide in Colorado's San Juan Mountains, and hiked deep into

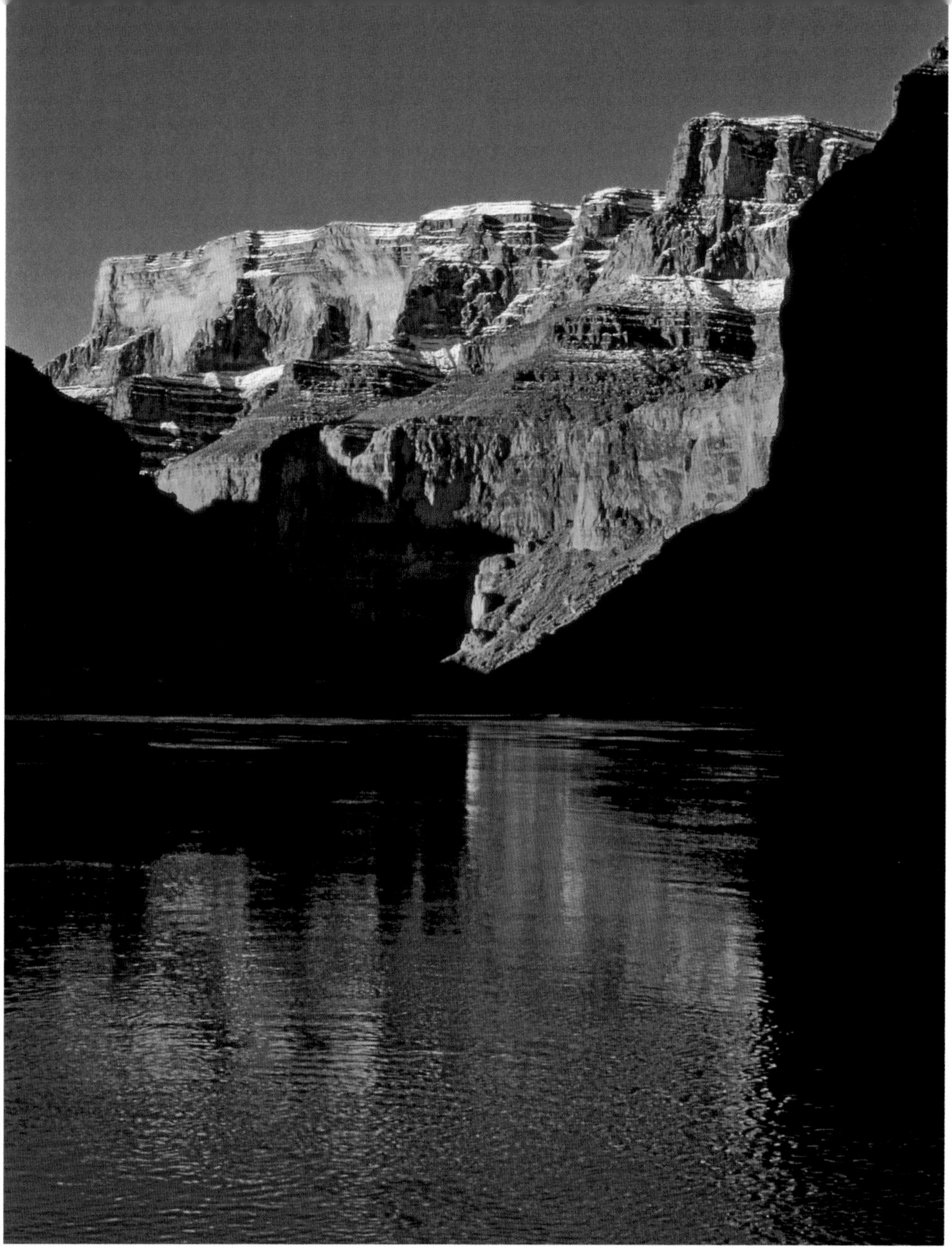

Winter on the Colorado River through Grand Canyon.

Canyonlands National Park. A life on the loose showed no signs of slowing down—my trail was still well marked.

The same bright, intense light that made Georgia O'Keefe exclaim, "The color! The color!"; the same magic that made author D. H. Lawrence write that a new part of his soul woke up in northern New Mexico and the old world gave way to the new; and the same golden light that brought the Taos Society of Artists together in the early 1900s always lured me back to my home on the rocky hillside beneath the mountain. I was a child of my landscape; it took control as I, by degrees, became my landscape. I became my house. My house was me.

New rooms with all the amenities joined tenuously to the original room, as if they were unsure that I should leave a simpler, more cohesive life behind—a time when I earned my water by carrying it from the creek, enjoyed a bath all the more because the water was heated on a cookstove; a time when I despised telephones and had few possessions. Did I own my house, or did it own me? It was now so comfortable that, at times, I felt like a prisoner—the beautiful house with the golden bars. But you can never go back. The original room metamorphosed into a library, gallery, and depository for memorabilia—a space through which I pass en route to spaces that I have become, spaces where large windows cast sunlight on new ways of seeing and being. Once I read DeVoto, Abbey, and Traven; now I read Montaigne, Rimbaud, and Milosz.

On a winter morning toward the end of the millennium, I heard the call of an old friend I hadn't seen in more than thirty years. Dave Brower was not well and I wanted to visit him—time was running out. I knocked on the same door high in the Berkeley hills of California that Terry and I had stood before with our bound manuscript of *On the Loose.* The old warrior had the same sparkle in his sky-blue eyes, though his armor was tarnished, and he was bent by years spent battling to preserve and protect wilderness.

Dave welcomed me with a smile and a hug. We sat at his kitchen table piled high with books and letters, a phone placed in the center—a place where he spent most of his time. He was reading Paul Hawken and Mark Hertsgard and titles like *The Biotech Century* and *The End of Work* that addressed the decline of global labor. Dave kept pace with the times, had mellowed and seemed at peace. He shared Tad Nichols' book *Glen Canyon, Images of a Lost World*. I thumbed through it in silence—there was no need for words. We sat quietly looking out at the Bay far below, where fog in every shade of gray played with shafts of light from a hidden sun. Through the mists San Francisco came and went, as fog cast the hard edges of concrete and steel into soft diffuse shapes like a dreamy watercolor.

Dave broke the silence, speculating on the trails Terry might have taken. We concluded he would have written a dozen books, eclipsing *On the Loose.* My brother was well on his way to losing his sociological innocence and becoming a hard-core radical, and may have in desperation taken up "monkey-wrenching" when all else failed. His fight for wilderness may have compelled him to question the very foundations of Western civilization. But for the many who hacked at the branches of the "evil empire," Terry may have struck the root. I conjectured with Dave that he probably would have taught at a university, lectured, married, and had a family. But who knows? Maybe he would have become so disillusioned he would have become a sour misanthrope who disappeared into a remote corner of wilderness, leaving no trace.

Dave had kept the bound manuscript of *On the Loose* all these years, and I had arrived bent on retrieving it—but I hadn't the heart to ask him about it, as I knew he considered his contribution to its publication a landmark. Tears arrived when I gave Dave a solid good-bye hug, knowing it would be the last time. The planet was on the edge of losing the irreplaceable, and the sun would never shine quite the same.

I left the Brower house in the rain and continued down the road of remembrance. Telegraph Avenue seemed benign—the fire of the '60s had gone out. I wondered in what kind of world the students at the University of California would raise their children, and where they would find the strength and vision to meet the challenges of the twenty-first century. In cyberspace? In wilderness? Would technology save the rogue primate from himself? Would technology provide the answers? The radiant smile of a young student with fire in her eye convinced me there was hope.

Had she hiked the John Muir Trail or run the Colorado through the Grand Canyon? Did she view the natural world as hostile and something to fear, requiring control and domination, or did she sleep blissfully beneath the stars? Did she care about renewable energy? Did she feel that the American political system needed an overhaul? Was she an anarchist, or passively following the herd? I wondered if, among the books she clutched to her breast, there were those by Howard Zinn, Derrick Jensen, John Livingston, or Paul Shepard. It's a rotten world my generation is leaving her; as Max Oelschlaeger noted, "We're caught between a failed story and a future powerless to be born." But she would give birth to it! She would help create a peaceful world and clean up the environment. But would she hear angels, and see a sky sparkling with diamonds? Her generation would prove Oelschlaeger dead wrong!

She and the swarms of students who passed were as much a mystery to me as the person I had been, dashing down Telegraph Avenue with my mind on fire or marching to the Oakland Draft Board to protest the war in Vietnam.

I sat on a bench outside Sproul Hall where musician Country Joe had once asked a question as pertinent today as in the Vietnam era, "One, two, three, what are we fighting for?" The Campanile chimed its familiar tones and a warm glow of memory surged through me.

The house where I lived during junior high school had been leveled for a park. The home seemed as remote as the entries in the lost leather-bound diary I had kept under lock and key beneath my bed. I stared blankly at a young couple entwined in the grass, concluding I may have dreamed the house. The College Avenue apartment remained standing, where in dawn's early light I had seen the flash in the street-lights of that Oldsmobile's hood emblem of the world, and wondered where and who my father was.

Then I visited 33 Canyon Road and walked up the long switchback trail to my brother's basement apartment where *On the Loose* was written, half expecting to see Terry smiling through the window. I walked down the trail in a trance and drove over the ridge to the community of Canyon. The house where I had lived nestled in the redwoods looked exactly the same, although the post office had burned to the ground. I had seen enough. *You can never go back.*

Next morning I left the Bay Area and headed back to New Mexico by way of Capitol Reef National Park in southeast Utah to revisit Fruita and its environs. The old stone Mormon church in Torrey had been leveled. I found the road to Fish Creek Ranch located at the foot of Boulder Mountain, where I had arrived broken in the dimming of my adolescence after my brother drowned. The ranch house had burned to the ground. I kicked through the ash and rubble searching for some memento—something familiar, perhaps a burned remnant of the cedar posts I had helped haul from the mountain that supported the entry. Maybe I would unearth an artifact from my uncle's studio. I found nothing. *You can never go back.*

I drove south down the highway to Capitol Reef National Park, past the new visitors' center, past the ruins of Ripple Rock Ranch where Dick Sprang drew Batman. Then on past the manicured orchards, where ashen-faced tourists wandered aimlessly among the pet deer, past the petroglyph panels that had once captured my imagination, past the swimming hole where in a dream I once swam with my brother, and on toward Hanksville on a road that tore the heart out of the canyon. *You can never go back.* Still, the towering sandstone domes were as grand, and the Fremont River still ran and will, one day, remember its way to the Colorado.

I reined in my truck at the Bureau of Land Management office in Hanksville, where I picked up a map of the Henry Mountains. Next to the office, I recognized the old waterwheel from the Wolverine Mine at the base of Mount Pennell that once crushed ore—the wheel my brother and I had spun one another around in as we clung to its gigantic spokes. I stared at it in bewilderment—a fragment of memory was out of place. *You can never go back.* I continued my drive up into the Henrys, and camped. In the morning I began my walk up Mount Ellen, which Terry and I had climbed in the early '60s.

The deep-orange light of early morning struck the peaks and inched its way down the ridges. I passed the turnout where Terry and I had parked our beat-up Jeep to climb the peak. There was a trail now, and I followed it up one long ridge after another. Near the summit I heard a rustling sound, like ten thousand birds in flight passing above me—a sound I hadn't heard for a long while. No wind stirred down the long bony ridges, where twisted pines grew from rocks.

From the summit, the enormity of the landscape assaulted me, just as it had decades before. Like a conduit that sparks with overload, I had to turn away lest I damage my system. From this altitude the canyons, mesas, ravines, and monoclines trail off in every direction to a horizon encircled by blue-gray mountains—country that teases, seduces, then overwhelms the senses. I saw nothing made by man for hundreds of square miles except an occasional flash of windshield. Some places you can return to and remain constant. I fell to my knees and embraced a mound of long, thin slabs of granite, peppered with black and white specks and covered over by orange, green, and black lichen.

Clouds swirled above, forming as quickly as they dissipated, reminding me of a photograph my brother had taken here in 1963. At ground level Terry had snapped photos of his brother overwhelmed by the magnitude of a landscape—a picture that found its way into *On the Loose* along with the words, "The wind goeth toward the south, and turneth about unto the north; it whirleth about continually, and the wind returneth again according to his circuits." My brother Terry was the wind, he was the light, and he was with me on the mountain.

Next day, I drove through Hite, where I had begun my Glen Canyon trip in the early '60s. The marina was closed due to drought. There was hardly enough water to fill a bucket, let alone a reservoir. The receding water had left behind rank, eerie mudflats and white high-water marks on the sandstone. The place seemed haunted—violated. At this rate of flow, Cathedral in the Desert would resurface, but its soul would be gone—like exhuming the dead. It is only a matter of time until the reservoir will be drained and the dam decommissioned.

Toward the end of the millennium, I felt the ground, which had once felt so solid beneath me, shift. The coyote and elk that once ran through my yard were gone. I had to go deeper into the woods where I measured time by how high the bear's claw marks were on the aspen trees, and where I still felt the eyes of Mountain Lion fixed on me. Behind my house, old trails were cut by bulldozers that pushed roads to timberline, where ATVs, snowmobiles, hunters, and deviants run rampant. A developer bought and subdivided large tracts of land in the valley below, and I witnessed subdivisions creeping up the hill, heard the rumble of generators, the pounding of metal, and traffic that diminished all the reasons I had settled here. I wondered if I had outgrown the place and it could no longer contain me. But like the willow I planted when I first arrived that now towers above the house, my roots, too, have grown deep.

It wasn't long after my return from Berkeley that I felt a burr under my saddle— I hadn't made peace with my father. I'd had a lifetime to ponder if Harvey was all my mother made him out to be. I drove north to Wyoming's Tetons to visit him. I had settled comfortably into agreement with what existential writer Jean Paul Sartre called the "burden of a father" who, he speculated, would "lie on me full length and crush me." My brother and I had no demanding authority figure to impose his wills on ours, so in a sense we were free to invent ourselves. We turned to wilderness. I really had no regrets not having grown up with a father, nor did I feel angry or deprived.

Rather, I was curious knowing if Harvey could shed light on my mother's character—was she a pathological liar, a misfit, an angel?—and if he and I shared some common ground.

I rolled into my dad's yard and found him in the corral with horses. Immediately I noticed our physical resemblance—his tall, lanky body, and his slow deliberate movements as he made his way through the herd. His pale-blue eyes leveled on mine. His tanned face was analogous to the Tetons—rugged and rich with character. I felt his strong steady grip as we shook hands. Next day we saddled the horses for an elk hunt and headed out for the high country. Right off he told me that he would have lassoed a star for my mom if she would have only told him what she wanted—what was in her heart. I sank deep in my saddle. I groped for explanation. That's not what she . . .

I rode in silence, admiring the fine tooling of my father's saddle and how he seemed part of his horse. Harvey's .30-30 Winchester caught my attention. He noticed and pulled the rifle from his saddle scabbard and handed it to me. He said it belonged to my grandfather and that it would be mine someday. A shiver shot down my spine.

In his laconic way he spoke of the early days with my mom in Jackson Hole and at Elk Springs Ranch. He said they didn't have horses when she lived there, a daunting revelation. It was clear that my mother had lied and invented a brutal and pitiless father—a man who mercilessly beat animals and who, she fantasized, would do the same with his children. My brother and I spent our childhood running from our mother's hallucinations.

I got off my horse, dazed, and tightened the cinch strap while Harvey told me how he fed alfalfa to the elk, deer, and moose that hunters had wounded. Then and there I realized that my father, though he couldn't express it, knew the subtle rite of the hunt. He was aware of the emotional and philosophical dilemma raised by the act of killing. To kill or be killed is significant only when the hunter is aware of the mysterious transformation of life and death—call it gifting the cosmos—of an unfathomable drama where one receives and gives, and in the final hour passes the gift on. When this awareness is lost, the killing of an animal is reduced to butchery in an abattoir.

I could tell something was eating at Harvey, and at length he asked point blank where his son was buried. I felt a connection with him blood direct that I haven't felt before or since and that nearly toppled me. I told him that I had packed Terry's ashes on my back to the rapid on the Green River where he drowned. He turned ash-white, rolled his eyes skyward, and fought back tears.

Arriving at "the truth" seems illusionary, nebulous, and subjective. It mattered less that I grew up with a lie, and more that I had a mother who all but drowned me in love. It seemed the more one knows, the less one knows, and the stranger life becomes. We all have our demons, our nemeses. There would be no more lamenting for the father who could have been. Harvey was uncomplicated and basic, and what we had in common was contained in silence. We were like two parallel rivers that could never find their confluence. A pragmatic, down-to-earth life on a Minnesota farm had cast Harvey's life. Mine was forged by the '60s, by loss, and by a lifetime of wanderings. He didn't know the difference between a genome and his jeans, ontogeny from neoteny, hadn't heard of psychopathy or ecological dysfunction, and couldn't care less. But he knew all about the Tetons, the wildlife, and the seasons, and consequently he was truly autochthonous—native to place.

The author with his father and Seedskeedee.

Father and son passed through the high country mostly in silence, with occasional observations about how he missed getting an antelope down by Pinedale that year; how there were too many god-damned tourists on the roads these days, and too many boaters on the Snake River.

My '88 Ford pickup spun gravel as I headed south past Hoback Junction where long ago, in the deep emerald green pools, I "became" a trout; past the store where the old Wurlitzer jukebox belted out Hank Williams songs; past the Broken Arrow Ranch and hunting camp on the Hoback that Harvey once owned. I streaked past the Wind River Mountains and Fremont Lake where I swam as a kid; past the Oregon Trail Lander Cut-Off and a monument celebrating Jim Bridger and Captain Fremont of the Reed–Donner party, which made the ghastly error of taking a shortcut to California; past Rock Springs. I found the elusive Highway 430, cruised past Dinosaur National Monument, crossed the Yampa River, endured the madness of Interstate 70, barreled through Leadville, slid over Poncha Pass into the San Luis Valley, and home again in the last light of day.

On the last day of the millennium, I loaded my pickup with firewood and headed west to the Rio Grande Gorge, which cuts through the savanna on the back side of Ute Mountain. A Texan had bought the mountain, and signs warned off trespassers. I drove through the fence anyway and parked, wondering how it was possible for anyone to own a mountain. I watched the last sun crawl up Ute Mountain and, in the fading light, built a fire that lit the sky. I leaned back against the volcanic rocks and saw sparks mingle with stars. I tried to separate the crack of the fire from the creaking of ice in the river just below the rim, and felt ten thousand light-years away from the hullabaloo at Times Square in New York. The light that passed through my crystal that evening set the rocks aglow with the same warm rainbow of colors I had seen all my life. Being outside, where I could hurl my lance at the sun, leap that rainbow, and follow the raven's call—that was truly my home, a place without walls under the roof of the sky.

A herd of fifty Outward Bound students thundered through Rock Creek Ranch and jolted me back to the orchard, where I still found myself wrapped around the limbs of the apple tree. What would the reclusive Seamounton brothers have thought of this crowd, or of the tree limbs pushing their way through the windows and doors into their home, toppling the stone blocks? Or of the fields they had toiled over being reclaimed by the desert, and of the worn-out horses that no one will ever ride grazing in the shade beneath the trees?

I unwrapped myself from the limbs of the grandfather of apple trees—we had become close—and walked back through

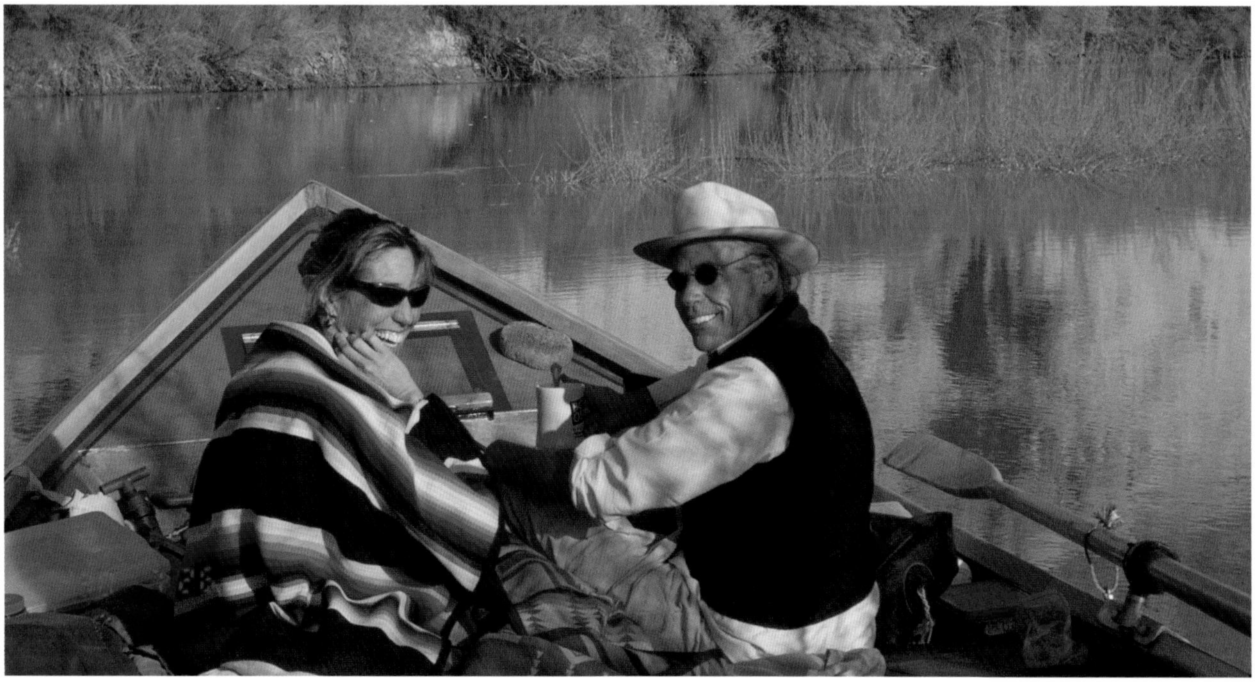

the parched grass and Russian thistle to the boat. A small crowd had gathered around *Seedskeedee,* and I noted with some jealousy that someone dared to fondle her gunwales. I gave an abbreviated class on building a wooden boat, and enjoyed some company after spending so much time navigating through my interior self.

They invited me to their camp for coffee and I obliged. I could no longer hold on to my arcane adventures and told them of my bear encounter. Stories were swapped. I heard of a young man who was sleeping out in the open not far from Rock Creek who had been attacked by a bear. His screams were heard and the bear was run off, but not before the young man had suffered puncture wounds and lacerations. A stretcher was improvised and the unfortunate fellow was loaded onto a boat and suffered the long boat ride to just north of Green River.

We all agreed that this was Bear's home and that we were only guests. We talked about boats, about rivers, about life and change, well into the morning. What we all had in common was love and respect for the Green River, which has an uncanny way of calling us back.

I felt the urge to move on, so I bid my friends adieu and let the water wash me down. The wind was tuning up for another performance: wind that sandblasted the face, leaving the eyes red and raw; wind to turn a boat over or even push it out of the water; and as an encore, wind to launch tents, chairs, and tables into orbit. Wind whipped *Seedskeedee* sideways, locked her there, and mercilessly slammed her against shore. I was battered and found protection for lunch in a clump of willows. Great oceanic waves, whipped up by wind, rolled upstream in long parallel rows. During a lull, I heard the next gale blowing upriver like a freight train. After lunch I took a nap and had a dream.

My ghostly counterpart floated through a grove of trees with a tattered blanket thrown over his bare shoulders. His skin was drawn tight over his ribs, and his glazed deep-blue eyes were fixed straight ahead. Curious, I followed, eventually arriving on the shore of an ocean where a solitary boat gently rocked on the water. A block of polished black marble rose from the sand, inlaid with designs of shell, lapis lazuli, and coral.

My ghostly other self fused with the marble, fracturing its surface. A figure emerged. It was Terry! I tried to force myself awake but couldn't. I reached out to embrace him but he was transparent. He could neither see nor hear me. My brother's elusive form drifted down to the water's edge. He looked down the long,

deserted beach, first one way, then the other, as though he were lost or searching for someone or something.

I ran after him, but the harder I tried to move the slower I went. Weightless now, I rose above the boat where Terry sat motionless, staring into infinity. Through the swirling mists I viewed the boat's deck shining like gold and a hull that flashed like silver. Its gunwales were made of ebony, and a thin line of turquoise-blue water ran through the center of the rails where tiny dolphins of azure and ivory swam. Powerful wings tucked under either side of the boat.

As the mists cleared, Terry was no longer alone. He was surrounded by a circle of children, knee deep in flowers, their faces beaming. My brother looked exactly as he had the last time I saw him, in his river shorts and old sneakers, with his Swiss army knife hanging from his belt. But his face was pale and expressionless. Beside him on the deck lay the autoharp he used to love to play and a stack of books. He picked one up, its golden-edged pages bound in deep red leather, and began reading. I ached to join them but was suspended above in an eerie flight of the imagination.

When my brother finished reading, the children dashed forward, smothering him with love. A young girl dressed in a white dress with blue and yellow ribbons braided in her hair looked up—I'd been discovered. Her soulful emerald-green eyes, like Terry's, locked with mine. I felt like I was falling headlong off a cliff—my chest was about to explode. She drifted toward me and whispered, "How did you find us . . . Are you . . .?" A pinpoint of light within a great dark grew brighter—and brighter . . .

I awoke with a jerk—or had I? Beside me was the black and red checked blanket from Rock Creek Ranch—the same blanket in my dream. I let out a scream and tumbled over a waterfall, and into the void, then slept a deep, dreamless sleep for what seemed an eternity. When I awoke I made sure with a prick. I had dreamt away most of the afternoon.

The wind blew harder than before as I untied the boat and headed downriver. I hadn't rowed more than a few miles when I was blown to shore to camp at mile 38. A fallen cottonwood offered a windbreak. I leaned against the old

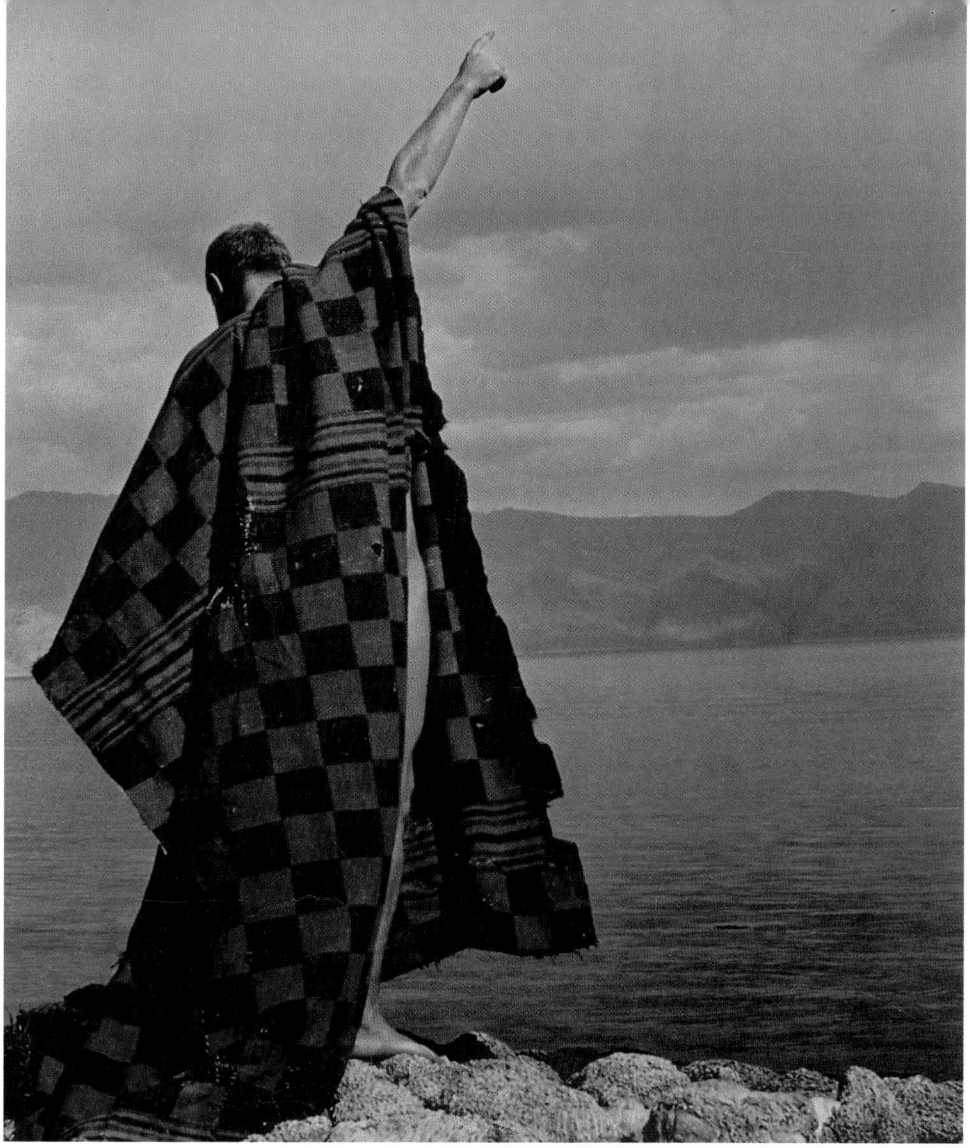

"Life is a dream . . . We sleeping wake and waking sleep." –Montaigne

giant, its smooth gray skin sculpted by floodwaters that once ran free from the Wind River Mountains to the sea. My emotions, inflamed by days of magic and madness, burned hot, so preparing dinner seemed meaningless. I made a raw entry in my journal from my guts, holding fast to the moment, knowing the fire would diminish, become cool and placid.

At last the wind showed mercy, and the sun made a feeble attempt to shine, so I set up camp. I took the makings from last night's dinner from the cooler and cooked quickly. From camp I could see for some distance, but I couldn't relax. Bear was everywhere. After dinner I walked warily to my tent, leery of every movement and shadow. The sky cracked open, releasing torrents of rain. Wind tugged at the cottonwood limbs where voices murmured through the leaves, and the songs of the river ushered me off into another dream.

CHAPTER EIGHTEEN

I've decided to make up my mind about nothing,

to assume the water mask, to finish life as a creek, an eddy,

joining at night the full, sweet flow, to swallow the heat and cold,

the moon and the stars, to swallow myself in ceaseless flow.

– JIM HARRISON

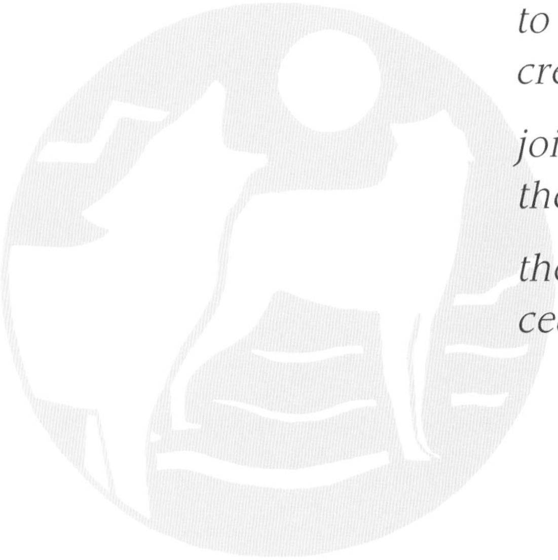

Rattlesnake Camp

Shafts of early sun poured into my tent. It was like waking up inside an orange. I hung on to the tail of my last dream and took a ride: Fog shrouded an island in the middle of the river. Above the island was a submerged driftwood log where a heron perched. He looked quite debonair smoking his pipe and wearing a black suit, red tie, and top hat. He put his book down and spoke. "Good morning, my friend. Are you lost? Would you like a cup of tea?"

I asked if he might know which side of the island would have more water, as I was concerned that my boat would run aground. He adjusted his hat, looked at me deliberately, and said, "Never having

been in a boat, I only can offer you this advice: As you can see, there are only two ways to go—if you take the wider channel believing there's more water, you may find the river is shallow and full of rocks, and if you take the narrow one you may find deep water, but around the bend it may split into many shallow channels and you'll still go aground." He began laughing and reminded me, "But no matter which channel you take, you end up in the same place. All rivers run to the sea, you know." As I passed, the heron tipped his hat good day and relit his pipe. I stood on the deck and confirmed what my friend had said.

The left-hand channel was more direct and did seem to have more water, but it was plain I'd go aground. The deep narrow channel on the right took a sharp turn, so I couldn't tell what lay ahead. I was torn between the two. The heron flew off. The dream evaporated and left me wondering if living a life of indecision and questioning was like trying to row across a river with an anchor still out.

I had survived the night without being crushed by a falling cottonwood, hit by lightning, dragged out of my tent by a bear, or washed away in a flash flood. Life was fine indeed. I stuck my head from the tent and took a deep breath of the new day. Yesterday's doomsday sky was now brilliant blue, and the air was sweet with the pungent scent of earth saturated with water. I bolted from my tent and began running, feeling the soft deep red earth under my feet. From a high ledge above camp, I could see the river sweeping around the corner upstream from Rain Canyon back at mile 38 and then down around the bend to Wire Fence Rapid.

It was so clear that behind me, along the rim, it seemed I could nearly touch Broken Finger Arch. I ran my fingers along the edges of the steep gullies lined with pine trees. This vantage point offered a dramatic view of the end of Desolation Canyon and the beginning of Gray Canyon. Upriver, the artist had used all his brilliant red, orange, and purple pigments, so downriver he was content to use more muted colors from his palette. The potholes on the high ledges overflowed, and I drank deeply of rainwater that was delicately flavored with juniper berries and minerals.

I took a leisurely, roundabout route back to the river—the morning was too good to let go. I dropped into a drainage cut by flash floods, and as I came around a bend, there they were—mustangs! Three of them—a colt, a mare, and a stallion. The stallion was magnificent—the color of smoke, the sky on a cloudy day, or the gray of a dreamless sleep. I froze as the mare and colt bolted out of sight down the wash, but the stallion stood motionless. His eyes were so forceful I imagined he could see through me and beyond, his hearing so acute he could hear my heart beating.

What happened next defied reason. The mustang walked slowly toward me—curious, absorbed, and with undeniable urgency. This was not the way of a wild horse. When he was within twenty feet, the tension was unbearable and I took off like a shot toward the river. Simultaneously, the stallion lunged sideways and charged up canyon, leaving in the dust lost opportunity.

Coward! said I to myself. I should have grabbed his long matted mane and swung onto his back, felt his hot steamy breath, searched his eyes for things only mustangs know! I felt my brother's spirit so strongly whenever I saw wild horses and felt their strength and independence. Had the elusive mustang appeared to test my moral fiber—to measure my fear of Death or the unknown? I looked around for Coyote. This could be the trickster's mischief! He could be atop the mesa laughing at the floundering mortal below who couldn't understand what he knew so well and would never tell. I vowed my next mustang encounter would be different—I would stay. I would listen. As I sauntered back to the river, I felt Coyote's eyes following me. He, too, would keep returning until I got it right—perhaps until I could dissolve in laughter and not take life so seriously!

I had a cup of coffee, a book of Taoist tales, and my guitar and held fast to the moment. Chuang Tzu's words jumped off the page and embedded themselves: "Manifest plainness, embrace simplicity, reduce selfishness, and have few desires." A fragment of cloud passed, wind rustled the leaves, a beaver swam upstream. Maybe in my next life I will arrive as a beaver, like the one I'd caught napping the other day in his womblike home sculpted into the riverbank. He lay on his back with his toes pointing up, deep in beaver dreams. I wanted to crawl into his den to rediscover my biological heritage, to become the river. To use my scaly tail as a rudder; to mate for life; to work with others to build my home of twigs and sticks; to plaster it inside to keep it warm in the winter and keep my enemies away; to eat fresh bark, water plants, fruit, and grasses; to live life at what the Indians call the "sacred center" by creating habitat for other animals, like fish, turtles, frogs, birds, and ducks.

It was late morning when I finally pushed off for a day of rapids. I cut *Seedskeedee* loose and we pounded through Wire Fence—the first of the day. Then we swept around the bend, rowing hard right, to take on Three Fords Rapid with its boulder-choked channel. Then came Last Chance, then Curry Rapid—named for outlaw George "Flat Nose" Curry, who was shot to death by lawmen in the early 1900s—followed by Rabbit Valley and Coal Creek Rapids. *Seedskeedee* met them all with style and grace.

"Yippee-ya-aye, yippee yi-yo, ghost riders in the sky." It was the song Terry sang on the tongue of Steer Ridge Rapid, and it thundered through me. I hadn't thought of it since. The song, filled with images of gaunt faces, burning eyes, shirts soaked with sweat, and horses snorting fire, reminded me that to save my soul from hell, I oughta change my ways pronto, or spend eternity chasing the devil's herd across an endless sky. I bellowed the song out so loud I bet ol' Flat Nose heard me!

By mile 22, just below Rattlesnake Rapid, we were played out, so I called it a day and pulled over to camp. The water was rising and cut me off from the east side of the river. I was on an island, and it suited me fine. Waves rolled up on the beach as *Seedskeedee* bucked and kicked in the wind. Now and then, a wave hit her side with a thump and sent a fine mist into the wind and over her deck. She was a wild thing. I tried to settle her down by telling her she was the most beautiful boat in the world, and when that didn't

work I tied her off from bow and stern, then threw out an anchor. I sensed something was eating at her. I had a hunch that *Seedskeedee* wanted to return to sedentary trailer life about as much as I wanted the trip to end.

I am a worshiper of flowing. The sound of running water has embedded itself in my subconscious. Without it I feel a vacancy, and my heart beats to a different rhythm. In the company of the water's many voices, I had reveled in simple acts. Like boat maintenance—replacing a bent oarlock or applying new hatch tape, making new lanyards, adjusting a foot brace, or sponging out a damp hatch. Like running along a beach feeling the warm sand between my toes—whooping with the joy of just being alive; like reading in the shade of cottonwoods and hearing their rustling leaves lull me to sleep. I would miss the mustangs, eagles, deer, and ducks, the big sky and the play of light on the water. But I was still on the river and pushed these thoughts away.

I looked out on the savage spectrum of the Green River, upon that unfathomable topography where all the colors of the world exploded soundlessly. In the late afternoon sun, the canyon walls were afire with deep, rich, vibrant colors—zinc and cadmium yellow, and burnt sienna with violet shadows that deepened as the sun climbed the canyon walls to begin its journey toward tomorrow.

Today I traced the route I had taken so long ago through the maze of canyons. How, without wings or shoes, I had passed the cliff face that juts from the river a mile above Rock Creek haunts me still. My thoughts as I stumbled through miles of steep, eroded gullies, threaded my way through a maze of ledges high above the river, and thrashed for miles through jungles of tamarisk and willow, I cannot access. I could never have guessed then that I would want to see a river again.

At Rattlesnake Camp, I would have been thirty-one miles below Rock Creek without any idea of where I was or when the canyon would release me. Another cliff on the west side of the river looks impassable. Downriver from this is a nearly vertical talus slope where only in late afternoon light can the faint thread of a game trail be seen. Below, water pounds and pulsates against house-size boulders; the slightest slip would have hurled me into the river. I imagined myself above the rapid as one trying to remember the lyrics of an old song when the music remains but the words are beyond reach. I had passed downriver into twilight.

I recalled my first night on the river with *Seedskeedee*, the immensity of the sky and infinite horizons, how blue-black clouds concealed kachinas that danced and worked their magic, bringing rain and life to the thirsty desert. Terry was in the circle of dancers. And how the cottonwoods stood like wise elders; among their leaves, my brother's spirit lingered still. And the chameleon moods of the river—how the light reflects golden-browns and silver-grays, and a thousand shades in between and beyond, like a thousand luminescent golden fish. Terry was the light on the water. He was the water that thundered over the rocks; he was the glassy smooth current pushing through an eddy.

Through my memory flew the eagle I had startled early in the trip—his wings transparent and golden in the sun as he rose and vanished on a thermal. He had soared with my brother. I thought of my wanderings on the high mesas and benches above the river, where floods exposed cobbles in old river channels, of the stones' warmth and smoothness, and of the deep-purple one that fit perfectly in my palm. Terry was the water that shaped the stone. He was the stone.

I remembered the grove of box elders where I had put away my pen and journal, unable to describe the light that illuminated the leaves. My brother was the light and the leaves. The memory of the morning I ran Steer Ridge Rapid flooded me; I was revisited by the raven who followed me through the day. My brother was the raven. He was the bear who tested my will and tumbled me into the spirit world when our eyes locked. Today Terry was Coyote, the joker, the truth-teller, the shape-shifter who as a mustang galloped toward me, challenging me to be strong and stand my ground— reminding me that fear of the unknown, even of

death itself, is only an illusion. Better to take chances and stay true to my own path, accepting that there are no shortcuts to the things I love.

Terry is omnipresent—his life an inspiration, his passing a benediction. A life such as his is never lost; it simply assumes other forms—as water turns to vapor to rise and fall as rain, joining the river again.

By crossing a continent and returning, Lewis and Clark transformed rumor, guess, and fantasy on a blank map into reality. Much of the untamed geography of the West remains as it was in 1806, and its quintessence endures. It has since metamorphosed into a repository for dreams, a place where another chance is given to begin—just over the next mountain range or across a river. My labyrinthine river journey had offered me another chance as well—to reconstruct, to forget and to celebrate, and to leave a scratch on the canyon wall before passing into the mystery.

But as it never has before, man's capacity for love reaches beyond the West and its geography out across the universe, to connect us all. We're reminded that we are not alone—we are all side streams that flow into rivers destined for the sea. The days of our lives should sparkle and shine, and if we listen they will whisper—*take your time.* Enjoy the perfection of what you are doing, revel in accomplishing it exquisitely, and remember those times when you sought and found, when you surrendered and were set free. Milosz said it well—

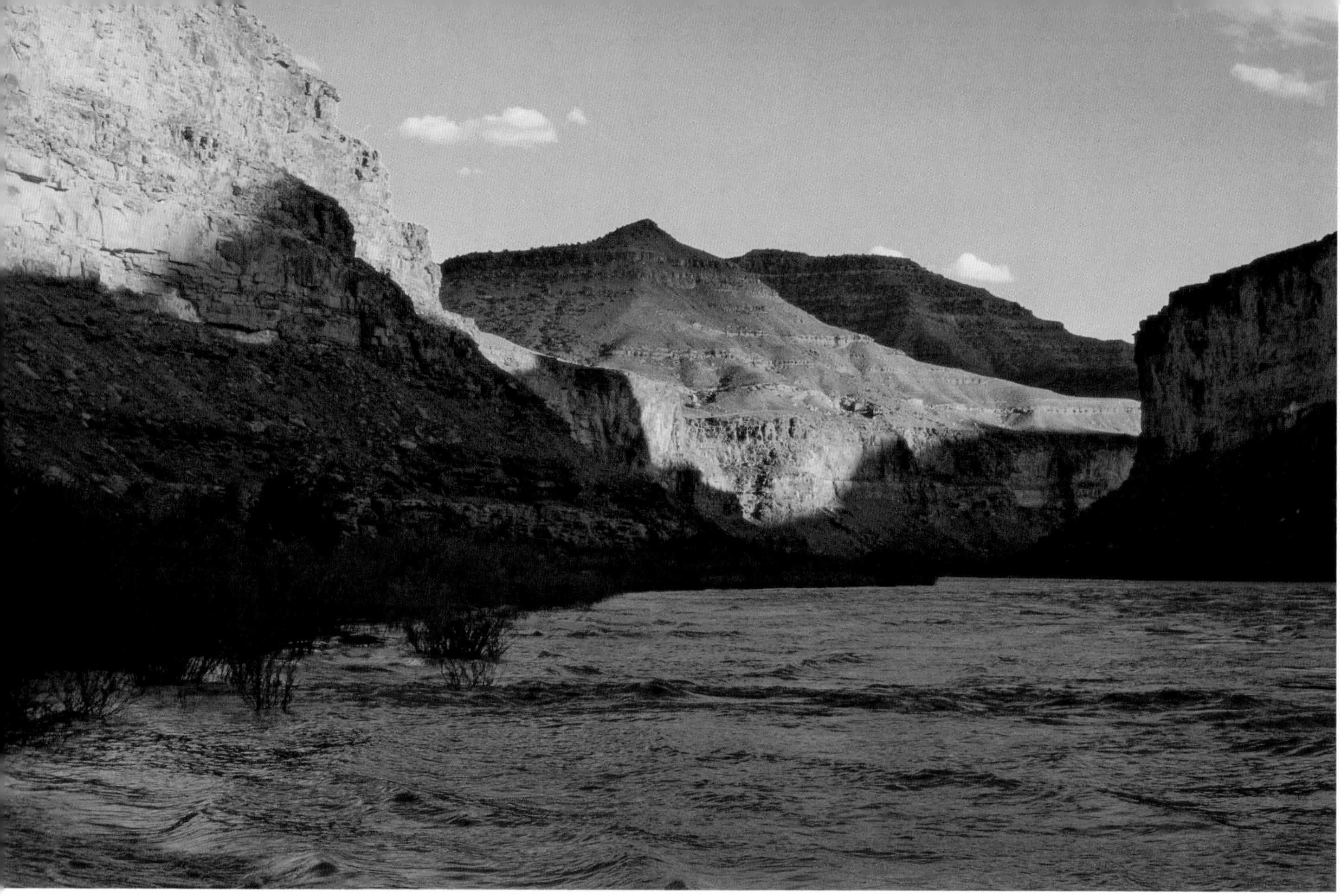

"Perhaps we should begin by worshiping a stone, an ordinary fieldstone, its very being, and pray without opening our lips."

On the final page of *On the Loose,* Terry essentially charted my course down the river—a journey he intuitively knew I would make alone. On that page is a photograph he took of his younger brother watching the sun sink into the Pacific—the water reflecting a zillion diamonds . . .

I walk down the beach and, with a stick smoothed by the river, write in the sand the words that accompany that picture: "So long as I can see I will keep looking. As long as I can walk I will keep moving. As long as I can stand I will keep fighting." This paean had resonated and endured for many of us, but now it truly lodged in my heart. The waters of the Green were on the rise, and I knew that in the morning Terry's words would be washed away. But the secret knowledge of the heart and of water is beyond language.

I lay in sand still warm from the afternoon sun and watched the stars appear, one by one. A coyote cackled in the distance. In the last light, big billowing clouds rolled across the sky like horses snorting fire. A new moon poked through the clouds like a tiny, luminous silver boat, sparks and spangles glittering in its wake, and I thought I heard the sound of laughing children. But it was probably the river. The boat cut across the sparkling night sky, and quiet did quiet remain.

INDIVIDUUM EST INEFFABILE

Photo Credits

Cover: Book jacket photograph of author—Used by permission, C. C. Lockwood.

Chapter 1: *Ouray ferry, Utah, 1930s*—Utah State Historical Society, all rights reserved; *Mill Valley, California, 1966*—Used by permission, Ephraim French.

Chapter 2: *Climbing Mount Eisenhower, Canadian Rockies, 1967*—Used by permission, Hobart Lenz; *La Paz, Baja, 1970s*—Used by permission, Ephraim French.

Chapter 5: *Author sketching*—Used by permission, Andy Hutchinson.

Chapter 6: *Dean Brimhall caught in a flood on the Fremont River; Georgie White and Harry Aleson swim the Colorado River;* and *Harry Aleson, breakfast in the desert*—Used by permission, Utah State Historical Society, all rights reserved.

Chapter 9: *Cathedral in the Desert, 1964; Hite ferry, Harry Aleson at the oars;* and *Crossing of the Fathers*—Used by permission, Utah State Historical Society, all rights reserved.

Chapter 10: *Sand Wash ferry, 1930s*—Used by permission, Utah State Historical Society, all rights reserved; *River and boat above Sand Wash*—Used by permission, Andy Hutchinson; *Utah's Canyonlands National Park*—Used by permission, Don Briggs.

Chapter 11: *Joan Baez* and *Sproul Hall*—Courtesy the Helen Nestor Collection, Oakland Museum of California. Gift of the artist; *Dancing hippies* and *Drop acid not bombs*—Used by permission, Robert Altman.

Chapter 12: *Author in boat* and *Author with guitar*—Used by permission, C. C. Lockwood.

Chapter 14: *Remains of Russell boat*—Photograph by Ken Slight from the Maston Collection, vol. 117 (40). This item is reproduced by permission of the Huntington Library, San Marino, California; *Harry Aleson threw me a lifeline*—Used by permission, Utah State Historical Society, all rights reserved.

Chapter 15: *Pickin' in Andreas Canyon, California, 1964*—Used by permission, Bill Wayne.

Chapter 17: Photograph of author and Mary Anne Griffin used by permission of M. Crabtree.

Quotes

I am grateful to the following authors and publishers for quotations used in this book:

"Sexual Water" by Pablo Neruda, from *Residence on Earth,* copyright © 1973 by Pablo Neruda and Donald D. Walsh. Reprinted by permission of New Directions Publishing Corp.

Frank Dobie, *The Mustangs,* used by permission of Little, Brown and Company.

The Immense Journey by Loren Eiseley. Used by permission of Random House, Inc. New York, 1956, 1957.

The Theory and Practice of Rivers and New Poems by Jim Harrison. Used by permission of Clark City Press. Livingston, Montana, 1989.

Listening to the Land: Conversations about Nature, Culture, and Eros by Derrick Jensen. Used by permission of Chelsea Green Publishing Company. White River Junction, Vermont, 2002.

June Jordan quote from *Moving Towards Home*, copyright June Jordan, reprinted with permission of the June M. Jordan Literary Estate Trust, www.junejordan.com.

On the Road by Jack Kerouac, used by permission of Penguin Putnam Inc.

I Feel Like I'm Fixin' to Die Rag by Joe McDonald, used by permission from Country Joe McDonald.

The Place No One Knew: Glen Canyon on the Colorado by Eliot Porter. Copyright 1963, 1966 by the Sierra Club. Reprinted by permission of Sierra Club Books.

The Birth of Reason and Other Essays by George Santayana, copyright 1968, Columbia University Press. Reprinted with the permission of the publisher.

Delmore Schwartz, from *Selected Poems: Summer Knowledge*, copyright © 1959 by Delmore Schwartz. Reprinted by permission of New Directions Publishing Corp.

Pygmalion by George Bernard Shaw. Used by permission of Dover Publishing Inc. Mineola, New York, 1994.

Last stanza from "The Rite" from *New and Collected Poems: 1931–2001,* Czeslaw Milosz, copyright © 1988, 1991, 1995, 2001 by Czeslaw Milosz Royalties, Inc. Reprinted by permission of HarperCollins Publishers.

Bibliography

Belknap, Buzz. *Desolation River Guide*. Evergreen, Colorado: Westwater Books, 1996.

Bryant, Felice and Boudleaux. "Bye Bye Love."

Cohen, Michael. *A Garden of Bristlecone.* Reno: University of Nevada Press, 1998.

Dingus, Lowell, and Timothy Row. *The Mistaken Extinction.* New York: W. H. Freeman, 1998.

Free Speech Movement Archives. www.fsm–a.org.

Gilbert, Cathy A., and Kathleen L. McKoy. *Capitol Reef National Park Administrative History,* Vol. 1.

Harry Le Roy Aleson Papers, 1918–1922, Utah State Historical Society.

Hölldobler, Bert, and Edward O. Wilson. *Journey to the Ants: A Story of Scientific Exploration*. Cambridge, Massachusetts: Belknap Press, 1994.

Howard, Walter. Department of Wildlife, Fisheries, and Conservation Biology. University of California, Davis.

Lavender, David. *River Runners.* Tucson: University of Arizona Press, 1985.

Lewis, David. *Utah History Encyclopedia*. "Uintah–Ouray Indian Reservation."

Lister, Robert, and Florence Lister. *Chaco Canyon.* Albuquerque: University of New Mexico Press, 1981.

Livingston, John. *The Fallacy of Wildlife Conservation*. Toronto: McClelland Stewart, The Canadian Publishers, 1981.

Powell, John Wesley. *The Exploration of the Colorado River*. Garden City, New York: Doubleday, 1961.

Rockwell, David. *Giving Voice to Bear*. Toronto: Key Porter Books, 1991.

Rumi, J. *The Masnavi.* London: Octagon Press, 1994.

Sierra Club Bulletin. San Francisco: James J. Gillick and Company, June 1950.

Sprang, Elizabeth. *Good Bye River.* Las Cruces, New Mexico: Kiva Press, 1992.

Stegner, Wallace. *Beyond the Hundredth Meridian*. Boston: Houghton Mifflin, 1962.

Webb, Roy. *If I Had a Boat*. Salt Lake City: University of Utah Press, 1996.

Wilderness Society. "Book Cliffs, Uinta Basin: In Big Oil's Cross Hairs."

Wilson, Edward O. *On Human Nature*. Cambridge, Massachusetts: Harvard University Press, 1978.

The Simply Healthy Lowfat Cookbook

University of California at Berkeley

THE Simply Healthy LOWFAT COOKBOOK

Over 250 lowfat recipes rich in the antioxidant vitamins that keep you healthy

By the Editors of The Wellness Cooking School
and The University of California at Berkeley WELLNESS LETTER

PUBLISHED BY REBUS, INC., NEW YORK
Distributed by Random House

THE UNIVERSITY OF CALIFORNIA AT BERKELEY WELLNESS LETTER

The Simply Healthy Lowfat Cookbook comes from the editors of the Wellness Cooking School and the editors of America's top-rated health newsletter, the *University of California at Berkeley Wellness Letter.*

The *Wellness Letter* is a monthly eight-page newsletter that delivers brisk, useful coverage on health, nutrition and exercise topics in language that is clear, engaging and nontechnical. It's a unique resource that covers fundamental ways to prevent illness.
For information on how to order this award-winning newsletter from the world-famous School of Public Health at the University of California at Berkeley, write to
Health Letter Associates, Department 1108, 632 Broadway, New York, New York 10012.

Library of Congress Cataloging-in-Publication Data

The simply healthy lowfat cookbook : over 250 lowfat recipes rich in the antioxidant vitamins that keep you healthy / by the editors of the Wellness Cooking School and the University of California at Berkeley, wellness letter.
p. cm.
At head of title: University of California at Berkeley.
Includes index.
ISBN 0-929661-28-1 : $24.95
1. Low-fat diet—Recipes. 2. Antioxidants.
I. Wellness Cooking School. II. University of California, Berkeley, wellness letter.

RM237.7.S575 1995 95-41527
641.5'638—dc20 CIP

Printed in the United States of America
10 9 8 7 6 5 4 3 2 1
Distributed by Random House, Inc.

This book is not intended as a substitute for medical advice.
Readers who suspect they may have specific medical problems should consult a physician about any suggestions made in this book.

Cover: California Pizza, page 176

Contents

Introduction

Scientists first discovered vitamins in the early part of the twentieth century. Once they understood the role vitamins play in human health, it was possible for them to establish recommended intakes to help maintain all functions of the body. Today, evidence is accumulating that intakes of certain vitamins above the levels needed to maintain general health may play a role in preventing or alleviating a wide variety of illnesses, especially heart disease and cancer, the leading causes of death in the United States.

These vitamins—beta carotene, vitamin C and vitamin E—are called antioxidants and they repair the damage cells incur during normal metabolic function. Researchers are just beginning to investigate the connection between antioxidant activity and disease prevention: Preliminary studies have found that people who eat a lot of foods rich in antioxidants are healthier than those who do not.

In "The Antioxidant-Rich Diet" chapter that follows, questions about this "new" role for these vitamins are answered in depth—including how much of each antioxidant you need, based on current knowledge, and which foods supply the greatest amounts. You may be surprised to discover that you can, in most cases, easily meet—and even surpass—the recommended intakes for these nutrients through diet alone.

The Recipes

The recipes in this book will teach you by creative example how to include high-antioxidant foods in your daily diet, both simply and deliciously. And as you browse through the chapters in this book (Soups & Stews, Poultry, Fish & Shellfish, Meat, Pasta, Meatless Main Courses, Main-Course Salads, Vegetables & Grains and Desserts) you will certainly discover that most high-antioxidant foods—such as broccoli, sweet potatoes, oranges, tomatoes, strawberries and cantaloupe–are already part of your daily routine.

You'll find clever tricks that help you add both nutrition and flavor to everyday fare. In California Pizza (page 176), for example, carrot juice is added to the pizza dough and shredded carrots are added to the tomato sauce for a beta carotene boost. These tricks work in desserts as well: Carrots are the hidden ingredient in Peach-Apricot Cobbler (page 246) and sweet potatoes add an incredible dense richness to a glazed chocolate cake (page 240). To add healthful doses of vitamin C to recipes, a salsa or uncooked sauce (vitamin C is partially destroyed by heat) made with such high-vitamin C ingredients as bell peppers, tomatoes, kiwi fruit and jalapeño peppers accompanies simple pastas, poultry, fish and meat.

The Nutritional Analyses

The nutritional analysis provided for each recipe gives information not only on the per-serving values of beta carotene and vitamin C, but also on total fat, saturated fat, calories, cholesterol, sodium, dietary fiber, calcium and iron (see the box on page 26 for the recommended daily intakes of all of these nutrients). For simplicity, all nutritional values above 10 have been rounded to the nearest whole number; all other values are rounded to the nearest tenth. Bear in mind that the values are averages. The nutritional content of any dish depends on the quality of the ingredients you use.

We do not include data for vitamin E because generally speaking the amounts of this vitamin in lowfat recipes are insignificant compared to the Wellness Recommended Intakes (page 11). In addition, nutritional data for the vitamin E content of foods is spotty, making an accurate vitamin E analysis difficult.

The Antioxidant-Rich Diet

By now, practically everyone knows that a diet low in fat and high in fiber is essential in helping to prevent chronic diseases. In fact, scientists estimate that as many as one-third of the cases of cancer and heart disease are attributable, at least in part, to dietary factors. As researchers gain a better understanding of the connection between diet and disease, however, it is becoming increasingly clear that fat and fiber are only two pieces of a much larger puzzle. In recent years, studies have shown that substances in vegetables and fruits called antioxidants can help the body protect itself from the molecular damage to cells that can lead to the development of chronic diseases—namely heart disease and cancer, but possibly also diseases associated with aging, such as cataracts, arthritis and senility.

But just what are antioxidants? How effective are they in preventing disease? What's the best way to get them? This chapter answers these and many more questions about the role antioxidants—and foods rich in them—play in chronic disease prevention.

What are antioxidants?

Antioxidants are chemical substances that protect the body from the adverse effects of oxygen. Oxygen is necessary for energy generation, and cells will die within minutes without it, but the chemical changes that take place when the body uses oxygen create unstable oxygen molecules called free radicals that can damage cells. Some antioxidants are enzymes and other compounds manufactured by the cells themselves. Others are nutrients that we eat—vitamin C, vitamin E and beta carotene.

Where do free radicals come from?

In the cells, oxygen is constantly involved in chemical reactions in which electrons (particles in atomic structure) are shifted around. To generate energy, cells remove electrons from sugars—that is, burn the sugars—and add these electrons to oxygen. This forms free radicals—highly reactive compounds, unstable and electrically charged in such a way as to combine quickly with other elements. Free radicals have unpaired electrons, and to create chemical balance must either acquire an additional electron from some other molecule or get rid of the odd one. As oxygen combines and recombines and electrons are exchanged, other unstable molecules are generated, thus setting off a chain reaction, creating still more free radicals.

Do free radicals cause disease?

Scientists now believe that free radicals are implicated in the development of many chronic diseases. Since the 1980s, accumulating research has pointed to free radicals as the culprits in a wide variety of disorders, from heart disease and cancer to Parkinson's and rheumatoid arthritis. Some studies even suggest that free radicals may be one cause of cataracts and macular degeneration (eye disorders that are leading causes of visual loss) by damaging the eye's lens and light-sensitive retina.

Can you stop free radicals from forming?

Since oxygen is the basic source of energy and therefore is necessary for every metabolic function in the body, you cannot halt the development of free radicals. However, you can decrease the damage they do to cells by supplying your body with antioxidants (which rapidly neutralize free radicals) and by avoiding external factors that stimulate free radical production—radiation, excessive sunlight, pollution (like ozone) and cigarette and cigar smoke.

How do antioxidants prevent cell damage?

Living cells don't just sit there allowing free radicals to beat them up. Just as our cells have methods of fighting infectious agents, they also have orderly systems for battling free radicals and repairing molecular damage—this is where antioxidants come in.

Antioxidants inactivate free radicals before they can do further damage to cells, cell structures and genetic material (such as DNA). Problems occur when free radicals outnumber the body's antioxidant defenses. Then widespread cell damage may occur, possibly disrupting a cell's normal cancer-prevention apparatus, for example, or impairing its ability to do other chemical work. And if genetic material damaged by free radicals isn't totally repaired, the damaged DNA is replicated in new cells.

Are foods or supplements the best sources of antioxidants?

You're far better off meeting your antioxidant needs by eating vegetables and fruits than by popping a pill. When you take a supplement you're only getting isolated vitamins and minerals. Numerous studies have linked fruit and vegetable consumption, but not isolated nutrients, to a reduced risk of disease. For example, researchers at the University of Hawaii found that a high consumption of vegetables—especially dark leafy green vegetables, vegetables in the cabbage family (called cruciferous vegetables) and tomatoes—was linked to a reduced risk of lung cancer. No association was found, however, between an intake of isolated nutrients—like vitamin C, folate (a B vitamin) or fiber—and reduced lung cancer risk.

In another lung cancer study, researchers at Yale University found that there was a reduced risk of lung cancer among nonsmoking men and women with the highest raw fruit and vegetable consumption. Fruits and vegetables also seem to protect against cancer overall, according to a study by U.C. Berkeley researcher Gladys Block. She reviewed 180 studies on the role vegetables and fruits—and antioxidants—play in cancer development and found that 156 of the studies reported a significant relationship between these factors and a reduced risk of cancer.

Most antioxidant supplements contain only beta carotene, but there are 50 to 60 other carotenoids—orange, red and yellow pigments—in fruits and vegetables that have antioxidant properties. For example, broccoli has 10 different carotenoids and tomatoes have five. Red fruits and vegetables, such as tomatoes and red peppers, are high in the carotenoid lycopene. Watercress and spinach don't just have beta carotene but also lutein. Oranges contain cryptoxanthin and dark leafy greens contribute zeaxanthin. Laboratory studies have shown that some carotenoids inhibit cancer cell growth. Additionally, preliminary research from Johns Hopkins University shows that patients with rectal, bladder and pancreatic cancer have low blood levels of various carotenoids, not just beta carotene.

In addition to antioxidants, fruits and vegetables contain hundreds of other substances that research has suggested may have disease-fighting potential. Of all these, fiber and folate have the best established record. Fiber has several health benefits: It can help prevent heart disease by lowering blood cholesterol levels; it may help prevent colon cancer; it speeds the transit of food through the digestive system, thus preventing constipation and hemorrhoids; and it can also play a role in a weight loss program, because high-fiber foods tend to make you feel full and are generally low in fat and calories.

Antioxidants: Wellness Recommended Intakes

Recommendations vary as to how much of each antioxidant is necessary to provide maximal health benefits without increasing the risk, however slight, of side effects. The amounts below are daily recommendations based on current research. The charts on pages 17 and 18 give the vitamin C and beta carotene contents of standard serving sizes of various foods.

Beta carotene	6 to 15 mg
Vitamin C	250 to 500 mg
Vitamin E	200 to 800 IU

Folate, when consumed in adequate amounts, has been shown to prevent the abnormal growth of cells in the cervix that may precede cancer, and to prevent spina bifida (a common birth defect) when consumed by women before or at least in the first few weeks of pregnancy. A low folate intake has also been linked to an increased risk of colon cancer. Folate is found in leafy green vegetables.

During the past few years, researchers have uncovered many chemicals in fruits and vegetables that have no nutritional value in the traditional sense, but can affect the body in various ways. Dubbed phytochemicals (from the Latin *phyto-*, referring to plant life), these substances have received a lot of attention in the press because studies have found that some of them may have the potential to protect against cancer and heart disease. Researchers aren't yet sure whether phytochemicals, which are often found in antioxidant-rich foods, work in tandem with antioxidants to lower the risk of disease or whether they have an independent effect. Phytochemicals currently showing disease-protective promise include: sulforaphane (found in broccoli, cabbage, Brussels sprouts, kale, carrots and scallions); indoles (found in broccoli, cabbage, cauliflower and other members of the cabbage family); flavonoids (found in citrus fruits, apples, tomatoes and onions); isoflavones (found in soybeans and soy products, such as tofu and soy milk); and allylic sulfides (found in garlic and onions).

A Daily Menu

The foods that are rich in vitamin C and beta carotene are already familiar to most people. The following menu is an example of how relatively easy it is to meet, and even surpass, the Wellness Recommended Intakes (see page 11) for these antioxidants simply by making a little extra effort to incorporate the fruits and vegetables rich in these nutrients into your daily meals. This sample menu is not intended to cover every food you might eat during the day—for example, you'd need to add some low- or nonfat dairy products to get enough calcium—but it does show how eating even one-antioxidant-rich meal a day can help you meet your antioxidant requirements through diet alone.

BREAKFAST	Beta carotene	Vitamin C
Glass of orange juice	0.2 mg	65 mg
Toasted corn muffin	0.1 mg	0 mg
LUNCH		
Green and Orange Minestrone (page 34)	12 mg	51 mg
Cantaloupe with fresh lime juice	3.1 mg	68 mg
SNACK		
1 medium carrot	12 mg	7 mg
DINNER		
Steak with Burgundy Sauce (page 117)	5.6 mg	58 mg
Baked potato	0 mg	26 mg
Steamed asparagus	0.3 mg	10 mg
Watercress, romaine and tomato salad	1.6 mg	33 mg
Sliced strawberries and oranges with vanilla yogurt	0.1 mg	83 mg
TOTAL	35 mg	401 mg

What foods are good sources of beta carotene and other carotenoids?

You can recognize carotenoid-rich foods by their color: They are orange or dark green (the chlorophyll in the green vegetables masks the orange color of the carotenoids). Among vegetables, sweet potatoes are rich sources, as are pumpkin, butternut squash, carrots, carrot juice, broccoli and dark leafy greens such as collards, kale and spinach. Good fruit sources include apricots (fresh and dried), cantaloupe and mangoes. The chart on page 18 lists the beta carotene content of typical serving sizes for various foods.

Where do we get vitamin C?

Many fruits and vegetables that contain carotenoids also provide vitamin C—mangoes, broccoli, peppers, spinach (and other dark leafy greens) and sweet potatoes. Other high-vitamin C foods include strawberries, blackberries, raspberries, grapefruit, oranges, papaya, kiwi fruit, tomatoes and potatoes. See the chart on page 17 for vitamin C content of typical serving sizes for various foods.

What foods contain vitamin E?

Vegetable oils (like safflower, sunflower and corn) and wheat germ are rich sources of vitamin E. So are nuts, seeds, whole grains and green leafy vegetables like kale, spinach and collards. You can also get vitamin E from avocados and fortified cereals.

Does this mean antioxidant supplements are unnecessary?

Ideally, you should get your antioxidant nutrients from foods, but supplements may be useful for people who do not consume enough vegetables or fruits. However, it's not difficult to get the amounts of beta carotene and vitamin C that have a protective effect against disease through diet alone (see page 11 for Wellness Recommended Intakes of antioxidants). For example, the recipes in this book are designed to go a long way toward helping you meet those recommendations (see "A Daily Menu" on the facing page). In fact, some recipes—such as Thanksgiving Salad (p. 201), Creamy Roast Garlic Pasta Primavera (p. 139) and Red Pepper and Black Bean Soup with Cilantro-Cream Swirl (p. 35)—supply at least enough beta carotene, vitamin C or both to provide you with the amounts currently recommended to help prevent disease. These amounts are higher than the Recommended Dietary Allowances, or RDAs, listed on page 26.

When it comes to vitamin E, however, you might want to consider taking a supplement. While it's possible to get enough vitamin E from foods to meet the RDA of 12 to 15 IUs, it is impossible to get the amount of vitamin E shown in studies to be protective against disease without consuming an inordinate amount of fat. Studies have shown that 100 IUs a day is the minimum amount of vitamin E needed to protect against chronic diseases. To get that amount you'd have to eat 3 cups of almonds or 22 cups of collard greens, not practical amounts at all, especially when you consider that the almonds would supply 2,430 calories and 214 grams of fat.

Is it enough to have a high intake of just one antioxidant nutrient?

No. To boost your overall disease-fighting potential you must increase your intake of all three antioxidant nutrients—vitamin C, vitamin E and beta carotene. Each antioxidant nutrient attacks different free radical reactions and in different parts of the cells as they try to prevent cellular damage. Vitamin E and beta carotene, both fat soluble nutrients, tend to work on the fat-containing cell membranes. Beta carotene seems to be most effective against singlet oxygen, an oxygen-derived free radical that can seriously damage cell membranes, cell enzymes and DNA. Vitamin C is water soluble and is more likely to be found in the watery interior of cells. Vitamin C has the important job of protecting vitamin E from oxidation. In the process of neutralizing free radicals, vitamin E becomes a free radical itself. Vitamin C converts vitamin E back to its original form so it can continue to function as an antioxidant.

Aside from combating free radicals, what other functions do antioxidants have in the body?

Beta carotene is often called provitamin A because the body can convert it to vitamin A. Excess beta carotene is stored in fat tissue, but is not converted to vitamin A beyond the needs of the body, thus preventing vitamin A toxicity. There are actually 50 carotenoids that can form vitamin A but beta carotene is the most potent. In its vitamin A role, beta carotene promotes good vision, particularly vision in dim light; maintains healthy skin, teeth, mucous membranes and skeletal and soft tissue; and may be essential for reproduction and lactation.

One of the key functions of vitamin C is to form collagen, the primary connective tissue in the body found in blood vessels, muscles and cartilage that surround the joints. It is also important in healing wounds, in bone structure and the health of teeth and gums. Other roles of vitamin C include enhancing iron absorption; activating folate; aiding in the formation of serotonin, a chemical important in nerve communication; and assisting the conversion of cholesterol to bile acids, which are needed for digestion.

Vitamin E protects tissues in the body from oxidation. In particular, vitamin E prolongs the life of red blood cells and protects the membranes of nerves, muscles and blood vessels. Vitamin E also preserves selenium, a mineral important in the production of the enzymes that function as antioxidants in the body.

Is preventing cell damage the only way antioxidants keep us healthy?

No. Antioxidants also seem to have a protective effect on the immune system as well. The immune system works on a system of checks and balances. When the body is invaded by bacteria, viruses or other organisms, immune cells, called T helper cells, signal other immune cells to mount an attack. In addition, the body produces other disease-fighting immune cells, such as natural killer cells (which fight viruses). Once the invader has been destroyed, suppressor cells make sure that the attacking immune cells retreat; otherwise healthy cells might get damaged. Too many suppressor cells, however, will dampen immune response.

Studies have suggested that antioxidants appear to counteract the increase in immune system suppressor cells that normally occurs with age, and also increase the number of disease-fighting immune cells in the body. In one study, immunity researcher R. K. Chandra found that people age 65 and over who took beta carotene and vitamin E supplements for a year experienced fewer infections than those who did not take supplements. In a University of Arizona study, people over 50 who took up to 60 milligrams of beta carotene a day had an increase in natural killer cells and T helper cells. In elderly subjects participating in a study at the USDA Human Nutrition Research Center on Aging at Tufts University, supplements of vitamin E (800 IUs per day) were found to boost levels of T helper cells and interleukin-2, a chemical that directs immune response.

What's the connection between antioxidants and heart disease?

Studies have found that people with low blood levels of vitamin E, vitamin C and beta carotene may be at increased risk for heart disease. A study by the World Health Organization, for example, found that a low level of vitamin E was the key predictor of death from heart disease in these people compared to more common risk factors like high blood cholesterol levels, high blood pressure and smoking (accounting for 20 percent of deaths combined).

Just how antioxidants fight heart disease is not yet clear, but some research suggests that they prevent the oxidation of LDL (bad) cholesterol in the bloodstream, which may be the first step in the development of plaque—a buildup of cholesterol, fat and other substances in the artery walls. As plaque grows, the spaces through which blood flows in the arteries get smaller and smaller. Blood clots can form on the surface of the plaque and become lodged in the artery. If this happens in an artery that supplies the heart muscle, a heart attack results; if a clot forms in an artery leading to the brain, the result is a stroke.

Vitamin E is very effective in preventing the oxidation of LDL cholesterol. The Nurses' Health Study, which has been following 87,245 women since 1980, found that women with the highest vitamin E intake had a 40 percent lower risk of heart disease than women with the lowest intake. The primary source of vitamin E was supplements. Women with high vitamin E intakes took 100 to 200 IUs of vitamin E a day for at least two years. A study by researchers at the University of Texas Southwestern Medical Center found that people taking a daily supplement of 800 IUs of vitamin E for three months had a 40 percent reduction in LDL oxidation.

While vitamin C and beta carotene both have the potential to prevent LDL oxidation, adding daily vitamin C (1,000 milligrams) and beta carotene (30 milligrams) supplements to the mix in the University of Texas study produced no additional improvement in LDL oxidation rate, probably because the high dose of vitamin E overshadowed the protective effect of the other nutrients. Other studies have provided convincing evidence for the benefit that vitamin C and beta carotene have on heart disease risk, however. When UCLA researchers looked at dietary records from the 11,348 adults participating in the National Health and Nutrition Examination Survey, they found that there were 42 percent fewer deaths from heart disease in the group of men with the highest intake of vitamin C—at least 50 milligrams a day from foods and supplements—than those with the lowest intake of vitamin C; for women, vitamin C reduced heart disease risk by 25 percent.

Preliminary results from the Physicians' Health Study—where 22,071 male physicians have been taking aspirin, beta carotene (50 milligrams), or both on a daily basis since 1983—found that in 333 doctors with a history of angina (chest pain) or heart surgery, such as coronary bypass, beta carotene alone reduced the number of strokes and heart attacks by more than 50 percent.

What role do antioxidants play in cancer prevention?

Free radicals are believed to promote cancer because they have the potential to damage genetic material and cell integrity and the ability to alter the immune system, which normally keeps cancer cells in check. Therefore, free radical-fighting antioxidants are one way the body protects itself from the chaotic growth of cancer cells.

Each antioxidant may protect against different types of cancer. For example, a low intake of vitamin C has been linked to a twofold increase in the risk of stomach, esophageal and oral cancer.

A low vitamin E intake was associated with an increased risk of stomach, esophageal and pancreatic cancers in a recent Finnish study. The same study also found that lung cancer risk was seven times higher in nonsmoking men with low blood levels of vitamin E than in nonsmoking men with high levels of vitamin E in the blood. In the Iowa Women's Health Study (which involved 35,215 women), women with the highest vitamin E intake had 68 percent lower risk of colon cancer than those with the lowest vitamin E intake.

Beta carotene, too, has a strong cancer-prevention record. Researchers at Albert Einstein College of Medicine found that low levels of beta carotene in the blood and in the cells of the cervix were associated with an increased risk of cervical cancer. Many studies have identified beta carotene's ability to reverse precancerous mouth lesions. A Yale University study found that a beta carotene-rich diet reduced lung cancer risk among nonsmokers. In a British study of cancer patients, those consuming more than 2.7 milligrams of beta carotene a day from food had half the lung cancer risk compared to those with lower intakes of beta carotene.

Didn't some studies find that antioxidants don't protect against cancer?

Two recent studies did find that antioxidant *supplements* had no cancer-preventive effects, but they had several flaws. The first study was designed to see if antioxidants would protect against lung cancer. It involved Finnish men who were heavy smokers and who had smoked for an average of 36 years. They were given either antioxidant supplements—20 milligrams of beta carotene, 50 IUs of vitamin E or both—or a placebo (a dummy pill) for six years. The researchers found no decrease in lung cancer cases among those who took the supplements, but, surprisingly, found an 18 percent increase in lung cancer incidence among the beta carotene group. (Interestingly, the participants who had high blood levels of antioxidants at the start of the study—suggesting that their antioxidant intake was high throughout their lives—did have lower rates of lung cancer.) In the second study, 864 individuals who previously had at least one potentially precancerous colon polyp removed were given antioxidant supplements (25 milligrams of beta carotene, 1,000 milligrams of vitamin C and/or 400 IUs of vitamin E) or a placebo. The supplements did not prevent the development of more of these potentially precancerous colon polyps.

Several scientists and researchers believe that these studies did not find a protective effect for antioxidants either because they didn't follow the study participants for a long enough period of time or because antioxidants may not be able to reverse the cancer process once it has begun. Because cancer develops over many years, it is possible that some of the participants in the Finnish study already had precancerous conditions that were not detected at the start of the study. Beta carotene may work only at the early, initiating stages of cancer development. In addition, all the people studied were heavy long-term smokers. It may be too much to expect that only six years of antioxidant therapy could wipe out the risks associated with a lifetime of heavy smoking. By comparison, even if the men had stopped smoking—by far the most important step they could take—there would have been only a tiny drop in cancer rates within the first six years.

The colon polyp study was also a short-term study. The results were discouraging, but not surprising given that other polyp and antioxidant studies have produced inconsistent results. While the antioxidants didn't prevent the development of new potentially precancerous polyps, the study did not investigate whether antioxidant supplements halted the progression of the polyps into cancer. Other population studies have found that antioxidants have a protective effect against colon and rectal cancers.

All in all, the accumulated evidence strongly suggests that antioxidants do protect against disease. However, as these two studies suggest, antioxidants are not a magic bullet; they cannot cancel out the effects of a lifetime of unhealthy habits. It is still necessary to exercise regularly, stop smoking (if you smoke) and have a healthy diet overall. As mentioned on page 12, antioxidants may work in tandem with other nutrients. The role antioxidants play in different diseases may vary. Perhaps they are extremely important in preventing the development of heart disease, for example, but only play a supporting role in the prevention of lung cancer. These questions will hopefully be answered by the many clinical studies now underway. Until these results are in, however, there is every reason to be sure to get enough antioxidants in your diet.

Are antioxidant supplements safe?

Yes. Beta carotene, vitamin C and vitamin E are relatively safe even when taken in substantial megadoses. There is no reason to stop taking supplements if you already do so and certainly no reason to cut back on antioxidant-rich foods.

The safety record of even high doses of beta carotene has been well established. For more than 20 years, doctors have used beta carotene in doses as high as 180 milligrams per day to treat erythropoietic protoporphyria (EPP), a photosensitivity disorder, with no reports of adverse side effects. Beta carotene is converted to vitamin A in the body, and what's not converted either acts as an antioxidant, is stored in body fat or is excreted. While high doses of vitamin A are extremely toxic—resulting in joint pain, headaches, vomiting and irritability—the worse thing you can expect from too much beta carotene is that the palms of your hands and feet

Vitamin C Sources

VEGETABLES	MG
Broccoli, fresh, chopped, cooked, 1 cup	116
Pepper, red, fresh, chopped, cooked, ½ cup	116
Brussels sprouts, fresh, cooked, 1 cup	97
Pepper, red, raw, chopped, ½ cup	95
Kohlrabi, fresh, cooked, 1 cup	89
Tomato purée, canned, 1 cup	88
Snow peas, raw, 1 cup	87
Broccoli, raw, chopped, 1 cup	82
Snow peas, fresh, cooked, 1 cup	77
Broccoli, frozen, chopped, cooked, 1 cup	74
Cauliflower, raw, florets, 1 cup	72
Brussels sprouts, frozen, cooked, 1 cup	71
Cauliflower, fresh florets, cooked, 1 cup	69
Mixed vegetable cocktail, 1 cup	67
Cauliflower, frozen florets, cooked, 1 cup	56
Tomatoes, fresh, cooked, 1 cup	55
Kale, fresh, chopped, cooked, 1 cup	53
Pepper, green, fresh, chopped, cooked, ½ cup	51
Asparagus, fresh, cooked, 1 cup	49
Collard greens, frozen, cooked, 1 cup	45
Pepper, green, raw, chopped, ½ cup	45
Tomato juice, canned, 1 cup	45
Bok choy, fresh, shredded, cooked, 1 cup	44
Sweet potato, 1 medium (8 ounces), baked	42
Cabbage, red, raw, shredded, 1 cup	40
Spinach, fresh, chopped, cooked, 1 cup	40
Salsa, bottled, ½ cup	39
Turnip greens, fresh, cooked, 1 cup	39
Beet greens, cooked, 1 cup	36
Cabbage, fresh, shredded, cooked, 1 cup	36
Tomatoes, canned whole, 1 cup	36
Turnip greens, frozen, cooked 1 cup	36
Tomatoes, raw, chopped, 1 cup	34
Snow peas, frozen, cooked, 1 cup	32
Butternut squash, baked, 1 cup cubes	31
Cabbage, green, raw, shredded, 1 cup	33
Kale, frozen, chopped, cooked, 1 cup	33
Tomato sauce, canned, 1 cup	32
Potato, baking, 1 medium, microwaved	31
Chestnuts, roasted, 4 ounces	30
Tomato paste, canned, ¼ cup	28
Potato, baking, 1 medium, oven-baked	26

FRUIT	MG
Black currant juice, ½ cup	203
Papaya, 1 medium	188
Orange juice, fresh, 1 cup	124
Currants, black, fresh, ½ cup	101
Orange juice, from frozen, 1 cup	97
Cranberry juice cocktail, 1 cup	90
Orange juice, canned, 1 cup	86
Strawberries, fresh, 1 cup	84
Grapefruit juice, from frozen, 1 cup	83
Orange, navel, 1 medium	80
Kiwi fruit, 1 medium	74
Cantaloupe, cubed, 1 cup	68
Strawberries, frozen, in light syrup, ½ cup	64
Strawberries, frozen unsweetened, 1 cup	61
Tangerine juice, from frozen, 1 cup	58
Grapefruit, pink, half	47
Mango, fresh, sliced, 1 cup	46
Mandarin oranges, canned juice-packed, ½ cup	43
Honeydew, cubed, 1 cup	42
Grapefruit, white, half	41
Raspberries, frozen, sweetened, 1 cup	41
Raspberries, fresh, 1 cup	31
Blackberries, fresh, 1 cup	30
Pineapple juice, from frozen, 1 cup	30
Tangerine, 1 medium	26
Pineapple, fresh, chunks, 1 cup	24

Beta Carotene Sources

VEGETABLES	MG
Sweet potato, canned, mashed, 1 cup	23
Sweet potato, baked, 1 medium (8 ounces)	22
Carrot juice, ½ cup	19
Carrots, fresh, sliced, cooked, ¾ cup	17
Pumpkin, canned purée, ½ cup	16
Carrots, raw, 1 medium	12
Spinach, fresh or frozen, cooked, 1 cup	8.9
Butternut squash, baked, 1 cup cubes	8.6
Hubbard squash, baked, 1 cup cubes	7.4
Collard greens, frozen, cooked, 1 cup	6.1
Kale, fresh, chopped, cooked, 1 cup	5.8
Kale, frozen, chopped, cooked, 1 cup	5.0
Dandelion greens, raw, chopped, 1 cup	4.6
Beet greens, fresh, cooked, 1 cup	4.4
Mustard greens, frozen, cooked, 1 cup	4.0
Turnip greens, frozen, cooked, ½ cup	3.9
Swiss chard, fresh, chopped, cooked, 1 cup	3.3
Pepper, red, fresh, chopped, cooked, 1 cup	3.1
Bok choy, fresh, cooked, 1 cup	2.6
Mustard greens, fresh, cooked, 1 cup	2.5
Turnip greens, fresh, cooked, ½ cup	2.4
Spinach, raw, chopped, 1 cup	2.3
Chicory greens, raw, chopped, ½ cup	2.2
Broccoli, frozen, cooked, 1 cup	2.1
Collard greens, fresh, cooked, 1 cup	2.1
Tomato purée, canned, 1 cup	2.0
Mixed vegetable juice, spicy, 1 cup	2.1
Mixed vegetable juice, 1 cup	1.9
Peppers, red, raw, chopped, ½ cup	1.7
Chili peppers, red, fresh, half a medium	1.5
Peppers, roasted, bottled, ½ cup	1.5
Tomato sauce, canned, 1 cup	1.4
Broccoli, fresh, cooked, 1 cup	1.3
Tomato paste, ¼ cup	1.0
Green peas, frozen, cooked, 1 cup	0.9
Romaine lettuce, fresh, chopped, 1 cup	0.9
Broccoli, raw, chopped, 1 cup	0.8
Pumpkin, fresh, cooked, mashed, ½ cup	0.8
Tomato juice, 1 cup	0.8
Brussels sprouts, fresh, cooked, 1 cup	0.7
Salsa, ¼ cup	0.7
Tomato, raw, chopped, 1 cup	0.7
Asparagus, fresh, cooked, 1 cup	0.6
Acorn squash, baked, 1 cup cubes	0.5

FRUITS	MG
Mango, 1 medium	4.8
Cantaloupe, cubed, 1 cup	3.1
Persimmon, Japanese, 1 medium	2.2
Apricot nectar, canned, 1 cup	2.0
Papaya, half a medium	1.8
Peaches, dried halves, 10	1.7
Apricots, fresh, 3	1.7
Apricots, dried halves, 10	1.5
Prunes, pitted, 10	1.0
Apricots, canned juice-pack, 3 halves	0.9
Tangerine juice, from frozen, 1 cup	0.8
Watermelon, cubed, 2 cups	0.7
Mandarin oranges, canned juice-pack, ½ cup	0.6
Nectarine, 1 medium	0.6

MISCELLANEOUS	MG
Paprika, 1 tablespoon	2.3
Chili powder, 1 tablespoon	1.6
Cayenne pepper, 1 teaspoon	0.5

may take on an orange appearance. The increase in lung cancer risk in the people taking beta carotene supplements in the Finnish study could be due to chance, according to the researchers.

Vitamin C is safe in doses of up to 1,000 milligrams a day. More than that can cause diarrhea and gas in some people. People with an inherited iron storage disease called hemochromatosis and those prone to calcium oxalate kidney stones should steer clear of megadoses of vitamin C.

Numerous controlled studies of people who took megadoses of vitamin E of up to 3,200 IUs for up to six months have shown few, if any, side effects. In uncontrolled studies, there have been reports of fatigue and changes in the immune system with doses of 300 to 800 IUs. In people who take anticoagulant medication or who have a deficiency of vitamin K, vitamin E supplements can interfere with the clotting ability of the blood, and so should not be taken.

Is is true that antioxidants can help slow the aging process?

It's a theory that free radicals are, at least partially, responsible for the aging of cells, tissues and organs in our body. In studies with mice, scientists have seen a relationship between a fast metabolism—which means a faster rate of oxygen use and an increase in free radical formation—and earlier aging and death. This is probably due to the damage caused by free radicals to genetic material in the cell. This may leave a cell unable to repair itself, leading to abnormal cell metabolic function and replication, resulting in degenerative disease and, ultimately, cell death. Free radical damage may be responsible not only for cancer and heart disease, but also other diseases we associate with old age, such as senility and arthritis. From this perspective, the effects of aging might be thought of as a buildup of unhealthy cells.

While antioxidants may help protect you from disease, there is no conclusive evidence that they can make you feel or look younger, by increasing energy or preventing wrinkles, for example. Even athletes taking antioxidants don't typically get a boost of energy from the vitamins. Some studies in animals and humans show that vitamins C and E when applied to the skin may reduce wrinkles, but these are extremely small studies and the results are very preliminary.

If vitamin A is necessary for good vision, can beta carotene improve vision?

Vitamin A, whether in its pure form or converted from beta carotene, does promote good vision, but it can only correct vision abnormalities if there is a true deficiency of the vitamin. So increasing your intake of beta carotene won't improve nearsightedness or make it easier for you to see at night.

However, antioxidants may prevent cataracts, one of the leading causes of visual loss. The development of cataracts is associated with aging and is believed to be due, at least in part, to free radical damage to the eye's lens. Scientists have noticed that many eye tissues, including the lens, have a high concentration of free radical scavengers, like vitamin C, presumably to prevent this damage. Cataract lenses contain a lot less vitamin C than healthy lenses.

There is some evidence to support the benefits of antioxidants on cataract risk. Women in the Nurses' Health Study who took vitamin C for at least 10 years had a 45 percent lower risk of cataracts than women who did not have a high intake of vitamin C. Beta carotene was also associated with a reduced cataract risk. Men in the Physicians' Health Study who took vitamins E and C had fewer cataracts as well, according to Harvard researchers.

And in a study at the USDA Human Nutrition Research Center on Aging at Tufts University, elderly subjects with low blood levels of carotenoids or vitamin C had an increased risk for different types of cataracts.

Can vitamin C protect against colds and other illnesses?

Vitamin C is needed for a properly functioning immune system, though it's still not clear whether megadoses can prevent infection. Most of the evidence in well-controlled studies indicates that vitamin C, if anything, can only reduce the severity and duration of a cold, by a barely perceptible degree. Nevertheless, when ultramarathoners—who are more susceptible to colds and upper respiratory infections because heavy-duty exercise depresses immune function—took 600 milligrams of vitamin C daily for three weeks before a race, only 33 percent got a cold compared with 68 percent in the control group.

Do athletes need extra antioxidants?

Exercise does not protect you against free radical formation. In fact, it may create more oxygen-derived free radicals because you take in more oxygen and your metabolic rate accelerates during exercise. Free radicals can also come from pollutants in the air that athletes breathe in during workouts, and from the hormones, such as adrenaline, released during exercise. Researchers at the University of Alberta in Canada found that people have higher levels of substances in the blood that indicate free radical formation *after* vigorous exercise than before exercise. Antioxidants can significantly reduce the levels of these substances, by as much as 25 percent according to an Australian study. In addition to the other damage that free radicals can cause, scientists suspect that free radicals are involved in the muscle damage that results in post-exercise strain and soreness, though it's not yet clear whether free radicals cause the muscle damage or the muscle damage leads to the formation of free radicals.

Because of this, researchers believe that anyone involved in vigorous exercise should make sure they're getting at least the recommended levels of vitamins C, E and beta carotene listed on page 11, if not more (a few studies have suggested that athletes need more antioxidants than other people, but the studies were small and the results only preliminary). Weekend athletes—who participate in infrequent concentrated periods of activity—may especially need to have an adequate antioxidant intake because their bodies' natural antioxidant defenses don't have time to adapt to the increased demands of exercise compared with people who exercise regularly.

What about smokers?

There's no evidence that smokers need more antioxidants than the Wellness Recommended Intakes for everyone listed on page 11, but smokers might be wise to opt for the higher end of these ranges. Smoking places a greater strain on the antioxidant systems of the body, thereby reducing antioxidant levels in the bloodstream and other tissues. In addition, surveys indicate that smokers eat fewer fruits and vegetables than nonsmokers. In a study by the Centers for Disease Control, smokers had carotenoid levels 21 to 29 percent lower than nonsmokers. Other research has found that smokers have lower blood levels of vitamin C and lower vitamin E levels in their lung tissue than nonsmokers.

Even people who don't smoke themselves but who are exposed to the smoke of others—passive smokers—may have trouble maintaining adequate antioxidant levels in the body. In one study involving 141 women, 12 percent of the passive smokers had low vitamin C levels compared with 24 percent of the smokers. Vitamin C levels were adequate in nonsmoking women who were not exposed to passive smoke. However, passive smokers who consumed more than 250 milligrams of vitamin C a day were able to maintain adequate vitamin C levels.

This doesn't mean, however, that boosting antioxidant intake makes it safe to continue smoking. While antioxidants may offer some protection against the damage cigar and cigarette smoke can cause, it pales in comparison to the protection provided by quitting smoking.

If I eat a high-antioxidant diet, can I eat more fat?

No, a high-antioxidant diet does not give you liberty to boost your fat intake. There isn't enough evidence to determine what level of antioxidant intake, if any, can offset the detrimental effects of a high-fat diet. Fortunately, eating more vegetables and fruits to increase your antioxidant intake generally means that you are eating less fat, since the vegetables and fruits often take the place of fatty foods. (Of course, vegetables doused with

Watching Your Fat Intake

The amount of fat you can eat each day depends on a number of factors: gender, level of physical activity and personal or family history of heart disease. Rather than calculating the percent calories from fat for the foods you eat, use the guidelines below to determine the approximate number of grams of fat you can eat each day. You are considered "active" if you exercise, walk, or perform active chores (such as gardening) in 20-minute stints for a total of at least 2½ hours a week, or if you have a physically demanding job. People with heart disease, or at high risk of developing it, should determine their category and then subtract 10 grams of fat a day from the recommendations below.

	SEDENTARY	ACTIVE
WOMEN	40 g/day	50 g/day
MEN	50 g/day	60 g/day

butter, cream, oil or cheese become high-fat foods.) All of the recipes in this book are low in fat. Each dish is designed to fit well within the daily fat goals in the box above, which meet the recommendations of all major health organizations.

Are antioxidants destroyed by cooking?

It depends on the cooking method you choose. Heat, light, water and even chopping vegetables and fruits can decrease the antioxidant content of a food to a degree. However, there are measures you can take to preserve these vitamins.

Vitamin C is very sensitive to heat and water. If you boil vitamin C-rich vegetables for long periods of time or cook them in a large quantity of water, you'll lose significant amounts of this nutrient. The high heat involved in frying results in a 90 percent loss of vitamin C. Microwaving results in the greatest retention of vitamin C; for example, broccoli that has been boiled loses 62 percent of its vitamin C, whereas microwaved broccoli loses just 10 to 20 percent. Steaming, too, is an excellent method for preserving vitamin C. For example, steamed asparagus loses just 17 percent of its vitamin C content, compared to a 55 percent loss when the vegetable is boiled. You can further preserve vitamin C by cooking vegetables whole when possible, or by cutting them into relatively large chunks.

Cooking beta carotene-rich foods makes more of the beta carotene available to the body, but *over*cooking destroys this nutrient. For example, boiling green beans for 20 minutes can reduce beta carotene levels by 30 percent.

Vitamin E is oxidized rapidly by heat and air. Heating vegetable oils for long periods of time—as in deep frying—or exposing oil to air will destroy the vitamin E and the oil will become oxidized, turning rancid. The vitamin E found in nuts and vegetables is also susceptible to oxidation.

In general, mild cooking methods and a minimum of water are best for preserving antioxidants. If you microwave, steam, stir-fry or blanch in a little water, there will be little decline in the amounts of vitamin C, beta carotene and vitamin E in your vegetables.

Is it ever too late to start consuming more antioxidants?

No, researchers believe that you're never too old to benefit from getting more antioxidants. Studies have shown that even short-term use of antioxidants has a positive effect on heart disease and immunity response. In the Physicians' Health Study, for example, the benefits of beta carotene on heart disease risk were already seen in the second year.

It would probably be better to have a high antioxidant intake throughout life. Indeed, antioxidants may have a greater effect in younger people, and certainly they would have more years to act against free radicals. But antioxidants have a wide range of effects at any age—and even if someone doesn't begin increasing antioxidant intake until the age of 60, that still leaves another 20 to 30 years of life that can be improved. Moreover, foods high in antioxidants have other health benefits as well, and antioxidant supplements taken at recommended doses are undoubtedly safe.

Foods High in Vitamin C

1

2

3

10

7

8

9

13

14

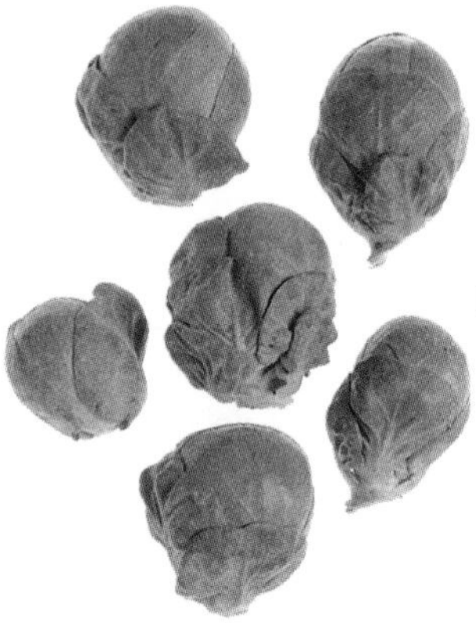

15

4

5

6

12

11

16

17

1 • BROCCOLI is a member of the cruciferous (cabbage) family that is thought to contain cancer-protecting substances. Broccoli is also rich in beta carotene and folate.
2 • POTATOES are also an excellent source of potassium.
3 • KIWI FRUIT is high in potassium and fiber.
4 • GRAPEFRUIT is a good source of potassium, and red and pink grapefruits supply beta carotene as well.
5 • RASPBERRIES contain ellagic acid, a substance that preliminary research suggests may help prevent certain types of cancer.
6 • STRAWBERRIES have just 45 calories per cup, and provide potassium, folate and a small amount of calcium in addition to vitamin C.
7 • PAPAYA is also rich in folate.
8 • CAULIFLOWER is a good source of folate and potassium.
9 • LEMONS are high in vitamin C, but too tart to eat out-of-hand. Fortunately, lemon juice is also a good vitamin C source, as is grated lemon zest—one tablespoon provides 13 percent of the RDA.
10 • ORANGES and their relatives tangerines, tangelos and clementines are high in vitamin C and provide folate and potassium as well.
11 • JALAPEÑO PEPPERS aren't usually eaten in large quantities, but even one-quarter of a pepper provides a good amount of vitamin C.
12 • MANGOES are also high in beta carotene.
13 • PINEAPPLE, when fresh, is a good source of vitamin C. Pineapple canned in juice has about a third less; pineapple canned in syrup has about half the vitamin C of fresh.
14 • BELL PEPPERS also contain folate and potassium, and the red ones are rich in beta carotene.
15 • BRUSSELS SPROUTS supply beta carotene, iron, potassium, folate and fiber in addition to vitamin C.
16 • TOMATOES—as well as tomato sauce, canned tomatoes and tomato paste—are good vitamin C sources.
17 • ASPARAGUS should be kept refrigerated to preserve its vitamin C content. It's an exceptional source of folate, and contains some beta carotene as well.

FOODS HIGH IN BETA CAROTENE

1 • Romaine Lettuce has twice as much beta carotene and three-and-a-half times more vitamin C than iceberg lettuce, and also contains folate and iron.
2 • Tomatoes are also high in vitamin C and lycopene, a carotenoid related to beta carotene.
3 • Dried Apricots are high in iron, fiber and potassium. Fresh apricots are also a good source of beta carotene, and contain some vitamin C as well.
4 • Red Bell Peppers, depending on variety, have up to 11 times more beta carotene—and one-and-a-half times more vitamin C—than green ones, ounce for ounce.
5 • Watermelon also contains some vitamin C and potassium.
6 • Kale also supplies hefty amounts of vitamin C, calcium, folate, iron and fiber.
7 • Carrots have more beta carotene by weight than any other food. They are also a good source soluble fiber, which some studies suggest lowers cholesterol levels.
8 • Persimmons are also a good source of vitamin C. The Hachiya variety (which is heart-shaped rather than round) has the most beta carotene.
9 • Mangoes are the leading fresh fruit source of beta carotene.
10 • Cantaloupe is the melon highest in beta carotene and vitamin C.
11 • Spinach is also rich in vitamin C, folate and potassium.
12 • Pumpkin, fresh or canned, is packed with beta carotene. Add canned pumpkin to muffin, quick bread and cookie recipes to boost the beta carotene content of these treats.
13 • Butternut Squash keeps for about three months uncut with no loss of beta carotene. In fact, the carotenoid content increases with storage. It is also a good source of vitamin C.
14 • Sweet Potatoes—which rival carrots in beta carotene density—are low in calories, despite their rich taste. For a quick healthy snack, bake a few sweet potatoes at a time and store in the refrigerator—they taste great cold.

Recommended Daily Intakes

To put the nutritional analyses that accompany the recipes on the following pages into perspective, the list below gives the recommended daily intakes for the nutrients featured in the analyses. Most of the values are based on the Recommended Dietary Allowances (RDA) and guidelines established by various health organizations and experts. The RDAs are designed to meet the overall nutrient needs of most people to maintain health and prevent deficiency diseases, such as scurvy. However, the RDAs for beta carotene, vitamin C and vitamin E are not high enough to have an antioxidant effect. The intakes for these antioxidant vitamins are based on the Wellness Recommended Intakes (page 11), followed by their RDAs in parenthesis. The recommendations are for adults and, unless otherwise noted, apply to both men and women.

Total fat: 40 to 60 grams per day depending on gender and activity level. See "Watching Your Fat Intake" on page 21.

Saturated fat: No more than a third of your daily fat intake.

Cholesterol: No more than 300 milligrams.

Sodium: No more than 2,400 milligrams.

Dietary fiber: 25 to 30 grams.

Calcium: 1,200 milligrams.

Iron: 10 milligrams for men; 15 milligrams for women.

Beta carotene: 6 to 15 milligrams (5 to 6 milligrams to meet the RDA for vitamin A).

Vitamin C: 250 to 500 milligrams (60 milligrams).

Vitamin E: 200 to 800 IUs (15 IUs for men; 12 IUs for women).

Soups & Stews

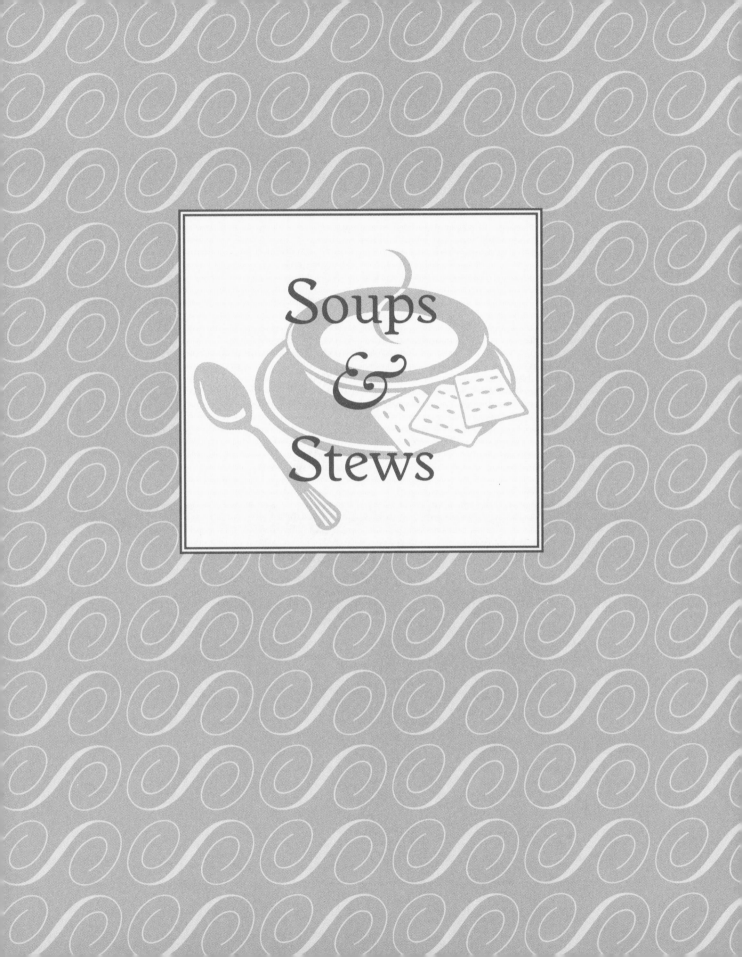

Creamy Spinach Soup

You will need only half a package of frozen spinach to make this creamy, but light, soup. Simply microwave the package, opened, until it just begins to thaw. Then saw it in half with a serrated knife. With the remainder wrapped and frozen, you are all set to make this lovely combination a second time.

Half a 10-ounce package frozen leaf spinach
1 large baking potato (8 ounces), peeled and thinly sliced
1 large carrot (12 ounces), shredded
4 scallions, coarsely chopped
2 garlic cloves, sliced
1 cup canned chicken broth diluted with 1¼ cups water, or 2¼ cups Homemade Chicken Broth (p. 54)
¼ teaspoon freshly ground black pepper
⅛ teaspoon salt
¾ cup lowfat (1%) milk
1 teaspoon unsalted butter
2 tablespoons grated Parmesan cheese
Half a small red bell pepper, slivered

1. In a large saucepan, combine the spinach, potato, carrot, scallions, garlic, diluted broth, pepper and salt. Cover and bring to a boil over high heat, then reduce the heat to medium-low and simmer until the potato and carrot are tender, about 15 minutes.

2. With a slotted spoon, transfer the solids to a food processor or blender and process to a smooth purée. Return the purée to the saucepan. Stir in the milk and butter and warm the soup over medium heat, stirring frequently.

3. Ladle the soup into bowls and sprinkle with the Parmesan. Garnish with the bell pepper.

Makes 4 servings

SUPER QUICK

Bahamian Pumpkin and Lime Soup

Working time: 10 minutes Total time: 30 minutes

1½ teaspoons cumin seed
¼ teaspoon freshly ground black pepper
¼ teaspoon nutmeg
⅛ teaspoon allspice
Pinch of cayenne pepper
1½ teaspoons olive oil
½ cup canned chicken broth diluted with ½ cup water, or 1 cup Homemade Chicken Broth (p. 54)
¾ cup water
1 medium onion, coarsely chopped
1 garlic clove, minced
1½ cups canned solid-pack pumpkin purée
2 tablespoons honey
1 tablespoon fresh lime juice
¼ cup plain nonfat yogurt
1 lime, cut into 4 wedges

1 In a small bowl, mix the cumin seed, black pepper, nutmeg, allspice and cayenne. In a medium saucepan, warm the oil over high heat until hot but not smoking. Add the spices and cook, stirring, for 30 seconds to release the flavors.

2 Immediately pour in the diluted broth and the ¾ cup water, then add the onion and garlic. Cover and bring to a boil. Reduce the heat to medium-low and simmer for 5 minutes.

3 Whisk in the pumpkin, bring to a simmer, cover and cook over low heat, stirring occasionally, for 15 minutes to blend the flavors.

4 Remove from the heat and stir in the honey and the lime juice. Ladle into soup bowls and top with a dollop of yogurt. Serve hot with a lime wedge.

Makes 4 servings

Values are per serving:
Calories: 117 Total fat: 2.4 g Saturated fat: .4 g Cholesterol: .3 mg Sodium: 142 mg
Dietary fiber: 2.4 g Beta carotene: 12 mg Vitamin C: 13 mg Calcium: 78 mg Iron: 2.1 mg

Nutrition Information
values are per serving

CALORIES 108	DIETARY FIBER 2.7 G
TOTAL FAT 2.7 G	BETA CAROTENE 6.2 MG
SATURATED FAT 1.4 G	VITAMIN C 37 MG
CHOLESTEROL 6.4 MG	CALCIUM 157 MG
SODIUM 426 MG	IRON 1.6 MG

Greek-Style Spinach and Lemon Soup

Fresh with the tang of lemon, this soup puts the traditional Greek culinary coupling of spinach and rice to yet another delicious use. Serve with toasted pita triangles.

1½ cups canned chicken broth diluted with 2½ cups water, or 4 cups Homemade Chicken Broth (p. 54)
½ cup converted rice
1 medium onion, chopped
2 garlic cloves, crushed through a press
¾ teaspoon oregano
½ teaspoon salt
¼ teaspoon freshly ground black pepper
1 cup shredded carrots
8 cups (loosely packed) stemmed spinach, cut into 1-inch-wide strips
1 egg
1 egg white
1 tablespoon water
¼ cup fresh lemon juice

1. In a flameproof casserole, combine the diluted broth, rice, onion, garlic, oregano, salt and pepper. Cover and bring to a boil over high heat. Reduce the heat to low and simmer until the rice is very tender, 25 to 30 minutes.

2. Stir in the carrots and cook for 5 minutes. Stir in the spinach and increase the heat to medium. Cook uncovered, stirring constantly, just until the spinach is wilted, 2 to 3 minutes.

3. In a small bowl, whisk together the whole egg, egg white and water. Whisk in a spoonful of the hot soup to warm the eggs. Stirring constantly, pour the warmed egg mixture into the soup. As soon as all of the egg has been added, remove the soup from the heat.

4. Stir in the lemon juice and serve hot.

Makes 4 servings

Nutrition Information
values are per serving

CALORIES 185	DIETARY FIBER 5.6 G
TOTAL FAT 2.5 G	BETA CAROTENE 10 MG
SATURATED FAT .5 G	VITAMIN C 52 MG
CHOLESTEROL 53 MG	CALCIUM 189 MG
SODIUM 796 MG	IRON 5.4 MG

Creamy Carrot and Rice Soup

The pleasure of this soup resides not only in its spicy carrot flavor, but also in its textures: a smooth purée served over grains of fluffy rice.

½ cup converted rice
1½ cups canned chicken broth diluted with 1¾ cups water, or 3¼ cups Homemade Chicken Broth (p. 54)
2½ cups sliced carrots
1 large leek, sliced (about 2 cups)
1 large onion, sliced
1 garlic clove, peeled
One ¼-inch slice fresh ginger, peeled
¼ teaspoon freshly ground black pepper
½ cup lowfat (1%) milk
2 tablespoons minced fresh dill

1. In a medium saucepan, combine the rice and 1¼ cups of the diluted chicken broth. Bring to a boil over high heat. Reduce the heat to low, cover and simmer until the rice is tender, about 20 minutes. Remove from the heat.

2. Meanwhile, in a large saucepan, combine the remaining 2 cups diluted chicken broth, carrots, leek, onion, garlic, ginger and pepper. Cover and bring to a boil over high heat. Reduce the heat to medium and simmer until the vegetables are very tender, about 10 minutes.

3. In a food processor or blender, purée the soup along with half of the rice until smooth. Return to the large saucepan, stir in the milk and heat over medium heat.

4. Scoop the remaining rice into soup bowls, ladle the soup on top and sprinkle with the dill.

Makes 4 servings

Nutrition Information
values are per serving

CALORIES 195	DIETARY FIBER 4.2 G
TOTAL FAT 1.3 G	BETA CAROTENE 12 MG
SATURATED FAT .3 G	VITAMIN C 17 MG
CHOLESTEROL 1.2 MG	CALCIUM 124 MG
SODIUM 424 MG	IRON 2.8 MG

Butternut and Sweet Potato Bisque

Fresh ginger and ground coriander spark this naturally sweet soup, fragrant with the flavors of sweet potato and squash. Should you be vegetarian, by all means substitute meatless broth and increase the seasonings accordingly.

1½ teaspoons olive oil
1 cup chopped onion
4 cups peeled and cubed butternut squash
1 medium sweet potato (8 ounces), peeled and cubed
1 cup corn kernels, fresh or frozen
1½ cups canned chicken broth diluted with 1½ cups water, or 3 cups Homemade Chicken Broth (p. 54)
2 tablespoons minced fresh ginger
1½ teaspoons light brown sugar
1 teaspoon ground coriander
¼ teaspoon freshly ground black pepper

1. In a large saucepan, warm the oil over medium-high heat until hot but not smoking. Add the onion and cook, stirring, until it begins to brown, 3 to 5 minutes.

2. Add the squash, sweet potato, corn, diluted chicken broth, ginger, brown sugar, coriander and pepper, and bring to a boil. Reduce the heat to low, cover and simmer until the squash is tender, 15 to 20 minutes.

3. With a slotted spoon, transfer the solids to a food processor or blender and process to a smooth purée. Return the purée to the saucepan and stir to blend with the liquid remaining in the pan. Serve hot.

Makes 4 servings

Nutrition Information
values are per serving

CALORIES 188	DIETARY FIBER 3.1 G
TOTAL FAT 3.0 G	BETA CAROTENE 12 MG
SATURATED FAT .3 G	VITAMIN C 44 MG
CHOLESTEROL 0 MG	CALCIUM 92 MG
SODIUM 389 MG	IRON 1.8 MG

Sweet Potato and Apple Soup

Serve this first-class, simple-to-make soup as a main course, with nothing more than a loaf of warm, crusty peasant bread and a vinaigrette-dressed green salad.

1¼ teaspoons cumin
1 cup canned chicken broth diluted with 1 cup water, or 2 cups Homemade Chicken Broth (p. 54)
2 tablespoons frozen apple juice concentrate
¾ pound sweet potatoes, peeled and cut into chunks
1 large Granny Smith apple, peeled and cut into chunks
1 medium onion, cut into chunks
¼ teaspoon freshly ground black pepper
⅛ teaspoon cinnamon
½ cup skim milk
2 tablespoons plain nonfat yogurt
1 tablespoon chopped cilantro or parsley

1. In a Dutch oven or flameproof casserole, cook the cumin over medium heat, shaking and stirring the pan frequently, until it is fragrant and toasted, 4 to 5 minutes.

2. Add the diluted chicken broth, apple juice concentrate, sweet potatoes, apple, onion, pepper and cinnamon; cover and bring to a boil over high heat. Reduce the heat to medium-low and simmer until the sweet potatoes and apple are tender, about 20 minutes.

3. Transfer the soup to a food processor or blender and purée. Return the purée to the pan and add the milk. Cook over medium heat, stirring frequently, until heated through.

4. Ladle the soup into bowls, top with the yogurt and sprinkle with the cilantro.

Makes 4 servings

NUTRITION INFORMATION
values are per serving

CALORIES 140	DIETARY FIBER 3.2 G
TOTAL FAT .9 G	BETA CAROTENE 7.4 MG
SATURATED FAT .1 G	VITAMIN C 26 MG
CHOLESTEROL .8 MG	CALCIUM 87 MG
SODIUM 281 MG	IRON 1.1 MG

Three Yellow Vegetable Soup

Three readily available, healthful vegetables combine here to make a luxurious, beautifully colored soup, perfect for cool fall dinners or late spring brunches. Feel free to toast the sesame seeds in advance.

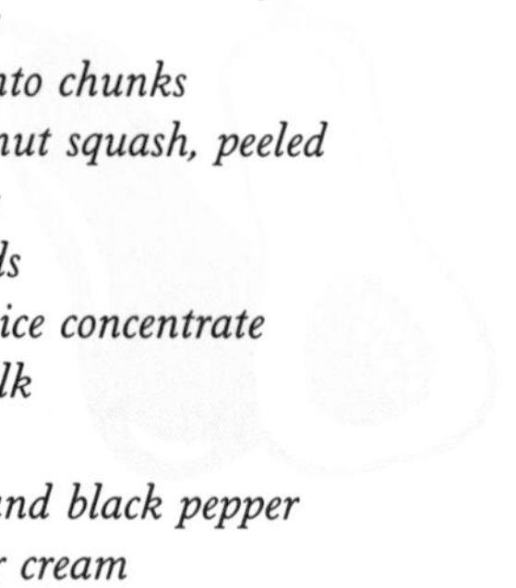

1 large sweet potato (12 ounces), peeled and cut into chunks
¾ pound carrots, cut into chunks
¾ pound seeded butternut squash, peeled and cut into chunks
2 teaspoons sesame seeds
½ cup frozen orange juice concentrate
2 cups lowfat (1%) milk
¼ teaspoon salt
¼ teaspoon freshly ground black pepper
3 tablespoons light sour cream
2 tablespoons minced chives, for garnish

1. Place the sweet potato, carrots and squash in a vegetable steamer. Cover and steam until tender, about 12 minutes.

2. Meanwhile, in a small ungreased skillet, toast the sesame seeds over medium heat, 3 to 5 minutes.

3. Place the cooked vegetables and the orange juice concentrate in a food processor or blender and process to a smooth purée.

4. Transfer the purée to a saucepan, add the milk, salt and pepper, and simmer over low heat until heated through.

5. Ladle the soup into 4 shallow bowls. Top with a dollop of sour cream and a sprinkling of toasted sesame seeds and chives.

Makes 4 servings

Nutrition Information
values are per serving

CALORIES 269	DIETARY FIBER 4.9 G
TOTAL FAT 4.0 G	BETA CAROTENE 27 MG
SATURATED FAT 1.7 G	VITAMIN C 88 MG
CHOLESTEROL 8.6 MG	CALCIUM 250 MG
SODIUM 238 MG	IRON 1.7 MG

Broccoli Chowder

This light chowder, flecked with the green of broccoli and the red of unpeeled new potatoes, is as delightful in appearance as it is in flavor.

1¼ pounds broccoli, broken into florets and stalks cut into ¼-inch-thick slices
½ pound unpeeled red-skinned potato, diced
1 small onion, chopped
¾ cup canned chicken broth diluted with ¾ cup water, or 1½ cups Homemade Chicken Broth (p. 54)
2 cups lowfat (1%) milk
¼ cup flour
½ teaspoon tarragon
½ teaspoon thyme
¼ teaspoon salt
¼ teaspoon freshly ground or cracked black pepper
3 ounces shredded Monterey jack cheese
½ cup minced red bell pepper

1. In a large saucepan, combine the broccoli, potato, onion and diluted broth. Cover and bring to a boil over high heat; reduce the heat to medium-low and cook until tender, about 6 minutes.

2. In a small bowl, whisk the milk into the flour. Add the milk mixture to the soup along with the tarragon, thyme, salt and black pepper. Stirring constantly, cook the mixture until it comes to a boil and is thickened, about 7 minutes.

3. Ladle the hot soup into bowls and sprinkle each serving with some of the cheese. Top with minced bell pepper.

Makes 4 servings

Nutrition Information
values are per serving

CALORIES 265	DIETARY FIBER 5.8 G
TOTAL FAT 8.7 G	BETA CAROTENE 1.7 MG
SATURATED FAT 4.6 G	VITAMIN C 168 MG
CHOLESTEROL 27 MG	CALCIUM 394 MG
SODIUM 539 MG	IRON 2.7 MG

Tomato-Garlic Soup with Pasta Shells and Fresh Mozzarella

Serve this Italian-inspired soup, resplendent with the flavor of garlic, as a main course with bread and a lush green salad.

1 tablespoon plus 1 teaspoon olive oil, preferably extra-virgin
1 cup finely chopped carrot
½ cup diced celery
¼ cup chopped shallots or onion
6 garlic cloves–2 minced and 4 thinly sliced
½ teaspoon basil
½ teaspoon sugar
One 28-ounce can tomatoes in purée

1 cup canned chicken broth diluted with 1 cup water, or 2 cups Homemade Chicken Broth (p. 54)
4 ounces small pasta shells
¾ teaspoon freshly ground black pepper
¼ teaspoon salt
3 ounces part-skim mozzarella cheese, cut into small cubes

1. In a large nonstick saucepan, warm 1 tablespoon of the oil over medium heat until hot but not smoking. Add the carrot, celery, shallots and minced garlic, and sauté until the vegetables are tender, about 8 minutes.

2. Stir in the basil and sugar. Add the tomatoes and diluted chicken broth and break up the tomatoes with a spoon. Bring to a boil over high heat. Reduce the heat to low, cover and simmer for 30 minutes to blend the flavors.

3. Bring the soup to a boil over medium-high heat. Stir in the pasta shells, pepper and salt. Reduce the heat to medium and cook until the pasta is tender, about 10 minutes.

4. Meanwhile, in a small nonstick skillet, warm the remaining 1 teaspoon oil over medium-high heat. Add the sliced garlic and sauté just until the garlic begins to turn brown, about 1 minute. Immediately scrape the garlic and oil into a small heatproof bowl to stop the cooking.

5. To serve, divide the mozzarella cubes among 4 soup bowls. Ladle the hot soup over the cheese, sprinkle each soup with some of the browned garlic and serve.

Makes 4 servings

NUTRITION INFORMATION
values are per serving

CALORIES 290	DIETARY FIBER 2.0 G
TOTAL FAT 8.9 G	BETA CAROTENE 5.5 MG
SATURATED FAT 2.9 G	VITAMIN C 37 MG
CHOLESTEROL 12 MG	CALCIUM 247 MG
SODIUM 823 MG	IRON 2.4 MG

SUPER QUICK

Green and Orange Minestrone

Working time: 25 minutes Total time: 30 minutes

- 2 teaspoons olive oil
- 1 large onion, chopped
- 3 garlic cloves, minced
- 1 cup diced carrots
- Two 10-ounce packages frozen spinach, thawed
- ½ teaspoon sugar
- ½ teaspoon dried basil
- ½ teaspoon oregano
- ¼ teaspoon salt
- 1½ cups canned chicken broth diluted with 1 cup water, or 2½ cups Homemade Chicken Broth (p. 54)
- ½ cup very small pasta shapes
- 1 cup canned chick-peas, rinsed and drained
- 1 cup diced plum tomatoes
- ¼ cup chopped fresh basil
- 1 tablespoon plus 1 teaspoon grated Parmesan cheese

1 In a large nonstick skillet, heat the oil over medium-high heat until hot but not smoking. Add the onion and garlic, and cook for 1 minute.

2 Stir in the carrot and cook for 2 minutes longer.

3 Add the spinach, sugar, dried basil, oregano and salt, and stir to coat. Stir in the diluted chicken broth and bring to a boil. Stir in the pasta and cook until tender, about 5 minutes.

4 Add the chick-peas and plum tomatoes and cook just until heated through. Stir the chopped fresh basil into the soup, sprinkle with Parmesan and serve.

Makes 4 servings

Values are per serving:
Calories: 248 Total fat: 5.5 g Saturated fat: .8 g Cholesterol: 1.3 mg Sodium: 739 mg
Dietary fiber: 7.8 g Beta carotene: 11 mg Vitamin C: 51 mg Calcium: 258 mg Iron: 5.8 mg

Red Potato Soup with Pasta and Peas

This marvelous soup is much like a minestrone: Vegetables combined with pasta in a light broth sprinkled with Parmesan.

1 tablespoon plus 1 teaspoon olive oil
1¾ cups sliced leek or onion
3 garlic cloves, minced
2 cups canned chicken broth diluted with 3½ cups water, or 5½ cups Homemade Chicken Broth (p. 54)
½ pound red-skinned potatoes, cut into chunks
4 ounces small elbow macaroni
1 ounce (not oil-packed) sun-dried tomatoes
1 cup frozen peas
½ teaspoon freshly ground black pepper
1 ounce grated Parmesan cheese

1. In a flameproof casserole or Dutch oven, warm the oil over medium heat. Add the leek and garlic, and sauté until the leek is tender, about 6 minutes.

2. Add the diluted chicken broth, potatoes and pasta; cover and bring to a boil over high heat. Reduce the heat to low and simmer until the potatoes and macaroni are tender, 20 to 25 minutes.

3. Meanwhile, place the sun-dried tomatoes in a small heatproof bowl. Ladle out about 1 cup of the hot broth and pour over the sun-dried tomatoes. Set aside for 10 minutes to soften. Then drain the tomatoes, returning the soaking liquid to the casserole. Cut the softened tomatoes into strips.

4. When the potatoes and macaroni are tender, add the sun-dried tomato strips, the peas and pepper to the soup and simmer until the peas are heated through, about 5 minutes. Ladle the soup into bowls, sprinkle with the Parmesan and serve.

Makes 4 servings

NUTRITION INFORMATION
values are per serving

CALORIES 319	DIETARY FIBER 5.1 G
TOTAL FAT 8.3 G	BETA CAROTENE 1.0 MG
SATURATED FAT 2.1 G	VITAMIN C 43 MG
CHOLESTEROL 5.6 MG	CALCIUM 156 MG
SODIUM 691 MG	IRON 3.9 MG

Red Pepper and Black Bean Soup with Cilantro-Cream Swirl

The flavors of the Southwest—roasted red bell peppers, cilantro and black beans—combine in this elegant, beautiful soup, spicy with cayenne and black pepper.

½ cup (loosely packed) cilantro sprigs
¼ cup light sour cream
1 tablespoon skim milk
5 large red bell peppers
1½ teaspoons olive oil, preferably extra-virgin
2 large onions, sliced
3 garlic cloves, sliced
¼ teaspoon salt
¼ teaspoon freshly ground black pepper
⅛ teaspoon cayenne pepper
½ cup canned chicken broth diluted with 2 cups water, or 2½ cups Homemade Chicken Broth (p. 54)
One 10½-ounce can black beans, rinsed and drained

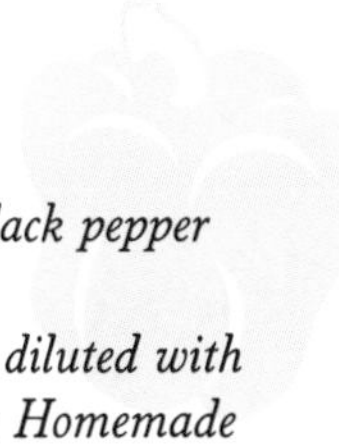

1. Preheat the broiler.

2. Meanwhile, in a food processor or blender, purée the cilantro, sour cream and milk. Transfer to a bowl and chill until serving time.

3. Cutting vertically, slice the bell peppers in 3

or 4 flat panels, leaving the core and seeds behind. Put the bell pepper pieces, skin-side up, in a single layer on a jelly-roll pan and broil 4 to 5 inches from the heat for 15 to 20 minutes, turning once, until the peppers are tender and lightly charred. Remove from the heat and let cool; peel off the skins.

4. In a Dutch oven, heat the oil over medium-high heat. Stir in the onions, garlic, salt, black pepper and cayenne, and sauté until the onions are softened slightly, about 2 minutes.

5. Add the diluted broth, and the bell peppers to the pan; cover and bring to a boil. Reduce the heat to medium-low and simmer until the peppers and onions are very tender, about 10 minutes.

6. In a food processor or blender, purée the soup. Return the purée to the saucepan. Add the beans and cook over medium heat until warmed through. Ladle the soup into bowls and top each serving with some of the cilantro cream.

Makes 6 servings

NUTRITION INFORMATION
values are per serving

CALORIES 167	DIETARY FIBER 5.9 G
TOTAL FAT 4.6 G	BETA CAROTENE 4.3 MG
SATURATED FAT 1.3 G	VITAMIN C 243 MG
CHOLESTEROL 5.1 MG	CALCIUM 62 MG
SODIUM 388 MG	IRON 1.8 MG

Chicken Noodle Soup with Browned Onions and Swiss Chard

When cooked until golden brown, onions take on a sweetness singularly their own, which here flavors this very uncommon—and delicious—chicken noodle soup.

1 tablespoon plus 1 teaspoon olive oil
1 large onion, thinly sliced
4 garlic cloves, minced
½ pound skinless, boneless chicken breast
½ teaspoon oregano
½ teaspoon freshly ground black pepper
¼ teaspoon salt
1½ cups canned chicken broth diluted with 2½ cups water, or 4 cups Homemade Chicken Broth (p. 54)
4 large carrots, sliced
4 ounces spaghetti, broken in thirds
4 cups (loosely packed) 1-inch pieces Swiss chard or spinach

1. In a large nonstick skillet, warm 2 teaspoons of the oil over high heat until hot but not smoking. Add the onion and garlic, then reduce the heat to medium-high and sauté until the onion is lightly browned, 4 to 5 minutes.

2. Push the onion mixture to one side of the skillet; add the remaining 2 teaspoons oil and the chicken. Sprinkle the chicken with ¼ teaspoon of the oregano, ¼ teaspoon of the pepper and ⅛ teaspoon of the salt. Cook the chicken breast until lightly browned on both sides, about 2 minutes per side.

3. Add ¼ cup of the diluted chicken broth and stir to loosen any browned bits on the bottom of the pan. Reduce the heat to medium and simmer the mixture until the chicken is no longer pink in the center, 3 to 4 minutes. Remove the chicken and half of the browned onion mixture to a plate and cover loosely to keep warm.

4. Transfer the remaining browned onion mixture to a large saucepan or Dutch oven and add the remaining 3¾ cups diluted broth, the carrots, spaghetti and the remaining ¼ teaspoon oregano, ¼ teaspoon pepper and ⅛ teaspoon salt. Cover and bring to a boil over high heat. Reduce the heat to medium-low and simmer for 5 minutes.

5. Stir in the Swiss chard or spinach, cover and simmer, stirring frequently, until the vegetables and pasta are tender, 4 to 6 minutes (spinach will cook faster).

6. Ladle the soup into bowls. Cut the reserved chicken on an angle into thin slices and arrange on top of each bowl. Spoon the reserved browned onion mixture over each and serve.

Makes 4 servings

Nutrition Information
values are per serving

CALORIES 296	DIETARY FIBER 4.8 G
TOTAL FAT 6.5 G	BETA CAROTENE 18 MG
SATURATED FAT .9 G	VITAMIN C 28 MG
CHOLESTEROL 33 MG	CALCIUM 86 MG
SODIUM 677 MG	IRON 3.3 MG

Curried Red Lentil Soup

Look for red lentils in Indian grocery stores and, at the same time, replenish your rack of Indian spices. The fresher the spices here, the fuller the remarkable curry flavor.

2 teaspoons olive oil
1 large onion, coarsely chopped
2 garlic cloves, minced
1½ teaspoons cumin
¾ teaspoon turmeric
½ teaspoon ground coriander
¼ teaspoon freshly ground black pepper
⅛ teaspoon cayenne pepper
2 cups canned chicken broth diluted with 2¼ cups water or 4¼ cups Homemade Chicken Broth (p. 54)
½ pound unpeeled all-purpose potatoes, cut into ½-inch chunks
7 ounces red lentils (about 1 cup), rinsed and picked over
2 medium carrots, sliced
1 bay leaf

1. In a large saucepan, warm the oil over medium-high heat. Add the onion and garlic and sauté until the onion is tender, 5 to 6 minutes. Stir in the cumin, turmeric, coriander, black pepper and cayenne, and stir-fry for 30 seconds.

2. Add the diluted chicken broth, potatoes, lentils, carrots and bay leaf; cover and bring to a boil over high heat. Reduce the heat to medium-low and simmer, stirring occasionally, until the lentils are tender, about 20 minutes. Remove and discard the bay leaf before serving.

Makes 6 servings

Nutrition Information
values are per serving

CALORIES 288	DIETARY FIBER 8.7 G
TOTAL FAT 3.8 G	BETA CAROTENE 6.1 MG
SATURATED FAT .4 G	VITAMIN C 21 MG
CHOLESTEROL 0 MG	CALCIUM 72 MG
SODIUM 518 MG	IRON 6.6 MG

Cold Carrot Soup with Red Pepper and Mint

Almost without fat and magnificent in both color and texture, this soup has yet another attribute to recommend itself: It must be made in advance.

2 cups sliced carrots plus ¼ cup grated carrot
1 small unpeeled Golden Delicious apple, cut into quarters
1 medium onion, sliced
1 cup canned chicken broth diluted with ¾ cup water, or 1¾ cups Homemade Chicken Broth (p. 54)
1 cup carrot juice
1 garlic clove, peeled

1¾ teaspoons cumin
¼ teaspoon ground coriander
¼ teaspoon freshly ground black pepper
⅛ teaspoon turmeric
1 large red bell pepper, diced
¾ cup plain nonfat yogurt
¼ cup chopped red onion
2 tablespoons chopped fresh mint or 1 teaspoon dried
1 small fresh red chili pepper, seeded and minced
⅛ teaspoon salt

1. In a large saucepan, combine the sliced carrots, apple, sliced onion, diluted broth, carrot juice, garlic, cumin, coriander, black pepper and turmeric. Cover and bring to a boil over high heat. Reduce the heat to low, cover and simmer until the vegetables are very tender and the flavors are blended, 15 to 20 minutes.

2. In a food processor or blender, purée the soup until smooth. Pour into a bowl, cover and chill. (Place in the freezer for a quicker chill.)

3. In a small bowl, stir together the bell pepper, yogurt, chopped red onion, grated carrot, mint, chili pepper and salt. Cover and chill until serving time.

4. Stir the yogurt mixture into the soup and serve.

Makes 6 servings

Nutrition Information
values are per serving

CALORIES 87	DIETARY FIBER 2.5 G
TOTAL FAT .7 G	BETA CAROTENE 14 MG
SATURATED FAT .1 G	VITAMIN C 49 MG
CHOLESTEROL .6 MG	CALCIUM 98 MG
SODIUM 262 MG	IRON 1.1 MG

SUPER QUICK

Minted Gazpacho

Working time: 25 minutes Total time: 25 minutes

2 pounds tomatoes
2 large red bell peppers, cut into large chunks
1 large green bell pepper, cut into large chunks
⅓ cup coarsely chopped sweet red or white onion
1 fresh jalapeño pepper, seeded and coarsely chopped
2 garlic cloves, peeled
One 5½-ounce can mixed vegetable juice
2 tablespoons fresh lemon juice
1 tablespoon extra-virgin olive oil
1 tablespoon red wine vinegar
¼ teaspoon salt
¼ teaspoon freshly ground pepper
1¼ cups shredded carrots
¼ cup chopped fresh mint

1 Bring a medium saucepan of water to a boil over high heat. One at a time, add the tomatoes and blanch for 10 to 20 seconds to loosen the skins. Cool under cold running water and slip off the skins. Core the tomatoes and then cut the tomatoes into big chunks.
2 In a food processor, combine the red and green bell peppers, the onion, jalapeño pepper and garlic, and process until coarsely chopped. Remove about half of the mixture and transfer to a large bowl.
3 To the mixture remaining in the food processor, add the tomatoes, in batches if necessary, and process until the gazpacho is finely chopped but still has some texture. Add to the mixture in the bowl.
4 Stir in the mixed vegetable juice, lemon juice, oil, vinegar, salt and black pepper; cover and chill until cold.
5 In a small bowl, mix the carrots and mint. Ladle the gazpacho into bowls; top each with some of the mint mixture.

Makes 6 servings

Values are per serving:
Calories: 98 Total fat: 3.0 g Saturated fat: .4 g Cholesterol: .1 mg Sodium: 200 mg
Dietary fiber: 4.2 g Beta carotene: 6.9 mg Vitamin C: 190 mg Calcium: 33 mg Iron: 1.5 mg

Cold Curried Mango Soup

A ripe mango should give slightly to the touch and have a splendid, full aroma. In general, mangoes are most affordable, available and at their peak of flavor during the late summer months—the very best time of all to make this exotic, cooling combination.

1 teaspoon olive oil
1 small onion, diced
2 teaspoons curry powder
½ cup canned chicken broth diluted with ½ cup water, or 1 cup Homemade Chicken Broth (p. 54)
3 large mangoes, peeled
1 tablespoon light brown sugar
½ teaspoon ground ginger
¼ teaspoon allspice
¼ teaspoon salt
1¼ cups plain nonfat yogurt
½ cup water
2 tablespoons fresh lime juice
2 tablespoons minced fresh basil

1. In a small nonstick skillet, warm the oil over medium heat until hot but not smoking. Add the onion and curry powder, and cook for 1 minute. Add ¼ cup of the diluted chicken broth and simmer gently until the onion has softened, about 4 minutes.

2. Remove the flesh from 2 of the mangoes and transfer to a food processor or blender along with the onion mixture, brown sugar, ginger, allspice and salt. Process to a smooth purée. Add 1 cup of the yogurt, the remaining ¾ cup diluted broth, the water and lime juice, and process to combine. Chill until serving time.

3. Before serving, cut the remaining mango into ½-inch cubes. Spoon the soup into 4 soup bowls, dollop with the remaining ¼ cup yogurt, spoon the diced mango on top and sprinkle the basil over the soup.

Makes 4 servings

NUTRITION INFORMATION
values are per serving

CALORIES 211	DIETARY FIBER 2.9 G
TOTAL FAT 2.2 G	BETA CAROTENE 4.6 MG
SATURATED FAT .4 G	VITAMIN C 59 MG
CHOLESTEROL 1.4 MG	CALCIUM 190 MG
SODIUM 319 MG	IRON 1.0 MG

Winter Vegetable Goulash

Goulash, a traditional Hungarian stew, should be thick and rich. In this case, richness comes from a variety of winter vegetables cooked until tender. Be sure to use good paprika here for true Hungarian effect.

1 tablespoon olive oil
2 large onions, sliced
1 tablespoon paprika
½ teaspoon salt
½ teaspoon freshly ground black pepper
4 cups coarsely shredded cabbage
2 cups peeled, coarsely chunked butternut squash
½ pound small red-skinned potatoes, each cut into 6 wedges
1½ cups carrot sticks
¼ cup canned chicken broth diluted with ¼ cup water, or ½ cup Homemade Chicken Broth (p. 54)
2 tablespoons dry white wine or dry vermouth (optional)
¼ cup light sour cream
1 tablespoon minced chives or scallion greens

1. In a Dutch oven or flameproof casserole, heat the oil over medium heat. Stir in the onions, paprika, salt and pepper, and reduce the heat to low. Cover and cook, stirring occasionally, until the onions are very tender, about 15 minutes.

2. Increase the heat to medium, stir in the cabbage and cook, tossing, until it is wilted, about 5 minutes.

3. Add the squash, potatoes, carrots, diluted broth and wine (if using), and bring to a boil over high heat. Reduce the heat to medium-low, cover and simmer, stirring occasionally, until the vegetables are very tender, about 30 minutes.

4. Spoon the goulash into bowls. Top each with a dollop of sour cream and a sprinkling of chives.

Makes 4 servings

Nutrition Information
values are per serving

CALORIES 227	DIETARY FIBER 6.6 G
TOTAL FAT 6.3 G	BETA CAROTENE 15 MG
SATURATED FAT 1.5 G	VITAMIN C 72 MG
CHOLESTEROL 5.0 MG	CALCIUM 114 MG
SODIUM 381 MG	IRON 2.3 MG

Summer Vegetable and White Bean Stew

Call this a summer harvest soup, if you will, filled as it is with vine-ripened tomatoes, zucchini, summer squash and bell peppers. If desired, serve this as a main course with grilled radicchio salad and Italian bread. For dessert, all you will need is a selection of fresh fruit and cheese.

1 tablespoon plus 1 teaspoon olive oil, preferably extra-virgin
4 scallions, cut into 1-inch pieces
4 garlic cloves, minced
3 large red bell peppers, cut into thin strips
1½ pounds tomatoes, cut into chunks
1 medium zucchini, sliced
1 small yellow summer squash, sliced
½ cup chicken broth, canned or homemade (p. 54)
One 19-ounce can cannellini or white kidney beans, rinsed and drained
½ cup coarsely chopped fresh basil or flat-leaf parsley

1. In a Dutch oven or flameproof casserole, warm the oil over medium-high heat until hot but not smoking. Add the scallions and garlic, stir to mix well with the oil and sauté until the scallions are wilted, 1 to 2 minutes. Stir in the bell pepper strips and sauté until they are crisp-tender, 5 to 7 minutes.

2. Add the tomatoes and increase the heat to high. Cover and cook, stirring often, until the tomatoes begin to release their juices, about 5 minutes.

3. Stir in the zucchini, summer squash and chicken broth, and bring to a boil. Reduce the heat to medium, cover and cook until the vegetables are tender, about 10 minutes.

4. Stir in the beans, cover and cook until heated through, 2 to 3 minutes. Sprinkle the soup with the basil and serve.

Makes 4 servings

Nutrition Information
values are per serving

CALORIES 221	DIETARY FIBER 10 G
TOTAL FAT 6.5 G	BETA CAROTENE 3.5 MG
SATURATED FAT .8 G	VITAMIN C 188 MG
CHOLESTEROL 0 MG	CALCIUM 122 MG
SODIUM 313 MG	IRON 4.0 MG

Provençale Fish Stew with Red Pepper Rouille

The cooking of Provence is heady with such ingredients as garlic and thyme and tomatoes and orange. This fish stew uses all of them and more, crowned as it is with the classic red pepper-tinged garlic mayonnaise known as rouille. Serve this stew as a main course, with a chilled bottle of white or rosé wine from Provence.

ROUILLE

1 large red bell pepper
⅓ cup reduced-calorie mayonnaise
⅛ teaspoon cayenne pepper
1 garlic clove, peeled

FISH STEW

1 tablespoon olive oil, preferably extra-virgin
2 large red bell peppers, thinly sliced
1½ cups thinly sliced fennel or celery
1 large onion, sliced
1 large carrot, thinly sliced
3 garlic cloves, thinly sliced
2 bay leaves, preferably imported
One 2-inch length of orange zest
¾ teaspoon freshly ground black pepper
½ teaspoon thyme
½ teaspoon fennel seed
¼ teaspoon salt
½ cup chicken broth, canned or homemade (p. 54)
1¾ pounds tomatoes, coarsely chopped
1 pound thick scrod or other firm-fleshed white fish fillets, cut into 1-inch pieces
2 tablespoons orange juice

1. To Make the Rouille Preheat the broiler. Cutting vertically, slice the bell pepper in 3 or 4 flat panels, leaving the core and seeds behind. Put the bell pepper pieces, skin-side up, in a single layer in a small baking pan and broil 3 to 4 inches from the heat source for about 10 minutes, turning once, until lightly charred and tender. Remove from the heat; let cool, then peel off the skin.

2. In a food processor or blender, combine the roasted pepper, the mayonnaise and cayenne. With the machine running, drop in the whole garlic clove and process the mixture to a smooth purée. Transfer to a small bowl and refrigerate until serving time.

3. To Make the Fish Stew In a Dutch oven or flameproof casserole, heat the oil over medium-high heat. Stir in the bell peppers, fennel, onion, carrot, garlic, bay leaves, orange zest, black pepper, thyme, fennel seed and salt. Sauté until the the vegetables start to soften, 2 to 3 minutes.

4. Stir ¼ cup of the chicken broth into the vegetables. Reduce the heat to medium-low; cover and simmer, stirring occasionally, until the vegetables are tender, about 8 minutes.

5. Add the tomatoes to the saucepan, increase the heat to high and bring to a boil. Reduce the heat to medium-high, stir in the remaining ¼ cup broth and cook, stirring and pressing down on the tomatoes occasionally, until the tomatoes cook down and make a sauce, 8 to 10 minutes.

6. Reduce the heat so the liquid is simmering gently, then stir in the fish. Cover and cook until the fish just flakes when tested with a fork, 3 to 5 minutes. Stir in the orange juice and remove from the heat. Ladle the soup into soup bowls and top with some of the rouille.

Makes 4 servings

Nutrition Information
values are per serving

CALORIES 293	DIETARY FIBER 6.0 G
TOTAL FAT 11 G	BETA CAROTENE 7.6 MG
SATURATED FAT 2.1 G	VITAMIN C 196 MG
CHOLESTEROL 55 MG	CALCIUM 94 MG
SODIUM 498 MG	IRON 2.9 MG

Manhattan Clam Chowder

The key to making any successful clam chowder that calls for fresh clams is not to overcook them. Add the littlenecks to the soup base and cook them as directed, then serve immediately in wide shallow bowls, preferably with a crusty loaf of bread for soaking up the delicious broth.

1 cup canned chicken broth diluted with 1 cup water, or 2 cups Homemade Chicken Broth (p. 54)
2½ cups diced carrots
½ pound peeled all-purpose potatoes, cut into ½-inch cubes
1 medium onion, diced
1 medium celery stalk with leaves, diced
2 garlic cloves, crushed through a press
2 bay leaves, preferably imported
¾ teaspoon thyme
½ teaspoon freshly ground black pepper
⅛ teaspoon celery seed
Two 14½-ounce cans no-salt-added stewed tomatoes
2 dozen littleneck clams, well scrubbed
2 tablespoons chopped parsley, preferably flat-leaf

1. In a Dutch oven or flameproof casserole, combine the broth, carrots, potatoes, onion, celery, garlic, bay leaves, thyme, pepper and celery seed. Cover and bring to a boil over high heat. Reduce the heat to medium and simmer until the vegetables are tender, about 8 minutes.

2. Add the tomatoes and bring to a boil over high heat. Reduce the heat to medium and simmer, uncovered, for 5 minutes to blend the flavors.

3. Add the clams, cover and cook over medium-low heat, stirring occasionally, until the clams open, 6 to 8 minutes. Discard any clams that do not open. Stir in the parsley and serve.

Makes 4 servings

Nutrition Information
values are per serving

CALORIES 225	DIETARY FIBER 8.8 G
TOTAL FAT 1.8 G	BETA CAROTENE 12 MG
SATURATED FAT .2 G	VITAMIN C 51 MG
CHOLESTEROL 31 MG	CALCIUM 163 MG
SODIUM 372 MG	IRON 16 MG

Shrimp and Vegetable Chowder

This satisfying and delicious chowder is filled with chopped shrimp and a host of vegetables—including the unusual addition of diced sweet potatoes.

1 tablespoon olive oil
½ cup chopped onion
2 tablespoons flour
1¼ cups canned chicken broth diluted with 1¼ cups water, or 2½ cups Homemade Chicken Broth (p. 54)
½ pound peeled and diced sweet potatoes
1 cup small broccoli florets
1 large red bell pepper, diced
1 teaspoon thyme
¼ teaspoon freshly ground black pepper
½ pound shrimp–shelled, deveined and coarsely chopped
1 cup lowfat (1%) milk
2 teaspoons fresh lemon juice
⅛ teaspoon cayenne pepper

1. In a medium saucepan, warm the oil over medium-high heat until hot but not smoking. Add the onion and cook, stirring, until softened, 1 to 2 minutes. Add the flour and cook, stirring, until the flour is no longer visible, about 30 seconds.

2. Add the diluted broth and sweet potatoes,

cover and bring to a boil over high heat. Reduce the heat to low and simmer until the sweet potatoes are just tender, about 3 minutes.

3. With a slotted spoon, remove about half of the sweet potatoes to a shallow bowl and lightly mash them with a fork. Return the mashed potatoes to the pan.

4. Add the broccoli, bell pepper, thyme and black pepper, and return the mixture to a boil over medium-high heat. Add the shrimp and milk, and cook, stirring gently, until the shrimp are just cooked through, 1 to 2 minutes.

5. Remove from the heat and stir in the lemon juice and cayenne. Serve immediately.

Makes 4 servings

NUTRITION INFORMATION
values are per serving

CALORIES 219	DIETARY FIBER 4.0 G
TOTAL FAT 5.6 G	BETA CAROTENE 8.8 MG
SATURATED FAT 1.0 G	VITAMIN C 128 MG
CHOLESTEROL 72 MG	CALCIUM 144 MG
SODIUM 424 MG	IRON 2.8 MG

Shrimp and Scallop Gumbo

Some gumbos are made rich with sausage and seafood; others are flavorful with duck and wild fowl. This modern gumbo boasts a light broth filled with the sweetness of shrimp and sea scallops and underscored with the heat of minced jalapeño pepper.

1 cup canned chicken broth diluted with 1 cup water, or 2 cups Homemade Chicken Broth (p. 54)
One 14½-ounce can no-salt-added stewed tomatoes
1 medium sweet potato (8 ounces), peeled and cut into ½-inch cubes
1 medium red bell pepper, cut into thin strips
1 small onion, cut into thin wedges
2 tablespoons minced fresh jalapeño pepper
2 tablespoons Worcestershire sauce
2 large garlic cloves, minced
1½ teaspoons oregano
1½ teaspoons rosemary, crumbled
1½ teaspoons thyme
½ pound medium shrimp
½ pound sea scallops
2 cups small broccoli florets
¼ cup chopped parsley

1. In a large saucepan or flameproof casserole, combine the diluted chicken broth, tomatoes, sweet potato, bell pepper, onion, half of the jalapeño pepper, the Worcestershire sauce, garlic, oregano, rosemary and thyme. Cover and bring to a boil over high heat. Reduce the heat to medium-low and simmer for 15 minutes to blend the flavors.

2. Meanwhile, shell and devein the shrimp. Halve or quarter any large scallops so they are all of uniform size.

3. Add the shrimp, scallops, broccoli and parsley and cook over medium heat until the shrimp and broccoli are just cooked, about 3 minutes. Stir in the remaining jalapeño and serve hot.

Makes 4 servings

NUTRITION INFORMATION
values are per serving

CALORIES 229	DIETARY FIBER 6.8 G
TOTAL FAT 2.2 G	BETA CAROTENE 6.7 MG
SATURATED FAT .3 G	VITAMIN C 122 MG
CHOLESTEROL 89 MG	CALCIUM 151 MG
SODIUM 531 MG	IRON 4.3 MG

Shrimp, Green Pepper and Sweet Potato Stew

Powerful flavors prevail in this sweet-potato-thickened shellfish stew. Serve as a main course, if desired, with an orange salad alongside.

2½ teaspoons cumin
¾ teaspoon ground coriander
½ teaspoon ground ginger
¼ teaspoon freshly ground black pepper
¼ teaspoon cayenne pepper
¾ pound medium shrimp–shelled, deveined and cut into 1-inch pieces
1½ pounds sweet potatoes, peeled and cut into 1-inch chunks
¾ cup canned chicken broth diluted with ¾ cup water, or 1½ cups Homemade Chicken broth (p. 54)
1 large onion, chopped
3 garlic cloves, crushed through a press
1 large green bell pepper, diced
2 tablespoons fresh lemon juice

1. In a small bowl or cup, combine the cumin, coriander, ginger, black pepper and cayenne.

2. In a medium bowl, toss the shrimp with 1 teaspoon of the spice mixture. Cover and let stand at room temperature while you simmer the soup.

3. In a Dutch oven or flameproof casserole, combine the remaining spice mixture, the sweet potatoes, diluted chicken broth, onion and garlic. Cover and bring to a boil over high heat. Reduce the heat to low and simmer, stirring occasionally, until the vegetables are tender, 15 to 20 minutes.

4. Remove 1 cup of the sweet potatoes to a bowl and mash. Stir the mashed potatoes back into the stew. Add the shrimp and bell pepper, cover and cook, stirring once, until the shrimp are just cooked through, 2 to 3 minutes.

5. Stir in the lemon juice and serve hot.

Makes 4 servings

Nutrition Information
values are per serving

CALORIES 247	DIETARY FIBER 5.0 G
TOTAL FAT 2.2 G	BETA CAROTENE 15 MG
SATURATED FAT .3 G	VITAMIN C 58 MG
CHOLESTEROL 105 MG	CALCIUM 96 MG
SODIUM 308 MG	IRON 3.6 MG

Shrimp and Black Bean Chili

In this chili, one of the all-time great comfort foods, the exquisite combination of flavors and textures includes shrimp, corn, tomatoes, a generous amount of cumin and chili powder, and not red beans, but black ones.

1 tablespoon olive oil
2 large red bell peppers, diced
1 large onion, diced
1 cup shredded carrot
2 fresh jalapeño peppers, diced, with some of the seeds
3 garlic cloves, minced
1 tablespoon chili powder
1½ teaspoons cumin
One 16-ounce can crushed tomatoes in purée
One 16-ounce can black beans, rinsed and drained
¼ cup chicken broth, canned or homemade (p. 54)
1 cup corn kernels, frozen or fresh (from 3 ears)
¾ pound medium shrimp–shelled, deveined and halved crosswise

1. In a Dutch oven or flameproof casserole, warm the oil over medium-high heat until hot but not smoking. Stir in the bell peppers, onion, carrot, jalapeño peppers, garlic, chili powder and cumin. Sauté until tender, 6 to 8 minutes.

2. Stir in the tomatoes, black beans and broth,

and bring to a simmer. Reduce the heat to low, cover and cook for 10 minutes, stirring occasionally, to blend the flavors.

3. Stir in the corn and shrimp, increase the heat to medium, cover and cook, stirring frequently, until the shrimp are cooked through, 6 to 8 minutes (the fresh corn should still be crunchy).

Makes 4 servings

NUTRITION INFORMATION
values are per serving

CALORIES 296	DIETARY FIBER 7.3 G
TOTAL FAT 6.2 G	BETA CAROTENE 7.3 MG
SATURATED FAT .8 G	VITAMIN C 143 MG
CHOLESTEROL 105 MG	CALCIUM 141 MG
SODIUM 562 MG	IRON 4.8 MG

Mama's Chicken Stew

A light broth-based sauce, a novel twist as most stews go, allows the wonderful flavors of the vegetables here to shine.

1 medium onion, coarsely chopped
⅓ cup sliced celery
3 garlic cloves, minced
1 cup canned chicken broth diluted with 1 cup water, or 2 cups Homemade Chicken Broth (p. 54)
1 pound sweet potatoes, peeled and cut into ½-inch chunks
½ cup thinly sliced carrots
½ teaspoon thyme
¼ teaspoon salt
¼ teaspoon freshly ground black pepper
1 pound skinless, boneless chicken thighs, cut into 2-inch pieces
1 pound stemmed spinach, coarsely chopped
2 teaspoons cornstarch blended with 1 tablespoon water

1. In a flameproof casserole or Dutch oven, combine the onion, celery, garlic and ½ cup of the diluted chicken broth. Simmer until the onion is tender and the liquid has almost evaporated, about 7 minutes.

2. Add the sweet potatoes, carrots, thyme, salt, pepper and the remaining 1½ cups diluted broth, and cook for 5 minutes.

3. Add the chicken, cover and cook until the chicken and sweet potatoes are tender, about 8 minutes. Stir in the spinach and cook until just wilted, about 3 minutes.

4. Stir the cornstarch mixture into the stew. Bring the stew to a boil and cook until the sauce is lightly thickened, about 2 minutes.

Makes 4 servings

NUTRITION INFORMATION
values are per serving

CALORIES 286	DIETARY FIBER 6.7 G
TOTAL FAT 5.5 G	BETA CAROTENE 17 MG
SATURATED FAT 1.2 G	VITAMIN C 59 MG
CHOLESTEROL 94 MG	CALCIUM 169 MG
SODIUM 595 MG	IRON 5.3 MG

Chicken Cacciatore

This chicken cacciatore, fragrant with herbs and filled with mushrooms in a simple tomato sauce, is especially good when accompanied with Arborio rice.

1 tablespoon olive oil, preferably extra-virgin
1 large onion, sliced
3 large carrots, sliced
¾ pound mushrooms, thickly sliced
3 garlic cloves, minced
1 fresh red chili pepper, minced, with some of the seeds

3/4 teaspoon freshly ground black pepper
1/2 teaspoon oregano
1/2 teaspoon rosemary, crumbled
1/4 teaspoon salt
1/4 cup dry white wine or chicken broth (canned or homemade, p. 54)
One 16-ounce can whole tomatoes in purée
One 8-ounce can no-salt-added tomato sauce
1 pound skinless, boneless chicken breast, cut into 1-inch chunks
Sprigs of fresh rosemary, for garnish (optional)

1. In a Dutch oven or flameproof casserole, warm the oil over medium-high heat until hot but not smoking. Stir in the onion, carrots, mushrooms, garlic, chili pepper, black pepper, oregano, rosemary and salt, and sauté until the vegetables are tender, 4 to 6 minutes; add the wine a little at a time as the pan gets dry.

2. Stir in the tomatoes and tomato sauce, and bring to a simmer, breaking the whole tomatoes up with a spoon. Reduce the heat to medium-low, cover and simmer for 10 minutes, stirring occasionally, to blend the flavors.

3. Stir in the chicken, cover and simmer until the chicken is cooked through, about 10 minutes.

4. Serve the cacciatore hot, garnished with sprigs of rosemary, if desired.

Makes 4 servings

NUTRITION INFORMATION
values are per serving

CALORIES 290	DIETARY FIBER 5.4 G
TOTAL FAT 5.8 G	BETA CAROTENE 14 MG
SATURATED FAT 1.0 G	VITAMIN C 70 MG
CHOLESTEROL 66 MG	CALCIUM 103 MG
SODIUM 435 MG	IRON 3.6 MG

Santa Fe Chicken and Squash Stew

Beans, hot peppers, and squash, the tried-and-true ingredients of much of the cooking of the southwestern United States, combine here with sautéed chicken for a nourishing, honest, homespun-style stew. Serve with warmed flour tortillas.

1 large butternut squash (about 3 1/4 pounds) –peeled, seeded and cut into 1-inch chunks
1 1/2 pounds chicken legs, split into drumsticks and thighs and skinned
2 large red bell peppers, cut into 1-inch chunks
1 large onion, cut into 1-inch chunks
1 1/2 cups canned chicken broth diluted with 1 1/2 cups water, or 3 cups Homemade Chicken Broth (p. 54)
2 fresh jalapeño peppers, halved, some seeds removed
1 tablespoon chili powder
1 tablespoon cumin seed
3/4 teaspoon freshly ground black pepper
One 15-ounce can black beans, rinsed and drained
1/2 cup chopped cilantro

1. In a Dutch oven or flameproof casserole, combine the squash, chicken, bell peppers, onion, diluted broth, jalapeños, chili powder, cumin seed and black pepper. Cover and bring to a boil over high heat. Reduce the heat to low and simmer until the squash and chicken are tender, about 20 minutes.

2. Remove the chicken from the stew and set aside to cool slightly. Meanwhile, mash some of the squash against the side of the pan to thicken the stew.

3. When the chicken is cool enough to handle, pull off the meat and return it to the stew. Stir in

the beans and warm the stew over medium heat until heated through. Stir in the cilantro and remove the jalapeños before serving.

Makes 6 servings

NUTRITION INFORMATION
values are per serving

CALORIES 251	DIETARY FIBER 3.6 G
TOTAL FAT 3.9 G	BETA CAROTENE 11 MG
SATURATED FAT .7 G	VITAMIN C 125 MG
CHOLESTEROL 52 MG	CALCIUM 149 MG
SODIUM 442 MG	IRON 4.2 MG

Mexican Pork Stew with Apricots and Almonds

Surprising ingredients—dried apricots, chili peppers, ground almonds and a combination of spices—render this stew marvelously rich and equally memorable.

2½ teaspoons cumin
¾ teaspoon ground coriander
½ teaspoon freshly ground black pepper
¼ teaspoon cinnamon
⅛ teaspoon salt
⅛ teaspoon cayenne pepper
½ pounds lean boneless pork loin, pounded to ½-inch thickness
1 tablespoon olive oil
½ cup canned chicken broth diluted with ½ cup water, or 1 cup Homemade Chicken Broth (p. 54)
1 large onion, chopped
1 large red bell pepper, diced
1 medium unpeeled Granny Smith apple, diced
One 4-ounce can chopped mild green chilies, rinsed and drained
2 garlic cloves, minced
½ cup dried apricots, preferably Turkish
2 tablespoons golden raisins
1 ounce whole unsalted almonds
½ teaspoon flour

1. In a small bowl or cup, combine the cumin, coriander, black pepper, cinnamon, salt and cayenne.

2. Cut the pork into ½-inch cubes.

3. In a Dutch oven or flameproof casserole, heat the oil over medium-high heat. Add the spices and sauté, stirring constantly, until fragrant, about 1 minute. Add the pork and sauté until it turns white, 1 to 2 minutes. With a slotted spoon, transfer the pork to a plate. Immediately pour ¼ cup of the diluted broth into the pan to deglaze it.

4. Add the onion, bell pepper, apple, chilies and garlic to the casserole and bring to a boil. Reduce the heat to medium, cover and simmer, stirring occasionally, until the vegetables begin to soften, about 5 minutes.

5. Add the remaining ¾ cup diluted broth, the apricots and raisins; increase the heat to high and bring to a boil. Reduce the heat to low, cover and simmer for 10 minutes, stirring once or twice, to blend the flavors.

6. Meanwhile, in a small food processor or in a nut mill, grind the almonds with the flour until the nuts are medium-fine.

7. Return the cooked pork (and any juices that have collected on the plate) to the casserole along with the ground almonds. Cover and simmer, stirring occasionally, until the stew is slightly thickened, 4 to 5 minutes.

Makes 4 servings

NUTRITION INFORMATION
values are per serving

CALORIES 269	DIETARY FIBER 4.8 G
TOTAL FAT 11 G	BETA CAROTENE 1.6 MG
SATURATED FAT 1.8 G	VITAMIN C 55 MG
CHOLESTEROL 36 MG	CALCIUM 76 MG
SODIUM 289 MG	IRON 2.9 MG

Pork Chili with Corn and Red Peppers

Chilis made with pork are invariably subtle, almost sweet. And this one is also intensely flavorful. Increase the cayenne if you like it fiery.

10 ounces lean pork tenderloin, cut into ½-inch cubes
2 tablespoons chili powder
1½ teaspoons cumin
1 tablespoon olive oil
3 large red bell peppers, diced
1 large onion, chopped
3 garlic cloves, crushed through a press
½ teaspoon basil
½ teaspoon salt
¼ teaspoon cayenne pepper
2 tablespoons flour
½ cup chicken broth, canned or homemade (p. 54)
1 cup low-sodium mixed vegetable juice
One 15-ounce can red kidney beans, rinsed and drained
1 cup corn kernels, frozen or fresh (from 3 ears)
2 large tomatoes, chopped
½ cup chopped scallions

1. Sprinkle the pork with 1 tablespoon of the chili powder and ¾ teaspoon of the cumin.

2. In a Dutch oven or flameproof casserole, warm the oil over high heat until hot but not smoking. Add the pork and sauté for 1 minute. With a slotted spoon, transfer the pork to a plate and cover loosely to keep warm.

3. Stir in the bell peppers, onion, garlic, the remaining 1 tablespoon chili powder, ¾ teaspoon cumin, the basil, salt and cayenne. Reduce the heat to medium-low, cover and simmer, stirring occasionally, until the vegetables are tender, about 10 minutes. Sprinkle in the flour and cook, stirring, for 1 minute.

4. Stir in the chicken broth, mixed vegetable juice and beans; increase the heat to high and bring to a boil. Reduce the heat to low, cover and simmer for 20 minutes to blend the flavors.

5. Return the pork (and any juices that have collected on the plate) to the saucepan and simmer 10 minutes longer to blend the flavors. Stir in the corn and cook to heat through, 2 to 3 minutes.

6. Remove from the heat, stir in the tomatoes and scallions, and serve hot.

Makes 4 servings

NUTRITION INFORMATION
values are per serving

CALORIES 338	DIETARY FIBER 10 G
TOTAL FAT 8.2 G	BETA CAROTENE 4.2 MG
SATURATED FAT 1.4 G	VITAMIN C 192 MG
CHOLESTEROL 46 MG	CALCIUM 96 MG
SODIUM 661 MG	IRON 4.8 MG

Meatball and Pepper Stew

There is no better way to make meatballs taste wonderful than to cook them in the sauce in which they will be served—a concept nicely demonstrated in this meatball stew.

½ pound skinless turkey breast, cut into cubes
6 ounces lean beef top round, cut into cubes
One 16-ounce can crushed tomatoes in purée
¼ cup plain dried bread crumbs
1 egg white
½ teaspoon basil
¼ teaspoon oregano
¼ teaspoon thyme
½ teaspoon freshly ground black pepper
2 large red bell peppers, cut into 1-inch pieces
1 large onion, sliced

½ cup canned chicken broth diluted with ¼ cup water, or ¾ cup Homemade Chicken Broth (p. 54)
2 garlic cloves, minced

1. Place the turkey and beef in a food processor and process until finely ground. Add 3 tablespoons of the crushed tomatoes, the bread crumbs, egg white, ¼ teaspoon of the basil, ⅛ teaspoon each of the oregano and thyme, and ¼ teaspoon of the black pepper. Process briefly just to mix.

2. Using about 1½ tablespoons of the meat mixture for each, shape into 24 small meatballs.

3. In a large saucepan, combine the bell peppers, onion, diluted chicken broth, garlic, the remaining ¼ teaspoon basil, ⅛ teaspoon each oregano and thyme, and ¼ teaspoon black pepper. Cover and bring to a boil over high heat. Reduce the heat to medium, cover and simmer until the vegetables are tender, 4 to 5 minutes.

4. Stir in the remaining crushed tomatoes and bring to a boil over high heat. Reduce the heat to medium-low, add the meatballs, cover and simmer, gently turning the meatballs once or twice, until the meatballs are cooked through and the flavors are blended, 5 to 6 minutes.

Makes 4 servings

NUTRITION INFORMATION
values are per serving

CALORIES 220	DIETARY FIBER 2.0 G
TOTAL FAT 2.5 G	BETA CAROTENE 2.2 MG
SATURATED FAT .7 G	VITAMIN C 117 MG
CHOLESTEROL 59 MG	CALCIUM 91 MG
SODIUM 428 MG	IRON 3.0 MG

SUPER QUICK

Moroccan Lamb Stew

Working time: 20 minutes Total time: 30 minutes

- ½ cup dried apricots
- 1 cup boiling water
- 2 teaspoons olive oil
- ½ teaspoon cinnamon
- ½ teaspoon ground ginger
- ½ teaspoon paprika
- ½ teaspoon turmeric
- ½ teaspoon freshly ground pepper
- 1 large onion, diced
- 1 cup thinly sliced carrots
- ⅔ cup thinly sliced parsnips
- ⅓ cup canned chicken broth diluted with ⅓ cup water, or ⅔ cup Homemade Chicken Broth (p. 54)
- 12 ounces well-trimmed lean lamb, cut into ½-inch pieces
- One 8-ounce can no-salt-added tomato sauce
- 1 cup canned chick-peas, rinsed and drained
- ¼ teaspoon salt
- 2 tablespoons chopped cilantro
- 1 tablespoon fresh lemon juice

1 In a small bowl, combine the apricots and boiling water. Set aside to soften.

2 In a flameproof casserole or Dutch oven, heat the oil over medium heat. Stir in the cinnamon, ginger, paprika, turmeric and pepper, and cook until fragrant, about 30 seconds. Stir in the onion, carrots, parsnips and broth, and cook, stirring frequently, until the vegetables have softened, about 5 minutes.

3 Stir in the lamb and cook until the lamb is no longer pink, about 5 minutes.

4 Meanwhile, reserving the soaking liquid, drain the apricots and coarsely chop.

5 Stir the chopped apricots, ¼ cup of the reserved soaking liquid, the tomato sauce, chick-peas, salt and cilantro into the stew and cook until the lamb is cooked through and the vegetables are tender, about 10 minutes. Stir in the lemon juice and serve.

Makes 4 servings

Values are per serving:
Calories: 295 Total fat: 7.9 g Saturated fat: 1.7 g Cholesterol: 54 mg Sodium: 378 mg
Dietary fiber: 6.9 g Beta carotene: 5.9 mg Vitamin C: 22 mg Calcium: 62 mg Iron: 4.4 mg

Spicy Beef and Lentil Stew

Two tablespoons of minced fresh hot chili pepper will make this one-pot dish spicy. If you feel the diners who will be sharing this hearty stew with you may lack fortitude, use the smaller amount of chili pepper suggested.

Two 14½-ounce cans no-salt-added stewed tomatoes
3 cups water
½ pound well-trimmed beef bottom round, diced
½ pound lentils, rinsed and picked over
1 large sweet potato (12 ounces), peeled and cut into ½-inch cubes
1 medium onion, cut into wedges
1 to 2 tablespoons minced fresh red or green chili peppers, to taste
2 teaspoons thyme
½ teaspoon salt
¼ teaspoon freshly ground black pepper
3 bay leaves

1. In a large saucepan, combine the stewed tomatoes, water, beef, lentils, sweet potato, onion, half of the minced chili peppers, the thyme, salt, black pepper and bay leaves. Cover and bring to a boil over medium-high heat. Reduce the heat to medium-low and cook, stirring occasionally, until the flavors are blended and the lentils are tender, about 40 minutes.

2. With a slotted spoon, remove about 1½ cups of the stew (but no meat) and purée in a blender or food processor. Return the purée to the stew and stir to combine. Stir in the remaining minced chili peppers and serve. Remove and discard the bay leaves.

Makes 4 servings

NUTRITION INFORMATION
values are per serving

CALORIES 413	DIETARY FIBER 14 G
TOTAL FAT 4.3 G	BETA CAROTENE 8.3 MG
SATURATED FAT 1.3 G	VITAMIN C 56 MG
CHOLESTEROL 33 MG	CALCIUM 144 MG
SODIUM 359 MG	IRON 9.7 MG

Beef, Carrot and Barley Stew

Creating a stew from the much-loved combination of beef and barley is a natural. It is the cooking of the meat at the end of the recipe, though, that makes this stew stand apart from all others in both flavor and texture.

2 cups canned beef broth diluted with 1½ cups water
⅓ cup pearl barley
2 garlic cloves, minced
1 bay leaf
½ teaspoon thyme
¼ teaspoon freshly ground black pepper
3 cups sliced carrots
2 celery stalks with leaves, sliced
1 medium onion, diced
2 teaspoons olive oil
12 ounces lean beef top round, cut into ½-inch cubes
2 cups diced tomatoes
¼ cup chopped parsley, preferably flat-leaf

1. In a large saucepan, combine the diluted beef broth, barley, garlic, bay leaf, thyme and pepper. Cover and bring to a boil over high heat. Reduce the heat to low and simmer for 20 minutes.

2. Add the carrots, celery and onion. Increase

the heat to medium and bring to a boil. Reduce the heat to low, cover and simmer, stirring occasionally, until the barley and vegetables are tender, 8 to 10 minutes.

3. Meanwhile, in a large nonstick skillet, warm the oil over high heat. Add the beef and sauté until browned and medium-rare, 3 to 4 minutes.

4. Add the beef to the stew, increase the heat to medium and bring to a boil, then simmer, uncovered, for 5 minutes to blend the flavors.

5. Remove from the heat and stir in the tomatoes and parsley. Serve hot.

Makes 4 servings

NUTRITION INFORMATION
values are per serving

CALORIES 276	DIETARY FIBER 7.6 G
TOTAL FAT 6.4 G	BETA CAROTENE 14 MG
SATURATED FAT 1.4 G	VITAMIN C 33 MG
CHOLESTEROL 48 MG	CALCIUM 64 MG
SODIUM 516 MG	IRON 3.8 MG

Homemade Chicken Broth

The carrot and vegetable juices used to make this homemade chicken broth not only contribute to its whopping amount of beta carotene, but also add substantially to its depth of flavor. One taste will convince you to make this frequently, and in double batches.

6 pounds whole chicken legs
8½ cups water
4 cups carrot juice
1 cup low-sodium mixed vegetable juice
2 large onions, unpeeled and halved
2 large carrots, peeled and thickly sliced
1 large leek, white and tender green part, thinly sliced
2 celery stalks, thinly sliced
8 garlic cloves, unpeeled
¾ teaspoon rosemary
¾ teaspoon thyme
10 sprigs of parsley
2 bay leaves

1. Preheat the oven to 450°. Spread the chicken legs in a large roasting pan and roast until browned and crisp, about 30 minutes.

2. With tongs or a slotted spoon, transfer the chicken to a large stockpot. Pour off all the fat from the roasting pan and pour ½ cup of the water into the pan, scraping up any browned bits clinging to the roasting pan. Add these juices to the stockpot along with the chicken.

3. Add the remaining 2 quarts water, the carrot juice and the mixed vegetable juice, and bring to a boil over high heat, skimming off the foam as it rises to the surface. Continue skimming until no foam remains.

4. Add the onions, carrots, leek, celery, garlic, rosemary, thyme, parsley and bay leaves. Return to the boil, continuing to skim any foam that rises. Reduce the heat to low and simmer until the broth is rich and flavorful, about 2 hours.

5. Strain the broth and discard the solids, Refrigerate and remove the fat that solidifies on the surface. Refrigerate for up to 3 days or freeze for longer storage.

Makes about 7 cups

NUTRITION INFORMATION
values are per half-cup

CALORIES 46	DIETARY FIBER .5 G
TOTAL FAT .3 G	BETA CAROTENE 12 MG
SATURATED FAT .1 G	VITAMIN C 14 MG
CHOLESTEROL 0 MG	CALCIUM 30 MG
SODIUM 47 MG	IRON .8 MG

Poultry

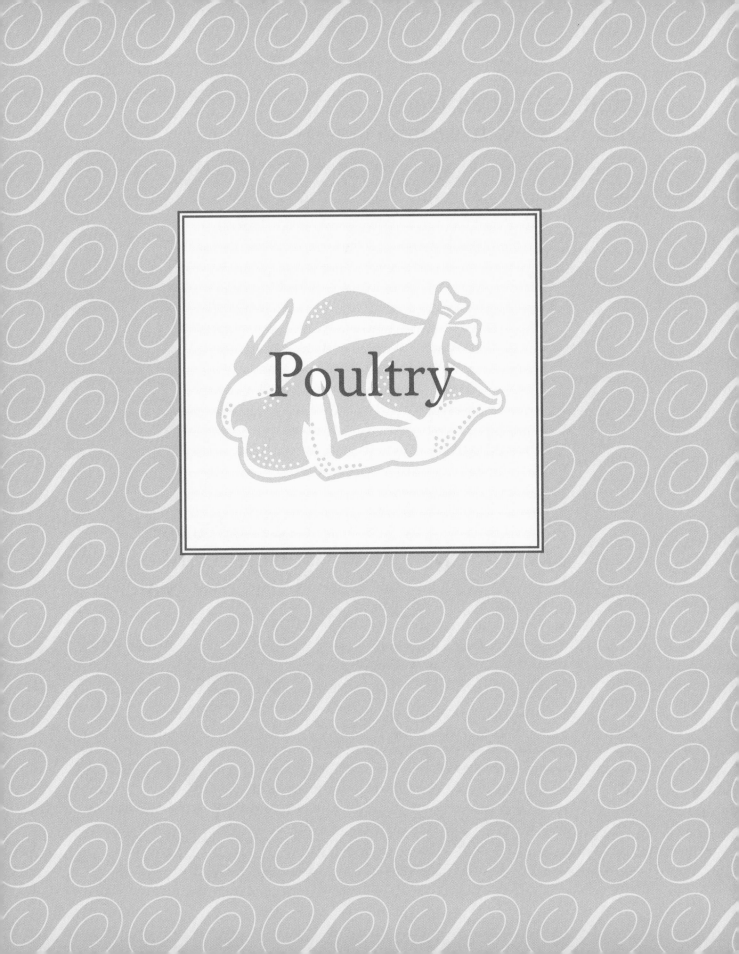

Honey-Brushed Hens with Fresh Citrus Salsa

Citrus fruits are available at their peak in most parts of the United States from October on, which is the perfect time to make this fragrant and stylish main course served with a pink grapefruit and fresh orange salsa. Accompany the hens with couscous studded with golden raisins.

Two 1½-pound Cornish game hens, split in half
½ teaspoon freshly ground black pepper
1 tablespoon grated orange zest
½ cup orange juice
3 tablespoons honey
1 tablespoon reduced-sodium soy sauce
1 tablespoon grated fresh ginger
2 large pink grapefruits
1 navel orange
1 tablespoon minced crystallized ginger (optional)
1½ teaspoons raspberry vinegar or 1 teaspoon red wine vinegar

1. Season the hens with the pepper.

2. In a bowl, combine the orange zest, orange juice, 2 tablespoons of the honey, the soy sauce and fresh ginger. Add the hens and turn to coat with the mixture. Let stand until ready to cook, but for at least 10 minutes.

3. Preheat the oven to 450°.

4. Meanwhile, remove the peel and white pith from the grapefruits and orange. Working over a bowl, cut out the sections from between the membranes, letting them drop into the bowl. Squeeze the juice from the membranes of the orange and 1 of the grapefruits into the bowl. Cut the grapefruit sections in half. Stir in the remaining 1 tablespoon honey, the crystallized ginger (if using) and the vinegar. Set the salsa aside.

5. Place the hens in a single layer in a baking pan and add the marinade. Bake for 25 to 30 minutes, basting with the pan juices, until the hens are cooked through.

6. When the hens are done, remove them to a serving platter and cover loosely to keep warm. Pour the pan juices into a gravy separator to remove the fat, then pour the degreased juices into a small skillet. Bring to a boil over high heat and boil rapidly until reduced to a light syrup, about 8 minutes.

7. Stir the pan juices into the salsa and serve with the hens. Remove the skin before eating.

Makes 4 servings

NUTRITION INFORMATION
values are per serving

CALORIES 325	DIETARY FIBER 1.0 G
TOTAL FAT 5.2 G	BETA CAROTENE .1 MG
SATURATED FAT 1.3 G	VITAMIN C 95 MG
CHOLESTEROL 114 MG	CALCIUM 65 MG
SODIUM 277 MG	IRON 1.9 MG

Chili-Rubbed Cornish Hens with Tangerine Sauce

Vary the spicy-but-sweet tangerine sauce that tops these chili-rubbed hens by substituting blood orange slices for the tangerine sections. The blood oranges, in markets in the early summer, will lend a slightly milder flavor and extraordinary ruby-red color to this dish.

1 tablespoon plus 1 teaspoon chili powder
½ teaspoon salt
Two 1½-pound Cornish game hens, cut into quarters
1 teaspoon olive oil, preferably extra-virgin
⅓ cup frozen tangerine or orange juice concentrate, thawed

1 cup water
2 tablespoons brown sugar
1 tablespoon light ketchup
1 tablespoon light molasses
1 teaspoon reduced-sodium soy sauce
1 tablespoon cornstarch
⅛ teaspoon cayenne pepper
3 tangerines, separated into sections
1 cup finely diced red bell pepper

1. Preheat the broiler. Spray the broiler pan rack with nonstick cooking spray.

2. In a small bowl or cup, combine the chili powder and salt. Rub the Cornish hens on the cut sides and under the skin with the chili powder mixture. Place the hens skin-side up in a single layer on the prepared broiler pan and drizzle with the oil.

3. Broil the hens 5 to 6 inches from the heat for 25 to 30 minutes, turning the pieces several times, until browned and cooked through.

4. Meanwhile, in a medium saucepan, whisk together the tangerine juice concentrate, water, brown sugar, ketchup, molasses, soy sauce, cornstarch and cayenne until smooth. Bring to a boil over high heat, stirring constantly, and cook until thickened. Remove from the heat and stir in the tangerine sections and bell pepper. Cover the sauce and let stand for at least 10 minutes, or until the hens are done.

5. Serve the sauce with the hens. Remove the skin before eating.

Makes 4 servings

Nutrition Information
values are per serving

CALORIES 335	DIETARY FIBER 2.5 G
TOTAL FAT 6.8 G	BETA CAROTENE 2.0 MG
SATURATED FAT 1.5 G	VITAMIN C 92 MG
CHOLESTEROL 114 MG	CALCIUM 64 MG
SODIUM 509 MG	IRON 2.5 MG

Lemon-Rosemary Roast Chicken with Pan Stuffing

Long ago wise cooks discovered how nicely the flavors of lemon, rosemary and roast chicken complement one another. Here, some delicious bonuses are added as well: a rub of apricot purée under the skin of the chicken before it roasts and a vegetable-filled stuffing as an accompaniment.

3 ounces sliced white bread, cut into cubes
½ cup dried apricots
⅓ cup plus 3 tablespoons water
3 tablespoons fresh lemon juice
1 tablespoon sugar
1 teaspoon rosemary
1 garlic clove
One 3½-pound chicken
½ teaspoon salt
1 teaspoon olive oil
½ cup minced scallions
1 large red bell pepper, diced
1 large green bell pepper, diced
1 cup frozen corn kernels
1 tablespoon no-salt-added tomato paste
2 teaspoons paprika
½ cup chicken broth, canned or homemade (p. 54)
1 tablespoon flour

1. Preheat the oven to 400°. Place the bread cubes on a baking sheet and bake until crisped, about 7 minutes. Leave the oven on and increase the temperature to 425°.

2. Meanwhile, in a food processor, combine the apricots, 3 tablespoons of water, 1 tablespoon of the lemon juice, the sugar, ½ teaspoon of the rosemary and the garlic. Process to a purée.

3. Rub the inside of the chicken with the salt and the remaining ½ teaspoon rosemary and 2 tablespoons lemon juice. With your fingers, carefully smear half of the apricot purée under the skin of the chicken. Place the chicken in a roasting pan, breast-side down, and roast for 30 minutes. Turn the chicken breast-side up and roast until the juices run clear and the chicken is cooked through, about 20 minutes.

4. Meanwhile, in a large nonstick skillet, warm the oil over medium heat until hot but not smoking. Stir in the scallions and cook until softened, about 1 minute.

5. Stir in the red and green bell peppers, and cook, stirring frequently, until softened, about 5 minutes.

6. Stir in the corn, tomato paste and paprika, and stir to coat. Stir in the bread cubes until moistened. Stir in the broth and the remaining apricot purée. Cook over medium heat until warmed through. Set aside and cover loosely to keep warm.

7. When the chicken is done, remove it to a carving board and let sit for 15 minutes before removing the skin and carving.

8. Meanwhile, pour the pan juices into a gravy separator and remove the fat. Transfer the degreased juices to a small saucepan and whisk in the flour. Cook over low heat, stirring constantly, until smooth, about 2 minutes. Stir in the remaining ⅓ cup water and cook until the gravy is thickened and no raw flour taste remains, about 3 minutes.

9. Carve the chicken and serve with the gravy and pan stuffing.

Makes 4 servings

Nutrition Information
values are per serving

CALORIES 463	DIETARY FIBER 3.9 G
TOTAL FAT 13 G	BETA CAROTENE 2.2 MG
SATURATED FAT 3.3 G	VITAMIN C 83 MG
CHOLESTEROL 127 MG	CALCIUM 79 MG
SODIUM 643 MG	IRON 4.3 MG

Broiled Carrot-Glazed Chicken

The look of this dish alone—the green of the spinach, the orange of the carrot sauce and the ivory of white-meat chicken—renders it captivating from the start. It is the carrot glaze, though, that gives the poultry a notable sweetness and resonance. Substitute Swiss chard for the spinach, if desired.

2 cups carrot juice
2 tablespoons honey
2 tablespoons red wine vinegar
½ teaspoon ground ginger
½ teaspoon salt
4 skinless, boneless chicken breast halves (1 pound total)
½ teaspoon thyme
1 teaspoon olive oil
1 garlic clove, minced
6 cups (loosely packed) stemmed spinach
½ teaspoon sugar
1 teaspoon cornstarch blended with 1 teaspoon water
⅛ teaspoon freshly ground black pepper

1. In a medium saucepan, stir together the carrot juice, honey, vinegar, ginger and ¼ teaspoon of the salt. Bring to a boil over medium heat and cook until reduced to 1¼ cups, about 10 minutes. Measure out ½ cup of the mixture to use as a glaze for the chicken; set the saucepan with the remaining carrot juice mixture aside.

2. Preheat the broiler with the broiler pan 5 inches from the heat. Rub the chicken with the thyme and the remaining ¼ teaspoon salt. Brush half of the carrot glaze over the chicken and broil for 4 minutes. Turn the chicken over, brush with the remaining carrot glaze and broil for 5 minutes, or until the chicken is golden and cooked through.

3. Meanwhile, in a large nonstick skillet, warm

the oil over medium heat until hot but not smoking. Add the garlic and cook until fragrant but not browned, about 2 minutes. Add the spinach, sprinkle with the sugar and cook until the spinach has wilted.

4. Stir the cornstarch mixture into the reserved carrot mixture in the saucepan. Cook the sauce over medium heat, stirring, until thickened, 1 to 2 minutes. Stir in the pepper.

5. To serve, spoon some spinach on a plate, top with the chicken and spoon the sauce over.

Makes 4 servings

NUTRITION INFORMATION
values are per serving

CALORIES 234	DIETARY FIBER 1.1 G
TOTAL FAT 2.9 G	BETA CAROTENE 21 MG
SATURATED FAT .6 G	VITAMIN C 24 MG
CHOLESTEROL 66 MG	CALCIUM 92 MG
SODIUM 417 MG	IRON 2.8 MG

Grilled Chicken with Tomato and Apricot Confit

Making confit—a jamlike reduction of fruits or vegetables—usually involves hours of cooking and stirring. Not so with this delicious mixture of fresh tomatoes, dried apricots and raisins, flavored with hot and sweet spices. Only thirty minutes of cooking, most of it unattended, is required: a very small investment for such a flavorful return.

1 cup coarsely chopped dried apricots (about 5 ounces)
¼ cup golden raisins
⅓ cup boiling water
2 cups diced tomatoes
½ cup sliced scallions

SUPER QUICK

Grilled Chicken Breast with Nectarine Salsa

Working time: 10 minutes Total time: 25 minutes

1 tablespoon sugar
¾ teaspoon salt
½ teaspoon ground ginger
½ teaspoon allspice
¼ teaspoon paprika
¼ teaspoon freshly ground black pepper
4 skinless, boneless chicken breast halves (1 pound total)
2 teaspoons olive oil
1 pound nectarines, cut into ½-inch dice
1 small red bell pepper, cut into ½-inch squares
½ cup diced red onion
1 teaspoon minced fresh or pickled jalapeño pepper
2 tablespoons fresh lime juice
2 tablespoons orange juice

1 In a small bowl, stir together ½ teaspoon of the sugar, ½ teaspoon of the salt, ¼ teaspoon of the ginger, ¼ teaspoon of the allspice, the paprika and black pepper. Rub the spice mixture onto the chicken, then rub in the oil. Let sit while you prepare the salsa.

2 In a medium bowl, stir together the nectarines, bell pepper, onion, jalapeño, lime juice, orange juice and the remaining 2½ teaspoons sugar and ¼ teaspoon each salt, ginger and allspice. Refrigerate until serving time.

3 Preheat the broiler or prepare the grill with the rack 6 inches from the heat. Broil the chicken about 4 minutes per side, or until golden brown and cooked through. Serve the chicken with the nectarine salsa spooned on top.

Makes 4 servings

Values are per serving:
Calories: 227 Total fat: 4.2 g Saturated fat: .7 g Cholesterol: 66 mg Sodium: 489 mg
Dietary fiber: 2.2 g Beta carotene: 1.0 mg Vitamin C: 43 mg Calcium: 32 mg Iron: 1.2 mg

¼ cup frozen orange juice concentrate, thawed
2 tablespoons honey
1 fresh red chili pepper, seeded and minced
2 teaspoons grated fresh ginger
½ teaspoon salt
½ teaspoon freshly ground black pepper
⅛ teaspoon allspice
4 skinless, boneless chicken breast halves (1 pound total)
2 tablespoons sliced unblanched almonds, toasted

1. Place the apricots and raisins in a medium bowl and add the boiling water. Let stand for 5 minutes or until the dried fruit has plumped and is tender. Drain and return to the bowl.

2. Stir in the tomatoes, scallions, orange juice concentrate, honey, chili pepper, ginger, ¼ teaspoon of the salt, ¼ teaspoon of the black pepper and half of the allspice. Cover and let the tomato-apricot confit stand for at least 20 minutes at room temperature.

3. Preheat the broiler and broiler pan.

4. Season the chicken on both sides with the remaining allspice, ¼ teaspoon salt and ¼ teaspoon black pepper. Place skinned-side down on the broiler pan rack and broil 3 to 4 inches from the heat for 5 to 6 minutes per side, or until cooked through.

5. Spread each piece of chicken with a heaping teaspoon of the confit and broil for 1 minute longer, or until the chicken is glazed.

6. Transfer the chicken to plates or a platter and brush with some of the juices from the confit. Sprinkle the almonds on top. Serve the chicken with the confit on the side.

Makes 4 servings

Nutrition Information
values are per serving

CALORIES 350	DIETARY FIBER 5.4 G
TOTAL FAT 4.1 G	BETA CAROTENE 2.7 MG
SATURATED FAT .6 G	VITAMIN C 74 MG
CHOLESTEROL 66 MG	CALCIUM 69 MG
SODIUM 364 MG	IRON 3.7 MG

Broiled Lemon Chicken with Carrot-Parsley Sauce

As main courses go, this one is exceptionally low in fat—a total of 1.5 grams per serving. It is also easy to prepare and would be particularly tasty served over spinach fettuccine, with steamed broccoli as an accompaniment. Keep it simple, with fruit ice and berries for dessert.

4 skinless, boneless chicken breast halves (1 pound total)
1½ teaspoons grated lemon zest
1 tablespoon plus 2 teaspoons fresh lemon juice
2 garlic cloves, crushed through a press
½ teaspoon thyme
¼ teaspoon salt
¼ teaspoon freshly ground black pepper
1 cup carrot juice
1 tablespoon cornstarch
Large pinch of cayenne pepper
2 tablespoons chopped parsley, preferably flat-leaf

1. Place the chicken on a plate. Sprinkle with the lemon zest, 1 tablespoon of the lemon juice, the garlic, ¼ teaspoon of the thyme, ⅛ teaspoon each of the salt and black pepper. Rub the seasonings into the surface. Cover loosely and set aside while you preheat the broiler and broiler pan.

2. Broil the chicken 4 to 5 inches from the heat for 5 minutes per side, or until cooked through. Transfer the chicken to a clean plate and cover loosely with foil to keep warm.

3. In a small saucepan, whisk the carrot juice and cornstarch until smooth. Stir in the cayenne and the remaining ¼ teaspoon thyme and ⅛ teaspoon each salt and black pepper.

4. Bring the carrot juice mixture to a boil over medium-high heat, stirring constantly. Cook until the sauce is lightly thickened. Remove from the heat, stir in the remaining 2 teaspoons lemon juice and the parsley. Stir in any juices that have collected on the plate under the chicken. Serve the sauce with the chicken.

Makes 4 servings

Nutrition Information
values are per serving

CALORIES 163	DIETARY FIBER .1 G
TOTAL FAT 1.5 G	BETA CAROTENE 9.6 MG
SATURATED FAT .4 G	VITAMIN C 13 MG
CHOLESTEROL 66 MG	CALCIUM 39 MG
SODIUM 228 MG	IRON 1.5 MG

Broiled Chicken with Mango–Avocado Chutney

Combining mango chutney with fresh mango and avocado makes a silky and complexly flavored accompaniment for the broiled chicken.

CHUTNEY

3 tablespoons prepared mango chutney (finely chop any large pieces)
2 tablespoons fresh lime juice
1 small fresh red chili pepper, seeded and minced
1 scallion, thinly sliced
¼ teaspoon salt
2 mangoes, diced
Half a medium avocado, diced
¼ cup chopped cilantro

CHICKEN

4 skinless, boneless chicken breast halves (1 pound total), lightly pounded
Grated zest of 1 lime
¼ teaspoon salt
⅛ teaspoon crushed red pepper flakes
1 teaspoon olive oil

1. To Make the Chutney In a medium bowl, mix the prepared chutney, lime juice, chili pepper, scallion and salt. Fold in the mangoes, avocado and cilantro. Cover and set aside.

2. To Cook the Chicken Preheat the broiler. Spray the broiler pan rack with nonstick cooking spray. Season the chicken on both sides with the lime zest, salt and red pepper flakes. Place on the prepared broiler pan and drizzle with the oil.

3. Broil 4 to 5 inches from the heat for about 6 minutes, turning once, until the chicken is cooked through. Serve with the chutney.

Makes 4 servings

Nutrition Information
values are per serving

CALORIES 258	DIETARY FIBER 1.2 G
TOTAL FAT 6.5 G	BETA CAROTENE 2.0 MG
SATURATED FAT 1.2 G	VITAMIN C 34 MG
CHOLESTEROL 66 MG	CALCIUM 30 MG
SODIUM 481 MG	IRON 1.2 MG

Country Captain Chicken

A classic curry recipe from the American south, Country Captain is said to have been named for a British officer who brought it back with him from a stay in India. Traditionally this is served with rice.

¼ cup flour
1 tablespoon plus 1 teaspoon curry powder
½ teaspoon thyme
¼ teaspoon salt

¼ teaspoon freshly ground black pepper
⅛ teaspoon cayenne pepper
2 pounds chicken drumsticks and thighs, skinned
2 teaspoons olive oil
Two 14½-ounce cans no-salt-added stewed tomatoes
1 large red bell pepper, diced
1 cup grated carrots
½ cup dried apricots
¼ cup dried currants
2 tablespoons apricot all-fruit spread
1 garlic clove, crushed through a press

1. Preheat the oven to 475°. Spray a 9-by-13-inch baking pan with nonstick cooking spray .

2. In a medium bowl, combine the flour, curry powder, thyme, salt, black pepper and cayenne. Measure out 2 tablespoons of the flour mixture and set aside. Dredge the chicken in the remaining mixture (using all of it) and arrange in a single layer in the prepared baking pan. Drizzle evenly with the oil.

3. Bake the chicken for about 10 minutes, turning once or twice, until lightly golden.

4. Meanwhile, in a medium saucepan, whisk the reserved flour mixture into the stewed tomatoes, taking care to not mash the tomatoes. Stir in the bell pepper, carrots, apricots, currants, apricot all-fruit spread and garlic. Bring to a boil over medium-high heat. Reduce the heat to medium-low and simmer, stirring frequently, until the sauce has thickened slightly and the flavors are blended, about 5 minutes.

5. Pour the sauce evenly over the chicken and cover the pan with foil. Reduce the oven temperature to 350° and bake for 30 minutes, or until the chicken is tender.

Makes 4 servings

SUPER QUICK

Chicken with Spinach and Cheese

Working time: 30 minutes Total time: 30 minutes

4 thin chicken breast cutlets (¾ pound total)
1 tablespoon flour
1 tablespoon plus 1 teaspoon olive oil
½ cup chopped scallions
2 garlic cloves, minced
⅓ cup chicken broth, canned or homemade (p. 54)
1 teaspoon oregano
¼ teaspoon salt
¼ teaspoon freshly ground black pepper
½ cup chopped mushrooms
1 pound spinach, stemmed
3 ounces part-skim mozzarella, shredded

1 Lightly dredge the chicken in the flour; reserve the excess. Preheat the broiler.

2 Meanwhile, in a large nonstick skillet, warm the oil over medium-high heat. Add the chicken and brown on both sides, about 6 minutes. Transfer to a plate and cover loosely.

3 Add the scallions, garlic and 2 tablespoons of broth to the skillet, and cook, stirring, until fragrant, about 1 minute. Sprinkle on the reserved flour and cook, stirring, until the flour is no longer visible, about 30 seconds. Add the remaining broth, the oregano, salt and pepper, and bring to a boil, stirring frequently.

4 Add the mushrooms and spinach, then cover and cook for 30 seconds. Uncover and stir until the spinach is just wilted, about 1 minute. Pour in any juices that have collected under the chicken on the plate.

5 Place the chicken on a broiler pan. Dividing evenly, spread the spinach-mushroom mixture on top of the chicken. Sprinkle the cheese on top and broil 4 inches from the heat for 3 minutes, or until the cheese is bubbly.

Makes 4 servings

Values are per serving:
Calories: 225 Total fat: 9.4 g Saturated fat: 3.1 g Cholesterol: 62 mg Sodium: 438 mg
Dietary fiber: 2.6 g Beta carotene: 3.4 mg Vitamin C: 27 mg Calcium: 248 mg Iron: 3.5 mg

Nutrition Information
values are per serving

CALORIES 370	DIETARY FIBER 8.7 G
TOTAL FAT 8.0 G	BETA CAROTENE 6.9 MG
SATURATED FAT 1.6 G	VITAMIN C 83 MG
CHOLESTEROL 104 MG	CALCIUM 124 MG
SODIUM 296 MG	IRON 5.3 MG

Roasted Chicken and Sweet Potatoes with Pepper Sauce

Some of the best flavors of Mexican cooking—chili peppers and cocoa, to be specific—flavor the spirited sauce on this otherwise simple sweet potato and chicken roast. Should you have trouble finding a poblano chili pepper, which can range in taste from mild to hottish, substitute a small green bell pepper; it will also lend depth to the dish, just somewhat less intriguingly.

2 teaspoons olive oil
6 garlic cloves–3 whole but peeled and 3 minced
¾ teaspoon rosemary, crumbled
2 pounds sweet potatoes, peeled and cut into ½-inch chunks
4 whole chicken legs (drumstick and thigh), skinned (2 pounds total)
½ teaspoon sugar
½ teaspoon paprika
½ teaspoon salt
¾ cup canned chicken broth diluted with ¾ cup water, or 1½ cups Homemade Chicken Broth (p. 54)
1 large onion, thinly sliced
1 large red bell pepper, cut into thin slivers
1 poblano pepper or small green bell pepper, thinly sliced
½ cup pitted prunes
1½ teaspoons minced pickled jalapeño pepper
2 teaspoons unsweetened cocoa powder

1. Preheat the oven to 375°. In a large roasting pan, combine the oil, the 3 whole garlic cloves and the rosemary. Heat in the oven for 5 minutes, or until fragrant.

2. Add the sweet potatoes and chicken, sprinkle with the sugar, paprika and ¼ teaspoon of the salt, and roast for 7 minutes, or until the sweet potatoes are lightly colored; stir the sweet potatoes and chicken once or twice for more even cooking.

3. Stir in ¼ cup of the diluted chicken broth, return to the oven and cook until the chicken and potatoes are cooked through, about 7 minutes.

4. Meanwhile, in a large nonstick skillet, combine the 3 cloves minced garlic, the remaining 1¼ cups diluted broth, the onion, red bell pepper, poblano pepper, prunes, jalapeño, cocoa and remaining ¼ teaspoon salt. Cook over medium heat until the vegetables are softened, about 7 minutes.

5. Transfer the mixture to a food processor or blender and process to a smooth purée.

6. Serve the chicken and sweet potatoes topped with the sweet and hot pepper sauce.

Makes 4 servings

Nutrition Information
values are per serving

CALORIES 449	DIETARY FIBER 8.1 G
TOTAL FAT 8.4 G	BETA CAROTENE 21 MG
SATURATED FAT 1.7 G	VITAMIN C 146 MG
CHOLESTEROL 104 MG	CALCIUM 94 MG
SODIUM 612 MG	IRON 3.7 MG

Red-Roasted Drumsticks with Spicy Red Pepper Purée

A dry rub—such as the Cajun-style one used on these drumsticks—can provides a powerful flavor component with an added benefit: It requires only a very little fat.

CHICKEN

1 tablespoon paprika
1 teaspoon garlic powder
1 teaspoon dry mustard
¾ teaspoon thyme
½ teaspoon onion powder
½ teaspoon salt
½ teaspoon freshly ground black pepper
2 pounds chicken drumsticks, skinned
2 teaspoons olive oil, preferably extra-virgin

RED PEPPER PUREE

2 large red bell peppers, cut into chunks
1 fresh jalapeño pepper, halved, some seeds removed
2 garlic cloves, sliced
½ cup chicken broth, canned or homemade (p. 54)
2 teaspoons fresh lemon juice

1. To Make the Chicken Preheat the oven to 325°. Spray a 9-by-13-inch baking dish with nonstick cooking spray.

2. In a small bowl or cup, combine the paprika, garlic powder, mustard, thyme, onion powder, salt and black pepper. Cut two or three deep, lengthwise slits in each drumstick and place in the prepared baking dish. Rub the spice mixture onto the chicken, pressing it into the slits. Let stand for 10 minutes.

3. Drizzle the chicken with the oil and bake, turning once or twice, for 35 to 45 minutes, or until well browned and cooked through.

4. To Make the Red Pepper Purée In a medium saucepan, combine the bell peppers, jalapeño, garlic and chicken broth. Stir well, cover and bring to a boil over high heat. Reduce the heat to medium-low and simmer, stirring occasionally, until the vegetables are tender, about 15 minutes (most of the liquid will evaporate).

5. Purée in a food processor or blender until very smooth. Stir in the lemon juice and serve with the chicken.

Makes 4 servings

Nutrition Information
values are per serving

CALORIES 199	DIETARY FIBER .9 G
TOTAL FAT 7.2 G	BETA CAROTENE 2.4 MG
SATURATED FAT 1.4 G	VITAMIN C 111 MG
CHOLESTEROL 94 MG	CALCIUM 36 MG
SODIUM 507 MG	IRON 2.4 MG

North African-Style Chicken Kebabs

For an authentic North African-style meal, serve these colorful chicken and vegetable kebabs over a bed of couscous, then present a platter of chilled orange slices sprinkled with rosewater and chopped almonds for dessert.

1 medium sweet potato (8 ounces)–peeled, halved lengthwise and cut crosswise into ½-inch-thick half-rounds
2 scallions, cut into 1-inch pieces
2 garlic cloves, peeled
4 thin slices (quarter-size) unpeeled fresh ginger
¼ cup (packed) cilantro leaves
½ teaspoon paprika, preferably sweet Hungarian
½ teaspoon salt
¼ teaspoon freshly ground black pepper
⅛ teaspoon cayenne pepper
Pinch of saffron or turmeric

2 tablespoons fresh lemon juice
1 tablespoon olive oil
1 pound skinless, boneless chicken breasts, cut into 1-inch chunks
1 medium zucchini, cut into ½-inch slices
8 cherry tomatoes
8 thin slices of lemon
8 bay leaves, preferably imported

1. Bring a medium saucepan of water to a boil. Add the sweet potato and cook until just barely tender but still firm enough to thread on a skewer, about 6 minutes. Rinse under cold water to stop the cooking.

2. In a food processor or blender, finely chop the scallions, garlic, ginger and cilantro. Add the paprika, salt, black pepper, cayenne, saffron, lemon juice and olive oil, and process until blended.

3. Place the sweet potato, chicken and zucchini in a large nonreactive mixing bowl and pour the saffron mixture over. Mix well, cover and marinate at room temperature while you preheat the broiler or prepare the grill. (For the most flavor, let the chicken and vegetables marinate for at least 30 minutes.)

4. Preheat the broiler or prepare the grill. On 4 skewers, alternately thread the sweet potato, chicken, zucchini, cherry tomatoes, lemon slices and bay leaves. Reserve any leftover marinade.

5. Broil or grill the skewers 3 to 4 inches from the heat for 6 to 8 minutes, turning the skewers once or twice, until the chicken and vegetables are just cooked through. Brush the skewers with any leftover marinade as they cook.

Makes 4 servings

NUTRITION INFORMATION
values are per serving

CALORIES 228	DIETARY FIBER 1.9 G
TOTAL FAT 5.3 G	BETA CAROTENE 5.3 MG
SATURATED FAT .9 G	VITAMIN C 41 MG
CHOLESTEROL 66 MG	CALCIUM 71 MG
SODIUM 359 MG	IRON 2.6 MG

Chicken and Roasted Root Vegetables

Herbed chicken with tomato overtones roasts alongside a wonderful combination of sweet potatoes, regular pototoes, carrots and parsnips—a perfect fall dinner that needs only a green salad, crusty bread and a simple dessert to be complete.

¼ cup no-salt-added tomato paste
2 teaspoons paprika
1 teaspoon rosemary, crumbled
¾ teaspoon salt
2 pounds chicken drumsticks and thighs, skinned
½ cup (not oil-packed) sun-dried tomatoes
1 cup boiling water
1½ cups peeled, diced sweet potatoes
1 cup diced unpeeled all-purpose potatoes
1 cup sliced carrots
1 cup sliced parsnips
4 garlic cloves, peeled
2 teaspoons light brown sugar
¼ teaspoon freshly ground black pepper

1. Preheat the oven to 400°. Spray a small baking dish with nonstick cooking spray.

2. In a small bowl or cup, stir together the tomato paste, paprika, ½ teaspoon of the rosemary and ½ teaspoon of the salt. Rub the chicken with the tomato paste mixture; place in the prepared baking dish and set aside.

3. In a small heatproof bowl, combine the sun-dried tomatoes and water. Let sit until the tomatoes have softened, about 10 minutes. Reserving the liquid, drain the tomatoes and coarsely chop.

4. In a 9-by-13-inch baking pan, stir together the sweet potatoes, all-purpose potatoes, carrots, parsnips, garlic, brown sugar, pepper and the remaining ½ teaspoon rosemary and ¼ teaspoon salt. Stir in the sun-dried tomatoes and their soaking liquid. Cover with aluminum foil and bake in the oven for 15 minutes. Uncover and bake until the vegetables are tender, about 15 minutes. Put the chicken in the oven for the last 20 minutes of the vegetable cooking time.

Makes 4 servings

Nutrition Information
values are per serving

CALORIES 333	DIETARY FIBER 7.0 G
TOTAL FAT 6.1 G	BETA CAROTENE 12 MG
SATURATED FAT 1.4 G	VITAMIN C 64 MG
CHOLESTEROL 104 MG	CALCIUM 79 MG
SODIUM 568 MG	IRON 3.8 MG

Baked Chicken with Tomatoes and Sweet Potatoes

The complementary flavors of tomato and feta cheese are a tangy counterpoint to the sweet potatoes in this satisyfing baked chicken dish.

2 tablespoons chicken broth, canned or homemade (p. 54)
1 tablespoon fresh lemon juice
1 teaspoon oregano
½ teaspoon freshly ground black pepper
¼ teaspoon salt
1¼ pounds unpeeled sweet potatoes, cut into ¾-inch chunks
1 pound plum tomatoes, cut into ½-inch chunks
8 skinless bone-in chicken thighs (1½ pounds total)
2 ounces crumbled feta cheese

1. Preheat the oven to 400°. Spray a 9-by-13-inch baking dish with nonstick cooking spray.

2. In a small bowl or cup, mix the broth, lemon juice, oregano, pepper and salt.

3. Arrange the sweet potatoes and tomatoes in the baking dish. Drizzle evenly with half of the broth mixture. Place the chicken on top of the vegetables and drizzle with the remaining broth mixture.

4. Cover with foil and bake for 45 minutes, occasionally spooning the pan juices over the chicken and vegetables. Uncover and bake for 15 to 20 minutes, or until the chicken is cooked through and the vegetables are tender.

5. Crumble the feta evenly over the top of the chicken and vegetables and bake for 3 to 4 minutes longer, or until the cheese is melted.

Makes 4 servings

Nutrition Information
values are per serving

CALORIES 364	DIETARY FIBER 5.8 G
TOTAL FAT 9.0 G	BETA CAROTENE 18 MG
SATURATED FAT 3.5 G	VITAMIN C 59 MG
CHOLESTEROL 116 MG	CALCIUM 128 MG
SODIUM 460 MG	IRON 3.0 MG

Chicken and Rice Casserole with Fresh Tomato Garnish

It is well worth the effort here to seek out basmati rice—an imported aromatic grain with a singular nutty flavor and wonderful chewy texture. Look for it in better supermarkets or in specialty food stores.

2 teaspoons olive oil
1 large onion, chopped
3 garlic cloves, minced
¾ cup basmati rice
1¼ cups canned chicken broth diluted with 1 cup water, or 2¼ cups Homemade Chicken Broth (p. 54)

1 pound skinless, boneless chicken thighs
1¾ pounds asparagus, cut on the diagonal into 2-inch lengths
1 cup frozen peas
¾ teaspoon marjoram
2 cups chopped tomatoes
3 tablespoons minced scallions
1 tablespoon red wine vinegar

1. In a Dutch oven or flameproof casserole, warm the oil over medium heat until hot but not smoking. Add the onion and garlic, and cook, stirring frequently, until softened, about 5 minutes.

2. Add the rice, stirring to coat. Add the diluted chicken broth and bring to a boil over medium heat. Reduce the heat to medium-low, cover and cook for 10 minutes.

3. Place the chicken on top of the rice mixture, cover and cook for 5 minutes. Add the asparagus, peas and marjoram, stir to combine, cover and cook until the chicken is cooked through and the asparagus is tender, about 5 minutes.

4. Meanwhile, in a medium bowl, stir together the tomatoes, scallions and vinegar.

5. Serve the chicken and rice casserole hot, with the fresh tomato garnish on top.

Makes 4 servings

NUTRITION INFORMATION
values are per serving

CALORIES 377	DIETARY FIBER 4.9 G
TOTAL FAT 8.5 G	BETA CAROTENE 1.1 MG
SATURATED FAT 1.6 G	VITAMIN C 67 MG
CHOLESTEROL 94 MG	CALCIUM 71 MG
SODIUM 475 MG	IRON 3.3 MG

SUPER QUICK

Stir-Fried Chicken with Shiitakes, Watercress and Carrots

Working time: 15 minutes Total time: 30 minutes

- 1 pound skinless, boneless chicken breasts, cut crosswise into ½-inch-wide slices
- 2 tablespoons dry sherry
- 1 tablespoon reduced-sodium soy sauce
- 1 tablespoon grated fresh ginger
- 4 teaspoons olive oil
- 2 large carrots, cut on the diagonal into long, thin slices
- 8 ounces fresh shiitake or large white mushrooms, sliced
- 6 cups watercress, tough stems removed
- 1 tablespoon cornstarch
- ½ cup chicken broth, canned or homemade (p. 54)
- 1 tablespoon oyster sauce
- ¼ teaspoon sugar

1 Toss the chicken with 1 tablespoon of the sherry, 2 teaspoons of the soy sauce and 2 teaspoons of the ginger.

2 In a large nonstick skillet, warm 2 teaspoons of the oil over high heat until hot but not smoking. Add the chicken and stir-fry until it turns white, 3 to 4 minutes. Transfer the chicken to a bowl.

3 Add the remaining 2 teaspoons oil to the pan and heat. Add the carrots and stir-fry until slightly softened, about 1 minute. Add the shiitake mushrooms and stir-fry until tender, about 2 minutes. Stir in the chicken (and any juices that have collected in the bowl) and the watercress and remove the pan from the heat.

4 In a small bowl, blend the cornstarch with the diluted chicken broth, the oyster sauce, sugar, the remaining 1 tablespoon sherry, 1 teaspoon soy sauce and 1 teaspoon ginger. Pour over the chicken mixture and toss to coat well.

5 Return the pan to high heat and stir-fry until the juices are thickened and the watercress is wilted, 2 to 3 minutes.

Makes 4 servings

Values are per serving:
Calories: 239 Total fat: 6.4 g Saturated fat: 1.0 g Cholesterol: 66 mg Sodium: 573 mg
Dietary fiber: 3.8 g Beta carotene: 10 mg Vitamin C: 35 mg Calcium: 109 mg Iron: 2.2 mg

Coq au Vin Blanc

White wine—not red—lends its inimitable flavor to this homespun, but classic, French dish. If you use chicken breasts for this, cut them into smaller serving pieces before cooking.

¼ cup flour
½ teaspoon freshly ground black pepper
¼ teaspoon salt
2 pounds bone-in chicken parts, skinned
2 teaspoons olive oil
1 ounce Canadian bacon, diced
2 garlic cloves, minced
¾ teaspoon thyme
2 bay leaves, preferably imported
½ cup canned chicken broth diluted with ½ cup water, or 1 cup Homemade Chicken Broth (p. 54)
1 cup dry white wine
3 cups carrot sticks
½ pound small mushrooms or quartered large mushrooms
1 cup frozen pearl onions

1. Preheat the oven to 450°. Spray a 9-by-13-inch baking pan with nonstick cooking spray.

2. On a sheet of wax paper, mix the flour with ¼ teaspoon of the pepper and ⅛ teaspoon of the salt. Dredge the chicken in the seasoned flour, reserving any leftover dredging mixture. Arrange the chicken in a single layer in the prepared pan and drizzle it with 1 teaspoon of the oil. Bake for 15 minutes, turning once or twice, until the chicken is lightly golden.

3. Meanwhile, in a Dutch oven or flameproof casserole, combine the remaining 1 teaspoon oil with the Canadian bacon, garlic, thyme and bay leaves. Stir-fry over medium heat just until the mixture is fragrant, 2 to 3 minutes.

4. Stir in the reserved dredging mixture and cook, stirring, until the flour is well incorporated, about 30 seconds. Whisk in the diluted broth, then stir in the wine until smooth.

5. Add the chicken (and any juices from the baking pan), the carrots, mushrooms, onions and the remaining ¼ teaspoon pepper and ⅛ teaspoon salt. Cover and bring to a boil over high heat, stirring occasionally. Reduce the heat to medium-low and simmer, stirring occasionally, until the chicken is cooked through and the vegetables are tender, about 30 minutes.

Makes 4 servings

Nutrition Information
values are per serving

CALORIES 268	DIETARY FIBER 3.6 G
TOTAL FAT 7.0 G	BETA CAROTENE 14 MG
SATURATED FAT 1.4 G	VITAMIN C 18 MG
CHOLESTEROL 80 MG	CALCIUM 77 MG
SODIUM 481 MG	IRON 3.5 MG

Sautéed Chicken with Lemon-Basil Pasta

From Greece, the world has learned just how appealing the rice-shaped pasta called orzo can be when it is flavored with lemon. Here, vegetables, chicken and fresh basil further enhance that delicious combination, and all in one dish.

1¼ cups canned chicken broth diluted with 1¼ cups water, or 2½ cups Homemade Chicken Broth (p. 54)
8 ounces orzo or other very small pasta shape
1 cup diced carrot
1 red bell pepper, cut into 1-inch pieces
1 cup small broccoli florets
1 tablespoon olive oil
½ cup chopped scallions
1 garlic clove, minced

1 pound skinless, boneless chicken breasts, cut into 1-inch cubes
3 tablespoons fresh lemon juice
3 tablespoons chopped fresh basil
1 teaspoon grated lemon zest
½ teaspoon freshly ground black pepper

1. In a medium covered saucepan, bring the diluted chicken broth to a boil over medium-high heat. Add the orzo and carrot, and return to a boil. Reduce the heat to low, cover and simmer for 12 minutes.

2. Add the bell pepper and broccoli and cook until the broccoli and pasta are tender, about 4 minutes.

3. Meanwhile, in a medium nonstick skillet, warm the oil over medium-high heat until hot but not smoking. Add the scallions and garlic, and cook, stirring, until the garlic is fragrant, about 30 seconds. Add the chicken and cook, stirring, until it is cooked through, about 8 minutes.

4. Stir 1 tablespoon of the lemon juice into the chicken mixture and remove from the heat.

5. Add the orzo mixture, the basil, lemon zest, black pepper and remaining 2 tablespoons lemon juice to the skillet and stir to combine.

Makes 4 servings

Nutrition Information
values are per serving

CALORIES 411	DIETARY FIBER 4.0 G
TOTAL FAT 6.3 G	BETA CAROTENE 5.7 MG
SATURATED FAT 1.0 G	VITAMIN C 71 MG
CHOLESTEROL 66 MG	CALCIUM 79 MG
SODIUM 406 MG	IRON 4.2 MG

Chicken and Red Vegetable Stir-Fry

The technique of stir-frying not only saves time for the cook, it also preserves the colors, flavors and textures of all the ingredients in the dish. In this delicious example, strips of chicken, red onion, red cabbage and red bell pepper are quickly cooked in a hot-and-sweet sauce.

1 tablespoon cornstarch
⅓ cup dry sherry
2 tablespoons reduced-sodium soy sauce
1 tablespoon minced garlic
1 tablespoon light brown sugar
½ teaspoon crushed red pepper flakes
2 tablespoons olive oil
1 pound skinless, boneless chicken breast, cut across the grain into ½-inch-wide strips
1 large red onion, halved lengthwise then sliced crosswise into half-rounds
1½ cups finely shredded red cabbage
2 medium red bell peppers, cut into strips
1 navel orange, peeled and cut crosswise into slices

1. In a small cup or bowl, blend the cornstarch with the sherry, soy sauce, garlic, brown sugar and red pepper flakes. Set aside.

2. In a large nonstick skillet, warm 2 teaspoons of the oil over medium-high heat until hot but not smoking. Add the chicken and stir-fry until just barely cooked, about 2 minutes. With a slotted spoon, transfer the chicken to a plate and cover loosely to keep warm.

3. Add 2 teaspoons of the oil to the skillet and heat. Add the onion and stir-fry until softened, about 3 minutes. Add the remaining 2 teaspoons oil and the cabbage and bell peppers, and stir-fry until crisp-tender, about 2 minutes.

4. Add the reserved sherry mixture to the skillet along with the chicken (and any juices that have collected on the plate). Cook over medium-high heat until the sauce thickens and the chicken is cooked through, about 3 minutes.

5. Serve the stir-fry topped with the orange slices.

Makes 4 servings

NUTRITION INFORMATION
values are per serving

CALORIES 303	DIETARY FIBER 3.0 G
TOTAL FAT 8.5 G	BETA CAROTENE 1.4 MG
SATURATED FAT 1.3 G	VITAMIN C 112 MG
CHOLESTEROL 66 MG	CALCIUM 74 MG
SODIUM 387 MG	IRON 1.8 MG

Apricot-Ginger Chicken with Sweet Potato Pancakes

Just as sweet potatoes can be used in bread dough, so can they be employed in batter for pancakes, which here are rolled to enclose an exceptional filling of chicken in an apricot-ginger sauce.

1 medium sweet potato (about 8 ounces), peeled and sliced
1 cup apple juice
½ cup dried apricots, diced
¼ cup dry white wine
2 tablespoons grated fresh ginger
1 clove
1 cup lowfat (1%) milk
2 eggs, lightly beaten
2 teaspoons unsalted butter, melted
½ cup flour
1 pound skinless, boneless chicken breasts
½ teaspoon vegetable oil

1. In a medium saucepan of boiling water, cook the sweet potato, covered, until tender, about 7 minutes. Drain well, place in a medium bowl and mash lightly with a fork (there should be about ½ cup).

2. In a large saucepan, combine the apple juice, apricots, wine, ginger and clove. Bring to a boil over high heat, then reduce the heat to low, cover and simmer while you prepare the sweet potato pancake mixture.

3. To the mashed sweet potato, add the milk, eggs and butter, and beat until well combined. Blend in the flour and set aside.

4. Add the chicken breasts to the simmering apricot-ginger mixture. Cover and poach until cooked through, 6 to 8 minutes. With a slotted spoon, remove the chicken from the poaching liquid and set aside to cool to room temperature.

5. Uncover the poaching liquid and cook over medium heat until reduced and syrupy, about 4 minutes. Remove the apricot-ginger sauce from the heat and set aside.

6. Meanwhile, in a medium nonstick skillet, warm the oil over medium heat. Add about ¼ cup of the sweet potato batter and cook for 2 minutes, then flip and cook until the second side is done, about 1 minute. Repeat with the remaining batter to make a total of 8 pancakes. As you cook them, keep the pancakes warm (and covered loosely with foil) in a low oven.

7. Cut the chicken breast into thin slices and add to the apricot sauce. Toss to coat well.

8. To serve, wrap the apricot-ginger chicken in a sweet potato pancake and serve two stuffed pancakes per person.

Makes 4 servings

NUTRITION INFORMATION
values are per serving

CALORIES 380	DIETARY FIBER 3.0 G
TOTAL FAT 7.4 G	BETA CAROTENE 5.6 MG
SATURATED FAT 2.9 G	VITAMIN C 38 MG
CHOLESTEROL 180 MG	CALCIUM 125 MG
SODIUM 146 MG	IRON 3.2 MG

Moo Shoo Chicken

Here are all the classic components of the great Chinese dish moo shoo pork—the pancakes, the mushrooms, the eggs and the filling—but in this dish the components are classically Western. Porcini mushrooms, not the traditional Chinese tree ear mushrooms, provide earthiness; tortillas act as wrappers instead of the famous thin Mandarin pancakes. Note, though, that there is no substitute for the singular garlicky soybean sauce known as hoisin.

½ ounce dried wild mushrooms, such as porcini
½ cup canned chicken broth diluted with ¼ cup water, or ¾ cup Homemade Chicken Broth (p. 54)
8 ounces skinless, boneless chicken breasts, cut crosswise into ½-inch strips
1½ teaspoons reduced-sodium soy sauce
1 teaspoon sugar
1 tablespoon olive oil
1 fresh jalapeño pepper, minced, with some of the seeds
1 tablespoon plus 1 teaspoon grated fresh ginger
3 large carrots, cut into long julienne strips
3 cups small broccoli florets
1 large red bell pepper, cut into thin strips
1 egg
1 egg white
½ cup diagonally sliced scallions
Eight 8-inch flour tortillas, heated
2 tablespoons plus 2 teaspoons hoisin sauce

1. In a small saucepan, combine the mushrooms and diluted chicken broth. Bring to a boil over high heat. Remove from the heat, cover and let stand until softened, about 5 minutes.

2. Lift the mushrooms from the broth with a slotted spoon. Strain the broth though a strainer lined with cheesecloth, leaving any sediment behind. Pour the broth into a medium skillet. Chop the mushrooms and set aside.

3. Place the broth over medium heat and bring to a boil. Stir in the chicken and simmer, turning frequently, until cooked through, 3 to 5 minutes.

4. With a slotted spoon, transfer the chicken to a plate and drizzle with ¾ teaspoon of the soy sauce and the sugar. Cover to keep moist.

5. Over high heat, reduce the broth in the skillet by half and set aside.

6. In a large nonstick skillet, warm the oil over high heat. Stir in the jalapeño and ginger, and stir-fry until fragrant, 20 to 30 seconds.

7. Add the carrots, broccoli, bell pepper and the remaining ¾ teaspoon soy sauce, and stir-fry until the vegetables begin to soften, about 2 minutes. Add the reduced broth, the chopped mushrooms and the chicken, and bring to a simmer. Reduce the heat to low, cover and simmer for 5 minutes.

8. Meanwhile, in a small bowl, beat the whole egg and egg white together until frothy.

9. Increase the heat under the skillet with the vegetables and chicken to medium-high. Pour in the eggs and scramble just until set, 1 to 2 minutes. Remove from the heat and sprinkle with the scallions.

10. To serve, spread each tortilla with 1 teaspoon of the hoisin sauce, add the chicken and vegetable mixture and roll up. Serve 2 tortillas per person.

Makes 4 servings

Nutrition Information
values are per serving

CALORIES 452	DIETARY FIBER 8.7 G
TOTAL FAT 11 G	BETA CAROTENE 14 MG
SATURATED FAT 1.8 G	VITAMIN C 137 MG
CHOLESTEROL 86 MG	CALCIUM 181 MG
SODIUM 994 MG	IRON 5.5 MG

Caribbean Chicken with Nectarines, Sweet Potatoes and Bananas

The cooking of the Caribbean Islands frequently uses fruits in savory dishes, often laced with a spiciness that could combat even the most withering heat. This sautéed chicken dish demonstrates the concept by combining the sweetness of bananas, nectarines and apricot jam with the heat of pickled jalapeño peppers. To relish every last drop of the delicious sauce, serve this over rice.

¾ pound sweet potatoes–peeled, halved lengthwise and cut crosswise into ½-inch half-rounds
1 tablespoon olive oil
½ pound lean ground chicken or turkey
1 large nectarine, cut into thin wedges
¼ cup orange marmalade or apricot all-fruit spread
¼ cup Dijon or grainy mustard
1 teaspoon thinly sliced fresh or pickled jalapeño pepper
2 medium firm-ripe bananas, sliced
¼ cup thinly sliced scallions

1. Bring a large saucepan of water to a boil. Add the sweet potatoes and return to a boil; then reduce the heat to medium-low, cover and simmer until tender, about 10 minutes. Drain well.

2. In a large nonstick skillet, warm the oil over medium-high heat until hot but not smoking. Add the chicken and sauté until opaque and cooked through, about 2 minutes.

3. Reduce the heat to medium and add the sweet potatoes, nectarine, marmalade, mustard and jalapeño pepper. Cook, tossing gently, until heated through, about 2 minutes.

SUPER QUICK

Smoked Turkey with Braised Greens

Working time: 15 minutes Total time: 30 minutes

½ cup (not oil-packed) sun-dried tomatoes
1 cup boiling water
1 teaspoon olive oil
1 ounce Canadian bacon, diced
2 large onions, cut into 1-inch cubes
3 garlic cloves, minced
¾ pound broccoli rabe
4 ounces Swiss chard, cut crosswise into ½-inch slices
½ cup golden raisins
½ cup reduced-sodium chicken broth
½ teaspoon crushed red pepper flakes
⅛ teaspoon freshly ground black pepper
9 ounces lean smoked turkey breast, cut into ½-inch dice

1 In a small heatproof bowl, combine the sun-dried tomatoes and boiling water. Set aside to soften, about 10 minutes. Reserving the soaking liquid, drain the tomatoes and coarsely chop.

2 In a large nonstick skillet, warm the oil over medium heat until hot but not smoking. Add the Canadian bacon and cook for 30 seconds. Stir in the onions and garlic, and cook, stirring frequently, until the onions have softened, about 5 minutes.

3 Stir in the broccoli rabe and Swiss chard, stirring to coat. Add the sun-dried tomatoes and the reserved soaking liquid, the raisins, chicken broth, red pepper flakes and black pepper. Cover and cook, stirring occasionally, until the greens have wilted and are tender, about 7 minutes.

4 Stir in the smoked turkey and cook until heated through. Serve hot.

Makes 4 servings

Values are per serving:
Calories: 242 Total fat: 3.4 g Saturated fat: .6 g Cholesterol: 31 mg Sodium: 944 mg
Dietary fiber: 6.9 g Beta carotene: 3.7 mg Vitamin C: 95 mg Calcium: 127 mg Iron: 3.9 mg

4. Add the bananas and cook until heated through, 1 to 2 minutes. Serve the mixture sprinkled with the sliced scallions.

Makes 4 servings

Nutrition Information
values are per serving

CALORIES 324	DIETARY FIBER 3.6 G
TOTAL FAT 10 G	BETA CAROTENE 7.6 MG
SATURATED FAT 1.9 G	VITAMIN C 27 MG
CHOLESTEROL 47 MG	CALCIUM 47 MG
SODIUM 517 MG	IRON 1.9 MG

Mexican-Style Chicken and Vegetables

Although most Americans think of chocolate as belonging in the dessert category, Mexican cuisine uses it to great effect in savory dishes, such as the classic sauce, *mole poblano.* You will find *mole*-like tones in the sauce for this chicken and vegetable dish, which uses both chocolate and cinnamon, another common ingredient in Mexican cuisine. You might also try making this dish with turkey, a frequent companion of *moles.*

1 pound skinless, boneless chicken breasts
2 teaspoons olive oil
1½ cups chopped red bell peppers
1½ cups chopped yellow summer squash
1½ cups chopped zucchini
1 cup medium-hot bottled salsa
2½ teaspoons light brown sugar
½ teaspoon cinnamon
Four 8-inch flour tortillas
½ ounce unsweetened chocolate, melted
1½ cups finely shredded Romaine lettuce
¼ cup light sour cream

1. In a covered skillet or a saucepan large enough to hold a cake rack, bring ½ inch of water to a boil. Place the chicken on a heatproof plate and place the plate on the cake rack in the skillet. Cover and steam until the chicken is cooked through, about 12 minutes. Set the chicken aside to cool to room temperature. When the chicken is cool enough to handle, shred it; reserve the cooking juices on the plate.

2. Meanwhile, in a large nonstick skillet, warm the oil over medium-high heat until hot but not smoking. Add the bell peppers, squash and zucchini, and cook, stirring, until beginning to soften. Stir in ¼ cup of the salsa, ½ teaspoon of the brown sugar and ¼ teaspoon of the cinnamon, and cook until the vegetables are tender, 3 to 4 minutes. Remove from the heat.

3. Preheat the oven to 400°. Place the tortillas directly on an oven rack and bake for 7 minutes, or until crisp (watch carefully; the tortillas can darken quickly).

4. In a small bowl, combine the chocolate with the remaining ¾ cup salsa, 2 teaspoons brown sugar, ¼ teaspoon cinnamon and the reserved cooking juices.

5. To assemble, place a tortilla in the center of each of 4 dinner plates. Top the tortillas with concentric rings of lettuce, sautéed vegetables and shredded chicken, starting in the middle with chicken and ending on the outside with lettuce. Dollop the chicken with sour cream and pass the sauce on the side.

Makes 4 servings

Nutrition Information
values are per serving

CALORIES 359	DIETARY FIBER 3.3 G
TOTAL FAT 10 G	BETA CAROTENE 2.1 MG
SATURATED FAT 3.2 G	VITAMIN C 128 MG
CHOLESTEROL 71 MG	CALCIUM 93 MG
SODIUM 608 MG	IRON 3.2 MG

Spicy Chicken Stir-Fry with Cherry Tomatoes and Carrots

Though not the most expected of ingredients in a Chinese stir-fry, the cherry tomatoes used here add their beautiful shape and color to strips of white chicken, carrot sticks and snow peas for a magnificent presentation.

2 cups water
1 cup brown rice
3 tablespoons reduced-sodium soy sauce
1 tablespoon plus 2 teaspoons cornstarch
1 tablespoon dry sherry or dry white wine
2 teaspoons sugar
1 teaspoon Oriental (dark) sesame oil
¼ teaspoon crushed red pepper flakes
¾ pound skinless, boneless chicken breasts, cut crosswise into ¼-inch strips
¼ cup chicken broth, canned or homemade (p. 54)
1 tablespoon vegetable oil
4 slices (quarter-size) fresh ginger, unpeeled
3 garlic cloves, minced
1 pint cherry tomatoes, halved
16 medium scallions, cut into 2-inch pieces
2 medium carrots, cut into ¼-by-3-inch matchsticks
4 ounces snow peas, trimmed

1. In a medium covered saucepan, bring the water to a boil over high heat. Add the rice and return the water to a boil. Reduce the heat to medium-low, cover, and simmer until the rice is tender and the water is absorbed, about 45 minutes.

2. Meanwhile, in a medium bowl, combine the soy sauce, 1 tablespoon of the cornstarch, the sherry, sugar, sesame oil and red pepper flakes. Add the chicken and toss to combine.

3. In a small bowl, combine the chicken broth and the remaining 2 teaspoons cornstarch.

4. In a large nonstick skillet, heat the vegetable oil over medium-high heat until hot but not smoking. Add the ginger and garlic, and stir-fry until the ginger is fragrant, about 30 seconds. Add the chicken and stir-fry until the chicken begins to brown, 2 to 3 minutes.

5. Add the tomatoes, scallions, carrots, snow peas and the broth-cornstarch mixture, and bring to a boil. Cook, stirring, until the carrots are crisp-tender, the sauce is lightly thickened and the chicken is cooked through, about 2 minutes.

6. Spoon the hot rice into 4 large bowls and top with the chicken stir-fry.

Makes 4 servings

NUTRITION INFORMATION
values are per serving

CALORIES 403	DIETARY FIBER 5.6 G
TOTAL FAT 7.4 G	BETA CAROTENE 6.5 MG
SATURATED FAT 1.2 G	VITAMIN C 43 MG
CHOLESTEROL 49 MG	CALCIUM 95 MG
SODIUM 599 MG	IRON 3.5 MG

Turkey and Broccoli Couscous with Red Pepper Harissa

The influence of North African cooking is apparent here in the use of couscous and harissa, a hot sauce from Tunisia. In Tunisia, harissa can be bewilderingly spicy, but our rendition of it has been tamed down for Western palates; increase the cayenne as you see fit.

HARISSA
2 garlic cloves, peeled
Two 4-ounce jars roasted red peppers, drained
⅛ teaspoon cayenne pepper
1 teaspoon olive oil

COUSCOUS

1 cup canned chicken broth diluted with 1 cup water, or 2 cups Homemade Chicken Broth (p. 54)
¾ teaspoon cumin
¾ teaspoon ground ginger
¾ teaspoon turmeric
½ teaspoon ground coriander
½ teaspoon paprika
⅛ teaspoon freshly ground black pepper
1 pound butternut squash–peeled, seeded and cut into 1-inch chunks
1 pound skinless turkey breast, cut into 2-inch chunks
1 large carrot, thinly sliced
2 cups small broccoli florets
⅔ cup couscous
1⅓ cups boiling water
1 tablespoon fresh lemon juice

1. To Make the Harissa In a small saucepan of boiling water, blanch the garlic for 3 minutes. In a food processor, combine the blanched garlic, roasted red peppers, cayenne and olive oil. Process to a smooth purée.

2. To Make the Couscous In a large saucepan, combine the diluted broth, cumin, ginger, turmeric, coriander, paprika and black pepper. Bring the broth to a boil over medium heat; then reduce to a simmer, cover and cook for 5 minutes to blend the flavors.

3. Stir in the squash and cook, uncovered, for 2 minutes. Stir in the turkey and carrot, and cook until the turkey is almost cooked through, about 3 minutes. Add the broccoli and cook until tender, about 3 minutes.

4. Meanwhile, place the couscous in a large heatproof bowl and pour the boiling water on top. Cover and let sit until the water has been absorbed and the couscous is tender, about 4 minutes.

5. Reserving the broth in the pan, transfer the vegetables and turkey with a slotted spoon to a serving platter. Arrange the turkey and vegetables around the outside of the platter, leaving a well in the center. Spoon the couscous into the center of the platter.

6. Bring the broth in the saucepan back to a simmer and stir in the harissa and the lemon juice. Spoon some of the harissa-enriched broth over the couscous, turkey and vegetables, and pass the remainder separately.

Makes 4 servings

Nutrition Information
values are per serving

CALORIES 354	DIETARY FIBER 3.1 G
TOTAL FAT 3.0 G	BETA CAROTENE 10 MG
SATURATED FAT .4 G	VITAMIN C 120 MG
CHOLESTEROL 70 MG	CALCIUM 114 MG
SODIUM 343 MG	IRON 4.5 MG

Turkey Scaloppine with Sautéed Melon

Sautéed fruit, like the cantaloupe here, can not only add enticing flavors to a dish, but can also enhance its eye appeal.

1½ teaspoons grated lemon zest
⅛ teaspoon crushed red pepper flakes
⅛ teaspoon salt
⅛ teaspoon freshly ground black pepper
Large pinch of nutmeg
4 turkey cutlets (1 pound total)
1 tablespoon olive oil
2 cups diced red bell peppers
¼ cup chicken broth, canned or homemade (p. 54)
1 tablespoon dry white wine

1 teaspoon cornstarch
2 teaspoons unsalted butter
1 small cantaloupe (2 pounds)—peeled, seeded and cut into thin wedges
1 lemon, cut into 4 wedges

1. In a small bowl or cup, combine the lemon zest, red pepper flakes, salt, black pepper and nutmeg. Season the turkey with the spice mixture.

2. In a large nonstick skillet, warm the oil over high heat until hot but not smoking. Add the turkey and sauté, turning once, until lightly browned and cooked through, about 4 minutes. Transfer the turkey to a platter and cover loosely to keep warm.

3. Add the bell peppers to the skillet and sauté until tender, 1 to 2 minutes. In a small bowl, whisk together the broth, wine and cornstarch until smooth. Pour over the peppers and cook over high heat, stirring to deglaze the pan. Cook, stirring, until the juices are reduced and thickened, 1 to 2 minutes. Pour the peppers and sauce over the turkey and re-cover.

4. Add the butter to the skillet and melt over medium heat. Add the melon slices and cook until just heated through, about 1 minute per side.

5. Serve the melon alongside the turkey and peppers, and accompany with lemon wedges for squeezing.

Makes 4 servings

Nutrition Information
values are per serving

CALORIES 235	DIETARY FIBER 1.6 G
TOTAL FAT 6.6 G	BETA CAROTENE 3.7 MG
SATURATED FAT 1.9 G	VITAMIN C 159 MG
CHOLESTEROL 76 MG	CALCIUM 47 MG
SODIUM 198 MG	IRON 2.0 MG

SUPER QUICK

Sweet-and-Sour Turkey Stir-Fry

Working time: 30 minutes Total time: 30 minutes

1⅓ cup water
⅔ cup rice
2 teaspoons vegetable oil
1 pound skinless turkey breast, cut into ½-inch-thick strips
1 tablespoon cornstarch
⅓ cup light ketchup
2 tablespoons rice wine vinegar or cider vinegar
1 tablespoon sugar
1 tablespoon reduced-sodium soy sauce
¼ teaspoon salt
1 tablespoon minced fresh ginger
3 garlic cloves, minced
2 large carrots, thinly sliced
2 cups sliced bok choy
2 cups cherry tomatoes
3 ounces snow peas, trimmed

1 In a medium covered saucepan, bring the water to a boil over high heat. Add the rice, reduce the heat to a simmer and cook, covered, until the water is absorbed and the rice is tender, about 20 minutes.

2 Meanwhile, in a large nonstick skillet, warm the oil over medium heat until hot but not smoking. Dust the turkey with the cornstarch, add to the skillet and sauté for 2 minutes. Transfer to a plate and cover loosely to keep warm.

3 In a small bowl, stir together the ketchup, vinegar, sugar, soy sauce and salt; set aside.

4 Add the ginger and garlic to the skillet and stir-fry until fragrant, about 30 seconds. Add the carrots, bok choy and cherry tomatoes, and stir-fry until the vegetables are crisp-tender, about 4 minutes. Add the snow peas and cook 30 seconds.

5 Stir in the ketchup mixture and bring to a boil. Return the turkey (and any juices that have collected on the plate) to the skillet and cook until just heated through. Serve the stir-fry over the hot rice.

Makes 4 servings

Values are per serving:
Calories: 343 Total fat: 3.6 g Saturated fat: .6 g Cholesterol: 70 mg Sodium: 534 mg
Dietary fiber: 3.1 g Beta carotene: 9.3 mg Vitamin C: 43 mg Calcium: 98 mg Iron: 4.1 mg

Turkey Scallops with Savory Fruit Compote

The mild flavor of turkey here serves as a brilliant foil for a cinnamony apricot-prune compote, one that would be equally good on chilled poached chicken breasts or grilled Cornish hens.

2 cups dried apricots, cut into 4 or 5 pieces
1 cup pitted prunes, diced
½ cup apricot nectar
¼ cup water
1 bay leaf, preferably imported
One 1-inch-long strip of lemon zest
1 cinnamon stick or ⅛ teaspoon ground cinnamon
¼ teaspoon freshly ground black pepper
4 turkey cutlets (1 pound total)
½ teaspoon oregano
¼ teaspoon salt
1 tablespoon olive oil
2 tablespoons fresh lemon juice
1 tablespoon frozen orange juice concentrate, thawed

1. In a medium saucepan, combine the apricots, prunes, apricot nectar, water, bay leaf, lemon zest, cinnamon stick and ⅛ teaspoon of the pepper. Cover and bring to a boil over high heat. Reduce the heat to medium-low and simmer, stirring occasionally, until the fruit is very tender, about 10 minutes. Remove the compote from the heat.

2. Meanwhile, sprinkle the turkey cutlets with the oregano, salt and remaining ⅛ teaspoon pepper. In a large nonstick skillet, warm the oil over high heat until hot but not smoking. Add the turkey and cook, turning once, until it is cooked through, 3 to 4 minutes. Transfer the turkey to a serving platter.

3. Remove the bay leaf, lemon zest and cinnamon stick from the compote and stir in the lemon juice and orange juice concentrate. Serve the fruit with the turkey.

Makes 4 servings

Nutrition Information
values are per serving

CALORIES 435	DIETARY FIBER 8.2 G
TOTAL FAT 4.6 G	BETA CAROTENE 3.6 MG
SATURATED FAT .7 G	VITAMIN C 30 MG
CHOLESTEROL 70 MG	CALCIUM 73 MG
SODIUM 200 MG	IRON 5.7 MG

Turkey and Red Onion Fajitas with Three-Fruit Salsa

The flour tortilla is a marvelous invention and is used here Mexican style to wrap around a filling of red onion and cumin-marinated turkey strips atop a delicious tomato, mango and avocado salsa. Try this same salsa on grilled fish, or even as a dipping sauce for steamed shrimp.

¾ pound thinly sliced turkey breast cutlets, cut into ½-inch strips
1 large red onion—halved lengthwise then sliced crosswise into thin half-rounds
2 tablespoons plus 2 teaspoons fresh lime juice
3½ teaspoons cumin
¼ teaspoon freshly ground black pepper
¼ teaspoon salt
1½ cups quartered red and yellow cherry tomatoes
1 mango, diced

¼ cup diced green bell pepper
¼ teaspoon crushed red pepper flakes
2 tablespoons canned chicken broth
Four 8-inch flour tortillas
Half a medium avocado, diced

1. In a 7-by-11-inch baking pan, combine the turkey, onion, 1 tablespoon of the lime juice, 2 teaspoons of the cumin, the black pepper and ⅛ teaspoon of the salt; toss to combine. Cover and let stand for 20 minutes.

2. Meanwhile, preheat the oven to 375° and start to prepare the salsa.

3. In a medium bowl, gently toss the cherry tomatoes, mango, bell pepper, red pepper flakes and the remaining 1 tablespoon plus 2 teaspoons lime juice, 1½ teaspoons cumin and ⅛ teaspoon salt. Cover and let stand at room temperature until serving time.

4. Drizzle the turkey with the chicken broth, cover loosely with foil and bake for 17 to 20 minutes, stirring several times, until the turkey is cooked through and the onion is crisp-tender. Halfway through the turkey cooking time, wrap the tortillas in foil and place them in the oven to warm up.

5. Gently fold the avocado into the salsa. Place the tortillas on warmed plates and top each tortilla with 2 tablespoons of the salsa. Top with the turkey and onion mixture and roll up. Top with the remaining salsa.

Makes 4 servings

Nutrition Information
values are per serving

CALORIES 326	DIETARY FIBER 3.6 G
TOTAL FAT 7.7 G	BETA CAROTENE 1.5 MG
SATURATED FAT 1.2 G	VITAMIN C 38 MG
CHOLESTEROL 53 MG	CALCIUM 98 MG
SODIUM 391 MG	IRON 4.1 MG

Turkey Burgers with Salsa

The benefits of grinding your own turkey, as is recommended below, are 1) that you know precisely when it was done—an important factor these days—and 2) you can be sure that no fat or flavorings have been added.

SALSA
Half a large green bell pepper, cut into chunks
2 tablespoons coarsely chopped red onion
1 or 2 fresh jalapeño peppers, cut into chunks, some seeds removed
½ pound tomatoes, cut into chunks
1 tablespoon fresh lemon juice
⅛ teaspoon salt
Large pinch of cayenne pepper (optional)

BURGERS
1 pound skinless turkey breast, cut into chunks
¼ cup plain dried bread crumbs
2 tablespoons reduced-calorie mayonnaise
½ teaspoon cumin
¼ teaspoon freshly ground black pepper
⅛ teaspoon salt
Four crusty whole wheat rolls (about 2 ounces each)

1. To Make the Salsa In a food processor, combine the bell pepper, onion and jalapeño, and pulse until finely chopped. Add the tomatoes and pulse until the salsa is finely chopped but still has some texture. Transfer to a medium bowl and stir in the lemon juice, salt and cayenne (if using).

2. To Make the Burgers Preheat the broiler and broiler pan.

3. In a food processor, process the turkey until finely chopped. Add ¼ cup of the salsa, the bread crumbs, mayonnaise, cumin, black pepper and salt, and pulse until blended. Shape the burger mixture into 4 patties.

4. Broil the patties 5 inches from the heat for 5 minutes per side, or until cooked through.

5. Place the patties on the rolls and serve with the salsa.

Makes 4 servings

NUTRITION INFORMATION
values are per serving

CALORIES 334	DIETARY FIBER 5.3 G
TOTAL FAT 5.8 G	BETA CAROTENE .3 MG
SATURATED FAT 1.4 G	VITAMIN C 38 MG
CHOLESTEROL 73 MG	CALCIUM 78 MG
SODIUM 598 MG	IRON 4.2 MG

Sidewalk Turkey and Pepper Heroes

If you think all hero sandwiches are layers of pink cold cuts on an oil-drenched loaf of Italian bread, think again. Here is an elegant but hearty hero that is as satisfying as it is flavorful, and that doesn't even come close to the original construction in grams of fat.

3 large red bell peppers, cut into 1-inch-wide strips
1 medium onion, sliced
1 tablespoon balsamic vinegar
1 teaspoon olive oil, preferably extra-virgin
¾ pound skinless turkey breast, cut into chunks
1 egg
6 to 8 sprigs of flat-leaf parsley
2 tablespoons plain dried bread crumbs
1 garlic clove, crushed through a press
¼ teaspoon fennel seed
⅛ teaspoon salt
⅛ teaspoon crushed red pepper flakes
3 ounces thinly sliced provolone cheese
2 tablespoons nonfat mayonnaise
½ teaspoon basil
¼ teaspoon oregano
¼ teaspoon thyme
Four crusty hero rolls (about 3 ounces each), split

1. Preheat the broiler. Spray a jelly-roll pan with nonstick cooking spray.

2. Place the red bell peppers and onion on the prepared pan. Drizzle with the vinegar and oil, and toss to coat. Broil 3 to 4 inches from the heat, stirring several times, for 15 minutes, or until the vegetables are tender and lightly charred. Set aside and cover loosely to keep warm. Keep the broiler on.

3. Meanwhile, in a food processor, coarsely grind the turkey breast. Add the egg, parsley, bread crumbs, garlic, fennel, salt and red pepper flakes. Process briefly just to combine. Shape the mixture into four thin oblong patties and place on a broiler pan.

4. Broil the turkey patties 4 to 5 inches from the heat, without turning, for about 5 minutes, or until cooked through. Top evenly with the cheese and broil for about 30 seconds, or until the cheese is melted.

5. Meanwhile, in a small bowl or cup, blend the mayonnaise with the basil, oregano and thyme. Brush the rolls with the seasoned mayonnaise and lightly toast the rolls.

6. Place a patty on one half of a roll; top with some of the peppers and the rest of the roll.

Makes 4 servings

NUTRITION INFORMATION
values are per serving

CALORIES 488	DIETARY FIBER 4.7 G
TOTAL FAT 12 G	BETA CAROTENE 2.7 MG
SATURATED FAT 5.1 G	VITAMIN C 147 MG
CHOLESTEROL 121 MG	CALCIUM 277 MG
SODIUM 895 MG	IRON 4.8 MG

Baked Moroccan Turkey Loaf

There are almost as many variations on meat loaf as there are cooks to create it, but here lowfat ground turkey is combined with special ingredients—dried apricots and cilantro—plus red bell peppers to take on Moroccan overtones and decidedly exotic flavors. Serve this with spiced-up ketchup, as suggested below, as well as grilled or roasted marinated vegetables and warmed pita pockets. Orange fruit ice, garnished with grated chocolate, would make a refreshing dessert.

½ cup dried apricots
1 cup boiling water
2 large red bell peppers, halved
1 pound ground turkey
¼ cup plus 1 tablespoon chopped cilantro
¼ cup apricot all-fruit spread
2 egg whites
2 tablespoons minced scallions
1¼ teaspoons cumin
¾ teaspoon salt
¼ teaspoon freshly ground black pepper
1 teaspoon ground coriander
1 teaspoon oregano
1 teaspoon paprika
2 ounces bread (about 2 slices), torn into fine crumbs (to yield 1 cup)
¼ cup lowfat (1%) milk
½ cup light ketchup

1. In a small heatproof bowl, cover the apricots with the boiling water and set aside to soften. When softened, drain and finely chop.

2. Meanwhile, preheat the broiler with the rack 5 inches from the heat. Cutting vertically, slice the bell peppers into 3 or 4 flat panels, leaving the core and seeds behind. Put the bell pepper pieces, skin-side up, in a single layer on a jelly-roll pan and broil 3 to 4 inches from the heat for 10 to 15 minutes.

3. Place the peppers in a bowl and cover. Set aside to steam for about 5 minutes to loosen the skins, then peel them. Finely chop the peppers and set aside.

4. Preheat the oven to 375°. Spray an 8-by-4-inch loaf pan with nonstick cooking spray.

5. In a large bowl, stir together the ground turkey, ¼ cup of the cilantro, 3 tablespoons of the fruit spread, the egg whites, scallions, 1 teaspoon of the cumin, the salt, black pepper and ¾ teaspoon each of the ground coriander, oregano and paprika.

6. Stir in the chopped apricots, bell peppers, bread crumbs and milk until the mixture is well combined.

7. Spoon the mixture into the loaf pan. Smooth the top and bake in the oven until the turkey is cooked through, about 25 minutes. Let sit for 10 minutes, then invert onto a platter.

8. Meanwhile, in a small bowl, blend the ketchup with 1 tablespoon of water and the remaining 1 tablespoon cilantro, 1 tablespoon fruit spread and ¼ teaspoon each cumin, ground coriander, oregano and paprika.

9. Serve slices of the turkey loaf with the ketchup sauce on the side.

Makes 4 servings

NUTRITION INFORMATION
values are per serving

CALORIES 331	DIETARY FIBER 2.5 G
TOTAL FAT 9.6 G	BETA CAROTENE 2.7 MG
SATURATED FAT 2.5 G	VITAMIN C 97 MG
CHOLESTEROL 84 MG	CALCIUM 96 MG
SODIUM 855 MG	IRON 3.8 MG

Fish & Shellfish

Baked Stuffed Flounder with Smoked Salmon

A small amount of smoked salmon goes a long, lovely way here, serving almost as a garnish and providing singular texture, taste and color to mild-flavored flounder. Substitute snow peas for the green beans for a different kind of crunch.

6 ounces green beans
3 large carrots, cut into long, slender strips the same length as the beans
1 large red bell pepper, cut into thin strips
4 flounder fillets (1 pound total)
1½ ounces thinly sliced smoked salmon, cut into 8 strips
2 tablespoons dry white wine
1 tablespoon fresh lemon juice
1 tablespoon extra-virgin olive oil
½ teaspoon thyme
¼ teaspoon salt
¼ teaspoon freshly ground black pepper
2 tablespoons minced fresh dill
1 lemon, cut into wedges

1. Preheat the oven to 400°. Spray a 9-by-13-inch baking dish with nonstick cooking spray.

2. Bring 1 inch of water to a boil in a deep medium skillet over high heat. Add the green beans, return to a boil and cook for 3 minutes, stirring occasionally. Stir in the carrots, return to a boil and cook for 2 minutes. Add the bell pepper and cook until all the vegetables are crisp-tender, about 1 minute. Drain in a colander and cool briefly under cold running water.

3. Cut each fillet of flounder in half lengthwise along the natural separation and lay out on a cutting board. Place some of the vegetables crosswise on the wide end of each piece of fish and roll up. Place the flounder rolls in the prepared pan. Drape a piece of smoked salmon crosswise over the fish rolls.

4. In a small bowl or cup, mix the wine, lemon juice, olive oil, thyme, salt and black pepper. Pour evenly over the fish and vegetables. Cover the pan with foil and bake for 10 to 12 minutes, or until the fish is just cooked through.

5. Sprinkle the fish with the dill and serve with lemon wedges and any pan juices.

Makes 4 servings

NUTRITION INFORMATION
values are per serving

CALORIES 213	DIETARY FIBER 3.6 G
TOTAL FAT 5.9 G	BETA CAROTENE 14 MG
SATURATED FAT 1.0 G	VITAMIN C 84 MG
CHOLESTEROL 57 MG	CALCIUM 89 MG
SODIUM 342 MG	IRON 2.0 MG

Spinach-Stuffed Flounder with Roasted Tomatoes

Chopped spinach has long served as a wonderful stuffing for savory dishes. In these flounder rolls it provides subtle flavor, beautiful color and lots of vitamins—no mean achievement for a lone vegetable. Sautéed potatoes sprinkled at the last minute with fresh herbs would make a delicious accompaniment.

1 large baking potato (8 ounces), peeled and thinly sliced
2 garlic cloves, peeled
½ teaspoon salt
2 tablespoons grated Parmesan cheese
⅛ teaspoon freshly ground black pepper
⅛ teaspoon nutmeg
One 10-ounce package frozen chopped spinach, thawed and squeezed dry

4 flounder fillets (1½ pounds total)
1 tablespoon plus 1 teaspoon fresh lemon juice
1 pound plum tomatoes, thickly sliced
1 teaspoon olive oil
½ teaspoon sugar
½ teaspoon tarragon
1 teaspoon paprika

1. Preheat the oven to 400°.

2. In a small saucepan, bring 2 cups of water to a boil over medium heat. Add the potato, garlic and ⅛ teaspoon of the salt, and cook until the potato is tender, about 10 minutes.

3. With a slotted spoon, transfer the potato and garlic to a medium bowl. Measure out 2 tablespoons of the cooking liquid and add to the bowl, then mash the potato and garlic with a fork or potato masher. Stir in the Parmesan, pepper, nutmeg and ⅛ teaspoon of the salt. Then stir in the spinach.

4. Lay the flounder fillets on a work surface with the skinned-side up. Sprinkle 2 teaspoons of the lemon juice evenly over the fish. Spoon the spinach mixture onto the fillets and roll them up.

5. In a 7-by-11-inch baking pan, toss the tomatoes with the olive oil, sugar and the remaining ¼ teaspoon salt.

6. Place the flounder rolls on top of the tomatoes, seam-side down. Sprinkle the flounder with the remaining 2 teaspoons lemon juice, the tarragon and paprika. Bake for about 10 minutes, or until the fish is cooked through and the tomatoes have started to give up their juices.

7. To serve, spoon the tomatoes onto 4 serving plates and place a flounder roll on top.

Makes 4 servings

NUTRITION INFORMATION
values are per serving

CALORIES 259	DIETARY FIBER 3.6 G
TOTAL FAT 4.6 G	BETA CAROTENE 3.9 MG
SATURATED FAT 1.2 G	VITAMIN C 50 MG
CHOLESTEROL 84 MG	CALCIUM 161 MG
SODIUM 524 MG	IRON 3.1 MG

Thai-Style Steamed Whole Fish with Vegetables

Certainly for those who will partake of it, as well as for the person who prepared it, there is an undeniable thrill that comes when a whole cooked fish, fragrant and beautifully garnished, arrives at the dinner table.

¼ cup chicken broth, canned or homemade (p. 54)
2 tablespoons coarsely chopped fresh ginger
1 tablespoon reduced-sodium soy sauce
1 tablespoon honey
1 tablespoon rice wine vinegar
4 anchovy fillets or 1½ tablespoons anchovy paste 4 garlic cloves, peeled
2 cups (packed) sliced broccoli rabe (2-inch lengths)
4 large carrots, cut into long, slender sticks
8 scallions, cut into 2-inch lengths
½ pound fresh shiitake mushrooms, stemmed and caps cut into ½-inch-thick slices
2 large fresh jalapeño peppers, cut into thin slivers, some seeds removed
Two 1-pound whole black bass or striped bass
½ cup cilantro sprigs

1. Preheat the oven to 450°.

2. Place the chicken broth, ginger, soy sauce, honey, vinegar and anchovies in a food processor. With the machine running, drop the garlic cloves through the feed tube and process until the ingredients are finely minced.

3. In the bottom of a broiler pan or in a large roasting pan, place the broccoli rabe, carrots, scallions, mushrooms and jalapeño peppers. Toss to combine the ingredients and then drizzle with half of the soy sauce mixture.

4. Place the fish on top of the vegetables and drizzle with the remaining soy sauce mixture.

Cover with foil and bake for 25 to 30 minutes, or until the fish flakes easily near the bone.

5. Transfer the fish, vegetables and cooking juices to a heated platter; garnish with the cilantro sprigs and serve.

Makes 4 servings

NUTRITION INFORMATION
values are per serving

CALORIES 213	DIETARY FIBER 6.0 G
TOTAL FAT 3.4 G	BETA CAROTENE 18 MG
SATURATED FAT .7 G	VITAMIN C 73 MG
CHOLESTEROL 80 MG	CALCIUM 103 MG
SODIUM 492 MG	IRON 3.7 MG

Baked Haddock with Swiss Chard and Tomatoes

To bake fish is often to risk drying it out. In this recipe, however, the problem is solved by layering the fish between a bed of Swiss chard and a topping aromatic with tomatoes and herbs. Serve the fish with creamy mashed potatoes.

1 pound Swiss chard
¼ cup chicken broth, canned or homemade (p. 54)
1¼ pounds haddock fillets, cut into 2-inch chunks
½ teaspoon salt
¼ teaspoon freshly ground black pepper
1 tablespoon olive oil
2 medium tomatoes—seeded, cubed and drained
1 large onion, cut into narrow wedges
½ cup minced parsley
2 tablespoons sliced garlic
1 teaspoon tarragon

1. Preheat the oven to 450°.

2. Separate the stems from the Swiss chard leaves. Slice the stems crosswise and set them aside. Shred the leaves and place them in a shallow 2-quart baking dish. Sprinkle the broth on top.

3. Place the fish on top of the chard and sprinkle with ¼ teaspoon of the salt and the pepper.

4. In a large nonstick skillet, warm the oil over medium-high heat until hot but not smoking. Add the chard stems, tomatoes, onion, parsley, garlic, tarragon and remaining ¼ teaspoon salt. Cook until the onion is crisp-tender, about 4 minutes.

5. Spoon the sautéed vegetables over the fish, cover the dish and bake for 10 to 15 minutes, or until the fish just flakes when tested with a fork.

Makes 4 servings

NUTRITION INFORMATION
values are per serving

CALORIES 222	DIETARY FIBER 2.1 G
TOTAL FAT 5.0 G	BETA CAROTENE 2.7 MG
SATURATED FAT .7 G	VITAMIN C 58 MG
CHOLESTEROL 81 MG	CALCIUM 145 MG
SODIUM 685 MG	IRON 4.6 MG

Stir-Fried Grouper with Sun-Dried Tomatoes and Broccoli

Grouper, more and more available these days, holds up superbly to the rigors of stir-frying because of its firm flesh. Monkfish would make a very reasonable substitute.

¼ cup (not oil-packed) sun-dried tomatoes
½ cup boiling water
2 teaspoons olive oil
1 ounce Canadian bacon, diced
2 teaspoons pine nuts

1½ pounds grouper fillet, cut into 2-inch chunks
1 tablespoon flour
¼ cup minced scallions
3 garlic cloves, minced
3 cups small broccoli florets
¼ cup golden raisins
¼ cup orange juice

1. In a small bowl, combine the sun-dried tomatoes and boiling water, and set aside until softened, about 10 minutes. Reserving the soaking liquid, drain and coarsely chop the tomatoes.

2. In a large nonstick skillet, warm the oil over medium heat until hot but not smoking. Add the bacon and pine nuts, and cook for 1 minute.

3. Dust the grouper with the flour, add it to the pan and cook until golden, about 3 minutes.

4. Stir in the scallions and garlic, and cook for 30 seconds. Add the broccoli, sun-dried tomatoes and reserved soaking liquid and the raisins. Cook, stirring frequently, until the fish and broccoli are tender, 4 to 5 minutes.

5. Remove the pan from the heat, stir in the orange juice and serve.

Makes 4 servings

NUTRITION INFORMATION
values are per serving

CALORIES 285	DIETARY FIBER 5.0 G
TOTAL FAT 5.7 G	BETA CAROTENE 1.4 MG
SATURATED FAT 1.0 G	VITAMIN C 92 MG
CHOLESTEROL 67 MG	CALCIUM 109 MG
SODIUM 221 MG	IRON 3.1 MG

SUPER QUICK

Bluefish with Spicy Vegetable Sauce

Working time: 20 minutes Total time: 30 minutes

- 1⅓ cups water
- ⅔ cup rice
- 2 teaspoons olive oil
- 1 large green bell pepper, diced
- 1 large carrot, diced
- ½ cup minced scallions
- 3 garlic cloves, minced
- 1 tablespoon minced fresh ginger
- ¼ teaspoon hot pepper sauce
- 2 teaspoons flour
- 1½ cups low-sodium mixed vegetable juice
- ½ teaspoon grated orange zest
- 3 tablespoons orange juice
- ½ teaspoon thyme
- 4 skinned bluefish fillets (1½ pounds total)

1 In a medium covered saucepan, bring the water to a boil over high heat. Add the rice, reduce the heat to a simmer and cook until the rice is tender and all the liquid is absorbed, about 20 minutes.

2 Meanwhile, in a large nonstick skillet, warm the oil over medium heat until hot but not smoking. Add the bell pepper, carrot, scallions, garlic, ginger and hot pepper sauce, and cook, stirring frequently, until the vegetables have softened, about 7 minutes. Stir in the flour and cook for 1 minute longer.

3 Stir in the mixed vegetable juice, orange zest, orange juice and thyme, and bring to a boil. Reduce to a simmer, place the fish on top, spoon some of the sauce over, cover and cook until the fish is cooked through, about 10 minutes.

4 Transfer the fish to serving plates and top with some of the vegetables. Spoon a mound of rice onto each plate and top with the remaining vegetables and sauce.

Makes 4 servings

Values are per serving:
Calories: 403 Total fat: 10 g Saturated fat: 2.0 g Cholesterol: 100 mg Sodium: 189 mg
Dietary fiber: 2.4 g Beta carotene: 5.0 mg Vitamin C: 65 mg Calcium: 59 mg Iron: 3.5 mg

Scalloped Salmon and Sweet Potatoes

Here is a highly nutritious take on one of this country's favorite comfort foods, scalloped potatoes. Replacing the usual white potatoes are beta carotene-rich sweet potatoes and, to make this casserole a satisfying main dish, flavorful fresh salmon has been added. Serve this with green salad and, for dessert, a still-warm-from-the-oven apple and pear crisp.

2 pounds sweet potatoes
2 cups lowfat (1%) milk
2½ tablespoons cornstarch
1 small onion, finely minced or grated
¾ teaspoon thyme
½ teaspoon salt
½ teaspoon freshly ground black pepper
¾ pound skinned center-cut salmon fillets
¼ cup plain dried bread crumbs
Large pinch of cayenne pepper
1 tablespoon unsalted butter, cut into small pieces
2 tablespoons grated Parmesan cheese

1. Cook the sweet potatoes in a large covered pot of boiling water until nearly tender, 25 to 30 minutes. Drain and rinse under running water.

2. When the sweet potatoes are cool enough to handle, peel them, halve them lengthwise and then cut them crosswise into ¼- to ⅓-inch slices. Arrange in overlapping rows in a 7-by-11-inch baking pan.

3. Preheat the oven to 350°.

4. Meanwhile, in a medium saucepan, whisk the milk, cornstarch, onion, thyme, salt and black pepper until smooth. Place over medium-high heat and bring to a boil, stirring constantly. Reduce the heat and simmer, stirring, until thickened (it will be quite thick), 3 to 4 minutes. Remove from the heat.

5. Cut the fish lengthwise in half along the natural separation. Then cut the fish crosswise into 1-inch-wide slices. In a small bowl, stir together the bread crumbs and cayenne.

6. Lay the salmon on top of the sweet potatoes and pour the sauce on top, trying to evenly cover the potatoes and fish. Sprinkle with the seasoned bread crumbs and dot with the butter.

7. Bake for 15 to 20 minutes, or until the fish is cooked through and the sauce is just bubbly. Turn the oven to broil, sprinkle the dish with the Parmesan and broil for 1 to 2 minutes, watching carefully, just until lightly browned.

Makes 4 servings

Nutrition Information
values are per serving

CALORIES 438	DIETARY FIBER 5.7 G
TOTAL FAT 11 G	BETA CAROTENE 20 MG
SATURATED FAT 4.1 G	VITAMIN C 40 MG
CHOLESTEROL 61 MG	CALCIUM 261 MG
SODIUM 500 MG	IRON 2.6 MG

Salmon with Braised Savoy Cabbage

Savoy cabbage, unlike plain green cabbage, has crinkly leaves and a loosely furled head, and often shares space in the produce department of supermarkets with Chinese cabbage and bok choy. Savoy cabbage is mild and sweetish in flavor—a good counterpoint to the slightly more assertive taste of kale that is also used in this simple-to-make, very pleasing salmon bake.

2 teaspoons olive oil
3 garlic cloves, minced
1 small Granny Smith apple, peeled and thinly sliced
¾ pound all-purpose potatoes, peeled and cut into ½-inch chunks

½ cup thinly sliced carrots
⅓ cup canned chicken broth diluted with ⅓ cup water, or ⅔ cup Homemade Chicken Broth (p. 54)
3 cups shredded Savoy cabbage (about 8 ounces)
2 cups shredded kale (about 4 ounces)
2 tablespoons balsamic vinegar
½ teaspoon salt
1¼ pounds salmon fillets, cut into 4 equal serving pieces
½ teaspoon sage

1. Preheat the oven to 425°. Spray a 7-by-11-inch baking pan with nonstick cooking spray.

2. In a large nonstick skillet, warm the oil over medium heat until hot but not smoking. Add the garlic and apple, and cook, stirring frequently, until the apple is golden, about 3 minutes.

3. Add the potatoes, carrots and diluted broth; cover and cook until the potatoes are almost tender, about 7 minutes.

4. Stir in the cabbage, kale, vinegar and ¼ teaspoon of the salt. Partially cover and cook until the cabbage has wilted and the potatoes are tender, about 10 minutes.

5. Meanwhile, place the salmon in the prepared baking pan. Rub with the remaining ¼ teaspoon salt and the sage. Bake for 10 minutes, or until the salmon just flakes when tested with a fork. Serve the salmon on a bed of the vegetables.

Makes 4 servings

NUTRITION INFORMATION
values are per serving

CALORIES 330	DIETARY FIBER 3.8 G
TOTAL FAT 12 G	BETA CAROTENE 4.2 MG
SATURATED FAT 1.7 G	VITAMIN C 67 MG
CHOLESTEROL 78 MG	CALCIUM 92 MG
SODIUM 455 MG	IRON 2.5 MG

Salmon on a Bed of Greens with Mango Salsa

This is dinner party fare—pretty to look at, splendid to taste and, as a bonus, requiring very little last-minute preparation (the salsa can be completely prepared in advance). Wild rice would make a nice accompaniment and large strawberries dipped in chocolate a special dessert.

1 pound skinned salmon fillets, cut into 4 equal serving pieces
1½ teaspoons cumin
1½ teaspoons ground coriander
½ teaspoon salt
½ teaspoon freshly ground black pepper
3 tablespoons fresh lemon juice
1 mango, diced
1 cup diced jicama or tart, crisp apple
1 cup diced red bell pepper
1 small fresh green or red chili pepper, seeded and finely chopped
1 tablespoon extra-virgin olive oil
4 cups (loosely packed) watercress, tough stems removed
1 cup shredded carrots

1. Season the salmon with 1 teaspoon of the cumin, ½ teaspoon of the coriander and ¼ teaspoon each salt and black pepper. Drizzle with 1 tablespoon of the lemon juice. Cover loosely and let the salmon stand for 20 to 30 minutes.

2. Preheat the broiler and broiler pan.

3. Meanwhile, in a medium bowl, mix the mango, jicama, bell pepper, chili pepper, 1 teaspoon of the olive oil, 1 tablespoon of the lemon juice, and the remaining ½ teaspoon cumin, 1 teaspoon coriander and ¼ teaspoon each salt and black pepper. Mix gently and set aside until serving time.

4. Place the salmon on the preheated broiler pan and broil 3 to 4 inches from the heat for 3 to 4 minutes, without turning, or until the fish is just opaque in the thickest part.

5. Meanwhile, in a small bowl or cup, whisk the remaining 1 tablespoon lemon juice and 2 teaspoons olive oil.

6. To serve, divide the watercress among four dinner plates and top with the carrots. Drizzle the olive oil and lemon juice dressing over the watercress and carrots. Top the greens with the salmon and spoon the salsa over the salmon.

Makes 4 servings

Nutrition Information
values are per serving

CALORIES 269	DIETARY FIBER 3.5 G
TOTAL FAT 11 G	BETA CAROTENE 7.9 MG
SATURATED FAT 1.7 G	VITAMIN C 104 MG
CHOLESTEROL 62 MG	CALCIUM 97 MG
SODIUM 356 MG	IRON 2.1 MG

Fillets of Sole with Fresh and Dried Tomato Coulis

The French term coulis means sauce, almost always a smooth purée, and is served frequently with fish or poultry. In this case, sole fillets seasoned with scallions and chili powder do the honors. Try this coulis with shrimp or scallops.

1/3 cup (not oil-packed) sun-dried tomatoes
1 cup boiling water
2 teaspoons olive oil
1 cup minced scallions
3 garlic cloves, minced
2 teaspoons paprika
3/4 teaspoon mild chili powder
2 cups chopped fresh tomatoes
1/4 cup chopped fresh basil
2 tablespoons frozen orange juice concentrate, thawed
4 sole fillets (1 1/2 pounds total)
1/2 teaspoon salt
1/4 teaspoon freshly ground black pepper
3 tablespoons grated Parmesan cheese

1. Preheat the oven to 400°. Spray a 7-by-11-inch baking dish with nonstick cooking spray.

2. In a small bowl, combine the sun-dried tomatoes and water and let stand until softened, about 10 minutes. When softened, drain and coarsely chop the tomatoes.

3. In a small nonstick skillet, warm the oil over medium heat until hot but not smoking. Add the scallions and garlic, and cook until the scallions are softened, about 2 minutes. Stir in 1 teaspoon of the paprika and the chili powder, and cook until fragrant, about 1 minute.

4. In a medium bowl, combine the chopped sun-dried tomatoes, half of the scallion mixture, the fresh tomatoes, 2 tablespoons of the basil and the orange juice concentrate. Set aside.

5. Lay the sole on a work surface, skinned-side up. Sprinkle with the salt and pepper. Then top with the remaining scallion mixture and 2 tablespoons basil. Fold the sole over the filling and place in the prepared baking dish in a single layer.

6. Sprinkle the remaining 1 teaspoon paprika and the Parmesan on top of the fish and bake until the fish just flakes when tested with a fork, about 7 minutes.

7. To serve, spoon the tomato coulis onto serving plates and top with the fish.

Makes 4 servings

Nutrition Information
values are per serving

CALORIES 263	DIETARY FIBER 3.2 G
TOTAL FAT 6.4 G	BETA CAROTENE 1.6 MG
SATURATED FAT 1.6 G	VITAMIN C 53 MG
CHOLESTEROL 85 MG	CALCIUM 147 MG
SODIUM 507 MG	IRON 2.7 MG

Pan-Fried Snapper Parmigiana

You don't need a lot of Parmesan cheese for flavoring as long as the one you are using is freshly grated and of good quality, meaning it has been aged. In this recipe, only three tablespoons of Parmesan lend inimitable flavor to a breading for snapper fillets.

1 cup chopped tomatoes
One 8-ounce can no-salt-added tomato sauce
1 large onion, diced
1 medium green bell pepper, diced
1 medium red bell pepper, diced
2 garlic cloves, minced
½ teaspoon salt
⅛ teaspoon cayenne pepper
3 tablespoons grated Parmesan cheese
2 tablespoons plain dried bread crumbs
2 tablespoons flour
1 tablespoon chopped parsley
½ cup lowfat (1%) milk
4 red snapper fillets (1½ pounds total)
1 tablespoon plus 1 teaspoon olive oil
1 lemon, cut into wedges

1. In a medium saucepan over medium heat, stir together the tomatoes, tomato sauce, onion, green and red bell peppers, garlic, salt and cayenne. Bring to a boil, reduce to a simmer, cover and cook until the vegetables are tender, about 7 minutes. Uncover and cook until thickened, about 5 minutes.

2. In a shallow bowl or pie plate, stir together the Parmesan, bread crumbs, flour and parsley. Place the milk in another shallow bowl or pie plate Dip the fish first in the milk, then in the Parmesan mixture, pressing to coat.

3. In a large nonstick skillet, warm 2 teaspoons of the oil over medium heat until hot but not smoking. Add half of the fish and sauté until golden brown, crisp and cooked through, about 2 min-

SUPER QUICK

Roasted Snapper with Curried Lime, Orange and Mango Purée

Working time: 15 minutes Total time: 25 minutes

- 4 red snapper fillets (1½ pounds total)
- 2 tablespoons fresh lime juice
- 2 tablespoons orange juice
- ½ teaspoon sugar
- ½ teaspoon salt
- 3 tablespoons chopped fresh mint
- 1 large mango, coarsely chopped
- ¼ cup apricot nectar
- 1½ tablespoons grated fresh ginger, squeezed to yield 1 tablespoon ginger juice
- 2 teaspoons curry powder

1 Preheat the oven to 425°. Spray a small baking sheet with nonstick cooking spray.

2 Season the snapper with 1 tablespoon of the lime juice, 1 tablespoon of the orange juice, the sugar and ¼ teaspoon of the salt. Top with 1 tablespoon of the mint. Bake until the fish is just cooked through, about 10 minutes.

3 Meanwhile, in a food processor or blender, combine the remaining 1 tablespoon each lime juice and orange juice, ¼ teaspoon salt and 2 tablespoons mint with the mango, apricot nectar, ginger juice and curry powder. Process to a smooth purée. Serve the fish topped with the fruit purée.

Makes 4 servings

Values are per serving:
Calories: 236 Total fat: 2.9 g Saturated fat: .5 g Cholesterol: 63 mg Sodium: 385 mg
Dietary fiber: 1.1 g Beta carotene: 1.7 mg Vitamin C: 33 mg Calcium: 72 mg Iron: .8 mg

utes per side. Transfer the fish to serving plates and repeat with the remaining 2 teaspoons oil and fish.

4. To serve, reheat the tomato sauce and spoon over the fish. Serve with the lemon wedges.

Makes 4 servings

NUTRITION INFORMATION
values are per serving

CALORIES 336	DIETARY FIBER 3.2 G
TOTAL FAT 9.0 G	BETA CAROTENE 1.4 MG
SATURATED FAT 2.1 G	VITAMIN C 95 MG
CHOLESTEROL 67 MG	CALCIUM 191 MG
SODIUM 517 MG	IRON 1.9 MG

Sweet-and-Sour Fish with Carrots, Broccoli and Mushrooms

This exotic combination of boy choy, fresh shiitake mushrooms and crispy strips of sea bass in a gingery sweet-and-sour sauce is best served over hot cooked rice. Dried shiitake mushrooms are not a substitute here; use fresh cremini or portobello mushrooms instead.

1/3 cup light ketchup
2 tablespoons reduced-sodium soy sauce
1 tablespoon brown sugar
1 tablespoon cider vinegar
1/2 teaspoon ground ginger
1/2 teaspoon Oriental (dark) sesame oil
2 teaspoons vegetable oil
1 1/4 pounds sea bass fillets, cut into 2-inch strips
1 tablespoon cornstarch
2 large carrots, cut into thin julienne strips
10 ounces bok choy, cut into 2-inch pieces (about 3 cups)
1/2 pound fresh shiitake mushrooms, thinly sliced
1/2 cup plus 1 tablespoon water
1/4 cup minced scallions
3 garlic cloves, minced
2 teaspoons minced fresh ginger

1. In a small bowl, stir together the ketchup, soy sauce, brown sugar, vinegar, ground ginger and sesame oil; set aside.

2. In a large nonstick skillet, warm the vegetable oil over high heat until hot but not smoking. Dust the sea bass with 2 teaspoons of the cornstarch. Add the fish to the skillet and cook until lightly golden, about 4 minutes. With a slotted spoon, transfer the fish to a plate and cover loosely to keep warm.

3. To the skillet, add the carrots, bok choy, mushrooms and 1/4 cup of the water, and cook until the vegetables are crisp-tender, about 2 minutes. Stir in the scallions, garlic and ginger, and cook until the scallions are softened, about 2 minutes.

4. Stir in the reserved ketchup mixture and 1/4 cup of the water, and simmer until the vegetables are almost crisp-tender, about 3 minutes. Return the fish to the skillet and simmer until cooked through, about 2 minutes.

5. In a small bowl, blend the remaining 1 teaspoon cornstarch and 1 tablespoon water. Stir into the skillet and cook until the sauce is lightly thickened, about 1 minute. Serve hot.

Makes 4 servings

NUTRITION INFORMATION
values are per serving

CALORIES 251	DIETARY FIBER 2.5 G
TOTAL FAT 6.2 G	BETA CAROTENE 9.7 MG
SATURATED FAT 1.1 G	VITAMIN C 40 MG
CHOLESTEROL 58 MG	CALCIUM 128 MG
SODIUM 611 MG	IRON 2.5 MG

Tandoori Tilefish

Tilefish fillets are cooked here tandoori style—an Indian method of cooking in which food is marinated in spiced yogurt and then baked at very high heat.

1½ cups plain nonfat yogurt
1½ teaspoons ground cumin
¾ teaspoon ground coriander
½ teaspoon salt
½ teaspoon freshly ground black pepper
¼ teaspoon turmeric
⅛ teaspoon cayenne pepper
Pinch of ground cardamom (optional)
1½ pounds skinned tilefish or red snapper fillets
3 cups diced cantaloupe
1 cup diced tomato
¼ cup chopped parsley, preferably flat-leaf
2 tablespoons raisins
1 tablespoon sugar

1. In a medium bowl, stir the yogurt until smooth. Stir in the cumin, coriander, salt, black pepper, turmeric, cayenne and cardamom (if using).

2. Place the fish in a single layer in a 9-by-13-inch baking dish. Add half of the yogurt mixture and turn to coat the fish with the mixture. Cover the fish and the remaining yogurt mixture separately and refrigerate for at least 30 minutes.

3. Preheat the oven to 475°.

4. Add the cantaloupe, tomato, parsley, raisins and sugar to the remaining yogurt mixture and toss gently. Cover and refrigerate the salad while cooking the fish.

5. Bake the fish for 10 to 15 minutes, or until it just flakes when tested with a fork.

6. Carefully lift the fish from the pan (leaving behind the yogurt liquid) and serve with the salad.

Makes 4 servings

Nutrition Information
values are per serving

CALORIES 294	DIETARY FIBER 2.0 G
TOTAL FAT 4.8 G	BETA CAROTENE 2.6 MG
SATURATED FAT .9 G	VITAMIN C 64 MG
CHOLESTEROL 1.7 MG	CALCIUM 247 MG
SODIUM 447 MG	IRON 1.9 MG

Striped Bass Provençale

One baking pan is all you need to bring the many flavors of Provence—garlic, thyme, basil and fennel—to your dinner table. Sea bass fillets are the fish of choice here, but could easily be replaced with swordfish steaks. The Pernod called for will add an ephemeral, licorice-like taste, underscoring the fresh fennel used in the dish.

2 teaspoons olive oil
3 cloves garlic, thinly sliced
1 teaspoon fennel seeds
¾ teaspoon thyme
1 bay leaf
1 large red bell pepper, cut into thin strips
1 large green bell pepper, cut into thin strips
1 medium red onion, halved and thinly sliced
2 cups chopped tomatoes
1 cup sliced fennel or celery
¼ cup coarsely chopped Calamata or other brine-cured black olives
3 tablespoons minced fresh basil
2 tablespoons no-salt-added tomato paste
1 tablespoon red wine vinegar
4 skinned striped bass fillets (1½ pounds total)
¼ teaspoon salt
¼ teaspoon freshly ground black pepper
1 tablespoon Pernod (optional)

1. Preheat the oven to 400°. In a 9-by-13-inch baking pan, combine the oil, garlic, fennel seeds, thyme and bay leaf. Place in the oven for about 5 minutes, or until fragrant.

2. Add the red and green bell peppers and onion, return to the oven and bake for 15 minutes. Stir in the tomatoes, sliced fennel, olives and basil, and bake for 10 minutes.

3. Meanwhile, in a small bowl, stir together the tomato paste and vinegar.

4. Place the fish on top of the vegetables, sprinkle with the salt, black pepper and Pernod (if using), and rub with the tomato paste mixture. Return the pan to the oven and bake for 10 minutes, or until the fish just flakes when tested with a fork.

Makes 4 servings

Nutrition Information
values are per serving

CALORIES 265	DIETARY FIBER 3.6 G
TOTAL FAT 7.8 G	BETA CAROTENE 1.5 MG
SATURATED FAT .7 G	VITAMIN C 99 MG
CHOLESTEROL 136 MG	CALCIUM 81 MG
SODIUM 373 MG	IRON 3.9 MG

Orange-Marinated Swordfish with Sautéed Peppers

Should the swordfish you buy for this fragrant dish have any flesh that is darkish in color, almost reddish-brown, remove it as it tends to be bitter when cooked. Also, for safety's sake, always remember to bring a marinade that is going to be used for a sauce to a full boil before serving.

⅓ cup frozen orange juice concentrate, thawed
½ cup water
2 teaspoons grated orange zest
1 teaspoon cumin
¼ teaspoon salt
¼ teaspoon freshly ground black pepper
1 pound skinned swordfish steak, cut into 4 equal serving pieces
2 teaspoons olive oil
3 large red bell peppers, thinly sliced
2 tablespoons chicken broth or water

1. In a shallow baking dish, mix the orange juice concentrate, water, 1 teaspoon of the orange zest, the cumin and ⅛ teaspoon each salt and black pepper. Add the swordfish and turn to coat with the juice mixture. Cover and let stand at room temperature for at least 15 and up to 45 minutes.

2. Preheat the broiler. Spray the broiler pan rack with nonstick cooking spray.

3. Meanwhile, in a large nonstick skillet, warm the olive oil over high heat. Add the bell peppers, broth, the remaining 1 teaspoon orange zest and ⅛ teaspoon each salt and black pepper. Toss to coat well, then bring the liquid in the pan to a simmer. Reduce the heat to medium and sauté the peppers until tender, 8 to 10 minutes. Transfer the peppers to a warmed serving platter and cover loosely to keep warm. (Keep the skillet for boiling the marinade in Step 5.)

4. Reserving the marinade, transfer the swordfish to the prepared broiler pan and broil 3 to 4 inches from the heat for 4 to 5 minutes per side, or until the fish is just opaque in the center.

5. Pour the marinade into the skillet, bring it to a boil and boil for 1 minute. Place the swordfish on top of the peppers and pour the hot marinade over both.

Makes 4 servings

Nutrition Information
values are per serving

CALORIES 221	DIETARY FIBER 1.4 G
TOTAL FAT 7.4 G	BETA CAROTENE 2.6 MG
SATURATED FAT 1.6 G	VITAMIN C 177 MG
CHOLESTEROL 44 MG	CALCIUM 27 MG
SODIUM 271 MG	IRON 1.7 MG

Swordfish with Roasted Corn and Pepper Salsa

The high, dry heat of a very hot (500°) oven here seals in the juices of these swordfish steaks, rendering them particularly moist. Try this method of cooking with any thick-cut fish steaks, such as halibut or tuna.

One 10-ounce package frozen corn kernels, thawed
1 medium red bell pepper, diced
4 ounces cremini or white mushrooms, diced
1 tablespoon canola oil
½ teaspoon salt
½ teaspoon freshly ground black pepper
¼ cup chopped cilantro
1 small fresh jalapeño pepper, seeded and minced
¼ teaspoon grated lime zest
2 teaspoons fresh lime juice
1 teaspoon white wine vinegar
½ teaspoon cumin
¼ teaspoon chili powder
4 swordfish steaks (1½ pounds total)
1 lime, thinly sliced

1. Preheat the oven to 500°.

2. In a medium bowl, toss the corn, bell pepper and mushrooms with the oil and ¼ teaspoon each of the salt and black pepper. Spread the vegetable mixture on a nonstick baking sheet and roast on the top rack of the oven for 15 minutes, stirring occasionally.

3. Transfer the vegetable mixture to a bowl and let cool. Meanwhile, return the baking pan to the oven to preheat (for cooking the fish).

4. Stir the cilantro, jalapeño, lime zest, lime juice and vinegar into the roasted vegetables.

5. In a small bowl or cup, stir together the cumin, chili powder and remaining ¼ teaspoon each salt and black pepper. Rub the spice mixture on both sides of the swordfish. Cover one side of the fish with lime slices and place the fish on the preheated baking sheet. Roast for about 8 minutes, or until just opaque in the center.

6. Serve the fish with the roasted corn and pepper salsa on the side.

Makes 4 servings

NUTRITION INFORMATION
values are per serving

CALORIES 298	DIETARY FIBER 2.3 G
TOTAL FAT 10 G	BETA CAROTENE .8 MG
SATURATED FAT 2.0 G	VITAMIN C 56 MG
CHOLESTEROL 59 MG	CALCIUM 25 MG
SODIUM 417 MG	IRON 2.3 MG

Fish Florentine with a Twist

When you see the word Florentine used gastronomically, it usually signals that spinach is part of the recipe and that it serves as a bed, usually for fish or poultry. Here cabbage and broccoli stand in for the spinach, and their crown is sea bass infused with orange and topped with Parmesan.

1 tablespoon olive oil
3 cups finely chopped green cabbage (about 8 ounces)
1 pound broccoli, coarsely chopped
2 large garlic cloves, minced
¼ teaspoon freshly ground black pepper
1 tablespoon grated orange zest
¼ teaspoon salt
4 striped bass fillets (1 pound total)
½ cup grated Parmesan cheese
2 navel oranges–1 halved and 1 cut into 8 wedges

1. Preheat the oven to 425°.

2. In a large nonstick skillet, warm the oil over high heat until hot but not smoking. Add the cabbage, broccoli, garlic and pepper, and sauté until the vegetables are wilted, 4 to 5 minutes. Stir in the orange zest and salt.

3. Transfer the vegetables to a 7-by-11-inch baking dish. Top with the fish fillets and sprinkle the Parmesan cheese on top. Bake for 20 minutes, or until the fish just flakes when tested with a fork.

4. Serve the fish on a bed of the vegetables. Just before serving, squeeze the halved orange on top and serve with 2 orange wedges per person.

Makes 4 servings

Nutrition Information
values are per serving

CALORIES 263	DIETARY FIBER 5.5 G
TOTAL FAT 9.6 G	BETA CAROTENE 1.2 MG
SATURATED FAT 3.0 G	VITAMIN C 163 MG
CHOLESTEROL 99 MG	CALCIUM 245 MG
SODIUM 441 MG	IRON 2.5 MG

Broiled Swordfish with Tomato-Arugula Salad

Contrast is the keynote of this clever combination of swordfish topped with arugula salad. The fish is mild; the salad tangy. The salad is cold; the fish is hot. And last but not least, the arugula wilts slightly from the heat of the broiled fish, adding yet another lovely dimension.

SWORDFISH

½ teaspoon grated lemon zest
2 teaspoons fresh lemon juice
1 teaspoon extra-virgin olive oil
½ teaspoon rosemary, crumbled
¼ teaspoon salt
½ teaspoon freshly ground black pepper
Pinch of cayenne pepper
4 skinned swordfish steaks (1½ pounds total)

SALAD

2 tablespoons plus 2 teaspoons fresh lemon juice
1 tablespoon plus 1 teaspoon Dijon mustard
1 tablespoon plus 1 teaspoon olive oil, preferably extra-virgin
¾ teaspoon rosemary, crumbled
½ teaspoon salt
½ teaspoon freshly ground black pepper
4 cups chopped arugula
3 cups diced plum tomatoes

1. Preheat the broiler and broiler pan or prepare the grill.

2. **For the Swordfish** In a small bowl, combine the lemon zest, lemon juice, olive oil, rosemary, salt, black pepper and cayenne. Brush the swordfish steaks with this mixture and set aside while preparing the salad.

3. **To Make the Salad** In a small bowl or cup, whisk together the lemon juice, mustard, oil, rosemary, salt and black pepper. Place the arugula and tomatoes in a medium bowl, pour the dressing on top and toss gently.

4. Broil the swordfish 2 to 3 inches from the heat, turning once, for 8 minutes, or until just opaque in the center.

5. Place a swordfish steak on each of 4 dinner plates and top with the tomato-arugula salad.

Makes 4 servings

Nutrition Information
values are per serving

CALORIES 278	DIETARY FIBER 2.7 G
TOTAL FAT 13 G	BETA CAROTENE 1.5 MG
SATURATED FAT 2.6 G	VITAMIN C 48 MG
CHOLESTEROL 59 MG	CALCIUM 64 MG
SODIUM 722 MG	IRON 2.1 MG

Cornmeal-Baked Snapper with Papaya and Corn Salsa

The flavors of the Southwest stand out here: Corn stars in the salsa that is spicy with chili powder and fresh with cilantro. Then corn appears again, as cornmeal, providing a wonderful crunchy crust on the snapper as it oven-bakes. Baked pepper halves, filled with black beans, would make a dramatic-looking and tasty accompaniment.

SALSA

1 papaya—peeled, seeded and diced
1 cup diced red bell pepper
½ cup corn kernels, thawed frozen or fresh (from 2 ears)
¼ cup minced cilantro
2 tablespoons fresh lime juice
¼ teaspoon chili powder

FISH

½ teaspoon garlic powder
½ teaspoon chili powder
¼ teaspoon salt
¼ teaspoon freshly ground black pepper
⅛ teaspoon cayenne pepper
4 skinned red snapper fillets (1 pound total)
1 egg white lightly beaten with 1 tablespoon water
⅔ cup cornmeal
1 tablespoon olive oil
1 lime, cut into wedges

1. To Make the Salsa In a medium bowl, gently mix the papaya, bell pepper, corn, cilantro, lime juice and chili powder; cover and set aside.

2. For the Fish In a small bowl or cup, mix the garlic powder, chili powder, salt, black pepper and cayenne. Sprinkle evenly over both sides of the red snapper.

3. Place the beaten egg white in a shallow bowl or pie plate. Place the cornmeal in another shallow bowl or pie plate.

4. Spray a baking sheet with nonstick cooking spray. One fillet at a time, dip the fish in the egg white mixture and then dredge in the cornmeal, pressing the cornmeal into the surface. Arrange in a single layer on the prepared pan. Cover with a sheet of wax paper and let stand while the oven preheats.

5. Preheat the oven to 450°.

6. Drizzle the fish with the oil and bake for 7 to 9 minutes, or it is until light golden brown and just flakes when tested with a fork.

7. Serve the fish with the salsa and lime wedges.

Makes 4 servings

Nutrition Information
values are per serving

CALORIES 297	DIETARY FIBER 3.1 G
TOTAL FAT 6.0 G	BETA CAROTENE 2.0 MG
SATURATED FAT .9 G	VITAMIN C 103 MG
CHOLESTEROL 42 MG	CALCIUM 69 MG
SODIUM 233 MG	IRON 1.6 MG

Orange-Glazed Broiled Tuna with Gingered Citrus Sauce

The clean, refreshing taste of citrus is remarkably compatible with fish, as this combination of fresh tuna, orange and grapefruit so ably demonstrates. Serve it with rice.

¼ cup orange juice
¼ cup grapefruit juice
2 tablespoons light brown sugar
2 tablespoons reduced-sodium soy sauce
1 tablespoon honey
2 garlic cloves, peeled and lightly smashed
2 slices (quarter-size) fresh ginger

4 tuna steaks (1¼ pounds total)
2 teaspoons cornstarch blended with 1 tablespoon water
1 cup diced orange sections
1 cup diced grapefruit sections
2 tablespoons chopped cilantro

1. In a small saucepan, stir together the orange juice, grapefruit juice, sugar, soy sauce, honey, garlic and ginger. Measure out half of the liquid (leaving the ginger and garlic in the saucepan) and place it in a nonreactive container big enough to hold all of the fish in a single layer. Set the saucepan with the rest of the citrus mixture aside.

2. Place the tuna steaks in the marinade and set aside to marinate for 30 minutes.

3. Preheat the broiler with the broiler pan 5 inches from the heat. Place the tuna steaks on the broiler pan and brush some of the marinade over them. Broil for 3 minutes, turn the tuna over, brush with the remaining marinade and continue broiling until the tuna is medium-rare, about 4 minutes longer.

4. Meanwhile, place the saucepan with the reserved citrus mixture over medium heat and bring to a boil. Discard the ginger and garlic. Stir in the cornstarch mixture and boil until lightly thickened, about 30 seconds.

5. Remove the sauce from the heat and stir in the diced orange and grapefruit sections and the cilantro.

6. Serve the tuna topped with the citrus sauce.

Makes 4 servings

NUTRITION INFORMATION
values are per serving

CALORIES 289	DIETARY FIBER 1.5 G
TOTAL FAT 6.3 G	BETA CAROTENE .1 MG
SATURATED FAT 1.6 G	VITAMIN C 55 MG
CHOLESTEROL 48 MG	CALCIUM 38 MG
SODIUM 353 MG	IRON 1.8 MG

SUPER QUICK

Grilled Tuna with White Beans

Working time: 25 minutes Total time: 30 minutes

¼ cup (not oil-packed) sun-dried tomatoes
½ cup boiling water
2 cups canned cannellini or other white beans, rinsed and drained
2 plum tomatoes, seeded and diced
½ cup diced red onion
¼ cup diced red bell pepper
¼ cup chopped flat-leaf parsley
3 tablespoons red wine vinegar
1 tablespoon plus 1 teaspoon extra-virgin olive oil
2 teaspoons coarsely cracked black pepper
1 garlic clove, minced
½ teaspoon salt
4 tuna steaks (1½ pounds total)

1 Preheat the broiler. Spray a broiler pan with nonstick cooking spray.

2 In a small bowl, combine the sun-dried tomatoes and boiling water, and set aside to soften, about 10 minutes. Drain and coarsely chop.

3 In a large bowl, combine the chopped sun-dried tomatoes, the beans, plum tomatoes, onion, bell pepper, parsley, 2 tablespoons of the red wine vinegar, 1 tablespoon of the olive oil, ½ teaspoon of the black pepper, the garlic and ¼ teaspoon of the salt. Mix well and set aside at room temperature to blend the flavors.

4 Rub the tuna with the remaining 1 tablespoon vinegar and 1 teaspoon olive oil. Sprinkle with the remaining 1½ teaspoons pepper and ¼ teaspoon salt. Broil the tuna 4 inches from the heat for about 8 minutes, or until just slightly pink in the center.

5 Divide the beans among 4 plates and place a grilled tuna steak on top.

Makes 4 servings

Values are per serving:
Calories: 383 Total fat: 13 g Saturated fat: 2.7 g Cholesterol: 58 mg Sodium: 604 mg
Dietary fiber: 6.4 g Beta carotene: .9 mg Vitamin C: 35 mg Calcium: 56 mg Iron: 4.4 mg

Tuna Cakes with Carrot-Pepper Slaw

Though not available everywhere, reduced-sodium water-packed tuna is well worth the search: Not only are the sodium levels better for you, but the flavors of the tuna are truer. If you can't find it, of course these fish cakes will be fine with regular water-packed tuna.

TUNA CAKES

One 6⅛-ounce can reduced-sodium water-packed tuna, drained and flaked
1 cup frozen corn kernels, thawed
½ cup shredded carrots
2 tablespoons minced red onion
2 egg whites
2 teaspoons grainy Dijon mustard
½ cup plain dried bread crumbs
½ teaspoon freshly ground black pepper
1½ teaspoons olive oil

SLAW

¼ cup plain nonfat yogurt
3 tablespoons reduced-calorie mayonnaise
1 tablespoon fresh lemon juice
¼ teaspoon freshly ground black pepper
4 cups shredded cabbage
1 cup shredded carrots
1 medium green bell pepper, thinly sliced

1. Preheat the oven to 375°. Spray a baking sheet with nonstick cooking spray.

2. To Make the Tuna Cakes In a medium bowl, mix the tuna, corn, carrots, onion, egg whites, mustard, ¼ cup of the bread crumbs and the black pepper. Form into four fairly flat patties. Dredge in the remaining ¼ cup bread crumbs, pressing the crumbs into the surface, and place on the prepared baking sheet. Drizzle with the oil.

3. Bake the patties for about 15 minutes, or until light golden brown.

4. Meanwhile, Make the Slaw In a medium bowl, whisk together the yogurt, mayonnaise, lemon juice and black pepper. Add the cabbage, carrots and bell pepper, and toss to blend well. Serve the slaw with the tuna cakes.

Makes 4 servings

Nutrition Information
values are per serving

CALORIES 238	DIETARY FIBER 4.9 G
TOTAL FAT 6.8 G	BETA CAROTENE 7.1 MG
SATURATED FAT 1.3 G	VITAMIN C 58 MG
CHOLESTEROL 19 MG	CALCIUM 115 MG
SODIUM 408 MG	IRON 2.2 MG

Broiled Scallops with Gingered Nectarine Sauce

The slightly sweet flavor and silken texture of sea scallops lend themselves well to simple broiling or grilling recipes. Here they are threaded with vegetables onto skewers, basted with a Chinese-inspired sauce and broiled. Be sure to serve these with rice in order to savor the marvelous nectarine sauce.

1 tablespoon plus 1 teaspoon olive oil
4 slices (quarter-size) fresh ginger, minced
2 small garlic cloves, minced
2 medium nectarines, coarsely chopped
¼ cup apricot preserves
2 tablespoons minced chives
2 tablespoons Dijon mustard
2 tablespoons cider vinegar
¼ teaspoon freshly ground black pepper
4 medium carrots, cut into 1-inch chunks
1¼ pounds sea scallops
1 large red bell pepper, cut into 1-inch squares

1. In a small saucepan, warm 2 teaspoons of the oil over medium-high heat until hot but not smoking. Add the ginger and garlic, and stir-fry until fragrant, about 30 seconds.

2. Add the nectarines, apricot preserves, chives, mustard, vinegar and black pepper. Bring to a boil, stirring. Reduce the heat to low, cover and simmer for 10 minutes. Remove from the heat.

3. Meanwhile, cook the carrots in a medium saucepan of boiling water until almost tender, 5 to 6 minutes. Drain and allow to cool slightly.

4. Preheat the broiler. Cut any large scallops so that all of the scallops are approximately the same size. Divide the carrots, scallops and bell pepper evenly among 8 skewers and place them on a nonstick broiler pan.

5. Transfer half of the nectarine mixture to a food processor or blender and purée until smooth.

6. Brush the skewers with half of the nectarine purée and drizzle with 1 teaspoon of the remaining oil. Broil the scallops 4 inches from the heat for 3 minutes.

7. Turn the skewers over, brush them with the remaining purée and drizzle with the remaining 1 teaspoon oil. Broil until cooked through, 3 to 5 minutes.

8. Serve the scallops with the reserved nectarine sauce on the side.

Makes 4 servings

NUTRITION INFORMATION
values are per serving

CALORIES 298	DIETARY FIBER 4.1 G
TOTAL FAT 6.6 G	BETA CAROTENE 13 MG
SATURATED FAT .7 G	VITAMIN C 61 MG
CHOLESTEROL 47 MG	CALCIUM 68 MG
SODIUM 488 MG	IRON 1.2 MG

Scallop, Pepper and Sweet Potato Skillet

A classic Creole gumbo begins with a roux—a cooked flour and butter mixture—and in addition to other components, which can range from shellfish to sausage, invariably includes okra. The gumbo-like dish below, also with okra, is much lower in fat than a traditional gumbo, but no less delicious. Salad is all you need as an accompaniment and, for dessert, try coffee frozen yogurt with crushed praline on top or stirred in.

2 teaspoons olive oil
1 large onion, chopped
4 garlic cloves, minced
1 large red bell pepper, diced
1 large green bell pepper, diced
1 medium sweet potato (8 ounces), peeled and cut into 2-inch chunks
⅔ cup rice
1½ cups water
One 14½-ounce can no-salt-added stewed tomatoes, chopped with their juice
One 10-ounce package frozen okra, thawed
½ teaspoon salt
½ teaspoon oregano
1 pound sea scallops, halved crosswise if large

1. In a large nonstick skillet, warm the oil over medium heat until hot but not smoking. Add the onion and garlic, and cook, stirring frequently, until softened, about 7 minutes.

2. Stir in the red and green bell peppers and the sweet potato, and cook until the peppers are softened, about 5 minutes.

3. Stir in the rice and water, bring to a boil, reduce to a simmer, cover and cook for 15 minutes.

4. Stir in the stewed tomatoes and their juice, the okra, salt and oregano; cover and cook until the rice is almost tender, about 7 minutes.

5. Place the scallops on top of the rice mixture, cover and cook just until the scallops are cooked through, about 5 minutes.

Makes 4 servings

Nutrition Information
values are per serving

CALORIES 364	DIETARY FIBER 7.8 G
TOTAL FAT 4.0 G	BETA CAROTENE 6.4 MG
SATURATED FAT .5 G	VITAMIN C 106 MG
CHOLESTEROL 37 MG	CALCIUM 162 MG
SODIUM 486 MG	IRON 3.5 MG

Garlic-Sautéed Shrimp and Spinach

Shrimp with garlic, and spinach with garlic are both natural combinations. To put them together, as here, is to have the best of both worlds.

1 pound medium shrimp, shelled and deveined
1½ teaspoons grated lemon zest
1 tablespoon fresh lemon juice
½ teaspoon salt
½ teaspoon freshly ground black pepper
1 tablespoon plus 1 teaspoon extra-virgin olive oil
6 garlic cloves, sliced
10 cups (loosely packed) stemmed spinach
1 tablespoon canned chicken broth
1 cup bottled roasted red peppers–rinsed, drained and cut into strips

1. Toss the shrimp with the lemon zest, lemon juice and ¼ teaspoon each of the salt and pepper.

2. In a large deep nonstick skillet, warm the oil over high heat until hot but not smoking. Add the garlic and sauté, stirring, until golden, 2 to 3 minutes. Immediately transfer the garlic with a slotted spoon to a plate.

3. Add the shrimp to the skillet and sauté until the shrimp are pink and just opaque in the center, 2 to 3 minutes. With tongs or a spoon, transfer the shrimp to a clean plate.

4. Add the spinach to the skillet in handfuls, adding another handful as the spinach cooks down; drizzle the spinach with the broth as it cooks. When all of the spinach has been added, season it with the remaining ¼ teaspoon each salt and black pepper. Add the roasted red peppers to the skillet and cook, stirring, just until heated.

5. Return the shrimp and the garlic to the skillet and toss to mix with the spinach and peppers.

Makes 4 servings

Nutrition Information
values are per serving

CALORIES 196	DIETARY FIBER 4.6 G
TOTAL FAT 7.0 G	BETA CAROTENE 7.8 MG
SATURATED FAT 1.1 G	VITAMIN C 94 MG
CHOLESTEROL 140 MG	CALCIUM 236 MG
SODIUM 571 MG	IRON 7.9 MG

Curried Shrimp and Peppers

Commercial curry powders vary in strength, so if you are concerned about the spiciness of this dish, add only half the curry powder called for, taste and then add the remainder if the dish seems mild. If, on the other hand, you prefer hot curry, do not increase the amount of curry powder, but add a bit of cayenne instead.

2 medium red bell peppers, cut into large pieces
½ pound unpeeled sweet potatoes, quartered
½ cup canned chicken broth diluted with ¼ cup water, or ¾ cup Homemade Chicken Broth (p. 54)
4 (not oil-packed) sun-dried tomato halves
2 teaspoons vegetable oil

1 cup chopped onion
2 garlic cloves, minced
2 tablespoons curry powder
½ teaspoon sugar
1 pound medium shrimp, shelled and deveined
1 medium green bell pepper, cut into 1-inch squares
1 cup sliced celery
3 tablespoons chopped cilantro
2 tablespoons nonfat sour cream

1. In a medium saucepan, bring the red bell peppers, sweet potatoes, diluted chicken broth and sun-dried tomatoes to a boil over medium-high heat. Reduce the heat, cover and simmer until the sweet potatoes are just tender, about 10 minutes.

2. Meanwhile, in a large nonstick skillet, warm the oil over medium-high heat until hot but not smoking. Add the onion and garlic, and cook, stirring, until lightly browned, about 2 minutes. Add the curry powder and cook, stirring, until the curry is fragrant, about 30 seconds. Remove the skillet from the heat.

3. Reserving the broth, transfer the cooked sweet potatoes and red bell peppers to a food processor. Add the sautéed onion mixture and process until smooth. Add the reserved broth and the sugar, and process the sauce until smooth.

4. Return the sauce to the skillet and bring to a boil over medium-high heat. Add the shrimp, green bell pepper and celery, and cook, stirring, until the shrimp are cooked through, about 4 to 6 minutes.

5. Stir the cilantro into the curry. Serve the curry dolloped with the sour cream.

Makes 4 servings

Nutrition Information
values are per serving

CALORIES 243	DIETARY FIBER 5.3 G
TOTAL FAT 5.0 G	BETA CAROTENE 8.5 MG
SATURATED FAT .6 G	VITAMIN C 113 MG
CHOLESTEROL 140 MG	CALCIUM 117 MG
SODIUM 306 MG	IRON 4.2 MG

Lime-Broiled Shrimp with Tropical Fruit Relish

In this light, appealing entrée, a colorful fresh fruit relish serves as background to broiled lime-marinated shrimp. This dish is simple to make, pretty and elegant, and could just as easily serve as a stunning appetizer for a dinner party.

½ teaspoon grated lime zest
3 tablespoons fresh lime juice
2 tablespoons reduced-sodium soy sauce
2 teaspoons light brown sugar
⅛ teaspoon cayenne pepper
1 pound large shrimp, shelled and deveined
2 cups diced pineapple, fresh or canned juice-packed
2 kiwi fruit, peeled and diced
½ cup diced jicama or tart, crisp apple
2 tablespoons honey
2 tablespoons chopped cilantro

1. In a large bowl, stir together the lime zest, 2 tablespoons of the lime juice, the soy sauce, brown sugar and cayenne. Add the shrimp, tossing to coat, and let marinate while you prepare the relish.

2. In a large bowl, stir together the pineapple, kiwi, jicama, honey, cilantro and remaining 1 tablespoon lime juice.

3. Preheat the broiler. Place the shrimp on a broiler pan, drizzle the marinade over them and broil 5 inches from the heat for about 5 minutes, or until the shrimp are just cooked through and browned.

4. Spoon the relish onto 4 serving plates and place the shrimp on top.

Makes 4 servings

Nutrition Information
values are per serving

CALORIES 214	DIETARY FIBER 2.5 G
TOTAL FAT 2.1 G	BETA CAROTENE .1 MG
SATURATED FAT .3 G	VITAMIN C 47 MG
CHOLESTEROL 140 MG	CALCIUM 71 MG
SODIUM 441 MG	IRON 3.0 MG

Shrimp with Carrot-Ginger Broth and Cilantro

If the remarkably healthful attributes of carrot juice were not enough (a half cup provides 100% of the Wellness Recommended Intake for beta carotene—see page 11), the subtly sweet flavor and glorious orange color it adds to this dish should be the final convincers. Though it is easily obtainable at health food stores, some supermarkets and even in take-out containers at juice bars, you can also make your own carrot juice in a juicer. Follow a super-light main course such as this with a salad of mesclun and grilled mushrooms and, for dessert, assorted fresh berries drizzled with wildflower honey.

1 cup carrot juice
½ cup chicken broth, canned or homemade (p. 54)
½ teaspoon ground ginger
1 teaspoon minced jalapeño pepper
¼ teaspoon salt
⅛ teaspoon ground cardamom
⅛ teaspoon cayenne pepper
1¼ pounds large shrimp, shelled and deveined
1 large red bell pepper, cut into slivers
1 medium yellow summer squash, thinly sliced
1½ teaspoons cornstarch blended with
1 tablespoon water
1 tablespoon fresh lime juice
3 tablespoons chopped cilantro

1. In a large skillet over medium heat, combine the carrot juice, chicken broth, ginger, jalapeño, salt, cardamom and cayenne. Bring to a boil, reduce to a simmer and cook for 5 minutes.

2. Add the shrimp, bell pepper and squash, and simmer gently until the shrimp and vegetables are cooked through, about 4 minutes.

3. With a slotted spoon, transfer the shrimp and vegetables to 4 deep serving plates or shallow bowls. Keep the cooking liquid at a simmer.

4. Stir the cornstarch mixture into the simmering broth. Bring to a boil and cook until the broth is slightly thickened and does not appear separated, about 1 minute. Stir in the lime juice and cilantro.

5. Pour the hot carrot-ginger broth over the shrimp and vegetables and serve.

Makes 4 servings

Nutrition Information
values are per serving

CALORIES 171	DIETARY FIBER .9 G
TOTAL FAT 2.4 G	BETA CAROTENE 11 MG
SATURATED FAT .4 G	VITAMIN C 59 MG
CHOLESTEROL 174 MG	CALCIUM 89 MG
SODIUM 448 MG	IRON 3.4 MG

Meat

Veal Scallops with Asparagus and Tomato Vinaigrette

As elegant combinations go, it is very hard to improve upon veal with asparagus. A sublime, light dish, perfect for entertaining, this would be especially good preceded by a fresh or wild mushroom risotto.

1¼ pounds asparagus, cut into 1½-inch pieces
½ teaspoon rosemary, crumbled
½ teaspoon salt
½ teaspoon freshly ground black pepper
1 pound thinly sliced veal scallops
1 tablespoons plus 1 teaspoon olive oil
4 medium shallots, minced
One 5½-ounce can low-sodium mixed vegetable juice
½ cup chicken broth, canned or homemade (p. 54)
1½ teaspoons cornstarch blended with 1 tablespoon water
1 tablespoon balsamic vinegar
1 teaspoon Dijon mustard
8 plum tomatoes, diced

1. In a vegetable steamer, steam the asparagus until it is crisp-tender, about 4 minutes. Transfer the asparagus to a plate and cover loosely.

2. In a small bowl, combine the rosemary, salt and pepper, and rub the veal with this mixture.

3. In a large nonstick skillet, warm 2 teaspoons of the oil over medium-high heat until hot but not smoking. Add half of the veal and sauté for about 1 minute per side. Transfer the veal to a plate and cover loosely to keep warm. Repeat with the remaining veal and 2 teaspoons oil.

4. Add the shallots to the skillet and cook for 1 minute. Add the mixed vegetable juice, chicken broth and cornstarch mixture, and cook, stirring, until the sauce is lightly thickened, 1 to 2 minutes.

5. Whisk in the vinegar and mustard, and cook for 30 seconds. Add the asparagus and tomatoes, and toss to coat with the sauce. Cook until the vegetables are heated through. Serve the veal topped with the asparagus and tomato mixture.

Makes 4 servings

Nutrition Information
values are per serving

CALORIES 232	DIETARY FIBER 2.6 G
TOTAL FAT 7.2 G	BETA CAROTENE 1.3 MG
SATURATED FAT 1.3 G	VITAMIN C 74 MG
CHOLESTEROL 89 MG	CALCIUM 54 MG
SODIUM 547 MG	IRON 2.7 MG

Flank Steak with Tomato Marmalade and Watercress

The flank steak here can just as easily be grilled on an outdoor barbecue as broiled. Wonderful al fresco fare, this entrée can be served hot or at room temperature, or even lightly chilled.

1 pound well-trimmed beef flank steak
1 medium yellow onion, coarsely chopped
2 garlic cloves, peeled
1 fresh jalapeño pepper, halved, some seeds removed
1 tablespoon coarsely chopped fresh ginger
1 tablespoon reduced-sodium soy sauce
1 tablespoon honey
¾ cup chopped red onion
¼ cup raisins
3 tablespoons red wine vinegar
2 tablespoons granulated sugar
2 tablespoons canned chicken broth
1½ teaspoons mustard seeds (optional)
¼ teaspoon freshly ground black pepper
2 medium tomatoes, diced

2 tablespoons chopped parsley, preferably flat-leaf
⅛ teaspoon salt
1 large bunch of watercress, tough stems removed

1. Score the flank steak on both sides with three or four ¼-inch-deep diagonal slashes.

2. In a food processor, place the chopped yellow onion, garlic, jalapeño, ginger, soy sauce and honey, and process until puréed. Rub the mixture onto both sides of the flank steak, pressing it into the slashes. Place the steak on a plate, cover and marinate for at least 30 minutes, and up to 8 hours.

3. Meanwhile, in a medium saucepan, combine the red onion, raisins, vinegar, sugar, chicken broth, mustard seeds (if using) and black pepper, and bring to a boil over high heat. Reduce the heat to medium-low, cover and simmer, stirring occasionally, until the onion is very tender and the raisins softened, about 15 minutes.

4. Remove the raisin mixture from the heat and stir in the tomatoes, parsley and salt. Cover the marmalade mixture and let stand while you preheat the broiler.

5. Preheat the broiler and broiler pan. Place the steak on the preheated broiler pan and spread with half the marmalade mixture. Broil 4 to 5 inches from the heat for 6 minutes. Turn the steak, spread with the remaining marmalade mixture, and broil for 6 minutes, or until medium-rare.

6. Spread the watercress on a platter and place the steak on the watercress. Let stand for 5 minutes (this will wilt the watercress slightly and make the beef juicier).

7. Carve the beef on an angle into thin slices and serve with the marmalade and watercress.

Makes 4 servings

Nutrition Information
values are per serving

CALORIES 301	DIETARY FIBER 3.9 G
TOTAL FAT 9.0 G	BETA CAROTENE 1.9 MG
SATURATED FAT 3.8 G	VITAMIN C 54 MG
CHOLESTEROL 57 MG	CALCIUM 107 MG
SODIUM 357 MG	IRON 3.3 MG

Grilled Flank Steak with Sweet-and-Sour Sauce

The dried-apricot based basting sauce for this marvelous steak also makes a delicious sauce to serve with the steak. Just be sure that you do not dip the basting brush—which has been used to coat the uncooked meat—back into the mixture to be used for the sauce.

½ cup chopped dried apricots
1¼ cups carrot juice
2 tablespoons apricot all-fruit spread
2 tablespoons honey
2 tablespoons red wine vinegar
1 tablespoon plus 1 teaspoon Dijon mustard
1 teaspoon ground ginger
¼ teaspoon salt
1 pound well-trimmed beef flank steak

1. In a small saucepan, combine the apricots and ¾ cup of the carrot juice. Bring to a boil over medium heat, reduce the heat to a simmer, cover and cook until the apricots are very soft and tender, about 20 minutes.

2. Transfer the apricots and liquid to a food processor. Add the remaining ½ cup carrot juice, the fruit spread, honey, vinegar, mustard, ginger and salt, and purée until smooth. Measure out ⅓ cup for brushing on the steak.

3. Preheat the broiler. Place the flank steak on a broiler pan and brush with the reserved ⅓ cup of apricot mixture. Broil 5 inches from the heat until lightly caramelized and medium-rare, about 15 minutes. Place on a carving board and let rest 15 minutes before slicing.

4. Slice the steak and pass the remaining sweet-and-sour sauce on the side.

Makes 4 servings

Nutrition Information
values are per serving

CALORIES 307	DIETARY FIBER 1.3 G
TOTAL FAT 9.1 G	BETA CAROTENE 13 MG
SATURATED FAT 3.7 G	VITAMIN C 7.0 MG
CHOLESTEROL 57 MG	CALCIUM 34 MG
SODIUM 380 MG	IRON 3.4 MG

Steak with Burgundy Sauce

To make a French Burgundy-style sauce in the classic manner requires a considerable investment in time and effort (including having homemade brown stock on hand) and relies on a good deal of butter. This streamlined version demands much less time, uses olive oil in place of butter and adds colorful and healthful vegetables to accompany the traditional mushrooms.

2 teaspoons olive oil
½ cup minced shallots
2 garlic cloves, minced
½ teaspoon thyme
½ teaspoon salt
½ teaspoon freshly ground black pepper
1 large red bell pepper, diced
1 cup diced carrots
½ cup beef broth
1 cup dry red wine
1 pound lean boneless sirloin steak
12 large mushroom caps, stems trimmed flat (about 1 pound)
1 tablespoon cornstarch blended with 2 tablespoons water
2 tablespoons chopped flat-leaf parsley

1. In a medium nonstick saucepan, warm the oil over medium heat. Stir in the shallots, garlic, thyme, and ¼ teaspoon each of the salt and black pepper, and sauté until the shallots start to brown and become tender, 1 to 2 minutes.

2. Add the bell pepper and carrots, and toss to coat well with the shallots. Sauté, stirring often, just until the vegetables start to soften, about 2 minutes.

3. Add the beef broth and bring to a boil. Reduce the heat to medium-low, cover and simmer, stirring once or twice, until the vegetables are tender, 5 to 7 minutes.

4. Preheat the broiler and broiler pan.

5. Meanwhile, stir the wine into the vegetables, increase the heat to medium and bring to a boil. Reduce the heat to medium-low and simmer, stirring once or twice, for 10 minutes to blend the flavors and remove the raw taste from the wine.

6. While the sauce simmers, season the steak with the remaining ¼ teaspoon each salt and black pepper. Place on the preheated broiler pan and arrange the mushrooms around the steak. Broil 4 to 5 inches from the heat, turning the steak and mushrooms once, for 10 minutes, or until the steak is medium-rare and the mushrooms are tender. Transfer the mushrooms and steak to a platter and let stand for 5 minutes.

7. Uncover the sauce and increase the heat to medium-high. Stir in the cornstarch mixture and bring to a boil, stirring constantly, until thickened and bubbly. Cover and remove from the heat.

8. Pour any juices from the platter into the sauce. Carve the steak into thin slices and spoon the sauce over the steak and the mushrooms; sprinkle with the parsley.

Makes 4 servings

Nutrition Information
values are per serving

CALORIES 304	DIETARY FIBER 3.1 G
TOTAL FAT 9.1 G	BETA CAROTENE 5.6 MG
SATURATED FAT 2.7 G	VITAMIN C 58 MG
CHOLESTEROL 76 MG	CALCIUM 48 MG
SODIUM 454 MG	IRON 5.4 MG

Rump Roast with Root Vegetables

Call it rump roast if you like, but this is pot roast, made particularly moist and juicy by the addition of six different vegetables that cook alongside the meat. This dinner in one pot deserves particularly good bread or dinner rolls for sopping up the pan juices.

3 garlic cloves, crushed through a press
1½ teaspoons rosemary, crumbled
1½ teaspoons coarsely cracked black pepper
1 teaspoon salt
One 2-pound well-trimmed beef rump roast
1½ pounds sweet potatoes, peeled and cut into 1-inch chunks
1½ pounds small red-skinned potatoes, cut into ¾-inch wedges
2 large onions, cut into ½-inch wedges
3 large carrots, cut into 1-inch chunks
3 medium parsnips, cut into 1-inch chunks
2 large celery stalks, cut into ½-inch pieces
½ cup chicken or beef broth
1 tablespoon extra-virgin olive oil

1. Preheat the oven to 375°.

2. In a small bowl or cup, combine the garlic, rosemary, 1 teaspoon of the pepper and ½ teaspoon of the salt. Rub the mixture over the roast.

3. Place the sweet potatoes, red potatoes, onions, carrots, parsnips and celery in a large roasting pan. Drizzle with the broth and olive oil and the remaining ½ teaspoon each pepper and salt. Toss to mix.

4. Place the roast on top of the vegetables and roast for about 1 hour and 15 minutes, stirring the vegetables occasionally, or until the meat is rare (135° on a meat thermometer).

5. Transfer the roast to a platter and set aside, loosely covered.

6. Continue roasting the vegetables, turning occasionally, for 15 to 20 minutes, or until they are lightly browned and tender.

7. Transfer the vegetables and pan juices to a large platter. Carve the meat into thin slices and arrange on the platter; pour any juices from the cutting board over the meat.

Makes 8 servings

Nutrition Information
values are per serving

CALORIES 381	DIETARY FIBER 7.5 G
TOTAL FAT 8.1 G	BETA CAROTENE 14 MG
SATURATED FAT 2.2 G	VITAMIN C 43 MG
CHOLESTEROL 66 MG	CALCIUM 68 MG
SODIUM 444 MG	IRON 4.2 MG

Tex-Mex Unstuffed Peppers

Several bell peppers here contribute flavor and tons of vitamin C to this spirited dish. The chili-style mixture that ordinarily is used to stuff whole peppers is here cooked along with strips of pepper and served over rice. If you are making this in advance and have added hot pepper sauce, remember that the longer it sits the spicier it will get.

1 cup converted rice
2 cups water
½ pound well-trimmed boneless beef top round, cut into chunks
1 tablespoon plus 1 teaspoon chili powder
2 teaspoons olive oil
2 garlic cloves, minced
¼ cup plus 2 tablespoons beef broth
3 large red bell peppers, cut into ¾-inch-wide strips
½ teaspoon oregano
½ teaspoon freshly ground black pepper
¼ teaspoon salt
One 14½-ounce can no-salt-added stewed tomatoes

One 8-ounce can no-salt-added tomato sauce
One 10½-ounce can kidney beans, rinsed and drained
Several drops of hot pepper sauce (optional)
1½ ounces sharp Cheddar cheese, shredded

1. Place the rice and water in a medium saucepan and bring to a boil over high heat. Reduce the heat to low, cover and simmer until the rice is tender and the water absorbed, about 20 minutes. Remove from the heat and set aside. (Covered, the rice will stay warm for quite a while.)

2. Meanwhile, place the beef in a food processor and process just until ground. Add 1 teaspoon of the chili powder and pulse just until mixed.

3. In a Dutch oven or flameproof casserole, warm 1 teaspoon of the oil over medium-high heat. Crumble in the beef; stir in the garlic and drizzle with 2 tablespoons of the broth. Cook, stirring, just until lightly browned, 1 to 2 minutes. With a slotted spoon, transfer the beef to a plate.

4. Add the remaining 1 teaspoon oil to the pan. Stir in the bell peppers, remaining 1 tablespoon chili powder, the oregano, black pepper and salt. Add the remaining ¼ cup beef broth and bring to a boil. Reduce the heat to medium, cover and cook, stirring frequently, until the vegetables are tender, 6 to 8 minutes.

5. Return the beef to the pan along with the stewed tomatoes, tomato sauce and beans; increase the heat to high and bring to a boil. Reduce the heat to medium-low, cover and simmer for 10 to 15 minutes, stirring occasionally, to blend the flavors. Add the hot pepper sauce (if using).

6. Spoon the rice into bowls, top with the chili and sprinkle with the cheese.

Makes 4 servings

NUTRITION INFORMATION
values are per serving

CALORIES 439	DIETARY FIBER 9.1 G
TOTAL FAT 9.3 G	BETA CAROTENE 3.9 MG
SATURATED FAT 3.3 G	VITAMIN C 168 MG
CHOLESTEROL 44 MG	CALCIUM 178 MG
SODIUM 460 MG	IRON 5.7 MG

SUPER QUICK

Hamburgers with Pepper Chutney

Working time: 10 minutes Total time: 25 minutes

- One 14½-ounce can no-salt-added stewed tomatoes, chopped
- 1 large red bell pepper, diced
- 1 large yellow bell pepper, diced
- ¼ cup (packed) dark brown sugar
- ¼ cup cider vinegar
- 1 pound lean ground beef
- ¼ cup thinly sliced scallions
- 1 tablespoon prepared mustard
- ¼ teaspoon oregano
- ¼ teaspoon salt
- ⅛ teaspoon freshly ground black pepper
- 4 cups shredded Romaine lettuce
- 1 large tomato, thinly sliced

1 In a large saucepan, combine the stewed tomatoes, the red and yellow bell peppers, sugar and vinegar. Bring to a boil over medium heat, reduce the heat to a simmer and cook until the chutney is thick and the peppers are tender, about 15 minutes.

2 Meanwhile, preheat the broiler or prepare the grill.

3 In a medium bowl, combine the beef, scallions, mustard, oregano, salt and black pepper. Shape into 4 patties and broil 5 inches from the heat for about 7 minutes, or until browned and cooked until medium.

4 Place the burgers on 4 serving plates along with the Romaine lettuce and sliced fresh tomato. Spoon the chutney over the burgers and serve.

Makes 4 servings

Values are per serving:
Calories: 335 Total fat: 15 g Saturated fat: 5.9 g Cholesterol: 70 mg Sodium: 279 mg
Dietary fiber: 4.8 g Beta carotene: 2.3 mg Vitamin C: 105 mg Calcium: 93 mg Iron: 4.0 mg

Spiced Beef Kebabs with Plums

Plum sauce, available in the Chinese foods sections of most supermarkets, combines plums cooked until thick with sugar, vinegar, ginger and spices. Used straight out of the bottle, it makes a good barbecue sauce, but enhanced, as it is below, it makes an even better one. If you can't find plum sauce, try a mixture of plum jam and soy sauce: Use 2 tablespoons jam and 1 teaspoon soy.

2 large carrots, cut into 1-inch lengths
2 tablespoons plum sauce
4 garlic cloves, minced
2 teaspoons oregano
½ teaspoon salt
½ teaspoon sugar
¼ teaspoon allspice
¼ teaspoon ground ginger
¼ teaspoon freshly ground black pepper
1 pound beef top round, cut into ¾-inch cubes
1 red onion, cut into 1-inch chunks
1 large red bell pepper, cut into 1-inch pieces
2 plums, cut into 1-inch wedges

1. In a large pot of boiling water, cook the carrots until crisp-tender, about 4 minutes. Drain and rinse under cold water.

2. In a large bowl, stir together the plum sauce, garlic, oregano, salt, sugar, allspice, ginger and black pepper.

3. Add the beef to the sauce and toss to coat. Add the onion, bell pepper and plums to the bowl, and stir to coat.

4. Preheat the broiler or prepare the grill.

5. Alternating ingredients, thread the meat, vegetables and plums onto eight 12-inch skewers. Broil or grill 6 inches from the heat, turning the skewers over midway, for about 8 minutes, or until the meat is browned and medium-rare.

Makes 4 servings

NUTRITION INFORMATION
values are per serving

CALORIES 237	DIETARY FIBER 3.4 G
TOTAL FAT 4.6 G	BETA CAROTENE 9.5 MG
SATURATED FAT 1.5 G	VITAMIN C 61 MG
CHOLESTEROL 71 MG	CALCIUM 76 MG
SODIUM 387 MG	IRON 3.5 MG

Taoseños Cornmeal Casserole

This New Mexican-style casserole of spicy meat atop cornmeal mush fits into the category of comfort food—a good Sunday supper kind of dish. Add a refreshing crunch by accompanying it with a salad of jicama and sliced oranges on a bed of watercress.

1 cup cornmeal
1½ cups lowfat (1%) milk
1 cup water
½ teaspoon salt
½ cup grated Parmesan cheese
1 tablespoon olive oil
½ pound lean ground beef, preferably from well-trimmed bottom round
3 red bell peppers, slivered
½ pound carrots, thinly sliced on the diagonal
¼ cup diced fresh jalapeño peppers, without seeds
4 ounces spinach leaves, cut crosswise into ¼-inch-wide strips
¼ teaspoon freshly ground black pepper

1. Preheat the oven to 400°. In a large saucepan, combine the cornmeal with the milk, water and ¼ teaspoon of the salt. Bring to a boil over medium heat; cook until the mixture reaches the consistency of mashed potatoes, 3 to 4 minutes.

2. Remove the cornmeal mixture from the

heat and stir in the Parmesan and oil. Spread the mixture in an even layer in the bottom of a shallow 2-quart baking dish.

3. In large nonstick skillet, sauté the beef with the bell peppers, carrots and jalapeño peppers over medium-high heat until cooked through and fragrant, about 6 minutes. Add the spinach, black pepper and remaining ¼ teaspoon salt, and cook until the spinach is wilted, about 1 minute.

4. Transfer the beef and vegetable mixture to the baking dish and spread over the cornmeal layer. Bake for 20 minutes, or until hot in the center.

Makes 4 servings

NUTRITION INFORMATION
values are per serving

CALORIES 371	DIETARY FIBER 5.3 G
TOTAL FAT 11 G	BETA CAROTENE 13 MG
SATURATED FAT 4.1 G	VITAMIN C 142 MG
CHOLESTEROL 45 MG	CALCIUM 307 MG
SODIUM 584 MG	IRON 4.3 MG

Broiled Pork Loin with Romesco Sauce

When served with simple, mild-in-flavor pork loin, the nuances of Romesco sauce—a beautiful roasted red bell pepper purée with garlic, ground almonds and cayenne—are especially notable and fine. Broccoli rabe with lemon and roasted herbed new potatoes would make good accompaniments. The sauce can be prepared well in advance, and it goes nicely with broiled or grilled poultry, too.

2 medium red bell peppers
3 garlic cloves, peeled
3 tablespoons orange juice
2 tablespoons no-salt-added tomato paste
2 teaspoons coarsely chopped unblanched almonds

S U P E R Q U I C K

Orange Pork Stir-Fry

Working time: 20 minutes Total time: 30 minutes

1⅓ cups water
⅔ cup rice
2 teaspoons vegetable oil
¾ pound well-trimmed pork loin, cut into ½-inch-thick strips
1 tablespoon flour
1 small onion, coarsely chopped
3 garlic cloves, slivered
1 tablespoon minced fresh ginger
2 teaspoons slivered orange zest
1½ cups diagonally sliced celery
2 large carrots, shredded
1 large red bell pepper, thinly sliced
¾ cup chicken broth, canned or homemade (p. 54)
¼ teaspoon salt
¼ teaspoon red pepper flakes
1½ teaspoons cornstarch blended with 1 tablespoon water
¼ cup thinly sliced scallions

1 In a medium covered saucepan, bring the water to a boil over high heat. Stir in the rice, reduce the heat to a simmer and cook, covered, until the rice is tender and the liquid is absorbed, about 20 minutes.

2 Meanwhile, in a large nonstick skillet, warm the oil over medium heat. Lightly dredge the pork in the flour. Add the pork to the skillet and sauté until cooked through, about 3 minutes. Transfer to a plate and cover loosely to keep warm.

3 Add the onion, garlic, ginger and orange zest to the skillet, and cook for 1 minute. Add the celery and cook for 1 minute. Stir in the carrots and bell pepper, and stir-fry until the vegetables are crisp-tender, about 3 minutes.

4 Stir in the broth, salt, red pepper flakes and cornstarch mixture, bring to a boil and cook until the sauce is lightly thickened, about 1 minute. Return the pork to the skillet and simmer gently until heated through, about 1 minute. Stir in the scallions and serve with the rice.

Makes 4 servings

Values are per serving:
Calories: 325 Total fat: 7.8 g Saturated fat: 2.0 g Cholesterol: 50 mg Sodium: 426 mg
Dietary fiber: 3.7 g Beta carotene: 9.4 mg Vitamin C: 61 mg Calcium: 76 mg Iron: 2.9 mg

⅛ teaspoon cayenne pepper
1 teaspoon paprika
¾ teaspoon oregano
½ teaspoon sage
¼ teaspoon salt
¼ teaspoon sugar
¾ pound well-trimmed pork loin, cut into 4 slices (about ¾ inch thick)

1. Preheat the broiler. Cutting vertically, slice the bell peppers in 3 or 4 flat panels, leaving the core and seeds behind. Put the bell pepper pieces, skin-side up, in a single layer on a jelly-roll pan and broil 4 to 5 inches from the heat for 7 to 10 minutes. Place the peppers in a covered bowl to steam, and when cool enough to handle, peel them. Leave the broiler on.

2. Meanwhile, in a small saucepan of boiling water, blanch the garlic for 3 minutes. Drain and rinse under cold water.

3. Transfer the bell peppers and garlic to a food processor along with the orange juice, tomato paste, almonds and cayenne. Process until well combined and smooth.

4. In a small bowl, stir together the paprika, oregano, sage, salt and sugar. Rub into the pork. Broil the pork 5 inches from the heat, turning once, for about 6 minutes, or until browned and cooked through.

5. Serve the pork topped with the sauce.

Makes 4 servings

Nutrition Information
values are per serving

CALORIES 171	DIETARY FIBER 1.1 G
TOTAL FAT 7.2 G	BETA CAROTENE 1.6 MG
SATURATED FAT 2.4 G	VITAMIN C 80 MG
CHOLESTEROL 50 MG	CALCIUM 34 MG
SODIUM 183 MG	IRON 1.3 MG

Roast Pork Loin Tonnato

Whether you prepare the classic veal tonnato or this delicious pork loin variation, the message you are conveying is the same: rich and subtle flavors. Here the traditional creamy tuna-based sauce is given texture, and a fair measure of beta carotene and vitamin C, by the addition of bell peppers and carrot. Serve this with herbed Arborio rice and an arugula salad.

1 pound well-trimmed boneless pork loin
¾ teaspoon freshly ground black pepper
1 teaspoon sage
2 bay leaves, preferably imported
2 large red bell peppers, cut into large pieces
½ cup shredded carrot
½ cup chicken broth, canned or homemade (p. 54)
2 garlic cloves, peeled
1 ounce drained water-packed tuna
3 tablespoons light sour cream
1 tablespoon fresh lemon juice
1 tablespoon drained capers

1. Preheat the oven to 375°. Spray a 9-inch square baking pan with nonstick cooking spray.

2. Season the pork with ½ teaspoon of the black pepper and the sage, and place the bay leaves on top. Place the pork loin in the prepared pan and roast for 40 to 45 minutes, or until the pork is cooked through but still juicy. Remove from the oven and cover loosely with foil to keep warm.

3. Meanwhile, in a medium saucepan, combine the bell peppers, carrot, chicken broth and garlic. Cover and bring to a boil over high heat. Reduce the heat to medium-low and simmer, stirring occasionally, until the peppers are very tender, about 10 minutes.

4. Transfer the pepper-carrot mixture to a food processor. Add the tuna and process to a fine purée. Add the sour cream, lemon juice and the remaining ¼ teaspoon black pepper and process until just mixed. Stir in the capers plus any cooking juices from the baking pan.

5. Carve the pork into thin slices. Serve the pork with the tonnato sauce.

Makes 4 servings

Nutrition Information
values are per serving

CALORIES 237	DIETARY FIBER 1.3 G
TOTAL FAT 10 G	BETA CAROTENE 4.1 MG
SATURATED FAT 3.8 G	VITAMIN C 99 MG
CHOLESTEROL 76 MG	CALCIUM 36 MG
SODIUM 254 MG	IRON 1.9 MG

Honey-Roasted Pork on a Bed of Sweet Potatoes

Pork tenderloin, in addition to being the leanest cut of pork and one that can be cooked with no added fat, is also convenient for time-pressured cooks. Here it roasts in just thirty minutes, on a bed of vegetables that are also used to make a delicious sauce to serve with the pork.

1 pound sweet potatoes, peeled and thinly sliced
1 large red bell pepper, cut into ½-inch squares
1 large green bell pepper, cut into ½-inch squares
3 cloves garlic, slivered
¼ teaspoon salt
¼ teaspoon freshly ground black pepper
⅔ cup chicken broth, canned or homemade (p. 54)
2 tablespoons honey
1 tablespoon prepared mustard
2 teaspoons fresh lemon juice
1 pound well-trimmed pork tenderloin

1. Preheat the oven to 425°.

2. In a large bowl, combine the sweet potatoes, red and green bell peppers, the garlic, salt and black pepper, and toss until well combined.

3. Spoon the vegetables into a 7-by-11-inch baking pan and toss with ⅓ cup of the chicken broth. Cover with foil and bake for 15 minutes.

4. Meanwhile, in a small bowl, stir together the honey, mustard and lemon juice.

5. Place the pork on top of the sweet potato mixture and brush with half of the honey mixture. Pour the remaining honey mixture over the vegetables. Roast uncovered for about 30 minutes, or until the pork is cooked through and the vegetables are tender.

6. Remove the pork to a cutting board and let stand 10 minutes before slicing.

7. Meanwhile, spoon 1 cup of the vegetable mixture into a food processor and purée with the remaining ⅓ cup chicken broth. Slice the pork and serve topped with the vegetable purée, with the roasted vegetables on the side.

Makes 4 servings

Nutrition Information
values are per serving

CALORIES 279	DIETARY FIBER 3.3 G
TOTAL FAT 4.6 G	BETA CAROTENE 11 MG
SATURATED FAT 1.4 G	VITAMIN C 91 MG
CHOLESTEROL 74 MG	CALCIUM 39 MG
SODIUM 419 MG	IRON 2.3 MG

Pork and Red Beans with Greens

Pork and beans is tried-and-true as culinary combinations go, but here has the added, and delectable, advantage of being combined with mustard and collard greens. For still more nourishing comfort, serve this with steamed rice.

1 cup chopped red onion
4 garlic cloves, minced
¼ cup canned chicken broth diluted with ¼ cup water, or ½ cup Homemade Chicken Broth (p. 54)
¾ pound collard greens, sliced
¾ pound mustard greens, sliced
½ teaspoon salt
¼ teaspoon savory, marjoram or sage
⅛ teaspoon nutmeg
2 cups chopped fresh tomatoes
1 cup reduced-sodium mixed vegetable juice
One 8-ounce can no-salt-added tomato sauce
One 19-ounce can red kidney beans, rinsed and drained
1 tablespoon red wine vinegar
2 teaspoons olive oil
¾ pound well-trimmed pork tenderloin, cut into ½-inch-thick slices
1 tablespoon flour

1. In a large skillet, combine the onion, garlic and chicken broth, and cook over medium heat until the onion has softened, about 5 minutes.

2. Stir in the collard and mustard greens, salt, savory and nutmeg, and cook, stirring frequently, until the greens have wilted. Stir in the fresh tomatoes, mixed vegetable juice and tomato sauce, and cook until the tomatoes have softened, about 5 minutes.

3. Stir in the beans and cook until the juices have reduced and are lightly thickened, about 8 minutes. Stir in the vinegar.

4. Meanwhile, in a large nonstick skillet, warm the oil over medium heat until hot but not smoking. Dust the pork with the flour, add to the skillet and sauté until no longer pink, about 3 minutes.

5. Stir the pork into the greens and cook until the pork is cooked through and the greens are tender, about 1 minute.

Makes 4 servings

Nutrition Information
values are per serving

CALORIES 348	DIETARY FIBER 12 G
TOTAL FAT 7.0 G	BETA CAROTENE 5.7 MG
SATURATED FAT 1.4 G	VITAMIN C 133 MG
CHOLESTEROL 55 MG	CALCIUM 179 MG
SODIUM 688 MG	IRON 5.4 MG

Sautéed Pork with Swiss Chard and Tomatoes

Although it may be well known to some, many people still don't realize how healthful Swiss chard is. Like other dark green leafy vegetables, it is an excellent source of beta carotene. It adds color, nutrients and its singular flavor to this appealing stir-fried dish that is served atop garlic-rubbed toast—all in all, a tasty idea.

½ cup (not oil-packed) sun-dried tomatoes
1 cup boiling water
½ pound well-trimmed boneless pork loin, cut into ½-inch-wide strips
½ teaspoon salt
½ teaspoon freshly ground black pepper

½ teaspoon thyme
¼ teaspoon crushed red pepper flakes
1 tablespoon plus 1 teaspoon extra-virgin olive oil
1 large onion, sliced
1 large red bell pepper, cut into thin strips
4 medium plum tomatoes, cut into thin wedges
½ pound Swiss chard or spinach, cut crosswise into 1-inch pieces
4 ounces French bread, cut on the diagonal into 16 thin slices
1 garlic clove, peeled and halved

1. Place the sun-dried tomatoes in a small heatproof bowl and pour the boiling water over them. Let stand until softened, about 10 minutes. Drain the tomatoes and cut into small pieces.

2. In a shallow bowl, mix the pork strips with ¼ teaspoon each of the salt, black pepper and thyme, and the red pepper flakes.

3. In a large, deep nonstick skillet, warm 2 teaspoons of the oil over high heat. Add the pork strips and stir-fry until lightly browned, 1 to 2 minutes. With a slotted spoon, transfer the pork to a plate and cover loosely to keep warm.

4. Add the remaining 2 teaspoons oil to the skillet and stir in the onion, bell pepper and the remaining ¼ teaspoon each salt, black pepper and thyme. Toss to coat well with the oil, reduce the heat to medium and sauté until the vegetables are tender and the onion golden, 6 to 8 minutes.

5. Stir in the sun-dried and plum tomatoes, reduce the heat to medium-low, cover and cook until the fresh tomatoes start to soften and release their juices, about 5 minutes.

6. Stir in the Swiss chard or spinach in batches, increase the heat to medium-high, cover and cook, turning the greens a few times, until wilted, 3 to 4 minutes (spinach will cook more quickly).

7. Return the pork (and any juices that have collected on the plate) to the skillet, cover and remove from the heat.

8. Preheat the broiler. Place the bread in a single layer on a baking sheet and broil about 30 seconds per side, or until toasted. Remove from the oven, let cool slightly, then rub each piece generously with a cut side of the garlic clove. Serve the toasts with the pork and vegetables.

Makes 4 servings

NUTRITION INFORMATION
values are per serving

CALORIES 275	DIETARY FIBER 4.4 G
TOTAL FAT 9.4 G	BETA CAROTENE 3.1 MG
SATURATED FAT 2.0 G	VITAMIN C 100 MG
CHOLESTEROL 33 MG	CALCIUM 93 MG
SODIUM 613 MG	IRON 3.6 MG

Jamaican Jerk Pork with Mango-Kiwi Relish

Hailing from the island of Jamaica, jerk is a combination of herbs and spices, frequently very hot ones indeed, that is rubbed into meats, like chicken or pork, to make them especially flavorful before they are grilled over the hot coals of big outdoor barbecues. Be careful not to get the jerk mix on your hands—it has jalapeños in it.

JERK PORK
1 pound well-trimmed boneless pork loin
2 fresh jalapeño peppers, halved, some seeds removed
4 garlic cloves, peeled
2 tablespoons canned chicken broth
1 tablespoon paprika
1 tablespoon distilled white vinegar
1½ teaspoons thyme
1 teaspoon olive oil
½ teaspoon allspice
½ teaspoon salt
⅛ teaspoon cayenne pepper

RELISH
1 mango, diced
1 large red bell pepper, diced
2 kiwi fruit, peeled and diced
1 tablespoon fresh lime juice
1 teaspoon sugar
⅛ teaspoon salt
⅛ teaspoon allspice
Pinch of cayenne pepper

1. For the Pork Thinly slice the pork crosswise into 12 slices (about ¼ inch thick). Place the pork in a shallow baking dish or pie plate.

2. In a food processor or blender, process the jalapeños, garlic, chicken broth, paprika, vinegar, thyme, olive oil, allspice, salt and cayenne until it forms a fine paste. Pour the jerk sauce over the pork and toss to coat well. Cover and marinate in the refrigerator for at least 20 minutes and up to 8 hours.

3. Meanwhile, Make the Relish In a medium bowl, combine the mango, bell pepper, kiwi, lime juice, sugar, salt, allspice and cayenne. Cover and set aside.

4. Preheat the broiler. Spray a broiler pan rack with nonstick cooking spray.

5. Place the pork on the prepared broiler pan and coat with any remaining marinade. Broil 4 inches from the heat, without turning, for 3 to 5 minutes, or until the pork is cooked through. Serve the pork with the relish.

Makes 4 servings

Nutrition Information
values are per serving

CALORIES 274	DIETARY FIBER 2.3 G
TOTAL FAT 10 G	BETA CAROTENE 2.8 MG
SATURATED FAT 3.3 G	VITAMIN C 113 MG
CHOLESTEROL 67 MG	CALCIUM 57 MG
SODIUM 434 MG	IRON 2.3 MG

Ham and Sweet Potato Kebabs with Orange-Mustard Glaze

Two well-known culinary partnerships are ham with mustard, and sweet potatoes with orange. Here you have each of those great flavors and ingredients, but they have been reshuffled in a most inventive way. The ham shares prominence on skewers with the sweet potatoes; the mustard mingles with orange in a glaze. How they all come together is particularly delicious.

1½ pounds sweet potatoes, peeled and cut into 1-inch chunks
½ pound reduced-sodium ham, in one piece, cut into 24 cubes
2 large green bell peppers, cut into 1-inch chunks
1 medium onion, cut into 1-inch chunks
3 tablespoons frozen orange juice concentrate, thawed
2 tablespoons honey
1 tablespoon grainy Dijon mustard
1 tablespoon canned chicken broth
½ teaspoon dry mustard
½ teaspoon freshly ground black pepper

1. Place the sweet potatoes in a medium saucepan and add cold water to cover. Cover and bring to a boil over high heat. Reduce the heat to medium and simmer until the sweet potatoes are tender but still firm, about 10 minutes. Drain in a colander and cool slightly.

2. Preheat the broiler. Spray the broiler pan rack with nonstick cooking spray.

3. Thread the sweet potatoes, ham, bell peppers and onion onto eight 12-inch skewers in the following order: bell pepper, onion, sweet potato and ham. Place the skewers on the prepared broiler pan.

4. In a small bowl, whisk together the orange

juice concentrate, honey, grainy mustard, chicken broth, dry mustard and black pepper.

5. Brush most of the glaze over both sides of the skewers. Broil 4 to 5 inches from the heat for 6 minutes. Turn the skewers and broil for 5 minutes, or until the vegetables are tender.

6. Remove from the broiler, brush with the remaining glaze and serve 2 skewers per person.

Makes 4 servings

NUTRITION INFORMATION
values are per serving

CALORIES 280	DIETARY FIBER 5.3 G
TOTAL FAT 2.7 G	BETA CAROTENE 15 MG
SATURATED FAT .8 G	VITAMIN C 94 MG
CHOLESTEROL 27 MG	CALCIUM 49 MG
SODIUM 616 MG	IRON 1.8 MG

Lamb Chops with Apricot-Ginger Chutney

Fruit chutneys are common companions to lamb in Indian cuisine. Here a homemade apricot chutney seasoned with ground ginger and cumin serves as a sauce for broiled lamb chops that have been rubbed with the same spices.

Four 5-ounce well-trimmed loin lamb chops
¾ teaspoon cumin
¾ teaspoon ground ginger
½ teaspoon freshly ground black pepper
2 teaspoons extra-virgin olive oil
2 large red bell peppers, diced
2 scallions, sliced
½ teaspoon sugar
¾ cup chicken broth, canned or homemade (p. 54)
½ cup diced dried apricots
½ cup apricot nectar
2 teaspoons cornstarch blended with 1 tablespoon water
⅛ teaspoon salt

1. Preheat the broiler and broiler pan. Rub the chops on both sides with ¼ teaspoon each of the cumin, ginger and black pepper. Set aside loosely covered and let stand while you make the chutney.

2. In a large nonstick skillet, warm the oil over medium heat until hot but not smoking. Add the bell peppers and scallions. Season with the sugar and the remaining ½ teaspoon cumin, ½ teaspoon ginger and ¼ teaspoon black pepper, and sauté until the vegetables begin to get tender, about 5 minutes.

3. Add the chicken broth, apricots and apricot nectar, and bring to a boil. Reduce the heat to medium-low and simmer, stirring occasionally, until the apricots are softened and the flavors blended, about 5 minutes.

4. Stir in the cornstarch mixture and return to a boil, stirring constantly. Cover and remove from the heat.

5. Sprinkle the chops with the salt and broil 5 inches from the heat for 5 minutes. Turn and broil for 2 minutes, then remove from the broiler.

6. Return the sauce to medium-low heat and bring to a simmer. Add the chops to the skillet, spoon some of the sauce over them, cover and cook until the chops are medium-rare to medium and the flavors blended, about 2 minutes.

Makes 4 servings

NUTRITION INFORMATION
values are per serving

CALORIES 287	DIETARY FIBER 2.5 G
TOTAL FAT 11 G	BETA CAROTENE 2.7 MG
SATURATED FAT 3.2 G	VITAMIN C 114 MG
CHOLESTEROL 79 MG	CALCIUM 42 MG
SODIUM 330 MG	IRON 3.3 MG

Indian-Style Lamb Chops

The beauty of this dish, aside from its most remarkable array of flavors, is that it requires very little preparation time. In fact, were you to serve it with basmati rice—the perfect accompaniment—you would need to start cooking the rice way in advance of the lamb. Add cucumber salad with yogurt dressing as a side dish, and chilled melon for dessert.

Four 5-ounce well-trimmed loin lamb chops
1 tablespoon flour
2 teaspoons olive oil
1 medium red onion, diced
1 large carrot, shredded
2 garlic cloves, minced
1 teaspoon cumin
¾ teaspoon ground coriander
½ teaspoon ground ginger
¼ teaspoon salt
¼ teaspoon freshly ground black pepper
1 cup chopped tomatoes
One 8-ounce can no-salt-added tomato sauce
½ cup chicken broth, canned or homemade (p. 54)
2 tablespoons chopped bottled mango chutney
2 tablespoons chopped cilantro
1 mango, cut into wedges

1. Lightly dredge the lamb in the flour. In a large nonstick skillet, warm the oil over medium heat until hot but not smoking. Sauté the lamb until golden brown, about 3 minutes per side. Remove from the pan and set aside.

2. Add the onion and carrot to the pan and cook, stirring frequently, until the onion begins to color, about 4 minutes.

3. Stir in the garlic, cumin, coriander, ginger, salt and pepper, and cook until fragrant, about 1 minute. Stir in the tomatoes, tomato sauce, chicken broth, mango chutney and cilantro, and cook until the sauce begins to thicken, about 4 minutes.

4. Return the lamb to the skillet and cook gently until just heated through, about 2 minutes.

5. Serve the chops topped with their sauce and wedges of mango.

Makes 4 servings

Nutrition Information
values are per serving

CALORIES 298	DIETARY FIBER 3.5 G
TOTAL FAT 9.2 G	BETA CAROTENE 6.1 MG
SATURATED FAT 2.5 G	VITAMIN C 40 MG
CHOLESTEROL 67 MG	CALCIUM 50 MG
SODIUM 448 MG	IRON 3.6 MG

Szechuan Lamb with Peppers and Spinach

A half teaspoon of red pepper flakes may not seem like much, but when combined with one tablespoon of grated fresh ginger, the dish lives up to the name Szechuan, the province in western China known for its incendiary style of cooking. Serve this with steamed brown rice and broccoli in garlic sauce.

¾ pound boneless lamb steak, cut crosswise into ½-inch-thick strips
1 tablespoon plus 1 teaspoon reduced-sodium soy sauce
1 tablespoon hoisin sauce
3 garlic cloves, crushed through a press
½ teaspoon crushed red pepper flakes
1 tablespoon olive oil

1 tablespoon grated fresh ginger
2 large red bell peppers, cut into thin strips
6 scallions, cut into 2-inch lengths
⅓ cup plus 1 tablespoon beef broth
1 tablespoon cornstarch
½ pound stemmed spinach

1. In a medium bowl, toss the lamb strips with 2 teaspoons of the soy sauce, the hoisin sauce, 2 of the garlic cloves and ¼ teaspoon of the red pepper flakes. Let marinate for at least 10 minutes.

2. In a large nonstick skillet, warm 1 teaspoon of the oil over high heat until hot but not smoking. Add the lamb and stir-fry until the pink color is gone, 2 to 3 minutes. Remove the lamb to a plate and cover loosely to keep warm.

3. Add the remaining 2 teaspoons oil to the skillet. Stir in the ginger, the remaining garlic clove and ¼ teaspoon red pepper flakes, and cook, stirring constantly, until fragrant, about 1 minute.

4. Stir in the bell peppers and scallions and the remaining 2 teaspoons soy sauce. Reduce the heat to medium and stir-fry for 1 minute. Drizzle in 1 tablespoon of the beef broth and stir-fry until the vegetables are tender, 2 to 3 minutes.

5. In a small bowl or cup, blend the cornstarch with the remaining ⅓ cup beef broth.

6. Add the spinach to the skillet, in batches, and stir-fry until wilted, 1 to 2 minutes. Stir in the cornstarch mixture along with the lamb (and any juices that have collected on the plate). Cook, stirring frequently, until the lamb is heated through and the juices are thickened, about 1 minute.

Makes 4 servings

NUTRITION INFORMATION
values are per serving

CALORIES 209	DIETARY FIBER 2.8 G
TOTAL FAT 9.6 G	BETA CAROTENE 4.1 MG
SATURATED FAT 2.5 G	VITAMIN C 116 MG
CHOLESTEROL 56 MG	CALCIUM 96 MG
SODIUM 518 MG	IRON 3.8 MG

Pasta

Pumpkin-Filled Wontons

The key to successfully serving these easy-to-make, tasty wontons is to preheat your dinner plates in a low oven while you are filling the dumplings. Cook only five wontons at a time to prevent them from sticking together and, as they are done, transfer them to the warmed plates. Cook the remaining wontons in the same small-batch manner. With the wontons finished, then all you have to attend to is the sauce.

1 cup canned solid-pack pumpkin purée
¼ cup grated Parmesan cheese
1 tablespoon finely ground almonds
1 tablespoon plus 1 teaspoon sugar
1 tablespoon plus 1 teaspoon plain dried bread crumbs
¼ teaspoon salt
1 egg, lightly beaten
40 wonton wrappers (3½-inch squares)
½ cup chicken broth, canned or homemade (p. 54)
1 tablespoon fresh lemon juice
½ teaspoon sage
⅛ teaspoon freshly ground black pepper
1 teaspoon cornstarch blended with 1 tablespoon water
3 tablespoons chopped parsley
1 tablespoon light sour cream

1. In a medium bowl, stir together the pumpkin, 2 tablespoons of the Parmesan cheese, the almonds, sugar, bread crumbs and salt. Add the egg and mix until well combined.

2. Spoon the mixture into the center of 20 wonton wrappers, moisten the borders of the wrappers with water and place another wonton wrapper on top of each, pressing down to seal the edges.

3. In a large pot of boiling water, cook the wontons (in small batches so they will cook evenly and not stick together) until al dente, about 8 minutes. Drain well, reserving ¼ cup of the pasta cooking liquid.

SUPER QUICK

Marco Polo Pasta

Working time: 15 minutes Total time: 30 minutes

4 cups (loosely packed) shredded spinach
1 cup bean sprouts, rinsed
2 medium carrots, cut into matchsticks
3 scallions, diagonally sliced
4 ounces snow peas, cut into lengthwise slivers
¼ cup reduced-sodium soy sauce
3 tablespoons smooth peanut butter
3 tablespoons dry sherry
2 tablespoons honey
One 14-ounce package firm tofu, cut into ½-inch cubes
8 ounces fresh spinach pasta

1 Place the spinach, bean sprouts, carrots, scallions and snow peas in a serving bowl. Set aside.

2 In a small saucepan, combine the soy sauce, peanut butter, sherry and honey, and heat gently, stirring often, until hot and bubbly. Add the tofu and toss gently with a rubber spatula to coat with the sauce. Remove from the heat and cover to keep warm.

3 Meanwhile, cook the pasta in a large pot of boiling water until tender, about 2 minutes.

4 Drain the pasta in a colander and add to the vegetables in the serving bowl. Pour the tofu and peanut sauce on top and toss to combine.

Makes 4 servings

Values are per serving:
Calories: 492 Total fat: 16 g Saturated fat: 2.6 g Cholesterol: 41 mg Sodium: 760 mg
Dietary fiber: 5.0 g Beta carotene: 9.1 mg Vitamin C: 46 mg Calcium: 339 mg Iron: 16 mg

4. In a large skillet, combine the reserved pasta liquid, the chicken broth, lemon juice, sage and pepper. Bring to a boil over high heat and boil for 2 minutes.

5. Stir the cornstarch mixture into the broth mixture and boil until lightly thickened, about 1 minute. Stir in the remaining 2 tablespoons Parmesan, the parsley and sour cream.

6. Spoon the wontons into 4 pasta bowls, spoon the sauce on top and serve.

Makes 4 servings

Nutrition Information
values are per serving

CALORIES 343	DIETARY FIBER 1.5 G
TOTAL FAT 5.7 G	BETA CAROTENE 8.2 MG
SATURATED FAT 2.0 G	VITAMIN C 6.9 MG
CHOLESTEROL 66 MG	CALCIUM 145 MG
SODIUM 849 MG	IRON 4.2 MG

Summer Noodles with Orange-Ginger Dressing

Oriental noodle salads make especially good summer food as many of them actually improve in flavor when prepared in advance. This variation, with the refreshing flavor and texture of fresh orange, is as lovely to look at as it is to eat.

½ pound capellini, broken into thirds
1 tablespoon peanut oil
2 navel oranges
2 tablespoons frozen orange juice concentrate
2 tablespoons reduced-sodium soy sauce
1 tablespoon grated fresh ginger
¼ teaspoon sugar
1½ cups shredded carrots
1 large red bell pepper, cut into thin strips
2 tablespoons thinly sliced scallions
2 tablespoons coarsely chopped unsalted, dry-roasted peanuts (½ ounce)

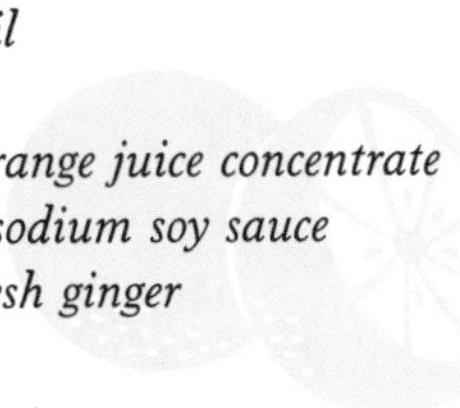

1. Cook the pasta in a large pot of boiling water until al dente, 3 to 4 minutes, or according to package directions. Drain in a colander and rinse briefly under cold running water and drain again. Place the pasta in a serving bowl and toss with ½ teaspoon of the oil.

2. Grate 2 teaspoons of zest from one of the oranges. With a serrated knife, remove the peel and white pith from both oranges. Working over a strainer set over a medium bowl, cut out the orange sections from in between the membranes, letting them drop into the strainer. Squeeze the juice from the membranes into the bowl.

3. To the freshly squeezed orange juice in the bowl, add the remaining 2½ teaspoons peanut oil, the orange zest, orange juice concentrate, soy sauce, ginger and sugar, and whisk with a fork to blend.

4. Pour the dressing over the pasta. Add the carrots, bell pepper and scallions, and toss to blend. Add the orange sections and toss again. Sprinkle with the peanuts.

Makes 4 servings

Nutrition Information
values are per serving

CALORIES 341	DIETARY FIBER 5.2 G
TOTAL FAT 6.2 G	BETA CAROTENE 7.9 MG
SATURATED FAT 1.0 G	VITAMIN C 106 MG
CHOLESTEROL 0 MG	CALCIUM 62 MG
SODIUM 321 MG	IRON 2.9 MG

Fettuccine and Vegetables with Almond-Orange Pesto

Beautiful fresh vegetables—carrots, yellow bell pepper and zucchini—color this pasta dish sauced with a clever variation on the renowned Italian basil sauce, pesto. To ensure that the pasta remains hot when you serve it, drain the water used for cooking the fettuccine directly into the serving bowl to warm it, then discard the water and place the pasta in the bowl.

1 cup (loosely packed) flat-leaf parsley sprigs
2 tablespoons frozen orange juice concentrate
2 tablespoons slivered almonds, toasted
2 tablespoons grated Parmesan cheese
1 teaspoon grated orange zest
½ teaspoon freshly ground black pepper
¼ teaspoon salt
1 garlic clove, peeled
3 cups carrot sticks
1 large yellow bell pepper, thinly sliced
1 medium zucchini, cut into sticks
½ cup chicken broth, canned or homemade (p. 54)
½ pound fettuccine

1. In a food processor, combine the parsley, orange juice concentrate, almonds, Parmesan, orange zest, black pepper and salt. With the machine running, drop the garlic through the feed tube and process until puréed. Place the pesto in a large serving bowl and set aside.

2. In a medium saucepan, combine the carrots, bell pepper, zucchini and chicken broth. Cover and bring to a boil over high heat. Reduce the heat to medium and simmer, stirring occasionally, until the vegetables are tender, 5 to 7 minutes. Remove from the heat.

3. Meanwhile, cook the pasta in a large pot of boiling water until al dente, 9 to 11 minutes, or according to package directions. Reserving ¼ cup of the pasta cooking liquid, drain the pasta.

4. Stir the reserved pasta cooking liquid into the pesto. Add the drained pasta and the vegetables in broth and toss to coat well.

Makes 4 servings

NUTRITION INFORMATION
values are per serving

CALORIES 333	DIETARY FIBER 6.3 G
TOTAL FAT 6.4 G	BETA CAROTENE 15 MG
SATURATED FAT 1.3 G	VITAMIN C 64 MG
CHOLESTEROL 56 MG	CALCIUM 130 MG
SODIUM 356 MG	IRON 4.8 MG

Fettuccine with Squash and Red Pepper Sauce

Winter squash and puréed red bell peppers combine here to make a mild but strikingly lovely sauce for fettuccine. The sauce can be made entirely in advance, and if you are feeling particularly colorful, you might use spinach pasta. A green salad, fresh bread and fruit for dessert would complete the menu very simply and nicely.

1 tablespoon olive oil
2 large red bell peppers–1 diced and 1 cut into strips
1 large green bell pepper, diced
1 tablespoon dry white wine
1 large onion, diced
¾ teaspoon freshly ground black pepper
½ teaspoon thyme
¼ teaspoon nutmeg
¼ teaspoon salt
1 cup chicken broth, canned or homemade (p. 54)
One 10-ounce package frozen winter squash, thawed

10 ounces fettuccine
1 tablespoon unsalted butter
2 tablespoons grated Parmesan cheese

1. In a large nonstick saucepan, warm the oil over medium heat. Stir in the diced red and green bell peppers and the wine, and sauté until tender, 4 to 6 minutes. With a slotted spoon, transfer the peppers to a bowl and set aside.

2. Add the red bell pepper strips, the onion, black pepper, thyme, nutmeg and salt. Cover and cook, stirring frequently, until the vegetables are very tender, 6 to 7 minutes; if the pan starts to get dry, add 2 or 3 tablespoons of the broth.

3. Stir in the remaining broth and the squash, and bring to a boil. Reduce the heat to medium-low, cover and cook, stirring occasionally, for 10 minutes to blend the flavors.

4. Meanwhile, cook the pasta in a large pot of boiling water until al dente, 9 to 11 minutes, or according to package directions. Drain the pasta in a colander and set aside in the colander.

5. Transfer the cooked squash mixture to a food processor or blender and purée to a smooth sauce. Add the sauce to the pasta cooking pot. Stir in the reserved diced peppers and the butter and stir over medium heat until the butter is melted and the sauce is warmed through.

6. Stir the drained pasta into the sauce, transfer to a serving dish and sprinkle with the Parmesan.

Makes 4 servings

Nutrition Information
values are per serving

CALORIES 428	DIETARY FIBER 4.1 G
TOTAL FAT 11 G	BETA CAROTENE 3.9 MG
SATURATED FAT 3.4 G	VITAMIN C 125 MG
CHOLESTEROL 77 MG	CALCIUM 105 MG
SODIUM 449 MG	IRON 4.8 MG

Ziti with Ratatouille Sauce

The famous vegetable stew of Provence, ratatouille, redolent of fresh herbs, plenty of garlic and a marvelous selection of late-summer produce, serves as an ideal topping for pasta. Pretty here over tubular-shaped ziti, this ratatouille sauce can also be layered with cooked lasagna noodles, sprinkled with cheese and briefly baked.

1 tablespoon olive oil
2 small Japanese eggplants, cut crosswise into ½-inch slices
1 large red bell pepper, cut into 4 or 5 large pieces
1 large green bell pepper, diced
2 medium zucchini, cut into ½-inch chunks
1 small sweet potato (6 ounces), peeled and diced
1 large onion, coarsely chopped
5 garlic cloves, minced
1½ cups fresh basil leaves, chopped
½ cup fresh mint leaves, chopped
¾ cup tomato juice
One 28-ounce can whole tomatoes
2 teaspoons red wine vinegar
¾ teaspoon freshly ground black pepper
½ teaspoon sugar
¼ teaspoon crushed red pepper flakes
12 ounces ziti or other tube-shaped pasta

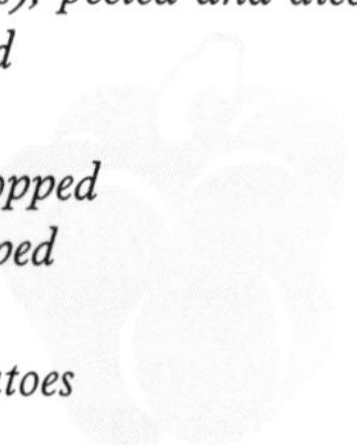

1. In a large nonstick skillet, warm the oil over medium-high heat until hot but not smoking. Stir in the eggplants, red and green bell peppers, the zucchini, sweet potato, onion and garlic. Stir-fry until the vegetables begin to soften, about 10 minutes. Stir in 2 tablespoons each of the basil and mint. Reduce the heat to medium-low, cover and cook until the vegetables are very tender, about 10 minutes.

2. Remove the large pieces of red bell pepper from the skillet and place them in a food processor. Add the tomato juice and 3 of the canned tomatoes to the processor and process to a purée.

3. Return the purée to the skillet along with the remaining canned tomatoes, the vinegar, black pepper, sugar and red pepper flakes, and bring to a boil over medium-high heat, breaking up the tomatoes with a spoon. Reduce the heat to low and simmer while you cook the pasta.

4. Cook the ziti in a large pot of boiling water until al dente, 10 to 12 minutes, or according to package directions. Drain the pasta in a colander and transfer to individual dinner plates.

5. Spoon the sauce over the ziti. Sprinkle the remaining basil and mint on top and serve.

Makes 4 servings

Nutrition Information
values are per serving

CALORIES 505	DIETARY FIBER 7.4 G
TOTAL FAT 5.9 G	BETA CAROTENE 5.0 MG
SATURATED FAT .8 G	VITAMIN C 132 MG
CHOLESTEROL 0 MG	CALCIUM 284 MG
SODIUM 508 MG	IRON 9.2 MG

Creamy Roast Garlic Pasta Primavera

Garlic that has been roasted is entirely different in flavor from its spirited fresh counterpart. Roasted, it lends a mild, almost sweet note here to the renowned Italian dish, pasta primavera—or pasta with vegetable sauce.

1 large head of garlic (about 4 ounces)
1 tablespoon olive oil
2 large red bell peppers, diced
2 large carrots, thinly sliced
3 tablespoons flour
1¼ cups canned chicken broth diluted with ¾ cup water, or 2 cups Homemade Chicken Broth (p. 54)
2 tablespoons fresh lemon juice
½ teaspoon freshly ground black pepper
½ teaspoon rosemary, crumbled
¼ teaspoon salt
½ pound radiatore pasta
4 cups small broccoli florets
½ cup frozen peas, thawed
3 tablespoons light sour cream

1. Preheat the oven to 425°. Wrap the garlic in aluminum foil and bake until the garlic is soft, about 30 minutes. When cool enough to handle, slice off the top of the garlic head and squeeze out the garlic pulp. Mash with a fork.

2. Meanwhile, in a large nonstick skillet, warm the oil over medium heat until hot but not smoking. Add the bell peppers and carrots, and cook, stirring frequently, until the vegetables are crisp-tender, about 4 minutes. Stir in the flour and cook, stirring constantly, until the vegetables are coated with flour, about 1 minute.

3. Gradually stir in the diluted chicken broth, lemon juice, black pepper, rosemary and salt. Stir in the mashed garlic and cook until the sauce is lightly thickened, about 4 minutes.

4. Meanwhile, cook the pasta in a large pot of boiling water until al dente, 9 to 11 minutes, or according to package directions.

5. Add the broccoli to the skillet and cook until crisp-tender, about 2 minutes. Add the peas and cook until heated through, about 1 minute. Swirl in the sour cream and remove from the heat.

6. Drain the pasta and place in a large serving bowl. Add the sauce and toss well to combine.

Makes 4 servings

Nutrition Information
values are per serving

CALORIES 417	DIETARY FIBER 9.1 G
TOTAL FAT 7.0 G	BETA CAROTENE 12 MG
SATURATED FAT 1.4 G	VITAMIN C 208 MG
CHOLESTEROL 3.8 MG	CALCIUM 141 MG
SODIUM 521 MG	IRON 4.9 MG

Radiatore Romesco

You will be amazed at how puréeing fresh tomatoes with canned tomato sauce can enliven the overall flavor of a red sauce. Add a touch of fresh or dried chili pepper, some homemade bread crumbs and ground almonds as thickeners, and you've made a simple Romesco sauce. Serve this pasta as a main course with steamed artichokes vinaigrette to start and for dessert present melon balls chilled in port, with a plate of biscotti for dipping into after-dinner espresso.

2 pounds tomatoes
2 tablespoons olive oil
1 cup cubed peasant or Italian bread (including crust)
4 garlic cloves, peeled
1 small fresh red chili pepper, minced, or ½ teaspoon crushed red pepper flakes
10 ounces radiatore pasta
12 unblanched whole almonds
One 8-ounce can no-salt-added tomato sauce
½ teaspoon salt

1. In a large pot of boiling water, blanch the tomatoes for 20 seconds. With a slotted spoon, remove the tomatoes and let cool slightly. (Keep the water hot for cooking the pasta.) When the tomatoes are cool enough to handle, peel them, halve them and set aside.

2. In a small nonstick skillet, warm 1 tablespoon plus 2 teaspoons of the oil over medium-low heat. Add the bread cubes and cook until golden brown, about 2 minutes. Transfer to a food processor and process to form fine crumbs.

3. To the skillet, add the remaining 1 teaspoon oil, the garlic and chili pepper; reduce the heat to low and cook until the garlic is golden and fragrant, about 4 minutes. Transfer to the processor.

4. Add the pasta to the boiling water and cook until al dente, 9 to 11 minutes, or according to package directions.

5. Meanwhile, add the almonds to the skillet and cook, stirring frequently, until toasted, about 5 minutes. Transfer to the processor.

6. Add the blanched tomato halves, the tomato sauce and salt to the processor, and process until not quite smooth, but some texture remains.

7. Drain the pasta in a colander and then toss with the sauce and serve.

Makes 4 servings

NUTRITION INFORMATION
values are per serving

CALORIES 433	DIETARY FIBER 5.8 G
TOTAL FAT 11 G	BETA CAROTENE 1.5 MG
SATURATED FAT 1.4 G	VITAMIN C 58 MG
CHOLESTEROL 0 MG	CALCIUM 46 MG
SODIUM 362 MG	IRON 4.6 MG

Fettuccine with Broccoli Rabe, Sweet Potatoes and Garlic

Broccoli rabe—also called broccoli di rape or rapini—is a relative of regular broccoli, but has longer stems and different-shaped leaves and buds. Should you have difficulty finding broccoli rabe—and it is really worth using for its wonderful, slightly bitter taste—use regular broccoli; separate the florets and stems, and cut the stems into thinner stalks for even cooking.

1 large sweet potato (12 ounces), peeled and cut into ½-inch cubes
10 ounces fettuccine
2 tablespoons olive oil
1 medium onion, coarsely chopped
4 garlic cloves, thinly sliced

1 pound broccoli rabe, cut into 2-inch lengths (about 7 cups)
½ cup chicken broth, canned or homemade (p. 54)
1½ ounces grated Parmesan cheese
½ teaspoon freshly ground black pepper
¼ teaspoon salt
¼ teaspoon crushed red pepper flakes

1. Place the sweet potato in a medium saucepan and add cold water to cover. Cover and bring to a boil over high heat. Reduce the heat to low and simmer until the sweet potato is tender but not mushy, about 10 minutes. Drain, return to the saucepan and cover to keep warm.

2. Meanwhile, cook the pasta in a large pot of boiling water until al dente, 8 to 10 minutes, or according to package directions. Drain the pasta in a colander.

3. In the pasta cooking pot, warm the oil over medium-high heat. Add the onion and garlic, and stir well to coat with the oil. Reduce the heat to medium-low, cover and cook until very tender, about 10 minutes.

4. Stir in the broccoli rabe and chicken broth, and bring to a boil over high heat. Reduce the heat to medium, cover and cook, stirring frequently, until the broccoli rabe is tender, about 5 minutes.

5. Add the fettuccine and sweet potato to the vegetables. Sprinkle with the Parmesan, black pepper, salt and red pepper flakes, and toss to coat well. Cook, tossing, just until heated through.

Makes 4 servings

Nutrition Information
values are per serving

CALORIES 499	DIETARY FIBER 7.9 G
TOTAL FAT 14 G	BETA CAROTENE 10 MG
SATURATED FAT 3.7 G	VITAMIN C 103 MG
CHOLESTEROL 76 MG	CALCIUM 284 MG
SODIUM 541 MG	IRON 5.9 MG

SUPER QUICK

Penne with Asparagus, Parmesan and Pecans

Working time: 10 minutes Total time: 25 minutes

½ pound penne pasta
1½ pounds asparagus, cut on the diagonal into 1½-inch lengths
1 medium red bell pepper, diced
⅔ cup canned chicken broth diluted with ⅔ cup water, or 1⅓ cups Homemade Chicken Broth (p. 54)
1 garlic clove, minced
½ teaspoon salt
¼ teaspoon freshly ground black pepper
1 teaspoon cornstarch blended with 1 tablespoon water
½ cup minced chives
3 tablespoons light sour cream
1 teaspoon grated lemon zest
⅓ cup grated Parmesan cheese
2 tablespoons coarsely chopped pecans, toasted

1 Cook the penne in a large pot of boiling water until al dente, 9 to 11 minutes, or according to package directions.

2 Meanwhile, in a large skillet, combine the asparagus, bell pepper, diluted broth, garlic, salt and black pepper. Cover and cook until the asparagus is crisp-tender, about 4 minutes. Uncover, increase the heat to high, bring to a boil and stir in the cornstarch mixture; cook until lightly thickened, about 1 minute.

3 Drain the penne and add the penne to the skillet along with the chives, sour cream and lemon zest, and toss well. Sprinkle on the Parmesan and pecans, and toss again.

Makes 4 servings

Values are per serving:
Calories: 335 Total fat: 7.3 g Saturated fat: 2.4 g Cholesterol: 9.0 mg Sodium: 570 mg
Dietary fiber: 3.8 g Beta carotene: 1.8 mg Vitamin C: 97 mg Calcium: 152 mg Iron: 3.7 mg

Penne with Broccoli and Roasted Carrot Sauce

The efficiency of using the pasta cooking water as part of the sauce that will top that same pasta cannot be denied. Here a half cup of cooking liquid smooths out a flavorful roasted carrot-garlic sauce that tops penne and broccoli for a colorful, low-fat, high-beta-carotene dish.

4 large carrots, cut into chunks
1 large onion, cut into chunks
4 garlic cloves, peeled
2 tablespoons extra-virgin olive oil
¼ teaspoon salt
½ teaspoon freshly ground black pepper
⅛ teaspoon cayenne pepper
½ cup chicken broth diluted with ¼ cup water, or ¾ cup Homemade Chicken Broth (p. 54)
½ cup carrot juice
½ pound penne pasta
3 cups small broccoli florets
One 15-ounce can red kidney beans, rinsed and drained

1. Preheat the oven to 425°. Place the carrots, onion and garlic cloves in a 7-by-11-inch baking pan. Drizzle with 2 teaspoons of the oil, the salt, ¼ teaspoon of the black pepper and the cayenne, and toss to mix. Bake, stirring several times, for about 45 minutes, or until the vegetables are tender and golden.

2. Transfer the vegetables to a food processor. Add the diluted chicken broth and the carrot juice, and process until puréed.

3. In a large pot of boiling water, cook the penne for 8 minutes, then add the broccoli and cook until the broccoli is crisp-tender and the pasta is al dente, 3 to 4 minutes longer. Add the beans and cook just until heated through, about 1 minute. Reserving ½ cup of the cooking liquid, drain the pasta, broccoli and beans in a colander.

4. Pour the carrot sauce, the reserved pasta cooking liquid, the remaining 1 tablespoon plus 1 teaspoon oil and ¼ teaspoon black pepper into the pasta cooking pot and warm over medium-high heat. Add the pasta-vegetable mixture and toss until combined and heated through. Serve hot.

Makes 4 servings

NUTRITION INFORMATION
values are per serving

CALORIES 461	DIETARY FIBER 13 G
TOTAL FAT 9.2 G	BETA CAROTENE 23 MG
SATURATED FAT 1.2 G	VITAMIN C 88 MG
CHOLESTEROL 0 MG	CALCIUM 130 MG
SODIUM 464 MG	IRON 4.9 MG

Fusilli and Broccoli with Tomato Pesto

This is a perfect dish for summertime, when tomatoes are drooping off the vines and lush, green basil leaves are begging to be picked. This lovely combination needs little more than good crusty bread and a salad as accompaniments, and peach crisp, still warm from the oven, for dessert.

1 cup (firmly packed) basil leaves
2 garlic cloves, peeled
½ cup chicken broth, canned or homemade (p. 54)
2 tablespoons no-salt-added tomato paste
½ pound short fusilli pasta
4 cups small broccoli florets
2 large red bell peppers, cut into thin strips
2 cups diced tomatoes
1 ounce grated Parmesan cheese
½ teaspoon salt
½ teaspoon freshly ground black pepper

Pumpkin Ravioli with Sweet Pepper Sauce

Both pumpkin- and spinach-filled ravioli are available at Italian markets or specialty foods stores. If you do not have access to a specialty food store, you can make this with another type of ravioli, though it would be best to find one that is not filled with cheese or meat, as they can be quite high in fat. The bell pepper sauce can be prepared almost entirely in advance, making this a very easy main course to put together at the last minute. A crisp green salad—Romaine, endive and fresh fennel—would make a fine accompaniment.

2 teaspoons olive oil
3 large red bell peppers, thinly sliced
1 large onion, halved and thinly sliced
3 garlic cloves, crushed through a press
1 cup vegetable or chicken broth
2 tablespoons no-salt-added tomato paste
½ teaspoon marjoram, oregano or sage
¼ teaspoon salt
½ teaspoon sugar
1¼ pounds pumpkin-, spinach- or vegetable-filled ravioli

1. In a large nonstick skillet, warm the oil over low heat. Add the bell peppers, onion and garlic, and cook until very soft, about 15 minutes.

2. Stir in the broth, tomato paste, marjoram, salt and sugar; cover and cook until the peppers and onion are meltingly tender, about 20 minutes.

3. Transfer the bell pepper mixture to a food processor and process to a smooth purée. Return the purée to the skillet.

4. Meanwhile, cook the ravioli in a large pot of boiling water until they float to the surface and the thickest part of the ravioli is al dente, 10 to 15 minutes, or according to package directions. Drain the ravioli in a colander, reserving ½ cup of the pasta cooking water.

5. Stir the reserved pasta cooking water into the pepper purée and bring to a simmer. Add the drained ravioli and cook until heated through, about 1 minute. Serve hot.

Makes 4 servings

NUTRITION INFORMATION
values are per serving

CALORIES 458	DIETARY FIBER 5.6 G
TOTAL FAT 11 G	BETA CAROTENE 2.7 MG
SATURATED FAT 5.1 G	VITAMIN C 150 MG
CHOLESTEROL 87 MG	CALCIUM 264 MG
SODIUM 901 MG	IRON 3.7 MG

Aegean Macaroni

There are many flavors and ingredients that come to mind when one thinks of the cooking of the countries that rim the Aegean Sea. Herbs such as mint and oregano and the inventive use of spinach, yogurt and feta cheese are reminiscent of Greece. At the mention of macaroni, there is only one possible association. So what we have here is a delightful Greco-Italian collaboration in a satisfying vegetarian entrée.

1½ cups plain nonfat yogurt
1 tablespoon cornstarch
½ pound elbow macaroni
1 tablespoon extra-virgin olive oil
1 cup thinly sliced scallions
4 garlic cloves, minced
1 teaspoon oregano
1 teaspoon dried mint
¾ teaspoon freshly ground black pepper
⅛ teaspoon salt

8 cups (loosely packed) stemmed spinach, cut into 1-inch-wide strips
2 ounces feta cheese, crumbled

1. Line a strainer with cheesecloth or a white paper towel and suspend it over a bowl. Spoon the yogurt into the strainer and let drain for 15 minutes. Discard the whey. Transfer the thickened yogurt to the bowl and whisk in the cornstarch until smooth.

2. Cook the macaroni in a large pot of boiling water until al dente, 8 to 10 minutes, or according to package directions. Drain in a colander.

3. Dry the pasta cooking pot. Add the oil to the pot and warm over medium-high heat until hot but not smoking. Stir in the scallions, garlic, oregano, mint, pepper and salt, and sauté until the scallions are wilted, 1 to 2 minutes.

4. Add the spinach in handfuls and cook until wilted, 1 to 2 minutes. Reduce the heat to low, stir in the yogurt and cook, stirring constantly, just until heated through. Do not boil.

5. Pour the pasta into a large serving bowl; add the spinach sauce and feta, and toss to coat well.

Makes 4 servings

Nutrition Information
values are per serving

CALORIES 378	DIETARY FIBER 5.7 G
TOTAL FAT 8.1 G	BETA CAROTENE 5.7 MG
SATURATED FAT 2.9 G	VITAMIN C 46 MG
CHOLESTEROL 14 MG	CALCIUM 420 MG
SODIUM 411 MG	IRON 6.8 MG

Pasta Gratin with Cheddar, Broccoli and Red Pepper

Serve this creamy, filling, cheese-rich pasta gratin with crusty whole-wheat Italian bread, an arugula salad with lemon vinaigrette and pears poached in white wine.

2 large red bell peppers
½ pound small pasta shells
2½ cups small broccoli florets
2 garlic cloves, peeled
½ teaspoon cayenne pepper
¼ teaspoon dry mustard
2 cups lowfat (1%) milk
2 tablespoons flour
1 cup shredded sharp Cheddar cheese
½ teaspoon salt
½ teaspoon freshly ground black pepper
⅛ teaspoon nutmeg
3 tablespoons grated Parmesan cheese

1. Preheat the broiler. Cutting vertically, slice the bell peppers in 3 or 4 flat panels, leaving the core and seeds behind. Place the bell pepper pieces, skin-side up, in a single layer on a jelly-roll pan and broil 4 to 5 inches from the heat for 10 to 15 minutes, or until blackened all over. Transfer to a bowl to cool. Preheat the oven to 400°.

2. Meanwhile, cook the pasta in a large pot of boiling water for 7 minutes. Add the broccoli and cook until the pasta is al dente and the broccoli crisp-tender, 2 to 3 minutes. Drain in a colander and set aside.

3. When the peppers are cool enough to handle, peel them and transfer to a food processor. Add the garlic, cayenne and mustard, and process until smooth.

4. In a large saucepan, whisk together the milk and flour, and cook over medium heat, whisking constantly, until lightly thickened, about 4 minutes. Whisk in the red pepper purée, ½ cup of the Cheddar cheese, the salt, black pepper and nutmeg. Gently fold in the broccoli and pasta.

5. Transfer the mixture to a 7-by-11-inch baking pan, sprinkle the remaining ½ cup Cheddar and the Parmesan on top. Bake for about 35 minutes, or until browned.

Makes 4 servings

Nutrition Information
values are per serving

CALORIES 462	DIETARY FIBER 5.8 G
TOTAL FAT 13 G	BETA CAROTENE 4.0 MG
SATURATED FAT 7.6 G	VITAMIN C 237 MG
CHOLESTEROL 38 MG	CALCIUM 466 MG
SODIUM 606 MG	IRON 3.8 MG

Pumpkin-Filled Lasagna Rolls

We have the chefs of Italy to thank for the wonderful use of pumpkin as a filling for stuffed pasta. This inventive variation on a theme employs pumpkin, subtly flavored with sage and lightened with egg white, as the filling for lasagna noodles that are then rolled, sauced and baked.

6 amaretti cookies (crisp Italian macaroons), finely ground (3 tablespoons)
1½ cups canned solid-pack pumpkin purée
¼ cup plus 2 tablespoons grated Parmesan cheese
3 tablespoons plain dried bread crumbs
1 egg white
2 teaspoons chopped fresh sage or ¼ teaspoon dried
2 teaspoons sugar
½ teaspoon almond extract
½ teaspoon salt
⅛ teaspoon freshly ground black pepper
8 lasagna noodles
¾ cup evaporated skimmed milk
2 tablespoons slivered almonds, finely chopped
2 teaspoons unsalted butter, cut into small pieces

1. In a medium bowl, stir together the amaretti crumbs, the pumpkin purée, ¼ cup of the Parmesan, the bread crumbs, egg white, 1 teaspoon of the sage, the sugar, almond extract, salt and pepper.

2. In a large pot of boiling water, cook the lasagna noodles until al dente, 10 to 12 minutes, or according to package directions.

3. Preheat the oven to 400°. With a paper towel, very lightly oil a gratin dish or baking dish large enough to fit the lasagna rolls in a single layer (about 7 by 11 inches).

4. Drain the lasagna noodles, rinse and drain again. Lay the lasagna noodles flat on a kitchen towel and pat dry. With a short end facing you, spread ¼ cup of the filling over each noodle and roll them up. Place the lasagna rolls seam-side down in the prepared baking pan.

5. In a measuring cup, combine the evaporated milk and remaining 1 teaspoon sage and pour over the rolls. Sprinkle the remaining 2 tablespoons Parmesan and the almonds on top and dot with the butter. Bake uncovered for 25 to 30 minutes, or until bubbly and lightly golden.

6. Transfer 2 rolls to each of 4 dinner plates.

Makes 4 servings

Nutrition Information
values are per serving

CALORIES 412	DIETARY FIBER 3.3 G
TOTAL FAT 8.9 G	BETA CAROTENE 12 MG
SATURATED FAT 3.3 G	VITAMIN C 4.5 MG
CHOLESTEROL 13 MG	CALCIUM 301 MG
SODIUM 534 MG	IRON 3.9 MG

Lasagna Rolls with Spinach and Ricotta in Creamy Tomato Sauce

Lasagna noodles here are spread—not layered—with a spinach and ricotta mixture, then rolled up, covered with tomato sauce and baked until bubbly. The colors, in particular, are beautiful, as is the presentation when served. This is dinner party fare, easy to make, but very impressive.

8 lasagna noodles
1 egg
1 egg white
Two 10-ounce packages frozen chopped spinach, thawed and squeezed dry
8 ounces part-skim ricotta cheese
¼ cup grated Parmesan cheese
3 garlic cloves, minced
¼ teaspoon freshly ground black pepper
⅛ teaspoon nutmeg
¾ teaspoon grated orange zest
1½ cups canned crushed tomatoes
2 teaspoons flour
½ teaspoon salt
¼ teaspoon sugar
¼ teaspoon cinnamon

1. Cook the lasagna noodles in a large pot of boiling water until al dente, 9 to 11 minutes, or according to package directions. Drain, rinse and set aside.

2. In a large bowl, beat together the whole egg and egg white. Beat in the spinach, ricotta, Parmesan, garlic, pepper, nutmeg and ¼ teaspoon of the orange zest.

3. Preheat the oven to 400°. Spray an 8-inch square baking pan with nonstick cooking spray.

4. Lay a lasagna noodle flat on a work surface, with a short end facing you. Spread one-eighth of the filling over the noodle and roll it up. Place the lasagna roll seam-side down in the prepared baking pan. Repeat with the remaining lasagna noodles and filling.

5. In a medium bowl, combine the remaining ½ teaspoon orange zest with the tomatoes, flour, salt, sugar and cinnamon. Pour the sauce over the lasagna rolls and bake uncovered for 25 minutes, or until bubbly.

Makes 4 servings

NUTRITION INFORMATION
values are per serving

CALORIES 376	DIETARY FIBER 5.0 G
TOTAL FAT 8.7 G	BETA CAROTENE 6.9 MG
SATURATED FAT 4.3 G	VITAMIN C 49 MG
CHOLESTEROL 75 MG	CALCIUM 429 MG
SODIUM 723 MG	IRON 6.0 MG

Lasagna Arrabbiata

The Italian word "arrabbiata" indicates a dish with tomato or bell pepper sauce, and by tradition the sauce often includes a hefty measure of red pepper flakes.

9 lasagna noodles
1 tablespoon extra-virgin olive oil
1 large red bell pepper, cut into thin strips
1 large green bell pepper, cut into thin strips
1 cup grated carrots
3 garlic cloves, minced
Three 8-ounce cans no-salt-added tomato sauce
½ teaspoon freshly ground black pepper
½ teaspoon crushed red pepper flakes
¼ teaspoon salt
8 ounces part-skim ricotta cheese
Half a 10-ounce package frozen chopped spinach, thawed and squeezed dry
2 egg whites
2 tablespoons grated Parmesan cheese

1 large tomato (about 9 ounces), halved lengthwise and cut crosswise into thin slices
1 ounce part-skim mozzarella cheese, shredded

1. Cook the lasagna noodles in a large pot of boiling water until al dente, 9 to 11 minutes, or according to package directions. Drain in a colander and rinse and cool under gently running cold water.

2. In a medium nonstick saucepan, warm the oil over high heat until hot but not smoking. Add the red and green bell peppers, the carrots and garlic, and sauté, stirring frequently, until the vegetables are tender, 5 to 6 minutes. Stir in the tomato sauce, ¼ teaspoon of the black pepper, the red pepper flakes and ⅛ teaspoon of the salt. Bring to a boil, reduce the heat to medium-low, cover and simmer for 5 minutes to blend the flavors. Remove from the heat.

3. Preheat the oven to 375°. Spray an 8-inch square baking dish with nonstick cooking spray.

4. In a medium bowl, mix the ricotta, spinach, egg whites, Parmesan and the remaining ¼ teaspoon black pepper and ⅛ teaspoon salt.

5. Spread 1 cup of the sauce in the bottom of the prepared baking dish. Top with three of the lasagna noodles, letting them hang over the edges of the dish. Spread half of the spinach filling over the noodles and layer the filling with half the tomato slices. Spoon 1 cup of the sauce over the tomatoes. Top with three more noodles; spread them with the remaining filling and top with the remaining tomatoes and 1 cup of the sauce. Fold the edges of the noodles over the top of the lasagna. Place the remaining three noodles on the top, tuck the edges down and under the lasagna. Top with the remaining sauce and sprinkle with the mozzarella.

6. Place the pan on a baking sheet to catch spillovers and bake for 25 to 30 minutes, or until the filling is heated through and the sauce is bubbly. Remove from the oven and let stand for 5 minutes before cutting into squares and serving.

Makes 4 servings

NUTRITION INFORMATION
values are per serving

CALORIES 473	DIETARY FIBER 7.2 G
TOTAL FAT 12 G	BETA CAROTENE 8.9 MG
SATURATED FAT 4.6 G	VITAMIN C 121 MG
CHOLESTEROL 24 MG	CALCIUM 307 MG
SODIUM 397 MG	IRON 5.3 MG

Linguine with Red Clam Sauce

A favorite Italian wedding of ingredients, this linguine with red clam sauce calls for fresh littleneck clams in their shells as well as for making your own sauce. More exciting to look at than a standard chopped-clam sauce, you could serve this either as an entrée, or in smaller portions as a first course followed by grilled fish and a summer salad. For dessert, stay in the warm-weather mode with fresh raspberries with lemon sorbet.

1 tablespoon plus 1 teaspoon extra-virgin olive oil
2 large red bell peppers, diced
1 medium onion, chopped
4 garlic cloves, minced
1 teaspoon oregano
½ teaspoon freshly ground black pepper
¼ teaspoon crushed red pepper flakes
¼ cup dry white wine or canned chicken broth
One 16-ounce can crushed tomatoes in purée
One 8-ounce can no-salt-added tomato sauce
½ pound linguine
2 dozen littleneck clams, scrubbed

1. In a Dutch oven or flameproof casserole, warm the oil over medium-high heat until hot but not smoking. Stir in the bell peppers, onion, garlic, oregano, black pepper and red pepper flakes, and sauté until the vegetables are tender, 4 to 6 minutes.

2. Stir in the wine and bring to a simmer. Stir in the crushed tomatoes and the tomato sauce, and bring to a boil. Reduce the heat to low, cover and simmer for 15 minutes, stirring occasionally.

3. Meanwhile, cook the linguine in a large pot of boiling water until al dente, 9 to 11 minutes, or according to package directions. Drain in a colander and transfer to a large serving bowl.

4. Add the clams to the sauce, cover and cook, stirring frequently, until the clams open, 10 to 12 minutes. (Discard any clams that do not open.) Pour the sauce and the clams over the pasta.

Makes 4 servings

NUTRITION INFORMATION
values are per serving

CALORIES 377	DIETARY FIBER 3.8 G
TOTAL FAT 6.5 G	BETA CAROTENE 2.7 MG
SATURATED FAT .9 G	VITAMIN C 126 MG
CHOLESTEROL 18 MG	CALCIUM 102 MG
SODIUM 230 MG	IRON 11 MG

Fettuccine with Mussels and Spinach

The small black tuft that protrudes from between the shell halves of a mussel is called the beard, and it needs to be removed before the mussels are cooked. As you scrub the shellfish, pull the beards out with your fingers, then rinse the mussels well.

½ pound fettuccine
½ cup dry white wine
½ teaspoon thyme
2 dozen mussels, scrubbed and debearded
1 tablespoon olive oil, preferably extra-virgin
4 garlic cloves, thinly sliced
12 cups (loosely packed) stemmed spinach
½ teaspoon freshly ground black pepper
¼ teaspoon salt

1. Cook the pasta in a large pot of boiling water until al dente, 8 to 10 minutes, or according to package directions. Drain in a colander.

2. Meanwhile, in a large saucepan, combine the wine and thyme. Cover and bring to a boil over high heat. Add the mussels, reduce the heat to medium-high, cover and cook, tossing and stirring frequently, until the mussels have opened, 4 to 6 minutes. Remove the pan from the heat. (Discard any mussels that do not open.)

3. After draining the pasta, add the oil and garlic to the pasta cooking pot. Cook over high heat, stirring constantly, until the garlic is golden, 1 to 2 minutes. Add the spinach, pepper and salt, and cook, stirring, until the spinach is just wilted, 3 to 4 minutes.

4. Add the drained pasta to the spinach mixture and toss just until heated through. Remove from the heat.

5. Reserving 4 mussels in their shells for garnish, shell the mussels and add to the pasta.

6. Line a small fine-mesh sieve with a piece of cheesecloth and set over a small bowl or measuring cup. Pour the mussel cooking juices through the strainer; then add the strained juices to the pasta and toss to mix well.

7. To serve, divide the pasta mixture among 4 pasta bowls and top with a mussel in the shell.

Makes 4 servings

NUTRITION INFORMATION
values are per serving

CALORIES 359	DIETARY FIBER 7.1 G
TOTAL FAT 7.7 G	BETA CAROTENE 8.5 MG
SATURATED FAT 1.3 G	VITAMIN C 60 MG
CHOLESTEROL 67 MG	CALCIUM 251 MG
SODIUM 452 MG	IRON 11 MG

Pasta with Shrimp, Fennel and Oranges

Fresh fennel, sometimes called anise, lends its incomparable licorice-like flavor to a medley of tastes in this light, citrusy shellfish and pasta dish.

2 navel oranges
¾ pound medium shrimp, shelled and deveined
½ teaspoon freshly ground black pepper
½ pound gnocchi-shaped or radiatore pasta
1 tablespoon extra-virgin olive oil
1 medium red onion, halved and thinly sliced
2 cups thinly sliced fennel
¼ cup chicken broth, canned or homemade (p. 54)
¼ teaspoon salt
6 Calamata or other brine-cured black olives, pitted and sliced
1 ounce Parmesan cheese, shaved into long strips

1. Grate 1 teaspoon of zest from one of the oranges and set aside. Peel both of the oranges, removing all of the bitter white pith. Working over a bowl, cut out the sections from in between the membranes, letting the sections drop into the bowl. Squeeze the juice from the membranes over the sections. Cover the oranges and set aside.

2. Toss the shrimp with the orange zest and ¼ teaspoon of the pepper. Let stand for at least 5 minutes.

3. Cook the pasta in a large pot of boiling water until al dente, 8 to 10 minutes, or according to package directions. Drain in a colander.

4. Meanwhile, in a large nonstick skillet, warm the oil over high heat. Add the onion and fennel, and sauté until tender, 3 to 4 minutes.

5. Add the shrimp, chicken broth, salt and the remaining ¼ teaspoon pepper, and sauté until the shrimp turn pink and are just cooked through, 3 to 4 minutes. Remove from the heat.

6. In a large serving bowl, toss the pasta with the shrimp mixture. Add the oranges (and the juice) and toss again. Sprinkle with the olives and the Parmesan and serve.

Makes 4 servings

NUTRITION INFORMATION
values are per serving

CALORIES 414	DIETARY FIBER 4.5 G
TOTAL FAT 8.6 G	BETA CAROTENE .1 MG
SATURATED FAT 2.3 G	VITAMIN C 51 MG
CHOLESTEROL 110 MG	CALCIUM 219 MG
SODIUM 544 MG	IRON 5.0 MG

Bow Ties with Green Chilies and Shrimp Sauce

Garlic-infused shrimp are puréed, then blended with mild green chilies to form a superb, one-of-a-kind sauce for spinach and pasta.

⅓ cup canned chicken broth diluted with ⅓ cup water, or ⅔ cup Homemade Chicken Broth (p. 54)
16 medium shrimp, unshelled
2 garlic cloves, peeled
⅓ cup light sour cream
¼ cup chopped fresh basil
½ pound bow-tie pasta
1½ cups carrot matchsticks
2 teaspoons olive oil
1 medium onion, chopped
One 4-ounce can diced mild green chilies, drained
4 cups (loosely packed) stemmed spinach, cut into ½-inch-wide strips
1 lemon, cut into wedges

1. In a medium saucepan, bring the diluted broth to a boil over medium-high heat. Add the shrimp and garlic, and return to a boil. Cover, reduce the heat to medium and simmer until the shrimp are just cooked, about 2 minutes. Reserving the cooking liquid, transfer the shrimp and garlic to a plate and set aside until cool enough to handle.

2. Shell and devein the shrimp, then place them in a food processor and process to form a paste. Add the sour cream and continue processing until smooth and well combined. Add the cooked garlic and about ⅓ cup of the reserved cooking liquid and process to purée the garlic. Stir in half of the basil and set the sauce aside.

3. Cook the pasta in a large pot of boiling water until al dente, 9 to 11 minutes, or according to package directions. About 2 minutes before the pasta is done, add the carrot matchsticks.

4. Meanwhile, in a small nonstick skillet, warm the oil over medium-high heat until hot but not smoking. Add the onion and green chilies and cook until the onion begins to soften, about 3 minutes. Stir in the shrimp sauce and the remaining 2 tablespoons basil and remove from the heat.

5. Place the spinach in a serving bowl. Drain the pasta and carrots in a colander, then add the hot pasta to the serving bowl. Add the shrimp sauce and toss to distribute the ingredients. Serve with the lemon wedges.

Makes 4 servings

NUTRITION INFORMATION
values are per serving

CALORIES 363	DIETARY FIBER 5.6 G
TOTAL FAT 7.0 G	BETA CAROTENE 9.9 MG
SATURATED FAT 1.9 G	VITAMIN C 48 MG
CHOLESTEROL 55 MG	CALCIUM 159 MG
SODIUM 256 MG	IRON 5.8 MG

SUPER QUICK

Wide Noodles with Curried Chicken

Working time: 15 minutes Total time: 25 minutes

- 1 tablespoon olive oil
- 3 garlic cloves, minced
- 1 teaspoon cumin
- 1 teaspoon ground coriander
- ¾ teaspoon ground ginger
- ¾ teaspoon turmeric
- ½ teaspoon paprika
- ¾ pound sweet potatoes, peeled and cut into ½-inch chunks
- 1 large carrot, thinly sliced
- ¾ cup canned chicken broth diluted with ½ cup water, or 1¼ cups Homemade Chicken Broth (p. 54)
- ½ pound skinless, boneless chicken breast, cut into ½-inch chunks
- ¼ teaspoon salt
- ¼ teaspoon freshly ground pepper
- ½ pound wide noodles
- ½ cup frozen peas
- ⅓ cup plain nonfat yogurt
- 1 tablespoon flour
- 1 teaspoon peanut buter
- 3 tablespoons chopped cilantro

1 In a large nonstick skillet, warm the oil over medium heat until hot but not smoking. Add the garlic and cook until fragrant, about 1 minute. Stir in the cumin, coriander, ginger, turmeric and paprika, and cook for 1 minute.

2 Add the sweet potatoes, carrot and ¼ cup of the diluted chicken broth, and cook, stirring frequently, until the carrot is almost tender, about 4 minutes.

3 Add the chicken, stirring to coat. Then add the remaining 1 cup chicken broth, the salt and pepper. Bring to a boil, reduce to a simmer and cook until the sweet potatoes and chicken are cooked through, about 5 minutes.

4 Meanwhile, in a large pot of boiling water, cook the noodles until al dente, 7 to 9 minutes, or according to package directions. Add the peas for the last minute or so to thaw them.

5 In a small bowl, blend the yogurt and flour. Whisk the yogurt mixture into the chicken mixture, then stir in the peanut butter. Drain the pasta and peas, and toss with the curried chicken mixture and the cilantro.

Makes 4 servings

Values are per serving:
Calories: 437 Total fat: 7.9 g Saturated fat: 1.3 g Cholesterol: 87 mg Sodium: 428 mg
Dietary fiber: 5.0 g Beta carotene: 12 mg Vitamin C: 22 mg Calcium: 101 mg Iron: 4.6 mg

Shells with Tomatoes, Peppers and Cod

The zesty flavors of Spain are at play in this dish of pasta shells topped with tomato sauce, fresh cod, peppers and green olives. If cod is unavailable, use scrod, haddock or another firm-fleshed white fish that has identity and that will flake easily. The fish's texture is important here.

1 tablespoon olive oil
¾ cup finely chopped onion
3 cloves garlic, finely chopped
1 medium red bell pepper, diced
2 cups chopped tomatoes
½ teaspoon grated orange zest
¼ cup orange juice
4 drops of hot pepper sauce
½ teaspoon salt
¼ teaspoon ground ginger
½ pound pasta shells
1¼ pounds cod fillets, cut into 4 pieces
2½ teaspoons cornstarch blended with
1½ teaspoons water
8 green olives, pitted and coarsely chopped
3 tablespoons chopped flat-leaf parsley

1. In a large nonstick skillet, warm the oil over medium-low heat. Add the onion and garlic, and cook, stirring frequently, until the onion has softened, about 7 minutes. Add the red bell pepper, increase the heat to medium and cook until the pepper has softened, about 5 minutes.

2. Stir in the tomatoes, orange zest, orange juice, hot pepper sauce, salt and ginger. Bring to a boil, reduce to a simmer and cook for 5 minutes to blend the flavors.

3. Meanwhile, cook the pasta in a large pot of boiling water until al dente, 7 to 9 minutes, or according to package directions. Drain in a colander.

4. Place the cod on top of the tomato-pepper mixture, cover and cook until the fish just flakes when tested with a fork, about 10 minutes.

5. Add the cornstarch mixture to the skillet, bring to a boil and cook until the sauce is lightly thickened, about 1 minute. Gently flake the cod with a fork, then stir in the olives and parsley. Toss with the hot pasta and serve.

Makes 4 servings

NUTRITION INFORMATION
values are per serving

CALORIES 419	DIETARY FIBER 3.7 G
TOTAL FAT 6.6 G	BETA CAROTENE 1.1 MG
SATURATED FAT .9 G	VITAMIN C 65 MG
CHOLESTEROL 61 MG	CALCIUM 61 MG
SODIUM 555 MG	IRON 3.6 MG

Whole Wheat Fettuccine with Chicken and Porcini Mushrooms

Both dried and fresh mushrooms act as the base for the sauce here that also includes Canadian bacon, broccoli and sautéed chicken. This is a grand dish for a small dinner party, which could begin with roasted red pepper and garlic crostini. Add green salad to the menu and chocolate-dipped strawberries for dessert.

⅓ cup dried porcini or other wild mushrooms
(about ½ ounce)
½ cup boiling water
1 tablespoon olive oil
1 ounce Canadian bacon, minced
6 ounces skinless, boneless chicken breast,
cut into ¼-inch-thick strips
½ pound fresh mushrooms, quartered
1¼ cups low-sodium mixed vegetable juice

¾ teaspoon salt
½ teaspoon sage
½ teaspoon freshly ground black pepper
5 cups small broccoli florets
1 teaspoon cornstarch blended with 1 tablespoon water
½ pound whole wheat fettuccine
½ cup part-skim ricotta cheese

1. In a small heatproof bowl, combine the porcini and the boiling water; set aside to soften.

2. In a large nonstick skillet, warm 2 teaspoons of the oil over medium heat until hot but not smoking. Add the Canadian bacon and cook, stirring frequently, until the bacon is crisped, about 4 minutes. Transfer the bacon with a slotted spoon to a plate.

3. Add the chicken to the skillet and cook, stirring frequently, until golden brown, about 4 minutes. Remove with a slotted spoon and add to the plate with the bacon.

4. Add the remaining 1 teaspoon oil and the fresh mushrooms to the skillet and cook, stirring frequently, until the mushrooms are lightly colored, about 4 minutes. Stir in the mixed vegetable juice, salt, sage and pepper.

5. Reserving the soaking liquid, remove the porcini and rinse them under cold running water. Coarsely chop the porcini and add them to the skillet. Line a fine-mesh sieve with cheesecloth or damp paper towels and strain the mushroom soaking liquid into the skillet.

6. Bring the mushroom sauce to a boil and add the broccoli and the reserved Canadian bacon and chicken. Reduce to a simmer, cover and cook until the broccoli is tender and the chicken is cooked through, about 3 minutes.

7. Stir the cornstarch mixture into the skillet, bring to a boil over medium heat and cook until lightly thickened, about 1 minute. Transfer the sauce to a large serving bowl.

8. Meanwhile, in a large pot of boiling water, cook the pasta until al dente, 9 to 11 minutes, or according to package directions. Drain well and toss with the sauce and ricotta cheese.

Makes 4 servings

NUTRITION INFORMATION
values are per serving

CALORIES 423	DIETARY FIBER 14 G
TOTAL FAT 8.3 G	BETA CAROTENE 2.1 MG
SATURATED FAT 2.4 G	VITAMIN C 148 MG
CHOLESTEROL 38 MG	CALCIUM 201 MG
SODIUM 679 MG	IRON 5.5 MG

Penne with Chicken, Spinach, Sun-Dried Tomatoes and Goat Cheese

Though 14 cups of spinach may seem astonishing, it actually is more or less the quantity of spinach that comes in a one-pound bag from the supermarket. Also, as most spinach devotees know, what seems like an impossible amount of spinach *before* it goes into the pan soon shrinks to more modest proportions. In any case, one taste of this lovely sauce will make the actual number of spinach leaves you have just handled simply fade away.

¼ cup (not oil-packed) sun-dried tomatoes
½ cup boiling water
2 teaspoons olive oil
6 ounces skinless, boneless chicken breast, cut into ¼-inch-thick strips
½ pound penne pasta
3 garlic cloves, minced
14 cups (loosely packed) shredded stemmed spinach
3 tablespoons chopped fresh basil
2 tablespoons balsamic vinegar

½ teaspoon salt
1½ teaspoons cornstarch blended with 1 tablespoon water
4 ounces soft goat cheese, crumbled

1. In a small heatproof bowl, combine the sun-dried tomatoes and boiling water, and set aside to soften, about 10 minutes. Reserving the soaking liquid, remove the tomatoes and coarsely chop them.

2. In a large nonstick skillet, warm the oil over medium heat until hot but not smoking. Add the chicken and cook, stirring occasionally, until the chicken is golden brown and almost cooked through, about 3 minutes. Transfer the chicken to a plate and cover loosely to keep warm.

3. Meanwhile, in a large pot of boiling water, cook the penne until al dente, 9 to 11 minutes, or according to package directions.

4. Add the garlic to the skillet and cook until softened, about 2 minutes. Add the sun-dried tomatoes and their soaking liquid, the chicken, spinach, basil, vinegar and salt, and cook until the spinach is wilted and the chicken is cooked through, about 4 minutes.

5. Stir the cornstarch mixture into the spinach mixture, bring to a boil and cook until lightly thickened, about 1 minute. Stir in the goat cheese until melted and transfer to a large serving bowl.

6. Drain the pasta and toss with the sauce.

Makes 4 servings

Nutrition Information
values are per serving

CALORIES 419	DIETARY FIBER 7.3 G
TOTAL FAT 11 G	BETA CAROTENE 8.4 MG
SATURATED FAT 4.8 G	VITAMIN C 69 MG
CHOLESTEROL 38 MG	CALCIUM 277 MG
SODIUM 571 MG	IRON 9.0 MG

Cajun Pasta

Louisiana's Cajun cooking is well known for its traditional use of bell peppers, onions and tomatoes, and here they form the basis of a sauce for pasta. Add spicy turkey—not pork—sausage and some additional fire in the form of both chili powder and hot sauce (preferably from Louisiana) and you have a delicious topping for linguine.

2 teaspoons olive oil
¾ pound spicy turkey sausage, cut into 8 pieces
1 teaspoon chili powder
1 teaspoon paprika
½ teaspoon oregano
3 garlic cloves, minced
1 large red onion, diced
¼ cup water
1 large red bell pepper, diced
1 large green bell pepper, diced
One 14½-ounce can no-salt-added stewed tomatoes, chopped with their juice
One 8-ounce can no-salt-added tomato sauce
¼ teaspoon hot pepper sauce
¼ teaspoon salt
¼ teaspoon freshly ground black pepper
½ pound linguine

1. In a large nonstick skillet, warm the oil over medium heat until hot but not smoking. Add the turkey sausage and cook until browned all over, about 5 minutes. Transfer to a plate and cover loosely to keep warm.

2. Add the chili powder, paprika and oregano to the skillet, and cook, stirring constantly, until fragrant, about 1 minute. Stir in the garlic and cook for 30 seconds.

3. Add the onion and stir to coat with the spices. Add the water and cook, stirring occasionally, until the onion has softened, about 7 minutes.

4. Stir in the red and green bell peppers and cook until they are crisp-tender, about 4 minutes.

5. Stir in the stewed tomatoes, tomato sauce, hot pepper sauce, salt, black pepper and the turkey sausages. Bring to a boil, lower to a simmer, cover and cook until the flavors have come together and the sausage is cooked through, about 5 minutes. Transfer to a large bowl.

6. Meanwhile, in a large pot of boiling water, cook the pasta until al dente, 9 to 11 minutes, or according to package directions. Drain well and toss with the sausage and pepper mixture.

Makes 4 servings

NUTRITION INFORMATION
values are per serving

CALORIES 452	DIETARY FIBER 5.0 G
TOTAL FAT 13 G	BETA CAROTENE 2.1 MG
SATURATED FAT 3.9 G	VITAMIN C 102 MG
CHOLESTEROL 51 MG	CALCIUM 81 MG
SODIUM 709 MG	IRON 5.4 MG

Angel Hair Pasta with Chinese Barbecued Pork and Vegetables

Dishes that combine a variety of cooked ingredients in broth are common in much of Asia. The meat, pasta and vegetables are savored on their own, but also add a great deal of flavor to the broth, which is often eaten afterwards.

½ pound lean boneless pork loin
2 tablespoons chili sauce
1 tablespoon reduced-sodium soy sauce
2 garlic cloves, crushed through a press
2 teaspoons grated fresh ginger
1½ teaspoons Oriental (dark) sesame oil
⅛ teaspoon crushed red pepper flakes
1 cup canned chicken broth diluted with 1 cup water, or 2 cups Homemade Chicken Broth (p. 54)
1 fresh jalapeño pepper, halved, some seeds removed
¾ pound bok choy, cut into 1-inch pieces (about 4 cups)
1 cup diagonally sliced carrots
1 cup diagonally sliced scallions
6 ounces angel hair pasta, broken into thirds

1. Place the pork on a cutting board with a cut end facing you. With a long, sharp knife, slice into the meat horizontally, cutting about three-fourths of the way through. Open the pork up like a book.

2. Preheat the broiler. In a small bowl or cup, mix the chili sauce, 1 teaspoon of the soy sauce, half of the garlic, 1 teaspoon of the ginger, 1 teaspoon of the sesame oil and the red pepper flakes. Spread this mixture over both sides of the pork and let stand at room temperature for 10 minutes.

3. Meanwhile, in a large saucepan, combine the diluted chicken broth, the remaining 2 teaspoons soy sauce, garlic, 1 teaspoon ginger and the jalapeño pepper. Cover and bring to a boil over high heat. Reduce the heat to low, cover and simmer for 5 minutes to blend the flavors.

4. Broil the pork 5 to 6 inches from the heat for 15 to 17 minutes, without turning, or until the pork is cooked through. Transfer the pork to a plate and let stand until ready to assemble the dish.

5. Meanwhile, add the bok choy and carrots to the broth and bring to a boil over high heat. Reduce the heat to medium, cover and simmer until the carrots are tender, 6 to 8 minutes. Stir in the scallions and remove from the heat.

6. Cook the angel hair pasta in a large pot of boiling water until al dente, 3 to 5 minutes, or according to package directions. Drain in a colander and toss with the remaining ½ teaspoon sesame oil.

7. Pour any juices that have collected under the pork into the broth. Carve the pork into thin slices. Stir the pasta into the broth, ladle the mixture into bowls and top with the sliced pork.

Makes 4 servings

Nutrition Information
values are per serving

CALORIES 307	DIETARY FIBER 2.5 G
TOTAL FAT 6.2 G	BETA CAROTENE 6.3 MG
SATURATED FAT 1.5 G	VITAMIN C 57 MG
CHOLESTEROL 33 MG	CALCIUM 140 MG
SODIUM 613 MG	IRON 3.6 MG

Rigatoni with Spicy Pumpkin-Tomato Sauce and Smoked Turkey

The cooking influences in this recipe are many, but the final nod goes to the American Southwest, for it is there that squash, fresh chili peppers and spices such as cumin and chili powder are used so inventively. Try to find the hulled pumpkin seeds called for—they are sometimes called *pepitas* and can be found in health food stores—as they add a wonderful rich touch.

One 16-ounce can whole tomatoes in purée
1 tablespoon extra-virgin olive oil
1 large onion, chopped
2 fresh jalapeño peppers, minced, some seeds removed
2 teaspoons cumin
1½ teaspoons chili powder
1½ teaspoons paprika
½ teaspoon turmeric
½ teaspoon freshly ground black pepper
⅛ teaspoon salt
⅛ teaspoon cayenne pepper
½ pound rigatoni
1 cup canned solid-pack pumpkin purée
One 8-ounce can no-salt-added tomato sauce
3 ounces smoked turkey, cut into matchsticks
2 tablespoons hulled, unsalted pumpkin seeds, toasted (optional)

1. In a blender or food processor, blend the canned whole tomatoes (and purée) to a smooth sauce.

2. In a medium nonstick saucepan, warm the oil over medium-high heat until hot but not smoking. Stir in the onion, jalapeño peppers, cumin, chili powder, paprika, turmeric, black pepper, salt and cayenne. Reduce the heat to medium and cook, stirring frequently, until the onion is tender, 3 to 4 minutes; add 1 tablespoon of water if the pan gets dry.

3. Cook the rigatoni in a large pot of boiling water until al dente, 12 to 14 minutes, or according to package directions. Drain in a colander and transfer to a large serving bowl.

4. Meanwhile, stir the puréed tomatoes, pumpkin purée and canned tomato sauce into the saucepan, and bring to a boil. Reduce the heat to low, cover and simmer for 10 minutes, stirring frequently. (If the sauce seems too thick or is beginning to scorch, stir in 2 to 3 tablespoons of water.)

5. Add the turkey to the sauce and heat through. Pour the sauce over the rigatoni and toss to coat well. Sprinkle with the pumpkin seeds (if using).

Makes 4 servings

Nutrition Information
values are per serving

CALORIES 371	DIETARY FIBER 4.7 G
TOTAL FAT 6.1 G	BETA CAROTENE 9.5 MG
SATURATED FAT 1.0 G	VITAMIN C 53 MG
CHOLESTEROL 11 MG	CALCIUM 96 MG
SODIUM 498 MG	IRON 5.3 MG

Picadillo-Style Radiatore

There is a Cuban rendition of *picadillo* as well as a Mexican one, and there are undoubtedly as many home versions of this warming, spicy ground meat combination as there are dedicated *picadillo*-makers. Though traditionally served on its own, *picadillo* is used here as a topping for pasta. Serve with a green salad topped with orange slices and frozen yogurt with caramel sauce and toasted almonds for dessert.

⅓ cup raisins
⅓ cup hot water
2 teaspoons olive oil
½ pound lean (10% fat) ground beef
1 large onion, diced
3 garlic cloves, minced
1 large red bell pepper, diced
1 large green bell pepper, diced
2 teaspoons minced fresh jalapeño pepper
10 ounces radiatore pasta
Two 8-ounce cans no-salt-added tomato sauce
2 tablespoons no-salt-added tomato paste
3 tablespoons chopped green olives
½ teaspoon oregano
¼ teaspoon salt
½ cup frozen corn kernels
1 tablespoon pine nuts

1. In a small bowl, combine the raisins and hot water and set aside to soften.

2. In a large nonstick skillet, warm the oil over medium heat until hot but not smoking. Add the beef and cook until no longer pink, about 4 minutes. With a slotted spoon, transfer the beef to a plate and cover loosely to keep warm.

3. Add the onion and garlic to the skillet and cook, stirring frequently, until the onion is soft, about 7 minutes.

4. Stir the red and green bell peppers and the jalapeño pepper into the skillet, and cook until the peppers have softened, about 4 minutes.

5. Meanwhile, cook the pasta in a large pot of boiling water until al dente, 9 to 11 minutes, or according to package directions. Drain in a colander.

6. Stir the raisins and their soaking liquid, the tomato sauce, tomato paste, olives, oregano, salt and reserved beef into the skillet and cook, stirring occasionally, until the sauce has thickened and the flavors have come together, about 5 minutes. Stir in the corn and cook until heated through, about 1 minute.

7. Toss the drained pasta with the sauce, spoon into 4 bowls and sprinkle the pine nuts on top.

Makes 4 servings

NUTRITION INFORMATION
values are per serving

CALORIES 539	DIETARY FIBER 6.7 G
TOTAL FAT 12 G	BETA CAROTENE 2.0 MG
SATURATED FAT 3.0 G	VITAMIN C 101 MG
CHOLESTEROL 35 MG	CALCIUM 51 MG
SODIUM 369 MG	IRON 6.1 MG

Broken Vermicelli and Meatballs

One of the best ways to make a meatball moist and juicy without using ground meat that is high in fat, is to cut the amount of meat used and replace it, as here, with spinach, bread crumbs and Parmesan. This mixture is seasoned with basil and black pepper, and then baked to produce an extraordinarily flavorful and tender meatball.

½ pound lean beef top round, cut into chunks
Half a 10-ounce packed frozen chopped spinach, thawed and squeezed dry
2 egg whites
⅓ cup plain dried bread crumbs
2 tablespoons grated Parmesan cheese

1½ teaspoons basil
½ teaspoon freshly ground black pepper
2 teaspoons olive oil
2 large red bell peppers, cut lengthwise into slivers and halved
1 large green bell pepper, cut lengthwise into slivers and halved
4 garlic cloves, minced
¼ cup chicken broth, canned or homemade (p. 54)
One 28-ounce can whole tomatoes
½ pound vermicelli, broken in half

1. Preheat the oven to 400°. Spray a jelly-roll pan with nonstick cooking spray.

2. In a food processor, finely grind the beef. Add the spinach, egg whites, bread crumbs, Parmesan, ¾ teaspoon of the basil and ¼ teaspoon of the black pepper, and pulse until blended. Shape into 20 meatballs, using about 1 tablespoon of the mixture for each.

3. Place the meatballs on the prepared jelly-roll pan and bake, turning once, for 12 to 15 minutes, or until no longer pink in the center.

4. Meanwhile, in a Dutch oven or flameproof casserole, warm the oil over high heat until hot but not smoking. Add the red and green bell peppers and the garlic, toss to coat well with the oil and sauté for 1 minute.

5. Add the broth, the remaining ¾ teaspoon basil and ¼ teaspoon black pepper, and sauté until the vegetables are tender, 8 to 10 minutes.

6. Reserving the liquid, drain the tomatoes. Stir the drained tomatoes into the casserole, breaking them up with a spoon. Bring to a boil. Add the meatballs, reduce the heat to medium-low and simmer, stirring frequently, for 10 minutes to blend the flavors. If the sauce gets too dry, use some of the reserved tomato liquid.

7. Meanwhile, cook the pasta in a large pot of boiling water until al dente, 8 to 10 minutes, or according to package directions. Drain in a colander and transfer to a serving bowl.

8. Pour the meatballs and sauce over the pasta and serve hot.

Makes 4 servings

NUTRITION INFORMATION
values are per serving

CALORIES 436	DIETARY FIBER 5.3 G
TOTAL FAT 7.3 G	BETA CAROTENE 4.2 MG
SATURATED FAT 1.7 G	VITAMIN C 157 MG
CHOLESTEROL 34 MG	CALCIUM 184 MG
SODIUM 598 MG	IRON 6.6 MG

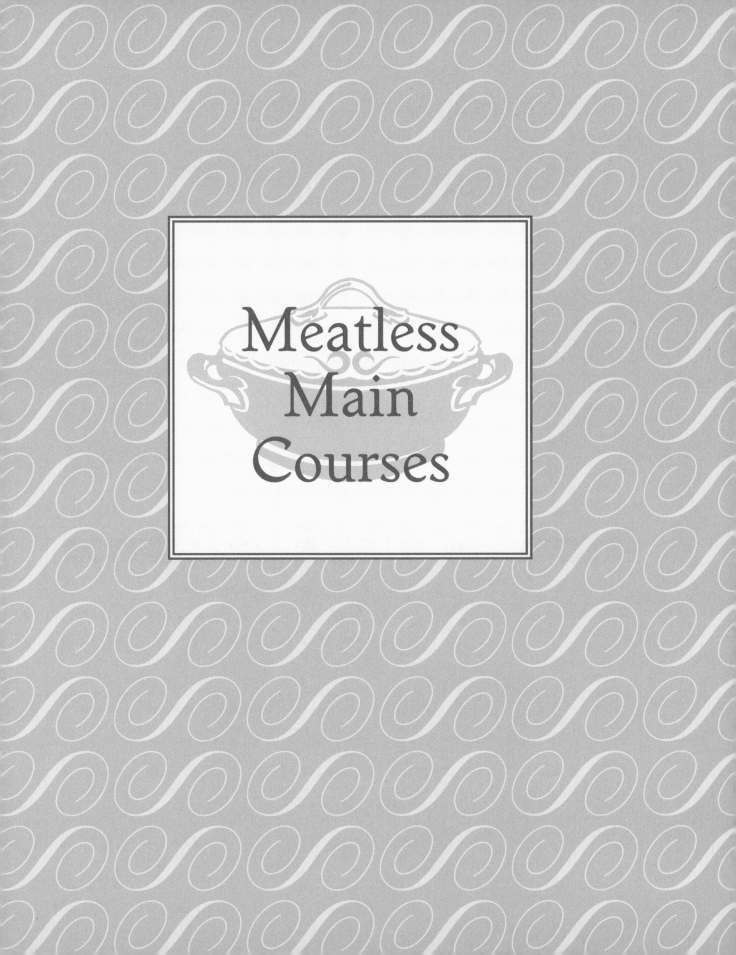

Meatless Main Courses

Vegetable Curry

Although the ingredient list for this dish may look daunting, most of it is made up of the spices used to flavor the curry sauce. These seasonings are actually included in most commerical curry powders, so if you are truly pressed for time or don't have all of the individual spices on hand, you can make this dish with 2 to 3 teaspoons of mild store-bought curry powder.

2¾ cups water
1 cup brown rice
1 tablespoon olive oil
1 large onion, coarsely chopped
1 tablespoon minced ginger
3 garlic cloves, minced
¾ teaspoon cumin
¾ teaspoon turmeric
½ teaspoon cinnamon
½ teaspoon ground coriander
½ teaspoon fennel seeds
½ teaspoon salt
¾ pound sweet potatoes, peeled and cut into 1-inch chunks
3 cups cauliflower florets
2 large carrots, thinly sliced
1 medium zucchini, thinly sliced
Two 8-ounce cans no-salt-added tomato sauce
1 tablespoon creamy peanut butter
1 cup plain nonfat yogurt

1. In a large pot, bring 2 cups of the water to the boil. Add the brown rice, reduce the heat to a simmer, cover and cook until the rice is tender and the water is absorbed, 40 to 45 minutes.

2. Meanwhile, in a large nonstick skillet, warm the oil over medium heat until hot but not smoking. Add the onion, ginger and garlic, and cook, stirring frequently, until the onion is translucent, about 7 minutes.

3. Stir in the cumin, turmeric, cinnamon, coriander, fennel seeds and salt, and cook until fragrant, about 2 minutes. Stir in the sweet potatoes, cauliflower and remaining ¾ cup water, cover and

SUPER QUICK

Sautéed Vegetables and White Beans Provençale

Working time: 25 minutes Total time: 25 minutes

1 tablespoon olive oil
1 large onion, diced
4 garlic cloves, minced
1 large red bell pepper, diced
1 medium zucchini, halved lengthwise and thinly sliced crosswise into half-rounds
6 ounces green beans, halved lengthwise
2 cups cherry tomatoes
½ cup chopped fresh basil
One 19-ounce can white beans, rinsed and drained

1 In a large nonstick skillet, warm the oil over medium heat until hot but not smoking. Add the onion and garlic, and cook until the onion is translucent, about 7 minutes.

2 Stir in the bell pepper and cook, stirring frequently, until the pepper is beginning to soften, about 3 minutes.

3 Add the zucchini and green beans, and sauté for 3 minutes. Stir in the cherry tomatoes, basil and white beans, and cook until the tomatoes have softened and the vegetables are tender, about 4 minutes.

Makes 4 servings

Values are per serving:
Calories: 189 Total fat: 5.9 g Saturated fat: .6 g Cholesterol: 0 mg Sodium: 160 mg
Dietary fiber: 6.5 g Beta carotene: 1.4 mg Vitamin C: 74 mg Calcium: 118 mg Iron: 3.6 mg

cook until the cauliflower and sweet potatoes are almost tender, about 10 minutes.

4. Add the carrots, zucchini and tomato sauce, cover and cook, stirring occasionally, until the vegetables are tender, about 10 minutes. Stir in the peanut butter until smooth.

5. Spoon the vegetables over the rice, dollop with yogurt and serve.

Makes 4 servings

NUTRITION INFORMATION
values are per serving

CALORIES 437	DIETARY FIBER 10 G
TOTAL FAT 8.1 G	BETA CAROTENE 17 MG
SATURATED FAT 1.2 G	VITAMIN C 99 MG
CHOLESTEROL 1.1 MG	CALCIUM 208 MG
SODIUM 405 MG	IRON 3.6 MG

Szechuan Vegetable Stir-Fry with Jasmine Rice

The reasons for using jasmine rice—a variety of rice frequently used in Thai and other Asian cuisines—are its wonderfully delicate fragrance and firm texture. Available at better supermarkets and specialty foods stores, it can be replaced by Texmati, basmati or any other of the so-called "aromatic" rices.

1½ cups water
⅔ cup jasmine or other aromatic rice
½ cup chicken broth, canned or homemade (p. 54)
¼ cup hoisin sauce
2 tablespoons sherry
2 tablespoons honey
¼ teaspoon crushed red pepper flakes
2 teaspoons Oriental (dark) sesame oil
⅓ cup sliced scallions
3 garlic cloves, minced
1 tablespoon minced fresh ginger
1 large red bell pepper, diced
2 large carrots, shredded
6 ounces snow peas, sliced on the diagonal
1 cup canned baby corn, rinsed and drained
One 8-ounce can sliced water chestnuts, drained
1 pound firm tofu, cut into 2-inch squares
2 teaspoons cornstarch blended with 1 tablespoon water

1. In a medium covered saucepan, bring the water to a boil. Add the rice, reduce the heat and simmer until all of the water is absorbed and the rice is tender, about 20 minutes.

2. Meanwhile, in a small bowl, stir together the chicken broth, hoisin sauce, sherry, honey and red pepper flakes; set aside.

3. In a large nonstick skillet, warm the sesame oil over medium heat until hot but not smoking. Add the scallions, garlic and ginger, and cook until softened, about 2 minutes. Stir in the bell pepper and carrots, and sauté until the vegetables are crisp-tender, about 2 minutes.

4. Add the snow peas, baby corn and water chestnuts, and cook, stirring frequently, until the snow peas are crisp-tender, about 2 minutes.

5. Add the hoisin mixture and tofu, bring to a boil and cook until the tofu is hot, about 1 minute. Stir in the cornstarch mixture, bring to a boil and boil until the sauce is lightly thickened, about 1 minute.

6. Serve the stir-fry on top of the rice.

Makes 4 servings

NUTRITION INFORMATION
values are per serving

CALORIES 478	DIETARY FIBER 5.1 G
TOTAL FAT 13 G	BETA CAROTENE 9.5 MG
SATURATED FAT 1.8 G	VITAMIN C 85 MG
CHOLESTEROL 0 MG	CALCIUM 294 MG
SODIUM 688 MG	IRON 16 MG

Vegetable Paella with Nectarines

The Spanish dish paella is known for its combination of shellfish and chicken or sausage atop saffron-colored rice. Here, in a healthful twist, broccoli, zucchini, bell pepper, tomato and nectarines are combined with turmeric-tinted brown rice enhanced with chopped fresh basil.

1½ cups brown rice
1½ cups canned chicken broth diluted with 1½ cups water, or 3 cups Homemade Chicken Broth (p. 54)
1 tablespoon olive oil
2 cups small broccoli florets
2 cups diagonally sliced zucchini
1 cup red bell pepper strips
1 large tomato, diced
2 medium nectarines, cut into thin wedges
¼ cup chopped fresh basil
¼ teaspoon salt
¼ teaspoon freshly ground black pepper
½ teaspoon turmeric

1. Cook the rice in the diluted chicken broth until all of the liquid is absorbed and the rice is chewy-tender, about 45 minutes.

2. Meanwhile, in a nonstick skillet, warm the oil over medium-high heat until hot but not smoking. Add the broccoli, zucchini and bell pepper, and stir-fry until the vegetables are slightly softened, about 4 minutes.

3. Add the tomato, nectarines, 2 tablespoons of the basil, the salt and black pepper. Cover and cook until the vegetables are crisp-tender, about 2 minutes.

4. When the rice is done, stir in the turmeric and the remaining 2 tablespoons basil.

5. Mound the rice on a platter and top with the vegetable-nectarine mixture.

Makes 4 servings

Nutrition Information
values are per serving

CALORIES 378	DIETARY FIBER 7.0 G
TOTAL FAT 6.7 G	BETA CAROTENE 2.1 MG
SATURATED FAT .9 G	VITAMIN C 112 MG
CHOLESTEROL 0 MG	CALCIUM 90 MG
SODIUM 532 MG	IRON 2.9 MG

Black and Gold Rice and Beans

In this colorful rendition of the classic pairing of rice and beans, black beans are combined with white rice, red and green peppers, red tomatoes and golden sweet potatoes, corn and Cheddar.

2 cups water
⅔ cup rice
⅓ cup minced scallions
2 garlic cloves, minced
½ teaspoon grated lemon zest
¼ teaspoon salt
1 tablespoon olive oil
1 medium red onion, minced
1 large red bell pepper, finely diced
1 large green bell pepper, finely diced
⅓ cup minced cilantro
1 teaspoon minced fresh jalapeño pepper
½ teaspoon cumin
1 large sweet potato (12 ounces), peeled and cut into ½-inch chunks
1½ cups chopped tomatoes
One 19-ounce can black beans, rinsed and drained
1½ cups frozen corn kernels, thawed
¼ cup shredded sharp Cheddar cheese

1. In a medium covered saucepan, bring 1½ cups of the water to a boil. Add the rice, scallions, garlic, lemon zest and salt. Return to a boil, reduce the heat to a simmer, cover and cook until the rice is tender, about 17 minutes.

2. Meanwhile, in a large nonstick saucepan or Dutch oven, warm the oil over medium heat until hot but not smoking. Add the onion and cook, stirring frequently, until tender, about 5 minutes. Stir in the red and green bell peppers, the cilantro, jalapeño pepper and cumin; cover and cook, stirring frequently, until the vegetables are tender, about 5 minutes.

3. Stir in the sweet potato and the remaining ½ cup water; cover and cook until the potato is almost soft, about 7 minutes. Stir in the tomatoes and black beans, and cook, uncovered, until the potato is tender and the flavors have blended, about 2 minutes. Stir in the corn and cook until heated through, about 2 minutes.

4. Serve the bean mixture over the rice and topped with the Cheddar cheese.

Makes 4 servings

NUTRITION INFORMATION
values are per serving

CALORIES 395	DIETARY FIBER 9.0 G
TOTAL FAT 7.5 G	BETA CAROTENE 6.2 MG
SATURATED FAT 2.2 G	VITAMIN C 106 MG
CHOLESTEROL 7.4 MG	CALCIUM 131 MG
SODIUM 419 MG	IRON 4.4 MG

Vegetable Picadillo Tortillas

The flavorful Hispanic spiced ground beef and raisin dish, *picadillo*, is not based here on meat but on beans and is served not with rice, as tradition would have it, but on tortillas.

2 teaspoons vegetable oil
1 large onion, diced
3 garlic cloves, minced
1 large red bell pepper, diced
1 large carrot, halved lengthwise and sliced crosswise
1¼ teaspoons mild chili powder
1 teaspoon unsweetened cocoa powder
1 teaspoon cumin
1 teaspoon oregano
One 16-ounce can small red beans, rinsed and drained
One 14½-ounce can no-salt-added stewed tomatoes, chopped with their juice
One 8-ounce can no-salt-added tomato sauce
½ cup raisins
Eight 8-inch flour tortillas
3 ounces soft goat cheese, crumbled

1. In a large nonstick skillet, warm the oil over medium heat until hot but not smoking. Add the onion and garlic, and cook, stirring occasionally, until the onion has softened, about 5 minutes.

2. Stir in the bell pepper and carrot, and cook, stirring frequently, until the vegetables have softened, about 7 minutes.

3. Stir in the chili powder, cocoa, cumin and oregano, and cook, stirring, until fragrant, about 1 minute. Add the beans, the stewed tomatoes, tomato sauce and raisins, and cook until the sauce is thickened and the flavors are blended, about 5 minutes.

4. Divide the mixture among the tortillas, crumble the cheese over, roll them up and serve.

Makes 4 servings

NUTRITION INFORMATION
values are per serving

CALORIES 536	DIETARY FIBER 12 G
TOTAL FAT 15 G	BETA CAROTENE 6.1 MG
SATURATED FAT 5.6 G	VITAMIN C 79 MG
CHOLESTEROL 17 MG	CALCIUM 245 MG
SODIUM 680 MG	IRON 6.5 MG

Black Bean Cakes with Spicy Vegetable Sauce

Here, meaty black beans are the main ingredient of patties that are topped with a puréed sweet-potato sauce seasoned with cayenne and fresh lime juice.

One small sweet potato (6 ounces)
One 19-ounce can black beans, rinsed and drained
1 medium red bell pepper, minced
¼ cup minced scallions
¼ cup chopped cilantro
¼ cup fresh lime juice
1¼ teaspoons cumin
½ teaspoon crushed red pepper flakes
1 egg white
½ cup flour
2 tablespoons cornmeal
1 tablespoon olive oil
¾ cup low-sodium mixed vegetable juice
⅛ teaspoon cayenne pepper
1 tablespoon plus 1 teaspoon light sour cream

1. Preheat the oven to 450°. Pierce the sweet potato and cook in the microwave at 100% for 5 to 6 minutes, or until tender. When cool enough to handle, scoop the flesh from the skin and set aside.

2. Meanwhile, in a large bowl, mash the beans with a fork. Stir in the bell pepper, scallions, 2 tablespoons of the cilantro, 2 tablespoons of the lime juice, the cumin and red pepper flakes. Blend in the egg white.

3. Form the bean mixture into 4 large patties. On a sheet of wax paper, combine the flour and cornmeal. Coat the patties with this mixture and place them on a nonstick baking sheet. Brush the cake with the oil and bake until heated through

SUPER QUICK

Pan-Fried Tofu in a Pita

Working time: 15 minutes Total time: 30 minutes

2 tablespoons reduced-sodium soy sauce
1 tablespoon plus 2 teaspoons cider vinegar
1 tablespoon plus 2 teaspoons minced fresh ginger
1 tablespoon light brown sugar
¼ teaspoon crushed red pepper flakes
1 pound firm tofu, cut into 8 triangles
1 tablespoon reduced-calorie mayonnaise
3 large carrots, shredded
1 large red bell pepper, slivered
1¼ cups alfalfa sprouts
2 teaspoons Oriental (dark) sesame oil
Four 6-inch pitas

1 In a medium bowl, stir together 1 tablespoon each of the soy sauce, vinegar and ginger, the brown sugar and the red pepper flakes. Add the tofu, turning to coat, and marinate for at least 20 minutes or for up to several hours.

2 In a large bowl, combine the mayonnaise with the remaining 1 tablespoon soy sauce, 2 teaspoons vinegar and 2 teaspoons ginger. Add the carrots, bell pepper and 1 cup of the sprouts, and toss to combine. Refrigerate until ready to serve.

3 In a large nonstick skillet, warm the oil over medium heat until hot but not smoking. Reserving the marinade, add the tofu to the skillet and sauté until crisp and golden brown, about 3 minutes per side. Add the marinade to the pan and cook until syrupy, about 2 minutes.

4 Slit open the pitas and spoon the carrot mixture in, then top with the tofu and any pan juices. Top with the remaining alfalfa sprouts.

Makes 4 servings

Values are per serving:
Calories: 422 Total fat: 14 g Saturated fat: 2.1 g Cholesterol: 1.2 mg Sodium: 687 mg
Dietary fiber: 4.0 g Beta carotene: 14 mg Vitamin C: 56 mg Calcium: 316 mg Iron: 14 mg

and crisped, 10 to 15 minutes. Transfer to 4 serving plates.

4. Meanwhile, in a food processor, combine the sweet potato, the remaining 2 tablespoons lime juice, the mixed vegetable juice and cayenne. Process to a smooth purée. Transfer the sauce to a small skillet and warm over low heat.

5. Stir the remaining 2 tablespoons cilantro into the sauce and spoon over the patties. Dollop with the sour cream and serve.

Makes 4 servings

Nutrition Information
values are per serving

CALORIES 247	DIETARY FIBER 5.9 G
TOTAL FAT 5.1 G	BETA CAROTENE 4.8 MG
SATURATED FAT .9 G	VITAMIN C 66 MG
CHOLESTEROL 1.7 MG	CALCIUM 57 MG
SODIUM 271 MG	IRON 3.4 MG

Caponata Turnovers

Made classically, the cold Sicilian eggplant salad *caponata* relies on olive oil for its texture and flavor. Here, no oil is used to make the *caponata*, but chili oil is used to paint the phyllo dough for these crispy turnovers. Made smaller, these would also make delicious appetizers.

2 tablespoons olive oil
2 teaspoons chili powder
Two 14½-ounce cans no-salt-added stewed tomatoes, chopped with their juice
5 garlic cloves, minced
2 large red bell peppers, diced
2 large carrots, diced
1 medium eggplant (about 12 ounces), peeled and cubed
½ teaspoon salt
¼ teaspoon cayenne pepper
½ cup golden raisins
¼ cup chopped fresh mint or basil
8 sheets (11 by 17 inches each) phyllo dough

1. In a small skillet, bring the oil and chili powder to a simmer over medium heat; remove from the heat and set aside.

2. In a large nonstick skillet, combine the stewed tomatoes, garlic, bell peppers, carrots, eggplant, salt and cayenne, and bring to a boil over medium heat. Reduce the heat to a simmer, cover and cook until the vegetables are tender, about 15 minutes.

3. Stir in the raisins and mint, and cook for 2 minutes longer to blend the flavors. Set aside to cool to room temperature.

4. Preheat the oven to 400°. Spray a baking sheet with nonstick cooking spray.

5. Lay one sheet of phyllo down on a work surface and brush with ½ teaspoon of the chili oil. Lay another sheet on top, brush with ½ teaspoon of the oil. With a short side facing you, cut the double sheet of dough crosswise into thirds. Using one-fourth of the caponata, and dividing evenly among the three phyllo strips, mound the filling at the end of the strips, then fold into turnover shapes as you would fold a flag. Place the turnovers on the prepared baking sheet.

6. Repeat with the remaining phyllo and filling, using 3 more teaspoons of the chili oil, to make 9 more turnovers (a total of 12). Brush the tops of the turnovers with the remaining 2 teaspoons chili oil and bake until crisp and heated through, about 10 minutes.

Makes 4 servings

Nutrition Information
values are per serving

CALORIES 347	DIETARY FIBER 9.5 G
TOTAL FAT 10 G	BETA CAROTENE 11 MG
SATURATED FAT 1.3 G	VITAMIN C 132 MG
CHOLESTEROL 0 MG	CALCIUM 139 MG
SODIUM 530 MG	IRON 4.2 MG

Spinach and Goat Cheese Strata

Stratas, traditional American layered casseroles, are appealing to cook and diner alike: Their preparation is relatively undemanding and the results are rewarding. Stratas are comforting, filling and even, on occasion, pretty—as it is in this strata, with its layers of bread and spinach topped with custard, then sprinkled with goat cheese and baked until puffed and golden. This is a perfect Sunday night supper type of dish that needs no more than a fresh fruit salad to go with it.

8 slices (1 ounce each) day-old white bread
2 teaspoons olive oil
3 tablespoons minced scallions
2 garlic cloves, minced
Two 10-ounce packages frozen chopped spinach, thawed and squeezed dry
1 teaspoon sugar
¼ teaspoon salt
⅛ teaspoon nutmeg
⅛ teaspoon freshly ground black pepper
2 eggs
4 egg whites
½ cup skim milk
4 ounces soft goat cheese, crumbled

1. Spray a 7-by-11-inch baking dish with nonstick cooking spray. Lay half of the bread slices in the prepared dish and set aside.

2. In a large nonstick skillet, warm the oil over medium heat until hot but not smoking. Add the scallions and garlic, and cook, stirring frequently, until the scallions have softened, about 2 minutes.

3. Stir in the spinach, sprinkle with the sugar, salt, nutmeg and pepper, and continue cooking until the spinach has softened and is heated through, about 4 minutes. Remove from the heat. Spoon half of the spinach mixture over the bread in the baking dish.

4. In a medium bowl, whisk together the whole eggs, egg whites and milk. Pour half of this mixture over the spinach layer. Sprinkle with half of the cheese. Top with remaining bread, spinach, egg mixture and cheese. Let sit for 30 minutes.

5. Preheat the oven to 350°. Bake the strata for about 30 minutes, or until golden, puffy and set. Let stand for 10 minutes before serving.

Makes 4 servings

NUTRITION INFORMATION
values are per serving

CALORIES 380	DIETARY FIBER 4.4 G
TOTAL FAT 16 G	BETA CAROTENE 6.6 MG
SATURATED FAT 7.5 G	VITAMIN C 36 MG
CHOLESTEROL 130 MG	CALCIUM 351 MG
SODIUM 794 MG	IRON 5.5 MG

Meatless Moussaka

Lamb is the meat called for in Greece's renowned layered eggplant dish moussaka. In this wonderful variation, a dish lined with broiled eggplant is filled with a warmly spiced vegetable ragout that is then topped with beaten egg whites and mild goat cheese and baked until golden. For a slightly less tangy variation, substitute crumbled feta cheese for the goat cheese.

½ cup balsamic vinegar
1 teaspoon sugar
⅓ cup chicken broth, canned or homemade (p. 54)
1 tablespoon olive oil
2 medium eggplants (about 12 ounces each), peeled and cut into ½-inch-thick slices
One 14½-ounce can no-salt-added stewed tomatoes, chopped with their juice
1½ cups peeled butternut squash chunks (½-inch)
1 large red bell pepper, cut into ½-inch squares
¾ teaspoon cumin
¾ teaspoon paprika
½ teaspoon cinnamon

½ teaspoon ground ginger
¼ teaspoon allspice
¼ cup finely chopped apricots
2 egg whites
¼ teaspoon salt
2 ounces soft goat cheese or farmer cheese, crumbled

1. Preheat the broiler.

2. Meanwhile, in a small skillet or saucepan, bring the balsamic vinegar and sugar to a boil over medium-high heat. Cook until the vinegar is reduced by half and is thick and syrupy, about 5 minutes. Remove from the heat.

3. In a small bowl, stir together the broth and olive oil. Brush the eggplant with the broth mixture, place on a broiler pan and broil 6 inches from the heat for 12 minutes, or until soft, turning the eggplant over halfway through. Brush the cooked eggplant with the reduced vinegar and set aside.

4. Preheat the oven to 375°. Spray a 6- to 8-cup casserole with nonstick cooking spray.

5. Meanwhile, in a large skillet, combine the stewed tomatoes, squash, bell pepper, cumin, paprika, cinnamon, ginger and allspice. Cover and cook over medium heat until the squash and bell pepper have softened, about 5 minutes. Stir in the apricots and cook for 5 minutes.

6. Line the prepared baking dish with the eggplant slices. Spoon in the vegetable mixture.

7. In a small bowl, beat the egg whites and the salt until stiff peaks form. Beat in the crumbled goat cheese. Spoon on top of the vegetable mixture and bake for about 15 minutes, or until the topping is puffy and golden.

Makes 4 servings

Nutrition Information
values are per serving

CALORIES 217	DIETARY FIBER 5.5 G
TOTAL FAT 8.5 G	BETA CAROTENE 4.2 MG
SATURATED FAT 3.4 G	VITAMIN C 75 MG
CHOLESTEROL 11 MG	CALCIUM 163 MG
SODIUM 346 MG	IRON 3.1 MG

Curried Stuffed Acorn Squash

The pleasure, to say nothing of the beauty, of using a vegetable as a container for serving is obvious, but there aren't many vegetables that can fill that bill as handsomely as the acorn squash. Here acorn squash halves are filled with a delicious curry-spiced mixture of fruit and vegetables and topped with Cheddar cheese.

1 cup brown rice
2 large acorn squash (about 1½ pounds each)
2 teaspoons olive oil
3 garlic cloves, minced
1 large carrot, shredded
¾ teaspoon ground ginger
¾ teaspoon curry powder
½ teaspoon salt
1½ cups chopped tomatoes
½ cup chopped pitted prunes
¼ cup chopped mango chutney
1 tablespoon fresh lemon juice
2 ounces Cheddar cheese, shredded
¼ cup plain nonfat yogurt

1. In a large pot of boiling water, cook the rice until firm-tender, about 30 minutes. Drain in a strainer.

2. Meanwhile, preheat the oven to 400°. Halve the squash lengthwise and remove the seeds. Cut off a thin sliver from the bottom of each half so that the squash will sit upright. Place the squash cut-side down in a baking dish with water to come ½ inch up the sides of the squash. Bake until softened, about 20 minutes. Remove from the oven, but leave the oven on.

3. Scoop out most of the flesh, leaving a sturdy shell. Cut the squash flesh into ½-inch chunks. In a large nonstick skillet, warm the oil over medium heat until hot but not smoking. Add the garlic and cook until fragrant, about 30 seconds. Add the

chunks of squash and cook, stirring frequently, until lightly colored, about 5 minutes.

4. Add the carrot and cook for 1 minute. Stir in the ginger, curry powder and salt, and cook until fragrant, about 1 minute. Stir in the tomatoes, prunes, chutney and lemon juice, and cook until the squash is tender, about 10 minutes. Stir in the rice and remove from the heat.

5. Turn the squash shells cut-side up in the baking dish. (Drain any liquid remaining in the pan.) Spoon the stuffing mixture into the shells, sprinkle with the Cheddar, cover with foil and bake until heated through, about 10 minutes.

6. Serve topped with a dollop of yogurt.

Makes 4 servings

Nutrition Information
values are per serving

CALORIES 489	DIETARY FIBER 14 G
TOTAL FAT 9.0 G	BETA CAROTENE 5.2 MG
SATURATED FAT 3.6 G	VITAMIN C 47 MG
CHOLESTEROL 15 MG	CALCIUM 255 MG
SODIUM 576 MG	IRON 3.7 MG

Pasta-and-Cheese-Stuffed Peppers

In this Italian-inspired variation on the stuffed pepper, red bell peppers hold small pasta shells in a creamy Parmesan-Gruyère sauce.

4 ounces very small pasta shells
4 large red bell peppers
1 tablespoon olive oil
¾ cup thinly sliced scallions
3 garlic cloves, minced
1 small zucchini, halved lengthwise and sliced
¾ cup evaporated skimmed milk
⅓ cup grated Parmesan cheese
2 tablespoons grated Gruyère or Swiss cheese
2 tablespoons dry sherry
½ teaspoon salt
⅛ teaspoon freshly ground black pepper
½ cup chicken broth, canned or homemade (p. 54)

1. Cook the pasta in a large pot of boiling water until al dente, 6 to 9 minutes, or according to package directions. Scoop the pasta out with a slotted spoon and drain in a colander; keep the water at a boil.

2. Trim the tops from the bell peppers and reserve. Discard the seeds and ribs. Shave a thin slice off the bottom of each pepper so they will stand upright. Add the peppers and the reserved tops to the boiling water and parboil until crisp-tender, about 4 minutes. Rinse under cold water, then invert the peppers onto paper towels to drain.

3. Meanwhile, in a large nonstick skillet, warm 1 teaspoon of the oil over medium-high heat. Add the scallions and cook until slightly softened, about 1 minute. Stir in the garlic and cook until fragrant, about 2 minutes. Add the remaining 2 teaspoons oil and the zucchini, and cook, stirring frequently, until tender, about 4 minutes.

4. Preheat the oven to 400°.

5. Stir the evaporated milk into the skillet and bring the mixture to a boil. Add the Parmesan, Gruyère, sherry, salt and black pepper, and stir to melt the cheese; remove from the heat. Add the drained pasta and toss to coat.

6. Divide the pasta mixture evenly among the 4 bell peppers and place them upright in an 8-inch square baking dish. Place the tops on the peppers and pour the broth into the dish. Cover with foil and bake for 20 minutes. Uncover and bake for 5 minutes longer, or until bubbly.

Makes 4 servings

Nutrition Information
values are per serving

CALORIES 265	DIETARY FIBER 2.9 G
TOTAL FAT 7.5 G	BETA CAROTENE 3.5 MG
SATURATED FAT 2.5 G	VITAMIN C 197 MG
CHOLESTEROL 11 MG	CALCIUM 305 MG
SODIUM 595 MG	IRON 2.2 MG

Pumpkin Frittata

This simple, open-faced Italian-style omelet glows with the golden colors of pumpkin, sweet potato and carrot.

1 medium sweet potato (8 ounces), peeled and sliced
1 tablespoon olive oil
1 large carrot, shredded
¼ cup thinly sliced scallions
2 garlic cloves, minced
2 eggs
3 egg whites
½ cup canned solid-pack pumpkin purée
½ teaspoon ground ginger
½ teaspoon salt
¼ teaspoon freshly ground black pepper
⅛ teaspoon nutmeg
½ cup shredded part-skim mozzarella

1. Cook the sweet potato in boiling water until tender, about 7 minutes. Drain well.

2. Preheat the oven to 400°.

3. In a large nonstick ovenproof skillet, warm 1 teaspoon of the oil over medium heat until hot but not smoking. Add the carrot, scallions and garlic, and cook, stirring frequently, until the carrot is soft, about 5 minutes. Set aside to cool slightly.

4. In a medium bowl, stir together the whole eggs, egg whites, pumpkin purée, ginger, salt, pepper and nutmeg. Stir in the carrot mixture.

5. In the same skillet, warm the remaining 2 teaspoons oil over medium heat until hot but not smoking. Add the sweet potato and stir to coat. Spoon the egg-carrot mixture on top and sprinkle with the mozzarella cheese. Cook until the bottom is set, about 5 minutes.

6. Transfer the skillet to the oven and bake until the frittata is set, about 10 minutes. Serve in wedges from the skillet.

Makes 4 servings

Nutrition Information
values are per serving

CALORIES 185	DIETARY FIBER 2.7 G
TOTAL FAT 8.4 G	BETA CAROTENE 13 MG
SATURATED FAT 2.7 G	VITAMIN C 15 MG
CHOLESTEROL 115 MG	CALCIUM 139 MG
SODIUM 429 MG	IRON 1.3 MG

Sweet Potato Pancakes with Creamy Dill Sauce

In these potato pancakes, shredded sweet potatoes add color, flavor and a substantial amount of beta carotene.

1 medium sweet potato (8 ounces), peeled and shredded
1 large baking potato (8 ounces), peeled and shredded
1 large carrot, shredded
1 small zucchini, shredded
½ cup grated onion
1 egg, lightly beaten
1 egg white, lightly beaten
¼ cup flour
3 ounces soft goat cheese
⅓ cup minced fresh dill
½ teaspoon salt
¼ teaspoon freshly ground black pepper
1 tablespoon olive oil
¼ cup light sour cream
2 tablespoons lowfat (1.5%) buttermilk

1. In a large bowl, combine the sweet potato, baking potato, carrot, zucchini and onion. Add the whole egg, egg white and flour, and stir to coat. Add half the goat cheese, 3 tablespoons of the dill, the salt and pepper, mixing until well combined. Form the potato mixture into 12 patties.

2. Preheat the oven to 400°.

3. In a large nonstick skillet, warm 1½ teaspoons of the oil over medium heat until hot but not smoking. Working in batches, sauté the patties until they are crusty and golden brown, about 2 minutes per side; add the remaining 1½ teaspoons oil to the pan as necessary. Transfer the patties to a nonstick baking sheet and bake for about 15 minutes, or until cooked through.

4. Meanwhile, in a small bowl, blend the remaining goat cheese and dill with the sour cream and buttermilk. Serve the pancakes with the creamy dill sauce.

Makes 4 servings

NUTRITION INFORMATION
values are per serving

CALORIES 268	DIETARY FIBER 3.4 G
TOTAL FAT 12 G	BETA CAROTENE 9.2 MG
SATURATED FAT 5.0 G	VITAMIN C 24 MG
CHOLESTEROL 68 MG	CALCIUM 93 MG
SODIUM 409 MG	IRON 2.3 MG

California Pizza

Carrot juice in the crust and shredded carrots in the tomato sauce are the secrets in this healthful vegetable-topped pizza.

BASIL OIL
⅓ cup (packed) fresh basil leaves
¼ cup chicken broth, canned or homemade (p. 54)
2 teaspoons olive oil

PIZZA DOUGH
1½ cups carrot juice
1 package (¼ ounce) active dry yeast
1 teaspoon sugar
3½ cups flour
½ teaspoon salt
¼ teaspoon cayenne pepper
Cornmeal, for dusting the baking sheet (optional)

SAUCE AND TOPPINGS
Two 8-ounce cans no-salt-added tomato sauce
1 large carrot, shredded
¼ cup chopped fresh basil
¼ teaspoon oregano
¼ teaspoon freshly ground black pepper
2 teaspoons olive oil
2 garlic cloves, minced
8 cups (packed) chopped stemmed spinach
1½ cups shredded part-skim mozzarella cheese
1 small red bell pepper, cut into thin slivers
1 cup yellow pear tomatoes, halved lengthwise
½ cup finely slivered red onion (optional)
¼ cup fresh jalapeño pepper rings

1. MAKE THE BASIL OIL In a food processor, purée the basil leaves with the chicken broth and olive oil. Set aside.

2. TO MAKE THE DOUGH In a small saucepan, warm ¼ cup of the carrot juice to lukewarm (105° to 115°); remove from the heat. In a small bowl, dissolve the yeast and sugar in the lukewarm carrot juice. Let sit until creamy, about 5 minutes.

3. In the large bowl, combine the flour, salt and cayenne, mixing until well combined. Beat in the yeast mixture and the remaining 1¼ cups carrot juice; knead until the dough is smooth and elastic. Transfer to a bowl that has been sprayed with nonstick cooking spray, cover and place in a warm spot until almost doubled in bulk, about 45 minutes.

4. MEANWHILE, MAKE THE SAUCE In a large nonstick skillet, combine the tomato sauce, carrot, 2 tablespoons of the chopped basil, the oregano and black pepper, and bring to a boil over medium heat. Reduce the heat to a simmer, cover and cook until the carrot is tender, about 5 minutes. Remove from the heat and set aside to cool.

5. In a large nonstick skillet, warm the oil over medium-high heat until hot but not smoking. Add the garlic and cook, stirring frequently, until soft, about 4 minutes. Stir in the spinach and remaining

2 tablespoons basil, and cook until the spinach is wilted, about 4 minutes. Drain in a strainer.

6. Preheat the oven to 500°. Punch the dough down and turn it out onto a lightly floured board. Roll the dough out to a 13-inch round. Fit the circle of dough onto a large baking sheet (if desired, sprinkle the sheet with cornmeal before placing the dough on top). Roll the dough inward all the way around to form a high edge.

7. Spoon the sauce evenly over the dough and bake on the lowest shelf of the oven for 10 minutes. Spoon the spinach over the tomato sauce and sprinkle the cheese over the spinach. Arrange the bell pepper, pear tomatoes, onion (if using) and jalapeño rings on top. Continue to bake the pizza on the lowest shelf of the oven until the crust is browned and the cheese is melted. Drizzle the basil oil over the hot pizza before serving.

Makes 6 servings

NUTRITION INFORMATION
values are per serving

CALORIES 472	DIETARY FIBER 6.1 G
TOTAL FAT 9.4 G	BETA CAROTENE 16 MG
SATURATED FAT 3.5 G	VITAMIN C 75 MG
CHOLESTEROL 16 MG	CALCIUM 327 MG
SODIUM 447 MG	IRON 7.5 MG

Crustless Tomato-Pepper Quiche

This unusual quiche, instead of being baked in a high-fat crust, incorporates flour into the filling. As the quiche bakes, the flour settles to the bottom of the pan to form a layer of "crust."

2 teaspoons olive oil
2 medium red bell peppers, diced
1 medium green bell pepper, diced
1 medium onion, minced
1 cup chopped tomato
2 eggs
3 egg whites
1 cup lowfat (1%) milk
¼ cup grated Parmesan cheese
¼ teaspoon salt
¼ teaspoon freshly ground black pepper
⅔ cup flour
1 cup bottled salsa

1. Preheat the oven to 350°. Spray a 9-inch quiche pan (*without* a removable bottom) or a 7-by-11-inch baking pan with nonstick cooking spray.

2. In a large nonstick skillet, warm the oil over low heat. Add the red and green bell peppers and the onion, and cook, stirring frequently, until the vegetables have softened, about 5 minutes.

3. Stir in the tomato and cook until almost all the liquid has evaporated, about 5 minutes. Transfer the vegetables to a large mixing bowl and set aside to cool to room temperature.

4. In a large bowl, beat together the whole eggs and egg whites. Stir in the milk, Parmesan, salt and black pepper, and mix until well combined. Whisk in the flour.

5. Transfer the vegetables to the prepared pan. Pour the egg mixture over the vegetables and bake until the eggs are just set, about 35 minutes.

6. Cool the quiche 10 minutes before cutting into 6 wedges. Serve topped with salsa.

Makes 6 servings

NUTRITION INFORMATION
values are per serving

CALORIES 169	DIETARY FIBER 1.8 G
TOTAL FAT 5.1 G	BETA CAROTENE 1.2 MG
SATURATED FAT 1.6 G	VITAMIN C 94 MG
CHOLESTEROL 75 MG	CALCIUM 119 MG
SODIUM 465 MG	IRON 1.3 MG

Vegetarian Burgers

The beef hamburger is appreciated for many reasons—its nutritional attributes, however, not being among them. Vegetarian "burgers," on the other hand, rarely have the meatiness many people crave. This meat-loaf-style burger seasoned with mint and scallions manages to bridge the gap.

1 cup water
¼ teaspoon salt
½ cup bulghur
2 large carrots, shredded
4 ounces firm tofu
1 egg white
3 tablespoons chopped fresh mint
3 tablespoons minced scallions
¼ teaspoon cayenne pepper
⅓ cup plain dried bread crumbs
⅓ cup flour
2 tablespoons light ketchup
2 teaspoons Dijon mustard
1 tablespoon olive oil
4 hamburger buns
4 Romaine lettuce leaves
4 large slices or 12 small slices of tomato
½ cup alfalfa sprouts

1. In a large covered saucepan, bring the water and salt to a boil over medium heat. Add the bulghur and carrots, remove from the heat, cover and let stand until the bulghur has softened and absorbed all the liquid, about 15 minutes. Drain well.

2. In a large bowl, mash the tofu. Stir in the bulghur mixture, egg white, mint, scallions and cayenne, stirring well. Stir in the bread crumbs, ¼ cup of the flour, the ketchup and mustard.

3. Preheat the oven to 400°. Form the bulghur mixture into 4 patties about 1 inch thick and 4 inches in diameter. Dredge the patties in the remaining flour.

4. In a large nonstick skillet, warm the oil over medium heat until hot but not smoking. Add the patties to the skillet and sauté until crusty, about 4 minutes per side. Transfer to a nonstick baking sheet and bake for about 5 minutes, or until heated through.

5. Serve the burgers on the hamburger buns with the lettuce, tomato and alfalfa sprouts.

Makes 4 servings

NUTRITION INFORMATION
values are per serving

CALORIES 367	DIETARY FIBER 6.8 G
TOTAL FAT 9.2 G	BETA CAROTENE 8.8 MG
SATURATED FAT 1.5 G	VITAMIN C 12 MG
CHOLESTEROL 0 MG	CALCIUM 176 MG
SODIUM 624 MG	IRON 6.4 MG

Golden Vegetable Risotto

The comforting and creamy Italian rice dish called risotto is turned into a filling main dish here by the addition of chick-peas, carrots and green beans.

2 teaspoons olive oil
1¼ cups brown rice
1 garlic clove, minced
¾ cup canned chicken broth diluted with ¾ cup water, or 1½ cups Homemade Chicken Broth (p. 54)
1 cup carrot juice
¼ cup chopped parsley
¼ teaspoon freshly ground black pepper
1 cup finely chopped carrots
1½ cups cut green beans, in 1-inch sections
1 cup canned chick-peas, rinsed and drained
½ cup finely chopped scallions
¾ cup grated Parmesan cheese

1. In a medium saucepan, warm the oil over medium-high heat until hot but not smoking. Add the rice and garlic, and sauté until the garlic is fragrant, about 1 minute.

2. Add the diluted chicken broth, carrot juice, parsley and pepper, and bring to a boil. Reduce the heat to low, cover and simmer for 25 minutes.

3. Stir in the carrots, green beans, chick-peas and scallions, and cook until the rice is tender and the liquid is absorbed, about 20 minutes.

4. Add the Parmesan, stir to combine and transfer to a serving dish.

Makes 4 servings

Nutrition Information
values are per serving

CALORIES 409	DIETARY FIBER 6.1 G
TOTAL FAT 10 G	BETA CAROTENE 15 MG
SATURATED FAT 3.6 G	VITAMIN C 21 MG
CHOLESTEROL 12 MG	CALCIUM 289 MG
SODIUM 582 MG	IRON 3.2 MG

Potato-Cheese Dumplings with Tomato-Basil Sauce

The very simple tomato sauce for these wonderful dumplings can easily be made in advance. Serve the dumplings with a simple salad and perhaps fruit ice and biscotti for dessert.

2 large carrots, thinly sliced
1 large baking potato (8 ounces), peeled and thinly sliced
1 cup water
3 garlic cloves, slivered
½ teaspoon salt
1 small red bell pepper, minced
1 egg
2 egg whites
1 cup shredded part-skim mozzarella cheese
2 cups flour
2 tablespoons grated Parmesan cheese
One 14½-ounce can no-salt-added stewed tomatoes, chopped with their juice
One 8-ounce can no-salt-added tomato sauce
2 tablespoons chopped fresh basil

1. In a large saucepan, combine the carrots, potato, water, garlic and ¼ teaspoon of the salt. Bring to a boil over medium heat, reduce to a simmer and cook until the vegetables are soft, about 12 minutes. Press the mixture through a sieve set over a bowl and set aside to cool slightly.

2. Preheat the oven to 425°. Spray a baking sheet with nonstick cooking spray.

3. Add the bell pepper, whole egg, egg whites, mozzarella and remaining ¼ teaspoon salt to the mashed vegetables and blend well. Stir in the flour until the mixture forms a dough stiff enough to pat out.

4. On a lightly floured board, pat the dough out to a 9-inch round about ½ inch thick. With a 2-inch round cutter, cut the dough into rounds and place them in a single layer on the prepared baking sheet. Gather the scraps, re-roll and cut for a total of 24. Sprinkle with the Parmesan and bake for 20 minutes, or until golden.

5. Meanwhile, in a large nonstick skillet, combine the stewed tomatoes and tomato sauce. Bring to a boil, reduce to a simmer and cook until lightly thickened, about 5 minutes. Stir in the basil and spoon the sauce over the dumplings.

Makes 4 servings

Nutrition Information
values are per serving

CALORIES 450	DIETARY FIBER 7.4 G
TOTAL FAT 7.9 G	BETA CAROTENE 9.8 MG
SATURATED FAT 3.9 G	VITAMIN C 64 MG
CHOLESTEROL 72 MG	CALCIUM 304 MG
SODIUM 548 MG	IRON 5.2 MG

Main-Course Salads

Broccoli, Black Bean and Bulghur Salad

A zesty dressing of lemon and orange juice with a good amount of fresh ginger enlivens this broccoli, black bean and bulghur combination.

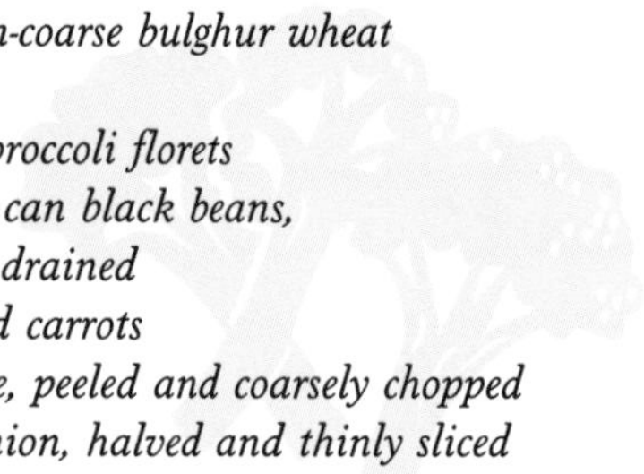

SALAD

¾ cup medium-coarse bulghur wheat
2 cups water
4 cups small broccoli florets
One 15-ounce can black beans, rinsed and drained
1 cup shredded carrots
1 navel orange, peeled and coarsely chopped
1 small red onion, halved and thinly sliced

DRESSING

3 tablespoons fresh lemon juice
2 tablespoons extra-virgin olive oil
2 teaspoons grated orange zest
2 tablespoons orange juice
2 teaspoons grated fresh ginger
1 garlic clove, crushed through a press
½ teaspoon salt
½ teaspoon crushed red pepper flakes

1. To Make the Salad In a medium saucepan, combine the bulghur and water, and bring to a boil over high heat. Reduce the heat to low, cover and simmer until the bulghur is tender and the liquid absorbed, 15 to 20 minutes. Spread the bulghur out on a jelly-roll pan and place in the freezer for 10 to 15 minutes to quick-cool.

2. Meanwhile, rinse the saucepan, fill with 1 inch of water and bring the water to a boil over high heat. Add the broccoli and return to a boil. Cook, stirring frequently, until the broccoli is crisp-tender, 3 to 4 minutes. Drain in a colander and cool briefly under cold running water.

3. Place the bulghur, broccoli, beans, carrots, chopped orange and onion in a large salad bowl.

4. For the Dressing In a small bowl, whisk together the lemon juice, olive oil, orange zest, orange juice, ginger, garlic, salt and red pepper flakes.

5. Pour the dressing over the salad and toss to coat. If there is time, let the salad sit at room temperature for at least 20 minutes before serving to blend and mellow the flavors.

Makes 4 servings

Nutrition Information
values are per serving

CALORIES 297	DIETARY FIBER 14 G
TOTAL FAT 8.3 G	BETA CAROTENE 6.0 MG
SATURATED FAT 1.1 G	VITAMIN C 130 MG
CHOLESTEROL 0 MG	CALCIUM 122 MG
SODIUM 494 MG	IRON 3.1 MG

Bruschetta Salad

In this clever variation on an Italian bread salad, the bread is toasted and rubbed with garlic before being tossed with marinated fresh tomatoes, mozzarella and basil. The best time to make this is in the late summer, when vine-ripened beefsteak tomatoes are available and basil is plentiful.

1½ pounds large tomatoes (about 3), cut into thin wedges
½ teaspoon salt
½ teaspoon freshly ground black pepper
1 tablespoon extra-virgin olive oil
1 tablespoon fresh lemon juice
2 teaspoons balsamic vinegar
3 ounces crusty Italian or French bread, preferably whole wheat, cut into 12 slices
1 garlic clove, peeled and halved
3 ounces part-skim mozzarella cheese, cubed
½ cup thinly sliced basil leaves

1. Place the tomatoes in a salad bowl; sprinkle with the salt and pepper, and toss gently. Then drizzle with the olive oil, lemon juice and vinegar. Cover and let stand at room temperature for 30 minutes.

2. Preheat the broiler. Arrange the bread on a baking sheet and broil 3 to 4 inches from the heat for 1 minute on each side, or until lightly toasted. Remove from the oven and let cool slightly. Then rub each slice of bread with a cut clove of garlic and cut the bread slices in half crosswise.

3. To the tomatoes, add the mozzarella, basil and the toasted bread and toss to blend well.

Makes 4 servings

Nutrition Information
values are per serving

CALORIES 186	DIETARY FIBER 2.9 G
TOTAL FAT 8.3 G	BETA CAROTENE .8 MG
SATURATED FAT 2.9 G	VITAMIN C 36 MG
CHOLESTEROL 12 MG	CALCIUM 215 MG
SODIUM 513 MG	IRON 2.4 MG

Spinach Salad with Creamy Carrot Dressing

Shallots lend subtle onion overtones to the creamy lemon and cumin flavored dressing made colorful (and rich with beta carotene) by the addition of carrot juice.

2 slices (1 ounce each) whole wheat bread, cut into ½-inch cubes
⅓ cup carrot juice
⅓ cup light sour cream
1 tablespoon fresh lemon juice
1 teaspoon cumin
½ teaspoon freshly ground black pepper
¼ teaspoon salt
1 large shallot, quartered
Half a small garlic clove, peeled
6 cups (loosely packed) stemmed spinach
One 16-ounce can chick-peas, rinsed and drained

SUPER QUICK

Crab Salad with Asparagus and Avocado

Working time: 25 minutes Total time: 25 minutes

¾ pound asparagus, cut into 2-inch sections
½ cup finely chopped scallions
¼ cup plain nonfat yogurt
3 tablespoons light sour cream
2 tablespoons chili sauce
1 tablespoon minced fresh dill
2 teaspoons grated lemon zest
2 teaspoons fresh lemon juice
2 teaspoons Dijon mustard
½ pound lump crabmeat, picked over to remove any cartilage
2 cups slivered bottled roasted red peppers
5 cups shredded Romaine lettuce
Half a medium avocado, thinly sliced
1 lemon, cut into 8 wedges

1 Cook the asparagus in a vegetable steamer until they are just cooked through, 1 to 2 minutes. Set the asparagus aside to cool.

2 Meanwhile, in a medium bowl, combine the scallions, yogurt, sour cream, chili sauce, dill, lemon zest and juice and mustard, and stir to blend.

3 Add the asparagus, crab and roasted peppers to the dressing and toss very gently to combine. Dividing evenly, line 4 salad plates with the lettuce. Top with fanned out avocado slices and top the avocado with a mound of the crab salad. Serve with lemon wedges.

Makes 4 servings

Values are per serving:
Calories: 200 Total fat: 7.2 g Saturated fat: 1.6 g Cholesterol: 61 mg Sodium: 385 mg
Dietary fiber: 2.8 g Beta carotene: 3.3 mg Vitamin C: 155 mg Calcium: 172 mg Iron: 4.2 mg

2 cups mixed yellow and red cherry tomatoes
2 tablespoons coarsely chopped walnuts, toasted

1. Preheat the oven to 350°. Place the bread in a 9-inch pie plate or baking pan and bake for 10 minutes, stirring several times, until the bread is very lightly toasted and crisp. Remove from the oven and let the cubes cool.

2. Meanwhile, in a food processor, combine the carrot juice, sour cream, lemon juice, cumin, pepper and salt. With the machine running, drop the shallot and garlic through the feed tube and process until puréed.

3. Place the spinach, chick-peas and tomatoes in a salad bowl. Add the croutons and the dressing, and toss to coat. Sprinkle with the walnuts and serve.

Makes 4 servings

NUTRITION INFORMATION
values are per serving

CALORIES 217	DIETARY FIBER 7.7 G
TOTAL FAT 8.0 G	BETA CAROTENE 7.6 MG
SATURATED FAT 1.8 G	VITAMIN C 44 MG
CHOLESTEROL 6.6 MG	CALCIUM 156 MG
SODIUM 430 MG	IRON 5.5 MG

Fusilli with Shrimp, Red Peppers and Dill

This glorious shrimp, pasta and red bell pepper salad is filled with flavor (as well as a great deal of vitamin C) and is very easy to make. Serve with assorted baby greens and crusty fresh bread.

6 cups water
Half a lemon, thinly sliced
2 garlic cloves, peeled and lightly smashed
1 teaspoon freshly ground black pepper
1 bay leaf, preferably imported
1 pound medium shrimp, shelled and deveined
10 ounces fusilli pasta
3 large red bell peppers, cut into thin strips
½ cup light sour cream
¼ cup minced fresh dill
2 tablespoons fresh lemon juice
½ teaspoon salt
8 scallions, thinly sliced

1. In a large saucepan, combine the water, lemon slices, garlic cloves, ½ teaspoon of the pepper and the bay leaf. Cover and bring to a boil over high heat. Reduce the heat to medium and simmer for 5 minutes to blend the flavors.

2. Add the shrimp to the saucepan and simmer just until the shrimp are pink and firm, about 2 minutes. With a slotted spoon, transfer the shrimp to a bowl to cool. Remove the garlic, place in a large salad bowl, mash with a fork and set aside. Discard the lemon slices and bay leaf.

3. Bring the shrimp cooking water back to a full rolling boil and add the pasta. Cook for 9 minutes. Add the bell peppers and cook until the pasta is al dente and the peppers are crisp-tender, about 2 minutes. Reserving 2 tablespoons of the cooking liquid, drain the fusilli and peppers in a colander. Rinse under cold running water to cool.

4. Whisk the sour cream, dill, lemon juice, salt, remaining ½ teaspoon black pepper and the reserved cooking liquid into the mashed garlic in the salad bowl. Add the shrimp, fusilli, bell peppers and scallions, and toss to mix.

Makes 4 servings

NUTRITION INFORMATION
values are per serving

CALORIES 448	DIETARY FIBER 3.7 G
TOTAL FAT 7.0 G	BETA CAROTENE 2.6 MG
SATURATED FAT 2.5 G	VITAMIN C 157 MG
CHOLESTEROL 150 MG	CALCIUM 113 MG
SODIUM 423 MG	IRON 6.3 MG

Roasted Salmon with Lentils and Lemon Cilantro Dressing

Here is a truly impressive main-course salad, with a variety of colors, textures and tastes. If you are preparing it for guests, make the lentils and greens combination and the dressing ahead of time, but postpone roasting the salmon until just before serving in order to serve it warm.

½ cup plus 3 tablespoons chicken broth diluted with 1½ cups water, or 2 cups plus 3 tablespoons Homemade Chicken Broth (p. 54)
1 cup lentils, rinsed and picked over
1 cup sliced carrots
¾ teaspoon freshly ground black pepper
1 bay leaf, preferably imported
1 pound skinned salmon fillet, cut into four pieces
3 tablespoons fresh lemon juice
¼ teaspoon salt
½ cup (packed) cilantro sprigs
1 tablespoon plus 1 teaspoon extra-virgin olive oil
1 garlic clove, peeled
1 bunch of watercress, tough stems removed
2 cups (loosely packed) stemmed spinach
1 large red bell pepper, cut into thin strips
2 tablespoons chopped red onion

1. In a medium nonstick saucepan, combine 2 cups of the diluted chicken broth with the lentils, carrots, ¼ teaspoon of the black pepper and the bay leaf. Cover and bring to a boil over high heat. Reduce the heat to medium-low and simmer until the lentils are tender, about 45 minutes. Drain off any excess liquid. Transfer to a large bowl and set aside to cool to lukewarm.

2. Preheat the oven to 450°. Spray a 7-by-11-inch baking pan with nonstick cooking spray.

3. Place the salmon in the pan and sprinkle with 1 teaspoon of the lemon juice, ¼ teaspoon of the black pepper and ⅛ teaspoon of the salt. Roast for 10 to 12 minutes, or until the fish is just opaque in the thickest part. Remove from the oven.

4. Meanwhile, in a food processor, combine the remaining 3 tablespoons chicken broth, 2 tablespoons plus 2 teaspoons lemon juice, ¼ tea-

SUPER QUICK

Tuna with White Beans and Minted Dressing

Working time: 15 minutes Total time: 15 minutes

½ cup chopped fresh mint
½ cup plain lowfat yogurt
3 tablespoons light sour cream
1 teaspoon grated lemon zest
3 tablespoons fresh lemon juice
1 garlic clove, minced
¾ teaspoon freshly ground pepper
Two 6⅛-ounce cans water-packed tuna—drained, flaked and rinsed
One 10½-ounce can cannellini beans, rinsed and drained
1 large red bell pepper, diced
1 cup shredded carrots
½ cup diced red onion
4 plum tomatoes, cut into wedges
1 bunch of arugula, tough stems removed

1 In a bowl, whisk together the mint, yogurt, sour cream, lemon zest, lemon juice, garlic and black pepper. Stir in the tuna, beans, bell pepper, carrots and onion.
2 Arrange the tomatoes and arugula on a platter and top with the tuna salad.

Makes 4 servings

Values are per serving:
Calories: 237 Total fat: 3.0 g Saturated fat: 1.2 g Cholesterol: 38 mg Sodium: 421 mg
Dietary fiber: 6.2 g Beta carotene: 7.0 mg Vitamin C: 87 mg Calcium: 155 mg Iron: 4.2 mg

spoon black pepper and ⅛ teaspoon salt with the cilantro and olive oil. With the machine running, drop the garlic clove through the feed tube and process until puréed.

5. Add the watercress, spinach, bell pepper and red onion to the lentils, and toss to combine. Add all but about 1 tablespoon of the dressing and toss to coat well.

6. Divide the salad among 4 plates. Top each with a piece of salmon and drizzle the salmon with the reserved dressing.

Makes 4 servings

Nutrition Information
values are per serving

CALORIES 409	DIETARY FIBER 8.8 G
TOTAL FAT 13 G	BETA CAROTENE 8.2 MG
SATURATED FAT 1.9 G	VITAMIN C 88 MG
CHOLESTEROL 62 MG	CALCIUM 146 MG
SODIUM 416 MG	IRON 6.8 MG

Broiled Scallop and Pepper Salad with Mustard Dressing

The rich flavors and silky textures in this salad seem almost sinful. Sweet sea scallops are matched with slices of avocado and roasted red peppers, all topped with a creamy mustard dressing. For best results, before cooking the scallops, remove the small, tough white tendon that is often found on their sides.

2 large red bell peppers, cut into ½-inch-wide strips
2½ teaspoons extra-virgin olive oil
¼ teaspoon salt
¾ teaspoon freshly ground black pepper
1¼ pounds sea scallops, halved crosswise
2 tablespoons fresh lemon juice
2 garlic cloves, minced
½ teaspoon paprika
8 cups (loosely packed) stemmed spinach
1 small avocado–halved lengthwise and cut crosswise into half-moon slices
¼ cup light sour cream
2 tablespoons plain nonfat yogurt
1 tablespoon Dijon mustard

1. Preheat the broiler. Place the peppers in a jelly-roll pan or large baking pan and toss with 1 teaspoon of the oil, ⅛ teaspoon of the salt and ¼ teaspoon of the black pepper. Broil 4 to 5 inches from the heat, stirring once, for 6 to 8 minutes, or until tender. Transfer the peppers to a plate. Keep the broiler on.

2. Place the scallops on the pan, drizzle with the remaining 1½ teaspoons oil, ⅛ teaspoon salt and ¼ teaspoon of the black pepper. Sprinkle with 1 tablespoon of the lemon juice, the garlic and paprika. Toss well, then spread out into a single layer. Broil 4 to 5 inches from the heat for 3 to 4 minutes, or until the scallops are just opaque in the center.

3. Divide the spinach among 4 dinner plates. Reserving the pan juices, place the broiled scallops on top of the spinach. Add the broiled peppers and avocado to the salad.

4. In a small bowl, combine the scallop cooking juices with the sour cream, yogurt, mustard and the remaining 1 tablespoon lemon juice and ¼ teaspoon black pepper. Drizzle the dressing over the salad and serve

Makes 4 servings

Nutrition Information
values are per serving

CALORIES 294	DIETARY FIBER 5.3 G
TOTAL FAT 13 G	BETA CAROTENE 7.6 MG
SATURATED FAT 2.5 G	VITAMIN C 142 MG
CHOLESTEROL 52 MG	CALCIUM 202 MG
SODIUM 597 MG	IRON 5.0 MG

Thai-Style Shrimp Salad

As is typical of many Thai salads, this beautiful shrimp salad has an almost fat-free dressing. A small amount (only ½ teaspoon) of sesame oil is added for its singular pungency and aroma.

VINAIGRETTE
¼ cup sugar
¼ cup water
2 garlic cloves, minced
½ teaspoon salt
½ teaspoon grated lime zest
⅓ cup fresh lime juice
½ teaspoon crushed red pepper flakes
½ teaspoon Oriental (dark) sesame oil

SALAD
1 scallion, thinly sliced on the diagonal
⅓ cup thinly sliced radishes
5 cups finely shredded nappa cabbage
⅓ cup cilantro leaves
1 pound large shrimp, shelled and deveined
2 seedless cucumbers or 6 kirby cucumbers, thinly sliced on the diagonal
1 medium carrot, cut into thin long strips with a vegetable peeler

1. Preheat the broiler and broiler pan or prepare the grill.

2. **Meanwhile, Make the Vinaigrette** In a small saucepan, combine the sugar, water, garlic and salt. Bring to a boil over high heat, stirring until the sugar dissolves, about 2 minutes. Remove from the heat, stir in the lime zest, lime juice, red pepper flakes and sesame oil, and set aside to cool.

3. **For the Salad** In a small bowl, combine the scallion with 3 tablespoons of the vinaigrette. In a large bowl, toss the radishes, cabbage and cilantro leaves with the remaining vinaigrette.

4. Broil or grill the shrimp 4 to 5 inches from the heat for about 4 minutes, or until cooked through. Place the shrimp in the bowl with the scallions and toss.

5. Line the edges of a platter with the cucumber slices. Mound the radish-cabbage mixture in the middle, place the shrimp and scallions on top and arrange the carrot around the outside.

Makes 4 servings

Nutrition Information
values are per serving

CALORIES 201	DIETARY FIBER 3.0 G
TOTAL FAT 2.6 G	BETA CAROTENE 3.8 MG
SATURATED FAT .4 G	VITAMIN C 43 MG
CHOLESTEROL 140 MG	CALCIUM 156 MG
SODIUM 431 MG	IRON 3.0 MG

Shrimp Salad with Orange Chive Dressing

For this coloful composed salad of shrimp, tomatoes, spinach, cucumber and red bell pepper, an unusual and flavorful dressing is made by combining sweet potato purée with orange juice, garlic, mustard and chives.

⅓ cup diced unpeeled sweet potato
1 garlic clove, peeled
1 pound medium shrimp, shelled and deveined
3 cups (loosely packed) torn stemmed spinach
3 plum tomatoes, diced
1 cup diced red bell pepper
1 cup thinly sliced cucumber
¼ cup sliced radishes
½ cup orange juice
2 tablespoons chopped chives or scallions greens
1 tablespoon olive oil
1 tablespoon Dijon mustard
¼ teaspoon freshly ground black pepper

1. In a medium saucepan, bring 1 cup of water to a boil. Add the sweet potato and garlic, and return to a boil. Reduce the heat to low, cover and simmer until the potato is tender, about 7 minutes.

2. With a slotted spoon, remove the sweet potato and garlic, and set aside to cool. Measure out 2 tablespoons of the cooking water and set aside. Return the remaining water to a boil over high heat and add the shrimp. Return to a boil, reduce the heat to medium, cover and cook just until shrimp are cooked through, 2 to 3 minutes. Drain the shrimp and set aside loosely covered while you prepare the other salad ingredients.

3. Divide the spinach among 4 large salad plates. Arrange the tomatoes, bell pepper, cucumber, and radishes on top of the lettuce. Top each salad with shrimp

4. In a food processor, purée the cooked sweet potato and garlic. Add the orange juice and about 1 tablespoon of the reserved sweet potato cooking water, and purée until very smooth. Blend in the chives, oil, mustard and black pepper. If necessary, thin the dressing with a little more potato cooking water.

5. When ready to serve, spoon the dressing over the salads.

Makes 4 servings

Nutrition Information
values are per serving

CALORIES 186	DIETARY FIBER 2.7 G
TOTAL FAT 5.6 G	BETA CAROTENE 4.1 MG
SATURATED FAT .8 G	VITAMIN C 84 MG
CHOLESTEROL 140 MG	CALCIUM 107 MG
SODIUM 289 MG	IRON 3.8 MG

Fennel and Pepper Pasta Salad

Here is a wonderful take on chicken salad, with the chicken taking a back seat to pasta, fresh vegetables and minced fresh basil. Serve with whole wheat bread sticks and, for dessert, orange sorbet.

3 large red bell peppers
1 pound skinless, boneless chicken breast
1 cup canned chicken broth diluted with 1 cup water, or 2 cups Homemade Chicken Broth (p. 54)
3 tablespoons balsamic vinegar

SUPER QUICK

Spinach and Almond Pasta Salad

Working time: 10 minutes Total time: 20 minutes

3 tablespoons red wine vinegar
2 tablespoons honey
2 tablespoons Dijon mustard
2 tablespoons nonfat mayonnaise
1½ teaspoons oregano
1 teaspoon minced garlic
6 ounces fusilli pasta
3 cups (loosely packed) torn stemmed spinach
2 cups diced tomatoes
One 10-ounce package frozen peas, thawed
1 tablespoon chopped dry-roasted almonds

1 In a small bowl or screwtop jar, combine the vinegar, honey, mustard, mayonnaise, oregano and garlic, and whisk or shake to blend.
2 Cook the pasta in a large pot of boiling water until al dente, 9 to 11 minutes, or according to package directions. Drain in a colander.
3 In a salad bowl, combine the pasta with the spinach, tomatoes, peas and almonds. Pour the dressing on top and toss well.

Makes 4 servings

Values are per serving:
Calories: 311 Total fat: 3.4 g Saturated fat: .3 g Cholesterol: 0 mg Sodium: 419 mg
Dietary fiber: 6.8 g Beta carotene: 3.2 mg Vitamin C: 48 mg Calcium: 107 mg Iron: 5.2 mg

1 large garlic clove, peeled and lightly smashed
½ pound penne or other small tubular pasta
2 tablespoons olive oil
¼ cup frozen orange juice concentrate, thawed
1 small fennel bulb (about ¾ pound), feathery tops removed and bulb thinly sliced
½ cup minced fresh basil
12 looseleaf lettuce leaves

1. Preheat the broiler. Cutting vertically, slice the bell peppers in 3 or 4 flat panels, leaving the cores and seeds behind. Put the bell pepper pieces, skin-side up, in a single layer on a jelly-roll pan and broil 4 to 5 inches from the heat for 10 to 15 minutes, or until well charred all over. Place the peppers in a bowl to steam. When cool enough to handle, pull off the skins and cut the peppers into 1-inch-wide strips.

2. Meanwhile, place the chicken in a large skillet with the diluted broth, 1 tablespoon of the vinegar and the garlic. Cover and bring to a boil over high heat. Reduce the heat to low and simmer, covered, until the chicken is cooked through, about 8 minutes; turn the chicken over about halfway through.

3. Reserving the broth, remove the chicken and garlic. Mash the garlic with a fork and set aside. Transfer the chicken to a plate to cool. When cool enough to handle, tear it into shreds.

4. Cook the pasta in a large pot of boiling water until al dente, 9 to 12 minutes, or according to package directions. Drain in a colander and rinse under cold running water.

5. In a large salad bowl, whisk together ¼ cup of the reserved chicken broth, the mashed garlic, the remaining 2 tablespoons vinegar, the oil and orange juice concentrate. Add the roasted peppers, shredded chicken, drained pasta, fennel and basil, and toss well.

6. Serve the salad on a bed of looseleaf lettuce.

Makes 4 servings

NUTRITION INFORMATION
values are per serving

CALORIES 471	DIETARY FIBER 3.7 G
TOTAL FAT 9.5 G	BETA CAROTENE 3.1 MG
SATURATED FAT 1.4 G	VITAMIN C 182 MG
CHOLESTEROL 66 MG	CALCIUM 139 MG
SODIUM 222 MG	IRON 5.4 MG

Sunbelt Chicken Salad

A cumin, honey and lime juice dressing complements the sunny flavors of cantaloupe and orange in this chicken salad. Unless you are a fan of the peppery, pungent flavors of arugula and watercress, use at least half looseleaf lettuce in the salad greens mixture.

1 pound skinless, boneless chicken thighs
2 teaspoons olive oil
1 small red onion, halved and cut into paper-thin slices
1½ teaspoons minced garlic
¾ teaspoon cumin
3 tablespoons reduced-sodium soy sauce
2 tablespoons honey
2 tablespoons fresh lime juice
4 cups (loosely packed) mixed greens: arugula, watercress and torn looseleaf lettuce
Half a cantaloupe, seeded and cut into narrow wedges
1 navel orange–peeled, halved and thinly sliced
2 limes, quartered

1. Cook the chicken in a vegetable steamer until cooked through, about 12 minutes. Transfer the chicken to a plate and set aside to cool. When cool enough to handle, shred or cut into strips (reserve any juices that have collected on the plate).

2. In a medium nonstick skillet, warm the oil over medium-high heat until hot but not smoking.

Add the onion and sauté until softened, about 1 minute. Add the garlic, ½ teaspoon of the cumin, 2 tablespoons of the soy sauce, 1 tablespoon of the honey, the reserved chicken juices and the shredded chicken. Cook, tossing lightly, for about 3 minutes to blend the flavors. Remove from the heat.

3. In a small bowl, blend the lime juice with the remaining ¼ teaspoon cumin, 1 tablespoon soy sauce and 1 tablespoon honey. In a large bowl, toss the greens, cantaloupe wedges and orange slices with the dressing.

4. Arrange the greens and fruit on individual dinner plates. Top with the chicken mixture. Serve with lime wedges.

Makes 4 servings

Nutrition Information
values are per serving

CALORIES 271	DIETARY FIBER 2.8 G
TOTAL FAT 7.2 G	BETA CAROTENE 2.5 MG
SATURATED FAT 1.4 G	VITAMIN C 86 MG
CHOLESTEROL 94 MG	CALCIUM 120 MG
SODIUM 573 MG	IRON 2.9 MG

Spinach Caesar with Chicken and Grilled Peppers

Caesar salad lovers are legion, and this variation on the theme should appeal to even the most discerning of them. Spinach replaces the original Romaine lettuce, and grilled peppers are added for vitamin C. The Parmesan remains, as do the croutons and anchovies, but missing, and with good reason, is the raw egg.

2 ounces crusty French bread, cut into ¼-inch-thick slices
2 large red bell peppers, cut into thin strips
1 teaspoon extra-virgin olive oil
½ pound skinless, boneless chicken breast, cut into 1-inch chunks
3 tablespoons chicken broth, canned or homemade (p. 54)
¾ teaspoon freshly ground black pepper
¼ cup reduced-calorie mayonnaise
3 tablespoons fresh lemon juice
1 ounce grated Parmesan cheese
4 anchovy fillets or 2 teaspoons anchovy paste
1 garlic clove, peeled
8 cups (loosely packed) stemmed spinach leaves

1. Preheat the broiler. Place the bread slices on a baking sheet and broil for 30 seconds, or until lightly toasted. Let cool slightly, then cut the croutons in half. Leave the broiler on.

2. Spray a jelly-roll pan with nonstick cooking spray. Place the bell pepper strips on the pan, drizzle with the olive oil, toss to coat well and broil 3 to 4 inches from the heat, stirring several times, for 4 to 5 minutes, or until the peppers are lightly charred in spots.

3. Add the chicken, 2 tablespoons of the chicken broth and ¼ teaspoon of the black pepper to the jelly-roll pan, and toss to mix. Broil for 3 to 4 minutes longer, stirring several times, until the peppers are tender and the chicken is cooked through. Cover loosely with a foil to keep warm.

4. Meanwhile, in a food processor, combine the remaining 1 tablespoon broth, the mayonnaise, lemon juice, all but 2 tablespoons of the Parmesan, the anchovies and remaining ½ teaspoon black pepper. With the machine running, add the garlic and process until puréed.

5. Place the spinach, chicken and bell peppers (and any juices that have collected on the pan) and the croutons in a large salad bowl. Add the dressing and reserved 2 tablespoons Parmesan, and toss to mix.

Makes 4 servings

Nutrition Information
values are per serving

CALORIES 243	DIETARY FIBER 4.9 G
TOTAL FAT 9.5 G	BETA CAROTENE 7.4 MG
SATURATED FAT 3.0 G	VITAMIN C 141 MG
CHOLESTEROL 46 MG	CALCIUM 271 MG
SODIUM 641 MG	IRON 5.2 MG

Pacific Rice Salad

You have the unique opportunity here to use apricot nectar, with its heavenly fragrance, in a dressing for chicken, mango and wild rice salad.

1 cup apricot nectar
2 tablespoons fresh lime juice
1 tablespoon chili powder
¾ teaspoon salt
½ teaspoon freshly ground black pepper
¾ pound skinless, boneless chicken breast, cut crosswise into ½-inch strips
1 cup brown rice
½ cup wild rice, rinsed
3 cups water
2 large red bell peppers, diced
1 mango, cut into ½-inch cubes
½ cup thinly sliced scallions
1 tablespoon honey
1 large lime, cut into 8 wedges

1. In a medium bowl, mix together the apricot nectar, lime juice, chili powder, salt and black pepper. Measure out ½ cup of the apricot mixture and set aside. Add the chicken to the remaining apricot mixture, cover and refrigerate while you cook the rice.

2. In a medium nonstick saucepan, combine the brown and wild rice with the water. Bring to a boil over high heat. Reduce the heat to low, cover and simmer until the rices are tender and the water is absorbed, 50 to 55 minutes. Spread the rice in a baking pan and place in the freezer for 15 to 20 minutes, or until cooled to warm.

3. Place the chicken and the marinade in a medium skillet. Place over medium-high heat and bring to a boil. Reduce the heat to medium-low and simmer, stirring frequently, until the chicken is cooked through, 4 to 6 minutes. Drain the chicken and place in a salad bowl.

4. Add the rices, bell peppers, mango and scallions to the bowl and toss gently. Whisk the honey into the reserved apricot mixture and pour over the salad. Toss to mix. Serve with 2 lime wedges per person for squeezing over the salad.

Makes 4 servings

Nutrition Information
values are per serving

CALORIES 453	DIETARY FIBER 5.4 G
TOTAL FAT 3.3 G	BETA CAROTENE 3.8 MG
SATURATED FAT .6 G	VITAMIN C 156 MG
CHOLESTEROL 49 MG	CALCIUM 64 MG
SODIUM 497 MG	IRON 2.9 MG

Cobb Salad with Buttermilk-Blue Cheese Dressing

The original Cobb salad, a classic American salad from California, was almost impossible not to like, composed as it was of cheese, hard-cooked eggs, bacon, turkey and avocado. The variation that follows is just as likable—and, not surprisingly, better for you.

DRESSING
⅓ cup buttermilk
¼ cup light sour cream
1½ ounces blue cheese, crumbled
2 tablespoons minced chives or scallion greens

1 tablespoon white wine vinegar
½ teaspoon freshly ground black pepper
⅛ teaspoon salt

SALAD

½ cup canned chicken broth diluted with ¼ cup water, or ¾ cup Homemade Chicken Broth (p. 54)
½ pound skinless, boneless chicken breast, diced
3 cups shredded Romaine lettuce (halved lengthwise before shredding)
3 cups (loosely packed) shredded spinach leaves
Half a medium avocado, diced
1 cup diced red or yellow bell pepper
One 10½-ounce can red kidney beans, rinsed and drained
1 cup shredded carrots
1 cup quartered cherry tomatoes

1. Make the Dressing In a small bowl, whisk together the buttermilk, sour cream, blue cheese, chives, vinegar, black pepper and salt. Mash any large lumps of cheese.

2. For the Salad In a medium saucepan, bring the diluted chicken broth to a boil over high heat. Add the chicken, reduce the heat to medium and cook, stirring frequently, until the chicken is cooked through, 1 to 2 minutes. Drain in a colander and set aside loosely covered.

3. In a large, wide salad bowl, toss the Romaine and spinach. Arrange the chicken, avocado, bell pepper, kidney beans, carrots and cherry tomatoes in separate piles or strips on top of the greens. Drizzle with the dressing. Toss just before serving.

Makes 4 servings

Nutrition Information
values are per serving

CALORIES 271	DIETARY FIBER 7.2 G
TOTAL FAT 11 G	BETA CAROTENE 8.5 MG
SATURATED FAT 4.0 G	VITAMIN C 84 MG
CHOLESTEROL 47 MG	CALCIUM 186 MG
SODIUM 490 MG	IRON 3.8 MG

Warm Madras Chicken Salad

Prepare the yogurt dressing, sweet potatoes and spinach for this salad in advance. Just before serving, cook the chicken, then enjoy the wonderful contrast in temperatures and flavors.

DRESSING

½ cup plain nonfat yogurt
¼ cup chopped cilantro
2 tablespoons minced red onion
1 tablespoon chopped fresh mint
⅛ teaspoon cayenne pepper
⅛ teaspoon salt

SALAD

2 teaspoons curry powder
¼ teaspoon ground ginger
⅛ teaspoon cayenne pepper
⅛ teaspoon salt
2 navel oranges
2 teaspoons olive oil
1 pound sweet potatoes, peeled and cut into 1-inch cubes
¾ pound skinless, boneless chicken breast
1 medium carrot, shredded
6 cups (loosely packed) shredded spinach leaves

1. Make the Dressing In a small bowl, whisk together the yogurt, cilantro, onion, mint, cayenne and salt. Refrigerate until serving time.

2. For the Salad In a heavy medium skillet, heat the curry powder, ginger and cayenne over medium-low heat until fragrant, about 30 seconds (be careful not to burn). Transfer to a small bowl or cup and stir in the salt.

3. With a sharp knife, remove the peel and white pith from the oranges. Working over a bowl to catch the juices, cut the orange segments away from the surrounding membranes, then gently squeeze the membranes to extract additional juice. Stir 1 teaspoon of the spice mixture and 1 tea-

spoon of the olive oil into the orange juice and set aside.

4. Cook the sweet potatoes in a vegetable steamer until tender, about 8 minutes. Remove the sweet potatoes, drain the water from the pan and return the sweet potatoes. Strain the orange juice over the potatoes; set the drained orange segments and the sweet potatoes aside separately.

5. Rub the remaining spice mixture onto both sides of the chicken. In a nonstick skillet, warm the remaining 1 teaspoon oil over medium-high heat. Add the chicken and cook until golden and cooked through, about 3 minutes per side.

6. Stir the carrot into the sweet potatoes. Line 4 dinner plates with the spinach and mound the vegetable mixture on top.

7. Cut the chicken into strips and arrange on top of the salads. Garnish with the reserved orange segments. Drizzle some dressing over each serving and pass the remainder on the side.

Makes 4 servings

Nutrition Information
values are per serving

CALORIES 318	DIETARY FIBER 8.8 G
TOTAL FAT 4.3 G	BETA CAROTENE 21 MG
SATURATED FAT .7 G	VITAMIN C 99 MG
CHOLESTEROL 50 MG	CALCIUM 237 MG
SODIUM 321 MG	IRON 4.7 MG

Asian Kiwi Chicken Salad

Kiwi fruit, with its lovely green color, was once an expensive imported fruit. Now grown extensively in this country, it is less pricey, though still most available in the summer.

¾ pound skinless, boneless chicken breast
2 teaspoons grated lime zest
¼ cup fresh lime juice
2 tablespoons honey
2 tablespoons reduced-sodium soy sauce
½ teaspoon ground ginger
8 cups (loosely packed) shredded Romaine lettuce
2 kiwi fruit–peeled, halved lengthwise and thinly sliced crosswise
½ cup canned sliced water chestnuts, rinsed and drained
¼ cup sliced scallions

1. Cook the chicken in a vegetable steamer until cooked through, 10 to 12 minutes. Transfer the chicken to a plate and set aside to cool. When cool enough to handle, cut the chicken into slices (reserve any juices that have collected on the plate).

2. In a small bowl, combine the lime zest, lime juice, honey, soy sauce, ginger and any reserved chicken juices. Pour ⅓ cup of this dressing over the chicken slices and set aside to marinate for at least 1 hour.

3. Line individual serving plates with shredded lettuce. Arrange the kiwi and water chestnut slices around the outside, mound the chicken in the center and sprinkle with scallions. Drizzle the remaining dressing over the salad (including any left in the bowl the chicken was marinating in).

Makes 4 servings

Nutrition Information
values are per serving

CALORIES 192	DIETARY FIBER 3.8 G
TOTAL FAT 1.5 G	BETA CAROTENE 2.2 MG
SATURATED FAT .3 G	VITAMIN C 70 MG
CHOLESTEROL 49 MG	CALCIUM 80 MG
SODIUM 371 MG	IRON 2.8 MG

Hacienda Salad

It wasn't too long ago that salad, no matter the kind, was dressed with either mayonnaise or oil-heavy vinaigrette. Those were the choices. Then, along came salsas, and they took the cooking world by storm, garnishing everything from tortillas to sundaes. Here see how a spirited papaya salsa makes a stand-out chicken salad.

4 skinless, boneless chicken breast halves (1 pound total)
1 medium papaya or 2 medium nectarines, peeled and coarsely chopped
1 medium red bell pepper, diced
Half a cucumber, peeled and coarsely chopped
2 tablespoons minced parsley
2 teaspoons grated lime zest
2 tablespoons fresh lime juice
1½ teaspoons minced fresh jalapeño pepper
1 teaspoon sugar
½ teaspoon salt
¼ teaspoon crushed red pepper flakes
1 cup finely shredded Romaine lettuce
1 cup finely shredded red cabbage
2 navel oranges, peeled and sliced
1 small avocado, peeled and sliced

1. Cook the chicken in a vegetable steamer until cooked through, 10 to 12 minutes. Transfer the chicken to a plate and set aside to cool. When cool enough to handle, slice each breast crosswise on the diagonal (reserve any juices that have collected on the plate). Cover the chicken loosely to keep it from drying out.

2. In a medium bowl, combine the papaya, bell pepper, cucumber, parsley, lime zest and juice, jalapeño pepper, sugar, salt and red pepper flakes. Stir in any reserved chicken juices.

3. To assemble, line a platter or plates with the shredded Romaine and cabbage. Arrange the sliced chicken breast, orange slices and avocado on top and serve with a mound of the papaya-pepper salsa.

Makes 4 servings

SUPER QUICK

Antipasto Salad

Working time: 30 minutes Total time: 30 minutes

¼ cup canned chicken broth
2 tablespoons extra-virgin olive oil
2 tablespoons red wine vinegar
2 teaspoons Dijon mustard
1 garlic clove, minced
½ teaspoon freshly ground pepper
¼ teaspoon oregano
½ cup thinly sliced red onions
4 cups stemmed spinach
½ cup shredded carrots
One 10½-ounce can chick-peas, rinsed and drained
1½ cups bottled roasted red peppers, cut into strips
1½ cups thinly sliced fennel
½ cup sliced radishes
2 plum tomatoes, cut into wedges
3 ounces roast turkey breast, sliced
1 ounce sliced provolone cheese, cut into quarters

1 In a small bowl, whisk together the chicken broth, olive oil, vinegar, mustard, garlic, black pepper and oregano. Stir in the onions and let marinate while you assemble the rest of the salad.

2 Arrange the spinach on a platter. Sprinkle with the carrots. Mound the chick-peas, roasted peppers, fennel, radishes, tomatoes, turkey and cheese in separate piles on the spinach. Spoon the onions and dressing over the salad.

Makes 4 servings

Values are per serving:
Calories: 228 Total fat: 11 g Saturated fat: 2.4 g Cholesterol: 23 mg Sodium: 399 mg
Dietary fiber: 5.2 g Beta carotene: 5.8 mg Vitamin C: 92 mg Calcium: 168 mg Iron: 4.7 mg

NUTRITION INFORMATION
values are per serving

CALORIES 271	DIETARY FIBER 4.2 G
TOTAL FAT 7.4 G	BETA CAROTENE 2.1 MG
SATURATED FAT 1.3 G	VITAMIN C 151 MG
CHOLESTEROL 66 MG	CALCIUM 90 MG
SODIUM 360 MG	IRON 1.9 MG

Turkey, Nectarine and Whole Grain Salad with Citrus Vinaigrette

Salads made with turkey seem to go unsung, but they shouldn't, for turkey contributes exceptional texture, subtle flavor, very few calories and a good measure of B vitamins. Here it combines beautifully with brown rice and nectarines.

¾ cup canned chicken broth diluted with ¾ cup water, or 1½ cups Homemade Chicken Broth (p. 54)
½ cup brown rice
¼ cup lentils
½ cup orange juice
2 tablespoons white wine vinegar
2 tablespoons mild olive oil
1 teaspoon grated lime zest
1 tablespoon fresh lime juice
1 tablespoon Dijon mustard
1½ teaspoons tarragon
½ pound unsliced roast turkey breast, cubed
2 medium nectarines, cubed
1 cup chopped carrots
¼ cup minced parsley
4 cups (loosely packed) torn looseleaf lettuce

1. In a medium saucepan, bring the diluted broth, brown rice and lentils to a boil over high heat, then reduce the heat to a simmer, cover and cook until the grains are tender, about 45 minutes. Fluff the grains into a medium bowl and set aside to cool slightly (if there is any liquid left in the saucepan, drain the mixture first).

2. Meanwhile, in a small bowl, whisk together the orange juice, vinegar, olive oil, lime zest, lime juice, mustard and tarragon.

3. To the grains, add the turkey, nectarines, carrots, parsley and vinaigrette, and toss well.

4. On each of 4 dinner plates, place some of the lettuce and top with the salad.

Makes 4 servings

SUPER QUICK

Caribe Turkey Salad

Working time: 15 minutes Total time: 15 minutes

16 large Romaine lettuce leaves
1 papaya—peeled, seeded and cut into thin slices
3 cups quartered strawberries
2 kiwi fruit, peeled and cut into thin slices
1 pound roast turkey breast, cut into ½-inch cubes
¼ cup dry-roasted cashews or peanuts, diced
⅓ cup frozen tropical fruit-juice-blend concentrate, thawed
¼ cup rice wine vinegar
1 tablespoon canola oil

1 Arrange the lettuce on 4 individual serving plates. Top with the papaya, strawberries and kiwi fruit. Mound the turkey in the center. Sprinkle with the nuts.

2 In a small bowl or screwtop jar, combine the fruit juice concentrate, vinegar and oil. Whisk or shake to blend. Pour over the salads and serve.

Makes 4 servings

Values are per serving:
Calories: 375 Total fat: 9.0 g Saturated fat: 1.4 g Cholesterol: 94 mg Sodium: 77 mg
Dietary fiber: 5.9 g Beta carotene: 1.9 mg Vitamin C: 180 mg Calcium: 91 mg Iron: 3.7 mg

Nutrition Information
values are per serving

CALORIES 350	DIETARY FIBER 5.1 G
TOTAL FAT 9.1 G	BETA CAROTENE 6.0 MG
SATURATED FAT 1.2 G	VITAMIN C 38 MG
CHOLESTEROL 47 MG	CALCIUM 98 MG
SODIUM 348 MG	IRON 4.1 MG

Chicken Tabbouleh

Tabbouleh—the Middle Eastern salad of bulghur (cracked wheat), tomatoes, fresh parsley and mint—is made more substantial in this variation by the addition of chicken, carrots and, for a special sweet-tart note, dried apricots.

1 cup medium-coarse bulghur
2 cups boiling water
¾ cup diced dried apricots
½ cup orange juice
½ cup chicken broth, canned or homemade (p. 54)
½ pound skinless, boneless chicken breast, cut into ¼-inch dice
2 cups shredded carrots
1½ cups chopped parsley, preferably flat-leaf
¼ cup finely sliced scallions
3 tablespoons fresh lemon juice
1 tablespoon plus 1 teaspoon extra-virgin olive oil
¾ teaspoon freshly ground black pepper
½ teaspoon salt
2 medium tomatoes, sliced

1. In a medium bowl, combine the bulghur and water. Let stand for 30 minutes, then drain in a fine-mesh sieve, pressing out the excess water.

2. Meanwhile, in a small bowl, combine the apricots and orange juice, and let stand while the bulghur is soaking.

3. In a small saucepan, bring the chicken broth to a boil over high heat. Add the chicken, reduce the heat to medium and simmer, stirring frequently, until the chicken is cooked through, 3 to 5 minutes. With a slotted spoon, transfer the chicken to a plate and cover loosely so it doesn't dry out.

4. Increase the heat under the saucepan to high and reduce the broth until it is caramel-colored, syrupy and reduced to about 1 tablespoon, about 10 minutes. Set the reduced broth aside.

5. In a large bowl, combine the drained bulghur, the apricots and their soaking liquid, the chicken, carrots, parsley and scallions. Toss to mix well.

6. In a small bowl or cup, whisk the reduced broth with the lemon juice, olive oil, black pepper and salt. Pour the dressing over the salad and toss to mix. Mound the salad on a platter and surround with the sliced tomatoes.

Makes 4 servings

Nutrition Information
values are per serving

CALORIES 347	DIETARY FIBER 12 G
TOTAL FAT 6.5 G	BETA CAROTENE 11 MG
SATURATED FAT 1.0 G	VITAMIN C 57 MG
CHOLESTEROL 33 MG	CALCIUM 89 MG
SODIUM 477 MG	IRON 4.6 MG

Melon-Berry Turkey Salad

For this delightful main-course salad, which is as lovely to look at as it is simple to prepare, cantaloupe and honeydew melon combine with red raspberries, turkey and watercress in a lemon-apricot dressing scented with sesame oil.

1 small cantaloupe (2 pounds), halved and seeded
Half a honeydew melon (2¼ pounds), seeded
½ cup apricot all-fruit spread

2 teaspoons grated lemon zest
1 tablespoon fresh lemon juice
1 teaspoon Oriental (dark) sesame oil
¾ pound unsliced roast turkey, cut into ½-inch cubes
4 ounces Romaine lettuce
4 ounces watercress, coarse stems removed
1 pint (6 ounces) raspberries
1 lemon, cut into 8 wedges

1. Cut the cantaloupe into thin wedges, remove the rind and cut the melon into 1-inch cubes. Place the cantaloupe in a bowl. Cut the honeydew melon into thin wedges, remove the rind and cut into 1-inch cubes. Add the honeydew to the cantaloupe and place in the refrigerator to chill.

2. In a small bowl, blend the all-fruit spread with the lemon zest, lemon juice and sesame oil.

3. Place the turkey in a medium bowl. Pour half of the dressing over the turkey and toss to coat well.

4. To assemble the salads, make a bed of Romaine and watercress on each of 4 plates. Top with the turkey and melon cubes. Drizzle the remaining dressing over the salads and top with the raspberries. Serve with the lemon wedges.

Makes 4 servings

Nutrition Information
values are per serving

CALORIES 354	DIETARY FIBER 5.1 G
TOTAL FAT 5.9 G	BETA CAROTENE 3.5 MG
SATURATED FAT 1.5 G	VITAMIN C 131 MG
CHOLESTEROL 66 MG	CALCIUM 113 MG
SODIUM 100 MG	IRON 2.6 MG

Thanksgiving Salad

All the flavors of Thanksgiving are combined in this superb salad, which not only provides a lowfat way to use leftover turkey, but also supplies over 100% of the Wellness Recommended Intake (see page 11) for beta carotene. The delicious lowfat dressing uses both cranberry and orange juices for an equally impressive amount of vitamin C.

1½ pounds sweet potatoes, peeled and cut into 1-inch chunks
2 navel oranges
3 cups sliced Romaine lettuce (tough inner ribs discarded, leaves cut crosswise into 1-inch-wide strips)
6 ounces roast turkey breast, torn into 1-inch pieces
½ cup thinly sliced scallions
3 tablespoons frozen cranberry juice concentrate, thawed
3 tablespoons frozen orange juice concentrate, thawed
1 tablespoon balsamic vinegar
1 tablespoon extra-virgin olive oil
½ teaspoon freshly ground black pepper
2 tablespoons coarsely chopped pecans, toasted (about ½ ounce)
2 tablespoons dried cranberries or dark raisins

1. Place the sweet potatoes in a medium saucepan and add cold water to cover by 1 inch. Cover and bring to a boil over high heat. Reduce the heat to medium-low and simmer until the sweet potato is fork-tender, 10 to 12 minutes. Drain in a colander and cool briefly under gently running cold water.

2. Meanwhile, with a serrated knife, remove the peel and white pith from the oranges. Cut each orange in half lengthwise, place the halves flat on a cutting board and cut crosswise into ¼-inch-thick slices.

3. Spread the lettuce on a platter. Top with the sweet potatoes, turkey and orange slices. Sprinkle with the scallions.

4. In a small bowl or cup, whisk together the cranberry juice concentrate, orange juice concentrate, vinegar, oil and pepper. Pour over the salad and sprinkle the salad with the pecans and the dried cranberries.

Makes 4 servings

Nutrition Information
values are per serving

CALORIES 393	DIETARY FIBER 8.2 G
TOTAL FAT 6.9 G	BETA CAROTENE 22 MG
SATURATED FAT .9 G	VITAMIN C 126 MG
CHOLESTEROL 35 MG	CALCIUM 103 MG
SODIUM 52 MG	IRON 2.6 MG

Penne Salad with Steak and Sautéed Spinach

Americans have learned from certain Oriental cuisines, China's most notably, that meat does not have to inevitably appear as a main course but can be served in smaller amounts, as a superb garnish. So it is with this salad. To maximize the flavor, grill the steak over hot coals.

1 lemon
¾ pound well-trimmed lean beef sirloin steak
2 garlic cloves, minced
2 tablespoons fresh oregano leaves, chopped, or ½ teaspoon dried
1 teaspoon coarsely ground black pepper
½ pound penne pasta
2 tablespoons olive oil
½ pound stemmed spinach
1 cup sliced scallions (about 16 medium)
2 cups cherry tomatoes
2 tablespoons balsamic vinegar
½ teaspoon salt

1. Grate the lemon to yield 2 teaspoons zest. Squeeze the lemon to yield 2 tablespoons juice.

2. Preheat the broiler. Rub the steak on both sides with the lemon zest, garlic, 1 tablespoon of the fresh oregano (or ¼ teaspoon of the dried) and ½ teaspoon of the pepper. Sprinkle with the lemon juice. Let stand while you cook the pasta.

3. In a large pot of boiling water, cook the penne until al dente, 10 to 12 minutes, or according to package directions. Drain in a colander and rinse under cold running water to prevent sticking. Transfer to a salad bowl.

4. Broil the steak 4 inches from the heat for about 5 minutes per side for medium-rare. Transfer to a plate and let cool to warm.

5. In a large nonstick skillet, warm the oil over medium-high heat until hot but not smoking. Add the spinach, in batches, stirring until the spinach is just wilted. Transfer the spinach to the salad bowl with the pasta.

6. Add the scallions and cherry tomatoes to the skillet and sauté, shaking the skillet often, until the cherry tomatoes just begin to split, about 3 minutes. Pour the mixture into the salad bowl.

7. Pour any beef juices that have collected on the plate into the salad bowl. Add the remaining 1 tablespoon fresh oregano (or ¼ teaspoon dried), ½ teaspoon pepper, the balsamic vinegar and salt, and toss to mix.

8. Divide the pasta salad among 4 dinner plates. Carve the steak into thin slices, arrange on top of the salad and serve.

Makes 4 servings

Nutrition Information
values are per serving

CALORIES 419	DIETARY FIBER 4.2 G
TOTAL FAT 12 G	BETA CAROTENE 2.5 MG
SATURATED FAT 2.4 G	VITAMIN C 35 MG
CHOLESTEROL 52 MG	CALCIUM 104 MG
SODIUM 381 MG	IRON 6.9 MG

Curried Pork Salad

Pork has always combined beautifully with potatoes and apples, as it does here in this memorable salad with exotic Indian overtones. The better your curry powder, the more rounded the flavor.

2 teaspoons curry powder
1 teaspoon ground ginger
1 teaspoon paprika
½ teaspoon salt
½ teaspoon sugar
1 pound boneless pork loin
½ pound all-purpose potatoes, peeled and cut into 1-inch chunks
½ pound sweet potatoes, peeled and cut into 1-inch chunks
1 cup plain nonfat yogurt
2 tablespoons frozen orange juice concentrate, thawed
2 tablespoons chopped mango chutney
1 cup thinly sliced radishes
1 celery stalk, cut into matchsticks
1 unpeeled Granny Smith apple, quartered and thinly sliced
1 bunch of watercress, coarse stems removed
1 large mango, diced
2 tablespoons coarsely chopped almonds

1. Preheat the oven to 425°.

2. In a small bowl, stir together the curry powder, ginger, paprika, salt and sugar. Measure out 2 teaspoons of the spice mixture and set aside. Rub the remaining spice mixture into the pork. Place the pork in a small baking pan and roast for 25 to 28 minutes, or until golden brown and cooked through. When the pork is cool enough to handle, thinly slice.

3. Meanwhile, in a large pot of boiling water, boil the all-purpose potatoes and the sweet potatoes until tender, about 10 minutes. Drain well.

4. In a large mixing bowl, stir together the reserved spice mixture, the yogurt, orange juice concentrate and chutney. Add the sliced pork, potatoes, radishes, celery, apple and watercress to the bowl, tossing to mix well.

5. Spoon onto serving plates and top with the diced mango and almonds.

Makes 4 servings

NUTRITION INFORMATION
values are per serving

CALORIES 415	DIETARY FIBER 6.0 G
TOTAL FAT 9.5 G	BETA CAROTENE 7.9 MG
SATURATED FAT 2.6 G	VITAMIN C 77 MG
CHOLESTEROL 68 MG	CALCIUM 236 MG
SODIUM 507 MG	IRON 2.6 MG

Lamb and Potato Salad with Carrot Vinaigrette

You don't often see kale as the main ingredient in salads. Pity, because this member of the cabbage family is notably high in beta carotene, vitamin C and vitamin E. Its full flavor works nicely with the lamb in this inventive salad.

½ teaspoon cumin
½ teaspoon ground coriander
½ teaspoon paprika
¼ teaspoon salt
¼ teaspoon sugar
1 pound well-trimmed boneless loin of lamb
1 large green bell pepper, diced
6 cups (loosely packed) torn kale (about 6 ounces)
⅓ cup (not oil-packed) sun-dried tomatoes, coarsely chopped

3/4 pound all-purpose potatoes, peeled and cut into 1-inch chunks
1/2 cup carrot juice
2 tablespoons red wine vinegar
1 tablespoon no-salt-added tomato paste
1 tablespoon plus 1 teaspoon Dijon mustard
1 tablespoon olive oil

1. Preheat the oven to 425°.

2. In a small bowl, stir together the cumin, coriander, paprika, salt, and sugar. Reserving ½ teaspoon of the mixture, rub the remainder into the lamb. Place the lamb in a small baking pan and bake until crusty and browned, about 20 minutes. Transfer the lamb to a cutting board and when cool enough to handle, thinly slice. Strain the pan drippings and remove all the fat; set aside.

3. Meanwhile, in a large pot of boiling water, blanch the bell pepper for 1 minute. Remove with a slotted spoon; drain. In the same water, blanch the kale and the sun-dried tomatoes until tender, about 4 minutes. Remove with a slotted spoon; drain. Add the potatoes to the water and cook until tender, about 10 minutes. Drain.

4. In a large mixing bowl, whisk together the carrot juice, vinegar, tomato paste, mustard, olive oil, the reserved ½ teaspoon spice mixture and the degreased pan juices from the lamb.

5. Add the bell pepper, kale, sun-dried tomatoes, potatoes and sliced lamb to the bowl and toss well to coat.

Makes 4 servings

NUTRITION INFORMATION
values are per serving

CALORIES 313	DIETARY FIBER 5.6 G
TOTAL FAT 11 G	BETA CAROTENE 7.9 MG
SATURATED FAT 2.9 G	VITAMIN C 107 MG
CHOLESTEROL 75 MG	CALCIUM 97 MG
SODIUM 404 MG	IRON 4.4 MG

Ginger and Sesame Steak Salad

A splendid combination of colors—deep green watercress, red bell pepper, pale bean sprouts and yellow corn—serve to enhance this stylish steak salad, a great choice for al fresco summer dining. Serve a mixture of fresh berries for dessert.

2 tablespoons reduced-sodium soy sauce
1 tablespoon coarsely chopped fresh ginger
2 garlic cloves, peeled
1/8 teaspoon crushed red pepper flakes
3/4 pound lean trimmed boneless beef sirloin steak
1 1/2 cups frozen corn kernels
2 tablespoons water
1 tablespoon canned chicken broth
1 tablespoon rice wine vinegar
4 cups (loosely packed) watercress sprigs, tough stems removed
1 large red bell pepper, thinly sliced
1/2 cup bean sprouts
1/4 cup thinly sliced scallions
1 tablespoon sesame seeds, toasted

1. In a small food processor, combine the soy sauce, ginger, garlic and red pepper flakes; process until the ginger and garlic are very finely chopped.

2. Preheat the broiler and broiler pan. Rub half of the soy sauce mixture over both sides of the steak and broil 4 to 5 inches from the heat for about 5 minutes per side for medium-rare. Transfer the steak to a plate and set aside.

3. Meanwhile, in a small saucepan, combine the corn and water, and bring to a boil over high heat. Reduce the heat to medium, cover and cook until the corn is heated through, 3 to 4 minutes. Drain the corn, cool under cold running water and drain again.

4. Pour the remaining soy sauce mixture into a salad bowl. Mix in the chicken broth and vinegar and any steak juices that have collected on the

plate. Add the drained corn, watercress, bell pepper, bean sprouts and scallions, and toss gently.

5. Carve the steak into thin slices. Sprinkle the salad with the sesame seeds, arrange the sliced steak on top and serve.

Makes 4 servings

Nutrition Information
values are per serving

CALORIES 203	DIETARY FIBER 3.1 G
TOTAL FAT 5.3 G	BETA CAROTENE 2.3 MG
SATURATED FAT 1.5 G	VITAMIN C 75 MG
CHOLESTEROL 52 MG	CALCIUM 80 MG
SODIUM 390 MG	IRON 3.3 MG

Southeast Asian Beef Salad

Fresh green chili pepper enlivens the dressing of this Southeast Asian beef salad that is served on a bed of watercress and spinach. If you can find Thai chili peppers, use them here for a note of authenticity. Be sure not to overcook the beef; it should still be pink in the center for the very best in texture, flavor and color.

DRESSING
2 tablespoons reduced-sodium soy sauce
1 tablespoon plus 1 teaspoon honey
1 tablespoon plus 1 teaspoon rice wine vinegar
1 tablespoon plus 1 teaspoon dry sherry
2 teaspoons Oriental (dark) sesame oil
¾ teaspoon minced fresh green chili pepper
¾ teaspoon minced garlic

SALAD
4 cups (loosely packed) mixed greens: watercress and torn spinach
3 cups (loosely packed) shredded nappa cabbage
2 medium carrots, coarsely grated
1½ cups bean sprouts
¾ pound well-trimmed lean beef sirloin, cut into narrow strips
1 tablespoon cornstarch blended with 2 tablespoons reduced-sodium soy sauce and 1 tablespoon water
2 teaspoons olive oil
¾ cup diagonally sliced scallion pieces (¾ inch long)

1. To Make the Dressing In a small bowl or cup, blend the soy sauce, honey, vinegar, sherry, sesame oil, chili pepper and garlic.

2. For the Salad Line a platter with the greens. At one end, arrange piles of nappa cabbage, carrots and bean sprouts.

3. Place the beef in a medium bowl, add the cornstarch-soy sauce mixture and toss to coat well.

4. In a medium nonstick skillet, warm the oil over medium-high heat until hot but not smoking. Add the beef and stir-fry until medium-rare, 2 to 3 minutes. Add the scallions and stir-fry just until slightly softened, about 30 seconds. Arrange the beef mixture at one end of the platter.

5. Drizzle the dressing over the greens and vegetables and serve.

Makes 4 servings

Nutrition Information
values are per serving

CALORIES 258	DIETARY FIBER 4.6 G
TOTAL FAT 8.8 G	BETA CAROTENE 9.2 MG
SATURATED FAT 2.2 G	VITAMIN C 60 MG
CHOLESTEROL 52 MG	CALCIUM 177 MG
SODIUM 723 MG	IRON 4.9 MG

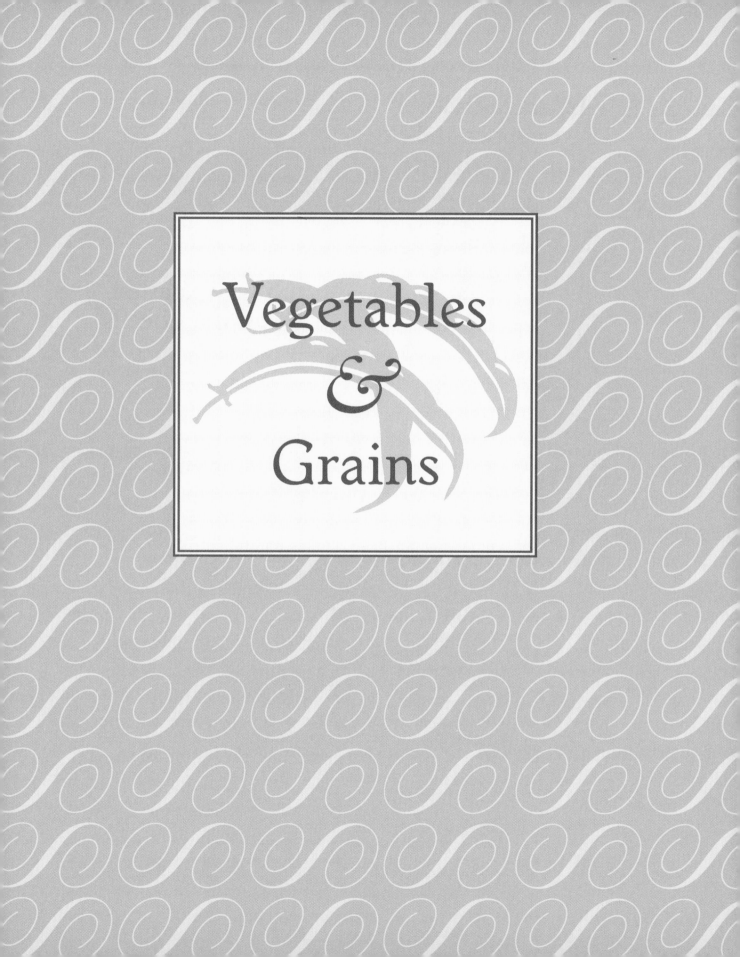

Vegetables & Grains

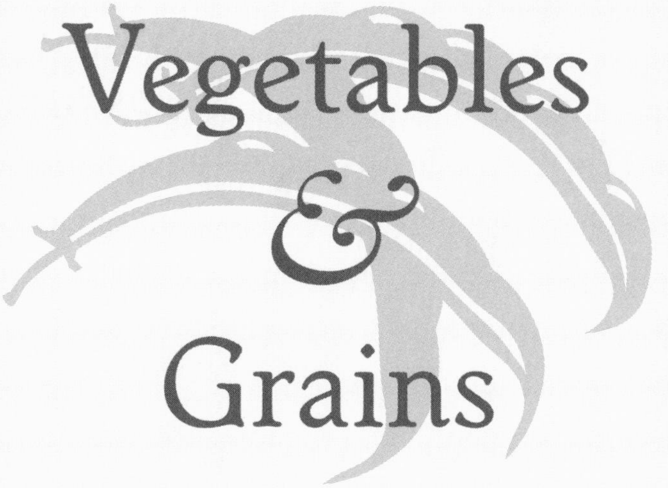

Asparagus with Red Pepper and Lemon Vinaigrette

If you have ever tried Vidalia onions, you know they do taste oniony but very subtly so. Indeed, they are quite sweet, and fans of the Vidalia claim you can eat them out of hand like an apple. If you cannot find Vidalias, look for other sweet onions, such as Maui or Walla Walla.

2 large red bell peppers, diced
½ cup shredded carrot
½ cup peeled, diced cucumber
¼ cup finely chopped sweet onion, such as Vidalia
¼ cup chicken broth, canned or homemade (p. 54)
¼ cup fresh lemon juice
2 tablespoons extra-virgin olive oil
2 teaspoons red wine vinegar
½ teaspoon salt
½ teaspoon freshly ground black pepper
2 pounds asparagus, trimmed

1. In a medium bowl, combine the bell peppers, carrot, cucumber, onion, chicken broth, 2 tablespoons of the lemon juice, the olive oil, vinegar, salt and black pepper. Cover and let stand at room temperature at least 15 minutes to blend the flavors.

2. In a large deep skillet, bring 1 inch of water to a boil over high heat. Add the asparagus and return to a boil; cook until the asparagus are crisp-tender, 3 to 4 minutes. Transfer the asparagus to a bowl of ice water to stop the cooking. When cool, lift from the ice water, pat dry and arrange on a platter.

3. Drizzle the asparagus with the remaining 2 tablespoons lemon juice. Then spoon the red pepper and lemon vinaigrette on top.

Makes 6 servings

Nutrition Information
values are per serving

CALORIES 79	DIETARY FIBER 1.8 G
TOTAL FAT 5.0 G	BETA CAROTENE 3.1 MG
SATURATED FAT .7 G	VITAMIN C 97 MG
CHOLESTEROL 0 MG	CALCIUM 30 MG
SODIUM 228 MG	IRON .8 MG

Orange-Roasted Beets and Greens

You use the entire beet in this beautiful side dish, making this not only cost-efficient but rich in beta carotene (from the greens).

4 pounds beets with tops (about 2½ pounds of beets weighed without the tops)
¾ cup orange juice
3 tablespoons vinegar, preferably raspberry-flavored
2 tablespoons brown sugar
1½ teaspoons fresh lemon juice
¼ teaspoon caraway seeds
Pinch of ground cloves
Pinch of allspice
½ teaspoon cornstarch
2 teaspoons olive oil

1. Preheat the oven to 400°.

2. Separate the tops from the beets. Wash well, trim the fibrous center ribs, coarsely shred, wrap in a towel and refrigerate until ready to use.

3. Wrap each beet in a double layer of foil, making sure they are well sealed. Bake for 1½ to 2 hours (depending on their size), until fork-tender. Remove from the oven and allow to cool.

4. Meanwhile, in a small nonreactive saucepan, combine the orange juice, vinegar, brown sugar, lemon juice, caraway, cloves and allspice. Measure

out 2 tablespoons of the mixture and combine in a small bowl with the cornstarch. Set aside.

5. Bring the remaining mixture to a boil over medium-high heat and cook for 1 minute. Stir the cornstarch mixture into the saucepan and cook until the dressing begins to thicken, about 30 seconds. Remove from the heat and set aside.

6. When the beets are cool enough to handle, peel them and cut into thin slices. Toss with the dressing and let stand at room temperature for at least 30 minutes to meld the flavors.

7. Shortly before serving, warm the oil in a large nonstick skillet over medium-high heat until hot but not smoking. Add the beet greens in batches and cook until wilted; add 1 or 2 tablespoons of water if the skillet gets too dry. Serve the beets on a bed of wilted greens.

Makes 4 servings

Nutrition Information
values are per serving

CALORIES 168	DIETARY FIBER 1.8 G
TOTAL FAT 2.6 G	BETA CAROTENE 4.5 MG
SATURATED FAT .3 G	VITAMIN C 74 MG
CHOLESTEROL 0 MG	CALCIUM 183 MG
SODIUM 369 MG	IRON 5.7 MG

Tex-Mex Broccoli

A simple cheese sauce sparked with the flavors of the Southwest dresses up nutritional broccoli florets here. Serve this as an accompaniment to turkey fajitas with black beans and rice.

1 cup lowfat (1%) milk
1 tablespoon flour
1 teaspoon Dijon mustard
½ teaspoon salt
¼ teaspoon freshly ground black pepper
⅛ teaspoon cayenne pepper
2 ounces pepper jack cheese, shredded
6 cups small broccoli florets

1. In a large saucepan, combine the milk and flour and whisk over medium heat until no lumps remain, about 1 minute.

2. Stir in the mustard, salt, black pepper and cayenne, and cook, stirring frequently, until lightly thickened and no floury taste remains, about 4

SUPER QUICK

Glazed Brussels Sprouts

Working time: 15 minutes Total time: 20 minutes

6 cups Brussels sprouts
2 teaspoons olive oil
1 garlic clove, minced
2 tablespoons sugar
⅓ cup red wine vinegar
3 tablespoons orange juice
½ teaspoon thyme
½ teaspoon salt
¼ teaspoon freshly ground black pepper

1 With a paring knife, make a small X in the stem end of each Brussels sprout. In a large pot of boiling water, cook the sprouts until crisp-tender, about 7 minutes. Drain well.

2 Meanwhile, in a large nonstick skillet, warm the oil over medium heat until hot but not smoking. Add the garlic and cook, stirring, until tender, about 2 minutes. Add the sugar and swirl in the pan until melted, about 2 minutes.

3 Add the vinegar, orange juice, thyme, salt, pepper and the drained sprouts, and continue cooking until the sprouts are richly glazed, about 5 minutes.

Makes 4 servings

Values are per serving:
Calories: 111 Total fat: 2.7 g Saturated fat: .4 g Cholesterol: 0 mg Sodium: 307 mg
Dietary fiber: 7.7 g Beta carotene: .7 mg Vitamin C: 117 mg Calcium: 64 mg Iron: 2.1 mg

minutes. Stir in the pepper jack cheese and remove from the heat.

3. Meanwhile, bring a large pot of water to a boil. Add the broccoli and cook until crisp-tender, about 3 minutes. Drain well and transfer to a serving dish. Pour in the cheese sauce and toss to coat well.

Makes 4 servings

NUTRITION INFORMATION
values are per serving

CALORIES 121	DIETARY FIBER 3.7 G
TOTAL FAT 5.5 G	BETA CAROTENE 1.0 MG
SATURATED FAT 2.9 G	VITAMIN C 75 MG
CHOLESTEROL 17 MG	CALCIUM 222 MG
SODIUM 461 MG	IRON .9 MG

Wilted Cabbage and Red Pepper Salad

If coleslaw is the first thing that comes to mind when you have cabbage on hand, try this simple combination, with its tart dressing, for an appealing, lowfat, high-vitamin C variation.

¼ cup apple cider vinegar
¼ cup water
3 tablespoons sugar
¼ teaspoon celery seed
¼ teaspoon salt
¼ teaspoon freshly ground black pepper
2 teaspoons olive oil
4 cups shredded cabbage
3 large red bell peppers, cut into thin strips
1 medium onion, halved and thinly sliced

1. In a small saucepan, combine the vinegar, water, sugar, celery seed, salt and black pepper. Bring to a boil over high heat, stirring to dissolve the sugar. Reduce the heat to medium-low and simmer for 5 minutes. Remove from the heat.

2. In a very large nonstick saucepan, warm the oil over medium-high heat until hot but not smoking. Add the cabbage, bell peppers and onion, and toss gently to mix. Sauté, tossing the vegetables often, until they begin to soften and cook down, 6 to 7 minutes.

3. Stir in the vinegar mixture, bring to a boil. Cover, reduce the heat to medium-low and cook, tossing occasionally, until the vegetables are very tender, 6 to 8 minutes.

4. Serve warm, at room temperature or chilled.

Makes 4 servings

NUTRITION INFORMATION
values are per serving

CALORIES 112	DIETARY FIBER 3.6 G
TOTAL FAT 2.6 G	BETA CAROTENE 2.6 MG
SATURATED FAT .3 G	VITAMIN C 178 MG
CHOLESTEROL 0 MG	CALCIUM 53 MG
SODIUM 151 MG	IRON 1.0 MG

Carrot-Apple Slaw

This refreshing, yogurt-dressed slaw makes a superb accompaniment to Indian curry or tandoori-baked chicken. Or, serve the slaw as a sort of salsa to top a well-peppered chili con carne.

1 cup plain nonfat yogurt
2 tablespoons dried currants
¼ cup boiling water
2 tablespoons frozen apple juice concentrate
⅛ teaspoon cinnamon (optional)
⅛ teaspoon cumin
⅛ teaspoon freshly ground black pepper
4 large carrots, coarsely shredded

2 medium unpeeled Golden Delicious apples, coarsely shredded

1. Line a small strainer with a paper towel (or line a coffee filter cone with a paper filter) and place over a small bowl. Spoon in the yogurt and let drain for 15 minutes. Discard the whey.

2. Meanwhile, place the currants in a small heatproof bowl or cup and pour the boiling water over them; set aside for 10 minutes to plump, then drain.

3. In a large bowl, combine the thickened yogurt with the apple juice concentrate, cinnamon (if using), cumin and pepper. Add the carrots, apples and drained currants, and toss well.

Makes 4 servings

NUTRITION INFORMATION
values are per serving

CALORIES 143	DIETARY FIBER 5.0 G
TOTAL FAT .6 G	BETA CAROTENE 17 MG
SATURATED FAT .2 G	VITAMIN C 22 MG
CHOLESTEROL 1.1 MG	CALCIUM 151 MG
SODIUM 81 MG	IRON .9 MG

Orange-Glazed Carrots

Note how little it takes—some honey, orange and lemon juices, a dab of butter and hints of spice—to render carrots extraordinary.

4 cups diagonally sliced carrots
2 tablespoons honey
1 tablespoon fresh lemon juice
1 tablespoon frozen orange juice concentrate
2 teaspoons unsalted butter
¼ teaspoon grated orange zest
¼ teaspoon freshly ground black pepper
⅛ teaspoon salt
Large pinch of cinnamon
Large pinch of nutmeg

1. In a large covered skillet, bring 1 inch of water to boil over high heat. Add the carrots and return to a boil, cover and cook, stirring occasionally, until the carrots are tender, 5 to 6 minutes. Reserving 1 tablespoon of the cooking liquid, drain the carrots in a colander.

SUPER QUICK

Carrots and Cucumbers with Sweet Chili Sauce

Working time: 15 minutes Total time: 30 minutes

¼ cup water
3 tablespoons sugar
3 tablespoons rice wine vinegar
1 garlic clove, minced
¼ teaspoon crushed red pepper flakes
¼ teaspoon salt
1 pound carrots, thinly sliced
1 seedless European or hot-house cucumber, halved lengthwise and thinly sliced (about 2½ cups)
¼ cup chopped cilantro
1 tablespoon plus 1 teaspoon fresh lime juice
1 teaspoon Oriental (dark) sesame oil

1 In a small saucepan, combine the water, sugar, vinegar, garlic, red pepper flakes and salt. Bring to a boil over high heat, stirring to dissolve the sugar. Reduce the heat to medium-low and simmer for 10 minutes, stirring occasionally.

2 In a salad bowl, toss together the carrots and cucumber, and add the sugar-vinegar syrup. Add the cilantro, lime juice and sesame oil; cover and chill until serving time.

Makes 4 servings

Values are per serving:
Calories: 108 Total fat: 1.4 g Saturated fat: .2 g Cholesterol: 0 mg Sodium: 179 mg
Dietary fiber: 4.3 g Beta carotene: 19 mg Vitamin C: 16 mg Calcium: 44 mg Iron: .8 mg

2. Wipe the skillet dry. Add the reserved cooking liquid, the honey, lemon juice, orange juice concentrate, butter, orange zest, pepper, salt, cinnamon and nutmeg, and place over medium heat. Cook the mixture, stirring, until heated through.

3. Add the carrots and toss until glazed and heated through. Serve hot.

Makes 4 servings

NUTRITION INFORMATION
values are per serving

CALORIES 105	DIETARY FIBER 3.6 G
TOTAL FAT 2.1 G	BETA CAROTENE 19 MG
SATURATED FAT 1.2 G	VITAMIN C 18 MG
CHOLESTEROL 5.2 MG	CALCIUM 34 MG
SODIUM 109 MG	IRON .6 MG

Sweet and Savory Carrots

Accompany roasted meats or poultry with this flavorful one-pot carrot and potato stew enlivened with a hint of brandy and sweet prunes.

1½ teaspoons vegetable oil
1 large onion, diced
4 garlic cloves, minced
¾ pound all-purpose potatoes, peeled and cut into 1-inch dice
3 large carrots, thinly sliced
¾ cup water
1 teaspoon grated orange zest
⅓ cup orange juice
2 tablespoons brandy
½ cup pitted prunes, coarsely chopped
½ teaspoon marjoram
¼ teaspoon salt
¼ teaspoon freshly ground black pepper
⅛ teaspoon cayenne pepper

1. In a large saucepan or Dutch oven, warm the oil over low heat. Add the onion and garlic, cover and cook, stirring frequently, until the onion is golden, about 10 minutes.

2. Add the potatoes and carrots, stir to coat, cover and cook until the potatoes and carrots begin to color, about 5 minutes.

3. Increase the heat to medium, stir in the water, orange zest, orange juice and brandy, and bring to a boil. Add the prunes, marjoram, salt, black pepper and cayenne. Cover and simmer until the vegetables are tender, about 15 minutes. Serve hot.

Makes 4 servings

NUTRITION INFORMATION
values are per serving

CALORIES 191	DIETARY FIBER 5.8 G
TOTAL FAT 2.1 G	BETA CAROTENE 13 MG
SATURATED FAT .3 G	VITAMIN C 34 MG
CHOLESTEROL 0 MG	CALCIUM 57 MG
SODIUM 168 MG	IRON 1.6 MG

Sautéed Peppers with Garlic and Balsamic Vinegar

We have Italy to thank for the creation of balsamic vinegar, which here adds its singular aroma to bell peppers. The more aged the vinegar is, the better, more rounded, its flavor.

4 garlic cloves, thinly sliced
1½ teaspoons extra-virgin olive oil
3 large red bell peppers, cut into ½-inch-wide strips
1 large green bell pepper, cut into ½-inch-wide strips
1 teaspoon sugar
¼ teaspoon salt

¼ teaspoon freshly ground black pepper
3 tablespoons chicken broth, canned or homemade (p. 54)
1 tablespoon balsamic vinegar
1 tablespoon chopped fresh oregano (optional)

1. In a large deep skillet, combine the garlic and olive oil. Place over medium-high heat and sauté, stirring constantly, until the garlic is golden brown, 2 to 3 minutes.

2. Add the bell peppers and sprinkle with the sugar, salt and black pepper. Toss to coat well, then add the chicken broth and bring to a boil. Reduce the heat to medium-low, cover and cook until the peppers are tender, 10 to 15 minutes.

3. Add the vinegar and simmer, uncovered, until the peppers are glazed, about 1 minute. Stir in the oregano (if using) and serve.

Makes 4 servings

Nutrition Information
values are per serving

CALORIES 53	DIETARY FIBER 1.6 G
TOTAL FAT 2.0 G	BETA CAROTENE 2.7 MG
SATURATED FAT .3 G	VITAMIN C 166 MG
CHOLESTEROL 0 MG	CALCIUM 16 MG
SODIUM 184 MG	IRON .6 MG

Maple-Glazed Sweet Potatoes

This sweet potato and dried fruit side dish makes a flavorful and elegant accompaniment to the Thanksgiving turkey and, better yet, can be prepared up to step 5 in advance.

3 pounds sweet potatoes, peeled and cut into 1-inch chunks
½ cup diced dried apricots
¼ cup diced prunes
½ cup apricot nectar
½ cup maple syrup
1 tablespoon fresh lemon juice
1 tablespoon unsalted butter
½ teaspoon cinnamon
½ teaspoon freshly ground black pepper
¼ teaspoon salt

1. Place the sweet potatoes in a large saucepan with water to cover. Cover and bring to a boil over high heat. Reduce the heat to medium and cook until fork-tender, 8 to 10 minutes. Drain in a colander and rinse gently under cold running water.

2. Preheat the oven to 400°. Spray a 7-by-11-inch baking pan with nonstick cooking spray.

3. Place the sweet potatoes in the prepared baking pan and sprinkle the diced apricots and prunes on top.

4. In a small saucepan, combine the apricot nectar, maple syrup, lemon juice, butter, cinnamon, pepper and salt. Bring just to a simmer over high heat, stirring to blend. Pour the mixture evenly over the sweet potatoes and fruit.

5. Cover the baking pan with foil and bake for 30 minutes, basting with the juices 2 or 3 times.

6. Uncover and bake for 5 to 10 minutes longer, basting 2 or 3 times, until the sweet potatoes are glazed.

Makes 8 servings

Nutrition Information
values are per serving

CALORIES 235	DIETARY FIBER 4.8 G
TOTAL FAT 2.0 G	BETA CAROTENE 15 MG
SATURATED FAT 1.0 G	VITAMIN C 38 MG
CHOLESTEROL 3.9 MG	CALCIUM 51 MG
SODIUM 87 MG	IRON 1.6 MG

Lacy Broiled Sweet Potatoes

These lacy broiled sweet potatoes go superbly with roasted meats and even grilled fish. For a colorful variation, use half sweet potatoes and half white. You could also vary the seasoning used: In place of the cumin, try about ½ teaspoon minced rosemary or crumbled tarragon.

1¼ pounds sweet potatoes, unpeeled
2 teaspoons olive oil
1 small garlic clove, minced
1 teaspoon cumin
½ teaspoon salt
¼ teaspoon freshly ground black pepper
¼ cup plus 2 tablespoons grated Parmesan cheese
1 tablespoon minced parsley or cilantro

1. Preheat the oven to 375°.

2. Meanwhile, in a food processor fitted with the largest shredding blade (or on the largest holes of a handheld box-style grater), shred the sweet potatoes.

3. In a large bowl, stir together the oil, garlic, cumin, salt and pepper. Add the shredded potatoes and toss to coat the potatoes thoroughly with oil.

4. Spread the potatoes in an even layer on two 9-by-13-inch nonstick baking sheets (if you use another size baking sheet, be sure to make the layer of potatoes as thin as possible).

5. Bake the sweet potatoes until just cooked through, about 10 minutes. Increase the oven temperature to broil. Combine the sweet potatoes on one baking sheet, spreading to make an even layer. Sprinkle with the Parmesan and broil 4 inches from the heat for about 2 minutes, or until golden brown. Sprinkle with the parsley and serve hot.

Makes 4 servings

NUTRITION INFORMATION
values are per serving

CALORIES 206	DIETARY FIBER 4.3 G
TOTAL FAT 5.0 G	BETA CAROTENE 17 MG
SATURATED FAT 1.8 G	VITAMIN C 33 MG
CHOLESTEROL 5.9 MG	CALCIUM 144 MG
SODIUM 433 MG	IRON 1.3 MG

SUPER QUICK

Cauliflower with Parsley-Mustard Dressing

Working time: 10 minutes Total time: 15 minutes

2 garlic cloves, peeled
2 tablespoons red wine vinegar
1 teaspoon anchovy paste
1 teaspoon Dijon mustard
1 teaspoon extra-virgin olive oil
1 head cauliflower (1¼ pounds), cut into florets
1 large red bell pepper, cut into slivers
3 tablespoons chopped parsley

1 In a small saucepan of boiling water, blanch the garlic for 2 minutes. When cool enough to handle, mince and then transfer to a large mixing bowl. Add the vinegar, anchovy paste and mustard; mix well to combine. Whisk in the olive oil.

2 Add the cauliflower, bell pepper and parsley, and mix well. Cover and refrigerate until serving time.

Makes 4 servings

Values are per serving:
Calories: 39 Total fat: 1.5 g Saturated fat: .2 g Cholesterol: .8 mg Sodium: 103 mg
Dietary fiber: 1.9 g Beta carotene: 1.0 mg Vitamin C: 90 mg Calcium: 28 mg Iron: .7 mg

Parmesan-Roasted Sweet Potato Skins

After making these irresistible sweet potato skins, you will have the scooped-out flesh of two pounds of sweet potatoes left over. You can make whipped sweet potatoes or glazed mashed sweet potatoes, or you can use them to make Glazed Chocolate Sweet Potato Cake (page 240).

2 pounds small sweet potatoes
2 ounces grated Parmesan cheese
3 tablespoons chopped parsley
2 garlic cloves, minced
½ teaspoon oregano
½ teaspoon rosemary, crumbled
¼ teaspoon salt
¼ teaspoon freshly ground black pepper

1. Preheat the oven to 400°.

2. If the potatoes are not small, halve them lengthwise to bake. Prick the sweet potatoes, place on a baking sheet and bake for about 35 to 45 minutes, or until they are tender but not mushy. Remove from the oven and set on a rack to cool. Increase the oven temperature to broil.

3. Meanwhile, in a medium bowl, combine the Parmesan, parsley, garlic, oregano, rosemary, salt and pepper.

4. When the potatoes are cool enough to handle, halve them lengthwise. Scoop the sweet potato flesh out of the skins, leaving a wall ¼ inch thick. (Reserve the scooped out flesh for another use.) Cut each sweet potato shell lengthwise into ½-inch-wide wedges.

5. Add the skins to the herbed Parmesan mixture and gently toss to combine. Place the sweet potato skins on a baking sheet and broil 4 to 5 inches from the heat for 4 to 6 minutes, or until the cheese is melted and bubbly. Serve hot.

Makes 6 servings

Nutrition Information
values are per serving

CALORIES 99	DIETARY FIBER 1.0 G
TOTAL FAT 2.9 G	BETA CAROTENE 6.8 MG
SATURATED FAT 1.8 G	VITAMIN C 15 MG
CHOLESTEROL 7.5 MG	CALCIUM 153 MG
SODIUM 272 MG	IRON .5 MG

Curried Sweet Potato Salad

Instead of cups of mayonnaise and white potatoes, this potato salad features sweet potatoes, pecans and a spicy-sweet curried dressing.

1½ pounds sweet potatoes
¼ cup plain nonfat yogurt
2 tablespoons reduced-calorie mayonnaise
2 tablespoons mango chutney, finely chopped
1 tablespoon frozen orange juice concentrate, thawed
1 to 1½ teaspoons curry powder, to taste
½ teaspoon cumin
½ teaspoon freshly ground black pepper
⅛ teaspoon salt
1 cup diced celery
1 tablespoon coarsely chopped pecans, toasted

1. Place the sweet potatoes in a large saucepan and add cold water to cover. Cover and bring to a boil over high heat. Reduce the heat to medium-low and simmer until the potatoes are fork-tender, 25 to 35 minutes. Drain in a colander and rinse under cold running water. Let stand until cool enough to handle.

2. In a salad bowl, blend the yogurt, mayonnaise, chutney, orange juice concentrate, curry powder, cumin, pepper and salt.

3. Peel the sweet potatoes and cut into ½-inch

chunks. Add to the dressing along with the celery and toss gently until well coated. Sprinkle with the pecans and serve.

Makes 4 servings

NUTRITION INFORMATION
values are per serving

CALORIES 208	DIETARY FIBER 4.6 G
TOTAL FAT 3.7 G	BETA CAROTENE 15 MG
SATURATED FAT .7 G	VITAMIN C 36 MG
CHOLESTEROL 2.8 MG	CALCIUM 76 MG
SODIUM 252 MG	IRON 1.3 MG

Mashed Root Vegetables

Mash these root vegetables as you would potatoes: Either smooth or lumpy, they are absolutely delicious.

1 pound all-purpose potatoes, peeled and cut into 1-inch chunks
½ pound sweet potatoes, peeled and cut into 1-inch chunks
½ pound carrots, peeled and cut into 1-inch chunks
½ pound white turnips, peeled and cut into 1-inch chunks
½ cup chicken broth, canned or homemade (p. 54)
2 tablespoons skim milk
2 tablespoons light sour cream
1 tablespoon grated Parmesan cheese
½ teaspoon freshly ground black pepper
¼ teaspoon salt
2 tablespoons thinly sliced scallions

1. Place the all-purpose potatoes, sweet potatoes, carrots and turnips in a large saucepan. Add the chicken broth and cold water to cover by 1 inch. Cover and bring to a boil over high heat, reduce the heat to medium-low and simmer until the vegetables are fork-tender, 15 to 20 minutes. Drain in a colander and return to the cooking pot.

2. Mash the vegetables with the milk and stir in the sour cream, Parmesan, pepper and salt. Transfer to a serving dish and sprinkle with the scallions.

Makes 4 servings

NUTRITION INFORMATION
values are per serving

CALORIES 169	DIETARY FIBER 5.2 G
TOTAL FAT 1.8 G	BETA CAROTENE 14 MG
SATURATED FAT .8 G	VITAMIN C 41 MG
CHOLESTEROL 3.6 MG	CALCIUM 74 MG
SODIUM 284 MG	IRON 1.4 MG

Double-Baked Potatoes with Salsa

Twice-baked potatoes are a great favorite, and here the potato-and-cheese-filled halves are made extra-special (and high in vitamin C) by a topping of fresh tomato salsa.

2 large baking potatoes (8 ounces each)
¼ cup lowfat (1%) cottage cheese
¼ cup lowfat (1.5%) buttermilk
2 tablespoons Neufchâtel cream cheese
2 scallions, minced
1 tablespoon minced fresh jalapeño pepper
¼ teaspoon freshly ground black pepper
¾ pound tomatoes, diced
1 small red bell pepper, diced
⅓ cup minced red onion
3 tablespoons chopped cilantro
1 tablespoon red wine vinegar
½ teaspoon sugar
¼ teaspoon salt

1. Preheat the oven to 450°. Prick the potatoes in several places. Bake for about 45 minutes, or until tender. When cool enough to handle, halve the potatoes lengthwise. With a fork, fluff the potato flesh inside and transfer to a bowl, leaving enough potato attached to the skin to form a sturdy shell (about ⅛ inch).

2. Add the cottage cheese, buttermilk, cream cheese, scallions, 1½ teaspoons of the jalapeño pepper and the black pepper. Mix well to combine, then spoon into the potato shells. Return to the oven and bake until the stuffing is piping hot, about 20 minutes.

3. Meanwhile, in a medium bowl, mix together the tomatoes, bell pepper, red onion, cilantro, vinegar, sugar, salt and the remaining 1½ teaspoons jalapeño pepper. Spoon the salsa over the potatoes and serve.

Makes 4 servings

NUTRITION INFORMATION
values are per serving

CALORIES 151	DIETARY FIBER 3.4 G
TOTAL FAT 2.3 G	BETA CAROTENE .9 MG
SATURATED FAT 1.3 G	VITAMIN C 62 MG
CHOLESTEROL 6.6 MG	CALCIUM 57 MG
SODIUM 254 MG	IRON 1.7 MG

Spinach and Potatoes with Hot Bacon Dressing

Be sure to serve this wilted salad as soon as you have dressed it, before the spinach wilts completely and while the dressing is just seeping into the potatoes.

1½ pounds all-purpose potatoes, peeled and cut into 1-inch chunks
1 tablespoon olive oil
1 ounce Canadian bacon, minced
11 cups (loosely packed) shredded stemmed spinach
3 large shallots, minced (about ½ cup)
1 tablespoon flour
⅔ cup water
¼ cup cider vinegar
1 tablespoon sugar
½ teaspoon freshly ground black pepper
2 tablespoons Dijon mustard

SUPER QUICK

Wilted Spinach and Kale

Working time: 15 minutes Total time: 20 minutes

2 teaspoons olive oil
3 garlic cloves, slivered
8 cups (loosely packed) torn kale
12 cups (loosely packed) torn spinach leaves
2 teaspoons sugar
1 teaspoon marjoram
¼ teaspoon salt
⅛ teaspoon cayenne pepper
2 teaspoons fresh lemon juice

1 In a very large nonstick skillet or Dutch oven, warm the oil over low heat. Add the garlic and cook until soft, about 3 minutes.

2 Increase the heat to medium and add the kale. Cover and cook, stirring occasionally, until the kale has softened, about 4 minutes.

3 Stir in the spinach, sprinkle with the sugar, marjoram, salt and cayenne, and cook, uncovered, until the spinach has wilted, about 3 minutes longer.

4 Sprinkle the lemon juice over and serve.

Makes 4 servings

Values are per serving:
Calories: 164 Total fat: 4.2 g Saturated fat: .6 g Cholesterol: 0 mg Sodium: 375 mg
Dietary fiber: 17 g Beta carotene: 18 mg Vitamin C: 265 mg Calcium: 445 mg Iron: 8.7 mg

1. In a large pot of boiling water, cook the potatoes until tender, about 10 minutes. Drain well and transfer to a large mixing bowl.

2. In a small nonstick skillet, warm the oil over medium heat until hot but not smoking. Add the bacon and cook until crisp, about 3 minutes. Remove with a slotted spoon and transfer to the bowl with the potatoes. Add the spinach to the bowl.

3. Add the shallots to the skillet and cook, stirring frequently, until tender, about 4 minutes. Whisk in the flour until blended. Add the water, vinegar, sugar and pepper, stirring to combine. Stir in the mustard. Bring to a boil and cook, stirring, until lightly thickened, about 1 minute.

4. Pour the hot dressing over the potatoes and spinach, mix well and serve.

Makes 4 servings

NUTRITION INFORMATION
values are per serving

CALORIES 230	DIETARY FIBER 7.3 G
TOTAL FAT 5.2 G	BETA CAROTENE 7.8 MG
SATURATED FAT .7 G	VITAMIN C 83 MG
CHOLESTEROL 3.5 MG	CALCIUM 210 MG
SODIUM 487 MG	IRON 6.7 MG

Baked Butternut Squash

Very little is asked of the cook in this recipe, but the rewards, both gustatory and nutritional, are superb. Just note the amount of fat.

2 small butternut squash (1¼ pounds each), halved lengthwise and seeded
⅓ cup orange juice
2 tablespoons apricot all-fruit spread
2 garlic cloves, minced
3 tablespoons chopped parsley
1 teaspoon olive oil
½ teaspoon salt
¼ teaspoon freshly ground black pepper

1. Preheat the oven to 425°. Cut a small piece off the bottom of each squash half so that it will sit in the pan.

2. In a small bowl, stir together the orange juice, apricot fruit spread, garlic, parsley, olive oil, salt and pepper. Spoon the mixture into the hollow of each squash half, cover with aluminum foil and bake until tender, about 45 minutes.

Makes 4 servings

NUTRITION INFORMATION
values are per serving

CALORIES 151	DIETARY FIBER .2 G
TOTAL FAT 1.4 G	BETA CAROTENE 11 MG
SATURATED FAT .2 G	VITAMIN C 61 MG
CHOLESTEROL 0 MG	CALCIUM 125 MG
SODIUM 285 MG	IRON 1.9 MG

Sautéed Winter Squash

Of the commonly available varieties of winter squash, butternut and Hubbard have the greatest amount of beta carotene.

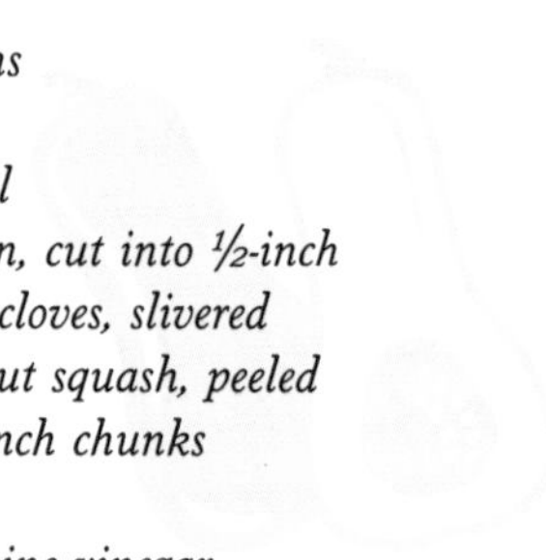

⅓ cup golden raisins
½ cup hot water
2 teaspoons olive oil
1 medium red onion, cut into ½-inch chunks 3 garlic cloves, slivered
1½ pounds butternut squash, peeled and cut into 1-inch chunks
¼ cup white wine
2 tablespoons red wine vinegar
1 tablespoon sugar

1. In a small bowl, combine the raisins and hot water; set aside to soften.

2. In a large nonstick skillet, warm the oil over medium heat until hot but not smoking. Add the onion and garlic, and cook, stirring frequently, until the onion has colored, about 7 minutes.

3. Add the squash and cook, stirring often, until the squash begins to color, about 5 minutes.

4. Add the raisins and their soaking liquid, the wine, vinegar and sugar. Bring to a simmer, cover and cook until the vegetables are tender, about 10 minutes.

Makes 4 servings

Nutrition Information
values are per serving

CALORIES 164	DIETARY FIBER 1.3 G
TOTAL FAT 2.5 G	BETA CAROTENE 6.7 MG
SATURATED FAT .3 G	VITAMIN C 36 MG
CHOLESTEROL 0 MG	CALCIUM 93 MG
SODIUM 13 MG	IRON 1.5 MG

Vegetable Slaw with Lemon-Mustard Dressing

All the vegetables for this tasty slaw can be prepared in a food processor fitted with the shredding blade. Just be sure to shred them separately and to press any excess juice from the shredded squash as it could water down the dressing.

3 cups small broccoli florets
3 tablespoons fresh lemon juice
3 tablespoons nonfat mayonnaise
3 tablespoons light sour cream
2 tablespoons plain nonfat yogurt
2 teaspoons grainy Dijon mustard
½ teaspoon freshly ground black pepper
4 medium carrots, shredded
1 medium yellow summer squash, shredded
1 medium zucchini, shredded

1. In a large skillet, bring 1 inch of water to a boil over high heat. Add the broccoli and return to a boil. Cook, stirring occasionally, until crisp-tender, 3 to 4 minutes. Drain in a colander and cool under cold running water.

2. In a salad bowl, whisk together the lemon juice, mayonnaise, sour cream, yogurt, mustard and pepper. Add the broccoli, carrots, yellow squash and zucchini, and toss to coat well.

Makes 4 servings

Nutrition Information
values are per serving

CALORIES 111	DIETARY FIBER 6.4 G
TOTAL FAT 2.2 G	BETA CAROTENE 13 MG
SATURATED FAT .8 G	VITAMIN C 89 MG
CHOLESTEROL 3.9 MG	CALCIUM 93 MG
SODIUM 210 MG	IRON 1.5 MG

Vegetable-Topped Baked Grits

In the South, cooked grits (very coarse cornmeal) are frequently served for breakfast. Their comforting texture, though, is especially appealing in this savory vegetable-topped side dish—a fine accompaniment to simple grilled poultry.

3⅓ cups water
⅔ cup grits
¾ teaspoon salt
2 teaspoons olive oil
1 large red onion, diced
3 garlic cloves, minced
1 large red bell pepper, diced

1 small unpeeled eggplant (8 ounces), cut into ½-inch cubes
1 medium zucchini, halved lengthwise and thinly sliced crosswise
One 8-ounce can no-salt-added tomato sauce
1 tablespoon red wine vinegar
¼ teaspoon freshly ground black pepper
2 tablespoons chopped fresh dill

1. In a medium saucepan, bring 3 cups of the water to a boil. Slowly stir in the grits and ½ teaspoon of the salt, stirring until the grits are thick and creamy, about 10 minutes. Spoon into a 9-inch square baking dish and set aside.

2. In a large nonstick skillet, warm the oil over medium heat until hot but not smoking. Add the onion and garlic, and cook, stirring occasionally, until the onion is soft, about 7 minutes.

3. Preheat the oven to 400°.

4. Add the bell pepper to the skillet and cook, stirring frequently, until almost tender, about 4 minutes. Stir in the eggplant, toss to coat and add the remaining ⅓ cup water and ¼ teaspoon salt. Cover and cook, stirring occasionally, until the eggplant is tender, about 7 minutes.

5. Stir in the zucchini, mixing well, and add the tomato sauce, vinegar, black pepper and dill. Cook, stirring occasionally, until the sauce is lightly thickened and the zucchini is tender, about 5 minutes.

6. Spoon the sauce over the grits, cover with foil and bake until the grits are piping hot, about 10 minutes.

Makes 4 servings

Nutrition Information
values are per serving

CALORIES 192	DIETARY FIBER 3.7 G
TOTAL FAT 3.0 G	BETA CAROTENE 1.4 MG
SATURATED FAT .3 G	VITAMIN C 68 MG
CHOLESTEROL 0 MG	CALCIUM 60 MG
SODIUM 436 MG	IRON 2.6 MG

Lentil Salad with Orange-Balsamic Dressing

You will find a minimum amount of oil but a maximum amount of flavor in this orange-scented lentil and spinach salad.

1 cup lentils, preferably green
¼ teaspoon salt
¼ cup frozen orange juice concentrate, thawed
2 tablespoons balsamic vinegar
1 tablespoon Dijon mustard
1½ teaspoons olive oil
¼ teaspoon freshly ground black pepper
⅛ teaspoon allspice
1 large carrot, finely diced
3 tablespoons minced scallion
4 cups (loosely packed) torn spinach leaves
4 teaspoons chopped pecans, toasted

1. In a saucepan, bring 3 cups of water to a boil over high heat. Add the lentils and ⅛ teaspoon of the salt, and cook until the lentils are tender but still hold their shape, about 25 minutes. Drain.

2. In a large mixing bowl, whisk together the orange juice concentrate, balsamic vinegar, mustard, olive oil, pepper, allspice and remaining ⅛ teaspoon salt.

3. Stir in the drained lentils, carrot and scallion. Add the spinach, tossing well to coat. Serve the salad sprinkled with the pecans.

Makes 4 servings

Nutrition Information
values are per serving

CALORIES 254	DIETARY FIBER 8.5 G
TOTAL FAT 4.2 G	BETA CAROTENE 7.1 MG
SATURATED FAT .4 G	VITAMIN C 50 MG
CHOLESTEROL 0 MG	CALCIUM 112 MG
SODIUM 318 MG	IRON 6.5 MG

White Bean and Tomato Salad with Roasted Garlic

Italian cooks have long understood the appetizing affinity between white beans and tomatoes. Here they are combined with fresh herbs and the mellowness of roasted garlic for a marvelous side dish to grilled fish or poultry.

1 medium head of garlic (about 3 ounces)
1½ teaspoons olive oil
¼ cup minced shallots
¾ teaspoon sage
3 cups diced plum tomatoes
⅓ cup diced celery
⅓ cup diced red onion
3 tablespoons chopped parsley
3 tablespoons minced chives
2 tablespoons fresh lemon juice
1 tablespoon balsamic vinegar
One 19-ounce can white beans, rinsed and drained

1. Preheat the oven to 375°. Wrap the garlic in aluminum foil, place on a baking sheet and bake until the garlic is soft, about 30 minutes. When cool enough to handle, unwrap, cut off the stem end and squeeze out the soft garlic that is inside. Set aside.

2. In a small nonstick skillet, warm the oil over low heat. Add the shallots and cook, stirring frequently, until the shallots are soft, about 3 minutes. Add the sage, stirring to coat.

3. Remove from the heat and transfer to a large bowl. Stir in the tomatoes, celery, onion, parsley, chives, lemon juice, vinegar and roasted garlic. Add the white beans and toss gently to combine.

Makes 4 servings

Nutrition Information
values are per serving

CALORIES 164	DIETARY FIBER 6.1 G
TOTAL FAT 2.9 G	BETA CAROTENE .7 MG
SATURATED FAT .3 G	VITAMIN C 43 MG
CHOLESTEROL 0 MG	CALCIUM 86 MG
SODIUM 245 MG	IRON 2.8 MG

Oven-Roasted Ratatouille

Made with very little oil and roasted instead of sautéed, this version of the classic Provençale dish is nonetheless filled with the exceptional and lusty flavors of the more traditional preparation.

1 teaspoon olive oil
4 garlic cloves, peeled
2 sprigs of fresh rosemary
1 strip (3 by ½ inch) orange zest
1 large onion, cut into 2-inch chunks
2 large red bell peppers, cut into 2-inch pieces
1 medium eggplant (12 ounces), peeled and cut into ½-inch chunks
1 medium zucchini, cut into 1½-inch-long pieces
One 8-ounce can no-salt-added tomato sauce
½ teaspoon salt
2 cups chopped plum tomatoes
¼ cup orange juice
⅓ cup chopped fresh basil

1. Preheat the oven to 400°. In a large baking pan, combine the oil, garlic, rosemary and orange zest. Place in the oven and cook until the oil is hot, about 5 minutes.

2. Add the onion, bell peppers, eggplant and zucchini, stirring to combine. Cover, return to the oven and cook, stirring occasionally, until the vegetables begin to soften, about 10 minutes.

3. Uncover, stir in the tomato sauce and salt. Return to the oven and cook, uncovered, until the vegetables are tender, about 7 minutes.

4. Remove from the oven, stir in the tomatoes, orange juice and basil. Discard the rosemary and orange zest.

Makes 4 servings

NUTRITION INFORMATION
values are per serving

CALORIES 140	DIETARY FIBER 5.9 G
TOTAL FAT 2.1 G	BETA CAROTENE 2.7 MG
SATURATED FAT .2 G	VITAMIN C 140 MG
CHOLESTEROL 0 MG	CALCIUM 119 MG
SODIUM 304 MG	IRON 2.9 MG

Sweet Red Pepper Rice

The addition of red bell peppers, red pepper flakes and paprika not only add interest to this side dish, they add vitamin C as well.

2 teaspoons olive oil
1 large onion, minced
3 cloves garlic, minced
1 teaspoon paprika
¼ teaspoon crushed red pepper flakes
2 large red bell peppers, finely diced
1 cup rice
2 cups water
¾ teaspoon grated orange zest
½ teaspoon salt
¼ cup finely chopped cilantro
2 tablespoons orange juice

1. In a large saucepan, warm the oil over low heat. Add the onion and cook, stirring frequently, until the onion has softened, about 7 minutes. Add the garlic, paprika and red pepper flakes, and stir to coat.

2. Stir in the bell peppers and cook, stirring frequently, until the peppers have softened, about 5 minutes.

3. Add the rice and stir to coat. Add the water, orange zest and salt. Bring to a boil, reduce to a simmer, cover and cook until the rice is tender and creamy, about 17 minutes.

4. Stir in the cilantro and cook until well combines, about 1 minute. Remove from the heat, stir in the orange juice and serve.

Makes 4 servings

NUTRITION INFORMATION
values are per serving

CALORIES 233	DIETARY FIBER 2.2 G
TOTAL FAT 2.8 G	BETA CAROTENE 2.0 MG
SATURATED FAT .4 G	VITAMIN C 103 MG
CHOLESTEROL 0 MG	CALCIUM 38 MG
SODIUM 279 MG	IRON 2.5 MG

Lemony Rice Pilaf with Raisins and Carrots

Serve this fragrant pilaf with grilled fish or shellfish. Or, once cooked and cooled, use it as a filling for red bell peppers.

¾ cup chicken broth diluted with 1¾ cups water, or 2½ cups Homemade Chicken Broth (p. 54)
1 teaspoon olive oil
1 cup shredded carrots
½ cup thinly sliced scallions
1¼ cups rice
¼ cup golden raisins
½ teaspoon freshly ground black pepper
⅛ teaspoon cinnamon
Pinch of ground cardamom (optional)
1½ teaspoons grated lemon zest
2 tablespoons fresh lemon juice

1. In a small saucepan, bring the diluted chicken broth to a boil; set aside.

2. In a medium nonstick saucepan, warm the oil over medium heat. Stir in the carrots and scallions, and sauté, stirring frequently, until the vegetables are tender, 2 to 3 minutes.

3. Add the rice, raisins, pepper, cinnamon and cardamom (if using), and stir to mix. Pour in the broth mixture and bring to a boil. Reduce the heat to low, cover and simmer until the rice is tender and the liquid absorbed, 20 to 25 minutes.

4. Stir the lemon zest and juice into the rice and let stand for 5 minutes before serving.

Makes 4 servings

Nutrition Information
values are per serving

CALORIES 272	DIETARY FIBER 2.4 G
TOTAL FAT 1.9 G	BETA CAROTENE 4.7 MG
SATURATED FAT .3 G	VITAMIN C 9.7 MG
CHOLESTEROL 0 MG	CALCIUM 43 MG
SODIUM 201 MG	IRON 3.1 MG

Toasted Couscous Pumpkin Risotto

The influences of several cuisines combine in this unique risotto made from quick-cooking couscous flavored with the sweetness of pumpkin and the richness of Parmesan.

PEPPER PURÉE

1 garlic clove, peeled
1 cup bottled roasted red peppers, rinsed and drained

RISOTTO

1½ cups couscous
1 large onion, minced
3 garlic cloves, minced
1 teaspoon sugar
1⅓ cups canned chicken broth diluted with 2 cups water, or 3⅓ cups Homemade Chicken Broth (p. 54)
½ cup sherry
¾ cup canned solid-pack pumpkin purée
2 tablespoons grated Parmesan cheese
¼ teaspoon freshly ground black pepper
1½ teaspoons unsalted butter

1. Make the Pepper Purée In a small saucepan of boiling water, blanch the garlic for 2 minutes. Transfer to a food processor, add the roasted peppers and process to a smooth purée. Set aside.

2. For the Risotto In a large skillet, heat the couscous over medium heat, stirring frequently, until golden, about 3 minutes. Remove the skillet from the heat.

3. In a large saucepan, combine the onion, garlic and sugar with ½ cup of the diluted broth. Cook over medium heat, stirring frequently, until the onion is wilted, about 7 minutes. Stir in the couscous and sherry, and cook until the sherry has evaporated, about 1 minute.

4. Gradually add the remaining diluted broth to the saucepan, ½ cup at a time, allowing the couscous to absorb all the liquid before adding any more. Continue cooking and adding liquid until all the liquid has been added and the couscous is creamy.

5. Stir in the pumpkin, Parmesan and black pepper, and cook until heated through, about 3 minutes. Stir in the butter. Serve topped with the pepper purée.

Makes 4 servings

Nutrition Information
values are per serving

CALORIES 364	DIETARY FIBER 1.8 G
TOTAL FAT 3.4 G	BETA CAROTENE 6.8 MG
SATURATED FAT 1.5 G	VITAMIN C 47 MG
CHOLESTEROL 5.9 MG	CALCIUM 89 MG
SODIUM 396 MG	IRON 2.6 MG

Desserts

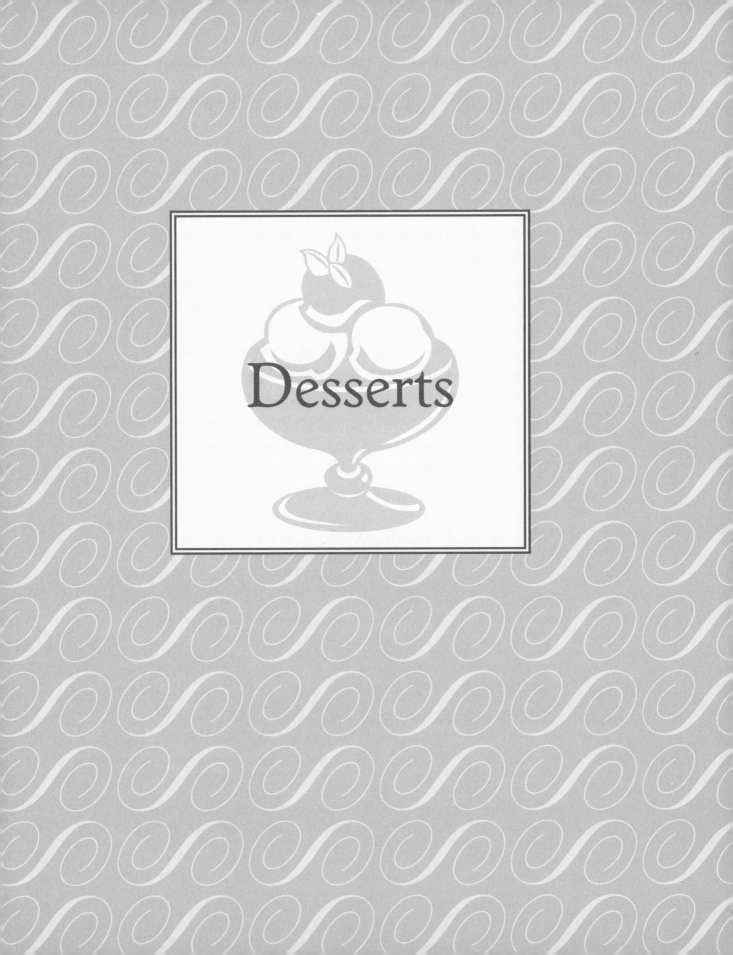

Fresh and Dried Fruit Compote

Serve this marvelous fruit compote for dessert or for a weekend brunch. Be sure to add the fresh fruits just before serving.

1 cup dried peaches, halved
1 cup dried apricots
1 cup pitted prunes, halved
Half a lemon–sliced, seeds removed and slices cut into half-moons
2 cups apple juice
1 cup water
¼ cup (packed) dark brown sugar
1 cinnamon stick
3 whole allspice berries
3 whole cloves
3 navel oranges
1 mango, peeled and cut into chunks

1. In a large nonstick saucepan, combine the dried fruit, lemon slices, apple juice, water, brown sugar, cinnamon stick, allspice and cloves. Stir to dissolve the sugar. Cover and bring to a boil over high heat. Reduce the heat to medium-low and simmer, stirring occasionally, until the fruit is very soft, 15 to 20 minutes. Remove from the heat and pour the dried fruit mixture into a serving bowl. Cool to warm (or place in the freezer to quick-chill), then remove the cinnamon stick, allspice berries and cloves.

2. Meanwhile, with a knife, remove the peel and white pith from the oranges. Working over a bowl, cut out the sections from between the membranes, letting the sections drop into the bowl, squeeze the juice from the membranes over the sections.

3. Stir the orange sections and juice and the mango into the fruit mixture. Serve at room temperature or lightly chilled.

Makes 8 servings

NUTRITION INFORMATION
values are per serving

CALORIES 232	DIETARY FIBER 5.9 G
TOTAL FAT .5 G	BETA CAROTENE 1.9 MG
SATURATED FAT 0 G	VITAMIN C 70 MG
CHOLESTEROL 0 MG	CALCIUM 63 MG
SODIUM 9.7 MG	IRON 2.6 MG

Oranges with Caramel Syrup

A simple caramelized sugar syrup can elevate fresh oranges to a memorable finale for almost any meal. Though the orange liqueur adds an extra dimension to this dessert, it will still be delicious without it.

4 navel oranges
1 tablespoon Grand Marnier, or other orange liqueur
⅓ cup sugar
½ cup water

1. Peel the oranges. Cut them crosswise into rounds, remove any seeds and cut the rounds in half. Arrange the oranges in a deep platter. Drizzle them with the Grand Marnier. Cover and set aside.

2. In a small heavy saucepan, combine the sugar and ¼ cup of the water. Stir over medium-high heat until the sugar dissolves. Bring to a boil and boil without stirring for 6 to 8 minutes, until the bubbles get larger and the syrup is golden around the edges.

3. Shake the pan gently to blend the colors and continue cooking the syrup until it is the color of weak iced tea. Immediately remove from the heat and let cool for 6 minutes.

4. Return the pan to medium heat and stir in the remaining ¼ cup water until blended and liquidy. Remove from the heat.

5. Gently pour the syrup over the oranges. Cover and refrigerate until chilled.

Makes 4 servings

Nutrition Information
values are per serving

CALORIES 139	DIETARY FIBER 3.4 G
TOTAL FAT .1 G	BETA CAROTENE .2 MG
SATURATED FAT 0 G	VITAMIN C 80 MG
CHOLESTEROL 0 MG	CALCIUM 56 MG
SODIUM 1.6 MG	IRON .2 MG

Gingered Cantaloupe and Kiwi with Toasted Almonds

Two kinds of ginger, crystallized and fresh, add singular spark and texture to this remarkably pretty and refreshing height-of-summer dessert.

2 tablespoons frozen apple juice concentrate, thawed
2 tablespoons water
1 tablespoon honey
3 tablespoons finely chopped crystallized ginger
½ teaspoon grated fresh ginger
1 small cantaloupe (about 2 pounds)–peeled, seeded and cut into ½-inch chunks
3 kiwi fruit–peeled, halved lengthwise and cut crosswise into ¼-inch-thick half-moons
2½ tablespoons slivered almonds (about 1 ounce), toasted

1. In a large serving bowl, whisk together the apple juice concentrate, water and honey. Stir in the crystallized ginger and fresh ginger. Fold in the cantaloupe and kiwi. Cover and refrigerate for at least 30 minutes, stirring several times, to blend the flavors.

2. Serve the fruit sprinkled with the toasted almonds.

Makes 4 servings

Nutrition Information
values are per serving

CALORIES 195	DIETARY FIBER 3.8 G
TOTAL FAT 4.4 G	BETA CAROTENE 2.7 MG
SATURATED FAT .4 G	VITAMIN C 112 MG
CHOLESTEROL 0 MG	CALCIUM 78 MG
SODIUM 25 MG	IRON 3.4 MG

Strawberries with Balsamic Vinegar and Pepper

Strawberries, black pepper and vinegar may seem odd companions, but their flavors work magically together to create a delicious and elegant dessert. Begin by adding the smaller amount of vinegar, taste and then add more if desired.

3 cups sliced strawberries
⅓ cup sugar
½ teaspoon vanilla extract
1½ to 2 teaspoons balsamic vinegar
⅛ teaspoon freshly ground black pepper
1 pint frozen vanilla nonfat yogurt

1. In a medium bowl, combine the strawberries, sugar and vanilla, and toss to combine. Cover and let stand for 20 minutes, stirring occasionally.

2. Just before serving, stir in the vinegar and pepper.

3. Scoop the frozen yogurt into individual serving bowls and top with the strawberries and their juices.

Makes 4 servings

Nutrition Information
values are per serving

CALORIES 200	DIETARY FIBER 3.0 G
TOTAL FAT .4 G	BETA CAROTENE .1 MG
SATURATED FAT 0 G	VITAMIN C 65 MG
CHOLESTEROL 0 MG	CALCIUM 116 MG
SODIUM 46 MG	IRON .4 MG

Glazed Cake with Fresh Berries

Old-fashioned desserts have never seemed more fashionable. Here sugar-dusted, toasted cake is topped, comfortingly, with a fresh compote of strawberies and blueberries.

3 tablespoons seedless strawberry jelly
½ teaspoon fresh lemon juice
2 cups sliced strawberries
1 cup blueberries
1 tablespoon granulated sugar
Four ½-inch-thick slices nonfat vanilla loaf cake (5 ounces total)
2 teaspoons confectioners' sugar

1. Preheat the broiler.

2. In a medium bowl, whisk the jelly with the lemon juice until syrupy. Add the strawberries and blueberries, sprinkle them with the granulated sugar and stir gently to coat. Cover and let stand for at least 15 minutes, stirring occasionally.

3. Place the cake slices on a baking sheet. Put the confectioners' sugar in a small strainer and dust the cake evenly with the sugar.

4. Broil the cake 4 to 5 inches from the heat for 2 to 3 minutes, watching carefully, until the slices are glazed and lightly browned.

5. Transfer to dessert plates and top each with some of the berries and their juices.

Makes 4 servings

Nutrition Information
values are per serving

CALORIES 192	DIETARY FIBER 3.4 G
TOTAL FAT .4 G	BETA CAROTENE .1 MG
SATURATED FAT 0 G	VITAMIN C 48 MG
CHOLESTEROL 0 MG	CALCIUM 24 MG
SODIUM 126 MG	IRON .4 MG

Upside-Down Spiced Fruit Sundaes

The heat from a small amount of jalapeño pepper adds a subtle kick to these delicious fresh fruit sundaes. If blackberries are not available, substitute blueberries. If nectarines are used in place of mango, be sure they are as ripe as possible.

2 teaspoons grated orange zest
¼ cup orange juice
2 tablespoons finely chopped fresh mint
2 tablespoons fresh lemon juice
1 tablespoon minced fresh ginger
1 tablespoon honey
2 teaspoons minced fresh jalapeño pepper
1 small cantaloupe (2 pounds)–seeded, peeled and cut into 1-inch cubes
2 medium mangoes, peeled and cubed, or 4 small nectarines, cubed
2 medium kiwi fruit, peeled and cubed
1 cup blackberries
3 cups frozen vanilla yogurt

1. In a small bowl, combine the orange zest, orange juice, mint, lemon juice, ginger, honey and jalapeño pepper.

2. In a serving bowl, combine the cantaloupe, mangoes, kiwi and blackberries. Add the dressing and toss to combine. The salad can be served immediately or chilled until serving time.

3. Spoon the fruit onto 6 dessert plates and top with vanilla frozen yogurt.

Makes 6 servings

NUTRITION INFORMATION
values are per serving

CALORIES 215	DIETARY FIBER 3.2 G
TOTAL FAT 1.6 G	BETA CAROTENE 3.0 MG
SATURATED FAT .1 G	VITAMIN C 81 MG
CHOLESTEROL 5.0 MG	CALCIUM 182 MG
SODIUM 64 MG	IRON .5 MG

4-Fruit Sorbet

In many parts of the country, limes are most affordable during the summer months, which is one reason, but certainly not the only one, to make this ambrosial fruit ice.

1 cup frozen pineapple juice concentrate, partially thawed
1 cup frozen orange juice concentrate, partially thawed
3 cups apricot nectar
¼ cup plus 2 tablespoons fresh lime juice
¼ cup light corn syrup

1. In a large bowl, combine the pineapple juice concentrate, orange juice concentrate, apricot nectar, lime juice and corn syrup. Pour into the container of an ice cream maker and freeze according to the manufacturer's directions.

2. Transfer to a freezer container and freeze until firm.

Makes 8 servings

NUTRITION INFORMATION
values are per serving

CALORIES 206	DIETARY FIBER .8 G
TOTAL FAT .2 G	BETA CAROTENE .8 MG
SATURATED FAT 0 G	VITAMIN C 119 MG
CHOLESTEROL 0 MG	CALCIUM 33 MG
SODIUM 17 MG	IRON .8 MG

Mango-Orange Sorbet

The unforgettable flavor and color of ripe mango make this sorbet the perfect dessert for an elegant luncheon or dinner. Mangoes are most plentiful during the late summer months.

1 cup sugar
1 cup water
3 medium mangoes (12 ounces each), peeled and cut into large chunks
1 small cantaloupe (2 pounds), halved and seeded
1 navel orange
1 cup fresh raspberries

1. In a small saucepan, combine the sugar and water, and bring to a boil over medium-high heat. Remove the sugar syrup from the heat and set aside to cool slightly. Place the syrup in the freezer to quick-cool while you prepare the fruit.

2. Purée the mango in a food processor and set aside. Cut the cantaloupe into thin wedges, remove the rind and cut the melon into chunks. Purée the cantaloupe in the processor. Grate the orange rind to yield 2 teaspoons zest. Squeeze the orange to yield ⅓ cup juice.

3. In a bowl, blend the mango and cantaloupe purées. Stir in the chilled sugar syrup and the orange juice and orange zest, and place in the refrigerator until well chilled, about 30 minutes.

4. Transfer the chilled mixture to an ice cream machine and freeze according to the manufacturer's instructions. Scoop the sorbet into a container and freeze until ready to serve. Let sit at room temperature to soften slightly before serving.

5. Serve topped with fresh raspberries.

Makes 6 servings

Nutrition Information
values are per serving

CALORIES 249	DIETARY FIBER 2.8 G
TOTAL FAT .7 G	BETA CAROTENE 4.2 MG
SATURATED FAT .1 G	VITAMIN C 77 MG
CHOLESTEROL 0 MG	CALCIUM 28 MG
SODIUM 9.6 MG	IRON .5 MG

Carrot-Hazelnut Ice Cream

Super-premium ice creams rely on fat for richness and flavor. Here, carrots, raisins, hazelnuts, frangelico and warm spices lend texture and wonderful flavors to a lowfat, vitamin-rich dessert.

⅔ cup raisins
3 tablespoons frangelico (hazelnut liqueur) or dark rum
2 large carrots, very thinly sliced
1 cup water
1 cup carrot juice
3 cups lowfat (2%) milk
⅔ cup sugar
½ teaspoon cinnamon
⅓ teaspoon ground cardamom
¼ teaspoon salt
⅛ teaspoon ground cloves
⅛ teaspoon ground white pepper
2 egg yolks
½ cup chopped hazelnuts, toasted

1. Place the raisins in a small bowl. In a small saucepan, warm the frangelico over low heat. Pour the warm liqueur over the raisins and set aside to plump, about 20 minutes.

2. In a medium saucepan, combine the carrots, water and carrot juice, and bring to a boil over medium heat. Reduce the heat to a simmer and cook, uncovered, until the carrots are very tender, about 15 minutes. Pour the mixture into a food processor and process to a smooth purée, about 2 minutes.

3. In a medium nonreactive saucepan, warm the milk, ⅓ cup of the sugar, the cinnamon, cardamom, salt, cloves and pepper over low heat until just scalded, about 5 minutes.

4. In a small bowl, whisk together the egg yolks and remaining ⅓ cup sugar. Whisking constantly, add about 1 cup of the warm milk mixture to the yolk mixture to warm it, then whisk the warmed yolk mixture and the carrot purée into the milk mixture in the saucepan. Cook over low heat, stirring constantly, until the mixture coats the back of a spoon, about 12 minutes. Remove from the heat and strain through a sieve into a bowl.

5. Chill the mixture, then transfer to an ice cream maker and freeze according to the manufacturer's instructions. When the ice cream is almost done processing, spoon the hazelnuts and the raisins and their soaking liquid into the ice cream canister and continue churning until firm.

Makes 8 servings

Nutrition Information
values are per serving

CALORIES 247	DIETARY FIBER 2.0 G
TOTAL FAT 7.7 G	BETA CAROTENE 9.0 MG
SATURATED FAT 1.8 G	VITAMIN C 6.3 MG
CHOLESTEROL 60 MG	CALCIUM 154 MG
SODIUM 135 MG	IRON 1.0 MG

Sweet Potato Ice Cream

Many ice creams, including the one below, begin with custard sauce—a milk and egg yolk mixture—to which you add flavoring, in this case sweet potato purée and ginger. The key to custard sauce is to keep stirring it while it cooks to prevent it from scorching on the bottom. This is a grand dessert for the holidays, and would make a superb accompaniment to hot baked apples.

2 small sweet potatoes (12 ounces total)
2 cups lowfat (1%) milk
1 cup whole milk
1/3 cup (firmly packed) dark brown sugar
2 strips (3-by-1/2-inch each) orange zest
1 vanilla bean, split lengthwise, or 3/4 teaspoon vanilla extract
1/8 teaspoon salt
2 egg yolks
1/3 cup granulated sugar
1/2 teaspoon ground ginger

1. Preheat the oven to 425°. Prick the sweet potatoes in several places and bake until very soft, about 1 hour. When cool enough to handle, peel and purée in a food processor or blender.

2. In a medium saucepan, combine the lowfat milk, whole milk, brown sugar, orange zest, vanilla bean (if using) and salt, and cook over low heat until just scalded, about 5 minutes.

3. In a small bowl, whisk together the egg yolks and granulated sugar.

4. Whisking constantly, whisk 1 cup of the warm milk mixture into the yolk mixture to warm it, then whisk the warmed yolk mixture into the milk mixture in the saucepan.

5. Whisk in the sweet potato and ground ginger, and cook over low heat, stirring constantly, until the mixture coats the back of a spoon, about 12 minutes. Remove from the heat, push through a strainer, discarding the orange zest and removing the vanilla bean. If using vanilla extract, stir it in at this point.

6. Chill the mixture, then transfer to an ice cream maker and freeze according to the manufacturer's instructions.

Makes 6 servings

Nutrition Information
values are per serving

CALORIES 213	DIETARY FIBER 1.2 G
TOTAL FAT 4.0 G	BETA CAROTENE 4.9 MG
SATURATED FAT 1.9 G	VITAMIN C 11 MG
CHOLESTEROL 80 MG	CALCIUM 177 MG
SODIUM 119 MG	IRON .7 MG

Mango Melba Parfaits

In French, the word *parfait* means perfect, which is an apt description of this colorful mango and raspberry dessert. The smooth and silken textures of the mango, raspberry and vanilla-flavored yogurt layers make every spoonful of this elegant parfait well worth the cook's efforts. If you do not have parfait glasses, serve this in wineglasses.

2 cups plain nonfat yogurt
2/3 cup sugar
1/2 teaspoon vanilla extract
1 teaspoon plain unflavored gelatin
1/4 cup water
2 large mangoes–peeled, sliced and puréed
2 teaspoons fresh lemon juice
One 10-ounce package unsweetened frozen raspberries–thawed, puréed and strained
Fresh raspberries and sliced mango, for garnish

1. Set a fine-mesh sieve lined with dampened cheesecloth or white paper towel over a bowl.

Spoon the yogurt in and strain in the refrigerator 8 hours or overnight. Transfer the thickened yogurt to a large bowl and stir in ⅓ cup of the sugar and the vanilla.

2. In a small bowl, sprinkle the gelatin over the water and set aside to soften.

3. In a small saucepan, warm ½ cup of the mango purée over medium heat. Stir in half of the gelatin mixture and stir to dissolve the gelatin, about 30 seconds. Stir in the remaining mango purée and the lemon juice, and remove from the heat.

4. Transfer the mango mixture to a bowl set in a larger bowl of ice and water and chill, stirring frequently, until thickened and the mixture starts to mound. Remove the bowl of thickened mango purée but keep the bowl of ice and water ready for the raspberry mixture.

5. Meanwhile, in another small saucepan, warm ½ cup of the raspberry purée with the remaining ⅓ cup sugar. Stir in the remaining gelatin mixture and stir to dissolve the gelatin, about 30 seconds. Stir in the remaining raspberry purée. Transfer the raspberry mixture to a bowl and quick-chill over the bowl of ice and water as for the mango mixture.

6. Dividing evenly among six 5-ounce parfait glasses, layer the mixture in the following order: raspberry, mango and thickened yogurt. Garnish with additional raspberries and mango, if desired.

Makes 6 servings

NUTRITION INFORMATION
values are per serving

CALORIES 214	DIETARY FIBER .9 G
TOTAL FAT .8 G	BETA CAROTENE 2.1 MG
SATURATED FAT .2 G	VITAMIN C 40 MG
CHOLESTEROL 1.5 MG	CALCIUM 179 MG
SODIUM 60 MG	IRON .7 MG

Citrus-Scented Rice Pudding

Comfort foods have never gone out of style, and certainly rice pudding has always been in the pantheon of comforting desserts. Rice pudding is also a most accommodating dish, allowing the cook to add any number of interesting ingredients. Here we add orange and lime zests for a delicate citrus flavor and shredded carrots and chopped apricots for marvelous color, flavor and, of course, beta carotene. For an added twist, try this with an aromatic rice such as basmati.

2⅓ cups water
1 cup long-grain rice
3½ cups lowfat (1%) milk
2 large carrots, shredded
1 teaspoon grated orange zest
1 teaspoon grated lime zest
½ cup sugar
¼ teaspoon cinnamon
⅛ teaspoon salt
1 egg
½ teaspoon vanilla extract
⅓ cup chopped dried apricots
3 tablespoons slivered almonds

1. In a large saucepan, bring the water to a boil. Add the rice, cover, reduce the heat to medium-low and cook until tender, about 20 minutes.

2. Stir in 2½ cups of the milk, the carrots and the orange and lime zests, uncover and cook over medium-low, stirring frequently, until the milk has been absorbed, about 10 minutes.

3. Stir in the sugar, cinnamon, salt and ½ cup of the milk, and cook, stirring frequently, until the rice is very tender and creamy, about 5 minutes.

4. In a small bowl, lightly beat the egg. Whisk some of the hot rice mixture into the egg to warm it, then whisk the warmed egg mixture into the saucepan along with the remaining ½ cup milk.

Cook, stirring constantly, until the rice pudding is very creamy and rich, about 5 minutes.

5. Remove from the heat and transfer to a bowl. Stir in the vanilla, apricots and almonds. Cool , then cover and refrigerate.

Makes 6 servings

NUTRITION INFORMATION
values are per serving

CALORIES 308	DIETARY FIBER 2.1 G
TOTAL FAT 4.8 G	BETA CAROTENE 5.9 MG
SATURATED FAT 1.4 G	VITAMIN C 5.6 MG
CHOLESTEROL 41 MG	CALCIUM 214 MG
SODIUM 142 MG	IRON 2.2 MG

Pumpkin Crème Brûlée

For many dessert lovers, crème brûlée is the ultimate indulgence, but one that they feel guilty about because of its formidable amounts of fat. If you are a crème brûlée lover, you are in luck with the recipe that follows. Lowfat milk replaces the cream and the number of egg yolks has been reduced, but the thick, rich texture of pumpkin purée makes up the difference.

2 cups lowfat (1%) milk
½ teaspoon cinnamon
⅛ teaspoon allspice
⅛ teaspoon ground cloves
⅛ teaspoon ground white pepper
3 eggs, lightly beaten
2 egg whites
⅓ cup granulated sugar
¼ teaspoon salt
½ teaspoon vanilla extract
⅔ cup canned solid-pack pumpkin purée
⅓ cup (packed) light brown sugar

1. In a medium saucepan, combine the milk, cinnamon, allspice, cloves and white pepper. Bring to a simmer over medium heat, remove from the heat, cover and let stand at room temperature for 20 minutes.

2. Preheat the oven to 350°.

3. In a medium bowl, whisk together the whole eggs, egg whites, granulated sugar and salt. Return the milk mixture to a simmer and, whisking constantly, add about 1 cup of the hot milk to the egg mixture to warm it. Then stir the warmed egg mixture back into the saucepan and continue cooking, stirring constantly, until the mixture coats the back of a spoon, about 10 minutes. Remove from the heat and stir in the vanilla.

4. Gently whisk the pumpkin purée into the custard mixture until well combined but not frothy and pour into six 8-ounce ramekins or custard cups. Line the bottom of a baking pan (large enough to comfortably hold all the ramekins) with paper towels and place the ramekins on top. Pour boiling water to come halfway up the sides of the ramekins and bake until the custard is set but still slightly wobbly, about 45 minutes. Cool on a wire rack, then refrigerate.

5. Just before serving time, preheat the broiler. Place the brown sugar in a fine-mesh sieve and sprinkle the tops of the custards evenly with the sugar. Place the custards on a baking sheet and broil 6 inches from the heat until the tops have caramelized, 2 to 3 minutes. Watch the custards carefully so they don't burn. Cool for several minutes before serving.

Makes 6 servings

NUTRITION INFORMATION
values are per serving

CALORIES 176	DIETARY FIBER .5 G
TOTAL FAT 3.4 G	BETA CAROTENE 3.6 MG
SATURATED FAT 1.3 G	VITAMIN C 2.0 MG
CHOLESTEROL 110 MG	CALCIUM 134 MG
SODIUM 187 MG	IRON 1.1 MG

Fresh Orange Gelatin with Strawberries

The flavorful combination of strawberry and orange is here enhanced by an interplay of textures: Smooth fresh orange jelly is punctuated by the crunch of sliced strawberries and mandarin orange sections. Mandarin oranges—which are actually tangerines—are high in vitamin C and have a decent amount of beta carotene as well.

1 envelope plain unflavored gelatin
2 cups fresh orange juice
1 teaspoon grated orange zest
¼ teaspoon vanilla extract
1 cup canned juice-packed mandarin oranges, well drained
1¼ cups sliced strawberries

1. In a small saucepan, sprinkle the gelatin over ½ cup of the orange juice. Warm the mixture over very low heat, stirring just until the gelatin is dissolved, then remove from the heat.

2. Let the gelatin mixture cool to lukewarm, then combine with the remaining juice, the orange zest and vanilla.

3. In parfait glasses, spoon alternating layers of mandarin oranges, orange gelatin and strawberies. Repeat the layering, ending with strawberries on top.

Makes 4 servings

Nutrition Information
values are per serving

CALORIES 100	DIETARY FIBER 1.5 G
TOTAL FAT .4 G	BETA CAROTENE .5 MG
SATURATED FAT 0 G	VITAMIN C 111 MG
CHOLESTEROL 0 MG	CALCIUM 29 MG
SODIUM 8.3 MG	IRON .6 MG

Cannoli Pudding with Strawberry Sauce

This inventive dessert takes the best part of the Italian pastry cannoli—the filling—and omits the deep-fried outer shell. Here a chocolate chip- and pistachio-flecked ricotta pudding is served topped with a fresh strawberry-orange sauce.

PUDDING
½ cup plain nonfat yogurt, stirred smooth
1 cup nonfat cottage cheese
1 cup part-skim ricotta cheese
⅓ cup confectioners' sugar
1½ teaspoons grated orange zest
1 teaspoon vanilla extract
1 ounce miniature semisweet chocolate chips
½ ounce shelled pistachios, coarsely chopped

STRAWBERRY SAUCE
2½ cups strawberries
3 tablespoons fresh orange juice
2 tablespoons granulated sugar

1. Make the Pudding Line a small strainer with cheesecloth or a white paper towel and suspend over a small bowl. Spoon the yogurt into the strainer and let drain for 15 minutes. Discard the whey and set the thickened yogurt aside.

2. In a food processor, combine the cottage cheese, ricotta, confectioners' sugar, orange zest and vanilla, and process to an almost smooth purée (do not process for too long, or the mixture will break down).

3. Add the thickened yogurt, chocolate chips and pistachios to the processor and pulse until just combined.

4. Divide the pudding among 6 dessert dishes, cover and chill until the pudding is set, at least 2 hours.

5. For the Strawberry Sauce Shortly before serving, place 1½ cups of the strawberries in a food processor or blender. Add the orange juice and granulated sugar, and process to a smooth purée. Slice the remaining berries and stir into the sauce.

6. Serve the pudding topped with the sauce.

Makes 6 servings

Nutrition Information
values are per serving

CALORIES 200	DIETARY FIBER 1.9 G
TOTAL FAT 5.9 G	BETA CAROTENE 0 MG
SATURATED FAT 3.0 G	VITAMIN C 41 MG
CHOLESTEROL 16 MG	CALCIUM 184 MG
SODIUM 200 MG	IRON .7 MG

Pumpkin Soufflé with Cranberry Purée

There is nothing quite like a soufflé. It is chemistry and magic all rolled into one, and when it puffs up to great heights it is as pleasing for the cook as it is for those who are waiting to enjoy it. These are individual soufflés, based on egg whites, not yolks, in a combination that is perfectly suited for Thanksgiving.

1 cup fresh or frozen cranberries
½ cup plus 1 tablespoon frozen apple juice concentrate, thawed
½ cup plus 1 tablespoon water
1 tablespoon plus 1 teaspoon maple syrup
½ teaspoon fresh lemon juice
2 tablespoons sugar
2 tablespoons cornstarch
¼ teaspoon allspice
¼ teaspoon cinnamon
1 cup canned solid-pack purmpkin purée
4 egg whites
¼ teaspoon cream of tartar

1. In a small nonreactive saucepan, bring the cranberries, 3 tablespoons of the apple juice concentrate and 3 tablespoons of the water to a boil over high heat and cook until the berries are soft. Reduce the heat to medium and cook until the sauce is syrupy, about 15 minutes. Remove from the heat and stir in the maple syrup and lemon juice.

2. Preheat the oven to 350°. Spray six 6-ounce ramekins with nonstick cooking spray and dust with 1 tablespoon of the sugar.

3. Meanwhile, in a medium saucepan, whisk together the cornstarch and the remaining 6 tablespoons apple juice concentrate, 6 tablespoons water and 1 tablespoon sugar. Whisking constantly, bring to a boil over medium heat and cook until the sauce thickens, about 5 minutes. Remove from the heat.

4. In a medium bowl, stir the allspice and cinnamon into the pumpkin purée. Stir in the thickened apple juice and mix well.

5. In another medium bowl with an electric mixer, beat the egg whites until foamy. Add the cream of tartar and beat until stiff peaks form. Fold one-fourth of the beaten whites into the pumpkin mixture to lighten it, then gently fold in the remaining whites until just mixed.

6. Spoon the soufflé mixture into the prepared ramekins, filling them three-fourths full. Place them in a roasting pan and pour in hot water to reach one-third of the way up the sides of the ramekins. Bake for 23 to 25 minutes, or until puffed and firm to the touch.

7. Meanwhile, transfer half of the cranberry mixture to a food processor or blender, and process until smooth. Return to the saucepan with the remaining cranberries and keep warm until serving time.

8. Serve the soufflés hot with a dollop of cranberry sauce on top.

Makes 6 servings

NUTRITION INFORMATION
values are per serving

CALORIES 120	DIETARY FIBER .8 G
TOTAL FAT .7 G	BETA CAROTENE 5.4 MG
SATURATED FAT .1 G	VITAMIN C 28 MG
CHOLESTEROL 0 MG	CALCIUM 23 MG
SODIUM 46 MG	IRON .9 MG

Carrot-Ginger Mousse

If the sweetness of carrots makes carrot cake delectable, it follows that carrot mousse, in this case spiced with ginger, would be very good, too.

1 large carrot, very thinly sliced
1 cup water
5 tablespoons sugar
¾ cup carrot juice
½ teaspoon ground ginger
⅛ teaspoon allspice
1 envelope plain unflavored gelatin
½ cup plain nonfat yogurt
⅓ cup plus 1 tablespoon light sour cream
1 teaspoon coarsely chopped crystallized ginger
Carrot curls, for garnish

1. In a small saucepan, combine the carrot, water and 2 tablespoons of the sugar. Bring to a boil, reduce the heat, cover and simmer until the carrot is very tender, about 15 minutes.

2. Transfer the carrot (and any liquid) to a food processor and add ½ cup of the carrot juice. Process to a smooth purée. Stir in the ground ginger and allspice; set the carrot purée aside.

3. In a small bowl, sprinkle the gelatin over the remaining ¼ cup carrot juice; set aside to soften.

4. In a small saucepan, bring ¼ cup of the carrot purée and the remaining 3 tablespoons sugar to a boil over medium heat, stirring constantly to dissolve the sugar. Remove from the heat and stir in the softened gelatin until dissolved, about 1 minute.

5. Pour the hot gelatin mixture into a large bowl, add the remaining carrot purée and stir to combine. Set the bowl into a larger bowl of ice and water, and whisk occasionally until the mixture is cooler than room temperature and slightly syrupy, about 5 minutes.

6. In a small bowl, stir together the yogurt and ⅓ cup of the sour cream and gently fold into the chilled carrot mixture. Spoon the mousse into four ½-cup ramekins and chill until set, about 2 hours.

7. To serve, top each mousse with some of the remaining sour cream and sprinkle the crystallized ginger on top. Garnish with carrot curls, if desired.

Makes 4 servings

NUTRITION INFORMATION
values are per serving

CALORIES 156	DIETARY FIBER .8 G
TOTAL FAT 3.3 G	BETA CAROTENE 11 MG
SATURATED FAT 1.6 G	VITAMIN C 7.0 MG
CHOLESTEROL 8.5 MG	CALCIUM 79 MG
SODIUM 48 MG	IRON .7 MG

Glazed Chocolate Sweet Potato Cake

Sweet potatoes and buttermilk render this chocolate cake remarkably moist and rich tasting. It will even satisfy serious chocolate lovers.

CAKE
1 pound sweet potatoes
2 cups flour
½ cup unsweetened cocoa powder
2 teaspoons baking powder
½ teaspoon baking soda
½ teaspoon cinnamon
½ teaspoon salt

¼ teaspoon nutmeg
⅛ teaspoon allspice
⅛ teaspoon ground cloves
⅓ cup granulated sugar
⅓ cup (firmly packed) light brown sugar
⅓ cup vegetable oil
3 egg whites
1 large carrot, shredded
⅔ cup lowfat (1.5%) buttermilk
½ cup carrot juice

GLAZE
1 cup confectioners' sugar
2 tablespoons orange juice
2 teaspoons grated orange zest

1. For the Cake Preheat the oven to 450°. Prick the sweet potatoes in several places, place on a baking sheet and bake until tender, about 45 minutes. When cool enough to handle, peel and mash with a fork. Reduce the oven temperature to 350°.

2. Generously spray a 9-by-13-inch baking pan with nonstick cooking spray; set aside. In a large mixing bowl, stir together the flour, cocoa powder, baking powder, baking soda, cinnamon, salt, nutmeg, allspice and cloves; set aside.

3. In the large bowl of an electric mixer, beat together the mashed sweet potatoes, the granulated sugar, brown sugar and vegetable oil until light and fluffy. Beat in the egg whites until well combined. Fold in the carrot.

4. In a small bowl, stir together the buttermilk and carrot juice. Alternately fold the buttermilk mixture and the flour mixture into the sweet potato mixture, beginning and ending with the flour mixture.

5. Spoon the batter into the prepared pan, smoothing the top. Bake for 35 minutes, or until a cake tester inserted in the center comes out clean. Cool on a rack in the pan.

6. For the Glaze In a medium bowl, stir together the confectioners' sugar, orange juice and orange zest. Drizzle over the cooled cake.

Makes 12 servings

Nutrition Information
values are per serving

CALORIES 268	DIETARY FIBER 2.7 G
TOTAL FAT 5.5 G	BETA CAROTENE 6.3 MG
SATURATED FAT 1.2 G	VITAMIN C 9.5 MG
CHOLESTEROL .5 MG	CALCIUM 88 MG
SODIUM 266 MG	IRON 1.9 MG

Carrot-Apricot Almond Cake

The traditional carrot cake relies on lots of butter or oil for it moist crumb. Here, almost no oil, but buttermilk, diced apricots and grated carrots provide moistness, as does the lemony cream cheese frosting. Slivered almonds add flavor, texture and vitamin E. If you are making this in advance to freeze it, freeze it unfrosted; thaw it at room temperature, then frost it before serving.

1⅓ cups flour
2 tablespoons wheat germ
2 teaspoons baking powder
1 teaspoon baking soda
1 egg
¾ cup granulated sugar
¾ cup lowfat (1.5%) buttermilk
2 tablespoons canola oil
3 tablespoons slivered almonds, coarsely chopped and toasted
2 cups coarsely grated carrots
12 dried apricot halves, diced

½ cup whipped cream cheese
1 tablespoon confectioners' sugar
2 teaspoons fresh lemon juice

1. Preheat the oven to 375°. Spray an 8-inch round cake pan with nonstick cooking spray.

2. In a small bowl, combine the flour, wheat germ, baking powder and baking soda. In a medium bowl, beat the egg and granulated sugar until light and lemon-colored. Beat in the buttermilk and oil. Add the dry ingredients in two batches, beating well after each addition.

3. Measure out 1 tablespoon of the toasted almonds and set aside. Add the grated carrots, dried apricots and the remaining almonds to the batter and stir to combine.

4. Spread the batter evenly in the prepared cake pan. Rap the pan on the countertop to remove any air bubbles, then bake for 30 to 35 minutes, or until a cake tester inserted in the center comes out clean and dry and the cake has begun to pull away from the sides of the pan. Let the cake cool in the pan for 5 to 10 minutes before turning out onto a rack to cool completely.

5. Meanwhile, in a small bowl, beat the whipped cream cheese, confectioners' sugar and lemon juice together.

6. When the cake is cool, frost with the cream cheese frosting. Sprinkle the remaining chopped almonds over the frosting.

Makes 8 servings

Nutrition Information
values are per serving

CALORIES 284	DIETARY FIBER 2.2 G
TOTAL FAT 9.6 G	BETA CAROTENE 4.9 MG
SATURATED FAT 2.7 G	VITAMIN C 3.6 MG
CHOLESTEROL 37 MG	CALCIUM 126 MG
SODIUM 358 MG	IRON 1.8 MG

Butternut Pie in an Almond Crust

Any winter squash—including pumpkin, of course—could be used for the filling of this autumnal crumb-and-nut crust dessert, but butternut is widely available and has one of the highest amounts of beta carotene. You might also look for Hubbard squash, although it is such a large squash that many markets sell it as pre-cut pieces.

1 cup graham cracker crumbs
2 tablespoons plus 2 teaspoon unsalted butter, melted
2 ounces almonds, finely chopped
2 cups cooked butternut squash
1 egg
1 egg white
⅓ cup (packed) brown sugar
2 teaspoons grated orange zest
½ teaspoon cinnamon
¼ teaspoon salt

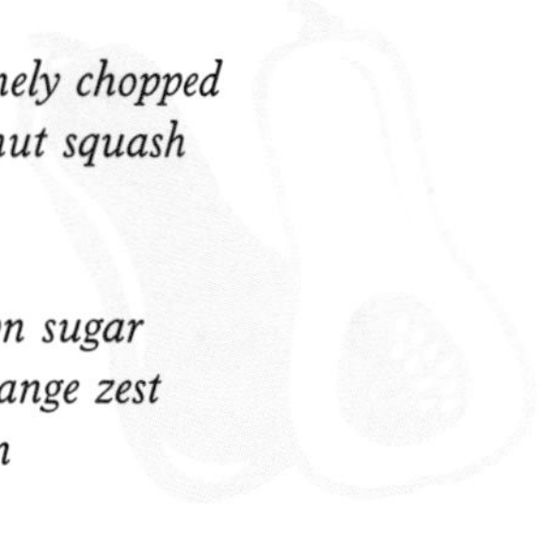

1. Preheat the oven to 375°.

2. In a bowl, combine the graham cracker crumbs, butter and almonds, and stir to blend. Transfer the nut-crumb mixture to an 8-inch pie plate and press into the bottom and up the sides of the plate.

3. In a food processor, purée the cooked squash. Add the whole egg, egg white, sugar, orange zest, cinnamon, and salt, and process until blended.

4. Pour the filling into the prepared pie shell and bake for 35 to 40 minutes, or until the filling is firm. Cool the pie on a rack.

Makes 6 servings

Nutrition Information
values are per serving

CALORIES 270	DIETARY FIBER 1.7 G
TOTAL FAT 12 G	BETA CAROTENE 3.0 MG
SATURATED FAT 3.9 G	VITAMIN C 11 MG
CHOLESTEROL 49 MG	CALCIUM 73 MG
SODIUM 239 MG	IRON 1.7 MG

Papaya-Tangerine Cheese Pie

There are lots of glorious flavors—ginger, tangerine, papaya and orange—at play in this marvelous summertime pie. You will need to start the yogurt cheese a day ahead.

3 cups plain nonfat yogurt
4 ounces (about 17) gingersnaps
2 tablespoons unsalted butter, melted
⅓ cup light sour cream
¼ cup sugar
2 teaspoons grated tangerine or orange zest
½ teaspoon vanilla extract
2 teaspoons unflavored gelatin
¼ cup frozen tangerine or orange juice concentrate, thawed
1¾ cups peeled, chopped papaya (about 2 medium)
1 cup canned juice-packed mandarin oranges, well drained

1. Set a large strainer lined with cheesecloth or white paper towels over a bowl. Spoon in the yogurt and allow to drain, loosely covered, in the refrigerator, until the yogurt has reduced to 1¾ cups and is the consistency of soft cream cheese.

2. In a food processor, process the gingersnaps to fine crumbs. Add the melted butter and process briefly to combine. Press the crumb mixture into the bottom and up the sides of an 8-inch pie pan.

3. In a medium bowl, beat together the yogurt cheese and sour cream until smooth. Beat in the sugar, tangerine zest and vanilla, and set aside.

4. In a small saucepan, sprinkle the gelatin over the tangerine juice concentrate. Warm the mixture over low heat, stirring just until the gelatin is dissolved, then remove from the heat. Beat the gelatin mixture into the yogurt cheese mixture.

5. Stir 1½ cups of the papaya into the yogurt cheese mixture. Pour the filling into the prepared crust. Refrigerate until the filling is set, 6 hours or overnight.

6. Just before serving, top the pie with the remaining papaya and the mandarin oranges.

Makes 8 servings

Nutrition Information
values are per serving

CALORIES 214	DIETARY FIBER .3 G
TOTAL FAT 5.8 G	BETA CAROTENE .6 MG
SATURATED FAT 2.8 G	VITAMIN C 39 MG
CHOLESTEROL 13 MG	CALCIUM 195 MG
SODIUM 162 MG	IRON 1.1 MG

Crunchy Carrot-Pistachio Biscotti

Biscotti are Italian cookies that are twice baked until crunchy. It is their crisp texture that makes them so perfect for dipping in coffee or tea. For an interesting variation, substitute dried cherries for the apricots.

1¼ cups all-purpose flour
½ cup sugar
2 tablespoons cornmeal

1½ teaspoons grated lemon zest
¾ teaspoon cinnamon
½ teaspoon baking powder
¼ teaspoon salt
1 large carrot, finely shredded
¼ cup coarsely chopped pistachio nuts
3 tablespoons finely chopped dried apricots
½ cup carrot juice

1. Preheat the oven to 350°. Spray a large cookie sheet with nonstick cooking spray.

2. In a large mixing bowl, whisk together the flour, sugar, cornmeal, lemon zest, cinnamon, baking powder and salt. Stir in the shredded carrot, pistachios and apricots. Add the carrot juice and stir until a firm dough forms.

3. Shape the dough into a log 15 inches long by 3 inches wide by ½ inch high. Place on the prepared cookie sheet and bake for 30 minutes, or until firmly set and golden brown.

4. Remove from the oven and cool slightly, then slice on the diagonal into ½-inch-thick cookies. Return to the oven and bake for 20 minutes, or until set, lightly colored and dry; turn the cookies over after 10 minutes.

Makes 6 servings

Nutrition Information
values are per serving

CALORIES 228	DIETARY FIBER 2.3 G
TOTAL FAT 3.1 G	BETA CAROTENE 6.2 MG
SATURATED FAT .4 G	VITAMIN C 4.1 MG
CHOLESTEROL 0 MG	CALCIUM 50 MG
SODIUM 144 MG	IRON 2.2 MG

Navajo Pumpkin-Nut Loaf

Serve this pumpkin-nut cake with apple butter for dessert or tea. It would even make a nice lunch or brunch dish topped with a mild-flavored cheese and toasted for open-faced sandwiches.

1½ cups flour
¾ cup sugar
1 teaspoon baking powder
1 teaspoon cinnamon
1 teaspoon nutmeg
¾ teaspoon salt
1 cup canned solid-pack pumpkin purée
¼ cup canola oil
1 egg
2 egg whites
½ cup grated carrot
¼ cup pine nuts
¼ cup chopped pistachio nuts

1. Preheat the oven to 350°. Spray a 9-by-5-inch loaf pan with nonstick cooking spray.

2. In a large bowl, blend the flour with the sugar, baking powder, cinnamon, nutmeg and salt. Add the pumpkin, oil, whole egg, egg whites, carrot, pine nuts and pistachios, and stir until evenly blended.

3. Transfer the batter to the prepared loaf pan and spread evenly. Bake for about 45 minutes, or until a cake tester inserted into the center comes out dry. Cool for 20 minutes in the pan, then invert onto a rack to cool completely.

Makes 12 servings

Nutrition Information
values are per serving

CALORIES 196	DIETARY FIBER 1.2 G
TOTAL FAT 8.1 G	BETA CAROTENE 3.5 MG
SATURATED FAT .9 G	VITAMIN C 1.3 MG
CHOLESTEROL 18 MG	CALCIUM 42 MG
SODIUM 196 MG	IRON 1.6 MG

Peach-Apricot Cobbler

Almost as American as apple pie, fruit cobblers are one of the all-time best comfort foods. In this example, a nutmeg-scented biscuit dough tops a combination of fresh peaches and dried apricots tossed with apricot nectar and apricot preserves. The surprise ingredient is shredded carrots, which taste as though they should have been in cobblers all along.

FILLING
¾ cup apricot nectar
¼ cup apricot all-fruit spread
3 tablespoons sugar
1 tablespoon fresh lemon juice
1½ teaspoons vanilla extract
1½ pounds peaches, cut into thin wedges
1½ cups dried apricot halves, snipped into thirds
1 cup shredded carrots

BISCUIT TOPPING
1½ cups flour
1 tablepoons plus 1 teaspoon sugar
2 teaspoons baking powder
¼ teaspoon baking soda
¼ teaspoon salt
3 tablespoons cold unsalted butter, cut into small pieces
¾ cup plain lowfat yogurt
¼ teaspoon nutmeg
1 teaspoon milk

1. Preheat the oven to 400°.

2. To Make the Filling In a medium bowl, whisk the apricot nectar, apricot all-fruit spread, sugar, lemon juice and vanilla until blended. Add the peaches, dried apricots and carrots, and toss to coat well. Pour the filling into a 9½-inch deep-dish pie plate and cover with foil. Place on a baking sheet to catch spillovers and bake for 25 to 30 minutes, or until the fruit starts to become tender.

3. Meanwhile, Make the Biscuit Topping In a medium bowl, stir together the flour, 1 tablespoon of the sugar, the baking powder, baking soda and salt. Cut in the butter with a pastry blender or your fingers until the mixture forms fine crumbs. Stir in the yogurt with a fork just until a dough forms.

4. Lightly dust a work surface with flour. Turn out the dough onto the surface and give it 10 to 12 kneads. Pat or roll the dough into a rough 9-inch circle, about ½ inch thick. Place the dough on top of the hot fruit and cut four slashes in the top to let the steam escape.

5. In a small bowl or cup, mix the remaining 1 teaspoon sugar with the nutmeg. Brush the dough with the milk and sprinkle with the sugar-nutmeg mixture.

6. Bake for 20 to 25 minutes longer, or until the crust is browned and the fruit is bubbly.

Makes 8 servings

Nutrition Information
values are per serving

CALORIES 294	DIETARY FIBER 4.1 G
TOTAL FAT 5.1 G	BETA CAROTENE 3.8 MG
SATURATED FAT 2.9 G	VITAMIN C 20 MG
CHOLESTEROL 13 MG	CALCIUM 132 MG
SODIUM 253 MG	IRON 2.6 MG

Index

Although all of the recipes in this cookbook provide a significant amount of beta carotene and vitamin C, there are a number of recipes that provide an exceptionally high amount of one or both of these antioxidants. These recipes are identified in the index by the following symbol: ◆

D

Q-R

S

T

U-V

W